COHABITATION AND TRUSTS OF LAND

AUSTRALIA
Law Book Co.
Sydney

CANADA and USA
Carswell
Toronto

HONG KONG
Sweet & Maxwell Asia

NEW ZEALAND
Brookers
Wellington

SINGAPORE and MALAYSIA
Sweet & Maxwell Asia
Singapore and Kuala Lumpur

COHABITATION AND TRUSTS OF LAND

Cohabitation and Trusts of Land and
Appointment of Trustees Act

Stephen Wildblood Q.C.
Elizabeth Darlington
Laura Heaton
Christopher Wagstaffe

Sweet & Maxwell Limited of
100 Avenue Road, London NW3 3PF
(http://www.sweetandmaxwell.co.uk)
Typeset by YHT Ltd, London

No natural forests were destroyed to make this product,
only farmed timber was used and replanted

ISBN 0 421 907 304
9780421907300

FOREWORD

The reader may wonder why I, a family lawyer, am commending a new title in an alien field. It is because the field is one I have frequently encountered but usually found difficult and unsympathetic. It is precisely because I have often struggled in the territory that I believe *Cohabitation and Trusts of Land* will provide an invaluable *vade mecum* to hosts of family lawyers whose needs must enter upon this adjacent country.

Again it may be said, why do we need guidance now that we are witnessing the dawn of a new day when judges will be more simply charged to do fairness in the exercise of a wide discretion? I refer, of course, to the Law Commission's Consultation Paper, *Cohabitation: the Financial Consequences of Relationship Breakdown* (Law Comm No. 179 of May 4, 2006). The paper is both scholarly and worldly; qualities reflected in its reception which has broadly been warm and supportive. But history shows how leisurely can be the progress from this stage in the process of reform to the commencement date of the ultimate Act. The Law Commission will clearly require a proper opportunity to analyse and reflect upon the responses. It will then have to prepare its report. If it decides to include a draft bill, further time must elapse. What happens thereafter depends on so many unpredictables, including government policy, public pressure, and the availability of a legislative slot. In short these difficult cases are likely to be decided according to present law and principle (so well summarised in the Law Commission's previous report) for years to come.

As a family lawyer my eye was drawn to Chapter 11, which deals with claims under section 15 and Schedule 1 to the Children Act 1989. Over 22 pages the statute and subsequent case law are clearly and comprehensively recorded. The subject is divided into practitioner friendly headings that spare the reader from wading through much irritatingly unhelpful learning in search of the particular answer he requires. The Chapter is as authoritative as it is comprehensive.

Stephen Wildblood Q.C. is a very experienced author and editor who has already covered a wide range of our family law. With the support of

Elizabeth Darlington, Laura Heaton and Christopher Wagstaffe, he has now confirmed his reputation for clarity and reliability.

The Rt Hon Lord
Justice Thorpe
Royal Courts of
Justice, London

ACKNOWLEDGEMENTS

The authors would like to thank Vikki Wagstaffe (for her tolerance) and Nicholas Allen, Catherine Knowles and Tina Abbott for their help.

Stephen Wildblood Q.C.
Elizabeth Darlington
Laura Heaton
Christopher Wagstaffe

October 17, 2006

CONTENTS

Table of Cases

TABLE OF CASES

Table of Statutes

Table of SIs

Table of CPR

Table of CPR PD

CHAPTER 1

INTRODUCTION

Contrary to popular misconception, there is no such thing as a "common **1–001** law marriage". Unlike the position upon divorce or the breakdown of a civil partnership, upon the breakdown of a relationship between cohabitees there is no coherent statutory machinery to adjust financial and property rights. When such relationships break down, the applicable legal principles are mainly found in trust and property law and the relevant procedural rules are the Civil Procedure Rules.

Where, however, a couple has a child or children a claim may be **1–002** brought under Sch.1 of the Children Act 1989 (see Chapter 11, below). In respect of engaged couples, an application may be made under the Married Women's Property Act 1882 (see Chapter 10). In both these cases the relevant procedural rules are those contained in the Family Proceedings Rules.

The aim of this book is to consolidate all the relevant principles of practice and procedure whether found in the civil or family jurisdiction in order to provide a practical guide to the practitioner advising upon the breakdown of a relationship of unmarried couples. The focus is upon issues concerning property and financial provision.

The following matters are dealt with:

(1) Express Declarations of Trust (Chapter 2);
(2) Constructive Trusts (Chapter 3);
(3) Resulting Trusts (Chapter 4);
(4) Quantification of Beneficial Interests (Chapter 5);
(5) Proprietary Estoppel (Chapter 6);
(6) Personal Obligations between Cohabitees (Chapter 7);
(7) The Trusts of Land and Appointment of Trustees Act 1996 — Substantive Provisions (Chapter 8);
(8) Practice and Procedure (Chapter 9);
(9) Engaged Couples (Chapter 10);
(10) Applications under Sch.1 of the Children Act (Chapter 11).

The appendices contain:

(1) Precedents and Forms;

(2) Digest of Leading Cases;

(3) Relevant Statutory Provisions.

1–003 In relation to ownership of the former home shared by the cohabiting couple questions of ownership are determined by reference to the law of trusts. It will often be necessary to make an application in respect of that property under s.14 of the Trusts of Land and Appointment of Trustees Act 1996. Where, for example, the property has been purchased in the sole name of one of the parties, it is necessary for the party claiming an interest in the property to establish an interest by way of constructive or resulting trust or by way of proprietary estoppel.

1–004   The leading case on whether a party who is not the legal owner of a property can establish that they have a beneficial interest in the property remains the House of Lords case *Lloyds Bank Plc v Rosset*.[1] The partner claiming a beneficial interest against the partner entitled to the legal estate has to establish that:

(1) there has, at any time prior to acquisition, or exceptionally at some later date, been any agreement, arrangement or under-standing reached between [the partners] that the property is to be shared beneficially. The finding of an agreement or arrangement to share in this sense can only be based on evidence of express discussions between the partners, however imperfectly remembered and however imprecise their terms may have been. Once a finding to this effect is made it will only be necessary for the partner asserting a claim to a beneficial interest against the partner entitled to the legal estate to show that he or she has acted to his or her detriment or significantly altered his or her position in reliance on the agreement in order to give rise to a constructive trust or a proprietary estoppel.[2]

(2) If the partner claiming a beneficial interest is not able to satisfy the requirements set out in (1) above, then according to Lord Bridge, direct contributions to the purchase price whether initially or by payment of mortgage instalments will readily justify the inference necessary to the creation of a constructive trust. But, it is at least extremely doubtful whether anything less will do (*per* Lord Bridge of Harwich at 132H to 133A).[3]

1–005 The strict application of the requirements necessary to establish a con-structive trust, as enunciated by Lord Bridge in *Lloyds Bank v Rosset*, can sometimes lead to unfairness. Often the partner claiming a beneficial interest by virtue of a constructive trust will have contributed to the household by looking after the couple's children, carrying out domestic

---

[1] [1991] 1 A.C. 107.

[2] *Per* Lord Bridge of Harwich at 132E to G.

[3] The House of Lords will have the opportunity to re-visit this vexed area of law in Spring 2007 when the case of *Stack v Dowden* [2005] EWCA Civ 857 is heard by their Lordships.

tasks, paying utility bills and other household expenses but will not satisfy the necessary requirements.[4]

Given the increasing numbers of heterosexual couples living together without getting married and in view of the perceived unfairness of outcome in cases where it is not possible to establish a beneficial interest in property by virtue of a constructive trust, the Law Commission has been charged with investigating proposals for reform.

In 2002 the Law Commission Discussion Paper *Sharing Homes* (Law Com No. 278, November 2002) considered the current position but failed to produce any proposals for reform, concluding inter alia that it was not possible to devise a statutory scheme for the determination of shares in the shared home which would operate fairly and evenly across the diversity of domestic circumstances and that the best course of action was to encourage those living together to make express written arrangements setting out clearly what they intend their rights to be.[5]

1–006

More recently, however, following the implementation of the Civil Partnerships Act 2004, the Law Commission has again been asked by Parliament to consider reform of the law governing the breakdown of cohabitees. In its Consultation Paper, *Cohabitation: The Financial Consequences of Relationship Breakdown,*[6] the Law Commission considers the implementation of a new statutory scheme to regulate the breakdown of those in a cohabiting relationship and invites comments on its proposals. It is suggested that such a scheme would apply only to those cohabiting couples that come within certain criteria, for example where there is a child or children of the relationship.[7] In addition, it is proposed that the scheme would be based upon economic advantage (paras 6.128) and economic disadvantage[8] at the point of separation. The Law Commission's final report is not expected until August 2007.

1–007

Unless and until a new statutory scheme is implemented, the current legal principles applicable to the breakdown of relationships of cohabitees remain diverse. It is hoped that this book will provide a useful summary of the relevant law in order to assist the practitioner advising upon the breakdown of such relationships.

---

[4] See for example, *Burns v Burns* [1984] 1 Ch. 317 where the female claimant made gifts of clothing to the defendant and the children; paid for the housekeeping; paid the rates; paid the telephone bills; paid for a number of chattels including a dishwasher, washing machine, tumble dryer, drawing room suite/three armchairs, bed together with certain door furnishings. In addition she decorated the interior of the property and did the housekeeping and domestic duties (including looking after the couple's two children). (See 328E to G and 330C to G.) The Court of Appeal found that these contributions could not give rise to a common intention that she would have a beneficial interest in the property.

[5] Part VI — Conclusions.

[6] Consultation Paper No. 179 completed on May 4, 2006.

[7] Paras 5.65 and 7.8.

[8] Paras 6.150–6.167.

CHAPTER 2

EXPRESS TRUSTS

In order for a declaration of trust to be enforceable, it must be in writing   **2–001**
and comply with the requirements of the Law of Property Act 1925,
s.53(1)(b). Section 53(1)(b) provides:

> "... a declaration of any trust respecting any land or any interest
> therein must be manifested and proved by some writing signed by
> some person who is able to declare such trust or by his will."

If the agreement is in writing but not signed then it is still valid but
unenforceable.[1]

For many years the Court of Appeal and others[2] have sought to encourage the use of express declarations of trust when dealing with property.

In *Carlton v Goodman*[3] Ward L.J. said: **2–002**

> "I ask in despair how often this court has to remind conveyancers
> that they would save their clients a great deal of later difficulty if
> only they would sit the purchasers down, explain the difference
> between a joint tenancy and tenancy in common, ascertain what they
> want and then expressly declare in the conveyance of transfer how
> the beneficial interest is to be held because that will be conclusive
> and save all argument. When are conveyancers going to do this as a
> matter of invariable practice? This court has urged that time after
> time. Perhaps conveyancers do not read the law reports. I will try
> one more time: ALWAYS TRY TO AGREE ON AND THEN
> RECORD HOW THE BENEFICIAL INTEREST IS TO BE
> HELD. It is not very difficult to do."[4]

---

[1] See, e.g. *Cowcher v Cowcher* [1972] 1 W.L.R. 425 at 430H to 431A. In *Roy v Roy* [1996] 1 F.L.R. 541 at 545 it was held that s.53(1) of the 1925 Act is irrelevant where a trust for sale arose only as result of a joint tenancy that had been expressly declared in a transfer. Section 53 may have to be considered in association with s.2 of Law of Property (Miscellaneous Provisions) Act 1989 — see *Yaxley v Gotts and Gotts* [1999] 2 F.L.R. 541, CA.

[2] See the Law Commission Discussion Paper "Sharing Homes" Law Com No. 278 November 2002.

[3] [2002] EWCA Civ 545 at para.44.

[4] See also *Goodman v Gallant* [1986] 1 F.L.R. 513 at 524F *per* Slade L.J.: "(This judgment) will also well illustrate the importance of the presence or absence of a declaration of trust in a conveyance into joint names and of the form of any such declaration — points which the draftsmen of such conveyances will no doubt carefully bear in mind."

2–003   The Land Registry form (TR1) (see Appendix I) now requires the parties to a property transaction to state whether they hold the property on trust for themselves beneficially as joint tenants, as tenants in common in equal shares or tenants in common in such shares as might be specified. All that is necessary is to tick the appropriate box. It is hoped that this will eventually lead to a reduction in the number of disputes on the grounds of constructive and/or resulting trusts.

Where there is an express declaration of trust the court must give effect to it, unless it is capable of rescission or rectification on the limited grounds of fraud or mistake (see further Chapter 6).[5]

2–004   In *Goodman v Gallant*[6] the Court of Appeal confirmed that in a case where there was an express declaration of trust which comprehensively declared the beneficial interests in the property or its proceeds of sale, there is no room for the application of the doctrine of resulting, implied or constructive trusts unless and until the conveyance is set aside or rectified; until that event the declaration contained in the document speaks for itself.[7] In *Goodman*, Mr and Mrs Goodman married and purchased a property in Mr Goodman's sole name but it was agreed between them that Mrs Goodman would have a 50 per cent beneficial interest in it. Mr Goodman subsequently left his wife and Mrs Goodman then began a relationship with the defendant, Mr Gallant. Mr Gallant ultimately moved into the property. Mr Goodman conveyed the freehold interest in the property to Mrs Goodman and Mr Gallant for £6,700 (the property being worth £17,000 to £18,000). The property was conveyed to them: "to hold the same unto the purchasers in fee simple as beneficial joint tenants." Clause 2 stated: "The purchasers hereby declare as follows: (a) the purchasers shall hold the property upon trust to sell the same with power to postpone the sale thereof and shall hold the net proceeds of sale and net rents and profits thereof until sale upon trust for themselves as joint tenants." The relationship between the parties then came to an end and Mrs Goodman served a written notice of severance on Mr Gallant which stated:

> "I hereby give you notice of my desire to sever as from this day the joint tenancy and equity of and in the property described in the schedule hereto now held by you and me as joint tenants both at law

---

[5] See Lord Upjohn in *Pettitt v Pettitt* [1970] A.C. 777 at 813: In the first place, the beneficial ownership of the property in question must depend upon the agreement of the parties determined at the time of its acquisition. If the property in question is land there must be some lease or conveyance which shows how it was acquired. If that document declares not merely in whom the legal title is to vest but in whom the beneficial title is to vest that necessarily concludes the question of title as between the spouses for all time, and in the absence of fraud or mistake at the time of the transaction the parties cannot go behind it at any time thereafter even on death or the break-up of the marriage. In *Gissing v Gissing* [1971] A.C. 886 at 905, Lord Diplock stated, "... Where the trust is expressly declared in the instrument by which the legal estate is transferred to the trustee or by a written declaration of trust by the trustee, the court must give effect to it."

[6] [1986] 1 F.L.R. 513.

[7] Per Slade L.J. at 517.

and in equity so that the said property shall henceforth belong to you and me in equal shares."

She then, however, issued an originating summons seeking an inquiry and declaration as to their respective shares on the basis that it was her belief that the effect of the purchase from Mr Goodman was to leave her owning three-quarters of the property and Mr Gallant one quarter. The Court of Appeal disagreed. Slade L.J. held that **2–005**

> "In the absence of any claim for rectification or rescission, the provision in the conveyance declaring that the plaintiff and the defendant were to hold the proceeds of sale of the property, 'upon trust for themselves as joint tenants' concludes the question of the respective beneficial interests of the two parties in so far as that declaration of trust, on its true construction, exhaustively declares the beneficial interests."[8]

Expressions which have been found to give rise to an express declaration of trust are: **2–006**

(i) That the purchasers "shall hold the said property upon trust to sell the same with power to postpone the sale thereof and shall hold the net proceeds of sale and other money applicable as capital and the net rents and profits thereof until sale upon trust for themselves as joint tenants" (*Wilson v Wilson*, above).

(ii) That the nominee was to hold the proceeds of sale "in trust for the purchasers as joint tenants beneficially" (*Leake v Bruzzi*).[9]

It is necessary, however, to contrast the above cases in which there have been found to be express declarations of trust with the following cases, in which the court has been unable to make such a finding.

In *Huntingford v Hobbs*[10] the transfer also contained a declaration by the parties in standard form that "the survivor of them can give a valid receipt for capital money arising on the disposition of the land." Sir Christopher Slade followed his previous judgment in *Harwood v Harwood*[11] where he had stated: **2–007**

> "In short, the form of declaration inserted in the transfer in the present case, though entirely consistent with the existence of a beneficial joint tenancy, is in our judgment no less consistent with the husband and wife holding the property as trustees for a single

---

[8] At 523D–E. The Court of Appeal followed the cases of *Wilson v Wilson* [1963] 2 All E.R. 447 (CA); *Leake v Bruzzi* [1974] 1 W.L.R. 1528 (CA) and *Pink v Lawrence* (1978) 36 P.C.R. 98 (CA).

[9] *Ibid.* at 1531.

[10] [1993] 1 F.L.R. 736.

[11] [1991] 2 F.L.R. 274.

third party. In these circumstances, we find it impossible to read the declaration as constituting, by necessary implication, the declaration of beneficial interests."[12]

In his Lordship's view, the words used in the transfer did not constitute a declaration of trust (*Harwood v Harwood* at 742G).

2–008   In *Stack v Dowden*[13] the Court of Appeal had to determine whether or not a declaration by the purchasers that the survivor of them was entitled to give a valid receipt for capital money was sufficient to give rise to an express trust that the parties held the beneficial interest as joint tenants in equity. The transfer stated:

"The Purchasers declare that the survivor of them is entitled to give a valid receipt for capital money arising from a disposition of all or part of the property."[14]

2–009   Lord Justice Chadwick held that it was not open to the court to depart from the position established by its earlier decisions in *Huntingford v Hobbs*[15] and *Harwood v Harwood*[16] and that this must be seen as a case in which the transfer of the property into the joint names of the parties contained *no* declaration of the trusts upon which they were to hold the proceeds of sale.[17]

2–010   It is suggested that the correct approach to be applied when considering a case in which the property has been purchased in the joint names of the parties is as follows:

   (i) Is there an express declaration of trust? Only when the declaration is clear, as set out at para. 2–006 above is there an express declaration that the parties intend to hold the property on trust for themselves as beneficial joint tenants or as otherwise provided. If the wording is merely to the effect that the survivor of the parties is entitled to give a valid receipt for capital money, there is no express declaration of trust to the effect that the parties hold the beneficial interest as joint tenants in equity;

---

[12] *Ibid.* at 289.

[13] [2005] EWCA Civ 857.

[14] A declaration in the above form is consistent with the right of survivorship, inherent in a joint tenancy, extending to the beneficial interests in the proceeds of sale (LPA 1925 s.36(2)). It is not apt in a case where there is a beneficial tenancy in common (LPA 1925 s.27(2)). The appropriate (and usual) declaration in a case where the parties intend from the outset that their beneficial interests shall be as tenants in common in equity — whether in equal or unequal shares — is that a valid receipt for capital monies cannot be obtained from the survivor alone. A declaration in that form will lead to a restriction on the register to that effect under s.58(3) of the Land Registration Act 1925 (*per* Chadwick L.J. at para.5).

[15] [1993] 1 F.L.R. 736.

[16] [1991] 2 F.L.R. 274.

[17] Above at para.11.

(ii) If there is no express declaration of trust, is there any evidence of what the parties said and did at the time of the acquisition, in relation to the extent of the parties' respective beneficial interests in the property?[18] In *Stack v Dowden* the Court of Appeal had to approach the appeal on the basis that there had been no discussion as to the respective shares of the parties in the property. Likewise the appellant in *Huntingford v Hobbs* was unable to argue that the parties had intended that the property would be shared equally as that submission had not been made in the lower court, and had not been the subject of cross-examination.

Where the property has been purchased in joint names, however, and particularly where there is some form of declaration to the effect that the survivor of the parties is able to give valid receipt for capital money, it is more likely that there will be some evidence which indicates that the purchasers intended themselves to be beneficial joint tenants.[19]

(iii) Only in the absence of any evidence as to an agreement as to the respective size of the parties' beneficial interests in the property should the court apply the test set out by Chadwick L.J. in *Oxley v Hiscock* (at 246F–H para.69): that is, that "each is entitled to that share which the court considers fair having regard to the whole course of dealing between them in relation to the property. And, in that context, 'the whole course of dealing between them in relation to the property' includes the arrangements which they make from time to time in order to meet the outgoings (mortgage contributions, council tax and utilities, repairs, insurance and housekeeping) which have to be met if they are to live in the property as their home."

---

[18] See *Stack v Dowden* para.25 and *Oxley v Hiscock* [2005] Fam. 211 at 246F–H.

[19] In *Stack v Dowden* Carnwath L.J., although concurring with the approach of Chadwick L.J., stated that if the Court of Appeal had been starting afresh, he could see attractions in the argument for distinguishing *Oxley* on the grounds that in the present case the parties had specifically agreed that the legal interest should be held as joint tenants. It is arguable that the presumption should be that beneficial interests should follow the legal interests in the absence of clear evidence of a contrary intention. The power of the survivor to give a receipt for capital monies points to the absence of any contrary intention (at para.78). It should be noted that *Stack v Dowden* is currently being appealed to the House of Lords.

CHAPTER 3

CONSTRUCTIVE TRUSTS

Constructive trusts are trusts imposed by the court acting in its equitable **3–001** jurisdiction to prevent unjust enrichment arising from fraud or unconscionable conduct.[1] The trust is imposed in a variety of situations, sometimes to circumvent the effects of fraud or other disreputable conduct. It has been described as "the formula through which the conscience of equity finds expression".[2] So far as cohabitation cases are concerned, the authorities in which a constructive trust has been found to exist almost exclusively concern the existence or otherwise of some intention or understanding, common to both parties, that both — not just the owner of the legal title — should have an interest in the relevant property, and reliance by the non-legal owner upon that understanding or arrangement to his/her detriment. Thus where cohabiting couples are concerned, the essence of the common intention trust is that the court will use the doctrine of the constructive trust to give effect to an imperfect agreement between one partner (C) and the other (D) to the effect that C will enjoy a beneficial interest in D's property (see *G v G (Matrimonial Property: Rights of Extended Family)* [2006] 1 F.L.R. 62 FD *per* Baron J. at 16 (para.85)). Such a trust will only arise, however, where C has acted to his detriment in reliance upon that agreement (or has acted in a way in which C and D agreed C should act in exchange for a share in the property). In this way, the constructive trust allows the successful claimant to rebut the prima facie position that the beneficial interests in the property follow the legal interests (*Crisp v Mullings* ((1976) 239 E.G. 119) *per* Russell L.J.).

A case based upon a constructive trust is most frequently deployed **3–002** where C asserts an interest in the property held in the sole name of the other (D). In cases where a property is held in the names of both parties, on the face of it the position is that each was intended to have an interest (*Crisp v Mullings* as above), though that starting point may be displaced in a case where only one of two legal title holders has in fact contributed to the purchase price.[3] Thus cases which turn on the question of whether

[1] *Binion v Evans* [1972] 1 Ch. 359 *per* Lord Denning M.R. at 368B–D, *Hussey v Palmer* [1972] 1 W.L.R. 1286 *per* Lord Denning M.R. at 1290A–B, *Van Laethem v Brooker & Anor* [2005] EWHC 1478 (Ch.), *G v G (Matrimonial Property: Rights of Extended Family* [2006] 1 F.L.R. 62 *per* Baron J. at 77 (para.86).
[2] *Beatty v Guggenheim Exploration Co* (1919) 225 N.Y. 380 *per* Cardozo J. at 386.
[3] See further Chapter 4 "Resulting Trusts", below.

a constructive trust has arisen tend to be cases where only one of two (or more) co-owners holds the legal title.[4]

3–003   As is discussed below, a claim that a constructive trust has arisen will generally involve reliance on some agreement, arrangement or understanding (whether spoken or otherwise) between the parties, or on a financial contribution to the purchase price being made by the party who does not enjoy any legal interest. In this latter case, it is equally possible for a claimant to pursue a claim to an interest under a purchase money resulting trust. However, one striking difference between the quantification of an interest under a constructive trust and of that under a resulting trust is that following the decision in *Oxley v Hiscock* ([2005] Fam. 211) the court has what amounts for practical purposes to a discretion in the quantification of the constructive trust (sometimes described as "quasi-discretionary powers"), whereas the resulting trust is quantified by reference purely to the quantum of the contributions made by each party to the purchase price. The practical result flowing from this is that where a claimant has provided less than 50 per cent of the purchase price, it will almost always be in his/her interests to advance a claim based upon the purported existence of a constructive trust rather than a resulting trust. Under a constructive trust, in most cases it will be unlikely that the extent of the interest recovered by the claimant will be less than that which (s)he would have recovered under a resulting trust — i.e. an interest commensurate with his/her contribution to the purchase price.[5] The resulting trust retains a residual role in a number of situations where a constructive trust will not arise.[6] However, the constructive trust — possibly with claims under a resulting trust or in proprietary estoppel advanced in the alternative — is the principal doctrine under which claims to proprietary interests between cohabiting couples now fall to be resolved.

Ingredients of a constructive trust

3–004   As Peter Gibson L.J. said in *Drake v Whipp* ([1996] 1 F.L.R. 826 at 830B), "all that is required for the creation of a constructive trust is that there should be a common intention that the party who is not the legal owner should have a beneficial interest and that that party should act to his or her detriment in reliance thereon." The two essential elements of a successful contention that an applicant holds an interest in the relevant property under a common intention constructive trust are therefore:

---

[4] The quantification of cases where legal title is held in the names of both parties but there is no agreement between them as to the extent of their respective interests is considered in Chapter 5 "Quantification of Beneficial Interests", below.

[5] See *Pettitt v Pettitt* [1970] A.C. 777 *per* Lord Upjohn at 814B, *Williams & Glyn's Bank v Boland* [1981] A.C. 487 *per* Lord Wilberforce at 502G; *c.f. Bull v Bull* [1955] 1 Q.B. 234.

[6] Considered further in Chapter 4 "Resulting Trusts", below.

> (i) that there was some meeting of minds (an "arrangement, agreement or understanding" — *Lloyds Bank v Rosset* [1990] 1 A.C. 107 HL *per* Lord Bridge of Harwich at 132F) as to the existence of a beneficial interest; and
>
> (ii) that the applicant has in some significant way shifted his/her position in reliance upon the commonly held intention.

Although the House of Lords has considered the question of when **3–005** constructive trusts can arise in cohabitation cases on a number of occasions (in particular in *Gissing v Gissing* ([1971] A.C. 886) and *Pettitt v Pettitt* ([1970] A.C. 777)), the most recent — and the most frequently cited — explanation of the law in the House of Lords is to be found in *Lloyds Bank v Rosset* ([1991] A.C. 107). This is the leading exposition of the circumstances in which a constructive trust will arise in cohabitation cases. Thus in *Hammond v Mitchell* ([1991] 1 W.L.R. 1127) Waite J. referred (at 1129F) to *Rosset* as providing the "template" for the court's approach to those cases where one cohabitee claims a beneficial interest in a property title to which is held in the sole name of the other.

The dispute in *Rosset* arose not between two putative co-owners, but between the spouse of the legal owner and the bank whose lending had been secured by the relevant property. The facts of *Rosset* were that the relevant property had been purchased on December 17, 1982 in the sole name of Mr Rosset. The property was on the same day charged with repayment of Mr Rosset's overdraft. In 1984, the bank's demand for repayment of the overdraft was not complied with and possession proceedings were commenced against both Mr and Mrs Rosset, who had by that time separated. Mrs Rosset, who remained living in the home, contended that she enjoyed a beneficial interest under a constructive trust. Her claim to a beneficial interest, if successful, would have provided a defence to the bank's claim for possession. The claim to an interest at first instance was based upon an express agreement, but that was rejected by the judge at trial. The judge held, however, that a common intention that Mrs Rosset should enjoy a beneficial interest could be inferred from her involvement in the renovation process which had taken place prior to completion of the purchase. Lord Bridge considered that the evidence simply did not warrant that inference. He considered that Mrs Rosset's input was perfectly consistent with a wife and mother who wanted to be in her new home before Christmas and did all she could to accelerate the process of making the house habitable.

In a speech with which the other four Law Lords simply agreed **3–006** without further comment, Lord Bridge of Harwich drew attention to what he regarded as a "critical distinction" to be drawn in cases involving disputes between former partners as to beneficial interests in the former family home. He said (at 132E–133B):

> "The first and fundamental question which must always be resolved is whether, independently of any inference to be drawn from the

conduct of the parties in the course of sharing the house as their home and managing their joint affairs, there has at any time prior to acquisition, or exceptionally at some later date, been any agreement, arrangement or understanding reached between them that the property is to be shared beneficially. The finding of an agreement or arrangement to share in this sense can only, I think, be based on evidence of express discussions between the partners, however imperfectly remembered and however imprecise their terms may have been. Once a finding to this effect is made it will only be necessary for the partner asserting a claim to a beneficial interest against the partner entitled to the legal estate to show that he or she has acted to his or her detriment or significantly altered his or her position in reliance on the agreement in order to give rise to a constructive trust or proprietary estoppel.

"In sharp contrast with this situation is the very different one where there is no evidence to support a finding of an agreement or arrangement to share, however reasonable it might have been for the parties to reach such an arrangement if they had applied their minds to the question, and where the court must rely entirely on the conduct of the parties both as the basis from which to infer a common intention to share the property beneficially and as the conduct relied on to give rise to a constructive trust. In this situation direct contributions to the purchase price by the partner who is not the legal owner, whether initially or by payment of mortgage instalments, will readily justify the inference necessary to the creation of a constructive trust. But, as I read the authorities, it is at least extremely doubtful whether anything less will do."

3–007   In other words, if both parties have contributed financially to the purchase price, the necessary "agreement arrangement or understanding" will be inferred from that fact; why else should the claimant have contributed to the purchase of a property by the defendant?[7] But if the claimant has not contributed financially to the purchase price, only express evidence of some specific discussion[8] will enable the court to find a constructive trust. In either case, a constructive trust will only arise if the claimant relied upon that agreement to his/her detriment. A claim based on non-financial contributions alone (no matter over what period of time) or based on indirect financial contributions (whereby the claimant meets certain necessary items of recurring expenditure, leaving the defendant better able to meet the mortgage payments) will — subject to the possible effect of the decision *Le Foe v Le Foe and Woolwich Plc*

---

[7] The possibility that the contribution is in fact in the nature of either a gift or a loan is considered below in Chapter 4 "Resulting Trusts".

[8] This need not necessarily amount to an agreement per se but sufficient to enable the court nonetheless to infer the existence of some agreement, arrangement or understanding — see below at 3–008 *et seq.*

([2001] 2 F.L.R. 970)[9] — seemingly fail, unless an agreement can be inferred that the indirect contributions should confer a beneficial interest.[10]

As the law appears to stand at the moment, therefore, the assertion that an interest under a constructive trust has arisen can only be justified by reference to the two situations envisaged by Lord Bridge in *Rosset* — express discussions justifying an inferred common intention ("*Lloyds Bank v Rosset* limb one") or imputation of a common intention based upon direct contributions to the purchase price ("*Lloyds Bank v Rosset* limb two").[11] Meritorious cases which do not fit within either limb of *Rosset* might give rise to a successful claim in proprietary estoppel even if no constructive trust is made out (see further Chapter 6 below, "Proprietary Estoppel").

Lloyds Bank v Rosset "limb one" — agreement evidenced by express discussions

At its simplest, determining whether there has been some agreement, arrangement or understanding to the effect that the beneficial interest in the property will be shared will be a straightforward matter of assessing the evidence before the court trying the claimant's application.   **3–008**

Perhaps the classic illustration of limb one is to be found in *Stokes v Anderson* ([1991] 1 F.L.R. 391). There, the relevant property was initially held in the name of Mr and Mrs Stokes, who were in the process of divorcing. The evidence of Mr Stokes' new partner, Miss Anderson, was that she had agreed with Mr Stokes that she would advance sums of £5,000 and £7,000 with which Mr Stokes would buy out his wife's share in the property. Mr Stokes contended that the payments had been by way of loans. The judge however accepted Miss Anderson's evidence, which included the suggestion that Mr Stokes had agreed that Miss Anderson's name "would go on the deeds when it was all sorted out". Once the judge had rejected Mr Stokes' case that the payments had been loan advances, it would on the face of it have been possible for Miss Anderson to establish an interest under limb two quite apart from the express agreement. Although the Court of Appeal allowed Mr Stokes appeal as to the quantification of Miss Anderson's share, Nourse L.J. assessed the case (at 398A) as being: **3–009**

"a clear example of what in *Grant v Edwards* [1986] Ch. 638 I thought, perhaps wrongly, was the rarer class of case ... where the parties have orally declared themselves in such a way as to make plain their common intention that the claimant should have a ben-

---

[9] Considered below at 3–073.

[10] See *Ivin v Blake* [1995] 1 F.L.R. 70, which placed considerable reliance upon the Northern Ireland decision of Lord MacDermott in *McFarlane v McFarlane* [1972] N.I.L.R. 59. These cases are referred to in more detail at para. 3–075.

[11] The phrases "limb one" and "limb two" were coined by Balcombe L.J. in *Halifax Building Society v Brown* [1996] 1 F.L.R. 103 at 107F.

eficial interest in the property ... it is unnecessary to look beyond the payments of £5,000 and £7,000 in order to find conduct which amounted to acting upon the common intention by Miss Anderson."

Similarly, in *Chapman v Chapman* ([1969] 1 W.L.R. 1367 CA) Edmund Davies L.J. observed[12] that where the parties had expressly agreed that H would pay for certain things (i.e. the mortgage repayments and other expenses of running the home), and W would pay for others (i.e. food and groceries) that arrangement "threw a flood of light on the intentions of the parties regarding the beneficial interests in the matrimonial home".

3–010   Logically, the first issue which falls to be determined in limb one cases is whether the agreement or promise which C relies upon was ever in fact made. It is however perhaps over-simplistic to say that this type of case always depends upon which is the more credible of two parties who disagree as to what was discussed and agreed at the relevant time, although many such cases turn on nothing else. In a number of cases it has been held in the higher courts that notwithstanding evidence that no agreement in terms was ever expressly reached, the discussions which did take place nonetheless manifest an intention common to both parties that the property should be held for the benefit of them both. These authorities illustrate that where there are discussions, the upshot of which is that one party should not join in the purchase or become a joint owner of the relevant property, the *nature* of the discussion rather than its conclusion might prove the best evidence as to the existence or otherwise of a common intention. Thus, as appears below, in a number of cases the Court of Appeal has overturned findings of fact made by the judge hearing the case that there was no common intention, on the basis of some agreed discussion which demonstrated the existence of some common intention albeit that no agreement was reached in terms.[13]

Reasons for not putting title in both parties' names

3–011   In particular, a discussion between the parties as to why a particular property should only be purchased in the name of one of the parties might of itself justify the inference that both would, but for that reason, have joined in the purchase. This phenomenon can be seen most clearly in operation where the parties were in a stable relationship prior to the acquisition of the property, but can also apply where, perhaps some time after the claimant has moved into the defendant's property, the parties discuss whether the property should be transferred into their joint names. In either case, where the parties expressly discuss ownership but conclude that for some reason or other title should be held in the names of one party only, the mere fact of the discussions might of itself amount to evidence from which the requisite common intention can be inferred. In

---

[12] At 1370H–1371B.

[13] It is not necessary that any agreement be recorded in writing: see above, Chapter 2 "Express Trusts" and see Law of Property Act 1925, s.53(2).

Grant v Edwards ([1986] Ch. 638) for instance, the Court of Appeal was concerned with a female partner who was told by the male partner that the property should be purchased in his name alone because if the property was bought in their joint names, that might operate to her prejudice in her ongoing divorce proceedings. The judge at first instance had held that there was no agreement "as such" between the parties and therefore no interest under a constructive trust could arise. On appeal, however, Nourse L.J. observed[14]:

> "these facts appear to me to raise a clear inference that there was an understanding between the plaintiff and the defendant, or a common intention, that the plaintiff was to have some sort of proprietary interest in the house; otherwise no excuse for not putting her name on to the title deeds would have been needed."

The same approach was adopted in *Eves v Eves* ([1975] 1 W.L.R. 1338) where the female partner's age (she was under 21 at the time of the purchase of the property) was advanced as a reason for the property being purchased in the male partner's name alone, and in *Heseltine v Heseltine* ([1971] 1 W.L.R. 342) where tax reasons were advanced as the reason for purchase in one party's name alone. *Hammond v Mitchell* ([1991] 1 W.L.R. 1127) is another illustration of a case in which tax reasons were advanced by D as a reason for purchasing the property in his sole name; he nonetheless assured C that the property would be "half yours once we are married". Waite J. held that those representations evidenced an intention that the property would be shared beneficially.

The important feature of these cases appears to be the mere fact of the **3–012** discussion between the parties, inasmuch as it evidences some expectation or understanding that both were in fact intended to have some share. In *Rosset* Lord Bridge clearly referred to the fact of the discussion, rather than any agreement which the parties expressly reached, as being the evidential basis of the common intention constructive trust. It is not necessary for a constructive trust to arise for the parties to have agreed in terms that each should have an interest. It *is* necessary however that the parties have at least talked about the subject. In *B v B (Real Property: Assessment of Interests)* ([1988] 2 F.L.R. 490), for instance, H caused W to become angry by suggesting at the time of the purchase that his name only should appear on the deeds. At trial, H suggested that W's anger was because she wanted to be seen by any third parties who had sight of the deeds as having a share in the responsibility for the house. That explanation was flatly rejected by the court as being unrealistic. Although purchased in H's name alone, W had been the driving force behind both the initial purchase and subsequent improvements, funded by H, to the property. The intention that each should have an interest was evidenced by W's provision of "stimulus and considerable personal effort". In that

---

[14] At 649.

case, it was the way in which W reacted to the suggestion that her name should not appear on the deeds which justified the inference of a common intention, not any agreement as to how the property should be held, as plainly W did not agree with H's proposal that the property should be in his name alone.

3–013   Nor is it the case that the court's ability to infer a common intention from the fact of discussions is affected by the validity (or otherwise) of the reasons for the conclusion that one party should alone be the legal titleholder, provided only that those were the factors which informed the decision to complete the purchase in the name of one party alone. In *Oxley v Hiscock* ([2005] Fam. 211) at first instance the judge found that the property had been purchased in D's name alone to guard against the possibility of C's ex-husband making a claim in the event of her death against her interest in the property. Chadwick L.J. observed (at 217 (para. 14)), however, that a purchase by D alone would, of itself, neither alter any interest in the property which C enjoyed by reason of her contribution to the purchase price, nor affect C's right to any share in the proceeds of sale which the parties might otherwise have agreed, nor defeat any claim by C's former husband in the event of her death to whatever interest in the property she did have. He continued (at 217–218):

> "The relevance of the judge's finding, as it seems to me, is not that, in the context of a possible claim by Mrs Oxley's former husband, the property was transferred into the sole name of Mr Hiscock so that it would not appear on the face of the register that Mrs Oxley was likely to have some beneficial interest in it; nor that the fact that the property was transferred into the sole name of Mr Hiscock 'in no way actually altered the reality of the situation'. Neither party had suggested that it did. The true relevance is that her finding that there was a discussion between the parties as to whose name should appear on the registered title in the context of a possible claim by Mrs Oxley's former husband is only explicable on the basis that they both intended — and expressed that intention to the other — that each should have a beneficial share in the property."

The crucial point is that the parties must have discussed the question of interests in the property, whether or not the upshot of the discussions was that the claimant would have an interest and whether or not the parties agreed with each other (e.g. *B v B (Real property: assessment of interests)*, above) as to what would appear on the face of the title deeds. The common intention must, in other words, be communicated between the parties even though there may not be agreement in terms (*Springette v Defoe* ([1992] 2 F.L.R. 388) *per* Dillon L.J. at 393).

Contemporaneous documentation

Even where the parties fail to recollect any particular discussion as to   **3–014**
beneficial ownership, a beneficial interest may be established if other
evidence makes it plain that there must have been some understanding
between the parties, whether the product of recollected discussions or
otherwise. In this respect, the evidential value of contemporaneous documentation can scarcely be overstated. The relevant conveyancing file in
particular can be of crucial importance (and will seldom be irrelevant) in
determining the presence or absence of a common intention. In *Re
Densham* ([1975] 1 W.L.R. 1519), for instance, the whole tenor of the
correspondence in the solicitors' conveyancing file demonstrated a plain
intention that the property should be shared beneficially, even though the
property was conveyed to a single purchaser. By contrast, in *Cowcher v
Cowcher* ([1972] 1 W.L.R. 425) a single letter from the legal purchaser to
the solicitors acting on the purchase, which contained reference to "we"
and "us", did not amount to satisfactory evidence of an intention to
share the property beneficially with his wife. Similarly, in *Otway v Gibbs*
((unreported) [2000] UKPC 39 (October 25, 2000)) Lord Millett said at
para.18:

> "Cohabiting couples, like married couples, speak of 'our home' and
> 'our money' meaning 'the home where we live' and 'the money we
> live on', without distinguishing between what belongs to one or the
> other or both."

While it will almost without exception be necessary to examine the   **3–015**
solicitor's conveyancing file (see further Chapter 8 below, "Practice and
Procedure"), that may not be the only source of contemporaneous doc-
umentary evidence as to the parties' intentions. Diary entries, correspondence (either between the parties or to others) and the like may be of
use in demonstrating an intention to share. The nature of the material is
probably of secondary importance provided the relevant documentation
is (a) genuinely contemporaneous, and (b) can be sensibly explained only
on the basis that some relevant discussions must have taken place in
circumstances where both parties understood that each would have a
beneficial interest.

That said, the execution of a will (indicating for instance that in the
event of D's death, C should inherit the relevant property) has been a
factor which has in many cases served more to obscure rather than clarify
the parties' true intentions. It is relatively common for the execution of,
for instance, mutual wills to be prayed in aid as evidence of an intention
that each party should have an interest in the property. However the
authorities do not generally support the conclusion that the creation of
an interest *inter vivos* is evidenced by a party's intentions for his/her
property post mortem. Thus in *Windeler v Whitehall* ([1990] 2 F.L.R. 505)
Millett J. was concerned with a Will executed by D leaving the bulk of his
estate to C. It was submitted on C's behalf that this was evidence which

illustrated the common intention that C should have some interest in the property. Millett J. said (at 515F):

> "It was nothing of the sort. It was a recognition of some moral obligation at that time on (D)'s part to provide for (C) if he should die unexpectedly and while circumstances remained the same. It was completely consistent with the absence of any intention on his part to make a present irrevocable disposition of an interest in his house."

Similarly, in *Lissimore v Downing* ([2003] 2 F.L.R. 308), D had executed a will which on his death would leave C with an interest in the relevant property. C relied on that as evidence of a common intention or conduct necessary to found an estoppel. HHJ Norris Q.C. (sitting as a Deputy High Court Judge) considered that what D intended on his death did not impact upon the position during his life.[15]

3–016   There is nonetheless a distinction to be drawn between on the one hand not mistaking a party's intentions for his property on his death for an intention as to what should happen in life, and on the other hand ensuring that justice is nonetheless done where certain arrangements are made on the basis of agreements or representations as to what will happen to the property on death, which are relied upon by the claimant to his detriment. In the latter case, the courts have demonstrated that even if no interest arises under a constructive trust, other remedies may be available. Thus in *Gillett v Holt* ([2001] Ch. 210) D had assured C that he would leave C his property in his Will. C relied on those assurances to his detriment. It was held in the Court of Appeal that it would be unconscionable for D to deal with his property in a way which was inconsistent with his earlier assurances and the doctrine of proprietary estoppel was invoked in circumstances to give effect to D's assurances (discussed further in Chapter 6 below, "Proprietary Estoppel"). Similarly, in *Parker v Clark* ([1960] 1 W.L.R. 286) the first Claimant was the niece of the Defendants. They had agreed that C and her husband should move in to the property and effectively act as D's carers (both of whom were elderly and in poor health), in return for which the property would be left to the claimants on the death of the survivor of the defendants. That agreement was held to be specifically enforceable as a contract and relief given in terms of a contractual remedy rather than on the basis of a proprietary interest.

---

[15] Different considerations apply in circumstances where, having made mutual wills, one testator dies and the second testator thereafter seeks to alter his will. A constructive trust may arise in relation to the estate of the second testator: see e.g. *In re Dale (deceased)* [1994] Ch. 31.

Ascertaining the true intentions of the parties

Even assuming that on the facts of a case, C can point to an ostensible **3–017** agreement or arrangement, a further difficulty confronts the practitioner in terms of establishing whether the agreement or similar relied upon by C was intended by D (and taken by C as such) to have the effect of conferring or varying proprietary rights. Since this type of constructive trust arises on the basis of what was C and D's common intention in relation to the property, it would appear to follow that the intention must be one which D genuinely held. It will perhaps rarely be the case that parties who are involved in an emotional relationship put their relationship as co-proprietors on any kind of formal footing by for instance drawing up formal express declarations of interest, unless perhaps this occurs during the process of purchasing the property on the specific advice of their conveyancing solicitor. Far more common are cases where the agreement is reached in relatively informal circumstances, often in the context of wider discussions about the parties' overall relationship. Thus as Waite J. observed in *Hammond v Mitchell* ([1991] 1 W.L.R. 1127) at 1139D:

> "The primary emphasis accorded by the law in cases of this kind to express discussions between the parties ('however imperfectly remembered and however imprecise their terms') means that the tenderest exchanges of a common law courtship may assume an unforeseen significance many years later when they are brought under equity's microscope and subjected to an analysis under which many thousands of pounds of value may be liable to turn on fine questions as to whether the relevant words were spoken in earnest or in dalliance and with or without representational intent."

The discussions relied on may even be conversations involving others, for **3–018** instance reference by D to "our house" or "our home" in conversations with friends or relatives. Although the use of the words "my" or "our" house might have been intended to mean "the house where I/we live"[16] it might equally have been intended to mean "the house I/we own". As HHJ Norris Q.C. (sitting as a Deputy Judge in the Chancery Division) observed in *Churchill v Roach* ([2004] 2 F.L.R. 989) at 996H, it is "dangerous to draw from social 'chit chat' the conclusion that parties are making irrevocable declarations as to in relation to their legal interests". Whilst this probably applies *a fortiori* where the words used are ambiguous, the difficulty in many cases is that there is little which readily enables the practitioner to differentiate between the tender exchanges which were intended to settle (or at least evidence) arrangements for future property interests on the one hand, and mere social "chit chat" on the other.

[16] As *per* Lord Millett's suggestion in *Otway v Gibbs* (unreported) [2000] UKPC 39 (October 25, 2000): see above at 3–014.

3–019   Equally, it is not difficult to imagine that in some cases the owner of the legal interest might aver that whatever may have been said during perhaps the early days of the couple's relationship, there was never any genuine intention on the part of the legal owner that the claimant would acquire an interest. Whether D allowed C to believe that he/she would have an interest in property which in fact D never intended should arise, or whether in the course of proceedings relating to the beneficial interests in the property D conveniently but falsely avers that there was never any such intention, is perhaps a somewhat academic distinction. In such cases, where there is agreement as to what was said, but there remains some question as to the genuine underlying intention, the courts apply effectively an objective test. In *Green v Green* ((2003) 5 I.T.E.L.R. 888 PC) Lord Hope of Craighead explained the matter in this way (at para.11):

> "The relevant intention is that which a reasonable man would draw from the parties' words or conduct. It is for the court to determine what inferences can reasonably be drawn, and each case must depend on its own facts."

3–020   In practice the courts have regard to the ordinary meaning of the words actually used as the guide to the real intention, rather than any suggestion to the contrary. It is unlikely therefore that, where D uses one of the phrases commonly found in the reports of cases of this type such as "it's half yours anyway" or "it's as much yours as it is mine" without genuinely intending that C should have any interest at all, that the court would allow the absence of a genuine intention on D's part at the relevant time to stand in the way of granting relief to C. This was Lord Denning's appraisal of the situation in *Eves v Eves* ([1975] 1 W.L.R. 1338), where D had led C to believe that she was too young to acquire a legal interest and had said that the property would be put into joint names when C was 21. The judge at first instance had described that as a trick. Lord Denning dealt with the issue (at 1342E) by observing that even though D had never actually intended that C should have a share, "he should be judged by what he told her — by what he led her to believe — and not by his own intent which he kept to himself." It is possible that the same result could be achieved by reference to the doctrine of proprietary estoppel even if on the facts of *Eves* no constructive trust had arisen.[17]

3–021   An important issue, where there are questions raised over the intention underlying the discussions or agreement relied on, is therefore the reasonableness of the claimant's belief that he/she would acquire an interest in the relevant property. If, having regard to the discussions etc. which took place between the parties, it was unreasonable for C to believe that what was said indicated/evidenced an intention that (s)he should acquire a beneficial interest, the constructive trust will not arise. Lord Diplock

---

[17] Although the decision in *Eves* appears to predate the landmark decision of the Court of Appeal in *Crabb v Arun DC* (see below Chapter 6 "Proprietary Estoppel").

made this point in *Gissing v Gissing* ([1971] A.C. 889) when he said at 906B–D:

> "the relevant intention of each party is the intention which was reasonably understood to be manifested by that party's words or conduct notwithstanding that he did not consciously formulate that intention in his own mind or even acted with some different intention which he did not communicate to the other party. On the other hand, *he is not bound by any inference which the other party draws as to his intention unless that inference is one which can reasonably be drawn from his words or conduct*" (emphasis added).

A defence advanced on that basis was plainly accepted by Mann J. as being well founded in law in *Cox v Jones* ([2004] 2 F.L.R. 1010 at 1035, para.44), but was not made out on the facts of that particular case. Where any ambiguity exists in relation to the legal owner's true intention, it may be possible to draw inferences as to the true intention held prior to purchase of the relevant property from the owner's conduct post-purchase (see *Burns v Burns* [1984] Ch. 317 *per* May L.J. at 344G–H).   **3–022**

The agreement or promise relied on must relate to proprietary interest rather than for instance mere occupation rights. In *Lloyds Bank v Rosset* ([1991] A.C. 107) the arrangements which existed as between Mr and Mrs Rosset were simply that they would occupy the property as their home. Lord Bridge considered (at 130D) that such an intention simply did not bear upon proprietary rights in the property.

Presumptions

The operation of presumptions, in particular the presumption of advancement, in cases where legal title is held in the name of one of two putative co-owners should not be overlooked, even though since *Pettitt v Pettitt* ([1970] A.C. 777 HL) there have been few if any cases where (in particular) the presumption of advancement has been of decisive effect. This issue is discussed below in Chapter 4 below, "Resulting Trusts".   **3–023**

Lloyds Bank v Rosset limb two — direct contributions to the purchase price

Where there is no express agreement, and no evidence of discussions from which an agreement, arrangement or understanding between the parties can be inferred, the court may nonetheless infer a tacit common intention from direct contributions to the purchase price by the non-owner.[18] The inference which should be drawn from the relevant conduct is that which a reasonable person would objectively draw from the words and conduct of the parties at the relevant time.[19] As Lord Bridge observed in *Rosset*,   **3–024**

---

[18] The phrase "tacit common intention" appears in Mustill L.J.'s judgment in *Grant v Edwards* [1986] Ch. 638 at 651G.

[19] *Burns v Burns* [1984] Ch. 317 at 336F *per* May L.J.; *c.f. Green v Green* (2003) 5 I.T.E.L.R. 888 P.C. *per* Lord Hope of Craighead at 894D–E (para.11).

direct financial contributions will "readily justify" the necessary inference.

Communication of intention between the parties

3–025 Given that the essence of the common intention constructive trust is that there is some meeting of minds on the question of beneficial interests, in both "limb one" and "limb two" cases it is necessary for the party asserting an interest to show that the common intention has in some way been communicated between the parties. This is relatively straightforward in limb one cases, where the relevant discussions will ordinarily satisfy the need for the relevant intention to have been communicated between the parties.[20]

In limb two cases, the relevant common intention is inferred from conduct. Whilst in such cases *ex hypothesi* there will not have been any express discussions between the parties as regards beneficial interests, this does not obviate the need to show that the relevant intention in some way has been communicated between the parties. The way in which this requirement is satisfied is generally by evidence that the conduct from which the common intention is inferred has been communicated between the parties. Where for instance C unilaterally takes it upon himself to make contributions towards mortgage repayments, that will not of itself justify the inference of a common intention: equity will not, according to the well-known maxim, assist a volunteer. Where D knows of and acquiesces in that arrangement, however, it will be much easier for the court to draw the necessary inference.

3–026 The absence of any communication was fatal to the appellant's case in *Lightfoot v Lightfoot Brown* [2005] 2 P. & C.R. 377 (discussed further below at 3–036) where, despite making a significant payment towards the capital debt, the appellant's claim to a beneficial interest failed in circumstances where the fact of that payment had not been communicated to the respondent. Arden L.J. commented that the decision of the Court of Appeal in *Oxley v Hiscock* [2005] Fam. 211 had not had the effect of dispensing with the need for a common intention to be communicated between the parties to a purported constructive trust (at para.27). In *Gissing v Gissing* ([1971] A.C. 886 at 906 B–D) (cited above) Lord Diplock had emphasised that an intention could be communicated by one party to another by way of words *or* conduct, and what was important was the intention which was reasonably understood by C to be manifested by D's words or conduct. Thus the fact that D might not have consciously formulated the necessary intention in his own mind, or even acted with some different intention which he did not communicate to D would not prevent C from reasonably concluding that D was of the same mind as regards beneficial interests.

---

[20] Albeit that it is not necessary that such communications result in a clear agreement in terms that C is to have an interest in D's property.

In *Ahmed v Gould* ([2005] EWCA Civ 1829) the parties (brother and **3–027** sister) had agreed that C would buy a property which D would occupy, and that D would be entitled to buy the property at market rate at some point in the future. Very shortly after the purchase of the property was completed by C, D paid a sum equal to around 50 per cent of the purchase price into C's bank account. He did not inform C of that. D contended that the payment either represented a contribution to the purchase price or a part payment towards the purchase of the property from C. It was held however that in the absence of any agreement as to the basis upon which the payment was made, it was impossible to say that there was a common intention that D was intended by both to enjoy a beneficial interest in the property.

Referability

In modern times it is comparatively rare that property is purchased by **3–028** cohabiting couples without the assistance of mortgage finance; thus cases under limb two generally involve either payment of at least part of the initial deposit or costs of purchase, or payment of mortgage instalments, or bringing about (either by financing or directly undertaking) improvements which add to the value of the property, or by some other financial contribution. Unfortunately it is not always clear what a party *has* paid for.

It is a fundamental requirement under limb two that the relevant contribution(s) must do more than merely relate generally to the property or to the relationship between the parties; the contribution must be directly referable to the *acquisition* thereof.[21] Equally, payments which might reasonably be made by one party in a relationship, e.g. for holidays, restaurants, theatre tickets, etc. on the basis that the other party pays the mortgage, do not evidence a contribution to the purchase price, even indirectly.

The classic statement of the law in this respect is perhaps that of Lord **3–029** Diplock in *Gissing v Gissing* ([1971] A.C. 886) who said (at 909):

> "Where the wife has made no initial contribution to the cash deposit and legal charges and no direct contribution to the mortgage instalments nor any adjustment to her contribution to the other expenses of the household *which it can be inferred was referable to the acquisition of the house*, there is in the absence of evidence of an express agreement between the parties no material to justify the court in inferring that it was the common intention of the parties that she should have any beneficial interest in a matrimonial home conveyed into the sole name of the husband, merely because she continued to contribute out of her own earnings or private income to other expenses of the household" (emphasis added).

---

[21] The possibility that funds are provided by way of a gift or a loan, neither of which would be consistent with a claim to an interest under *Lloyds Bank v Rosset* limb two, is discussed in detail in Chapter 4 below, "Resulting Trusts".

In *Richards v Dove* [1974] 1 All E.R. 888 Walton J. rejected the suggestion that C's contributions towards monthly expenses evidenced a common intention that she should enjoy an interest: he categorised the financial relationship between the parties as simply one of mutual convenience.[22] In *Winkworth v Edward Baron Developments* ([1986] 1 W.L.R. 1512) the House of Lords considered the payments made by C to reduce the overdraft of the company in which he was a major shareholder were not specifically referable to the acquisition of the property, even though the company had purchased the property which had been used by C and her husband as their matrimonial home.[23] Equally, general support by one cohabitant of another in various walks of life will not give rise to a beneficial interest without more (see below, "mortgage contributions").

3–030   In *R. v Robson* ((1991) 92 Cr.App.R. 1) the Court of Appeal was concerned with the beneficial interests in a property held in the name of the defendant's mother, in the context of an order for confiscation pursuant to the Drug Trafficking Offences Act 1986. The defendant had made a periodic contribution which was in fact applied by his mother towards the mortgage repayments. The Court of Appeal held that in the circumstances of that case, the mere fact of a financial contribution was not enough to establish a beneficial interest per se. The fundamental question was whether the intention of the parties was that the payments should be allocated towards the cost of capital acquisition. That would appear to be an issue of fact which can only be resolved by reference to all the circumstances in which the contribution is made.

One issue which frequently arises is the purchase of furniture, domestic appliances or the like for the home by the non-legal owner. Whilst such purchases may be relevant in terms of the analysis (post *Oxley v Hiscock*, discussed further below in Chapter 5 "Quantification of Beneficial Interests") of the extent of any beneficial interest, the cost of buying such items has not in the reported cases enabled the court to impute a common intention to the parties that the claimant beneficial interest. Domestic appliances and the like can, after all, be taken away by the purchaser on the breakdown of the relationship. Thus in *Gissing v Gissing* ([1971] A.C. 886) Lord Diplock said:

> "The court is not entitled to infer a common intention (as to beneficial interests) from the mere fact that she provided chattels for joint use in the new matrimonial home; and there is nothing in the conduct of the parties at the time of the purchase which supports such an inference."[24]

---

[22] In *Eves v Eves* [1975] 1 W.L.R. 1338 at 1342C Lord Denning M.R. expressed the view that *Richards v Dove* had been decided on its own special facts and was not of any general application.
[23] c.f. *Lightfoot v Lightfoot Brown* [2005] 2 P. & C.R. 377 at 384 (para.24).
[24] At 910G–H. Even though contribution towards the purchase of chattels does not of itself justify the inference of a contribution towards the purchase of the relevant property, plainly questions of ownership of the chattels arise in these circumstances. This is considered in detail below in Chapter 7 "Personal Obligations Between Co-owners".

Likewise, payment of bills and so forth will not without more justify **3–031** the inference of a common intention[25]: only payments directly referable to the acquisition of the property (rather than payments relating to the ongoing occupation of that property) will suffice.[26]

In *Burns v Burns* ([1984] Ch.317) Fox L.J. considered that C's contributions towards various household expenses (including payment of grocery bills, rates, telephone bills and purchase of domestic "white goods" and soft furnishings) did not demonstrate a common intention of the sort which would, to put the matter in post-*Rosset* terms, suffice in terms of limb two. "What is needed," Fox L.J. continued (at 328H) "is evidence of a payment or payments by the plaintiff which it can be inferred was referable to the acquisition of the house." He added (at 329C):

> "a payment could be said to be referable to the acquisition of the house if *for example* the payer either (a) pays part of the purchase price, or (b) contributes regularly to the mortgage instalments, or (c) pays off part of the mortgage, or (d) makes a substantial financial contribution to the family expenses so as to enable the mortgage instalments to be paid" (emphasis added).

The italicised words indicate that Fox L.J. did not appear to consider that this is an exhaustive list of payments which could be considered referable to the acquisition of the relevant property.

The decision in *Burns* has been criticised in a number of quarters[27] as **3–032** producing an unfair result, bearing in mind the domestic contribution made by Mrs Burns over 19 years (including devoting much of her time to the care of the parties' children). However, the authorities demonstrate that sympathy alone is no basis on which to found a beneficial interest. As Millett J. said in *Windeler v Whitehall* ([1990] 2 F.L.R. 505), "it is not enough for (C) to persuade me that she deserves to have such a share. She must satisfy me that she already owns it."

The claim, and the contribution on which the claim is based, must relate to a specific property: the court does not enjoy a general discretion to divide the assets of one partner so as to achieve a fair overall result other than in matrimonial cases. The interest must flow from a specific contribution to the acquisition or preservation of specific property. As Scott J. said (in *Layton v Martin* ([1986] 2 F.L.R. 227) at 237B), the need to demonstrate specific contributions relating to a specific property "lies at the heart of the circumstances which create the claimant's equitable

---

[25] See *Mollo v Mollo* [2000] W.T.L.R. 227.

[26] Although again, this is not to say that where an interest can be established for other reasons, that payment of household bills cannot be taken into account in quantifying such interest: see further Chapter 5 "Quantification of Beneficial Interests".

[27] E.g *Sharing Homes* Law Com No 217 at paras 2.108, *Cohabitation: The Case for Reform* Law Society, July 2002, Bridge, *The Property Rights of Cohabitants — Where do We Go From Here?* [2002] Fam. Law 743, Burles, *Promises, Promises — Burns v Burns 20 years On* [2003] Fam. Law 834.

interest in the specific assets in question". This requirement however will not necessarily be elevated to the point whereby an otherwise meritorious claim is effectively defeated by a technicality. In *Chan Pui Chun v Leung Kam Ho* ([2003] 1 F.L.R. 23), for example, C and D agreed (while D was in prison) that D would share "everything he had" with C if she would look after certain business ventures which were on foot during D's incarceration and organise his bail and appeal. Despite the absence of any specific promise relating to the property in which C later claimed a half interest, and some uncertainty as to whether D's promise extended to other projects undertaken by D, Jonathan Parker L.J. considered that the agreement was not so vague as to preclude the court from granting equitable relief in relation to it.

Payment of a deposit etc.

3–033   An initial cash contribution at the time of the original purchase of a property is perhaps the clearest instance of a case where the existence of a common intention will be "readily" inferred.[28] Although evidential difficulties about where the cash deposit originates will frequently arise in practice, the authorities do not indicate any distinction between a contribution made by the non-legal owner from his/her own resources, and a gift from others (such as parents or relatives) to the non-legal owner which is then used in the purchase of the property.

3–034   *Midland Bank v Cooke* ([1995] 2 F.L.R. 915) and *McHardy v Warren* ([1994] 2 F.L.R. 338) are both examples of cases where the relevant contribution was treated as having emanated from the parties, even though the monies in fact originated from others. In *Midland Bank v Cooke* the relevant property had been purchased in H's sole name, but the deposit was at least in part funded by a wedding gift made by H's parents. There had been no discussion or agreement between H and W at the time of the acquisition as to the basis upon which the property was held, or as to the extent of their respective beneficial interests. It was held that the wedding gift should be treated as having been made to H and W equally, and therefore each was regarded as having contributed half of that gift. In *McHardy & Sons v Warren* again the property was purchased with a deposit which had been a wedding gift from H's father. Dillon LJ held that it was an "irresistible conclusion" that all three — H, W and H's father — had intended that W should have a equal share in the property purchased in H's sole name. A similar conclusion was reached in *Halifax Building Society v Brown* [1996] 1 F.L.R. 103. The difficulty which faces the claimant who relies on a contribution made from joint resources is likely to be an evidential one; findings of fact that the wedding gifts had been made to one party alone would have left each of Mrs Warren, Mrs Cooke, and Mrs Brown without any interest in their respective properties, much less 50 per cent.

[28] As in *Gissing v Gissing* [1971] AC 886 at 907; see also *Re Densham* [1975] 1 W.L.R. 1519 and *Halifax Building Society v Brown* [1996] 1 F.L.R. 103 *per* Balcombe L.J. at 109D.

McHardy v Warren ([1994] 2 F.L.R. 338) and *Halifax Building Society*   **3–035**
v Brown ([1996] 1 F.L.R. 103) (in particular *per* Balcombe L.J. at 108B)
also demonstrate that where the deposit relates to one property which is
later sold and the proceeds of sale are used to purchase a further property, the contribution to the purchase of the first house can justify the
imputation of a common intention in relation to the second. Equally,
evidence of some specific agreement or arrangement in relation to the first
property will, in the absence of any evidence of a contrary intention,
generally lead to the conclusion that the same intention was held in
relation to the later property.[29]

The factual difficulty as to whether a contribution has been made by
way of a gift or loan is discussed in detail below in Chapter 4 "Resulting
Trusts".[30] Ordinarily, however, money provided by way of a loan will not
give rise to a proprietary interest save insofar as the property may be
security for the loan (*Re Sharpe* ([1980] 1 W.L.R. 219)). Nonetheless,
funds which are initially advanced by way of loan may nonetheless
become contributions which would justify the inference of a common
intention, if the intention of the parties is that a proprietary interest in the
relevant property should arise in the place of the contractual obligation
to repay the loan. This is essentially the situation which arose in *Risch v
McFee* [1991] 1 F.L.R. 105. In that case, a loan made from C to D was
neither repaid, nor was any demand for repayment or offer of payment
made. A beneficial interest was established by reason of a further advance
which enabled D to repay the mortgage. It was held that although the
earlier payment "started life" as a loan (*per* Balcombe L.J. at 110G), once
it was established that C had a beneficial interest in the house, the loan
advance would be regarded as part of her contribution.

There are few reported cases where a financial contribution at around   **3–036**
the time of purchase does not give rise to a constructive trust. However, it
can be dangerous to assume, from the mere fact that some payment has
been made, that the suggestion that a constructive trust has arisen is
incapable of being successfully resisted. Thus in *Ahmed v Gould* ([2005]
EWCA Civ 1829) Jacob L.J. pithily observed (at para.7) that "you
cannot create a beneficial interest by just paying money into somebody's
bank account". A similar point arose in *Lightfoot v Lightfoot Brown*
([2005] 2 P. & C.R. 377). There, the parties had been married, and the
relevant property was transferred to W as part of the divorce settlement.
The parties reconciled (but did not remarry) and H moved back in to the
property. He paid about £24,000 towards mortgage repayments and paid
a lump sum of £41,000 to reduce the capital debt owed under the
mortgage. The relationship between the parties broke down, and H
asserted that the payments justified the inference of a common intention
constructive trust. At first instance, the judge found that the mortgage

---

[29] *Muetzel v Muetzel* [1970] 1 W.L.R. 188, *c.f. Bothe v Amos* [1976] Fam 46, *Protheroe v
Protheroe* [1968] 1 W.L.R. 519.
[30] See Chapter 4 para.4–010 *et seq.*

repayments were paid in lieu of a maintenance award in W's favour made during the divorce proceedings which H had not paid. The £41,000 reduction was found by the judge to have been made so that the outstanding balance of the mortgage debt qualified for tax relief, and was further made without the knowledge of W. The judge therefore rejected H's claim to a beneficial interest. The Court of Appeal accepted that these were findings which were open to the judge to make on the evidence before him, and dismissed H's appeal against the finding that he had no interest in the property, despite his conduct in substantially reducing the capital debt.

Discounts to the purchase price

3–037 A number of reported cases contain consideration of the effect of discounts under the "right to buy" scheme (under the Housing Act 1985) whereby local authority tenants are able to take advantage of periods spent as tenants of a local authority in quantifying any discount which might be available on the purchase of the relevant local authority property. The existence of the discount is generally regarded as a relevant factor in the quantification of beneficial interest.[31] However, there is no reason to conclude that the existence of a discount and the circumstances in which it arose cannot also be taken into account in terms of identifying a contribution in terms of limb two of *Lloyds Bank v Rosset*.[32] That, after all, underscored the reasoning of the Court of Appeal in *Springette v Defoe* ([1992] 2 F.L.R. 388).[33] Although *Springette* has been held to have been wrongly decided insofar as it concerns the quantification of beneficial interests[34] there is no reason to doubt the decision insofar as it establishes, in terms of *Lloyds Bank v Rosset* limb two, that a discount to the purchase price can amount to a contribution to the purchase price just as easily as can a cash contribution.

In practice, it is perhaps unlikely that a local authority discount would inform the question of the existence of a common intention. There can be no question that the tenant who exercises his right to buy does *not* have a beneficial interest: plainly he does. However it is *only* the local authority tenant entitled to occupy the property who is entitled to exercise the right to buy. The tenant cannot feasibly join with any other person in exercising the right to buy, because a disposition of any part of his interest in the property (including a disposition in fact made at the time of the purchase from the local authority) within three years of purchase on the face of it gives rise to the obligation to repay (at least in part) the discount available on the initial purchase.[35] This plainly encompasses any

---

[31] See Chapter 5 below, "Quantification of Beneficial Interests".

[32] Although whether it *should* be taken into account will be a question of fact for determination by the trial judge: see e.g. *Ashe v Mountford* [2000] T.L.R. 802.

[33] E.g *per* Steyn L.J. at 395F.

[34] See below, Chapter 5 "Quantifying the Interest" and see *Oxley v Hiscock* [2005] Fam 211 *per* Chadwick L.J. at 241.

[35] See Housing Act 1985, s.155 as amended.

prospective purchaser seeking to join with a local authority tenant in exercising the right to buy, for instance by advancing funds which the tenant will use to effect the purchase in his/her sole name.

This situation was in fact confronted by the claimant in *Oxley v His-* **3–038** *cock* ([2005] Fam. 211). There, C exercised her right to buy her local authority accommodation with a discount of around 45 per cent. D provided the entire balance of the purchase monies. Notwithstanding the parties' execution of an agreement which charged the property with the sums advanced by D, at first instance the judge found that the parties had both intended to hold the property beneficially in equal shares. Chadwick L.J. simply dismissed that conclusion as "plainly wrong" (see para.18 at 219D), holding that the property was owned beneficially by C, subject to the charge securing the monies advanced by D.

However, beyond the scope of local authority discounts, there appears to be no good reason why such discounts cannot be taken into account in terms of evidence from which the inference of a common intention can be drawn. In *Marsh v von Sternberg* ([1986] 1 F.L.R. 526) a private landlord sought to dispose of a property which was subject to a secure tenancy. The respondent was the tenant entitled to statutory protection against eviction, and negotiated a discount attributable to the loss of that protection in the course of purchasing with the applicant the property from the landlord. Bush J. said (at 531):

> "Though the respondent's situation only had a financial value in a given set of circumstances and did not have a market price in the world at large, it was a financial benefit nevertheless and, in my view, it is possible to infer and I do infer that as part of their agreement or arrangement the parties regarded the realization of that financial benefit by way of discount as a contribution by the respondent to the purchase of the flat."

In *Evans v Hayward* ([1995] 2 F.L.R. 511 at 516N) Staughton L.J. said **3–039** that it was difficult to see how a discount could be regarded as part of the purchase money provided by either party when it is not money which is in fact provided at all. However, he proceeded to say:

> "But I do consider that the facts as to the existence of a discount and the source from which it is derived must be taken into account, and are capable of leading to the inference that the parties have made an agreement as to how the purchase price is provided."

In terms of *Lloyds Bank v Rosset* limb two, therefore, there would appear to be no difference in principle between drawing from the circumstances of the discount inferences as to the parties' intentions on the one hand as regards the *extent* of their respective beneficial interests, and as regards the *existence* of a beneficial interest on the other.

Payment of costs of purchase

3–040   Lord Bridge's reference in *Rosset* to nothing less than "payments to the purchase price" being satisfactory (in terms of establishing a common intention absent sufficient evidence of agreement under limb one) might be thought to mean that the partner who pays nothing towards the purchase price, but who nonetheless pays ancillary cost such as professional fees or stamp duty, does not acquire an interest absent an express understanding. In fact, there is almost universal acceptance that a contribution to the proper costs of purchase stands on the same footing as a direct contribution to the purchase price, in terms of establishing an interest under limb two. In *Gissing v Gissing* ([1971] AC 886) Lord Diplock had referred (at 907H) to a common intention evidenced by contribution towards "the cash deposit *and legal charges*" (emphasis added).[36]

3–041   There does not appear to be any reported authority where a beneficial interest has been founded upon a contribution to the legal fees or other costs of purchase alone.[37] Care should be taken, if reliance is placed on such a contribution alone in the context of limb two, that the *de minimis* principle is not offended (discussed below at 3–068 *et seq.*). On the other hand, many courts would undoubtedly adopt the position that where D pays the deposit and C pays the surveyor's and solicitor's fees, is probably simply a matter of their own internal accounting and convenience, rather than indicative of an intention that D was intended to have a beneficial interest and C was not.

Mortgage repayments

3–042   As Lord Bridge observes in *Lloyds Bank v Rosset*, the payment of mortgage instalments will usually — but not necessarily invariably — justify the inference that the parties have agreed that both cohabitees should have an interest. Lord Reid considered in *Gissing v Gissing* ([1971] A.C. 886 at 896G) that the interest is presumed even where nothing was ever said or agreed about beneficial interests at the relevant time.

Thus in *Re Nicholson* ([1974] 1 W.L.R. 476) the initial arrangement was that H would be responsible for mortgage repayments. W, however, agreed that she would repay the mortgage from the proceeds of an inheritance the receipt of which she anticipated. It was held that the parties had intended that each would have an equal share in the property. In *Huntingford v Hobbs* ([1993] 1 F.L.R. 736 CA) the relevant property was bought in joint names but without a declaration as to their respective shares. Sir Christopher Slade considered that the parties must have had a common intention that both cohabitees should have an interest in the property where the property was conveyed into the names of both, and

---

[36] See also *Law of Trusts & Trustees* Underhill & Hayton (16th edn, 2003, p.352).
[37] In *Huntingford v Hobbs* [1993] 1 F.L.R. 736, for instance, the payment of legal fees was included in the quantification of the parties' respective interests in a case where it was plain that both parties enjoyed some beneficial interest: see also *Curley v Parkes* [2004] EWCA Civ 1515 *per* Sir Peter Gibson at para.22.

both had accepted joint and several liability for the mortgage repayments. However, occasional payments made by the claimant where the payments are usually discharged by the other party may not suffice (e.g. *Cowcher v Cowcher* [1972] 1 W.L.R. 425).

One significant issue of fact arises in the situation where D pays the **3–043** mortgage instalments on a periodic basis and receives a financial contribution from C on a similar periodic basis. The question of fact for the court to resolve, in essence, is whether on the one hand C's contribution is a contribution to the mortgage payment per se, which opens the door to an interest under either limb two or by reason of a purchase money resulting trust, or on the other hand simply a contribution by way of rent in relation to C's occupation of the property. The latter plainly would not evidence or otherwise give rise to a beneficial interest.[38] In such circumstances, the fundamental question is that of referability (discussed above). Thus where D advertises that he has a room to let and C moves in and makes periodical financial payments to D, there would appear little prospect of persuading the court that a common intention should be imputed to the parties that C was understood to have a beneficial interest. Where, however, a relationship between C and D leads to C moving in to D's residence, it might be more difficult to characterise an ongoing contribution as equivalent to an occupation rent.[39]

The determination of that issue of fact may be assisted by considera-   **3–044** tion of how, in the absence of C's contributions, D would otherwise have been able to meet the mortgage payments. In a case where there is agreement in terms that C's payments are a contribution towards the mortgage, it would not on the face of it be difficult for C to establish a common intention in terms of *Lloyds Bank v Rosset* limb two. Where in the absence of C's contribution D would not have been able to obtain or maintain the mortgage, again that would tend to suggest a common intention that C should share in the beneficial interest,[40] but all will depend on the particular facts of the case. It might be more difficult to reach the conclusion that C was understood by both parties to be entitled to a share however where D would have been perfectly able to manage without C's contribution. In *Barton v Wray* (Lawtel May 10, 2002), for instance, although C's payments assisted D in paying the mortgage, no common intention was inferred in circumstances where the payments had not been specifically identified as mortgage contributions, and where D

---

[38] See e.g. *Savage v Dunningham* [1974] 1 Ch. 181 *per* Plowman J. at 184H–185A, *c.f. Annen v Rattee* [1985] 1 E.G.L.R. 136; *c.f. Buggs v Buggs* [2003] EWHC 1538 (Ch).

[39] In *Savage v Dunningham* [1974] 1 Ch. 181 Plowman J. said at 185C–E: "It is in my judgment unrealistic to suggest that (flatsharing) is an area in which the law of trusts comes into play — an area where the existence of a trust is said to depend not on any express agreement but on inference from the facts. The application of the law of trusts to flat-sharing agreements would give rise to all sorts of problems. The occupants of shared flats are constantly changing. People come and go for one reason or another without any thought of legal consequences and without reference to lawyers. They are not likely to have heard of s.53 of the Law of Property Act 1925."

[40] How else would C have been able to acquire or preserve the property at all?

would have been able to maintain the mortgage even in the absence of such payments.

Quite apart from any fact-based question of referability, where reliance is placed by a claimant on mortgage contributions, two cautionary notes should be sounded.

First, contributions to an "interest only" mortgage (whether that mortgage is linked to an endowment policy or pension or otherwise) may not justify the inference of a common intention as readily, or possibly at all. This is due to a well charted distinction between capital applied towards the purchase of the property, and interest on that capital.

3–045   The distinction can be traced back at least to *Leake (formerly Bruzzi) v Bruzzi* ([1974] 1 W.L.R. 1528). Payments of interest under a mortgage are not usually taken to be contributions to the purchase price in that the capital debt owing under the mortgage is not reduced by reason of such payments. Thus where one cohabitee leaves the property and the entire mortgage burden falls on the other, only the repayment of capital falls to be taken into account as a contribution to the purchase price (as in *Leake v Bruzzi* itself). Equally, where one co-owner continues to pay both the capital and interest elements of the mortgage post separation, in quantifying the parties' respective interests it is common to give credit for capital contributions but to treat interest payments as akin to an occupation rent.[41]

3–046   With an endowment mortgage, or similar, it is at least arguable that no capital repayment is made until the mortgage is redeemed in full. The mortgage interest is paid, but that does not reduce the capital debt, and stands on a different footing to capital payments. Payment of premiums in relation to the endowment policy are payments which might confer or evidence a beneficial interest in the proceeds of that policy,[42] but do not necessarily extend so as to confer or evidence an interest in a property which was *not* purchased with those contributions, even though a contractual connection exists between the two assets. At the heart of this issue lies the distinction between direct contributions to the purchase price (as in for instance *Re Nicholson*) and indirect contributions (as identified in *Burns v Burns*). The higher courts do not appear to have indicated on which side of the fence contributions to a mortgage endowment policy fall.

Similar considerations might arise in cases where the legal owner holds an "offset" mortgage, namely where his mortgage account also acts as his current account, into which his salary is paid each month and out of which not only the monthly interest payment under the mortgage is made but also from which many other household obligations are discharged. There is no capital repayment as such save to the extent that the original

---

[41] See further Chapter 7 "Personal Obligations Between Cohabitants" and see *Re Pavlou* [1993] 1 W.L.R. 1046.
[42] See below, Chapter 7 "Personal Obligations Between Cohabitants".

borrowing may be higher than the current balance of what is in effect a very large, secured overdraft.

It is not difficult to imagine that the higher courts would be sympa-   **3–047** thetic to the argument that it was somewhat unsatisfactory for questions of entitlement under an asserted beneficial interest to turn on basis of the potentially arbitrary choice between a repayment mortgage, an offset mortgage or an endowment mortgage. On the other hand, if what counts is a contribution to the purchase price per se, it seems difficult to maintain that paying the interest on money borrowed to enable the purchase to take place, or money paid to an insurance company under an endowment policy, can properly be said to be a contribution to the cost of buying a property. The money borrowed becomes the property of the borrower,[43] subject to a personal liability to repay the loan, that liability being secured against the property itself. Whilst a reduction in the amount due to be repaid to the lender will often justify the inference of a limb two common intention, it is by no means clear that payments which defray only the contractual liability to interest will have the same effect. Plainly an interest in the surrender value of the policy might arise, but that does not necessarily equate to a contribution to the purchase price in limb two terms. Equally, the fact that the mortgage deed may provide that unpaid interest can be added to the capital debt does not necessarily equate to a contribution to the purchase price.

Where an interest can be established otherwise, there would appear to   **3–048** be no difficulty in principle in taking into account payments of interest under the mortgage in quantification of the interest (see below, Chapter 5 "Quantification of Beneficial Interests" and see *Passee v Passee* ([1988] 1 F.L.R. 263 at 271B) *per* Nicholls L.J.). There do not however appear to be any reported authorities which deal directly with the question whether a contribution to an interest-only mortgage coupled with a contribution to the premium payable in relation to a related endowment policy would suffice in terms of establishing an interest under *Lloyds Bank v Rosset* limb two.

The case of *Huntingford v Hobbs* ([1993] 1 F.L.R. 736) featured an endowment policy, but the ratio for the decision related to the capital borrowed by way of mortgage finance, rather than to the arrangements for repayment. In that case, the mortgage advance equated to 39 per cent of the total purchase price. D would not have been able to raise such a mortgage without C, and C had agreed to be solely responsible for the mortgage repayments and the payments of the premiums on the endowment policy. The mortgage advance was accordingly treated as being C's contribution to the purchase price. On sale of the property, the parties' respective interests were calculated by reference to the proceeds of sale without any account being taken of the mortgage advance. Thus the Court of Appeal, although aware of the existence of the endowment

---

[43] See *Halifax Building Society v Brown* [1996] 1 F.L.R. 103 *per* Balcombe L.J. at 109D and see below, Chapter 4 "Resulting Trusts".

policy (as is apparent from, for example, the judgment of Sir Christopher Slade at 738G), treated the mortgage advance as though it had been a cash contribution from C, and regarded him as solely responsible for repayment of the mortgage. It would plainly have been inconsistent with that approach to give C credit either for interest payments or for payments of the insurance policy premiums.

3–049   It is clear from cases such as *Powell v Osbourne* ([1993] 1 F.C.R. 797) and *Smith v Clerical Medical and General Life Assurance Society and others* ([1993] 1 F.L.R. 47)[44] that the higher Courts are not generally slow to recognise the economic and social realities of endowment mortgages. This might indicate a willingness on the part of appellate judges to look at the reality of the situation in the context of cohabitation cases, rather than confine itself to a technical equitable assessment of a contribution to the relevant purchase price. However, it may be of significance that both *Powell* and *Smith* concerned one co-owner with an undisputed beneficial interest in the relevant property in dispute with the personal representatives of the deceased co-owner. The reluctance of the court in those cases to confer a windfall on the deceased's estate at the expense of the surviving co-owner may not translate into a willingness to find that payments which evidence an interest in the proceeds of an endowment policy also evidence an interest in real property held in the name of the policyholder simply because of a contractual connection between the two.[45]

3–050   Even with a repayment mortgage, the combination of the *de minimis* principle (discussed below at 3–068 *et seq.*) and the interest/capital distinction can prove fatal to a claim to a beneficial interest. In *Young v Young* ([1984] F.L.R. 375 CA) May L.J. observed (380D) that in the early years of the mortgage term, the lion's share of the monthly instalment represents the payment of interest; only a small proportion of the capital loan is repaid. Thus although the appellant in that case had paid two-thirds of the mortgage for 16 months, the reduction in the capital balance of the mortgage was so small that the inference of a common intention was not justified.

The second cautionary note is that a mere assumption of liability under a mortgage will not necessarily justify the inference of a common intention that both parties should share beneficially.

3–051   The reality of modern homebuying at least in modern Britain is that the overwhelming majority of house purchases involve mortgage

---

[44] Both of which concerned claims to beneficial interests in endowment policies — considered further in Chapter 7, below, "Personal Obligations Between Cohabitants".

[45] The ability of the courts to deal with endowment policies under the jurisdiction conferred by the Trusts of Land and Appointment of Trustees Act 1996 seems questionable — see s.14(1), which provides "any person who is *a trustee of land or who has an interest in property subject to a trust of land* may make an application to the court for an order under this section" (emphasis added): see further, below, Chapter 9 "Practice and Procedure".

finance.[46] For many mortgage lenders, the decision as to how much they are willing to lend to a prospective purchaser or purchasers is arrived at, at least in part, on the basis of a multiple of the purchaser's income or their combined incomes. A common multiple might be three times a single person's income, or 2.5 times the income of a couple. Thus a purchaser (D) who seeks to borrow more than the relevant lender could be persuaded to advance on the basis of his income alone, may well join with another person (C) in the mortgage application and purchase. Sometimes this would be because D preferred to buy with C (and to share the beneficial interest with C) rather than not buy at all. In other cases, even though C joined in the purchase and mortgage application to put D in a position whereby he could bring about the purchase, D alone was the "real" purchaser. In other words, mere status as a party might not necessarily resolve the issue one way or the other. The following cases appear to establish the proposition that whilst assumption of liability under a mortgage is plainly not irrelevant in terms of demonstrating an intention to share the beneficial interest, neither is it — of itself — necessarily conclusive.

In *Crisp v Mullings* ((1976) 239 E.G. 119) Russell L.J. held that **3–052** assumption of liability under a mortgage could justify the inference of a common intention (*c.f. Young v Young* [1984] F.L.R. 375 *per* May L.J. at 378E–H), but there are several reported cases where of itself status as a party to the mortgage has fallen some way short of enabling the court to find the necessary common intention. In *Re Share (Lorraine)* ([2002] 2 F.L.R. 88), although the property was purchased by A alone, B had in fact paid the entire deposit and all of the mortgage repayments. A had simply been B's nominee and enjoyed no beneficial interest accordingly. Equally, in *Carlton v Goodman* ([2002] 2 F.L.R. 259) the property was purchased in joint names but was for the use and occupation of only one purchaser. It was held that while assumption of liability under the mortgage *might* be treated as a contribution to the purchase price, on the facts of that particular case it had never been intended that the claimant should pay anything; she had not paid anything and would have been entitled as a trustee to an indemnity had she been required to pay anything. Her involvement had been so temporary and of such a limited nature that the assumption of liability under the mortgage alone could not justify the inference of a common intention that she should share the beneficial ownership of the property. In *Allied Irish Banks v McWilliams* [1982] N.I. 156 Murray J. was not persuaded that, in circumstances where H had not provided financially in any way (whether in terms of mortgage repayments, provision of groceries or otherwise) an assumption of personal liability under a mortgage of itself did not evidence an intention to share the property beneficially, as the claimant would have been entitled

---

[46] See, if authority were needed, e.g. *Pettitt v Pettitt* [1970] A.C. 777 at 824–5 *per* Lord Diplock, *Curley v Parkes* [2004] EWCA Civ 1515 *per* Sir Peter Gibson at para.15 and see *Burns v Burns* [1984] Ch. 317 at 344E *per* May L.J.

in the event of personal liability to an indemnity from the proceeds of sale of the trust property (see 161D).

In *Kyriakides v Pippas* ([2004] 2 F.C.R. 432) the defendant's acceptance of liability under the relevant mortgage as a surety did not evidence any intention that she was to share in the beneficial interests in the relevant property.[47]

3–053   Nevertheless, the assumption of joint liability is by no means *inconsistent* with an intention to share the beneficial interest. There is no reason in principle why a "joint advance" case could not be construed in terms of C and D joining together in order to benefit each of them in terms of strengthening their joint purchasing power, which would tend to demonstrate an intention that both should enjoy an interest. This is in fact what happened in *Crisp v Mullings* ((1976) 239 E.G. 119). There, the parties needed to raise a mortgage of £5,700 which D alone was unable to raise. The mortgage (and also the property) were taken in joint names, the arrangement between the parties being that D would pay the expenses of running the house (including mortgage repayments) and C would pay for groceries. D contended that since he alone had contributed to the deposit, and he alone had paid the mortgage instalments, C did not have any beneficial interest in the property, and had been a party to the transaction purely to enable a mortgage to be obtained. Russell L.J. disagreed, and said:

> "We do not think that that (C's inability to raise the necessary mortgage on his own) demonstrates that the plaintiff was a mere nominee. It is, we think, a *non sequitur*. On the contrary, the fact that the house for 'the family' could not be bought without the plaintiff incurring some liability, or some potential liability, would be some ground for inferring that the plaintiff was to beneficially interested."

3–054   It is suggested that each case will depend on its own facts, and the wider circumstances surrounding the transaction and the course of dealings between the parties will be of greater significance in such a case than the simple question whose name appears on the mortgage. Assumption of liability under a mortgage of itself is not necessarily conclusive either way.[48]

---

[47] *c.f. McKenzie v McKenzie* [2003] 2 P. & C.R.D.G. 6). Finally, in *Young v Young* [1984] F.L.R. 375 the Court of Appeal regarded C's actual contribution to the mortgage repayments as *de minimis* and upheld the finding of the judge below that C's status as a legal owner and party to the mortgage did not of itself necessarily indicate a beneficial interest in C's favour. These cases clearly demonstrate that participation by C in D's application for a mortgage does not necessarily evidence an intention that C should enjoy an interest in the property subsequently purchased.

[48] The apparent inconsistency between those constructive trust cases where a party to the mortgage has been found not to have an interest, and resulting trust cases where liability under the mortgage is taken to demonstrate a contribution to the purchase price in direct proportion to liability under the mortgage (see below, Chapter 4 "Resulting Trusts") can only sensibly be explained on the basis that in each case the court is making a decision of fact as to the intentions of the parties on the basis of the evidence before it.

Improvements and capital contributions made subsequent to purchase

One situation commonly encountered is that a party who asserts that a **3–055** constructive trust arose at the time of purchase on either a limb one or limb two basis, fortifies his/her argument (either as evidence of the agreement or evidence of detrimental reliance) by reference to works undertaken by him/her or at his/her cost which have a beneficial effect on the value of the property. This is precisely what happened in *Eves v Eves* ([1975] 1 W.L.R. 1338), where having been told that the property would have been purchased in joint names had she not been too young, the claimant wielded her 14lb sledgehammer to such good effect. The later improvements merely evidenced the unspoken understanding which the Court of Appeal imputed to the parties as at the date of purchase (see above), absent which there would have been no need for D to explain to C why her name did not appear on the deeds. Equally, where the fact of a beneficial interest is established, such improvements may have a very real bearing in determining the share of an otherwise unquantified beneficial interest.[49]

Less common, however, is the situation where a party, who otherwise **3–056** would have no basis for mounting a claim to an interest in the property, undertakes at his/her own expense works on the property which have the same effect. Such a situation might arise where the parties embark upon a relationship sometime after the legal owner has purchased his/her property. Ordinarily, the beneficial interests in a property will be determined by the common intention of the relevant parties as at the time of purchase. This however does not preclude the court from drawing inferences as to the intention of the parties at the time of acquisition from their conduct after the purchase has completed. Moreover, there would appear to be no logical basis for concluding that a defendant who alone holds the beneficial interest in the relevant property is incapable in law of allowing a claimant to obtain a beneficial interest in his/her property on such a basis.

Arguably, this is what happened in *Stokes v Anderson* ([1991] 1 F.L.R. **3–057** 391). In *Rosset*, Lord Bridge observed that the "agreement, arrangement or understanding between them that the property is to be shared beneficially" would normally arise prior to acquisition (see also *Burns v Burns* [1984] Ch. 317 *per* Fox L.J. at 327A) but "exceptionally" might arise "at some later date". In *Grant v Edwards* ([1986] 1 Ch. 638) Mustill L.J. referred to the parties' intention at the time of acquisition but added (at 651G) in parenthesis:

"I use the expression 'on acquisition' for simplicity. In fact, the event happening between the parties which, if followed by the relevant type of conduct on the part of the claimant, can lead to the creation

---

[49] See Chapter 5, below, "Quantification of Beneficial Interests" and see in particular e.g. *Cooke v Head* [1972] 1 W.L.R. 518 *per* Karminski L.J. at 522H, *Passee v Passee* [1988] 1 F.L.R. 263 *per* Nicholls L.J. at 270F *Midland Bank v Cooke* [1995] 2 F.L.R. 915 *per* Waite L.J. at 917D–F and *Drake v Whipp* [1996] 1 F.L.R. 826 *per* Peter Gibson L.J. at 831D–E.

of an interest in the claimant, may itself occur after acquisition. The beneficial interests may change in the course of the relationship."

3–058   There are a number of instances of the Courts accepting the general proposition that a beneficial interest could be inferred from post-acquisition conduct even where at the time of acquisition it was plain that the requisite common intention had not existed, albeit that on the facts of the reported cases the inference has only seldom been justified. In *Churchill v Roach* ([2004] 2 F.L.R. 989 at 1001C) HHJ Norris Q.C. (sitting as a Deputy Judge of the Chancery Division) observed that although property interests were fixed rather than fluid, where the evidence demonstrated an expression of intention subsequent to the purchase of the property, or an agreement subsequent to that purchase which could be inferred from the parties' conduct, that would properly give rise to an interest on the part of the claimant even though none was contemplated at the time of the original purchase. In *Bernard v Josephs* ([1982] 1 Ch. 391 at 404E) Griffiths L.J. gave the example of one partner (the man) purchasing the house in the first place, and the other (the woman) later using a legacy to build an extra floor to make more room for the children. "In such circumstances," said Griffiths L.J., "the obvious inference would be that the parties agreed that the woman should acquire a share in the greatly increased value of the house produced by her money."[50] In *Burns v Burns* ([1984] Ch. 317 at 344F) May L.J. said that a common interest might be inferred from the financial contributions made by the parties "or their real and substantial equivalent". It follows that renovations, interior improvements, construction of extensions, even garden improvements, all *might* evidence a common intention formed *subsequent to* the purchase of the property. It will be a matter for the trial judge whether such works will in fact have the effect of enabling the court to draw the necessary inference.

3–059   One important distinction to be drawn in such cases is that between on the one hand married or engaged couples and on the other their cohabiting counterparts. In the context of married or engaged couples, it can be important to keep in mind the effect of s.37 of the Matrimonial Proceedings and Property Act 1970. This provides that:

> "where a husband or a wife contributes in money or money's worth to the improvement of real or personal property in which or in the proceeds of sale of which either or both of them has or have a beneficial interest, the husband or wife so contributing shall, if the contribution is of a substantial nature, and subject to any agreement to them to the contrary express or implied, be treated as having then acquired by virtue of his or her contribution a share or an enlarged share as the case may be in that beneficial interest."

---

[50] *c.f. Jansen v Jansen* [1965] P. 478.

By s.2(2) of the Law Reform (Miscellaneous Provisions) Act 1970 this provision is extended so as to apply to engaged as well as married couples.[51]

In practical terms, these provisions amounts to a presumption that **3–060** either a spouse or a fiancé(e) contributing in money or money's worth to the improvement of the property acquires thereby a beneficial interest in that property if (s)he did not have one previously. In for instance *Kowalczuk v Kowalczuk* ([1973] 1 W.L.R. 930) the relevant property had been bought well before H and W were married. As Buckley L.J. pointed out (at 934G), at the date of marriage the property was legally and beneficially undoubtedly H's sole property. In those circumstances W would not be able to establish any beneficial interest unless she could point to subsequent contributions of a substantial nature in money or money's worth. On the facts of that case, W had contributed "her own physical help" to the repair, alteration and improvement of the property. The Court of Appeal accepted (see 934E) that her contributions demonstrated an interest within the scope of s.37, and remitted the case for a determination of the extent of that interest. It is perhaps surprising that although Mrs Rosset prayed in aid principally her relatively modest contributions to the renovation of the relevant property (supervising builders and some decorating and wallpapering) s.37 of the 1970 Act does not appear to have been relied upon in argument, nor does it feature in the speech of Lord Bridge.

The difficulty which arises for the practitioner in this respect lies in **3–061** terms of characterising the nature of the contribution made. A claim to a beneficial interest, giving rise to property rights of a substantial and valuable nature may turn on nothing more than the judge's subjective characterisation of those works around the house either as being in the nature of running repairs, or being works which have some intrinsic value and add value to the property. The authorities are perhaps understandably vague as to the distinction in practical terms between on the one hand run of the mill maintenance, and on the other improvements which allow the imputation of some common intention; those, in short, which (to use the language of s.37) are "of a substantial nature". There is no obvious test which in practical terms demarcates the first situation from the second. As Lord Hodson said in *Pettitt*:

> "the husband does not become entitled to a share in the wife's property by occupying his leisure hours in the house or the garden even though he enhances the value of the property ... a husband should not be entitled to a share in the house simply by doing the 'do it yourself' jobs which husbands often do. This is not only good law but good sense which, in my opinion, should normally be applied to this sort of situation."

---

[51] See *Mossop v Mossop* [1989] Fam. 77 CA at 82G *per* Balcombe L.J. See further Chapter 10 "Engaged Couples".

3–062   Similarly, in *Gissing v Gissing* ([1971] A.C. 886 at 900) Viscount Dilhorne said (of the decision in *Pettitt*) "(p)ayment for a lawn and provision of some furniture and equipment for a house does not of itself point to the conclusion that there was (the necessary) intention". Mrs Gissing herself had redecorated the entire house; that was held to be insufficient evidence on which to base the inference of a common intention. In *Burns v Burns* ([1984] Ch. 317) Mrs Burns' decoration of the property was described as being undertaken simply because she wanted the house to be wall-papered, and could not justify the inference of a common intention (see 330B–D *per* Fox L.J.). (*c.f. Button v Button* [1968] 1 W.L.R. 457).

An important question of fact will be whether the relevant works have been financed by the claimant (whether or not in addition to being personally undertaken by him) or by contrast whether the contribution relied on is simply the physical/manual work done on the property. Where the married or engaged claimant funds such improvements, the provision of funding strengthens the claim to an interest to the point where even if the improvements per se would not justify the necessary inference, the combination of funding and effecting those improvements may suffice. In *Davis v Vale* ([1971] 1 W.L.R. 1022) the claimant wife paid for a water heater, a sink unit, fireplaces, a wall and iron gates. Had the claimant simply effected those improvements without paying for them, it is doubtful whether the necessary common intention could have been demonstrated, even bearing in mind the effect of s.37. The combination of paying for and performing the relevant improvements, however, was held to evidence a common intention that she should have an interest. In *Stokes v Anderson* the claimant's capital contributions (considered above) were in fact augmented by a further £2,500 spent on decorations and improvements to the grounds. Given the other contributions, the Court of Appeal did not need to decide whether those improvements would of themselves justify the inference of a common intention.

3–063   In *Griffiths v Griffiths* ([1973] 1 W.L.R. 454 FD) the substance of the improvements was largely demonstrated by reference to the cost of the improvements and the effect of such improvements on the value of the property. Arnold J. considered that H had spent about £4,500 on improvements to the property between about 1959 and 1969, and that these had increased the value of the house from about £45,000 (had the improvements not been undertaken) to the sale price achieved of £60,000. Often, as in *Anderson* and in *Cowcher v Cowcher* ([1972] 1 W.L.R. 425 at 440E–G) a contribution by way of funding or executing improvements or renovations will be one of a number of factors prayed in aid by C in seeking to establish an interest.

3–064   In the case of couples who cohabit without marrying or becoming engaged, the authorities demonstrate that a heavy burden rests upon a litigant whose claim rests solely on contributions by way of improvements physically undertaken, but not paid for, by the claimant. In *Stack v Dowden* ([2005] 2 F.C.R. 739) Chadwick L.J. bluntly said (para.38 at 757A), "What will not do in that context (of *Lloyds Bank v Rosset* limb two) is work done in and about the property (including decoration and renovation) after the property has been acquired."[52] In *Windeler v Whitehall* ([1990] 2 F.L.R. 505) C claimed an interest based upon what she contended were substantial works of improvement to the relevant property. Millett J. found that these were in fact relatively trivial in nature, consisting of minor building works, such as "repointing, carpentry, redecoration and renovation of drains". Completion of these works by builders had been supervised by C, who let the builders in each day, made them tea and coffee and transported them around when further supplies were needed, but the works had been paid for by D. Millett J., having held that "any wife or mistress would have done the same", made the devastating (and cautionary) observation that:

> "only a lawyer versed in the authorities but lacking all sense of proportion would consider that such conduct gave her any kind of proprietary interest in the house".

The combination of *Windeler* and *Rosset* would appear to establish that whether C and D are married or not, the simple supervision of building works will rarely if ever suffice in terms of demonstrating the necessary common intention.

In *Thomas v Fuller Brown* ([1988] 1 F.L.R. 237) C (who was unem-   **3–065**
ployed) undertook substantial improvements to the property owned by D. The improvements were in fact funded by D who had received an improvement grant. Slade L.J. accepted the general proposition that improvements to another's property in reliance upon an *implicit* promise that an interest in the land would be created following such expenditure, might suffice to give rise to an interest under a constructive trust. It is all too easy to see why it was submitted on D's behalf that his personal investment of labour evidenced a common understanding that he enjoyed an interest in the property. On the facts, however, the trial judge had concluded that the arrangements between C and D had not included any understanding that C should obtain an interest in D's property. The trial judge categorised the labours of C as equivalent to "keep", in lieu of payment for board and lodging. The Court of Appeal refused to upset the trial judge's conclusion, even though in the absence of C's labours, D could not otherwise have afforded to have the works completed by private contractors.

This is not to say that improvements undertaken by a cohabitee will never justify the inference of a common intention. In *Ungurian v Lesnoff* ([1990] 2 F.L.R. 299) C undertook various works including the partitioning of certain bedrooms, removal of fireplaces and cleaning and decorating a property which, when purchased by D, was in a poor state of repair. The various works in that case were funded by D but undertaken by C and her

---

[52] At the time of writing, an appeal to the House of Lords in *Stack v Dowden* is still pending.

sons. It was held that these improvements illustrated a common intention that the property was held by D on constructive trust for himself and C, though on the facts of that case D's interest under the trust was a life interest in occupation, not an interest in the equity in the property per se.

3–066   Questions arise, where C meets the cost of improvements, as to whether the improvements were funded because C thought she was beneficially entitled to a share in the property, or whether the improvements were funded because she wanted to live in a nicer property. These are simple matters of evidence which are decisions for a judge hearing such a case. It is axiomatic that a beneficial interest is not "earned" by reason of the improvement: the improvement is merely the evidence from which a common intention may be inferred. Thus not every case where C funds and/or personally undertakes the improvements of D's property will result in the inference that C and D held a common intention that C should have a beneficial interest. As Griffiths L.J. said in *Bernard v Josephs* ([1982] Ch. 391 at 404F) "the mere fact that one party has spent time and money on improving the property will not normally be sufficient to draw such an inference."

Nonetheless, while the claims of unmarried cohabitees based on improvement works alone face significant difficulties, that is not to say that such cases are doomed to fail in every case. In principle, if there could be no objection to the parties *expressly* reformulating their intentions as to beneficial ownership some time after the purchase, it follows that such an agreement must, in certain circumstances, be capable of being inferred from conduct; (indeed Slade L.J. expressly accepted that proposition in *Thomas v Fuller Brown* [1988] 1 F.L.R. 237 at 241H). Whilst the statutory presumption under s.37 is not available to the unmarried/non-engaged claimant, there may nonetheless be cases where so substantial is C's contribution (in non-financial terms) to the renovation of a property that the only sensible explanation is that C and D agreed or understood that C was to have a beneficial interest in the property. A high evidential hurdle would, the authorities would seem to indicate, need to be cleared; however those authorities do not appear to establish the proposition that such conduct can never justify the inference of a common intention, no matter what the circumstances.

3–067   *Ungurian v Lesnoff* and *Thomas v Fuller Brown* perhaps illustrate the reality of cohabitation cases, namely that the courts appear far more willing to infer or impute some common intention to a party whose claims otherwise attract the court's sympathy than to one whose conduct attracts some censure. In *Fuller Brown* itself, Slade L.J. recorded the trial judge's acceptance of the submission (see 243G) that C, being "well versed in these matters, had an ulterior motive in doing what he did to the house and was covertly seeking to establish a beneficial title to it, without letting (D) understand what he was trying to achieve." Millett J.'s frequent references to the claimant in *Windeler v Whitehall* as "immature"[53]

---

[53] "She never shook off an adolescent desire to avoid being tied down". See 514C.

highlight the lack of sympathy with which he viewed her claims. On the other hand, in *Ungurian*, the Court's willingness to afford the claimant relief may well have been strengthened by the extent of the reliance, and the detriment to herself (the claimant had given up secure accommodation and a stimulating academic career to join the defendant) placed by the claimant on the putative intention (discussed further below at 3–087). The admiration of the Court of Appeal for Janet Eves (said to have done "more than most wives would do") is self-evident. It comes as little surprise that Mrs Eves was able to demonstrate an interest under a constructive trust whereas Ms Windeler was not.

The de minimis *principle*

The authorities are unanimous that not every contribution, even if in money rather than money's worth, will justify the inference of a common intention (just as not every contribution to the purchase price gives rise to the presumption of a resulting trust). In *Rosset* itself the monetary value of Mrs Rosset's contribution — as a proportion of the overall purchase cost of £70,000[54] was described (at 131G) as being "trifling". In *Burns v Burns* [1984] Ch. 317 Fox L.J. outlined the contributions made by C as being gifts of clothing to D, payment of housekeeping, rates and telephone bills, purchase of a number of domestic appliances and provision of doorknobs and door furnishings of no great value. Fox L.J. considered that all but the provision of door fittings simply could not be described as referable to the purchase of the property, and that "the provision of doorknobs etc. is of very small consequence" (at 329D). In *Windeler v Whitehall* ([1990] 2 F.L.R. 505) C's claim to an interest was based upon what Millett J. found to be relatively trivial matters such as "repointing, carpentry, redecoration and renovation of drains". There, however, C's role had principally been supervision and assistance, in terms of letting builders in each day, providing them with tea and coffee and transporting them around when further supplies were needed. The relevant improvement works were actually paid for by D.

There is even case law suggesting that payment of mortgage instalments will not justify the inference of a common intention in a case where the *de minimis* principle applies. In *Young v Young* ([1984] F.L.R. 375) the appellant paid two-thirds of the mortgage instalments for a period of about six months in the early stages of a 20-year mortgage term. May L.J. assessed the actual capital contribution to the repayment of the mortgage debt to be around £175 as opposed to the £4,000 initially contributed by the respondent. "It would I think" he continued (at 380E) "be wholly unrealistic to decide that even a very small proportion of the equity was held beneficially for the interest of the appellant".

3–068

3–069

---

[54] A property worth £70,000 in 1982 would, according to Halifax Plc's house price index, have been worth around £450,000 by 2005.

While both case law[55] and statute[56] indicate that the contribution must be of a substantial nature in order to justify either the inference of a common intention or the presumption of a resulting trust, there are (unsurprisingly) few pointers as to where the line between a substantial and an insubstantial contribution is drawn. Perhaps, rather like the elephant, a judge knows a substantial contribution when (s)he see one; perhaps also, in some cases judges are more inclined to look for one than in others.

Claims based on indirect contributions alone

3–070 There are many cases in which one party makes what in the context of a marriage would be regarded as a full contribution to a relationship without parting with a penny or ever wielding a sledgehammer in earnest. Undertaking domestic or childcare tasks is an obvious example, but for instance working without remuneration in a cohabitee's business might be analogous, where the business provides financial support for both parties. Equally, in many cases, one party shoulders a significant financial burden without actually contributing to the purchase price. Thus one partner's willingness to purchase groceries or pay school fees enables the other party to meet the mortgage repayments and utility bills.

3–071 In neither case is there a direct contribution to the purchase price, which on the face of it is fatal to any claim to an interest based on a constructive trust. As observed above, the speech of Lord Bridge of Harwich in *Rosset* would appear to leave no room for doubt that a claimant who can demonstrate only non-financial or indirect financial contributions alone will not be able to satisfy the court that a common intention existed. One of the most (in)famous cases on this point is *Burns v Burns* [1984] Ch. 317 (referred to above at 3–031). In *Cohabitation: The Financial Consequences of Relationship Breakdown* the Law Commission described *Burns* as "the leading authority on the law's refusal to base a beneficial share on non-financial contributions alone" (see para 4.18). In that case, despite a relationship of almost 20 years' duration Mrs Burns[57] was not able to establish a proprietary interest in the relevant property as she could neither point to an agreement to share the beneficial interest in the property nor to evidence which would justify the inference of such an agreement. Fox L.J. commented (327H–328A) that domestic contributions, such as childcare and housekeeping,

"do not carry with them any implication of a common intention that the plaintiff should have an interest in the house. Taken by

---

[55] E.g. *Falconer v Falconer* [1970] 1 W.L.R. 1333 CA, *Burns v Burns* [1984] Ch. 317 at 329E *per* Fox L.J.
[56] s.37 Matrimonial and Property Proceedings Act 1970, discussed above at 3–059.
[57] In the context of a marriage Mrs B would undoubtedly be described as a "fully entitled wife".

themselves they are simply not strong enough to bear such an implication".

He added (at 331A):

"The mere fact that parties live together and do the ordinary domestic tasks in, in my view, no indication at all that they thereby intended to alter the existing property rights of either of them."

In *Hall v Hall* ((1982) 3 F.L.R. 379) the claimant relied on indirect financial contributions alone in establishing an interest under (as the court described it) a resulting trust but the existence of a resulting trust had been conceded by the defendant and the question for the court to decide was simply the extent of the interest (*per* Dunn L.J. at 383E). May L.J. later describe that concession as having been wrongly made (see *Burns v Burns* [1984] Ch. 317 at 341G). The approach adopted by Lord Denning M.R. in the 1970s and early 1980s, to infer the existence of a "constructive trust of a new model" on the basis of domestic or indirect contributions to the purchase price (e.g. *Hazell v Hazell* [1972] 1 W.L.R. 301) did not meet with universal approval and was disapproved in *Burns v Burns* ([1984] Ch. 317). In that case May L.J. said:

3–072

"I respectfully think that the dictum of Lord Denning MR that the woman's contribution to the family well-being by keeping the house and looking after the children can be taken into account in assessing the extent to which a resulting trust has arisen in her favour was wrong."[58]

That said, it must be acknowledged that there is at least some judicial support for the contention — notwithstanding Lord Bridge's observation that it is "at least extremely doubtful whether anything less will do" — that indirect contributions towards the purchase price will after all justify the inference of the necessary common intention. In particular, the case of *Le Foe v Le Foe and Woolwich Plc* ([2001] 2 F.L.R. 970) Nicholas Mostyn Q.C. (sitting as a Deputy Judge of the Family Division) considered that it was important that Lord Bridge's reference to it being "at least extremely doubtful whether anything less will do" had not been stated in absolute terms. He continued (at 980–982):

3–073

"In my view what Lord Bridge of Harwich is saying is that in the second class of case to which he is adverting, namely where there is no positive evidence of an express agreement between the parties as to how the equity is to be shared, and where the court has fallen back

---

[58] At 342G. *C.f. Lloyds Bank v Rosset* [1991] A.C. 107 *per* Lord Bridge of Harwich at 133: this does not however amount to a *carte blanche* to disregard each and every pronouncement of Lord Denning's in the field of equity and co-ownership.

on inferring their common intention from the course of their conduct, it will only be exceptionally that conduct other than direct
contributions to the purchase price, either in cash to the deposit or
by contribution to the mortgage instalments, will suffice to draw the
necessary inference of a common intention to share the equity."

3–074   Mr Mostyn Q.C. continued to say that he did not believe that in using the
words "direct contributions" Lord Bridge of Harwich meant to exclude
the situation with which he was confronted:

> "namely, where there was no initial cash contribution but only an
> indirect contribution to the mortgage ... such a state of affairs
> should suffice to enable the necessary inference to be drawn.
> Otherwise these cases would be decided by reference to mere acci-
> dents of fortune, being the arbitrary allocation of financial respon-
> sibility as between the parties".

Here, Mr Mostyn Q.C. echoed the judgment of Griffiths L.J. in *Bernard v
Josephs* ([1982] 1 Ch. 391) who observed that who paid for what might be
no more than a matter of the parties' internal accounting (see 403H–
404A). *Le Foe* itself was a case where the parties were in fact married, and
the real issue was whether the wife had an interest in the matrimonial
home to which the Woolwich could not look in order to secure repayment of the sums it had lent to the husband. On the facts therefore it is
very different from the line of cases which concern a dispute as between
former cohabitees as regards their respective interests in what has
hitherto been their family home.

3–075   It does not appear from the report of *Le Foe* that the Court was
referred to the earlier decision of the Court of Appeal in *Ivin v Blake*
([1995] 1 F.L.R. 70). In that case, Glidewell L.J. (with whom the other
members of the court agreed) referred to the Northern Ireland case of
McFarlane v McFarlane [1972] N.I. 59.[59] In particular, Lowry J. had said
in *McFarlane* (at 74):

> "where the husband is the legal owner and the wife has an income,
> whether from employment, from her own business, or from other
> sources, or works in the husband's business and in one way or
> another eases the husband's financial position, and thereby indirectly
> augments the fund out of which the husband buys the property ... in
> such a case the wife acquires a beneficial interest if, and only if, there
> is an agreement or arrangement between the spouses that she is to
> have such an interest."

---

[59] The judgments in that case had been cited with approval by Lord Bridge in *Lloyds Bank v
Rossett* and were adopted by Chadwick L.J. more recently in *Oxley v Hiscock* [2004] 2
F.L.R. 669.

In *Ivin v Blake* Glidewell L.J. dealt with the contribution made by the claimant by saying:

> "her contribution to the purchase price ... was indirect. She does not allege that there was an express agreement that she should have a beneficial interest. Accordingly, applying the principles set out in the speech of Lord Bridge in *Lloyds Bank v Rosset* and in the judgments of the court in *McFarlane, which in my opinion accurately state the law of England as well as of Northern Ireland,* Mrs Ivin had failed to establish that she has, or ever had, a beneficial interest in the house." (Emphasis added.)

On the face of it, therefore, *Le Foe* was decided *per incuriam*. In any **3–076** event, it seems clear that the decision in *Le Foe* does not reflect the mainstream of judicial thinking in this area. Mr Mostyn Q.C. for instance referred in giving judgment in *Le Foe* to *Burns v Burns* ([1984] Ch. 317) and appeared to draw some support from the judgment of May L.J. in that case. The result of *Burns* was however to deny Mrs Burns' claim to a beneficial interest in the relevant property, yet the logic of *Le Foe* would suggest both Mrs Burns and Mrs Rosset should both have been able to demonstrate a common intention that each in their respective situations should have an interest. May L.J.'s observations in relation to indirect contributions to the mortgage in *Burns* were plainly made in the context of the claimant *also* making a direct prior contribution to the purchase price (see 344H). Moreover, in *Midland Bank v Cooke* ([1995] 2 F.L.R. 915) Waite L.J. specifically observed (in a passage also cited, though in a different context, by Mr Mostyn Q.C. in *Le Foe*) that in determining the extent of any beneficial interest, the court was not obliged to "limit itself to the limited range of acts of direct contribution of the sort that are needed to found a beneficial interest in the first place" (see 926).

In its discussion paper *Sharing Homes* the Law Commission considered **3–077** the situation where the non-legal owner has not made any financial contribution to the purchase price or mortgage repayments, but has shouldered other financial responsibilities which better enable the legal owner to meet mortgage instalments, and said:

> "In our view an indirect contribution to the mortgage of this kind should be sufficient to enable the courts to infer that the parties had a common intention that the beneficial entitlement to the home to be shared."

The decision in *Le Foe* was specifically cited by the Law Commission in contrast to the general trend of the courts which had, in the opinion of the Law Commissioners, made it too difficult for a person to establish a beneficial entitlement in the shared home (see *Sharing Homes* Law Com No. 278 at para.4.26). It does not appear as though *Ivin v Blake* was drawn to the Law Commissioners' attention.

Assuming *Le Foe* is not good law, the difficulty perceived in *Sharing Homes* is that a beneficial interest might be inferred in circumstances where the parties agree to bear equally the cost of every individual outgoing (including the mortgage) relating to the home, but not in the case where the totality of the outgoings is also split equally but the legal owner pays for certain items and the claimant pays for the rest, but those items paid for by the claimant do not include the mortgage repayments. The difference between the two situations may arise from nothing more scientific than the convenience of the parties in terms of the times of the month at which the parties each receive their wages/salaries and the dates upon which various payments fall to be made. As the Law Commissioners point out, it seems somewhat unsatisfactory that the existence or otherwise of beneficial interests may turn on what in reality are accidents of fortune.

3–078   Moreover, a claimant's interest in the disputed property arises because it is the common intention of the parties (tacit or express) that both should have an interest. The contribution — whatever its nature — is merely the evidence which entitles a judge to reach the conclusion that the parties must have had the requisite common intention at some time in the past. A restrictive interpretation of *Rosset* (which *Ivin v Blake* would appear to require) would necessarily lead to the conclusion that a judge was never in any circumstances entitled to find a tacit agreement as to shared beneficial ownership absent a qualifying contribution to the purchase price; yet the existence or otherwise of a common intention is clearly a question of fact.[60] It is difficult to discern any logical reason which should prevent a judge from finding a common intention due to the absence of either express discussions or financial contributions if the evidence in the case otherwise seems to the judge to justify amply that finding.

As the law stands, no matter what the circumstances of the case, C's claim fails unless she can tick one of the *Rosset* boxes. This seems an unnecessary fetter upon the judge's ability to reach appropriate findings on the evidence before him.

Thus the views expressed by the Deputy Judge in *Le Foe* might well be founded on firm foundations of principle, if perhaps inconsistent with the mainstream of authority on the point.

3–079   Perhaps the conclusion to be drawn from this is that *if* the decision in *Le Foe* does not reflect the law at present, then a change in the law to enable the courts to find that indirect contributions justify the inference of a common intention in an appropriate case, would seem (at least in the opinion of the Law Commissioners) to be a positive development. By way of a tailpiece, the Commission also commented upon the advantages of a holistic approach to the quantification of the beneficial interest, having regard to the whole course of dealings between the parties. *Oxley v Hiscock* ([2005] Fam. 211) was the first occasion on which the Court of

---

[60] See e.g. *Gissing v Gissing* [1971] A.C. 886 at 901 *per* Lord Pearson.

Appeal had to consider the quantification of the beneficial interest following the publication of the Law Commission paper. Though *Sharing Homes* was not cited in the judgment of Chadwick L.J. (despite having been referred to extensively in argument) the conclusion of *Oxley* as to quantification was essentially that advocated by the Law Commission (see further Chapter 5, "Quantification of Beneficial Interests", below). It is not perhaps too difficult to anticipate some development of the law so far as establishing an interest under a constructive trust is concerned, even without direct contribution to the purchase price and absent an express agreement, in the not too distant future.

See also the Law Commission Consultation Paper "Cohabitation: The Financial Consequences of Relationship Breakdown", No. 179 completed on May 4, 2006.

Proving reliance

A constructive trust does not come into existence simply because D **3–080** makes some promise or forms some intention to transfer an interest to C or create an interest for C (*G v G (Matrimonial Property: Rights of Extended Family* [2006] 1 F.L.R. 62 *per* Baron J. at 78 (para 87). It is necessary for C to demonstrate also that he/she has placed reliance on that agreement to his/her detriment, or at least has significantly altered his/her position in reliance upon the agreement (see *Lloyds Bank v Rosset* [1991] 1 A.C. 107 at 133). The importance of this second requirement can easily be overlooked, in the quest to demonstrate a common intention; yet so important is the necessity of demonstrating reliance upon the common intention that even an express common intention that the claimant should have a beneficial interest will not give rise to any such interest if, as Scott J. said in *Layton v Martin* ([1986] 2 F.L.R. 227 at 237A), the express agreement is "unsupported by any quid pro quo moving from the claimant" (*c.f. Eves v Eves* ([1975] 1 W.L.R. 1338) *per* Brightman J. at 1345 A–D). Thus in *Midland Bank v Dobson* ([1986] 1 F.L.R. 171) the relevant property was held in the name of the husband alone, although he and his wife had agreed expressly that the beneficial interests should be shared equally (the Court of Appeal accepted that it could not go behind the finding of the trial judge in this regard). The wife was not however able to establish an interest under a constructive trust so as to defend a claim by the claimant bank for possession of the property which had been used by the husband as security for his business borrowings, since she had not in any way acted to her detriment in reliance upon that agreement. Her contributions to the household and periodic decorating were not acts done in reliance upon the agreement with her husband as regards any interest in the property; they were characterised (*per* Fox L.J. at 177A) as the sort of things that members of a family do in a house.

It must be acknowledged that there are few discernable rules or prin- **3–081** ciples which can be gleaned from the authorities in this area. In *Sharing*

Homes the Law Commission commented that "the precise limits of the concept of detrimental reliance remain somewhat unclear" (at para.2.74, citing A Lawson, *The Things We Do For Love: Detrimental Reliance in the Family Home* (1996) Legal Studies 218; see further *Eves v Eves* [1975] 1 W.L.R. 1338 at 1345A–D *per* Brightman J.; see also *Chan Pui Chun v Leung Kam Ho* ([2003] 1 F.L.R. 23) at 46 (para.93)).

The evidence which a claimant must advance, therefore, in order to establish an interest under a constructive trust, must not only enable the court to base a finding of a common intention on that evidence, but must also justify the conclusion that (s)he has relied on that common intention to his/her detriment. Thus in *Grant v Edwards* ([1986] 1 Ch. 638 at 651G) Mustill L.J. explained (at 651G):

> "the inquiry must proceed in two stages. First, by considering whether something happened between the parties in the nature of a bargain, promise or tacit common intention at the time of the acquisition. Second, if the answer is Yes, by asking whether the claimant subsequently conducted herself in a manner which was (a) detrimental to herself, and (b) referable to whatever happened on acquisition."[61]

Since the burden of proof rests on the claimant to demonstrate the necessary intention and the necessary reliance, it is important in formulating or responding to a claim to an interest under a constructive trust for attention to be paid to the respective contentions of the parties from two perspectives: first, in relation to whether, absent an express agreement, the conduct concerned evidences a common intention; second, in relation to whether sufficient reliance has been placed on that intention.

3–082   The fact that the inquiry proceeds in two stages does not necessarily mean that evidence relevant to the first stage will not also be relevant to the second. In *Grant v Edwards* itself, Nourse L.J. referred (at 647B) to the case where the existence of an agreement is inferred from the claimant's contribution to the purchase price, and observed:

> "If it is found to have been incurred, such expenditure will perform the two-fold function of establishing the common intention and showing that the claimant has acted upon it."[62]

Just as in *Oxley v Hiscock* ([2005] Q.B. 211) Chadwick L.J. held that in quantifying beneficial interests the court should take into account the entire course of dealings between the parties relevant to the property, in

---

[61] The use of the phrase "on acquisition" is explained above at 3–057.

[62] In *Lightfoot v Lightfoot Brown* [2005] 2 P. & C.R. 377 Arden L.J. observed (at 384 para.24) that contributions might be relevant not only to the demonstration of a common intention and evidence or detrimental reliance, but also to corroboration of direct evidence of an agreement, and also as regards quantification of any interest.

Chan Pui Chun v Leung Kam Ho ([2003] 1 F.L.R. 23) Jonathan Parker L.J. considered (at 47 para.96) that the court was entitled to look at the entirety of the parties' relationship from the date of the agreement onwards in determining whether C had altered her position to her detriment in relation to the promise of an interest. Nonetheless, even though the same evidence can fulfil more than one function it is helpful to keep in mind the distinction between the need to prove the common intention on the one hand, and the need to prove reliance on the other. Certain matters will properly relate to one but not the other.

While the authorities tend to concentrate on this requirement in terms **3–083** of the need for a claimant to establish detrimental reliance, it would not be correct to conclude that a constructive trust will only arise in cases where C is in some way worse off by relying on the imperfect agreement with D. There will be many such cases where some major shift in position is arguably of itself beneficial to C and therefore does not fulfil the requirement of *detrimental* reliance. Thus for instance moving to a new country in the light of some promise or representation[63] might conceivably be something which a claimant does in search of a better life, or might be something which costs the claimant the security of life in his/her homeland. It is suggested that whether of itself beneficial or detrimental to the claimant, provided that the shift in position or alteration in circumstances is of a significant nature, and is related to the promise or agreement which is at the heart of the claim in constructive trust, the claimant ought to be able to rely on Lord Bridge of Harwich's observation in *Lloyds Bank v Rosset* ([1991] A.C. 107 at 133) that a significant alteration of position will, for these purposes, suffice.

In considering the authorities dealing with detrimental reliance/significant shift in position, it is convenient to consider separately financial and non-financial conduct.

Financial conduct

Proof of a direct financial contribution to the purchase price is almost **3–084** always conclusive evidence that a claimant has a beneficial interest under a constructive trust (*Grant v Edwards* at 647B *per* Nourse L.J.; *c.f. Stokes v Anderson* ([1991] 1 F.L.R. 391) *per* Nourse L.J. at 398A). The same questions arise as in relation to the establishment of a common intention based on a financial contribution, namely whether the financial contribution was truly intended to be a gift or a loan[64] or whether the contribution is referable to the acquisition of the property[65]

It will frequently be the case that a claimant who has not made a financial contribution to the purchase price nonetheless acts in a way which has financial repercussions for him/her. Whether these amount to

---

[63] As in, for instance, *Ungurian v Lesnoff* [1990] 2 F.L.R. 200.
[64] Discussed in greater detail in Chapter 4, "Resulting Trusts", below, and see *Sekhon v Alissa* [1989] 2 F.L.R. 94.
[65] See e.g. *Winkworth v Edward Baron Development Co Ltd* [1986] 1 W.L.R. 1512.

detrimental reliance will be a matter of fact for the trial judge. Thus in *Cox v Jones* [2004] 2 F.L.R. 1057 C, a barrister, significantly reduced her practice at the bar in order to concentrate her energies on the joint property enterprise she was undertaking with D. That was held to be conduct which evidenced a detrimental reliance on the common intention that the beneficial interests in the relevant property should be shared. In *Banner Homes Plc v Luff Developments Ltd* ([2000] Ch. 372) Chadwick L.J. discusses (see 383–399) a number of authorities (largely commercial cases) and concluded (at 398E) that the reliance element of a constructive trust claim required that:

> "the non-acquiring party should do (or omit to do) something which confers an advantage on the acquiring party in relation to the acquisition of the property; or is detrimental to the ability of the non-acquiring party to acquire the property on equal terms".

In other words, an advantage conferred upon D will satisfy the requirement of an alteration of position or detrimental reliance just as readily as C acting to her direct detriment in the ordinary way.

Non-financial conduct

3–085 As the Court of Appeal made clear in *Grant v Edwards* ([1986] Ch. 638) reliance is not only established by expenditure referable to the acquisition of the house: conduct which does not necessarily involve direct financial outlay will just as readily suffice. In that case, Sir Nicholas Browne-Wilkinson V.C. was plainly of the view that reliance was not established by financial outlay only, but left open the question (see 656C) whether the conduct needed to be directly referable to the acquisition of the house, such as physical improvements to it or contributions to the purchase price. In his judgment in the same case, Nourse L.J. was less hesitant. He approached the issue in the following way (at 648E–H):

> "a distinction is to be made between conduct from which the common intention can be inferred on the one hand and conduct which amounts to acting upon it on the other. There remains this difficult question: what is the quality of the conduct required for the latter purpose? … In my judgment it must be conduct on which the woman could not reasonably have been expected to embark unless she was to have an interest in the house. If she was not to have an interest, she could reasonably be expected to go and live with her lover, but not, for example, to wield a 14lb sledgehammer in the front garden."

This last sentence is of course a reference to the facts of *Eves v Eves* ([1975] 1 W.L.R. 1338), where having been told that the property would have been purchased in joint names had she not been too young, the claimant wielded her 14lb sledgehammer to such good effect. That case in fact illustrates a wider proposition so far as improvements and renovations to the relevant property are concerned, namely that evidence which of itself would not necessarily justify the inference of a common intention may nonetheless suffice in terms of demonstrating detrimental reliance upon an intention which is established by other evidence.

The conduct must however go beyond that which might be ordinarily **3–086** expected from a person in C's circumstances who did *not* profess an interest in the relevant property. In *Cox v Jones* ([2004] 2 F.L.R. 1010) Mann J. considered that C had clearly acted to her detriment in reliance upon the agreement in that case, not only by supervising an extensive programme of renovations, but also by significantly reduced her practice at the bar in order to do so. By contrast, in *Lloyds Bank v Rosset*, Mrs Rosset had supervised and helped with the renovations to her home, in an attempt to get her home ready for occupation before Christmas. Lord Bridge remarked that far from evidencing any detrimental reliance on any common intention, or significant shift in her position, Mrs Rosset's actions in seeking to hasten the works to her house were "the most natural thing in the world" (at 131). In *Windeler v Whitehall* ([1990] 2 F.L.R. 505 at 511D) Millett J. accepted that Miss Windeler had supervised the builders renovating the relevant property, but held that "any wife or mistress would do the same".

Despite the Vice Chancellor's reservations in *Grant v Edwards*, there **3–087** are even instances in the reported cases of a shift in circumstances or change in the financial dealings between the parties which satisfy the reliance requirement even though the conduct relied on is wholly removed from any question of proprietary interests. In *Ungurian v Lesnoff* ([1990] 2 F.L.R. 200) for instance the claimant had given up secure accommodation and an academic career in Poland (described as "stable and stimulating" by the trial judge) in reliance upon the tacit agreement she had with the defendant. Although not directly related to the relevant property, Vinelott J. accepted without difficulty that the reliance requirement was more than satisfied by the claimant's conduct in irrevocably foresaking her settled life in Poland — at that time still a communist state.

Having said that, simply moving in with one's partner is unlikely to satisfy that requirement. As Nourse L.J. observed in *Grant v Edwards* (see 648G), "the law is not so cynical as to infer that a woman will only go to live with a man to whom she is not married if she understands that she is to have an interest in their home". Something further — conduct which can only be reasonably explained by an intention that (s)he was to have an interest in the relevant property — is required.

In terms of Lord Bridge's formulation of the test in *Rosset*, it does not **3–088** appear to be enough that a claimant can demonstrate some financial contribution to the running of the household or some significant shift in her position at about the time of the formulation of the common intention: (s)he must demonstrate a causal link between the two — in other words that her contribution was made in reliance upon the agreement, or that her shift in position was brought about by the common intention. Thus in *Green v Green* (2003) 5 I.T.E.L.R. 888 P.C. Lord Hope of Craighead considered (at 895A (para.12)) that there "must be a sufficient link between the common intention and the conduct relied on to show that the claimant has acted on the common intention to his detriment". To take the facts of *Ungurian v Lesnoff* for example, giving up a stable career and secure accommodation on the strength of an express or a tacit agreement that C should share the beneficial interest in the relevant property is one thing: giving up life behind the iron curtain in order to seek a better life in the UK (to alter the facts of that case slightly) and thereafter moving in with D because she loves him is quite another. In this respect the latter, the authorities seem to indicate, will not suffice.

3–089 A distinction must however be drawn in this regard between the usual case of the tacit common intention, and the more unusual case of a specific agreement between C and D that C would have an interest if she acted in a certain way. There, it is not necessary that the conduct in question relates to the property or its acquisition. It is sufficient to establish the reliance element necessary for the imposition of a constructive trust that it is the conduct agreed on by the parties:[66] Thus in *Bannister v Bannister* [1948] 2 All E.R. 133 an agreement that D would sell the relevant property to C subject to being able to remain living there for life was upheld as a constructive trust in D's favour even though there was no obvious detrimental reliance upon that agreement on D's part.

As with financial contributions, in cases where the claim to an interest is founded on an express agreement or understanding, the evidence establishing that agreement may also be relevant on the question of reliance. In for instance the situation where the parties discuss particular reasons why the claimant should not have a legal interest (e.g. to guard against claims from an ex spouse, as in *Oxley v Hiscock* [2005] Fam. 211) those discussions[67] plainly justify — though perhaps do not compel — the inference that both parties had intended that each should in fact have an interest. However, those discussions might also evidence detrimental reliance upon that common intention, if for instance the claimant acquiesced in the arrangement whereby she was not named as one of the legal owners, even though it was understood by both parties that she was to have an interest. In *Cox v Jones* ([2004] 2 F.L.R. 1010), for example D purchased the relevant property as C's nominee. At 1035 (para.45) Mann J. quoted with approval the remarks of Megarry J. in the earlier case of *Pallant v Morgan* [1953] Ch. 43 who had said:

"if A and B agree that A shall acquire some specific property for the joint benefit of A and B on terms yet to be agreed, and B, in reliance on A's agreement, is thereby induced to refrain from attempting to

---

[66] See *Grant v Edwards* at 657 *per* Sir Nicholas Browne-Wilkinson.
[67] See above at 3–011 *et seq.*

acquire the property, equity ought not to permit A when he acquires the property to insist on retaining the whole benefit for himself to the exclusion of B."[68]

The concept of detrimental reliance is discussed further in Chapter 6, **3–090** "Proprietary Estoppel", below. However, whilst the concept of reliance insofar as concerns constructive trust cases has much in common with the requirement of detrimental reliance for the purposes of establishing an estoppel, the two are not necessarily synonymous.

---

[68] In *Pallant v Morgan* [1953] Ch. 43 A and B agreed that A would not bid at auction for one of two plots bought by B on the basis that if B's bid for both plots was successful, he would sell one plot to A. In *Banner Homes Group Plc v Luff Developments Ltd* [2000] Ch. 372 Chadwick L.J. refers to a "*Pallant v Morgan* equity".

CHAPTER 4

RESULTING TRUSTS

As with constructive trusts, resulting trusts arise in a variety of different **4–001** circumstances and provide the means to achieve a just conclusion in many different situations. In cohabitation cases, the most commonly encountered version of this species of trust is the "purchase money" resulting trust. Briefly stated, this doctrine involves the assumption (rebuttable with appropriate evidence) that where C provides all or part of the purchase money in relation to a property acquired in D's name, then unless C's contribution was by way of a gift or a loan, the parties intended that C should have an interest commensurate with his/her contribution to the purchase price. The classic statement of the law in this respect is the observation of Eyre CB in *Dyer v Dyer* (1788) 2 Cox Eq. Cas. 92, who said:

> "The trust of a legal estate ... results to the man who advances the purchase money".[1]

A resulting trust may also arise where C transfers property in which he hitherto has enjoyed the undivided legal and beneficial interest into either D's sole name, or the joint names of C and D, in circumstances in which he does not intend to divest himself of his beneficial interest (or his entire beneficial interest) in the property. In such a case, there is no presumption that a resulting trust has arisen, but its existence can be established where the transferor demonstrates an intention, notwithstanding the transfer of legal title, to retain all or part of the beneficial interest for himself. In the absence of direct evidence of that intention, in parting with the legal interest the transferor is taken to have intended to part also with the beneficial interest in the property.[2] Direct evidence of an intention to retain a beneficial interest however places a claimant in the same situation as that enjoyed by a claimant in whose favour a resulting trust is presumed to have arisen.

---

[1] See also *Gross v French* (1975) 238 E.G. 39.
[2] An absence of an express declaration that the property is conveyed to A for his own use and enjoyment is not enough to give rise to the presumption of a resulting trust: see s.60(3) of the Law of Property Act 1925; see also *Hodgson v Marks* [1971] Ch. 892 and *Lahia v Lahia* (2000) LSG July 7.

4-002   For many years, the purchase money resulting trust was the principal vehicle utilised by claimants in cohabitation cases.[3] In a number of cohabitation cases before the appellate courts, the observation was made — perhaps inaptly — that it did not much matter whether an interest arose under a resulting trust or under a constructive trust. In *Gissing v Gissing* ([1971] A.C. 886 HL) Lord Diplock considered (at 905B–D) for the purposes of that appeal it was unnecessary to distinguish between a resulting trust and a constructive trust (*c.f. Hussey v Palmer* ([1972] 1 W.L.R. 1286) *per* Lord Denning M.R. at 1289H). More recent authority, however, clarifies that the resulting trust and the constructive trust are not merely interchangeable terms. Thus in *Drake v Whipp* ([1996] 1 F.L.R. 826 at 827C) Peter Gibson L.J. considered that the suggestion that it mattered not whether the terminology used was that of the resulting or the constructive trust was a "potent source of confusion". He drew in clear terms a distinction between "the constructive trust, to which the intention, actual or imputed, of the parties is crucial" and "the resulting trust, which operates as a presumed intention of the contributing party in the absence of rebutting evidence of actual intention".[4]

4-003   The fundamental distinction between the two situations appears to be that in the case of a resulting trust, it is C's contribution to the purchase price which of itself gives rise to the interest under the trust, unless evidence is deployed to the effect that the contribution was *not* intended to give rise to a beneficial interest. In the case of a constructive trust, the contribution is merely evidence which justifies the court in concluding that the parties have reached some imperfect agreement that both should share the beneficial interest in the property. In short, with a constructive trust, C gets what it was agreed/understood C should have. With a resulting trust, C gets what (s)he paid for.

Many academic commentators have criticised Lord Bridge's speech in *Lloyds Bank v Rosset* ([1991] A.C. 107) as wrongly characterising as a constructive trust the interest which arises where C and D both provide the funds with which the relevant property is purchased in D's name alone. That situation, it is argued, gives rise to a purchase money resulting trust rather than a constructive trust.[5] However, as Peter Gibson L.J. observed in *Drake v Whipp* ([1996] 1 F.L.R. 826 at 828H–829A) the principle of the resulting trust cannot arise if (a) there is a common intention to share the property beneficially, and (b) the claimant acts to his/her detriment on that common intention. In other words, any interest which might be established under a purchase money resulting trust is irrelevant if the claimant can make out a case based on a constructive trust.

4-004   Moreover, since the decision of the Court of Appeal in *Oxley v Hiscock* ([2005] Fam. 211), unless the parties have agreed what their respective

---

[3] As it was in matrimonial cases at least until the early 1970s, at which time the divorce courts were conferred with the power to adjust property rights on divorce.

[4] See also *Walker v Walker* (unreported) April 12, 1984 C.A. *per* Browne-Wilkinson L.J.

[5] See e.g. Underhill & Hayton, *Law Relating to Trusts and Trustees* (16th edn, 2003, p.414).

interests under a constructive trust should be, their interests will be determined in accordance with the court's view of what is fair having regard to the whole course of dealings between the parties in relation to the property (see *Oxley v Hiscock per* Chadwick L.J. at 246F–H (para.69) and see Chapter 5 "Quantification of Beneficial Interests", below). For practical purposes, the court is clothed with a discretion in this regard in all but name.[6] It is difficult to conceive of circumstances where a claimant's interest might be quantified as being less extensive under a constructive trust than under a resulting trust[7] and all too easy to conceive of circumstances where the interest under a constructive trust will be found to be greater than the interest which would arise under a resulting trust. For this reason, few claimants are likely to advance their claims on the basis of a resulting trust only.[8]

There are two further points of distinction between the two situations. First, in the case of a constructive trust, a claimant must show not only that each intended that each should have an interest, but also that C acted on that common intention to his/her detriment. The absence of any detrimental reliance would be fatal to both a claim founded in either the doctrine of the constructive trust or the doctrine of proprietary estoppel.[9] By contrast, in the case of a purchase money resulting trust, the presumption which arises on proof of a contribution to the overall purchase price (where there is an absence of evidence that the contribution was not intended to give rise to an interest) is that each party intended that the parties' respective shares were proportionate to their respective contributions to the purchase price. Nothing more therefore needs to be proved by the claimant alleging that a resulting trust has arisen in his/her favour. It must be acknowledged that in many constructive trust cases the contribution to the purchase price evidences not only the agreement or intention but also reliance upon it (see *Grant v Edwards* ([1986] Ch 638) *per* Nourse L.J.) but this will not invariably be the case.

The second point of distinction is this. A resulting trust arises by reference to contributions to the purchase price upon or prior to completion of the purchase.[10] Thus a claim based on a resulting trust cannot on the face of it succeed where the contribution prayed in aid is made after the purchase has been completed. Where a property is bought with the assistance of a mortgage, the party liable for the mortgage is, by reason of his liability under the mortgage, treated as having contributed the mortgage advance as though from his own funds.[11] Thus, as noted by

4–005

---

[6] See e.g. *Supperstone v Hurst* [2005] EWHC 1309 (Ch.)
[7] Where, as observed above, the claimant's interest is directly proportionate to his/her contribution to the purchase price.
[8] See also Law Commission paper *Cohabitation: the Financial Consequences of Relationship Breakdown* at para.3.24)
[9] As in *Midland Bank v Dobson* [1986] 1 F.L.R. 171.
[10] Described by Sir Peter Gibson in *Curley v Parkes* [2004] EWCA Civ 1515 at para.14 as arising "once and for all" at the time of the purchase.
[11] See also *Kowalczuk v Kowalczuk* [1973] 1 W.L.R. 930 at 935; *c.f. McKenzie v McKenzie* [2003] 2 P. & C.R. DG 6.

Sir Peter Gibson in *Curley v Parkes* ([2005] EWCA Civ 1515 at para.15), where the basis for C's claim to an interest in D's property arises from her contributions towards mortgage repayments,[12] reliance is generally placed on the common intention constructive trust identified in *Lloyds Bank v Rosset* ([1991] A.C. 107). Moreover, non-financial contributions, or indirect financial contributions, will by definition not give rise to a purchase-money resulting trust, even where the effect of such contribution is to enable or better enable the legal purchaser to complete the purchase.

The role of the resulting trust in cohabitation cases may therefore be seen, post *Oxley v Hiscock*, as somewhat residual[13] but it is submitted that there are still situations where a claimant may succeed in demonstrating an interest under a resulting trust even if a claim to a constructive trust cannot be made out. These are considered further below.

The presumption of the resulting trust

4–006   An interest under a resulting trust arises because the presumption of a resulting trust is not displaced. The presumption of a resulting trust however only arises where an earlier presumption — that the legal and beneficial interests in land coincide[14] — is rebutted. Whether the presumption of a resulting trust is itself rebutted will of course depend entirely on the evidence adduced.

4–007   Determining where the beneficial interests truly lie therefore depends on which in a series of consequential presumptions can successfully be rebutted. The somewhat tortuous route by which equity arrives at the answer to the question[15] "who *really* owns this property?" can be summarised in the following series of propositions:

1.   The beneficial interest in any land is presumed to correspond to the legal interests in that land. Where D holds the legal title to any land, in the absence of evidence to the contrary he is presumed also to enjoy the beneficial interest in property.[16]

2.   The presumption described in (1) can be rebutted with evidence that:

---

[12] Or from a contribution to the costs of the purchase — *ibid.* para.22.

[13] See e.g. Simon Edwards, *Property Rights in the Family Home — Clarity at Last* [2004] Fam. Law 524.

[14] As reflected in the maxim "equity follows the law", *c.f. Pettitt v Pettitt* [1970] A.C. 777 HL *per* Lord Upjohn at 813H–814A, *Vandervell v IRC* [1966] Ch 261 CA *per* Diplock L.J. at 287G, *Crisp v Mullings* (1976) 239 E.G. 119, *Grimes v Grimes* [2003] 2 F.L.R. 510 *per* Wilson J. at para.35, *Walker v Hall* [1984] F.L.R. 126 *per* Dillon L.J. at 133E.

[15] To put it in the way in which the man on the Clapham omnibus might.

[16] *Pettitt v Pettitt* [1970] A.C. 777 at 814A *per* Lord Upjohn, *Crisp v Mullings* (1976) 239 E.G. 119 *per* Russell L.J., *Gissing v Gissing* [1971] A.C. 886 *per* Lord Pearson at 902B, *Bernard v Josephs* [1982] Ch. 391 *per* Griffiths L.J. at 403D–F.

(a) C (a person other than the legal purchaser) provided the whole of, or contributed to, the purchase price[17]; or

(b) the land in question was conveyed from C to D without any intention that D should become the beneficial owner.[18]

3. The presumption described in (1) will not be rebutted where valuable consideration (e.g. some lesser interest in, or rights over, the land in question) is conferred upon C.[19]

4. Where the presumption in (1) is rebutted in the circumstances mentioned in either (2)(a) or (b) above, a resulting trust is presumed to arise in favour of C.[20]

5. C is presumed in the circumstances described in (2(a)) to enjoy a beneficial interest in the land in proportion to his contribution to the purchase price.[21]

6. C is presumed in the circumstances described in (2(b)) to enjoy the entire beneficial interest in the property, unless the evidence establishes that C only intended to retain a partial interest for himself, in which his case his interest will be commensurate with that intention.[22]

7. In the circumstances described in (2(a)) above, the presumption of a resulting trust in C's favour can be rebutted by evidence that the relevant funds were provided to D by way of a gift or a loan.[23]

8. In the circumstances described in (2(b)) above, the presumption of a resulting trust either does not arise or can be rebutted by evidence that the relevant land was conveyed to D by way of a gift.[24]

9. In the circumstances described in either (5) or (6) above, where the relationship between C and D is such as to give rise to the

---

[17] *Pettitt v Pettitt* [1970] A.C. 777 *per* Lord Upjohn at 815G, *Cowcher v Cowcher* [1972] 1 W.L.R. 425 *per* Bagnall J. at 431B, *Kyriakides v Pippas* [2004] 2 F.C.R. 432 *per* Gabriel Moss Q.C. (sitting as a deputy judge of the Chancery Division) at 447 (para.74)

[18] *Lavelle v Lavelle* [2004] 2 F.C.R. 418 *per* Lord Phillips M.R. at 421 (para.13), *Hodgson v Marks* [1971] Ch. 892, *Fowkes v Pascoe* (1875) 10 Ch. App. 343. The mere absence of any expression in the relevant instrument to the effect that the property is conveyed to the transferee for his use or benefit will not of itself give rise to the presumption of a resulting trust: see s.60(3) of the Law of Property Act 1925.

[19] *Collier v Collier* (2002) 6 I.T.E.L.R. 270 *per* Chadwick L.J. at 292H–293A (para.70)

[20] *Dyer v Dyer* (1788) 2 Cox Eq. Cas. 92, *Gissing v Gissing* [1971] A.C. 886.

[21] *Crisp v Mullings* (1976) 239 E.G. 119 *per* Russell L.J., *Walker v Hall* [1984] F.L.R. 126 *per* Dillon L.J. at 133G, *Pettitt v Pettitt* [1970] A.C. 777 *per* Lord Upjohn at 814B, *Williams & Glyn's Bank v Boland* [1981] A.C. 487 *per* Lord Wilberforce at 502G; *c.f. Bull v Bull* [1955] 1 Q.B. 234.

[22] *Hodgson v Marks* [1971] 1 Ch. 892, *Lavelle v Lavelle* [2004] 2 F.C.R. 418 *per* Lord Phillips M.R. at 421 (para.13)

[23] *Sekhon v Alissa* [1989] 2 F.L.R. 94 at 99D–E *per* Hoffman J.

[24] *Fowkes v Pascoe* (1875) 10 Ch. App. 343 *per* Mellish L.J. at 352–3, *Cowcher v Cowcher* [1972] 1 W.L.R. 425 *per* Bagnall J. at 431C and *Winkworth v Edward Baron Development Co Ltd* [1986] 1 W.L.R. 1512 *per* Lord Templeman at 1516E.

presumption of advancement, that presumption displaces the earlier presumption of a resulting trust.[25]

4–008   One consequence of the importance of presumptions in this field is that the burden of proof shifts from one party to the other and back again at various stages of the court's analysis. Where D holds the legal title, the burden is first on C to deploy evidence which gives rise to the presumption of a resulting trust. Where C successfully does so, the burden shifts to D to show that the presumption of a resulting trust is rebutted by evidence of an intention on C's part to the effect that any funds advanced were by way of a gift or loan.[26] The presumption of the resulting trust is however displaced by the presumption of advancement, if it arises, in which case the burden shifts back to C to demonstrate that the advance or transfer was *not* intended to be by way of a gift.

In *Pettitt v Pettitt* ([1970] A.C. 777) Lord Upjohn made the important point (at 814G) that the various presumptions were capable of being rebutted with "comparatively slight evidence". It does not follow however that in every case "comparatively slight evidence" will in fact rebut the presumption. Where the presumption arises, the weight of the evidence required to rebut it will vary from case to case. In *Fowkes v Pascoe* ((1875) 10 Ch. App. 343) Melish L.J. said:

> "(T)he presumption must, beyond all question, be of different weight in different cases. In some cases it would be very strong indeed. If, for instance, a man invested a sum of stock in the name of himself and his solicitor, the inference would be very strong indeed that it was intended solely for the purpose of a trust and the court would require very strong evidence on the part of a solicitor to prove that it was intended as a gift ... On the other hand, a man may make an investment of stock in the name of himself and some other person, although not a child or wife, yet in such a position to him as to make it extremely probable that the investment was intended as a gift."

Lord Upjohn accepted in *Pettitt* (at 813G) that the operation of presumptions in this area (particularly the presumption of advancement) had been "criticised as being out of touch with the realities of today" but considered that "when properly understood and properly applied ... they remain as useful as ever in solving questions of title".

The nature of the contribution

4–009   The circumstances in which a contribution to the relevant purchase price gives rise to the presumption of a resulting trust do not in practice tend (with the exception of contributions post-purchase to the mortgage

[25] E.g. *Moate v Moate* [1948] 2 All E.R. 486 Ch. D. *per* Jenkins J. at 487D–G.
[26] See *Sekhon v Alissa* [1989] 2 F.L.R. 94 at 99D–E *per* Hoffman J.; *c.f. Dewar v Dewar* [1975] 1 W.L.R. 1352 *per* Goff J. at 1535G.

repayments) to be notably different from the circumstances which justify the inference of a common intention in terms of *Lloyds Bank v Rosset* limb two.[27] In either case, evidence that a person other than the legal owner has contributed to the purchase price will on the face of it evidence an intention to share the beneficial interests. Where the relevant contribution is made in the nature of a gift or a loan, however, no beneficial interest will arise either under a constructive trust or under a resulting trust. This is because where the contribution is made by way of a gift or a loan, the intention of the contributor is either that the advance should be returned (with or without terms as to, for instance, interest or security) notwithstanding any fluctuation in the value of the property, or that the advance is intended solely to benefit the recipient. Neither is consistent with an intention to share in the beneficial interest in the property. Equally, evidence however of an intention to make a gift of the land in question will displace the presumption of a resulting trust.

The analysis of the basis upon which a contribution to the purchase price was made is therefore of crucial importance in both constructive trust and resulting trust cases In either case, a finding that the relevant contribution was advanced by way of a gift or loan will be fatal to the claim to share the beneficial interest, just as a finding that land was transferred as a gift will be fatal to a claim to an interest under a resulting trust.

Loans

Ordinarily, where one party advances to another part or all of the pur- **4–010** chase price relating to the relevant property, if that advance is by way of a loan, the funds advanced become the property of the borrower (see *Halifax Building Society v Brown* ([1996] 1 F.L.R. 103) *per* Balcombe L.J. at 109D). The lender generally does not retain any beneficial interest in the funds advanced. Whilst the borrower is fixed with a liability to repay the loan on whatever terms are agreed (or even on terms imposed by statute) he is absolutely beneficially entitled to any property he purchases using the loan advance (save in the exceptional case of the *Quistclose* trust,[28] discussion of which is beyond the scope of this work). Thus where C lends money to D which is used by D to purchase a property, the money C has provided specifically by way of a loan will not give rise to a proprietary interest in that property in C's favour save insofar as the property may be security for the loan (*Re Sharpe* [1980] 1 W.L.R. 219).[29]

The importance of the distinction between a loan advance and a contribution to the purchase price cannot therefore be easily understated. The nature of the advance will have a crucial role to play in establishing

---

[27] See above, and see Chapter 3 "Constructive Trusts", below.
[28] See *Barclays Bank v Quistclose Investments Ltd* [1970] A.C. 567 HL.
[29] This would not of course be the case where the parties agree in terms that a contribution which started life as a loan should thereafter be regarded as a contribution to the purchase price — see *Risch v McFee* [1991] 1 F.L.R. 105, discussed below.

whether C now enjoys a beneficial interest in the property.[30] The importance of the proper investigation of the factual issue is perhaps illustrated by the case of *Risch v McFee* ([1991] 1 F.L.R. 105). There, what started out as a loan from C to D was neither repaid, nor was any demand for repayment or offer of payment made. A beneficial interest was established by reason of a further advance which enabled D to repay the mortgage. It was held that although the earlier payment "started life" as a loan (*per* Balcombe L.J. at 110G) once it was established that C had a beneficial interest in the house, the loan advance would be regarded as part of her contribution.

4–011   The possibility that the funds provided were intended to be repayable as a loan does not only arise at the point of purchase: subsequent cash injections can also give rise to the possibility. In *Hussey v Palmer* ([1972] 1 W.L.R. 1286) Cairns L.J. said (at 1292E–G):

> "As it was a loan, I think it is quite inconsistent with that to say that it could create a resulting trust at the same time ... that proposition is equally applicable where it is not a matter of the property being purchased, but a matter of a builder being paid for an extension to a property which already belongs to the borrower of the money."[31]

While of course in general terms a resulting trust arises at the point of purchase, so that contributions towards mortgage repayments do not for instance give rise to the presumption, where for instance one party funds substantial improvements to the property, the "purchase" for that purpose might properly be regarded as the point at which the property becomes substantially different in nature to the unimproved property, even though there may be no transfer of title or other transaction in the nature of a purchase. It is submitted however that such a contribution is perhaps more appropriately regarded as evidence of a common intention such as to give rise to a constructive trust.

Gifts

4–012   As with a loan, evidence that a contribution to, or payment of, the purchase price in relation to the relevant property will not give rise to an interest under a resulting trust if the payment/contribution was made by way of a gift. The essence of a gift is that the recipient of the gift receives something for nothing: Bagnall J. described the necessary intention on the part of the donee[32] as being an intention "to confer bounty". An interest under a resulting trust is on the face of it incompatible with a finding that the relevant contribution was made by way of a gift. Thus

---

[30] See e.g. *Richards v Dove* [1974] 1 All E.R. 888 where the court characterised the funds advanced by C in that case as a loan which did not give rise to any beneficial interest.

[31] Although this statement was made in the course of a dissenting judgment, as a concise statement of the general law on this point it is submitted that the above is unimpeachable.

[32] See *Cowcher v Cowcher* [1972] 1 W.L.R. 425 at 431C.

where for instance land is conveyed by C to D without consideration in return either in terms of money or money's worth, the only logical possibilities would appear to be either that C intended to confer a beneficial interest upon D without seeking anything in return, in which case no resulting trust can arise, or that he did not, in which case a gift does not arise.[33]

In practice, one of the areas in which the question of whether a gift was intended most frequently arises is in the context of a claim by the extended members of the family of the owners of the relevant property to a beneficial interest in the relevant property arising by way of a contribution to the purchase price. Where for instance H and W are provided by H's parents with a 10 per cent deposit in relation to the property then purchased by H and W, there might be a number of situations in which the nature of that contribution might arise for determination: W may for instance seek financial provision from H on the breakdown of their marriage, with H's parents intervening to protect their interest; if H's parents are declared bankrupt; a threat to H and W's property may be posed by the parents' creditors. Each case would require the court to determine whether the contribution made by H's parents gives rise to the presumption of a resulting trust, and whether that presumption is rebutted. In for instance *Sekhon v Alissa* ([1989] 2 F.L.R. 94) a mother and daughter both contributed towards the purchase price of a property conveyed into the daughter's sole name, in respective proportions of (approximately) 60/40. The 40 per cent contributed by the daughter was in fact raised by way of a mortgage; the mother's contribution came from her savings. Hoffman J. held on the facts that neither party considered the mother's contribution to be a gift, inter alia because the finding of a gift would mean that the mother had intended to part with the entirety of her life savings.

In such cases, written records of the relevant intention of the parties **4–013** tend to be incomplete or vague when they exist at all; this is a common trait in "gift" cases which naturally tend to involve informal family arrangements rather than arms' length commercial transactions. *In re Gooch* (1890) 62LT 384[34] is therefore an unusual case in that there was some written record of the alleged donor's intention. In that case, a father purchased stock in a certain company in his son's name. The stockholding ensured that the son was qualified to act as a director of the company. However the father kept the relevant certificates in an envelope on which he had written "belonging to me", which was accepted as evidence that he had not intended to confer a gratuitous benefit on his son.

In cases where the presumption of advancement does not apply, the absence of any direct evidence of a donative intent will usually, but not

---

[33] Even in cases where it is common ground that the transferor intended to retain a partial interest, the same question arises in relation to the balance of the interest as to whether or not the transfer was intended to be a gift.

[34] Cited by Lord Upjohn in *Pettitt v Pettitt* [1970] A.C. 777 at 814G.

necessarily, be fatal to an assertion that the relevant contribution is a gift. In for instance *Fowkes v Pascoe* ((1875) 10 Ch. App. 343),[35] stock in a company which was paid for by C was conveyed to D, the son of C's daughter in law by a previous marriage. After C's death, the question arose as to whether the stock in D's name was subject to a resulting trust in favour of C's estate. Since there was no conceivable reason for C's putting the stock in D's name, the presumption of a resulting trust was rebutted and the stock was held to be a gift to D. Had the relationship between C and D been such as to give rise to the presumption of advancement, the outcome of the case would have been no different.

The presumption of advancement

4–014 This presumption carries, at least potentially, particular significance in certain cases in the determination of whether a contribution was made with the intention of conferring a gratuitous benefit. Where the presumption of advancement operates, it has the effect of shifting the burden to the party asserting a beneficial interest to show that funds he provided towards the purchase price of the relevant property (or that the property was transferred by him to the legal titleholder for no or no adequate consideration) were *not* provided by way of a gift. The burden therefore rests upon the party asserting a beneficial interest to show that the transaction was *not* intended to be a gift.[36] Thus, unless the presumption of advancement can be rebutted, even in a case where it is accepted that C provided all or part of the purchase money in relation to the property held in D's name, he will not be able to make out his claim to a resulting trust, or indeed to a limb two constructive trust unless C can show that he did *not* intend his contribution to the purchase price to be a gift to D.

It is not every relationship which gives rise to the presumption of advancement: the rules relating to the presumption in general were formulated in the nineteenth century and earlier, when very different social attitudes existed towards family relationships and obligations.[37] The presumption therefore operates against a father where the relevant property is conveyed into the name of a child,[38] but not against a mother in otherwise indistinguishable circumstances.[39] Whilst comparatively slight evidence might be needed to show that a mother's intention had

---

[35] Also cited by Lord Upjohn in *Pettitt*.

[36] See *Warren v Gurney* [1944] 2 All E.R. 472, *Stock v McAvoy* (1872) L.R. 15 Eq. 55; *Gross v French* [1976] 1 E.G.L.R. 129.

[37] *Pettitt v Pettitt* [1970] A.C. 777 at 824C *per* Lord Diplock; in *Falconer v Falconer* [1970] 1 W.L.R. 1333 Lord Denning suggested at 1335H–1336A that the presumption emanated from "Victorian days when a wife was utterly subordinate to her husband" — see also *per* Megaw L.J. at 1337G.

[38] *Dyer v Dyer* (1788) Cox Eq. Cas. 92 at 93F, *Re Roberts* [1946] Ch. 1.

[39] *Gross v French* [1976] 1 E.G.L.R. 129 *per* Scarman L.J., *Bennet v Bennet* (1879) 10 Ch. D. 474 at 478 *per* Sir George Jessel M.R., *Sekhon v Alissa* [1989] 2 F.L.R. 94.

been to make a gift of the relevant property (or purchase monies) to her child,[40] the presumption per se does not apply.[41] The presumption does not apply "in reverse", i.e. where as between a father and his child, the relevant property is purchased using the child's money but is conveyed into the name of the father.[42]

Similarly, the presumption applies as between a husband and a wife[43] if   **4–015**
the relevant property is purchased using the husband's funds but conveyed into the wife's name,[44] but does not apply where the roles are reversed and the property is conveyed to the husband where the wife has provided the purchase monies.[45] The presumption even applies where a man funds the purchase of property in the name of a woman, if in express contemplation of a marriage which does in fact later take place[46] but again not where the sexes of the parties are reversed. The presumption does not apply to cohabitees who do not marry,[47] or to transactions involving siblings, children in law, nephews or nieces or parents in law (*Hoare v Hoare* (1982) 13 Fam. Law 142).

From the perspective of the 21st century practitioner, the principles and authorities dealing with the presumption of advancement appear paternalistic and arcane, their impact in practice arbitrary and liable to lead to injustice. In *Pettitt v Pettitt* ([1970] A.C. 777) Lord Reid observed at 793F that the presumption of advancement between husband and wife had been much diminished given changing social attitudes. Lord Diplock made the same point in *Gissing v Gissing* ([1971] A.C. 886 at 907D–E).[48] In *McGrath v Wallis* ([1995] 2 F.L.R. 114) Nourse L.J. expressed the view that since *Pettitt*, the presumption had been "reclassified as a judicial instrument of last resort". In that case, the decision made at first instance, which had treated the presumption as determinative, was decisively reversed. Ordinarily, as Nourse L.J. observed in *McGrath*, comparatively slight direct evidence of an absence of an intention to make a gift of the relevant property would suffice to rebut the presumption in those cases where it applied.[49] Equally, in *Ali v Khan* ((2002) 5 I.T.E.L.R. 232 CA) Sir Andrew Morritt V.C. acknowledged (at 245B) that the presumption could not be used to override admissible evidence of a contrary intention.[50]

---

[40] *Bennet v Bennet* (1879) 10 Ch. D. 474 *per* Sir George Jessel M.R. at 478.
[41] In *Re Cameron, dec'd* [1999] Ch. 386 Lindsay considered at 405D (para.51) that the presumption arose whether the donor was a father or a mother, though in the context of whether a legacy under a will had been satisfied by an *inter vivos* disposition.
[42] *Binmatt v Ali* (unreported) October 6, 1981.
[43] But see below at 4–016.
[44] *Pettitt v Pettitt* [1970] A.C. 777 at 824B and see *Christ's Hospital v Budgin* (1712) 2 Vern. 683 at 684.
[45] *Mercier v Mercier* [1903] 2 Ch. 98.
[46] *Moate v Moate* [1948] 2 All E.R. 486 at 487E–H; *c.f. Mossop v Mossop* [1989] Fam. 77 at 84F–H *per* Balcombe L.J.
[47] *Diwell v Farnes* [1959] 1 W.L.R. 624 *per* Hodson L.J. at 627.
[48] *c.f. Falconer v Falconer* [1970] 1 W.L.R. 1333 *per* Lord Denning at 1335H–1336A.
[49] *c.f. Pettitt v Pettitt* [1970] A.C. 777 *per* Lord Upjohn at 814G.
[50] See also *Anson v Anson* [1953] 1 Q.B. 636 *per* Pearson J. at 641, 645.

4–016   Nevertheless, despite the nature and history of the presumption, it remains part and parcel of the law which governs cohabitation claims, and therefore cannot simply be cavalierly disregarded. Thus Slade L.J. said in *Harwood v Harwood* ([1991] 2 F.L.R. 274 at 294B):

> "Though the presumption of advancement as between husband and wife must be applied with caution in modern social conditions, we see nothing sufficient to displace it in the present case".

It should be noted that whilst the above represents the law at the time of going to press, the Family Law (Property and Maintenance) Bill was introduced before Parliament in late 2005. If this Bill becomes law, it is proposed that the presumption of advancement should be abolished insofar as it applies as between husband and wife. The Bill makes no proposals — at least as presently drafted — as regards the presumption insofar as it applies to fathers. The gender bias demonstrated above would seem to indicate that it is only a matter of time until it is declared incompatible with the European Convention on Human Rights. In a written answer to a question in the House of Lords,[51] the Government acknowledged a strong case for concluding that the apparent gender bias surrounding the presumption contravenes Article 5 of the Seventh Protocol to the European Convention on Human Rights in terms of equality of rights and responsibilities between spouses. Whilst the Bill presently before Parliament may correct that, the inequality as between fathers and mothers and their children remains.

4–017   In practice the presumption only rarely affects the outcome of a case.[52] Nonetheless, there is one situation in which the presumption takes on a particular significance. This is where the reason for the conveyance into the name of D alone, even though C funds or contributes to the purchase, or conveys his property ostensibly gratuitously to D, is to further some unlawful or illegitimate purpose of C's. One illustration of this would be where the reason for the transfer giving rise to the trust is to enable the true beneficial owner to shield an asset from the view of actual or potential creditors. In such circumstances, equity will not allow a claimant to rely on evidence of his own wrongdoing in order to displace the prima facie position that the legal and beneficial interests coincide. This issue requires consideration in some detail.

Claims made in furtherance of an unlawful agreement or purpose

4–018   The distinguishing feature of the common intention constructive trust it is that equity interposes itself to uphold the imperfect agreement reached between the parties.[53] The respective intentions of the relevant parties is

---

[51] *Hansard* HL April 21, 1998 vol. 588 col. 197, and see *Sharing Homes* Law Com 278.
[52] In *McGrath*, Nourse L.J. confessed at 115B that he had been unable to recollect any reported case since 1970 in which the presumption had been decisive.
[53] See above, Chapter 3 "Constructive Trusts".

therefore of fundamental importance. Yet where the parties' agreement itself furthers an illegal purpose, any claim that a constructive trust has arisen must fail on the application of the general principle of law which prevents a claimant to benefit from his own wrongdoing. This principle is of course reflected in maxims such as "he who comes to equity must come with clean hands", and "*ex turpi causa non oritur actio*" (see *Holman v Johnson* (1775) 1 Cowp. 341, 343).[54] Public policy prevents a claimant from relying on his own unlawful intention, thus he is unable to demonstrate the common intention necessary to give rise to a constructive trust. In *Tribe v Tribe* ([1996] Ch. 107 at 133F) Millett L.J. described this as "the primary rule".

In such cases, however, where two parties contribute towards the purchase of a property conveyed into the name of only one of them, the necessary intention (namely that the parties intended that each should have an interest commensurate with his contribution to the purchase price), is presumed. There is therefore no need to lead evidence which would establish the necessary intention (albeit formed for an unlawful purpose); the claimant must merely demonstrate that the contribution to the purchase price was actually made. Even direct uncontested evidence that an illegal purpose was intended will not prevent such a contribution from giving rise to the presumption of a resulting trust. It is in this situation, perhaps, where the property enjoyed by C and D is held in D's sole name to avoid some actual or potential claim against C, or to confer some illegitimate benefit upon D, that the doctrine of the resulting trust is likely to be of greatest significance in the context of cohabiting couples.

The leading case on this point is undoubtedly the decision of the House **4–019** of Lords in *Tinsley v Milligan* ([1994] 1 A.C. 340). In that case, C and D jointly purchased a house which was registered only in D's name. Although both C and D understood the beneficial interests to be shared between themselves, both made applications for various social security benefits which would not have been paid to them had the Department of Social Security been made aware that both in fact had an interest in the relevant property. On C's claim (after her relationship with D had broken down) to a 50 per cent interest in the property, D's defence was that C was not entitled to rely upon her own illegal purpose in claiming equitable relief. By the time the litigation reached the House of Lords, C had made a full disclosure of her wrongdoing to the Department of Social Security. D had been prosecuted, convicted, fined and required to repay certain sums to the Department. By a majority of 3:2, the House of Lords decided that C was entitled to an interest in the property by reason of the

---

[54] In fact, to characterise this situation as an application of the "clean hands" doctrine might be a convenient shorthand description but that would in fact be slightly misleading: the House of Lords held by a majority in *Tinsley v Milligan* [1994] 1 A.C. 340 that the clean hands doctrine only applied to an applicant seeking discretionary relief such as specific performance or an injunction, rather than to an applicant seeking to establish a proprietary right: see further *Lowson v Coombes* [1999] 1 F.L.R. 799 *per* Robert Walker L.J. at 807D–808B.

interest which arose in her favour under a resulting trust, not by reason of any constructive trust. As Lord Browne-Wilkinson said (at 371G):

> "Where the presumption of resulting trust applies, the plaintiff does not have to rely on the illegality. If he proves that the property is vested in the defendant alone but that the plaintiff provided part of the purchase money, or voluntarily transferred the property to the defendant, the plaintiff establishes his claim under a resulting trust unless either the contrary presumption of advancement displaces the presumption of resulting trust, or the defendant leads evidence to rebut the presumption of resulting trust. Therefore, in cases where the presumption of advancement does not apply, a plaintiff can establish his equitable interest without relying in any way on the underlying illegal transaction."[55]

In other words, if it had been necessary for C to rely upon her own illegality, for instance in a case where a constructive trust was alleged to have arisen on the basis of express discussions, her claim would have failed. However, having made a contribution to the purchase price, her claim to an interest succeeded on the basis of a resulting trust in the absence of evidence that C's contribution was made by way of a gift or a loan. Similarly, in *Lowson v Coombes* ([1999] Ch. 373) the Court of Appeal considered the situation where C and D had using joint funds bought a property which was conveyed into D's name alone to avoid claims against C brought by his former wife. The Court of Appeal accepted that the intention to defeat the claims of C's wife was an illegal purpose, but in order to establish a resulting trust C did not need to rely upon that purpose. The provision by C of part of the purchase monies itself gave rise to the presumption of a resulting trust.

4–020   Lord Browne-Wilkinson's reference in *Tinsley v Milligan* to the presumption of advancement in the context of some illicit underlying purpose calls for particular consideration. Ordinarily, the claim to a resulting trust arises in circumstances where the evidence established that C provided the purchase money in relation to the property bought in D's name, or transferred the relevant property to D for no consideration. Evidence of such facts alone will give rise to the presumption of a resulting trust, unless and until evidence is put before the court tending to show that C's advance was by way of a loan or a gift. If, however, the relationship between C and D gives rise to the presumption of advancement (see above) the only way in which C can rebut the presumption is by leading

---

[55] In *Collier v Collier* (2002) 6 I.T.E.L.R. 270 Mance L.J. accepted at para. 106 that the distinction between allowing a claim to a proprietary interest to succeed in the teeth of the claimant's illegality but not a claim to a discretionary remedy was tenuous, but considered that the rationale was that "the existence of objective and neutral facts preserves a limited distance between the court and the illegality".

evidence of the illicit underlying purpose. This he cannot do[56] because of the primary rule which operates so as to prevent him from leading evidence of such purpose. The claimant is thereby disabled from discharging the burden of proof upon him on that issue.[57]

The authorities dealing with this point all tend to illustrate that one particularly common reason for placing the relevant property in the hands of another — that is, to defeat actual or potential creditors — is generally regarded as a purpose which offends the "clean hands" doctrine and the underlying rule of public policy. As noted above, in *Lowson v Coombes* ([1999] Ch. 373) the Court of Appeal accepted that an intention to defeat the claims of C's wife was an illegal purpose, though on the facts of that case C did not need to rely upon that purpose. In *Gascoigne v Gascoigne* ([1918] 1 K.B. 223) C used his own funds to build a house which he then transferred into the name of D, his wife. The intention of both parties had been to defeat present and future creditors. C for instance refused to pay tax in relation to the property on the basis that it belonged to his wife. C later brought an action to recover the property which failed, on the basis that he was not entitled to rely on his own illegality in seeking to rebut the presumption of advancement which arose as between husband and wife.

In *Tinker v Tinker* ([1970] P. 136) C moved to Cornwall having purchased a garage business there. He also bought a house there, which was conveyed into his wife's name, in order to defeat potential creditors in the event that the business was not a success and he was indebted to creditors. On the breakdown of the marriage between C and D, C argued that the house belonged to him under a resulting trust. At first instance, the registrar made the finding that C had not acted dishonestly. In the Court of Appeal it was held that there was nothing objectionable about placing the house in his wife's name to protect it from the claims of creditors if the wife held the beneficial interest as well as the legal interest. The significance of the finding that C had *not* acted dishonestly was that if C had intended to place the property in D's name whilst retaining the beneficial interest himself, that would plainly indicate a dishonest intention. The finding of an honest intention was consistent only with an actual intention (to protect the house from the claims of creditors) that D should enjoy the beneficial interest as well as the legal interest. In those circumstances, evidence as to C's reasons for placing the house in D's name in no way went displaced the presumption of advancement: rather, the evidence tended to strengthen the presumption that C had intended D to enjoy the beneficial interest as well as the legal interest. The Court of Appeal made clear in that case its distaste for the prospect of a claimant maintaining as against his creditors that he had no interest in the

4–021

---

[56] at least not if the purpose has been carried into effect; see *Tribe v Tribe* [1996] Ch. 107, discussed below.

[57] In *Ali v Khan* (2002) 5 I.T.E.L.R. 232 Sir Andrew Morritt V.C. stressed (at 245B) that *admissible* evidence was required to rebut the presumption.

property, yet claiming a beneficial interest as against the person in whose name the property had been purchased.[58]

4–022   In *Tribe v Tribe* ([1996] Ch. 107), the Court of Appeal drew a distinction, however, between an unlawful purpose which had actually been carried into effect, and one which had not been implemented. In that case, the property with which the Court of Appeal was concerned was in fact shares in a company rather that real property, although that did not give rise to a material distinction in terms of the applicable principles.[59] The facts of *Tribe* were that C was the majority shareholder in the company through which he conducted a clothing business. The premises from which the company traded, however, were rented by C in his own name. C's obligations under the lease included a full repairing covenant, and he was served with a schedule of dilapidations which he was not in a position to make good. In order to protect the company in the event of an attempt to any enforcement action against him arising from his liability under the lease, C transferred the majority of his shares to his son D. The stated consideration for the transfer was £89,000 though this was never in fact paid. C was able in the event to resolve his dispute with the landlord by (inter alia) surrendering the lease, without making good the dilapidations. Subsequently, D refused to transfer the shares back to C. On C's claim for a declaration that D held the shares on trust for C, it had been contended for D that although no consideration had been paid for the shares, the presumption of advancement arose in D's favour. On the facts of the case, it was argued, the presumption could not be rebutted by C since in order to do so, he would need to rely on his own illegal purpose, namely an improper attempt to defeat his creditors. At first instance, C's claim was upheld. Dismissing D's appeal against the order made at first instance, Nourse L.J. held that *Tinsley v Milligan* had not decided that a claimant could not lead evidence of an illegal purpose to rebut the presumption of advancement in any circumstances. He considered (see 121F) that where the presumption of advancement prima facie arose, the claimant was precluded from leading evidence of his own illegality to rebut that presumption only if the illegal purpose had been carried out.[60] Where, as here, the unlawful intention had not actually been implemented, there was no actual benefit to the party asserting an interest under the trust. As such, the principle that the law should not assist a party to benefit from his own wrongdoing was not engaged.

4–023   At some risk of repetition, the law in this area might be summarised in this way:

---

[58] Per Lord Denning at 141G–H.

[59] There are some modest distinctions in trusts arising in relation to personal property, for instance the fact that s.53(1) of the Law of Property Act 1925 does not apply. These are discussed further in Chapter 8 "Personal Obligations between Co-Owners", below.

[60] See also *per* Millett L.J. at 134134E–135B; *c.f. Sekhon v Alissa* [1989] 2 F.L.R. 94 *per* Hoffman J. at 96C, *Chettiar v Chettiar* [1962] A.C. 294 P.C. *per* Lord Denning.

1. A party ("C") cannot advance a claim to an interest under a constructive trust in property held by another party ("D") where the property is held or acquired in D's name in furtherance of some illicit purpose, including any attempt to shield assets from creditors.
2. C can however establish an interest under a resulting trust from a contribution to the purchase price (or on a transfer from C to D without consideration) because there the intention that C should have an interest does not have to be proved by, as one might term it, "tainted evidence"; rather, it is presumed from the fact of the contribution/absence of consideration.
3. Different considerations apply where the relationship between C and D gives rise to the presumption of advancement. There, an intention to confer bounty is presumed in favour of D. Ordinarily, C cannot rebut this presumption since to do so would involve him relying on his own unlawful purpose.
4. If, however, C has not actually carried out his illicit purpose, he can nonetheless give evidence of his unlawful intention since there he has not benefited from the illicit purpose.

It might be concluded, from all of the above, that the law is in a somewhat unsatisfactory state. Where the relationship the transferor has with X would give rise to the presumption of advancement and the relationship with Y would not, the selection of X rather than Y to act as the nominal titleholder is vested with a significance which is in all probability entirely unforeseen. Even where the illegality has been relied on, if the claimant is the defendant's mother a resulting trust can be established, but not if the claimant is the defendant's father. If a husband and wife transferred joint property to their son to defeat the claims of creditors, the mother would on the face of it be able to recover the property from her son but the father would not.

As between partners living together, the presumption arises (at least for **4–024** the time being) between those who have married but not between those who have not. If a man transfers his property to the woman he lives with to protect it from creditors, on her death the woman's estate is entitled to the property if the man and woman were married (even, in certain circumstances, where the parties were not married at the time of the transfer), but not if they simply lived together. Had the parties in *Lowson v Coombes* been married, C's claim to an interest in the property, where he had provided half the purchase money, would have failed.[61] Thus property rights in such circumstances are decided almost exclusively by reference to the parties' married state, or their relationship of father and

[61] Although undoubtedly on a dissolution of any later marriage by divorce rather than death C would have been entitled to apply for relief under the Matrimonial Causes Act 1973.

child rather than the actual circumstances which existed and the intentions of the parties at the time of the conveyance.

4–025   This places those cases which involve some illicit element, such as a desire to shield assets improperly from creditors, in an almost unique situation. In the majority of cases, the presumption of advancement has little effect on the outcome of a case. Where however the case involves a relationship between the parties giving rise to the presumption, and the circumstances of the transfer reveal some dishonest intention or design, the presumption is virtually irrebuttable. This state of affairs led the trial judge in *Tribe v Tribe* ([1996] Ch. 107 at 118C) to observe that he found it difficult to see why the outcome in such cases depended "to such a large extent on arbitrary factors such as whether the claim is brought by a father against a son or a grandfather against a grandson". In the same case, Nourse L.J. commented, somewhat acerbically, that "in times when the presumption has for other purposes fallen into disfavour there seems to be some perversity in its elevation to a decisive status in the context of illegality" (see 118D–E).

Consideration for some lesser interest

4–030   Plainly, no resulting trust will arise if in fact what appears to be a contribution to the purchase price is in fact consideration for some interest in or licence over the land in question which does not amount to a proprietary interest. Thus where, for instance, A purchases land through which a river flows, B might, prior to or immediately upon the purchase make a contribution to the purchase price in exchange for the right to fish in the river. B does not acquire a proprietary interest in the property, since A has provided valuable consideration for the funds advanced by A. The arrangement may give rise to rights to fish (and perhaps rights ancillary thereto) which can be protected in equity, but no beneficial interest in the land will arise. This (as discussed above) was precisely what happened in *Collier v Collier* ((2002) 6 I.T.E.L.R. 270) where a lease of freehold property was granted by D to his daughter.

Chapter 5

QUANTIFICATION OF BENEFICIAL INTERESTS

Once it is established that an applicant does have some beneficial interest **5–001** in the disputed property, the court is then required to determine the extent of that interest. The principles which govern the quantification of a beneficial interest are not, however, of uniform application in all circumstances. First of all, the way in which the legal interests in the property are held will inform (at least to a certain extent) the quantification of the beneficial interest. The existence of an agreement between the parties as regards who should own what shares in property will also, where present, have a very significant impact on the quantification of their respective interests. The legal basis upon which the claimant establishes an interest is an extremely important factor, as the correct approach to quantification in resulting trust cases is quite different from the correct approach in cases involving a constructive trust or proprietary estoppel.

Since different factual scenarios involve different approaches to the issue of quantification, it is convenient to consider in turn the following cases:

- Where legal title to the property is held by both parties
- Where legal title to the property is held in the name of one party only but at some point agreement is reached as to what the parties' respective shares should be
- Where legal title to the property is held by one of the parties only and an interest is established under a constructive trust, without agreement between the parties as to the extent of their respective interests
- Where legal title to the property is held by one of the parties only and an interest is established under a resulting trust
- Where legal title to the property is held by one of the parties only and the conduct of the legal owner is such that he is estopped from denying the interest of the other party.

In addition to questions of general principle regarding quantification, examination of the authorities is instructive as regards certain issues which frequently arise in cohabitation cases. These are set out and discussed further below.

Cases where title is held in the names of both parties

5–002   As is discussed above,[1] ordinarily the beneficial interests in a property reflect the legal interests in the property.[2] The mere fact that the property is held in joint names indicates, albeit not necessarily conclusively, that both parties are intended to have a beneficial interest.[3] All however depends of the intention of the parties at the time the legal interests were created: thus in *Hodgson v Marks* ([1971] Ch. 892) the Court of Appeal considered that if land was conveyed from C to D without any intention that D should become the beneficial owner, C would retain the entire beneficial interest notwithstanding the transfer of title. The task of the court is to seek to ascertain the parties' intentions rather than simply to rely on any presumptions or prima facie positions.[4]

Where a property has been purchased (or subsequently transferred into) joint names, in quantifying the respective shares of the co-owners the first issue to consider will be the terms of the conveyance or other transfer instrument.[5] Where the relevant instrument contains an express declaration of trust, it is only rarely that such a declaration will *not* be determinative of the extent of the parties' respective interests. As Fox L.J. observed in *Roy v Roy* ([1996] 1 F.L.R. 541 at 546F), in cases where there is such an instrument, it either reflects the intention of the parties at the time it was executed, or it does not. If it does, there is generally no rational basis for interfering with it[6]; if it does not, the appropriate remedy lies in rectification of the instrument to give effect to the true intention of the parties.[7] An express declaration of trust cannot normally be disturbed by the application of constructive trust principles.[8] There may be situations, however, where the original agreement is renegotiated or the parties' subsequent conduct is so inconsistent with what was agreed that the only sensible conclusion must be that the agreement has been varied or cancelled.[9]

5–003   In recent years, declarations made by multiple-purchasers in relation to their respective interests have become commonplace, and modern Land Registry forms specifically enquire as to whether the property is to be held as tenants in common (if so enquiring as to the respective shares of the purchasers) or joint tenants. Many of the claims which come before the courts thus relate to properties acquired in the era before such

[1] See above, Chapter 4, "Resulting Trusts".
[2] *Crisp v Mullings* (1976) 239 E.G. 119 *per* Russell L.J.
[3] See Chapter 3 "Constructive Trusts" above and see *Stack v Dowden* [2005] EWCA Civ 857 *per* Chadwick L.J. at paras.17 and 25, and *Crossley v Crossley* [2005] EWCA Civ 1581 *per* Sir Peter Gibson at para.28.
[4] *Crossley v Crossley* [2005] EWCA Civ 1581 *per* Sir Peter Gibson at para.9.
[5] *Bernard v Josephs* [1982] Ch 391 *per* Griffiths L.J. at 403C.
[6] *Godwin v Bedwell The Times*, March 10, 1982
[7] Discussed further in Chapter 7, below, "Personal Obligations Between Co-owners". The Court of Appeal accepted in *Bykiert v Jones* (1981) 125 Sol. Jo. 323 that an express declaration was conclusive as to the parties' beneficial interests absent any issue of fraud or mistake.
[8] *Pink v Lawrence* (1978) 36 P. & C.R. 98 *per* Buckley L.J. at 101.
[9] *The Mortgage Corporation v Shaire* [2001] Ch. 743 *per* Neuberger J. at 750D.

declarations became commonplace.[10] This is not to say that cases where the relevant property is acquired in circumstances where the modern TR1 is completed do not ever come before the courts. The declaration may not be signed, for instance; the parties may specify that they are to hold the property as tenants in common without indicating the respective shares that they have agreed, or the conveyancing solicitors may have misunderstood their instructions or not acted upon them. In such cases it is important to remember that the TR1 form is simply the mechanism by which, having acquired a property, the purchasers inform HM Land Registry of that fact. The transfer instrument itself may constitute evidence which is influential or even determinative even if the TR1 is silent as to the parties' respective interests and intentions. In such cases, there may be scope for a party who feels aggrieved at the failure of his/her solicitor to protect his/her interests by ensuring the form is properly completed, to institute a negligence action against the culpable conveyancing solicitor. Such claims are outside the scope of this work and the reader is referred to specialist texts on the subject. Where this is a possible course of action, the requirements of the Limitation Act 1980 should particularly be borne in mind. The temptation to make good the deficiencies of the conveyancing process via proceedings seeking declarations as to beneficial interests under the Trusts of Land and Appointment of Trustees Act 1996 may mean that a negligence action is statute barred by the time the latter proceedings are launched.

Where the relevant transfer instrument does not contain any specific and express declaration of trust[11] an important distinction exists between cases where the parties hold as joint tenants, and cases where they hold as tenants in common. It is necessary to consider this issue in some detail.

Purchase by joint tenants — the decision in Goodman v Gallant

Where parties purchase a property as joint tenants, in general terms their **5–004** status as joint tenants is determinative of the extent of their respective beneficial interests. Each joint tenant holds an equal aliquot share in the property. Thus if two co-owners own the property, each owns the entire beneficial interest in the property and will acquire the entire property under the doctrine of survivorship on the death of the other. The severance of the joint tenancy automatically produces a tenancy in common equal shares. Similarly, three joint tenants on severance each become beneficially entitled to a one third share as tenants in common; on the death of one of three joint tenants, the interest each would enjoy (in the event of the joint tenancy being severed) increases from a third to a half.[12]

---

[10] See e.g. *Crossley v Crossley* [2005] EWCA 1581 *per* Sir Peter Gibson at para.5
[11] Express declarations of trust are discussed in greater detail in Chapter 2 "Express Trusts", above.
[12] The word "moiety", previously used to describe an equal share, appears to have been consigned to the history books.

Since at least the decision of the Court of Appeal in *Goodman v Gallant* ([1986] Fam. 106), it has been clear that the fact that one co-owner may have made substantially greater contributions to the purchase price is immaterial to the determination of the parties respective interests where the parties hold as joint tenants. The facts of that case were that the appellant and her husband had owned a property in equal shares. After their marriage broke down, an agreement was reached whereby the appellant and her new partner would purchase the appellant's husband's interest in the property. The property was conveyed to the appellant and her partner as joint tenants. On the breakdown of their relationship, the appellant claimed that she was beneficially entitled to three quarters of the relevant property, on the basis that she owned half of the property in any event and had joined equally with her new partner in the purchase of the other half. The Court of Appeal rejected the submission that on severance the parties were entitled to anything other than an equal share of the equity. Slade L.J. (giving the judgment of the Court) said (at 117D):

> "in the absence of any claim for rectification or rescission, the provision in the conveyance declaring that the plaintiff and the defendant were to hold the proceeds of sale of the property 'upon trust for themselves as joint tenants' concludes the question of the respective beneficial interests of the two parties insofar as that declaration of trust, on its true construction, exhaustively declares the beneficial interests."

He continued (at 118H):

> "quite apart from authority, it seems to us that it is the very nature of a joint tenancy that, upon a severance, each takes an equal *aliquot* share according to the number of joint tenants."

5–005 Thus, where a property is held by co-owners as joint tenants, the mere fact of purchase as joint tenants constitutes a declaration of trust. An equal division of the proceeds of sale in those circumstances is not necessarily automatic, but a high hurdle faces those seeking to persuade the court to the contrary. The fact that one co-purchaser has contributed significantly less than the other(s) towards the purchase price may attract the sympathy of the court, and whilst that sympathy may find an outlet in terms of any account or enquiry that the court conducts,[13] the fact that the parties hold as joint tenants has a decisive status in quantifying their respective interests.[14]

---

[13] See Chapter 7 "Personal Obligations Between Cohabitants".
[14] *Huntingford v Hobbs* [1993] 1 F.L.R. 736 at 753E *per* Dillon L.J., *Turton v Turton* [1988] 1 Ch. 542 where one co-owner contributed nothing at all but was still held to be entitled to a half share.

Exceptions to Goodman v Gallant

In cases where practitioners have the luxury of finding out what the **5–006** prospective co-purchasers have in mind prior to completion (as opposed to the burden of unearthing evidence some time afterwards which justifies the presumed intention later ascribed to the parties) it is plainly possible to draft the transfer so as to leave the parties enjoying the benefits of holding as joint tenants prior to severance, but providing that something other than equal *aliquot* shares should follow if the joint tenancy should be brought to an end by severance rather than survivorship. That much was specifically envisaged by Slade L.J., who said ([1986] Fam. 106 at 119C):

> "It would no doubt be possible for a trust in terms to provide that the beneficial interests of the two parties should be equivalent to those of joint tenants unless and until severance occurred, but that in the event of severance their interests should be otherwise than in equal shares".

Where the transfer indicates that the parties hold as joint tenants on a conventional basis, there are two established routes to a challenge to an equal division of the proceeds of sale. These are first, a challenge to the agreement/understanding which gave rise to the joint tenancy (or the document which purports to reflect that agreement), the second being a claim to an equitable account. Those possibilities are essentially *in personam* remedies which may be available to one co-owner as against the other.[15]

Purchase as tenants in common

The essential feature of a purchase as joint tenants is that since a joint **5–007** tenancy is inconsistent with anything other than equal beneficial interests on the part of the co-owners, a declaration that a property is held by the parties as joint tenants is determinative of the parties' respective beneficial interests. This is so even though the relevant instrument may be silent as to the beneficial share each party is to have. Where, however, a property is purchased by co-owners as tenants in common, the reasoning in *Goodman v Gallant* is plainly inapplicable. Unlike a declaration of joint tenancy, a declaration that the parties hold as tenants in common is of itself no more indicative of an intention to hold in shares 50/50 than it is of an intention to hold in shares 90/10.

Where parties expressly purchase as tenants in common in defined/ declared shares, again in the absence of a claim to rectification or rescission that declaration will be conclusive of their interests (see below, and see *Mortgage Corporation v Shaire* ([2001] Ch. 743 *per* Neuberger J.

---

[15] Considered in detail in in Chapter 7, below, "Personal Obligations Between Cohabitants".

at 750B–D)). It is far more common for contested litigation between joint legal owners to concern the situation whereby no declaration has been made at all.

5–008   In many cases, the parties will, possibly without ever agreeing in terms what their interests are, nonetheless reach a consensus which is expressed to third parties, whether by way of informal discussions with friends or relatives or in the context of arms' length relationships with for instance bankers or creditors. Statements to third parties as to the extent of the parties' interests will in general be accorded significant weight and may have a decisive impact on the outcome of a case. In for instance *Supperstone v Hurst* ([2006] 1 F.C.R. 352) H and W owned their house jointly in unascertained shares. H, who was in financial difficulties, entered into an Individual Voluntary Arrangement with his creditors, in the course of which both he and W made written statements indicating that the property was held in equal shares. In the course of H's subsequent bankruptcy, W asserted that she was beneficially entitled not to 50 per cent of the proceeds of sale but 85 per cent. Mr Michael Briggs Q.C. (sitting as a Deputy Judge in the Chancery Division) held that whilst the IVA statements did not amount to declarations of trust, they were compelling evidence (though not of themselves determinative) of the parties' intentions. The facts of that case can be contrasted with the circumstances considered by Neuberger J. in *Mortgage Corporation v Shaire* [2001] Ch. 743, where a statement made by one co-owner was not considered to be evidence of the common intention of both co-owners.

In cases where there is no evidence that the parties ever reached any consensus as to their respective interests, or positive evidence that they never reached any consensus (or even, as in *Supperstone v Hurst* where there is unsatisfactory evidence of a consensus) the principles outlined by the Court of Appeal in *Oxley v Hiscock* are applicable.[16] The decision in *Oxley* is considered in detail below; however, whether the court is dealing with joint legal owners or a claimant who establishes an interest in property held in another's name, the effect of *Oxley* is relatively clear: if the parties have not agreed what their respective interests should be, the issue will be resolved on the basis that the court has a broad discretion to decide what is fair, having regard to the whole course of dealing between the parties in relation to the property.

Purchase by one party alone where the parties agree what their respective interests should be

5–009   As with cases where the property has been bought in joint names without any express declaration of trust, where the relevant property is acquired in the name of one party alone, but a cohabitant can demonstrate an interest under either limb of *Lloyds Bank Plc v Rosset*, the question of what (if anything) the parties have agreed between themselves again

[16] See *Stack v Dowden* [2005] EWCA Civ 857 *per* Chadwick L.J. at para.26 and see *Cox v Jones* [2004] 2 F.L.R. 1010.

assumes central importance. In a case where the parties have at some point agreed on not just the fact of an interest but also the extent of that interest, that agreement is generally conclusive, notwithstanding any question of who has contributed what. Thus in *Mortgage Corporation v Shaire* ([2001] Ch 743) Neuberger J. said (at 750B–D):

> "When determining the respective beneficial interests of two persons who are living in a house together either as man and wife or in a close relationship, the law appears to be as follows:
> 1.   Where the parties have expressly agreed the shares in which they hold, that is normally conclusive.
> 2.   Such an agreement can be in writing or oral.
> 3.   Where the parties have reached such an agreement, it is open to the court to depart from that agreement only if there is very good reason for doing so, for instance a subsequent renegotiation or subsequent actionswhich are so inconsistent with what was agreed as to lead to the conclusion that there must have been a variation or cancellation of the agreement."

These general principles are illustrated in a number of cases. In *Oxley v Hiscock* ([2005] Fam. 211) Chadwick L.J. observed (para.69). that the extent of each party's share might well be governed by what the parties said and did at the time of acquisition. In *Cox v Jones* ([2004] 2 F.L.R. 1010) Mann J. said (para.80 at 1050):   **5–010**

> "Had I found that ... it was expressly agreed that (C) should have 50 per cent of the beneficial interest in the Mill, then that would be the appropriate interest for her to have."

In *Clough v Killey* ((1996) 72 P. & C.R. D22) C transferred to D £12,500 from her divorce settlement which was used by D to clear an overdraft and, in part, fund improvements to the relevant property. C and D had agreed that C would have a half share in the property. At first instance, C recovered only 25 per cent and appealed against the order of the County Court Judge. In the Court of Appeal, D argued that an interest of 50 per cent was completely disproportionate to C's contribution of £12,500. Peter Gibson L.J. however considered that even if that were correct, there was still no justification for allowing D to resile from what he had agreed with C, namely that they should share the property equally. Similarly, in *Pascoe v Turner* [1979] 1 W.L.R. 431 the agreed share was upheld even though it was arguably disproportionate to the proved intention and reliance.

It may be possible for the court to infer agreement between the parties as to the extent of their respective shares, even where no agreement in terms was ever reached. In *Chapman v Chapman* ([1969] 1 W.L.R. 1367   **5–011**

CA), for instance, Edmund Davies L.J. observed (at 1370H–1371B) that where the parties had expressly agreed that H would pay for certain things (i.e. the mortgage repayments and other expenses of running the home), and W would pay for others (i.e. food and groceries) that arrangement "threw a flood of light on the intentions of the parties regarding the beneficial interests in the matrimonial home". In *Sekhon v Alissa* ([1989] 2 F.L.R. 94 Hoffman J. held at 100F) that the conduct and conversations between the parties gave rise to an understanding as regards the extent of each party's interest, which the parties were held to notwithstanding the absence of any agreement in terms.

It is important to distinguish between on the one hand cases where the parties agree in terms with each other what their respective interests should be, and on the other cases where the parties for instance give similar or even identical accounts of their respective interests to third parties. An agreement in terms between the parties will engage the principles summarised in *Shaire*. By contrast, declarations to third parties, even in identical terms, will simply be evidence which informs (albeit perhaps to a very great extent) the court's determination of fairness.[17]

Purchase by one party alone where the parties have not agreed what their respective interests should be

5–012   Where the parties have not agreed at some point in the past on the extent of the claimant's interest, the question "what is the claimant's interest in this property" will of necessity need to be determined by the court. The answer will depend at least in part on the basis upon which the claim to any interest at all is made out. In short, where an interest is established under a constructive trust or by reason of proprietary estoppel, the extent of the interest will be determined by reference to what the court considers fair: in resulting trust cases, the interest will be in proportion to the claimant's contributions to the purchase price alone. Each possibility is considered further below.

Claimant establishing an interest under a constructive trust

5–013   Where the parties reach agreement as to what their respective shares should be, the question for the court is essentially whether effect should be given to that agreement. Generally, the answer will by "Yes". However, where there is no agreement, the court is required not simply to endorse or otherwise fix a figure ostensibly agreed by the parties themselves, but to impose a solution upon them.

This may arise in a number of situations. Even in cases where an interest on the claimant's part is acknowledged by the legal owner, the parties may not have agreed what the extent of that interest should be. In

---

[17] Contrast *Shaire* for instance with *Supperstone v Hurst* [2006] 1 F.C.R. 352

cases where the parties agree for some reason that the property should be held in one party's name only (such as where the other party faces the potential claims of creditors or a former spouse) the fact of such discussions demonstrates a common intention[18] that the claimant should have an interest, but not necessarily any common intention as to what that interest should be. In cases where a common intention is inferred under limb two of *Lloyds Bank Plc v Rosset*, it follows *ex hypothesi* that the parties are most unlikely to have agreed what the claimant's share should be.

In all three situations, the extent of the claimant's interest falls to be resolved in the light of the principles set out by the Court of Appeal in *Oxley v Hiscock* ([2005] Fam. 211).

The background against which this case was decided is of some his-   **5–014** torical interest, if no longer of great legal significance. Throughout the late 1990s and into the early years of the 21st century there was some tension between two lines of authority in the Court of Appeal, that represented on the one hand by the decision in *Springette v Defoe* [1992] 2 F.L.R. 388 and on the other hand that represented by *Midland Bank v Cooke* [1995] 2 F.L.R. 915. The issue, simply stated, was this. In a case where the claimant was agreed or found to have a beneficial interest in the defendant's property, but there was no agreement between the parties as to the extent of that interest, was the interest of the non-legal owner to be calculated by reference to resulting trust principles, namely by reference to the contribution made to the original purchase price, or by reference to constructive trust principles, namely that the claimant's interest would be determined by the court with reference to financial contributions but not to the exclusion of all other factors? The state of the law was such that advice could not be given with any degree of certainty not only in relation to the outcome of a case, but even on the question of which principles would be applied. One cynical view that emerged was that wherever a bank or other lending institute sought to enforce its security against a family home, the court was more willing to give greater weight to non-financial contributions at the expense of the bank (thus preserving a greater share of the equity in the relevant property to enable a family to rehouse) but where the issue before the court was as between co-owners, the court was more inclined to attach more significance to who had contributed what.[19]

The tension between these two lines of authority was resolved in *Oxley v Hiscock* ([2005] Fam. 211). The effect of the decision in that case is that where an interest can be established under *constructive* trust principles, in assessing the extent of that interest the court is not constrained by the mathematical computation of the claimant's contribution to the purchase

---

[18] See *Grant v Edwards* [1986] Ch. 638 and see Chapter 3 "Constructive Trusts", above)
[19] See also, e.g. *Le Foe & Le Foe v Woolwich Plc* [2001] 2 F.L.R. 970 and *Drake v Whipp* [1996] 1 F.L.R. 826.

price. Wider questions such as financial contributions to the household not strictly referable to the purchase price, and non-financial contributions can also be taken into account. It is instructive to consider, before examining the reasoning in *Oxley*, a number of authorities which were relied on by Chadwick L.J. in giving the lead judgment in that case. In *Grant v Edwards* ([1986] Ch. 638) Sir Nicholas Browne-Wilkinson V.C. said (at 655A):

> "Once it has been established that the parties had a common intention that both should have a beneficial interest *and* that the claimant has acted to his detriment, the question may still remain 'what is the extent of the claimant's beneficial interest?' This last section of Lord Diplock's speech (in *Gissing v Gissing* [1971] A.C. 886 at 908D–909) shows that here again the direct *and indirect* contributions made by the parties to the cost of acquisition may be crucially important" (emphasis added).

5–015   The weight given to Lord Diplock's speech in *Gissing v Gissing* by Sir Nicholas Browne-Wilkinson was specifically noted by Chadwick L.J. in *Oxley*. In *Gissing* Lord Diplock had said (at 909):

> "If the contribution of the wife in the early part of the period of repayment [of a building society mortgage] is substantial but is not an identifiable and uniform proportion of each instalment, because her contributions are indirect or, if direct, are made irregularly, it may well be a reasonable inference that their common intention at the time of acquisition of the matrimonial home was that the beneficial interest should be held by them in equal shares and that each should contribute to the cost of its acquisition whatever amounts each could afford in the varying exigencies of family life to be expected during the period of repayment. In the social conditions of today this would be a natural enough common intention of a young couple who were both earning when the house was acquired but who contemplated having children whose birth and rearing in their infancy would necessarily affect the future earning capacity of the wife...
>
>   The relative size of their respective contributions to the instalments in the early part of the period of repayment, or later if a subsequent reduction in the wife's contributions is not to be accounted for by a reduction in her earnings due to motherhood or some other cause from which the husband benefits as well, may make it a more probable inference that the wife's share in the beneficial interest was intended to be in some proportion other than one half. And there is nothing inherently improbable in their acting on the understanding that the wife should be entitled to a share which was not to be quantified immediately upon the acquisition of the home but should be left to be determined when the mortgage was

repaid or the property disposed of, on the basis of what would be fair having regard to the total contributions, direct or indirect which each spouse had made by that date. Where this was the most likely inference from their conduct it would be for the court to give effect to that common intention of the parties by determining what in all the circumstances was a fair share." (Emphasis added.)

In *Lloyds Bank Plc v Rosset* ([1991] 1 A.C. 107) Lord Bridge discussed   **5–016** both *Grant v Edwards* and the earlier case of *Eves v Eves* [1975] 1 W.L.R. 1338, and said:

"It is significant to note that the share to which the female partners in *Eves v Eves* and *Grant v Edwards* were held entitled were one quarter and one half respectively. In no sense could these shares have been regarded as proportionate to what the judge in the instant case described as a 'qualifying contribution' in terms of the indirect contributions to the acquisition or enhancement of the value of the houses made by the female partners."

In *Stokes v Anderson* ([1991] 1 F.L.R. 391) Nourse L.J. said (at 400C) "there is no practicable alternative to the determination of a fair share. The court must supply the common intention by reference to that which all the material circumstances have shown to be fair". In *Mortgage Corporation v Shaire* ([2001] 1 Ch. 743) Neuberger J. pointed out (at 750) that the extent of the respective financial contributions was a relevant factor in determining the extent of a claimant's beneficial interest, but was no means decisive. Thus in *Midland Bank v Cooke* a wife who had made a financial contribution of around 6 per cent to the original purchase price was held to have a 50 per cent interest under constructive trust principles.

The decision in Oxley v Hiscock

The facts of *Oxley* are relatively straightforward. C purchased the   **5–017** property which she occupied from the local authority under the "right to buy" scheme. Her occupation history meant she was entitled to a significant discount to the purchase price. The balance of the purchase price was entirely met by a loan from D. Some years later, C's property was sold, and the proceeds of sale were entirely applied towards the purchase of a subsequent property, in D's name only. D provided significant further capital towards the purchase of the second property, and a small proportion of the purchase price was raised by way of a mortgage. At first instance, the trial judge found that the parties had been involved in a classic pooling of resources, and held that the parties' common intention had been to hold the property in equal shares. On appeal, it was held that the trial judge had given insufficient weight to the capital contribution made by D, and reduced the order in C's favour from a half share to 40 per cent.[20]

5–18   It is perhaps not so much the outcome of the appeal in *Oxley* itself but the reasons given by Chadwick L.J. in allowing the appeal which are of particular significance. Of central importance are the observations at paras 68–71 which are worthy of citation at some length:

> "(68) I have referred, in the immediately preceding paragraphs, to 'cases of this nature'. By that, I mean cases in which the common features are: (i) the property is bought as a home for a couple who, although not married, intend to live together as man and wife; (ii) each of them makes some financial contribution to the purchase; (iii) the property is purchased in the sole name of one of them; and (iv) there is no express declaration of trust. In those circumstances the first question is whether there is evidence from which to infer a common intention, communicated by each to the other, that each shall have a beneficial share in the property. In many such cases — of which the present is an example — there will have been some discussion between the parties at the time of the purchase which provides the answer to that question. Those are cases within the first of Lord Bridge's categories in *Lloyds Bank Plc v Rosset*. In other cases — where the evidence is that the matter was not discussed at all — an affirmative answer will readily be inferred from the fact that each has made a financial contribution. Those are cases within Lord Bridge's second category. And, if the answer to the first question is that there was a common intention, communicated to each other, that each should have a beneficial share in the property, then the party who does not become the legal owner will be held to have acted to his or her detriment in making a financial contribution to the purchase in reliance on the common intention.
>
> (69) In those circumstances, the second question to be answered in cases of this nature is "what is the extent of the parties' respective beneficial interests in the property?" Again, in many such cases, the answer will be provided by evidence of what they said and did at the time of the acquisition. But, in a case where there is no evidence of

---

[20] A number of commentators have observed that this in effect simply conferred on C the interest which she would have established under a resulting trust. This is in fact an over-simplification. At para.23 at 220 Chadwick L.J. said, "There is obvious scope for debate about the figures. The defendant's approach treats Mr Hiscock as having contributed the whole of the monies (£30,000) advanced by the building society — no doubt on the basis that as the person in whose sole name the property was registered, he was solely responsible for the mortgage debt ... But *making all assumptions in Mrs Oxley's favour the amount of her share based on financial contributions could not exceed 40 per cent*" (emphasis added). In other words a strict resulting trust analysis may well have led to the conclusion that C's share was much lower (D contended on appeal that her share was no more than 22 per cent — see para.22) but in view of Chadwick L.J.'s conclusion that the trust which arose was a constructive trust, not a resulting trust, his final conclusion (para.74) was that it would be fair to treat them as having approximately equal contributions to the purchase price insofar as it was funded by way of a mortgage advance.

any discussion between them as to the amount of the share which each was to have — and even in a case where the evidence is that there was no discussion on that point — the question still requires an answer. It must now be accepted that (at least in this Court and below) the answer is that each is entitled to that share which the court considers fair having regard to the whole course of dealing between them in relation to the property. And, in that context, "the whole course of dealing between them in relation to the property" includes the arrangements which they make from time to time in order to meet the outgoings (for example, mortgage contributions, council tax and utilities, repairs, insurance and housekeeping) which have to be met if they are to live in the property as their home...

(71) (I)f it were their common intention that each should have some beneficial interest in the property — which is the hypothesis upon which it becomes necessary to answer the second question — then, in the absence of evidence that they gave any thought to the amount of their respective shares, the necessary inference is that they must have intended that question would be answered later on the basis of what was then seen to be fair. But, as I have said, I think that the time has come to accept that there is no difference in outcome, in cases of this nature, whether the true analysis lies in constructive trust or in proprietary estoppel. ... The right question, in the circumstances of this case, was "*what would be a fair share for each party having regard to the whole course of dealing between them in relation to the property?*" (Emphasis added.)

Thus, in quantifying the extent of a claimant's interest in circumstances where such was not agreed between the parties, the court is not, as for instance *Springette v Defoe* ([1992] 2 F.L.R. 388) would suggest, obliged only to declare that each party enjoys an interest commensurate with his/her contribution to the purchase price. The court is required to take into account the whole course of dealing between the parties in relation to the property, and from that history reach a conclusion on the basis of what is perceived to be fair.[21]

There are perhaps three important consequences of the judgment in **5–019** *Oxley* for the practitioner. First, the language used by Chadwick L.J. in his judgment ("*includes* the arrangements ...") makes it clear that the factors he refers to in considering the whole course of dealings in relation to the property is not an exhaustive list. Thus, whilst Chadwick L.J. seemed to have financial contributions at the forefront of his mind, there appears no reason why non-financial contributions in terms of child care or home-making cannot be taken into account. Certainly, in *Grant v Edwards* Sir Nicholas Browne-Wilkinson considered that it was not

---

[21] Chadwick L.J.'s judgment was described in *Lightfoot v Lightfoot-Brown* [2005] EWCA Civ 201 as reviewing the authorities with "great clarity and thoroughness". Similarly, in *Stack v Dowden* [2005] EWCA Civ 857 Carnwath L.J. described the judgment of Chadwick L.J. in *Oxley* as a "comprehensive and authoritative" review.

improbable that H and W might agree at the time of purchase that each should have an equal share in the knowledge that W's future ability to contribute towards mortgage repayments would be curtailed by child-rearing. Thus, although it is clear from *Burns v Burns* ([1984] 1 Ch. 317) that domestic contributions will not of themselves justify the inference of a common intention,[22] if a claimant in Mrs Burns' position can otherwise establish an interest under either limb of *Lloyds Bank Plc v Rosset*, in quantifying her interest her domestic contributions can be taken into account and weighed, even if they are of no relevance in establishing the *fact* of an interest.

Second, whilst the decision in *Oxley* frees the court from the straitjacket of the arithmetic or mechanical calculation, it also involves the practitioner in educated guesswork. Having regard to the relevant course of dealings between the parties, Judge A may conclude a fair share is 33 per cent. Judge B may conclude the fair share is only 25 per cent. Neither is necessarily wrong.[23] Much therefore will depend upon the judge's own subjective view of the merits of the case. This makes it difficult to advise with confidence as to the outcome of any case where quantum is in issue: in terms of advising on settlement, the "litigation risk" discount appears broadly analogous to that encountered when dealing with ancillary relief claims between former spouses.[24]

5–020 Third, in practical terms, where a claim to a beneficial interest is based on a financial contribution to the purchase price, there may be a significant advantage (at least where the contribution amounts to less than 50 per cent of the purchase price) to the claimant in asserting a case based on a constructive trust rather than a resulting trust. Any financial contribution which might give rise to a resulting trust would prima facie also satisfy the second strand of Lord Bridge's reasoning in *Lloyds Bank Plc v Rosset* ([1991] A.C. 107), and thus demonstrate the existence of a constructive trust.[25] The fact of payment evidences not only the common intention but also, following *Grant v Edwards* ([1986] Ch. 638), reliance thereon.[26] There may be cases where for some reason a constructive trust will not arise notwithstanding a financial contribution (e.g. positive evidence that a financial contribution did *not* evidence detrimental reliance, or possibly some question of illegality, as to which see Chapter 4

---

[22] Subject perhaps to the effect of the decision in *Le Foe v Le Foe & Woolwich Plc* [2001] 2 F.L.R. 970: see above, Chapter 3 "Constructive Trusts".

[23] See *Supperstone v Hurst* [2006] 1 F.C.R. 352 *per* Michael Briggs Q.C. at 369D–E (para.60)

[24] This is not however to say that the judge truly enjoys a discretion: any appeal court reconsidering a judge's decision as to quantum would for instance not necessarily be bound by the constraints which exist in relation to any challenge on appeal to the exercise of a true discretion, as to which see *G v G (Minors: Custody Appeal)* [1985] 1 W.L.R. 647 HL.

[25] See for instance Elizabeth Cooke's analysis at [2005] Conv. 79 at 84.

[26] Indeed, Arden L.J. pointed out in *Lightfoot v Lightfoot-Brown* [2005] P. & C.R. 22 EWCA Civ 201 that an analysis of the non-legal owner's contributions to the purchase price might also act as corroboration of evidence of an express understanding and would plainly be relevant to the quantification of any interest.

"Resulting Trusts", above) in which case the resulting trust would have a residuary role. In the overwhelming majority of cases, however, there would appear to be no advantage to the non-legal owner in casting his/her application on the basis of a resulting trust rather than on the basis of a constructive trust.[27] It was even held in *Drake v Whipp* ([1996] 1 F.L.R. 826) that a resulting trust could not arise in circumstances where the elements necessary to give rise to a constructive trust are made out (*per* Peter Gibson L.J. at 828H–829A). Thus where there is a common intention between C and D that C should have an interest in D's property, and C acts on that intention to her detriment, the doctrine of the resulting trust simply has no application.

Limits to the application of Oxley v Hiscock

It is perhaps important to recognise that whilst *Oxley v Hiscock* is plainly an important decision, its application is limited to those cases where the parties have not agreed, as between themselves, the extent of their respective interests. In *Crossley v Crossley* ([2005] EWCA 1581) Sir Peter Gibson said (at para.32)   **5–021**

> "The task of determining the fair share having regard to the whole course of dealing in accordance with *Oxley v Hiscock* need only be performed in the absence of an agreement, arrangement or understanding as to the nature and extent of the respective beneficial interests of the parties. As Chadwick L.J. said at para.66 (of his judgment in *Oxley*) what the court is doing when performing that task is to supply or impute a common intention as to the parties respective shares in circumstances in which there was in fact no common intention. Where a common intention has been found in the agreement, arrangement or understanding of the parties, that is unnecessary."

At para.68 of his judgment in *Oxley*, Chadwick L.J. referred to "cases of this nature", and indicated that by that he had in mind cases where:

(i)   the property is bought as a home for a couple who, although not married, share a home as though they were,
(ii) each of them makes some financial contribution to the purchase,
(iii) the property is purchased in the sole name of one of them; and
(iv) there is no express declaration of trust.

It might be thought at first blush that *Oxley* was of no assistance, therefore, in "limb one" cases where no financial contribution was made by the claimant to the purchase price, or where the parties bought the property as co-owners in unspecified shares. Nonetheless, the cases which   **5–022**

---

[27] See e.g. Edwards, *Property Rights in the Family Home* [2004] Fam. Law 524.

have followed *Oxley* appear to indicate that the crucial features are in fact (i) and (iv), that is to say, the property is occupied as a home (rather than say as an investment for instance on a "buy-to-let" or similar basis) and, as suggested, the parties do not agree as between themselves what the share of each is intended to be. In *Cox v Jones* ([2004] 2 F.L.R. 1010) for instance Mann J. considered (at 1050 para.80) that there was no reason why *Oxley* principles should be limited to cases where both parties had contributed to the purchase price. Certainly, if a common intention can be ascertained from express discussions, relied on by the claimant to his/her detriment, it is difficult to see why the test of fairness should not govern "limb one" cases just as it governs "limb two" cases. As to point (iii) above, in *Stack v Dowden*[28] the Court of Appeal considered that *Oxley* principles were equally applicable where the property was bought in the names of both parties but without any express declaration of their respective shares.

Nor is there any reason in principle to limit the applicability of *Oxley v Hiscock* to cases where the parties lived together as cohabitants, even though Chadwick L.J. clearly indicated that he had in mind unmarried cohabitants when he referred to "cases of this nature". The availability of relief under the Matrimonial Causes Act 1973 will usually mean that there is no need for parties who are married to consider the precise extent of their legal/beneficial entitlement to the relevant property. However, this is not to say that where for instance the creditors of one spouse look to co-owned property in satisfaction of outstanding liabilities, *Oxley v Hiscock* would be inapplicable where the parties neither held as joint tenants nor otherwise agreed what their respective interests were to be. In such cases, the authorities seem to demonstrate that a married cohabitee will find it rather easier to establish an equal share than her unmarried counterpart.[29]

Cases where the claimant establishes an interest under a resulting trust

5–023   In resulting trust cases, since the time of *Dyer v Dyer* ((1788) 2 Cox Eq. Cas. 92) (and even before) the courts have presumed, in resulting trust cases, that the parties will each enjoy a beneficial interest in proportion to their respective contributions to the purchase price.[30] unless the parties have otherwise agreed to hold the beneficial interests in some other proportions. (The question of whether mortgage repayments amount to a contribution towards the purchase price is considered below.) Since the same principle is not necessarily determinative of the parties' interests in constructive trust case, identification of the applicable equitable princi-

---

[28] See above at 5–008 and see *Stack v Dowden* [2005] EWCA Civ 857 *per* Chadwick L.J. at para.26 (but note that there is to be an appeal to the House of Lords in this case).
[29] See for instance *Midland Bank Plc v Cooke* [1995] 2 F.L.R. 915, *Le Foe v Le Foe & Woolwich Plc* [2001] 2 F.L.R. 970, *Kubiangha v Ekpenyong* [2002] B.C.L.C. 597.
[30] See also *Bull v Bull* [1955] 1 Q.B. 234 at 236, *Pettitt v Pettitt* [1970] A.C. 777 at 814B, *Heseltine v Heseltine* [1971] 1 W.L.R. 342, *Williams & Glyn's Bank v Boland* [1981] A.C. 487 at 502F–G.

ples is of particular significance.[31] In *Drake v Whipp* [1996] 1 F.L.R. 826 the claimant had contributed about 20 per cent of the purchase price, and under a purchase money resulting trust could not have recovered a greater share. The Court of Appeal, however, observed that her interest arose under a constructive, not a resulting trust, and so the court, in holding that her interest was 33 per cent, was not restricted to a pure arithmetic reckoning of her interest.

Proprietary estoppel cases

The circumstances in which a claim based in proprietary estoppel is made out, and effect of such a finding in terms of the relief which may be afforded to the claimant, are considered below (see Chapter 6 "Proprietary Estoppel"). In essence, however, the same two-stage process of determining first whether the elements of the claim are made out and then considering how the claim is satisfied is involved. It is significant that in cases where an estoppel has arisen, the court is not bound to satisfy the equity which arises thereby purely by way of a declaration that the claimant enjoys a beneficial interest in the property. Where however the court is satisfied that nothing short of such a declaration will do justice to that equity, the court is required to consider also the extent of such an interest.   **5–024**

In a number of cases the courts have remarked upon the broad analogy between the equity arising under a constructive trust and that arising in proprietary estoppel cases (see below, Chapter 6 "Proprietary Estoppel"). In *Oxley v Hiscock* ([2005] Fam. 211) Chadwick L.J. went further, and remarked (at para.71):

"I think that the time has come to accept that there is no difference in outcome, in cases of this nature, whether the true analysis lies in constructive trust or in proprietary estoppel"

This is not to say however that there is no difference at all between constructive trust and proprietary estoppel cases. In an estoppel case, the fundamental principle on which the court acts is that it should interfere with the legal owners' rights only to the extent necessary to "satisfy the equity" arising in the claimant's favour.[32] However in those cases where a beneficial interest does arise, there is no fundamental difference between the determination of a fair share under a constructive trust in the *Oxley* sense and the determination of the interest which would satisfy the equity which arises by reason of an estoppel.   **5–025**

Chadwick L.J.'s observation would tend to suggest that the requirement in proprietary estoppel cases that the relief ordered should be proportionate to the detriment suffered[33] should apply with equal force in

---

[31] See Chapter 4, above, "Resulting Trusts".
[32] See *Crabb v Arun District Council* [1976] Ch. 179 *per* Scarman L.J. at 198.
[33] See e.g. *Jennings v Rice* [2002] EWCA Civ 159 *per* Robert Walker L.J. at paras 44–52.

constructive trust cases. Thus it is not automatic that the relief granted by the court will simply compensate the Claimant for the detriment suffered;[34] nor will the court necessarily compensate the claimant by restoring to him/her that which he/she thought she would acquire — see e.g. *Madison v Alderson* ((1883) 8 App. Cas. 467). In *Jennings v Rice* Robert Walker L.J. observed that the "essence of the doctrine of proprietary estoppel is to do what is necessary to avoid an unconscionable result, and a disproportionate remedy cannot be the right way of going about that." (at para.56).

The range of options open to the court in terms of satisfying an equity arising by reason of proprietary estoppel other than by way of a declaration of a beneficial interest are considered below in Chapter 6 "Proprietary Estoppel".

5–026   There is an intriguing argument as to whether, since it is possible for the conveyance to specify in terms that joint tenants should not have equal shares following severance, a claimant can in an appropriate case invoke equity to supply the missing words from the transfer instrument under the doctrine of proprietary estoppel. In *Crabb v Arun* ([1976] 1 Ch. 179) Lord Denning said that under the doctrine, equity would:

"... prevent a person from relying insisting on his strict legal rights — whether arising under a contract, *or on his title deeds*, or by statute, when it would be inequitable for him to do so having regard to the dealings between the parties." (emphasis added.)

Such an argument might find some support in the observation of Slade L.J. (523) that where parties declare that they are joint tenants, that "concludes the question of the respective beneficial interest of the two parties in so far as *that declaration of trust* on its true construction *exhaustively* declares the beneficial interests." (Emphasis added.) That observation plainly permits an assertion that the relevant declaration does not in fact exhaustively declare those interests. On the other hand, Slade L.J. may have had in mind no more than the recognised exception in relation to cases of fraud or mistake: that would follow from the observation of Lord Upjohn in *Pettitt v Pettitt* that fraud or mistake would allow an appropriate court to go behind the joint tenancy, though Slade L.J. commented (at 522) that the Court in *Goodman v Gallant* thought that fraud and mistake provided the only such exception.

5–027   Moreover, perhaps the chief difficulty with such an argument is the proximity between the doctrine of proprietary estoppel and the doctrine of the constructive trust. In *Grant v Edwards* Sir Nicholas Browne-Wilkinson V.C. commented (99) that the principles underlying proprietary estoppel were "closely akin" to those underlying the doctrine of the resulting trust. In *Pink v Lawrence* ((1978) 36 P. & C.R. 98) the Court of

---

[34] As would for instance be the position in Australia — see e.g. *Public Trustee v Wadley* [1997] 7 Tas. L.R. 35

Appeal (relying on *Wilson v Wilson* [1969] 3 All E.R. 945) rejected an attempt to assert as between joint tenants that one had a beneficial interest in excess of 50 per cent on the basis of a constructive trust. That was a point specifically noted by Slade L.J. in *Goodman v Gallant*. As Chadwick L.J. observed in *Oxley v Hiscock* ([2005] Fam. 211) (at para.71), there is little difference in outcome whether the true analysis of an interest lies in terms of an interest under a constructive trust or an interest arising by way of a proprietary estoppel. (See Chapter 6 for a discussion of proprietary estoppel generally.) If there is no difference for practical purposes between a claim in trust and a claim based on an estoppel, the decision in *Goodman v Gallant* may have the effect of disposing of any attempt to go behind a declaration that the parties hold as joint tenants based upon the doctrine of proprietary estoppel.

Specific issues relating to the quantification of beneficial interests

Thus far the discussion has concentrated on the broad principles applied by the courts when assessing the extent of a claimant's interest in the relevant property. There are however a number of specific issues which frequently arise in litigation of this nature, which are worthy of consideration. **5–028**

Treatment of mortgage advance

Given the modern reliance on mortgage finance, an extremely important question arises as to how the courts should treat any mortgage advance, or outstanding mortgage liability, when quantifying the parties' respective interests in the relevant property. Surprising as it may seem, there is no clear principle to be discerned from the authorities as to how this question should be answered. It is possible to approach this question in two ways, and neither approach is necessarily wrong in principle. **5–029**

The first, and most common, approach, is simply to disregard the mortgage insofar as the valuation of the property is concerned, so that the parties' respective shares in the property are calculated by reference to the net equity in the property (i.e. the notional value after repayment of the mortgage and payment of costs of sale). Thus if a property was worth £210,000, subject to a mortgage of £150,000 and notional costs of sale of £10,000, the value of a 20 per cent interest in that property would, in cash terms, be £10,000.

In this case, the effect of the mortgage is to reduce the effective value of the asset which is the subject of the parties' dispute. In such circumstances, the payment by one party or the other of mortgage contributions (whether interest or capital in nature) will be of considerable significance in cases where *Oxley v Hiscock* determines the court's approach to quantification, but will usually be[35] of marginal relevance only where

---

[35] Subject to any question of equitable accounting — see below, Chapter 7 "Personal Obligations Between Cohabitants".

Goodman v Gallant is in point. In either case, whether the parties hold in shares 50/50 or otherwise, the interest of each is characterised as a share in the net equity only.

This is in one way the most realistic approach, in that on the sale of the property, unless there are reasons why the mortgagor's interest is subject to the prior interest of a co-owner[36] the net equity is all that the parties would be left with on a sale. It is also broadly analogous to the way in which most judges consider the equity in the matrimonial home when exercising their functions under Part II of the Matrimonial Causes Act 1973.

5–030   However, it is certainly not the only approach. The alternative is to treat a mortgage advance as a contribution to the purchase price made by the party or parties who are liable under the mortgage. This is the approach which the court is obliged to adopt in considering cases where the interest is established under a resulting trust. In *Curley v Parkes* ([2004] EWCA Civ 1515) Sir Peter Gibson described the position in this way (at para.14):

> "The relevant principle is that the resulting trust of a property purchased in the name of another in the absence of a contrary intention arises once and for all at the date on which the property is acquired. Because of the liability assumed by the mortgagor in a case where monies are borrowed by the mortgagor to be used on the purchase the mortgagor is treated as having provided the proportion of the purchase price attributable to the monies so borrowed. Subsequent payments of the mortgage instalments are not part of the purchase price already paid to the vendor but are sums paid for discharging the mortgagor's obligations under the mortgage."

In this way, the court essentially disregards the existence of the mortgage in quantifying the parties' respective interests: their interests are quantified by reference to the gross value of the property, and the party or parties liable under the mortgage are fixed with the repayment of the mortgage from their share of the proceeds of sale.

5–031   Examples of both approaches are evident in the reported cases. In *Savill v Goodall* ([1993] 1 F.L.R. 755) the parties had agreed that C and D would each have a half share in the relevant property, on the basis that C was contributing 40 per cent of the purchase price (by way of a discount) and the rest would be raised by way of a mortgage, D being solely liable for the repayments. The Court of Appeal held that the parties held the property in equal shares as to its gross value, D being solely liable for the repayment of the outstanding mortgage from his share of the gross sale

---

[36] See e.g. *City of London Building Society v Flegg* [1988] 1 A.C. 54, detailed discussion of which is beyond the scope of this work.

value.[37] A similar approach was adopted in *Huntingford v Hobbs* ([1993] 1 F.L.R. 736), and in *Crisp v Mullings* ((1975) 239 E.G. 119) the mortgage advance was treated as being a contribution from both parties, given that both were liable under the mortgage. In *Midland Bank v Cooke* [1995] 2 F.L.R. 915 by contrast the court adopted the more conventional practice of deducting the mortgage from the gross sale price and assessing the parties' interests by reference to the equity in the property.

In cases where the claimant's interest arises under a resulting trust, *Curley v Parkes* provides clear authority for the way in which a mortgage advance (and, it follows, liability under the mortgage) should be treated when quantifying the parties' respective interests: that is to say, there is no room for any adjustment of the parties shares under the resulting trust on the basis that C funded mortgage repayments which D would otherwise have been liable to pay.[38]

In constructive trust cases, the courts have adopted whichever **5–032** approach best suited the justice of the case. Thus in *Huntingford v Hobbs* ([1993] 1 F.L.R. 736) where C's contribution to the purchase was a mortgage contribution for which he had agreed to be solely responsible, his interest in the property was quantified by reference to the gross value of the property, with the mortgage notionally being repayable from his share of the gross value. Sir Christopher Slade observed (at 747B) that in those circumstances he could not claim credit for mortgage interest and repayments, since his share "came into being on the footing that he would be paying all such sums".

It is submitted that although there is no guidance in the higher courts to this effect, a case-by-case approach to this question is inevitable, since the circumstances of this type of case can vary so widely, and the justice of the case can be affected by circumstances outside the control of the parties.

Mortgage repayments

Where a mortgage in the name of one party is repaid or reduced in **5–033** circumstances where the parties have pooled their resources, the courts will in quantifying the respective shares generally treat the repayment or reduction of the capital debt as a contribution made by both parties. As Griffiths L.J. pointed out in *Bernard v Josephs* ([1982] 1 Ch. 391 at 403H), in such circumstances who actually pays the mortgage may simply be a matter of internal accounting between the parties.[39] Ordinarily, therefore, the court will generally treat the mortgage repayments as having been

---

[37] Presumably, on the redemption of the mortgage on any later sale, D would have been personally liable to C had she recovered following such sale less than 50 per cent of the gross sale value.

[38] Though there may be in such cases some personal liability as between C and D in this respect.

[39] Referred to by Nicholas Mostyn Q.C. sitting as a deputy judge of the Family Division as the arbitrary allocation of financial responsibility as between the parties: see *Le Foe v Le Foe & Woolwich Plc* [2001] 2 F.L.R. 970 at 982 (para.49).

made by the parties in equal or other appropriate shares (see also *Oxley v Hiscock* ([2005] Fam. 211) *per* Chadwick L.J. at 220 (para.23)). This however is very much a matter of practice rather than law, and the approach adopted by the court to this question will essentially depend upon how the court perceives the justice of the case.

Date of valuation

5–034   One issue which seems clearly decided by authority relates to the date at which the court must determine the extent of the beneficial interest. Even where a claimant can establish a 50 per cent interest, in a rising property market it would plainly prejudice the claimant for his/her interest to be quantified at the date on which the parties ceased cohabitation. However, the authorities make it plain that it is a matter of discretion for the court as to the date at which the interest should be valued (see *Walker v Hall* ([1984] F.L.R. 126) *per* Dillon L.J. at 132B–C and see *Hall v Hall* ((1982) 3 F.L.R. 379 at 382F) *per* Lord Denning M.R. and *Gordon v Douce* ((1983) 4 F.L.R. 508) *per* Fox L.J. at 512B).

In practice, it is extremely rare for the court to value the respective interests in the property at anything other than the date of trial, or if the property has already been sold, by reference to the sale price achieved (as in for instance *Oxley v Hiscock*; see also *Turton v Turton* ([1988] Ch. 542)). As Lawton L.J. said in *Walker*, a beneficial interest in property, once created, cannot be brought to an end by the happening of an event unrelated to the property itself such as the parties ceasing to live together. Where, however, the court values the interest at some earlier date[40] interest ought to be ordered (if sought in the relevant pleadings) from the date on which the trust was extinguished.

Discounts

5–035   A number of reported cases contain consideration of the effect of discounts under the "right to buy" legislation (Housing Act 1985) whereby local authority tenants are able to take advantage of periods spent as tenants of a local authority in quantifying any discount which might be available on the purchase of the relevant property.

There is no doubt that one way or another, the fact that a party has been able to purchase a property at a significant discount is not simply ignored either in considering the existence of or indeed the extent of a beneficial interest. What is not clear is the precise way in which that conclusion is reached. As Staughton L.J. said in *Evans v Hayward* ([1995] 2 F.L.R. 511 at 516H) it is difficult to accept that a discount is part of the

---

[40] For instance pursuant to a finding that the trust was extinguished at the date of separation — as in *Munday v Robertson* (unreported) April 18, 1973 CA — cited with approval by Dillon L.J. in *Walker v Hall* at 132C.

purchase money provided by either party when it is not money which is in fact provided at all. However, he proceeded to say:

"But I do consider that the facts as to the existence of a discount and the source from which it is derived must be taken into account, and are capable of leading to the inference that the parties have made an agreement as to how the purchase price is provided."

It is at least arguable that in *Marsh v von Sternberg* ([1986] 1 F.L.R. 526) Bush J. shared this approach. There, a private landlord sought to dispose of the relevant property. The respondent was a sitting tenant entitled to statutory protection against eviction, and on purchasing the property from the landlord, negotiated a discount attributable to the loss of that protection. Bush J. inferred that the parties regarded that discount as a contribution by the respondent to the purchase of the property. In *Springette v Defoe* [1992] 2 F.L.R. 388 Steyn L.J. regarded the discount in that case (41 per cent) as a direct contribution by the person entitled to the discount. In *Evans v Hayward*, Dillon L.J. observed that it was open to the court to credit a discount to the plaintiff on either the approach of Bush J. or that of Steyn L.J.

Capital improvements

It frequently happens that one cohabitee meets the costs of (or even **5–036** undertakes) work on the relevant property which increases its' value. Whether or not this would give rise of itself to the inference of a common intention constructive trust.[41] where the existence of an interest is otherwise established or not disputed, there is no reason why such improvements cannot be taken as part of the overall course of dealings or contributions made by one party, insofar as these are relevant. Thus where the court is assessing the overall contributions made by a party as part of the *Oxley v Hiscock* exercise, the cost of improvements (or, if lower, the value added to the property by such works. *Re Pavlou* [1993] 1 W.L.R. 1046) can perfectly properly be taken into account as one of the relevant dealings between the parties.[42]

"Equality is equity"

Fittingly this equitable maxim is dealt with last of all. The maxim is "not **5–037** to be applied unthinkingly" (*per* Waite J. in *Hammond v Mitchell* ([1991] 1 W.L.R. 1129 at 1137F)). The preponderance of recent authority is to

---

[41] See above, Chapter 3 "Constructive Trusts"
[42] See also *Cooke v Head* [1972] 1 W.L.R. 518 *per* Lord Denning M.R. at 522H, and *Passee v Passee* [1988] 1 F.L.R. 263 *per* Nicholls L.J. at 271B). In cases where the parties' interests have been agreed, as where the principles explained in *Goodman v Gallant* are applicable, the paying party may be able to recover part of the cost of the improvements from the other party under an equitable account (see below Chapter 7 "Personal Obligations Between Cohabitants").

the effect that this maxim should be used only as a last resort (see e.g. *Midland Bank v Cooke* [1995] 4 All E.R. 562 at 574E *per* Waite L.J. and see *Mortgage Corporation v Shaire* [2001] Ch. 743 at 750H *per* Neuberger J.).

The possibility of setting off the sum owed by one party to the other in relation to his/her beneficial interest against the costs of meeting that party's obligations in relation to the occupation of the property is considered below in Chapter 7 "Personal Obligations Between Cohabitants". A number of issues arising from the quantification of beneficial interests, including possible consequences and stamp duty issues, are also dealt with there.

CHAPTER 6

PROPRIETARY ESTOPPEL

When considering whether a client has a claim in respect of a property by **6–001** virtue of a constructive or resulting trust, the related doctrine of proprietary estoppel should also be considered. This chapter sets out the three elements historically required to establish a claim based on proprietary estoppel (assurance, reliance and detriment) before going on to consider the remedies available. The doctrines of constructive trust and proprietary estoppel have much in common. In *Grant v Edwards* Sir Nicholas Browne-Wilkinson V.C., when considering a claim for a beneficial interest in a property by virtue of a constructive trust, said:

> "...useful guidance may in the future be obtained from the principles underlying the law of proprietary estoppel which in my judgment are closely akin to those laid down in *Gissing v Gissing* [1971] A.C. 886. In both, the claimant must have acted to his or her detriment in reliance on such belief. In both, equity acts on the conscience of the legal owner to prevent him from acting in an unconscionable manner by defeating the common intention. The two principles have been developed separately without cross-fertilisation between them: but they rest on the same foundation and have on all other matters reached the same conclusions."[1]

The House of Lords has not yet, however, gone so far as to assimilate expressly the principles of constructive trust and those of proprietary estoppel, as was recognised by Nourse L.J. in *Stokes v Anderson*. His Lordship said that the Court of Appeal:

> "must continue to regard cases such as the present (being a claim for a beneficial interest in a property) as being governed by the principles of Gissing v Gissing, at any rate until we come to one where we

---

[1] [1986] Ch. 638, 656F–H. See also *Lloyds Bank Rosset* [1991] 1 A.C. 107, 132 *per* Lord Bridge and *Yaxley v Gotts* [1999] 3 W.L.R. 1217, 1227 *per* Robert Walker L.J. See also *Chan Pui Chun v Leung Kam Ho* [2003] 1 F.L.R. 23 at para.91 in which the Court of Appeal (Jonathan Parker L.J.) held that the result in that case would have been the same whether the claim was framed in terms of proprietary estoppel or constructive trust, citing Robert Walker L.J. in *Jennings v Rice and Ors* [2002] EWCA Civ 159 at para.45.

cannot be confident that their application will produce a just result."[2]

6–002   In *Oxley v Hiscock*[3] the Court of Appeal considered the overlap between the constructive trust and proprietary estoppel. *Oxley* concerned the situation where both parties contribute financially to the purchase price of a property which is bought in the sole name of one of the parties and there is no discussion as to the size of the parties' respective interests at the time of the purchase. The question was whether the court was confined to applying strict resulting trust principles when determining the size of the beneficial interests. The Court of Appeal found that it was not and that the test to be applied is that each is entitled to that share which the court considers fair having regard to the whole course of dealing between the parties in relation to the property. See further the discussion set out in Chapter 5 "Quantification of Beneficial Interests", para.5–017 *et seq*. The question of the assimilation of the principles of proprietary estoppel and constructive trust was therefore *obiter*.

Having considered all the relevant authorities, Chadwick L.J. turned his attention to the similarities between the constructive trust and proprietary estoppel and said:

> "Once it is recognised that what the court is doing, in cases of this nature, is to supply or impute a common intention as to the parties' respective shares (in circumstances in which there was, in fact, no common intention) on the basis of that which, in the light of all the material circumstances (including the acts and conduct of the parties after the acquisition), is shown to be fair, it seems to me very difficult to avoid the conclusion that an analysis in terms of proprietary estoppel will, necessarily, lead to the same result; and that it may be more satisfactory to accept that there is no difference, in cases of this nature, between constructive trust and proprietary estoppel."[4]

6–003   It might be thought, therefore, that there is little to be gained by arguing that the claimant is entitled to an interest in the property by virtue of proprietary estoppel, as an alternative to a claim by virtue of constructive trust. There are nevertheless certain situations where it remains advantageous and advisable to do so:

>   (i) A claim founded on proprietary estoppel does not require proof of such a clear *agreement, arrangement or understanding*[5] as is usually required for a claim based on a constructive trust. Relevant assurances in the context of proprietary estoppel can

---

[2] [1991] 1 F.L.R. 391, 399 E.
[3] [2004] 3 W.L.R. 715.
[4] Above, at para.66.
[5] *Lloyd's Bank v Rosset* [1991] 1 A.C. 107, 132 E–G *per* Lord Bridge.

even include "standing by in silence" whilst another acts to his/her detriment.[6]

(ii) In a claim based on constructive trust principles, where there is no express or inferred *agreement, arrangement or understanding*, the claimant has to show that there have been direct financial contributions made to the purchase price.[7] In cases based on proprietary estoppel, there is no requirement for the detriment to take the form of financial contributions. As Robert Walker L.J. said in *Gillett v Holt*:

> "The detriment need not consist of the expenditure of money or other quantifiable financial detriment, so long as it is something substantial. The requirement must be approached as part of a broad inquiry as to whether repudiation of an assurance is or is not unconscionable in all the circumstances."[8]

(iii) The remedy granted in a claim based on proprietary estoppel need not necessarily be for a beneficial interest in the property, but may be for some lesser right, for example, an "equitable licence" to remain in the property.[9]

Requirements of proprietary estoppel

Proprietary estoppel arises most commonly when an owner of property   **6–004**
encourages another to act to his detriment in the belief that he will obtain an interest in that property. The underlying principle is that it would be unconscionable for the maker of the assurance not to give effect to his promise.

In *Crabb v Arun District Council*[10] the Court of Appeal set out the rationale underlying claims based on proprietary estoppel. The case concerned a dispute over a right of access that had been promised by the defendants to the claimant. The defendants subsequently reneged on their promise leaving one section of the claimant's land land-locked and thus impossible to sell. Lord Denning M.R. said:

> "The basis of this proprietary estoppel — as indeed of promissory estoppel — is the interposition of equity. Equity comes in, true to form, to mitigate the rigours of strict law. The early cases did not speak of it as 'estoppel'. They spoke of it as 'raising an equity'. If I may expand what Lord Cairns LC said in *Hughes v Metropolitan Railway Co* (1877) 2 App. Cas. 439, 448: 'It is the first principle upon which all courts of equity proceed, 'that it will prevent a person from

---

[6] *Taylor's Fashions Ltd v Liverpool Victoria Trustees Co. Ltd* [1982] Q.B. 133 (Note), 148 E–F.
[7] *Lloyd's Bank v Rosset*, above at 132G to 133A.
[8] [2001] Ch. 210, 232D.
[9] *Inwards v Baker* [1965] 2 Q.B. 29 (see *Remedies* below, at para.6–012 *et seq*).
[10] [1976] 1 Ch. 179.

insisting on his strict legal rights — whether arising under a contract, or on his title deeds, or by statute, when it would be inequitable for him to do so having regard to the dealings which have taken place between the parties."[11]

Proprietary estoppel, unlike the related doctrine of promissory estoppel, gives rise to a cause of action and does not merely operate as a defence.[12] Proprietary estoppel has traditionally required (i) an assurance, (ii) reliance and (iii) detriment.

6–005 More recently, however, the courts have taken a "holistic" approach when determining whether an estoppel is made out, as shown by the following cases. In *Gillett v Holt*[13] the claimant, Mr Gillett, met the defendant, Mr Holt, when Mr Gillett was a school boy aged 12 and Mr Holt was a gentleman farmer aged 38. A close relationship developed between them and at one stage Mr Holt considered adopting Mr Gillett, although this did not happen. When Mr Gillett left school he began to work for Mr Holt and became his farm manager. Mr Holt made repeated assurances over many years, usually on family occasions, that Mr Gillett would succeed to his farming business including the farmhouse in which Mr Gillett and his family had lived for over 25 years. After 1992 relations between Mr Holt and Mr Gillett deteriorated rapidly. In 1995 Mr Gillett was dismissed and Mr Holt made lifetime dispositions to the second defendant, Mr Wood. He also altered his will in Mr Wood's favour, making no provision for Mr Gillett. The Court of Appeal allowed Mr Gillett's appeal, granting him the freehold of the farmhouse together with a sufficient sum of money to compensate him for his exclusion from the rest of the farming business.

Robert Walker L.J. said:

"...it is important to note at the outset that the doctrine of proprietary estoppel cannot be treated as subdivided into three or four watertight compartments. Both sides are agreed on that, and in the course of the oral argument in this court it repeatedly became apparent that the quality of the relevant assurances may influence the issue of reliance, that reliance and detriment are often intertwined, and that whether there is a distinct need for a 'mutual understanding' may depend on how the other elements are formulated and understood. Moreover, the fundamental principle that equity is concerned to prevent unconscionable conduct permeates all the elements of the doctrine. In the end the court must look at the matter in the round."[14]

[11] Above, at 187 G–H.
[12] Above, at 187 E.
[13] [2001] Ch. 210.
[14] Above, at 225 B–D.

This dictum was subsequently cited with approval by Arden L.J. in *Ottey*   **6–006**
v Grundy.[15] This case concerned a dispute under the Inheritance (Provision for Family and Dependants) Act 1975 and also a claim by way of proprietary estoppel. The claimant, Miss Ottey and the deceased, Mr Andreae began a relationship in 1996. Mr Andreae did not work, having a private income. He also had a severe alcohol problem. Miss Ottey was an actress and originally came from Jamaica, a country with which Mr Andreae had strong links. He treated Miss Ottey as his wife and she was financially dependent on him. She also looked after him and tried to help him with his alcohol problem. Miss Ottey sought an award of an apartment in Kingston and a life interest in a house boat in Chelsea, the total capital value of which was approximately £240,000/£250,000. Mr Grundy, the executor of Mr Andreae's estate, sought an award of around £20,000. The judge at first instance dismissed the Inheritance Act claim but made an award out of the estate of £50,000 and ordered that Mr Grundy should use his best endeavours to secure a transfer of the Jamaica apartment to Miss Ottey, in default of which to pay her a further £50,000. Both sides appealed. The Court of Appeal upheld the decision of the judge at first instance and dismissed both appeals.

Lady Justice Arden said:

> "It is common ground that proprietary estoppel can arise where an owner of property encourages another to act to his detriment in the belief that he will obtain an interest in that other property. The underlying rationale is that it would be unconscionable for the maker of the assurance not to give effect to his promise. The matter must be looked at in the round."[16]

It remains necessary, however, to examine the three elements traditionally required to establish a claim based on proprietary estoppel as when pleading a claim based on proprietary estoppel, each of the three requirements should be specifically pleaded.[17]

(i) Assurance

The assurance can take a number of different forms, including an express   **6–007**
representation, passive or active encouragement of expenditure or alteration of legal position. In *Taylors Fashions Ltd v Liverpool Trustees*[18] Oliver J. said:

---

[15] [2003] EWCA Civ 1176, para.52.
[16] Above, para.52. See also *Uglow v Uglow* [2004] EWCA Civ 987, a case which also concerned a challenge to a will, in which Mummery L.J. said: "The overriding concern of equity to prevent unconscionable conduct permeates all the different elements of the doctrine of proprietary estoppel: assurance, reliance, detriment and satisfaction are all intertwined (at para.9). See also *Murphy v Burrows* [2004] EWHC 1900 (Ch.).
[17] See *Gillett v Holt* [2001] Ch. 210 at 232F in relation to detriment and *Churchill v Roach* [2004] 2 F.L.R. 989 at 1004A in relation to assurance.
[18] [1982] 1 Q.B. 133 (Note) at 148 E–F.

"It may take the form of standing by in silence whilst one party unwittingly infringes another's legal rights. It may take the form of passive or active encouragement of expenditure or alteration of legal position upon the footing of some unilateral or shared legal or factual supposition. Or it may, for example, take the form of stimulating, or not objecting to, some change of legal position on the faith of a unilateral or a shared assumption as to the future conduct of one or other party. I am not at all convinced that it is desirable or possible to lay down hard and fast rules which seek to dictate, in every combination of circumstances, the considerations which will persuade the court that a departure by the acquiescing party from the previously supposed state of law or fact is so unconscionable that a court of equity will interfere."[19]

6–008   An example of a case in which the claimant was able to rely merely upon the actions of the defendant in circumstances where no specific representations had been made is *Clark v Clark and GW Clark and Sons Ltd.*[20] The second defendant was a haulage company run by two brothers, the claimant and the first defendant. For a number of reasons it was necessary to move the site on which the company operated and the claimant was willing to make available more than half of his land to be used as part of the yard and to also allow a new access way over his land, which was essential to the relocation. The brothers subsequently fell out and the claimant issued a claim for a declaration that a notice served by the claimant on the second defendant company terminated any right that the company had to use his land. The Court[21] held that there was a proprietary estoppel in the Defendants' favour. His Lordship stated that, whether or not anything specific was said about the Company's use of the claimant's land, the fact was that he made it available and did so without objection and without anything being said to indicate that its use was merely temporary, terminable upon notice by the claimant.[22] His Lordship added that it would have been quite unconscionable of him, having allowed the company to commit itself to the new haulage yard and lay out £38,000 in the process, he had then suddenly terminated the company's use of his land as a means of access.

---

[19] See also *Inwards v Baker* [1965] 2 Q.B. 29 *per* Lord Denning M.R. at 36G–37A. In *Chan Pui Chun v Leung Kam Ho* [2002] EWCA Civ 1075 the Court of Appeal held that the existence of a degree of uncertainty as to whether the male partner's promise extended to other business projects did not mean that his promise in relation to two specific business projects should be treated as so uncertain as to preclude the court from equitable relief in respect of it (para.88) *per* Jonathan Parker L.J.

[20] [2006] EWCH 275 (Ch.).

[21] Blackburne J. sitting in the Chancery Division.

[22] At para.31.

The general rule is that the representation or assurance relied upon by the claimant must relate to some specific property, or to some part of the property which is objectively ascertainable.[23] In *Layton v Martin*[24] the deceased wrote to the claimant offering her, "what emotional security I can give, plus financial security during my life, and financial security on my death." The court held that this assurance was insufficient to give rise to either a constructive trust or proprietary estoppel.[25]

In contrast, however, in *Re Basham (Deceased)* ([1986] 1 W.L.R. 1498) it was held that the representation could relate to the whole of the estate. Also in *Wayling v Jones*[26] the statement, "you'll get everything after I'm gone" was understood to relate to a particular hotel. In *Jennings v Rice*[27] the phrase "this will all be yours one day" was understood to relate to the deceased's house and furniture and in *Gillett v Holt*[28] "It's all yours" was understood to relate to a particular part of the farming business.

(ii) Reliance

The principles concerning reliance were summarised by Balcombe L.J. in **6–009** *Wayling v Jones*.[29] The deceased had promised the claimant, his long-term partner with whom he cohabited, that he would inherit his business upon his death. The parties had met in 1967 and began to cohabit in 1971 when the claimant was aged 21 and the deceased was aged 56. The deceased had owned a series of businesses. In 1980 he had purchased a café and flat in London W1. In 1981, having sold the café and flat he purchased a grocery shop in Aberystwyth. In 1982 he bought the Glen-y-Mor Hotel, also in Aberystwyth. The claimant acted throughout this time as the deceased's companion and chauffeur and helped run the businesses. In return he received pocket money, living and clothing expenses and the assurance that he would inherit the business. The deceased made wills to this effect. In 1985 the deceased sold the Glen-y-Mor Hotel and purchased the Royal Hotel, Barmouth, telling the claimant that it was for him to run and inherit after his death and that he would alter his will accordingly. The deceased failed to do so and, following his death, the claimant brought an action based on proprietary estoppel or alternatively under the Inheritance (Provision for Family and Dependants) Act 1975. The Court of Appeal upheld the claimant's appeal from the decision of

---

[23] See *Lissimore v Downing* [2003] 2 F.L.R. 308 in which representations that "she would never want for anything" or that the defendant would "take care of her" or that "she did not need to worry her pretty little head about money" or that "his other girlfriends had never wanted for anything" or that he had "looked after his other girlfriends and she would not be different" were insufficient to found a claim based on proprietary estoppel.

[24] [1986] 2 F.L.R. 227.

[25] See also *Murphy v Burrows*, above, in which the representations made were found to be equivocal in that it was not clear whether they related solely to the pigs or to the timber yard as a whole.

[26] (1993) 69 P. & C.R. 170.

[27] [2002] EWCA Civ 159.

[28] [2001] Ch. 210.

[29] (1993) 69 P. & C.R. 170.

the circuit judge. The Court of Appeal[30] held that in order to satisfy the requirements of reliance the following were necessary:

6–010

(i) a sufficient link between the promises relied upon and the conduct which constitutes the detriment. The Court of Appeal referred to the case of *Eves v Eves*[31] in which Brightman J. said that it was:

> "difficult to suppose that (the claimant) would have been wielding the 14 lb. sledge hammer, breaking up the large area of concrete, filling the skip and doing the other things which were carried out when they moved in except in pursuance of some expressed or implied arrangement that she had an interest in."

(ii) The promises relied upon do not have to be the sole inducement for the conduct: it is sufficient if they are an inducement.[32]

(iii) Once the claimant has established that promises were made and that there has been conduct by the claimant which is detrimental to him/her, there is a rebuttable presumption that the claimant adopted that course of conduct in reliance upon the assurances. The burden of proof then shifts to the defendant to establish that the claimant did not rely on the promises.[33]

(iii) Detriment

6–011 Detriment is an essential requirement of proprietary estoppel, but it has to be approached as part of a broad inquiry as to whether the repudiation of a promise or representation could be unconscionable in all the circumstances, looking at the claim in the round.

In *Gillett v Holt*[34] Robert Walker L.J. stated:

> "... the authorities show that [detriment] is not a narrow or technical concept. The detriment need not consist of the expenditure of money or other quantifiable financial detriment, so long as it is something substantial. The requirement must be approached as part of a broad inquiry as to whether repudiation of an assurance is or is not unconscionable in all the circumstances."[35]

---

[30] Above, *per* Balcombe L.J. at 173.
[31] [1975] 1 W.L.R. 1338, 1345 C–F. See also *Grant v Edwards* [1986] Ch. 638, 648–649, 655–657, 656 G–H *per* Nourse L.J. and *per* Browne-Wilkinson V.C.
[32] *Amalgamated Property Co. v Texas Bank* [1982] Q.B. 84, 104–105.
[33] *Coombes v Smith* [1987] 1 F.L.R. 352 at 366C; *Greasley v Cooke* [1980] 1 W.L.R. 1306; *Grant v Edwards* [1980] Ch. 638, 657.
[34] [2001] Ch. 210 at 232D; [2000] 2 F.L.R. 266
[35] At 232E.

Claims based on too insubstantial a detriment will fail. For example, in *Beale v Harvey*,[36] the Court of Appeal was concerned with a boundary dispute. In 1998 some disused farm buildings in Otterton, Devon were developed and converted into three residential units. The defendant, Mrs Harvey, was the first to move into the development, having purchased plot one. A fence was erected by the developers and Mrs Harvey obtained the agreement of the developer to make the fence stock proof. She then planted nearly 50 plants and shrubs alongside the fence. The developer's agent saw and expressed his approval of what she was doing. The claimants, Mr and Mrs Beale, then purchased plot two. It emerged that the fence had been placed in the wrong place with the effect that the western end of the Beales' garden was 2.2 metres narrower at the western end than at the eastern end. The developers agreed that the fence between the two plots was in the wrong place and sought to obtain Mrs Harvey's consent to its realignment and offered to make good any damage or disturbance. Mrs Harvey refused. The Beales sought a mandatory injunction requiring her to realign the fence. The injunction was granted and Mrs Harvey appealed. Her appeal was dismissed. Lord Justice Peter Gibson said,

"... the detriment suffered by Mrs Harvey by acting on Country-wide's promise or representation for so short a period is too insubstantial a detriment to make it unconscionable for Country-wide to seek to rectify its mistake at its own expense. Putting it another way, to treat what has occurred as giving Mrs Harvey the right to a permanent enlargement of her garden at the expense of the Beales with their smaller garden would be, in my view, quite disproportionate."[37]

In *Coombes v Smith*,[38] Mr Jonathan Parker Q.C., sitting as a Deputy High Court Judge, held that the claimant's acts of allowing herself to become pregnant by the defendant and giving birth to a daughter; leaving her husband and moving into a property purchased by the defendant; looking after the property and the daughter and decorating the property were not done in reliance upon some mistaken belief as to her legal rights and did not constitute detriment.[39]

[36] [2003] EWCA Civ 1883.
[37] Above, at para.39.
[38] [1986] 1 W.L.R. 808.
[39] At 364H to 365E. See also *Windeler v Whitehall* [1990] 2 F.L.R. 505 in which Millett J. held that the spending of some of a legacy on living expenses and supervision of minor building works did not constitute detriment as "any wife or mistress would do the same." *Lissimore v Downing* [2003] 2 F.L.R. 308 in which the "present advantage" of moving in to live with the defendant, a founder member of the band "Judas Priest" outweighed the prospective detriment. *Churchill v Roach* [2004] 2 F.L.R. 989 in which the creation of an easily reversible doorway, a pond and the undertaking of some of the DIY work which had to be done were found to be insufficient to amount to give rise to a proprietary estoppel.

Remedies

6–012   Once a claim to equitable relief has been established, the court has to determine the appropriate form of remedy. It is important to note that the court is not limited to making a finding that the claimant has a beneficial interest in the property in dispute, but has a much broader range of remedies at its disposal.[40]

Even if it is not possible to establish that the claimant has a beneficial interest in a property, it may be possible to argue that the claimant has a lesser right, for example a licence, to remain in the property. This is demonstrated by the case of *Kay v Mills*.[41] The case concerned an application for possession of a property by Mr Kay against his daughter, Mrs Mills. The property had been purchased in the joint names of Mr Kay and Mrs Mills, but a trust deed stated that the property was held upon an express trust for the sole benefit of Mr Kay. Mr Kay paid the entirety of the purchase price. Relations between the parties soured and Mr Kay sought possession of the property. In her defence and counterclaim, Mrs Mills argued that she and her family had a right to remain in the property on the basis of oral representations made both at the time of the purchase and subsequently. She claimed that she had a beneficial interest in the property.

Mr Kay applied to strike out the defence and counterclaim on the basis that in early 2003 Mrs Mills' previous mortgagee sought a charging order on her share of the property on the footing that she was a beneficial owner. In those proceedings she denied that she had any interest in the property. She could not now seek to argue that she had such an interest. The judge at first instance found for Mr Kay and struck out the defence and counterclaim. Mrs Mills appealed. It was conceded on her behalf that as at the time of the charging order proceedings she did not have a beneficial interest in the property. It was argued, however, that Mrs Mills and her family had the right to remain in the property on the basis of proprietary estoppel. Mrs Mills was entitled to rely on oral and written assurances to the effect that she would have a "home for life" and that her children would have a home "for as long as they require it" and that there had been detrimental reliance upon those representations. Mr Kay was therefore estopped from denying that she had a licence to remain in the property. The Court of Appeal agreed that there were triable issues and held that the claim should not have been struck out.

6–013   Examples of remedies available to the court include:

(i) a beneficial interest in the property;
(ii) the payment of a lump sum[42];

---

[40] See *Gray and Gray Elements of Land Law* (4th edn, para.10.286).
[41] [2005] EWCA Civ 1537.
[42] E.g. *Jennings v Rice* [2002] EWCA Civ 159, para.15.

(iii) a licence to occupy a property rent free for life[43]; See also *Matharu v Matharu* ((1994) 68 P. & C.R. 93) where the Court of Appeal substituted the judge at first instance's order that the defendant had a beneficial interest in the property with an order that she had a licence to remain in the property for her life or such shorter period as she may decide;

(iv) transfer of the freehold title.[44]

The court will look at all the circumstances of the case when deciding how to satisfy the equity. In *Gillett v Holt*, Robert Walker L.J. said:

> "The aim is, as Sir Arthur Hobhouse said in *Plimmer v Wellington Corporation* (1884) 9 App. Cas. 699 714, to 'look at the circumstances in each case to decide in what way the equity can be satisfied.' The court approaches this task in a cautious way, in order to achieve what Scarman L.J. in *Crabb v Arun District Council* [1976] Ch. 179, 198, called 'the minimum equity to do justice to the plaintiff.' "[45]

This includes the conduct of the parties. In *Pascoe v Turner*[46] the defendant went to live with the plaintiff as his housekeeper in 1963. In 1964 they began living together as husband and wife. In 1973 the plaintiff began an affair with another woman. Three years later he gave the defendant two months' notice to quit. The defendant had however relied upon the plaintiff's assurance upon separation that the house and everything in it was hers, by spending money on the house. The Court of Appeal upheld the decision of the court below and found that the defendant was entitled to have the promise and expectations satisfied by having the property conveyed to her. In so doing, Cumming-Bruce L.J. looked at all the circumstances and had regard to the history of the conduct of the plaintiff in relation to the proceedings which "leads to an irresistible inference that he is determined to pursue his purpose of evicting her from the house by any legal means at his disposal with a ruthless disregard of the obligations binding upon conscience (above, at 151)."

In *Crabb v Arun District Council*,[47] the Court of Appeal also had regard to the "history of delay, and indeed highhandedness" (above, at 199) displayed by the defendant council when awarding the claimant an easement without payment.

The remedy must be proportionate to the detriment suffered. Proportionality may be more easily satisfied where there is an assurance to transfer specific property. Sometimes, however, the claimant's expecta-

6–014

6–015

---

[43] *Inwards v Baker* [1965] 2 Q.B. 29, 37G.
[44] *Pascoe v Turner* [1979] 1 W.L.R. 431, 439B.
[45] *Gillett v Holt*, above at 235E.
[46] [1979] 2 All E.R. 945.
[47] [1976] Ch. 179.

tions will be out of proportion to the detriment suffered. *Jennings v Rice*[48] concerned a claim under the Inheritance Act (Provision for Family and Dependants) Act 1975, in contract and also under the doctrine of proprietary estoppel. Mrs Royle died in August 1997 leaving no family. Her estate was sworn for probate at £1.285 million net with the house and furniture being valued at £435,000. The estate was administered by the defendant, Mr Rice. The claimant, Mr Jennings, was a self-employed brick-layer who lived in the same village as the deceased. He began working for her as a gardener but then his job extended to running errands, taking Mrs Royle shopping and minor maintenance work around the house. In 1993 Mrs Royle had a burglary and sought to persuade Mr Jennings to stay overnight to provide security. He did so, sleeping on a sofa for most nights from 1994 until her death in 1997. She had not paid him since the late 1980s but when Mr Jennings asked Mrs Royle about this she would tell him that he need not worry and that "this will all be yours one day". She died intestate. The claims under the Inheritance Act and in contract failed, but the claim under proprietary estoppel succeeded. The judge ordered that the estate pay the sum of £200,000 to Mr Jennings. Mr Jennings appealed contending that he was entitled to the whole of the estate or alternatively to a sum equal to the value of the property and furniture. The appeal was dismissed on the grounds that the claimant's expectations were out of proportion to the detriment which he had suffered.

Robert Walker L.J. said:

> "Sometimes the assurances, and the claimant's reliance on them, have a consensual character falling not far short of an enforceable contract ... In a case of that sort both the claimant's expectations and the element of detriment to the claimant will have been defined with reasonable clarity ....[49]
>
> ... But if the claimant's expectations are uncertain, or extravagant, or out of all proportion to the detriment which the claimant has suffered, the court can and should recognise that the claimant's equity should be satisfied in another (and generally more limited) way."[50]

6–016   A further example of a case in which the claimant's expectations were disproportionate to the detriment suffered is *Sledmore v Dalby*.[51] The claimant and her husband purchased the property in dispute in 1962. In 1965 the defendant, Dalby, married the Sledmore's daughter and they had moved into the property as tenants of the Sledmores. The Sledmores accepted rent from them until 1976 when their daughter became ill and Dalby unemployed. Between 1976 and 1978 Dalby carried out substantial

---

[48] [2002] EWCA Civ 159.
[49] Above, para.45.
[50] Above, para.50
[51] 72 P. & C.R. 196.

works to the property to improve it as a family home and was encouraged to do so by Mr Sledmore. Mr Sledmore had told them that one day he intended to give the property to them. Mr Sledmore died in 1980. Mrs Dalby died in 1983. Dalby continued to live in the property and refused to pay rent. In 1990 Mrs Sledmore brought proceedings for possession. The Court of Appeal allowed her appeal, making an order for possession. The Court of Appeal held that the minimum equity to do justice to Dalby was an equity which had now expired. The extent of the equity was to have made good, so far as may fairly be done between the parties, the expectations of Dalby which the Sledmores had encouraged. Dalby had expended money in 1976 to 1978 upon his then family home and he and his family had enjoyed the benefits of such expenditure. He had also enjoyed rent-free occupation of the property for over 15 years. The effect of any equity that he had once had had therefore been exhausted.[52]

It should always be borne in mind, however, that the court will take into consideration whether or not the claimant can be said to have come to the court with "clean hands". In certain circumstances, if the claimant cannot be said to have done so, the court may dismiss the claimant's claim.

Claims against third parties

Where property has been transferred from the person upon whose unconscionable conduct the claimant seeks to rely to a third party, the claimant may have a potential claim against that third party. Section 116(a) of the the Land Registration Act 2002 provides that, in relation to registered land, an "*equity by estoppel*" has effect "from the time the equity arises as an interest capable of binding successors in title (subject to the rules about the effect of dispositions on priority)".[53]

6–017

It is doubtful whether the claimant in these circumstances (ie. where property has been transferred to a third party) would have a personal claim against the person responsible for the unconscionable conduct.[54]

---

[52] A further example is *Uglow v Uglow* [2004] EWCA Civ 987 where the Court of Appeal refused to make an order conveying the deceased's entire farm to the claimant. See also *Dodds v Messruther* March 1, 2006 HHJ Kaye Q.C. (unreported) in which the court held that as the claimant had had her debts paid by the defendant and had enjoyed almost two years rent-free occupation of the property her claim based on proprietary estoppel should be dismissed.

[53] It is unclear, however, whether s.116(a) includes every interest arising by virtue of proprietary estoppel or only those equities which are satisfied by the grant of a proprietary interest in the property. The editors of *Snell's Equity* by J. McGhee (31st edn, 2005) at para.10–28 take the view that it is only those equities which will be satisfied by the award of a proprietary interest that will bind third parties and that the position relating to estoppel licences remains unchanged.

[54] See *Lloyd v Dugdale* [2001] EWCA Civ 1754 *per* Sir Christopher Slade at 55, although contrast *Personal Liability in Proprietary Estoppel* by Susan Bright and Ben McFarlane, Conveyancer and Property Lawyer [2005] 14–31.

Conclusion

6–018   Proprietary estoppel still has a significant role to play in disputes between cohabitees, in spite of repeated assertions by the Court of Appeal that there is no difference in this type of case between the principles applicable to proprietary estoppel and constructive trusts.[55] Unless and until this is modified by the House of Lords or Parliament, proprietary estoppel should always be considered when advising in this context.

---

[55] *Grant v Edwards* [1986] 638, 656 F–G; *Yaxley v Gotts* [1999] 1217, 1227 and *Oxley v Hiscock* [2004] 3 W.L.R. 715.

CHAPTER 7

PERSONAL OBLIGATIONS BETWEEN COHABITANTS

There are a number of situations in which obligations arise as between   **7–001**
cohabitants which do not necessarily affect or give rise to direct interests
in real property, but arise out of the parties' cohabitation and are
nonetheless enforceable either at law or in equity. The parties' respective
beneficial interests in the property they have shared as a home may not be
much affected by questions of ownership of personal property (such as
household contents or the funds held in a joint bank account), however
disputes of that nature for obvious reasons tend to co-exist alongside
disputes relating to the interests in real property. Such disputes are frequently of considerable importance to the parties, albeit disproportionately so on occasion. The question, for instance, "who owns
this car?" requires an answer whether or not that answer mirrors the
beneficial interests in the family home, and whether or not the value of
the car in question would of itself justify litigation concerning its
ownership.

A claimant who fails to establish an interest in a relevant real property
may nonetheless establish an interest in other property, such as an
endowment policy, or may establish that the defendant is personally
indebted to him/her. The range of obligations and personal remedies
which might arise as between cohabitants (whether or not co-owners) is
wide and perhaps incapable of being exhaustively itemised. However, the
discussion which follows considers a number of commonly encountered
issues which arise on the breakdown of a relationship between those who
have cohabited without marrying.

Perhaps the first issue to consider relates to the situation where the   **7–002**
parties reach an agreement which on the face of it governs their respective
beneficial interests in the relevant property, but one party later asserts
that the relevant agreement is vitiated by reason of some misconduct on
the part of the other, such as fraud, undue influence or mistake. That
misconduct may have a bearing on questions of title and beneficial
interest, but the remedy in relation to such misconduct is a personal
remedy as between one party and the other. It is therefore convenient to
consider such questions alongside other personal remedies which may lie
between the parties. The difficulties in pleading and making out a case
based on fraud should not be underestimated, but where fraud can be

made out, the court is left in the position of deciding the extent of the claimant's beneficial interest without assistance from the declaration contained in the title deeds. Thus the principles explained in *Oxley v Hiscock* ([2005] Fam. 211) and *Stack v Dowden* ([2005] EWCA Civ 857) would prima facie apply.

Beyond cases of fraud, mistake or the like, where a trust instrument does not give effect to the intentions of the parties it can be rectified by the court so that it does. Whereas in the case of rescission the court must seek to identify the relevant shares without reference to the rescinded declaration, in a case of rectification, the deed, as rectified by the court, is conclusive of the parties' respective shares (subject to the question of an equitable account) in the same way as would a deed in a case where no claim to rectification was made. A deed might be rectified, for instance so as to exclude one party who had hitherto been a joint tenant from any beneficial interest (as in e.g. *Wilson v Wilson* ([1969] 3 All E.R. 945 at 949A–B)) or to provide for the parties to hold as tenants in common rather than joint tenants (as in *In re Colebrook's Conveyance* [1972] 1 W.L.R. 1397 at 1398H). A claim to rectification does not open the door to the exercise of discretionary or even quasi-discretionary powers. The court's power to rectify extends only to amend the relevant instrument so that it accords with what the parties truly intended at the time it was executed; the court cannot exercise its power to rectify in order to give effect to the court's overall view of the justice of the case.

Rescission/rectification

7–003   It is one of the cardinal principles of co-ownership that property held subject to a joint tenancy is beneficially held by the joint tenants in equal *aliquot* shares (*Goodman v Gallant* ([1986] Fam. 106) and see Chapter 5 "Quantification of Beneficial Interests", above). This rule admits only one exception, namely that parties are free to agree in terms that on severance they will hold in shares other than 50/50; for this purpose[1] only clear words to that effect will do.

This is not to say that a co-owner who feels aggrieved that his/her ex partner will receive a half share having made considerably less than an equal contribution is necessarily without redress of any form. Quite apart from any *in personam* claim in the nature of an account or enquiry (as to which, see below) it may be possible to challenge the legitimacy or accuracy of the original declaration of joint tenancy. The authorities on the point envisage two possible avenues by which the agreement underpinning the joint tenancy could be impeached. These are firstly, a claim to rescission on the grounds that some irregularity such as fraud or mistake vitiates the agreement between the parties, and secondly, to rectification of the trust instrument itself. It ought, however, to be possible to impugn the agreement underpinning the declaration on other recognised grounds

---

[1] Subject to the interesting academic argument as to whether the relevant intention can be supplied under the doctrine of proprietary estoppel, as to which see Chapter 5, above.

such as undue influence. A detailed analysis of these essentially contractual remedies is beyond the scope of this work, however the following propositions can be offered as a general guide.

Rescission and rectification

Where there is an express declaration of trust, which conforms with the requirements of s.53(1)(b) of the Law of Property Act 1925, it will only be rescinded or rectified in very limited circumstances.[2] Claims for rectification, setting aside or cancellation of deeds or other written deeds are assigned to the Chancery Division: Supreme Court Act 1981, s.61, Sch.1, para.1. Every judge of every Division must, however, recognise and give effect to all equitable rights, obligations and defences and must grant all such remedies as the parties maybe entitled to in respect of any legal or equitable claim, so that as far as possible all matters in controversy between the parties may be completely and finally determined and all multiplicity of legal proceedings avoided (see Supreme Court Act 1981, s.49). If seeking rectification, it is important to note that the general equity jurisdiction of the County Court is limited to £30,000 (see County Courts Act 1984, s.23 (b),(d) and (g); see also County Courts Jurisdiction Order 1981 (SI 1981/1123)). However, the county court has jurisdiction under s.14 TLATA whatever the amount involved and whatever the value of any fund or asset connected with the proceedings.[3] Of course, there are a number of other important factors which will inform the question of where to issue proceedings, such as High Court or County Court, and Family Division or Chancery Division. Further, s.24 of The County Courts Act 1984 provides for the extension of the county court jurisdiction by agreement in the terms set out in that section. This issue is discussed at greater length below in Chapter 9 "Practice and Procedure".

7–004

In *Pettitt v Pettitt* Lord Upjohn stated[4]:

7–005

> "In the first place, the beneficial ownership of the property in question must depend upon the agreement of the parties determined at the time of its acquisition. If the property in question is land there must be some lease or conveyance which shows how it was acquired. If that document declares not merely in whom the legal title is to vest but in whom the beneficial title is to vest that necessarily concludes the question of title as between the spouses for all time, and **in the absence of fraud or mistake at the time of the transaction** the parties cannot go behind it at any time thereafter even on death or the break-up of the marriage."

---

[2] A claim for rectification should normally be pleaded *Blay v Pollard* [1930] 1 K.B. 628 but *c.f. Butler v Mountview Estates Ltd* [1951] 1 K.B. 563. Where this is not initially done it may be possible to amend the pleadings at a later stage in the proceedings, though this may involve terms as to costs.

[3] High Court and County Courts Jurisdiction Order 1991, SI 1991/724, art.2, as amended by SI 1996/3141.

[4] [1970] A.C. 777 at 813.

Examples of where such a situation may arise are:

    i. Where the client insists that the express declaration on the transfer does not represent an agreement that the parties reached between themselves as to the size of their respective shares.

    ii. Where the client insists that both parties were not advised properly or at all as to the meaning of what they were signing, where he or she has contributed a larger amount to the purchase price of the property.

In cases where there is a dispute about the advice given at the time of drafting the express declaration it may be appropriate to consider an action for professional negligence on the part of the legal adviser engaged to deal with the conveyancing of the property. Such matters are outside the scope of this work and other specialist texts should be consulted. Solicitors ought to be aware of the potential implications this situation might have for their firm if the adviser who dealt with the conveyance also works for the firm which is now asked to advise on the potential remedies available to the client. In such circumstances the client should usually be advised to seek advice from a different firm.

7–006   The difficulties of setting aside an express declaration of trust were highlighted in *Pink v Lawrence*.[5] Mr Pink and Mr Lawrence purchased a property as joint tenants in law and in equity which was given effect by a document under seal executed by the vendor. The claimant, Mr Lawrence, brought an action seeking a declaration that he and the defendant, Mr Pink, held the property upon trust for sale for Mr Lawrence absolutely, since the Mr Pink had contributed nothing to the purchase price. The Court of Appeal found that even though the two gentlemen may not have understood at all clearly the implications of the transaction into which they entered[6] they were bound by the express declaration of trust. Buckley L.J. stated at 101:

"Once a trust has been effectively declared, it can only be got rid of either by rescinding the document containing the declaration of trust on the ground of fraud or mistake, or rectifying it in the appropriate manner to vary or delete the declaration of trust."[7]

[5] (1978) 36 P. & C.R. 98.
[6] At 99.
[7] See also *Goodman v Gallant* [1986] Fam. 106 *per* Slade L.J. at 116B, *Huntingford v Hobbs* [1993] 1 F.L.R. 736 *per* Sir Christopher Slade at 740F. See also, for example, *Bowser v Caley and Ors* LTL 19/4/06 in which HHJ Behrens Q.C. sitting as a judge of the High Court found that the claimant was unable to set aside a transfer on the grounds of undue influence, misrepresentation or lack of capacity owing to drunkenness, although he did find that the claimant was entitled to a life interest in the proceeds of sale by virtue of a constructive trust or proprietary estoppel.

Fraud

Where actual fraud is proved the court will set aside an express **7–007** declaration of trust. As Denning L.J. observed in *Lazarus Estates v Beasley*,[8, 9] "fraud unravels everything".

It is important to note that the CPR requires that any allegation of fraud must be specifically set out in the particulars of claim where the claimant wishes to rely on them in support of his claim.[10] In addition, the fact of any illegality; the details of any misrepresentation; details of all breaches of trust; notice or knowledge of a fact; details of unsoundness of mind or undue influence; details of wilful default and any facts relating to mitigation of loss or damage, must also be specifically set out in the particulars of claim.

Undue Influence

Undue influence is one of the grounds of relief developed by the courts of **7–008** equity as a court of conscience.[11] Cases of undue influence can be divided into two classes: (i) actual undue influence and (ii) presumed undue influence.

(i) Actual undue influence

Actual undue influence is an equitable wrong committed by the dominant **7–009** party which makes it unconscionable for the dominant party to enforce his legal rights against the other. It is typically some express conduct overbearing the other party's will. It is capable of including conduct which might give a defence at law, e.g. duress and misrepresentation. Actual undue influence does not depend upon some pre-existing relationship between the two parties though it is most commonly associated with and derives from such a relationship. He who alleges actual undue influence must prove it.[12]

---

[8] [1956] 1 Q.B. 702, 712.
[9] See also *London v General Omnibus Co. Ltd v Holloway* [1912] 2 K.B. 72 at 81, and *Standard Chartered Bank v Pakistan National Shipping Corp (No. 2)* [1998] 1 Lloyd's Rep. 684 at 704 *per* Cresswell J. cited in *Niru Battery Manufacturing Co. v Milestone Trading Ltd* [2003] EWCA Civ 1443: "The tort of deceit involves a false representation made by the defendant, who knows it to be untrue, or who has no belief in its truth, or who is reckless as to its truth. If the defendant intended that the plaintiff should act in reliance on such representation and the plaintiff in fact does so, the defendant will be liable in deceit for the damage caused." The editors of *Snell's Equity* (31st edn) define fraud as, "A false statement of fact which is made by D to C knowingly, or without belief in its truth, or recklessly, without caring whether it is true or false, with the intent that it should be acted upon and which is in fact acted upon by C" (see para.8–006 and the further cases cited therein.).
[10] CPR 16 P.D. 8.2.
[11] *Royal Bank of Scotland v Etridge (No. 2)* [2001] U.K.H.L. 44 *per* Lord Nicholls at para.6.
[12] *Etridge No. 2* at paras 13 and 103.

(ii) Presumed undue influence

7–010   Presumed undue influence necessarily involves some legally recognised, pre-existing relationship between the two parties. As a result of that relationship one party is treated as owing a special duty to deal fairly with the other. Typically they are fiduciary or closely analogous relationships.[13]

In this type of case the influence of one person over another provides scope for misuse without any specific overt acts of persuasion.[14]

If the complainant proves that

(i) he/she placed trust and confidence in the other party in relation to the management of the complainant's financial affairs, and

(ii) there is a transaction which calls for explanation,

then an inference of undue influence can be drawn and the legal burden is also satisfied, unless the other party can produce evidence to counter the inference which would otherwise be drawn.[15]

7–011   In some cases, however, the law has adopted a sternly protective attitude towards certain types of relationship in which one party acquires influence over another who is vulnerable and dependent and where substantial gifts by the influenced or vulnerable person would not normally to be expected.[16] In these circumstances, the complainant need not prove that he actually reposed trust and confidence in the other party; it is sufficient for him to prove the existence of the type of relationship (*Etridge No. 2* at para.18). These types of relationship include parent and child; guardian and ward; trustee and beneficiary; solicitor and client and medical adviser and patient.[17]

Engaged couples formerly fell into this category,[18] but given that it is now well established that husband and wife is not a relationship which falls within this category of case, and given that Lord Nicholls in *Etridge No. 2* does not include engaged couples in the list of examples given[19] it is doubtful that engaged couples remain within this category of relationships.

7–012   The principles contained in *Etridge No. 2* were usefully summarised in *Papouis v Gibson-West* [2004] EWHC 396 by Lewison J. at para.5:

(1) The objective of the doctrine of undue influence is to ensure that the influence of one person ("the donee") over another ("the donor") is not abused (*Etridge No. 2*, para.6);

---

[13] *Etridge No. 2* para.104. See further *Irvani v Irvani* [2000] 1 LILR 412 at 424 *per* Buxton L.J. and *Singla v Bashir* [2002] EWHC 883 (Ch.).
[14] *Etridge No. 2*, para.9. See *Allcard v Skinner* (1887) 36 Ch. D. 145 at 181.
[15] *Etridge No. 2* paras 14, 21 and 156 and see *Papouis v Gibson-West* [2004] E.W.H.C. 396.
[16] *Etridge No. 2* at para.18.
[17] *Etridge No. 2* at para.18.
[18] See Maugham J. in *Re Lloyds Bank Ltd* [1931] 1 Ch. 289 at 302.
[19] At para.18.

(2)   If the donor intends to enter into a transaction, but the intention was produced by means which lead to the conclusion that the intention thus procured ought not fairly to be treated as the expression of the donor's free will, the law will not permit the transaction to stand (*Etridge No. 2* para.7);

(3)   Leaving aside cases of improper pressure or threats, undue influence may arise where the donee has acquired over the donor a measure of influence or ascendancy of which he takes unfair advantage (*Etridge No. 2* para.8);

(4)   Disadvantage to the donor is not a necessary ingredient of undue influence (*Etridge No. 2* para.12). However, it may have an evidential value, because it is relevant to the questions whether any allegation of abuse of confidence can properly be made, and whether any abuse actually occurred (*Etridge No. 2* para.104);

(5)   Whether a transaction has been brought about by undue influence is a question of fact (*Etridge No. 2* para.13);

(6)   The legal burden of proving undue influence rests on the person alleging it (*Etridge No. 2* para.13);

(7)   If the claimant proves (a) that the donor placed trust and confidence in the donee in relation to the management of the donee's financial affairs, and (b) that the transaction calls out for explanation, the claimant has discharged an evidential burden, which will also enable an inference of undue influence to be drawn, and thus satisfy the legal burden, unless the donee produces evidence to counter the inference which would otherwise be drawn (*Etridge No. 2* paras 14, 21 and 156);

(8)   This is simply a question of evidence and proof. At the end of the day, after trial, there will either be proof of undue influence or that proof will fail and it will be found that there is no undue influence. In the former case, whatever the relationship between the parties and however the influence was exerted, there will have been found to have been an actual case of undue influence. In the latter there will be none (*Etridge No. 2* para.93);

(9)   Proof that the donor received advice from a third party before entering into the impugned transaction is one of the matters a court takes into account when weighing all the evidence. The weight, or importance, to be attached to such advice depends on all the circumstances. In the normal course, advice from a solicitor or other outside adviser can be expected to bring home to a donor a proper understanding of what he or she is about to do. But a person may understand fully the implications of a proposed transaction, for instance, a substantial gift, and yet still be acting under the undue influence of another. Proof of outside advice does not, of itself, necessarily show that the subsequent completion of the transaction was free from the exercise of undue influence. Whether it will be proper to infer

that outside advice had an emancipating effect, so that the transaction was not brought about by the exercise of undue influence, is a question of fact to be decided having regard to all the evidence in the case (*Etridge No. 2* para.20);

(10) The nature of the advice required is that someone free from the taint of undue influence should put before the donor the nature and consequences of the proposed transaction. It is not necessary for the adviser to recommend the transaction. An adult of competent mind is entitled to enter into a financially unwise transaction if he or she wants to (*Etridge No. 2* paras 60 and 61).

(iii) Defences

7–013   The usual equitable defences of delay, acquiescence and confirmation are available to defeat a claim brought on grounds of undue influence — see *Snell's Equity* (31st edn) at 13–16.

Unconscionable Bargain

7–014   It is now doubtful as to whether there is any relevant distinction between a claim based on undue influence and one based on unconscionable bargain. In *Williams v Williams*,[20] the judge proceeded on the basis that there was no difference between the two, following dicta in *Etridge No. 2*, that:

> The principle [of undue influence] is not confined to cases of abuse of trust and confidence. It also includes, for instance, cases where a vulnerable person has been exploited.[21]

There is, however, a distinct line of authority relating to unconscionable bargains and in an appropriate case the doctrine should be relied upon. In *Irvani v Irvani*[22] Buxton L.J. stated:

> "It is particularly important to keep these distinctions [between a case of undue influence and a case of unconscionable bargain] clear, because otherwise there may be a tendency to think that a case that has some elements of undue influence, but is not a case of undue influence; and which has some elements of unconscionable bargain, but which is not in law a case of unconscionable bargain; can by the combination of these different and inadequate claims be turned into a case that attracts relief on a vaguer basis of general equity."[23]

---

[20] [2003] EWHC 742. In *Williams*, a donor who made a gift of half of his house had to understand not just that he was giving away half of his property but also the general implications of becoming a joint owner by way of a tenancy in common at para.43.

[21] *Etridge No. 2 per* Lord Nicholls at para.11.

[22] [2000] 1 Lloyd's Rep. 412 at 423.

[23] See also *Singla v Bashir* [2002] EWHC 883 (Ch.) at para.30.

It is important, therefore, to be clear about what constitutes an unconscionable bargain. Buxton L.J. in *Irvani*, adopted from *Chitty on Contracts*[24] the following definition of the doctrine of unconscionable bargain:

> "The doctrine of unconscionable bargain seems to be limited in three ways. The first is that the bargain must be oppressive to the complainant in overall terms; the second is that it may only apply when the complainant was suffering from certain types of bargaining weakness; and the third that the other party must have acted unconscionably in the sense of having knowingly taken advantage of the complainant."

A relevant disability or "bargaining weakness" need not equate to a lack   **7–015**
of capacity but could instead encompass someone suffering a significant mental decline or exhibiting eccentric behaviour leading an objective observer to question the judgment and understanding of that person (*Qutb v Hussain*, [2005] EWHC 157 (Ch.) at para.40).

The doctrine requires a very strong case before the courts will intervene. The bargain has to be more than hard, unreasonable or foolish. It must be proved to be unconscionable in the sense that one of the parties has imposed the bargain in a morally reprehensible manner. His behaviour must be characterised by some moral culpability or impropriety. There needs to be unconscientious or extortionate abuse of power.

An example of the court's reluctance to intervene is the case of *Singla v Bashir* where the High Court (Chancery Division) refused to set aside an agreement on this ground even though the transferor was 66 years old, had a very poor grasp of English and had not worked for 20 years due to ill health. In contrast, the transferee was a medical doctor by profession and was therefore well educated.[25] Where the transaction is one which "shocks the court", unconscionable conduct can be inferred in the absence of an innocent explanation: see *Credit Lyonnais Bank Nederland NV v Burch* [1997] 1 All E.R. 144 *per* Millett L.J. at 153.

Setting aside gifts due to lack of capacity

The courts may set aside a transaction where there is a lack of capacity on   **7–016**
the part of a donor of a gift. The leading case is *Re Beaney*.[26] Here the judge held that the question to be addressed is whether the person concerned is capable of understanding what he does by executing the

---

[24] 28th edn. but now in its 29th edn.
[25] *Singla v Bashir* [2002] EWHC 883 (Ch.).
[26] [1978] 2 All E.R. 595.

deed in question when its general purport has been fully explained to him.[27, 28]

The degree of understanding required in respect of any instrument is relative to the particular transaction. In the case of a will the degree required is always high. In the case of a contract, a deed made for consideration or a gift *inter vivos* (whether by deed or otherwise), the degree required varies with the circumstances of the transaction. If the subject matter and value of the gift are trivial in relation to the donor's other assets a low degree of understanding will suffice. If on the other hand the effect is to dispose of the donor's only asset of value then the degree of understanding required is high (see *Re Beaney*, above at 601).

Williams v Williams[29] is a good example of where the court will intervene due to lack of capacity. The claimant was the brother of the first defendant and brother-in-law of the second defendant. The experts agreed that he had learning disabilities which meant that he had "significant sub-average intellectual functioning, with concurrent deficits or impairments in present adaptive functioning."[30] He had lived with his mother in the family home but in 1986 she died. She left a will leaving the family home to the claimant. The claimant's brother and wife then came to live with him in the family home. The claimant then executed a deed of gift to himself and his brother and wife to hold upon trust for the three of them in the shares 50:25:25. Relations between them soured and the claimant moved out. He brought proceedings seeking a declaration that the gift was void or in the alternative, an order setting aside the deed of gift on the grounds of his lack of capacity. The court held that in order for the gift to be valid, the claimant must have been capable of having an understanding of the general nature and effect of a gift of this kind and not just that he was giving away half of his property but also of what the general implications of becoming a joint owner by way of a tenant in common.[31] The court granted the relief sought.

7–017   Where there is, prima facie, a lack of capacity at the time the transaction was entered into, the burden of proof passes to the defendant to demonstrate that the claimant did have the requisite capacity.[32] Where a donor is found to lack capacity the transaction will be void[33]

---

[27] Mr Martin Nourse Q.C. as he then was, sitting as a Deputy Judge of the High Court at 600.

[28] See also *The Special Trustees for Great Ormand Street Hospital for Children v Rushin* April 19, 2000 (unreported) *per* Rimer J.: "having found, as I have, that by 1996 [the donor] was suffering from a material degree of dementia occasioned by Alzheimer's disease, I consider that the burden of proving that [she] had the requisite degree of capacity shifted to [the defendants]. See also *Qutb v Hussain and Anr* (above) *per* Warren J. at para.21.

[29] [2003] EWHC 742 (Ch.).

[30] At para.37.

[31] At para.43.

[32] *The Special Trustees for Great Ormond Street Hospital v Rushin*, above and *Williams v Williams*, above at para.45.

[33] See *In re Beaney*, above, *The Special Trustees for Great Ormond Street Hospital for Children v Rushin*, above and *Williams v Williams*, above.

Mistake

Where the claimant can establish that the written agreement was entered **7–018**
into on the grounds of mistake, then the court will set aside or rectify the
document. It may be possible for the court to give effect to the true
position between the parties without rectifying the declaration, by
granting some more direct form of relief, for example, a declaration.[34]

(i) Common mistake

Where the parties enter into a written agreement in the mistaken belief **7–019**
that the terms of the written agreement represent their prior agreement,
then in certain circumstances the court will either set aside or rectify the
written agreement.

The relevant principles were considered in *Joscelyne v Nissen* ([1970] 2
Q.B. 86). This case concerned a dispute between a father (claimant) and
daughter (defendant). The claimant's mother and father were tenants of a
house, "Martindale" in Enfield. The father operated a car hire business
from the property. In 1960 the father was served with notice to quit. In
order to help her parents, the daughter and her husband purchased the
house and moved in. The mother and father lived on the ground floor
and the daughter and son-in-law on the first floor. The daughter helped
to run the business. The mother unfortunately suffered two strokes and
returned to the house unable to look after herself. The father and
daughter therefore agreed that the daughter would take over the business.
In conversation she agreed to pay the mother and father expenses,
including the gas, electricity and coal bills, and the cost of home help. It
was not in issue that there was an express agreement between the parties
in relation to these items. The written agreement however simply stated:

> "[The defendant] shall discharge all expenses in connection with the
> whole premises ... and shall indemnify [the claimant] from and
> against any claim arising in respect of the same."

The daughter paid the gas, electricity and coal bills for a time. The father
and daughter then had a disagreement in relation to whether the mother
and father should move to the first floor and allow the daughter and her
husband to occupy the ground floor. The daughter stopped paying the
bills, arguing that the written agreement did not require her to do so. The
father sought a declaration that she should pay the bills, alternatively,
rectification of the agreement.

It was argued before the Court of Appeal that in order to rectify the **7–020**
written agreement there had to be a complete antecedent concluded oral
contract. The Court of Appeal rejected this argument. Russell L.J.

[34] *Pink v Lawrence* (1978) 38 P. & C.R. 98 at 101–102 citing *Wilson v Wilson* [1969] 3 All
E.R. 945 (at 949A–B).

considered the relevant case law. His Lordship adopted the principles set out by Simonds J. in *Crane v Hegeman-Harris Co Inc.*[35]:

> "...in order that this court may exercise its jurisdiction to rectify a written instrument, it is not necessary to find a concluded and binding contract between the parties antecedent to the agreement which it is sought to rectify ... it is sufficient to find a common continuing intention in regard to a particular provision or aspect of the agreement. If one finds that, in regard to a particular point, the parties were in agreement up to the moment when they executed their formal instrument, and the formal instrument does not conform with that common agreement, then this court has jurisdiction to rectify..."

Russell L.J. added one qualification: that some outward expression of accord is required.[36]

Where rectification is sought on the grounds of mutual mistake, the burden on the party seeking rectification is particularly onerous where there have been prolonged negotiations leading to a formal instrument. The more detailed and lengthy the document, the more difficult it will be to show that it did not represent the parties' intentions (*James Hay Pension Trustees Ltd and Ors v Hird and Ors* ([2005] EWHC 1093 (Ch.)).

Examples of cases of "mistake" where the courts have refused to go behind the written agreement

7–021   *Wilson v Wilson:*[37] a property had been conveyed into the joint names of the husband and wife in law and in equity. The husband had provided the deposit for the property and paid the mortgage payments. The wife contended she was entitled to an equal share in the net proceeds of sale. The Court of Appeal agreed.[38]

Re John's Assignment Trusts; Niven v Niven[39]: The parties married in 1936. In 1948, they purchased a property known as 15 Henfaes Road, Tonna. By an assignment dated April 19, 1948, a Mr Johns assigned to the parties his leasehold interest of 99 years in the premises together with the goodwill of the business being carried on by him in the premises for a

---

[35] [1939] 1 All E.R. 662 at 664.

[36] At 98C. The Court of Appeal rejected the statement of Denning L.J. in *Frederick E. Rose (London) Ltd v William H. Pim Jnr & Co. Ltd* [1953] 2 Q.B. 450 (the "horsebeans" case) insofar as it could be taken to suggest that an antecedent complete contract is necessary (at 97E).

[37] [1963] 1 W.L.R. 601. NB. Contrast the different case of *Wilson v Wilson* [1969] 3 All E.R. 945.

[38] *Per* Donovan L.J. at 607: By the conveyance the husband and wife, who were the purchasers thereunder, were to hold the property upon trust to sell the same with power to postpone the sale thereof and to hold the net proceeds of sale and other money applicable as capital and the net rents and profits thereof until sale upon trust for themselves as joint tenants. Thus the entire beneficial interest in the property was declared at the outset. While it was the matrimonial home the spouses owned it as joint tenants. If it should be sold, they were to hold the net proceeds of sale as joint tenants, which I construe as meaning that on a division of these proceeds the division was to be in equal shares." See also Russell L.J. at 609.

[39] [1970] 2 All E.R. 210.

sum of £2,000. The assignment contained an express declaration of trust for the claimant and defendant as beneficial joint tenants. The purchase price comprised the proceeds of sale of the parties' previous property which had been in the husband's sole name and the remainder was borrowed from the bank on mortgage. The claimant wife relied upon the express declaration of trust.

Goff J. (having referred to *Pettitt v Pettitt* [1969] 2 All E.R. 385 at 405 (above) and to *Wilson v Wilson* [1963] 2 All E.R. at 452) found that, on the facts of the case, there was no sufficient ground entitling the defendant husband to go behind the express trust.

Leake v Bruzzi[40]: The wife applied for an order under s.17 of the   7–022
Married Women's Property Act 1882 that the former matrimonial home be sold and the proceeds divided equally between herself and her husband. There was an express declaration which provided that the husband and wife had equal beneficial interests in the former matrimonial home. The Court of Appeal[41] held that the wife was entitled to one half of the net proceeds of sale.

Examples of cases of "mistake" where the courts have been prepared to go behind the written agreement

Wilson v Wilson:[42] The defendant wished to purchase a property, but   7–023
because his own income was insufficient to qualify for a loan, he requested his brother to join him on the loan application, which his brother, the claimant, duly did. The purchase of the property proceeded. The transfer, which was executed by the brothers as prepared by their solicitor, declared that they were beneficial joint tenants. This was quite inconsistent, however, with the true intention of the brothers that the beneficial ownership should be solely vested in the defendant and that the claimant was joined in the transaction merely in order to enable him to assist the defendant in obtaining a mortgage loan (*per* Buckley J. at 947I–948A and 949A). Neither of the two brothers appreciated the effect of the declaration of the beneficial interest. As the declaration was quite contrary to the real intention of the parties, the Court of Appeal rectified the deed by striking out the part of it which declares the beneficial interests.

Re Colebrook's Conveyances[43]: Farmland was conveyed to the claimant

---

[40] [1974] 1 W.L.R. 1528.

[41] Following the case of *Wilson v Wilson* [1963] 1 W.L.R. 601.

[42] [1969] 3 All E.R. 945 at 949A–B. Not to be confused with *Wilson v Wilson* [1963] 1 W.L.R. 601, above.

[43] [1973] 1 All E.R. 132. See also *Standley v Stewkesbury* [1998] 2 F.L.R. 610 where an agreement did not state that the provision of a new motor vehicle by the husband for the wife every three years was would terminate upon her remarriage or cohabitation and the trial judge had preferred the husband's evidence that it was agreed by the parties that it should include such a limitation, the judge was correct to order rectification of the agreement. See also *Hussain v Bahadir* (2005) Ch. D. (Judge Behrens) LTL 16/11/2005: there was convincing evidence of mutual mistake where B had had rent review discussions and had been aware and accepted that the underlease would contain such provisions. In the circumstances the underlease was rectified.

father and his son as joint tenants. The son died and the claimant sought rectification of the conveyance on the basis that it did not reflect their intention that they would hold the land as tenants in common. The High Court held that on the evidence it was quite clear that at the date when the conveyances were executed, they did not accurately represent the agreement of the parties that the land should be held as tenants in common and made the order for rectification.

(ii) Unilateral mistake

7–024   It is now recognised by the courts that an agreement can, in certain circumstances, be set aside or rectified not only where there is a common mistake between the parties but also where only one of the parties is mistaken. This appears to be a form of equitable estoppel.[44]

The three requirements for the granting of equitable relief on the grounds of unilateral mistake were set out by the Court of Appeal in *Thomas Bates & Son Ltd v Wyndham's (Lingerie) Ltd* [1981] 1 W.L.R. 505 *per* Buckley L.J. (with whom Brightman L.J. agreed):

> "For this doctrine [of unilateral mistake] to apply I think it must be shown: first, that one party A erroneously believed that the documents sought to be rectified contained a particular term or provision, or possibly did not contain a particular term or provision which, mistakenly, it did contain; secondly, that the other party B was aware of the omission or the inclusion and that it was due to a mistake on the part of A; thirdly, that B has omitted to draw the mistake to the notice of A. And I think there must be a fourth element involved, namely, that the mistake must be one calculated to benefit B. If these requirements are satisfied, the Court may regard it as inequitable to allow B to resist rectification to give effect to A's intention on the ground that the mistake was not, at the time of execution of the document, a mutual mistake."[45]

See also *Kemp v Neptune Concrete*.[46] Purchas L.J. considered *A Roberts & Co. Ltd v Leicestershire County Council*, above; *Riverplate Properties Ltd v Paul* [1975] 1 Ch. 133 and *Thomas Bates Ltd v Wyndham's Ltd* (above) before setting out the relevant principles:

> (1) A mistake by the party seeking relief in executing the deed which does not translate that party's subjective intention at the time of the execution of the deed. The moment of time at which the

---

[44] *Kemp v Neptune Concrete Ltd* 57 P. & C.R. 369 at 376 citing *A Roberts & Co. Ltd v Leicestershire County Council* (1961) 1 Ch. 555 at 570 *per* Pennycuick J., citing *Snell on Equity*.

[45] In *George Wimpey UK Ltd v VIC Construction Ltd* [2005] EWCA Civ 77 the Court of Appeal adopted Buckley L.J.'s analysis as the authoritative statement of the requirements for rectification for unilateral mistake *per* Peter Gibson L.J. at para.38.

[46] Above.

subjective intention of the party seeking relief must be determined is at or immediately before, executing the deed (at 14H–15A);

(2) There has been no mistake by the party against whom relief is being sought, but who intends the result achieved by the deed, or has merely accepted that deed by execution (at 15C);

(3) There must be established awareness on the part of the party against whom relief is being sought of the other party's mistake at the time of executing the deed; and further, that in so standing back and allowing the other party to execute the deed, the conduct of the party against whom relief is sought was unconscionable behaviour on his part in inducing the party who is seeking rectification to execute the deed, or in standing by allowing him so to execute it (at 15D–F). Equity will only intervene if all three criteria are satisfied (at 15F).

In *Hurst Stores and Interiors Ltd v ML Europe Property Ltd* ([2004] EWCA Civ 490): for example the judge at first instance was entitled to rectify a document where evidence before him that one party was mistaken as to the nature of the document he had signed and that given the lack of evidence before him there was nothing to show that he was wrong to conclude that the other party had knowledge of that mistaken belief.

It is necessary to provide convincing proof that the party relying upon the agreement had actual knowledge of the other party's mistake.[47]   **7–025**

"Actual knowledge" includes not only actual knowledge of the other party's mistaken belief, but also a case where, objectively viewed, there has been a wilful shutting of eyes to the fact that the other party is acting under a mistaken belief or a wilful failure to make such enquiries as a reasonable and honest person would make.[48,49]

Non est factum

In certain limited circumstances, it may be possible to rely upon the doctrine of "*non est factum*". This doctrine applies where a person sought to be held liable did not in fact sign the document. It also applies in certain cases where the person who signed the document can establish that it was "not his deed" (see *Saunders v Anglia Building Society* [1971] A.C. 1004 *per* Lord Reid at 1015).   **7–026**

---

[47] *Per* Brightman L.J. in *Thomas Bates*, above at 521F–H and Buckley L.J. at 514G–H referring to *Hornal v Newberger Products Ltd* [1957] 1 Q.B. 247 at 258 *per* Denning L.J.). See also *Templis Properties Ltd v Hyams* (1999) E.G.C.S. 60: "The jurisdiction, particularly to rectify on the ground of unilateral mistake, is one to be exercised cautiously, and clear evidence is required before an order is made. This is consistent with the basis of the jurisdiction being misconduct on the part of the defendant: the standard of proof must reflect the gravity of the charge."

[48] *Witney Golf Club Ltd v Parker and Strainge* LTL 25/4/2006 at para.52

[49] Above *per* Sedley L.J.

Where a person is illiterate, or blind or lacking in understanding the law may provide relief if satisfied that consent was truly lacking (*Saunders*, above *per* Lord Wilberforce at 1027. See also *Qutb v Hussain* ([2005] EWHC 157 (Ch.) at paras 28–30)).

Equitable accounting

7–027 Whenever the court exercises its equitable jurisdiction it has the discretion to order further or other relief, beyond a mere declaration as to the existence and extent of beneficial interests. In cohabitation cases, the principal form of relief sought is the account and inquiry.

A monetary award following upon the taking of an account and inquiry does not impact upon the parties' respective interests in the relevant property. Rather, their interests remain unchanged and the equitable compensation stands as a personal liability owed by one party to the other. In practice this tends to be set off against that party's property rights (see *Bernard v Josephs* ([1982] Ch. 391 at 405 F–G) *per* Griffiths L.J.). The importance of this distinction is that, if the equitable compensation remains unpaid, a fall in the value of the property ought not to be met with a corresponding reduction to the equitable compensation which is payable.

For example, C's interest in the property is quantified at 25 per cent. She has, however, spent £5,000 on installing a bathroom which has added £10,000 to the value of the property. She is entitled to be compensated for the 75 per cent of the cost of the works (i.e. £3,750) which D ought to have paid, if the parties had contributed to the works in proportion to their respective interests. A subsequent fall in the value of the property will cause the value of C's 25 per cent share to fall, but she will remain entitled to recover £3,750 from D as a debt owed to her.

In *Bernard v Josephs* (above) C and D purchased a property in joint names with the benefit of a 100 per cent mortgage. D contributed £650 and C £200 to the costs of purchase. The intention was that the mortgage would be paid by taking in tenants. D spent £2,000 on decorations and repairs to enable part of the house to be let. The income from the tenants was paid to D, who applied it towards the mortgage costs. On the breakdown of the relationship, the Court of Appeal held that the parties were prima facie entitled to an equal share in the property, but D was to be credited with his greater contribution towards purchase costs, the cost of renovations and payment of the expenses after the couple separated. Thus C's 50 per cent interest was subject to an account in favour of D in a sum equal to half the amount spent by D on improvements, half of the difference between the contributions made by C and D to the initial purchase costs, and half of the mortgage costs he had paid after the separation. D's violence towards C appears to have been a significant factor in the decision not to credit D with all of the mortgage payments post separation; essentially, D was required to pay C an occupation rent (see further below at 7–033 *et seq.*).

Account and Inquiry

The account and the inquiry are two separate remedies, though often the **7–028**
facts of a case will necessitate relief in both forms.

Duty to account

The account simply refers to the duty of a trustee to account to the **7–029**
beneficiaries in full in respect of the property held on trust. To the extent
that one beneficiary is disadvantaged by the trustees' actions, the beneficiary is entitled to call upon the trustee to account to him (the
beneficiary) in relation to his loss. Thus in cohabitation cases, where both
parties are beneficiaries under the relevant trust and either one party or
both of them is the trustee of that trust, each cohabitee is entitled to an
account from the trustee(s) in relation to the trusts upon which the
property is held.

A clear illustration of the duty to account in the context of cohabitation cases is to be found in *Savill v Goodall* ([1993] 1 F.L.R. 755). There,
the Court held that although the parties had agreed that they should hold
the property in equal shares, they had also agreed that D should pay the
entire mortgage, C having contributed more towards the initial capital
payment. D failed to do so from the time he left the property. C paid the
mortgage alone from that time onwards. The Court of Appeal accepted
that there should be some reckoning in C's favour, describing the
agreement that D would pay the mortgage as "the quid pro quo for [D's]
acquisition of a half share" (at 762C). It was accepted that the interest
element of the mortgage was in effect an occupation rent which C alone
should bear, but so far as the capital element was concerned Nourse L.J.
said:

> "[D's] cessation of occupation cannot diminish his liability for
> anything other than interest, about which there is no dispute. Equity
> will not allow him both to assert a claim to his half share and to deny
> the liability subject to which it was acquired".

Whilst D remained beneficially entitled to 50 per cent of the net proceeds
of sale, his share of the proceeds of sale was accordingly debited with a
figure equal to the amount by which the capital balance owed under the
mortgage had been reduced by C following her assumption of the
mortgage payments.

The inquiry

The determining feature of the account is that the extent to which D is **7–030**
liable to C (or vice versa) is already known to the court. D is called to
account to C to the extent that C is owed equitable compensation in
relation to a breach of D's duty as trustee. The inquiry, by contrast, is
ordered where the court is satisfied that some reckoning is due to C (or,

again, vice versa) but the evidence at that stage before the court does not enable it to proceed to order an account. In the case of building works for instance, where C funds such works, she is entitled to credit for the lesser of the cost of the works or the value added to the property thereby (see *Re Pavlou* ([1993] 1 W.L.R. 1046 at 1049A–B)). Where the evidence before the court does not establish which is in fact the lesser of the two sums, an inquiry might be ordered accordingly. Thus the defining characteristic of a claimant's request for an inquiry is that the court is invited to direct a further round of litigation, the object of which is to determine the amount for which one party will be ordered to account (i.e. pay) to the other.

Often the costs of carrying out an inquiry and the court time involved will prove disproportionate to the sums in issue. In *Cox v Jones* ([2004] 2 F.L.R. 1010 at 1054) Mann J. held that it would be disproportionate to the sums involved (£1,500 at most) for the court to order an inquiry in relation to C's allegedly extravagant use of D's funds. In reaching that conclusion, Mann J. had regard to the sums which the parties had spent on the litigation generally. He also considered that the inquiry sought by D was not deserving of the court time which it would take to be conducted.

Repairs and improvements

7–031   In the taking of an account or inquiry, there is no distinction between a beneficial tenancy in common and a beneficial joint tenancy (see *In re Pavlou*, above at 1048F). The guiding principle is that neither party can take the benefit of an increase in the value of the property without making an allowance for what had been expended by the other to obtain it (see (*Leigh v Dickeson* (1884) 15 Q.B.D. 60)).

In *Re Pavlou*, Millett J. stated:

> "the proportions in which the entirety should be divided between former co-owners must have regard to any increase in its value which has been brought about by means of expenditure by one of them. (Above, at 1048H.)"

His Lordship went on to state that the wife was entitled to credit for one half of any repairs or improvements that she had carried out and that there would have to be an inquiry as to the amount expended and the increase, if any, in the value of the property thereby realised. It was observed that much expenditure on property is not reflected in any increase in value and most expenditure on property results in a much smaller increase in value than the amount expended (above, at 1049A–B). The wife will be entitled to credit only for one half of *the lesser* of the actual expenditure and any increase in the value realised thereby (above, at 1049B).

Capital element of the mortgage instalments

As with any claim for an account or inquiry in respect of improvements   **7–032**
or repairs to a property, the party who pays the mortgage instalments is
entitled to credit for one half of the increase in value of the equity of
redemption which results from the capital (as opposed to the interest)
payments of the mortgage (above, at 1049B–C). This is because the
repayment of the capital element in each instalment increases the value of
the equity of redemption to the benefit of both joint tenants.

Interest element of the mortgage instalments and occupation rent

More difficult questions as to whether the party that has remained in the   **7–033**
property paying the mortgage instalments is entitled to credit for payment of the mortgage instalments and/or whether the party that has
moved out of the property is entitled to credit for an occupation rent.

Leake (formerly Bruzzi) v Bruzzi[50] concerned an application by the
wife under s.17 of the Married Women's Property Act 1882 for
the determination of her beneficial interest in the matrimonial home. The
registrar declared that the wife was entitled to one-third and the husband
to two-thirds of the proceeds of sale, taking into account the parties'
respective financial contributions towards the purchase. The wife
appealed contending that the husband should not be given credit for the
mortgage repayments made after she had left him because the marriage
had irretrievably broken down because of his behaviour. The Court of
Appeal allowed the appeal, finding that as the husband had had sole use
of the property since his wife's departure he was not entitled to credit for
mortgage payments in respect of interest, although he was so entitled in
respect of the capital mortgage payments.

In *Suttill v Graham*[51] the Court of Appeal followed its approach in   **7–034**
Leake v Bruzzi[52] and held that the correct approach was to firstly
establish the rights of the parties on conventional trust principles[53] and
that secondly, applying those principles a beneficiary entitled to an equal
share in equity of the property of which he is a trustee and which he
himself occupies is to be charged with "*at least an occupation rent*".
Stamp L.J. concluded:

"so ... if as here he seeks to charge his co-beneficiary trustee with
half the out-goings he should be charged with half the occupation
rent."

---

[50] [1974] 2 All E.R. 1196
[51] [1977] 3 All E.R. 1117; *Cracknell v Cracknell* [1971] distinguished
[52] Above
[53] Eg. *Pettitt v Pettitt* [1969] 2 All E.R. 385, [1970] A.C. 777 and *Gissing v Gissing* [1970] 2
All E.R. 780, [1971] A.C. 886.

By contrast, in both *Davis v Vale*[54] and *Cracknell v Cracknell*[55] credit was given for both the capital element of the mortgage repayments made by the party who remained in occupation and the interest element: in other words, no occupation rent was payable in those cases to the party who had vacated the property.

Where both parties are entitled to occupy a property, and one party actually or constructively excludes the other, on the face of it, the excluding party is liable to pay an occupation rent to the excluded party.[56]

7–035   In *Re Pavlou (A Bankrupt)*[57] a husband and wife had purchased a property in 1973 as beneficial joint tenants. They lived together in the matrimonial home until January 1983 when the husband left. The wife remained in sole occupation and paid the mortgage instalments. In 1986 she petitioned for divorce. In 1987 a bankruptcy order was made against the husband. It was agreed that there would have to be an order for sale and an equitable accounting between the parties. Millett J. set out the relevant principles:

- a court of equity will order an inquiry and payment of *occupation rent* not only where the co-owner in occupation has ousted the other, but in any other case in which it is necessary to do equity between the parties that an occupation rent should be paid (at 1050C–D);

- where it is a matrimonial home and the marriage has broken down, the party who leaves the home will, in most cases, be regarded as excluded from the family home, so that an occupation rent should be paid by the co-owner who remains. This is not a rule of law but a statement of the prima facie conclusion to be drawn from the facts. The true position is that if a tenant in common leaves the property voluntarily, but would be welcome back and would be in a position to enjoy his or her right to occupy, it would normally not be fair or equitable to the remaining tenant in common to charge him or her with an occupation rent (at 1050D–F);

- As to the *interest element of the mortgage* prima facie the wife is entitled to reimbursement of the interest element of the mortgage from the date on which the husband left the property (the date on which she began paying the mortgage instalments);

- In many cases the court will simply set off the interest element in the mortgage repayments against an occupation rent, but this is a rule of convenience and more readily applies between husband

[54] [1971] 1 W.L.R. 1022.
[55] [1971] 3 W.L.R. 490.
[56] E.g. *Dennis v McDonald* [1982] Fam. 63.
[57] [1993] 1 W.L.R. 1046.

and wife or co-habitees than between a spouse and a trustee in bankruptcy of the other co-owner.[58]

- If the trustee in bankruptcy insists on the strict accounts being taken he is entitled to do so, unless it can be seen in advance that the amounts are likely to be so similar that the taking of the two accounts would be a waste of time and the costs would outweigh any possible advantage to be gained. In such a case, the court might well impose its own solution of directing the interest element in the mortgage instalments to be set off against the use and occupation without any further inquiry (at 1051C).

The case of *Byford v Butler*,[59] unlike *Re Pavlou*[60] concerned the situation   **7–036** where there was no breakdown of the marriage and the husband continued to reside in the matrimonial home until his death nearly ten years after the bankruptcy, whilst his wife maintained all the mortgage repayments. Lawrence Collins J. stated:

"What the court is endeavouring to do is broad justice or equity as between co-owners. As Millett J. said in *Re Pavlou*, the fact that there has not been an ouster or forcible exclusion is not conclusive."[61]

His Lordship added that he did not consider that the policy expressed in the new s.283A of the Insolvency Act 1986 would have been of any assistance even if it had been in force.

Timing of the inquiry

When considering an application for an account and inquiry the court is   **7–037** endeavouring to do broad justice or equity between the parties. It appears from the decided cases that where one party has left the property voluntarily and where the party in occupation remains willing to have that party back then it would not normally be fair or equitable to charge the party who remains in the property with an occupation rent (see *Re Pavlou* at 1050E). Often, however, in order to avoid disproportionate costs and court time, the court will simply treat mortgage interest paid by the party in occupation as equal to an occupation rent — see e.g. *Leake v Bruzzi* (above) and *Suttill v Graham* (above). A great deal will depend upon how the individual judge exercising the discretionary jurisdiction views the overall justice of the case.

In many cases, such as *Leake v Bruzzi*, the court will achieve broad equality by determining that the occupation rent and the interest payable under the mortgage equate to each other, so that there is an exact set-off between the mortgage interest paid by the party remaining in occupation

---

[58] *In re Gorman (A Bankrupt)* [1990] 1 W.L.R. 616, 626.
[59] [2003] EWHC 1267 Ch.
[60] And also *Re Gorman*, above.
[61] At para.40.

and the occupation rent payable to the other owner. Evidence as to what the market rent payable would be, or as to the rent actually paid by the ousted party for alternative accommodation, might all inform the exercise of the court's discretion.

7–038   The discretion enjoyed by the court in terms of the jurisdiction to order accounts and inquiries relates to the period over which the account or inquiry will be taken, just as it does to the quantification of the amount payable for instance by way of occupation rent. In some cases, there will be no need to order an inquiry relating to expenditure during the period prior to separation.[62] In other cases, such an inquiry will be absolutely necessary where for instance the parties do not agree as to the value that improvement works funded by one party prior to the separation have actually added to the property.

In a case where the parties have not agreed the extent of their respective interests, the court's quasi-discretionary adjudication can take such matters into account.[63] Where, however, the interests of the parties are fixed (e.g. where there is a declaration of joint tenancy) an account and inquiry might be the only way of ensuring that justice can be done as between two parties who for instance had agreed to share all outgoings equally just as they agreed to share the beneficial interests equally. (The position whereby the existence of a beneficial interest, rather than its quantification, is inferred from improvements to a property is dealt with above in Chapter 3 "Constructive Trusts".)

Taxation

7–039   One aspect of dealing with co-ownership disputes which should not be overlooked is the incidence of taxation. Where taxation issues arise it may be appropriate for the court to do justice between the parties, where for instance a tax burden would fall unfairly on one party alone, by way of an account and inquiry. For this reason, taxation questions, whilst of general application in cohabitant disputes, are dealt with under this head.

Capital Gains Tax

7–040   Capital Gains Tax is payable on the accrual of chargeable gains to an individual who is ordinarily resident in the UK during the relevant year of assessment (Taxation of Chargeable Gains Act 1992). In general terms, this tax impacts upon any case where an asset is disposed of for a higher price than that for it was initially acquired.

On the face of it, wherever residential properties increase in value between acquisition and sale, CGT is therefore payable. The reason that (in the overwhelming majority of cases) no CGT is payable on the sale of a private dwelling is because such sales are largely exempted from the

---

[62] See *Clarke v Harlowe* (2005) 149 S.J. 1087, and see *Joint Spending* (Mark Pavlowski) (2005) 149 S.J. 1198.
[63] See e.g. *Oxley v Hiscock* [2004] 3 W.L.R. 715 at 750C *per* Chadwick L.J.

charge to tax, not because the charge does not apply in the first case. Considering whether a tax liability arises is therefore a question of whether a particular case fits within the established exemptions, not a question of whether the charge applies at all.

The reason CGT does not impact upon the vast majority of sales of residential property is because of the particular exemption set out at ss.222–6 of the Taxation of Chargeable Gains Act 1992. In summary, the effect of these provisions is that where a property has been the principal private residence of the taxpayer, the whole or part of the gain on disposal is likely to be exempt from capital gains tax.

There are however a number of caveats to this general proposition. The first is that the exemption only applies to gains whilst the property is the principal private residence of the taxpayer. Thus if a property is first used as a home, and later let to tenants, only the gain during the time that the property was the taxpayers' principal residence avoids the charge to tax.[64]

The second is that a taxpayer may only enjoy one principal private   **7–041** residence for the purpose of this exemption (TCGA 1992, s.222(6)). This also applies to married couples, who between them may only enjoy one principal private residence even though they are taxed independently. Unmarried partners however may enjoy separate principal residences.[65]

The third caveat is that generally, only 0.5 hectares of land (around 1.25 acres) will qualify for principal private residence relief.[66] This is not an absolute rule; where the grounds inasmuch as they exceed 0.5 hectares are reasonably required for the enjoyment of the property as a residence (having regard to the size and character of the property) the larger area may not be subject to the tax.[67]

The final main caveat is that it frequently happens that on the termination of a relationship, one party leaves the property which is later the centre of the dispute. In those circumstances, that party is still entitled to relief on the basis of the principal private residence exemption provided that the property is sold within three years (see s.223) or that the property is (a) later transferred to the other partner, (b) is in the meantime the other partner's principal residence, and (c) the taxpayer does not acquire

---

[64] In practice the Revenue tend not to look at the precise rise in value during particular periods of residence and non-residence, but apply a pro-rata reduction to the overall gain in proportion to the length of time the property was in use as the taxpayer's main residence. Thus if a property was lived in by A for two years and then let out for a further three, three-fifths of the overall gain during the five years of ownership would be subject to the charge to tax.

[65] Where a taxpayer acquires a second property and spends time in each so that each could properly be described as a "principal" residence, he is entitled to serve a notice in writing on the Inland Revenue (provided this is done within two years of the acquisition of the later property) and may vary the notice in respect of any period beginning not more than two years before the variation (see s.222(5)(a) of the Taxation of Chargeable Gains Act 1992. See also *Griffin v Craig-Harvey* [1994] S.T.C. 54.

[66] S.222(2) of the Taxation of Chargeable Gains Act 1992.

[67] See s.222(3).

a further property during that time on which he claims principal private residence relief.[68]

Stamp Duty

7–042   It will frequently arise that the despatch (by compromise or otherwise) of an application under TLATA will involve either the transfer of the property from both names into a single person's name, or vice versa. One issue to consider will be the incidence of Stamp Duty Land Tax in any such arrangement. Stamp Duty Land Tax is charged on any "land transaction", which means any *acquisition* of a chargeable interest.[69] (Emphasis added.) A chargeable interest includes a beneficial interest in the land (*ibid.* s.48(1)). All land transactions are chargeable transactions unless exempted from the charge to tax (*ibid.* s.49). In general terms, transfers of interests between co-owners will incur *Ad Valorem* Stamp Duty Land Tax. Thus where for instance one co-owner pays the other a lump sum to purchase the other's interest in the property, that is a transaction which on the face of it will be subject to the duty. Equally, where one party acquires an interest, whether by way of a "limb one" agreement or a "limb two" contribution, on the face of it Stamp Duty Land Tax is payable at the point of creation if that occurs after the commencement date.[70]

In practical terms, therefore, the charge to Stamp Duty Land Tax seems likely to arise where existing interests in property are altered in circumstances where some consideration is paid. This would appear to apply in principle firstly at the point of acquisition of an interest in the property, and secondly at the point of disposal. Where in particular disputed proceedings are resolved on the basis that C transfers her beneficial interest in the property to D who pays a corresponding lump sum, the fact that C will be liable to pay Stamp Duty Land Tax should not be overlooked.

The position would appear to be otherwise, however, where a transfer is simply ordered or agreed so as to reflect existing beneficial interests. Under para.1 of Sch.3 (which sets out exemptions to the duty), a land transaction is exempt from charge if there is no chargeable consideration for the transaction. Where a claimant is not *acquiring* any chargeable interest — that is, because he/she already enjoys that interest and the transfer of legal title simply reflects the prior existence of the claimant's interest — or where no consideration is paid on the transfer, it follows that no charge to tax will arise (see s.42).

---

[68] This derives from the Inland revenue's Extra-Statutory Concession ESC D06.
[69] Finance Act 2003, ss.42, 43(1)).
[70] The charge arises in respect of any land transaction which takes place on or after 1/12/03 (see para.2 of Sch.19 to the 2003 Act and see Stamp Duty Land Tax (Appointment of Implementation Date) Order 2003 (SI 2899/2003).

Property other than real property

Fundamentally, save the application of s.53 of the Law of Property Act   **7–043**
1925, the nature of the property concerned does not impact upon the
considerations which will govern the question of whether the property is
held by one party absolutely or subject to an implied trust in favour of
another. It might appear, therefore, that perhaps a less onerous burden
rests on those claiming an interest in personalty than realty.

In practice, there is little difference as regards the applicable principles
whatever the nature of the property concerned. In *Heseltine v Heseltine*
[1971] 1 W.L.R. 342 Lord Denning M.R., referring to the speech of Lord
Diplock in *Gissing v Gissing* ([1970] 3 W.L.R. 255) said, "What Lord
Diplock said about land applies also to shares, money or chattels".
Similarly, in *Tribe v Tribe* ([1996] Ch. 107) the same questions arose in
relation to whether an unlawful intention could defeat a claim based
upon a constructive trust as in *Tinsley v Milligan* ([1994] 1 A.C. 340) even
though the former case concerned personal property (shares) and the
latter concerned real property. *Windeler v Whitehall* ([1990] 2 F.L.R. 505)
and *Cox v Jones* ([2004] 2 F.L.R. 1010) both concerned claims relating to
beneficial interests in both real and personal property, without distinction
being drawn between the relevant equitable principles to be applied in
each case. *Rowe v Prance* ([1999] 2 F.L.R. 787) was a claim to a share in a
boat based firmly upon *Lloyds Bank Plc v Rosset* ([1991] 1 A.C. 107)
principles.

Where personal property is held by two co-owners as joint tenants,
there is no practical difference when it comes to the severance of the joint
tenancy. In for instance *Burgess v Rawnsley* ([1975] 1 Ch. 429 at 440A)
Lord Denning said that it would be absurd if there was a difference
between real and personal estate.

What follows is an analysis of the way in which frequently arising
issues have been regarded by the courts.

Endowment policies

The widespread use of mortgage finance in the purchase of family homes   **7–044**
has already been remarked upon (see above, Chapter 3 "Constructive
Trusts"). Where repayment mortgages are concerned, the issues which
arise for consideration are relatively straightforward, in terms of who has
paid, or contributed to, the mortgage instalments: each such instalment
consists to a certain extent of both capital and interest, and so the sorts of
problems which might arise in relation to interest-only mortgages tend
not to create problems in practice. Where endowment mortgages are
concerned, however, not only can questions arise as to whether the
premia relating to such policies properly be described as "referable to the
purchase price" but also issues might arise as to the interests of the
parties in the policy (or perhaps more relevantly the proceeds or surrender value of the policy).

Two particular issues arise in relation to such policies. The first concerns the circumstances in which a beneficial interest might arise in the proceeds of the policy on behalf of a non-policyholder. The second relates to the interests in the proceeds of the policy which arise on death.

As to the first, ordinarily, life insurance policies (including endowment policies) are the property of the proposer, namely the person who first entered into the contract of insurance. Thus in cases where title to the relevant property is held in one party's sole name, it is likely that an endowment policy will have been proposed by the legal owner only and that he will be prima facie entitled to the proceeds of the policy if sold or surrendered (irrespective of who would be the nominated beneficiary under the policy in the event of his death). Likewise, in the case of a property held in joint names it is probable that the policy will be a joint policy, with the consequence that the parties are equally entitled to the proceeds of the policy.

7–045   That said, an interest under a policy is a chose in action and like other forms of property can be assigned or become subject to equitable interests. Generally, endowment policies are charged in favour of a mortgage lender[71] but since it is usual practice for the capital debt to be discharged from the proceeds of any sale, it is quite common for endowment policies to become freestanding assets. The intended beneficiaries under such policies will often be those with beneficial interests in the proceeds of any such policy, but this will not always be the case.

As with the establishment of beneficial interests in other assets, the crucial issue is the intentions of the parties. Where for instance one party pays the premia in fact payable by another (being the policyholder) that may be for instance because it is commonly intended that both should share in the proceeds or the surrender value of the policy. In that case, the proceeds become subject to a beneficial interest in favour of the non-policyholder, This might arise even though the non-policyholder is neither an intended beneficiary under the policy nor an insured person.

On the other hand, there may be sound practical reasons why a person other than the policyholder would want the premia to be paid. It might be for instance in a person's favour to ensure that the policy remains in force and is not cancelled due to missed payments. In such circumstances, payment of the premia would be unlikely to give rise to or evidence any beneficial interest, but the non-policyholder may be entitled to the return of the payments made together with interest on those sums (see e.g. *Foskett v McKeown* [1998] Ch. 265).

7–046   As regards the second issue, one scenario which is relatively common is where one of two co-owners dies with the benefit of life insurance under such a policy. In such cases, the remaining co-owner of course would manifestly become the sole owner of any property previously held by the parties as joint tenants. The issue which has concerned the courts is

---

[71] See e.g. *Cowcher v Cowcher* [1972] 1 W.L.R. 425 *per* Bagnall J. at 442A.

whether the benefits under the policy are payable to the estate/personal representatives of the deceased or to his co-owner.

This was the issue which concerned the Court of Appeal in *Powell v Osbourne* ([1993] 1 F.C.R. 797). The issue arose in the context of an application under the Inheritance (Provision for Family and Dependants) Act 1975, s.9 of which deals specifically with the relationship between the state of the deceased for the purposes of the Act, and the benefits payable on the death of the insured under an insurance policy. The proceeds of the endowment policy were charged in the ordinary way with repayment of the mortgage relating to the family home, which was held in joint names. The terms of the policy required the death benefits to be paid to the deceased's personal representative. The deceased's former partner brought an action against the personal representatives seeking the recovery of the death benefits in accordance with the terms of the charge to which they were subject. Dillon L.J. said (at 803C–D):

> "If the deceased had in fact severed the joint tenancy immediately before the date of death, he would have thereupon become entitled to a half-share in the property subject to the mortgage but with the benefit of a half share in the policy monies, and, accordingly, on his death his net estate would have been left with the clear half-share of the property, half the policy monies having gone to discharge his half-share of the mortgage."[72]

In *Smith v Clerical Medical and General Life Assurance Society and others*   **7–047** ([1993] 1 F.L.R. 47) the Court of Appeal were concerned with an endowment mortgage in circumstances where the purchasers had obtained a 100 per cent mortgage at the time of the initial acquisition. On the death of one co-owner, the property was sold and the proceeds used to repay the mortgage, even though the policy was charged to the mortgage company. The issue for the court was whether the death benefits under the policy should be paid to the personal representatives of the deceased or to the co-owner. Scott L.J. described the situation as (at 52C) a "common lending arrangement with which thousands of homeowners throughout the country will be very familiar". His view (at 53C–D) was that the case was:

> "... a simple one. The parties bought the property. They borrowed the purchase price from the building society, entered into an endowment mortgage and effected the policy with the intention that the policy proceeds should be applied in repayment of the mortgage loan. Equity will not permit either party, or the personal representatives of either party for that matter, to defeat that intention

---

[72] These observations are also perhaps worth noting in terms of the argument that payment of the premia might justify the inference of a limb one common intention constructive trust.

upon which both parties acted and upon the basis of which both parties entered into substantial financial commitments".

Parker L.J. was of the same view, observing (at 51D–F):

> "The entire purpose of the transfer was that this money should be used to pay off the mortgage so that in the event of either the assured dying before the mortgage was paid off, the survivor would be left not only with the title to the property by survivorship, but with that property free of mortgage. That that was the joint intention of the parties appears to me to be beyond all doubt. That being the case, if the building society for some reason chose not to demand the policy monies in order to pay off the mortgage, there can be no possible ground upon which the personal representatives could claim to be beneficially entitled to the money."

It would appear to follow from the logic of *Powell* and *Smith* that where the relevant policy simply matures (rather than becomes payable on death) the same position will arise. The proceeds of the policy will be charged in the first instance to the mortgage lender, but assuming that either the mortgage is repaid from the proceeds of sale of the property, or in the case where after the policy proceeds are used to discharge the mortgage debt a surplus remains, on the face of it the parties would be entitled to those proceeds in the same proportions as the beneficial interests were held in the relevant property.

Bank accounts — one party's sole name

7–048   On the face of it, cash held in a cohabitant's personal bank account is the property of that cohabitant, absent an intention that the funds were intended to belong (in whole or in part) to another. Evidence for instance that the funds of the other cohabitant were simply deposited with the account holder for some convenient purpose or other (e.g. where the owner of the cash does not have access to his/her own account) would leave the account holder in the position of a bare trustee without any interest in the relevant funds.

The funds in an account may however be in reality joint property, even though the account is in the name of one party only, where there has been an oral declaration to that effect. In *Paul v Constance* ([1977] 1 W.L.R. 527) the Court of Appeal was concerned with circumstances where D had repeatedly told C that the funds in D's bank account were "as much yours as they are mine". The Court of Appeal held that the judge had been entitled to find that those words constituted an express declaration of trust with the effect that the Claimant was entitled to a half share of the funds held in the account. By contrast, no such trust necessarily arises where the account holder simply allows a non-account holder access to the funds in his account, even if the access is unlimited. Such an arrangement might easily be properly characterised as a gift or series of gifts.

Mere access to the account of another will not, however, of itself necessarily indicate that both parties are beneficially entitled to the funds in the account. Such an arrangement might on the facts be equally consistent with an intention on the part of the account holder to make a gift of the funds held in the account.

Joint accounts

Just as funds in an account held by one person alone can in reality be joint property, so can funds held in a joint account in fact remain beneficially owned by one of the account holders only. In other words, the mere fact that an account is held in joint names does not mean that both account holders are necessarily beneficially entitled to those funds (see e.g. *Stoeckert v Geddes (No. 2)* [2004] UKPC 54, considered below). Again, all depends on the intention of the parties concerned. In the case of *In re Figgis (deceased)* [1969] 1 Ch. 123 the court was concerned with a joint account opened when the deceased had been about to go overseas on active service with the armed forces. It was contended that the opening of a joint account was a simple matter of convenience and that it had never been the deceased's intention that his wife (the joint account holder) should be beneficially entitled to the funds in the account. Whilst on the facts Megarry J. rejected that contention (not least in view of the effect of the presumption of advancement — see 144C), it was accepted that as a matter of law the mere fact that the account was held in joint names was not conclusive of the beneficial interests in the property.

Ordinarily, however, funds held in a joint account will be the joint property of the account holders. In *Jones v Maynard* [1951] 1 Ch. 572 Vaisey J. rejected C's claim that since he had contributed more towards the funds in the joint account, that he should receive a greater share of the closing balance, in proportion to his greater contribution. The essential feature of *Jones*, however, is perhaps the absence of any settled agreement as to the parties' respective rights in the funds held in the account.

One additional feature of the decision in *Jones v Maynard* is Vaisey J.'s analysis of what happens to the funds after they are drawn down from the account. Ordinarily, even if personal property is purchased using funds drawn from a joint account, it remains the personal property of the person who actually purchases that property (see e.g. *In re Young* ((1885) 28 Ch. D. 705) *c.f. Gage v King* ([1961] 1 Q.B. 188), *Stoeckert v Geddes (No. 2)* ([2004] UKPC 54, (2004) 7 I.T.E.L.R. 506)). Vaisey J. however considered that the position was otherwise in the case of investments purchased in one party's name using funds drawn from a joint account. He said (at 575):

7–049

"In my view the money that goes into the pool becomes joint property ... if follows that the investments paid for out of the joint account, although made in the name of the husband, were in fact made by him in his own name as a trustee as to a moiety for his wife."

A different conclusion was however reached in *In re Bishop (deceased)* ([1965] 1 Ch. 450). In that case, although *Jones v Maynard* had been cited with approval in the Court of Appeal,[73] Stamp J. said (at 464G):

"Mrs Bishop authorised Mr Bishop to draw on the account for making investments he thought fit in his own name, in order if he thought fit to benefit himself, and that the investments in his name belonged to him beneficially."

7–050   Although very different conclusions were reached in *Jones v Maynard* on the one hand and *In re Bishop* on the other, both cases illustrate that this sort of question, fundamentally, depends upon the assessment by the trial judge of the parties' intentions in relation to the funds in the joint account.

The same point can be illustrated by reference to the conclusion of the Privy Council in *Stoeckert v Geddes (No. 2)* ([2004] UKPC 54). In that case, funds held in a joint account remained beneficially owned by the account holder, D, who had initially provided the funds. C had no beneficial interest in the sums standing to the credit of the account until funds were actually drawn from the account. Prior to that time, the funds remained in D's beneficial ownership under resulting trust principles.

Household contents

7–051   In principle, assets in the nature of household chattels bought by one party to a relationship are the absolute property of that party, even where (as observed above) the source of the funds used to purchase such chattels was a joint account; that at least is the conventional approach to such matters (see *In re Bishop*). *Perhaps the principal distinction between such chattels and larger items of personal property such as the boat in issue in Rowe v Prance* ([1999] 2 F.L.R. 787) is that it is inherently more likely that a relatively minor purchase of for instance a domestic electrical appliance was intended to be the purchaser's sole property. This logic does not necessarily extend to larger purchases concerning perhaps a boat or a caravan.

So far as more day to day purchases are concerned, one issue which causes particular difficulty in applying cases such as *In re Bishop* is the changing reality of modern banking and the gradual progression moves towards an economy less dependent on cash. Where one party draws

---

[73] See *Rimmer v Rimmer* [1953] 1 Q.B. 63.

funds out of a joint account which are used to purchase an asset which is not in the nature of an investment, it is not difficult to understand that the person who goes to the bank, draws the cash, goes to the shop and purchases the relevant item is in reality the absolute owner of that item.

In the 21st century, however, the overwhelming majority of transactions are not made that way. The overwhelming majority of household purchases involve the use of credit, debit or store cards. In each case, potential difficulties arise. Where the relevant purchase is made by the use of a debit card issued in relation to an account in the name of one party only, subject to any argument either that the item was bought as a gift to the other party, or that the account was the subject of a declaration similar to that made in *Paul v Constance* [1977] 1 W.L.R. 527, the asset would appear to be the undisputed property of the account holder. The same would appear to be the case where a store or credit card held in the sole name of the account holder is used, where the card balance is repaid solely from the account holder's undisputed personal resources.

The realities of cohabitation, however, are that there is usually at least some mingling of funds and in many cases joint bank accounts are matched by either joint debit/credit cards or store cards or, failing that, the parties both holding credit or store cards in relation to an account in the name of one party only.

So far as joint accounts are concerned, difficulties arise in simply applying *In re Young* and similar decisions in an indiscriminate fashion to purchases using debit cards. Where for instance the parties are together when the relevant item is bought, it may be a matter of simple convenience as to which of them actually hands over the card to the cashier. There may be significance attached to the fact that the relevant item was purchased by the parties together. On the other hand, it may be that one party returns at a later stage to purchase an item both had selected. As a rule of thumb it might be thought that the more expensive the purchase, the more likely it is that if it was purchased using funds in a joint account, the relevant item was intended to belong to both parties.

7–052

Other difficulties arise in relation to telephone or internet purchases. Again, the question of who makes the telephone call or visits the relevant website may be a simple matter of convenience or (by contrast) may be extremely cogent evidence as regards the identity of the owner of the item in question. Difficulties also arise where joint credit/store cards are used to purchase an item where the credit balance relating to that card is then paid off using funds from an account in the name of one party older, or vice versa. The extent to which a particular item was intended to be one person's property or joint property will depend on the intentions of the parties at the relevant time. For this reason, it can be dangerous simply to assume that whoever physically carries out the transaction is by definition the absolute owner of the item in question. It is necessary to consider all the relevant circumstances insofar as they cast light on the parties' intentions.

7-053   The essential difficulty which confronts the practitioner in cases such as this is neither legal or evidential. The principal difficulty is that in the overwhelming majority of cases litigation will simply not be proportionate to the value of the items in question.[74] The experienced practitioner will need no warnings as to the level of judicial irritation which can be encountered in cases where former partners genuinely do engage in litigation about household contents.

The authorities, it must be said, are replete with instances of judges dispensing what might be perceived as very rough justice when it comes to chattels. In *Windeler v Whitehall* [1990] F.C.R. 268 Millet said at 279 that parties ought to be able to divide chattels between themselves by agreement. In *Hammond v Mitchell* ([1991] 1 W.L.R. 1127 at 1138H) Waite J. said:

> "While no-one suggests that English law recognizes or should develop a doctrine of community of property regarding household goods of those who settle for an unmarried union, the parties must expect the court in ordinary cases to adopt a robust allegiance to the maxim that 'equality is equity', if only in the interests of fulfilling the equally salutary maxim '*sit finis litis*'."

Bearing the above in mind, when it comes to disputes about chattels, practitioners should perhaps pay particular regard to the matter of proportionality as dealt with under the Civil Procedure Rules (with particular reference to costs) and also, for instance, to public funding criteria regarding merits and cost/benefit analysis.

[74] Particularly on a "resale" valuation basis rather than a valuation based on cost at purchase.

CHAPTER 8

THE TRUSTS OF LAND AND APPOINTMENT OF TRUSTEES ACT 1996 SUBSTANTIVE PROVISIONS

(Appendix II sets out the
Trusts of Land and Appointment of Trustees Act 1996)

The Trusts of Land and Appointment of Trustees Act 1996 ("TLATA") **8–001** came into force on January 1, 1997.[1] Prior to the implementation of TLATA, property owned by more than one person, not held on a strict settlement, was held on trust for sale and s.30 of the Law of Property Act 1925 applied.

The Law Commission report, *Transfer of Land, Trusts of Land*,[2] recommended, inter alia, that s.30 of the Law of Property Act 1925 should be amended (a) so as to enable any trustee or other interested person to apply to the court to intervene in any dispute relating to a trust of land and (b) to include guidelines for the exercise of the court's discretion.[3] Rather than simply amend s.30 LPA the legislature responded by enacting the Trusts of Land and Appointment of Trustees Act 1996. The principal recommendations of the Law Commission were adopted.[4]

The purpose of this chapter is to summarise the provisions contained within TLATA and to focus on those provisions which most often arise in litigation and raise the most controversial issues: ss.12 and 13 — the right of beneficiaries to occupy trust land and ss.14 and 15 — the powers of the court upon an application to the court for an order under s.14 and the matters relevant in determining such applications, as set out in s.15. The issue which will most frequently arise under s.14/15 is whether or not the court should make an order for sale.

---

[1] The Trusts of Land and Appointment of Trustees Act 1996 (Commencement) Order 1996 (SI 1996/2974).
[2] (1989) (Law Com No. 181)
[3] *Ibid.*
[4] See the observations of Neuberger J. in *Mortgage Corporation Plc v Shaire* [2001] 3 W.L.R. 639 at 655E–F.

OVERVIEW

8–002   The Act has the effect of rendering trusts for sale obsolete and replacing them with the less arcane and simpler trusts of land.[5]

Section 1 of TLATA defines a trust of land as *"any trust of property which consists of or includes land"*.[6] It includes a trust for sale and a bare trust and includes a trust created or arising before the commencement of TLATA.[7] It does not include land which is settled land or which is land to which the Universities and College Estates Act 1925 applies.[8]

Sections 6–11 are concerned with the powers and duties of trustees. When exercising their functions as trustees, the trustees of land have in relation to the land subject to the trust, all the powers of an absolute owner.[9] The trustees' powers must be exercised unanimously. Where there is a dispute between the trustees then an application should be made to the court under s.14 (see below at para.8–007 *et seq.*). The powers conferred by TLATA on the beneficiaries must not be exercised in contravention of any other enactment or any rule of law or equity (s.6(6)).

The trustees' powers may be excluded by express provision in a disposition creating the trust of land.[10] When exercising their powers, the trustees must, so far as practicable, consult the beneficiaries of full age and beneficially entitled to an interest in possession in the land and, so far as consistent with the general interest of the trust, give effect to the wishes of those beneficiaries, or in the case of dispute, of the majority.[11]

Sections 12 and 13 are concerned with the rights of beneficiaries to occupy the trust property (see 8–003 *et seq.*, below). Sections 14 and 15 provide the mechanism for applications to be made to the court in respect of any exercise by the trustees of any of their functions or declaring the nature or extent of a person's interest in the property subject to the trust (see para.8–007 *et seq.* below).

Where a person purports to convey a legal estate in land to a minor, or two or more minors alone, the conveyance is not effective to pass the legal estate, but operates as a declaration that the land is held in trust for the minor or minors (TLATA, Sch.1, para.1(1)).

Section 16 contains provisions relating to purchaser protection and ss.17 and 18 contain supplementary provisions relating to proceeds of sale. Part II of TLATA contains provision relating to the appointment and retirement of trustees.

---

[5] *Mortgage Corporation Plc v Shaire* [2001] 3 W.L.R. 639 at 653D.
[6] S.1(1)(a).
[7] S.1(2).
[8] S.1(3).
[9] S.6(1).
[10] S.8(1).
[11] S.11(1).

Rights of Occupation

Section 12

The right of a beneficiary under a trust of land to occupy the property is **8–003** now largely, if not exclusively derived[12] from TLATA. A beneficiary who is beneficially entitled to an interest in possession in land subject to a trust of land is entitled by reason of his interest to occupy the property at any time — s.12(1) TLATA. The right of the beneficiary to occupy the land is subject to the requirements that:

(a) the purposes of the trust include making the land available for his occupation (or for the occupation of beneficiaries of a class of which he is a member or of beneficiaries in general), or

(b) the land is held by the trustees so as to be so available.[13]

The beneficiary does not have a right to occupy the land if the land is either unavailable for occupation, for example because it has been rented to a third party or unsuitable for occupation, for example because it is unfit for habitation (s.12(2) TLATA).

Section 13

The right of occupation conferred by s.12 of TLATA is subject to: **8–004**

(a) the power of the trustees of land to exclude or restrict the entitlement of any one or more (but not all) of the beneficiaries[14] and

(b) the power of trustees to impose conditions on any beneficiary in relation to his occupation of land.[15]

Power to exclude or restrict the entitlement of a beneficiary to occupy trust property

The power to exclude or restrict the entitlement of any one or more beneficiaries to occupy land contained within s.13(1) has been interpreted broadly by the Court of Appeal. In *Rodway v Landy*[16] the Court held that where a single building lends itself to physical partition, there was no reason why the trustees could not exclude or restrict one beneficiary's entitlement to occupy one part and at the same time exclude or restrict the other beneficiary's entitlement to occupy the other part. So construed, s.13(1) provides a useful power which trustees might wish to exercise in

---

[12] Law Commission Discussion Paper, Sharing Homes Law Com No. 278 para.2.34.
[13] S.12(1)(a) and (b) of TLATA.
[14] S.13(1).
[15] S.13(3).
[16] [2001] EWCA Civ 471.

appropriate circumstances so as to be even-handed between beneficiaries.[17]

The power to exclude any beneficiary's entitlement to occupy land may not be exercised unreasonably.[18] Nor should any restriction of beneficiary's entitlement to occupy be restricted to an unreasonable extent.[19]

Power to impose reasonable conditions

8–005 The trustees may also from time to time impose reasonable conditions on any beneficiary in relation to his occupation of land.[20] The power to impose reasonable conditions can include conditions requiring the beneficiary to pay any outgoings or expenses in respect of the land or to assume any other obligation in relation to the land or to any activity which is or is proposed to be conducted there.[21]

Where the entitlement of any beneficiary to occupy land has been excluded or restricted, the conditions which may be imposed on any other beneficiary include conditions requiring him to:

(a) make payments by way of compensation to the beneficiary whose entitlement has been excluded or restricted; or
(b) forgo any payment or other benefit to which he would otherwise be entitled under the trust so as to benefit that beneficiary.[22]

So where a cohabitee moves out of a property in which he or she has a beneficial interest, he or she is therefore entitled to claim compensation in respect of their exclusion from the property under s.13(6) of TLATA.

Matters to be taken into consideration under s.13

8–006 When exercising their powers under s.13 of TLATA, the trustees should have regard to the following matters:

(a) the intentions of the person or persons (if any) who created the trust;
(b) the purposes for which the trust is held, and
(c) the circumstances and wishes of each of the beneficiaries who is (or apart from any previous exercise by the trustees of those powers would be) entitled to occupy the land under s.12.[23]

The powers of the trustee to exclude or restrict the entitlement of any one or more beneficiary may not be exercised so as to prevent any person who

---

[17] *Per* Peter Gibson L.J. at para.33.
[18] S.13(2)(a).
[19] S.13(2)(b).
[20] S.13(3).
[21] S.13(5).
[22] S.13(6).
[23] S.13(4).

is in occupation of land (whether or not by reason of an entitlement under s.12) from continuing to occupy the land unless that person consents or the court has given approval (s.13(7)). In determining such an application, the matters which the court is to have regard to include the matters set out at s.13(4) as set out above.[24]

APPLICATIONS FOR ORDERS UNDER TLATA

Section 14

Section 14 is the key provision within TLATA, providing the mechanism   **8–007** under which a cohabitee who does not appear upon the legal title to the property can apply to the court for an appropriate order.[25] The court is given jurisdiction to make any order:

    (a) relating to the exercise by the trustees of any of their functions (including an order relieving them of any obligation to obtain the consent of, or to consult, any person in connection with the exercise of any of their functions, or

    (b) declaring the nature or extent of a person's interest in property subject to the trust

    as it thinks fit: s.14(2) of TLATA.[26]

Section 15 — Considerations

Section 15 contains the relevant factors that the court will take into   **8–008** consideration when determining applications made under s.14. When considering any application under the TLATA, the court is to have regard to:

    (a) the intentions of the person or persons (if any) who created the trust,

    (b) the purposes for which the property subject to the trust is held,

    (c) the welfare of any minor who occupies or might reasonably be expected to occupy any land subject to the trust as his home, and

    (d) the interests of any secured creditor of any beneficiary (s.15(1) of TLATA).

The court is also to have regard to the circumstances and wishes of the beneficiaries of full age and entitled to an interest in possession in

---

[24] S.13(8). Section 15(2) of TLATA also provides that in the case of an application relating to the exercise in relation to any land of the powers conferred on the trustees by s.13, the matters to which the court is to have regard also include the circumstances and wishes of each of the beneficiaries who is … entitled to occupy the land under s.12.

[25] S.14(1).

[26] The court may not under s.14 make any order as to the appointment or removal of trustees: s.14(3).

property subject to the trust or (in case of dispute) of the majority (according to the value of their combined interests).[27] Section 15 does not apply to an application if s.335A of the Insolvency Act 1986 which concerns applications by trustees in bankruptcy applies (see below).[28]

In *Mortgage Corporation v Shaire*[29], the question arose as to whether s.15 had changed the law. In applications brought by either a creditor or a trustee in bankruptcy pre-TLATA the normal rule was that, save in exceptional circumstances, the wishes of the person wanting the sale would prevail. The interests of children and families in occupation would be unlikely to prevail.[30]

The facts of the case were that Mrs Shaire and Mr Fox lived together as a married couple and each had a beneficial interest in their home. Following Mr Fox's death in 1992 it emerged that he had forged Mrs Shaire's signature on a charge in favour of the claimant to secure the sum of £118,000. Repayments on the charge were not met and the bank applied for possession and sale of Mrs Shaire's home under s.14(1) TLATA. Mrs Shaire defended the claim on the grounds that she had no knowledge of or liability in respect of the claimant's mortgage. She also argued that s.15 now required the court to take into account a wider range of factors other than the interest of a chargee and that the bank's desire for sale should not necessarily prevail over her wish to remain in her home. Neuberger J. accepted that she was not bound by the charge.

8–009 His Lordship gave a number of reasons for his opinion that s.15 of TLATA represented a change in the law. These included the fact that, while the interest of a chargee is one of the four specified factors to be taken into account in s.15(1)(d), there is no suggestion that it is to be given any more importance than the interests of the children residing in the house: see s.15(1)(c).[31] The court is not limited to taking into consideration those matters set out in s.15 and can take other factors into account depending on the circumstances of each individual case. Once the relevant factors to be taken into account have been identified, it is a matter for the court as to what weight to give each factor in a particular case (see *Mortgage Corporation v Shaire* at 656D).

Cases decided pre-TLATA are unlikely to be of much assistance when considering whether the court is likely to make an order for sale under s.14 of TLATA, although it would be wrong not to pay them any regard. Such cases should nevertheless be treated "with caution" (*Mortgage Corporation v Shaire* at 656H–657A).

There are relatively few decided cases as to the effect of s.15 and it therefore remains useful to consider the pre-TLATA case law:

[27] S.15(3), except where the application is made under s.13 (see above) or s.6(2) (see *Mortgage Corporation v Shaire* [2001] 3 W.L.R. 639 at 657 E–F.
[28] S.15(4).
[29] [2001] 3 W.L.R. 639.
[30] *Mortgage Corporation v Shaire* at 653B.
[31] *Mortgage Corporation v Shaire* at 654E.

Section 15(1)(a): the intentions of the person or persons (if any) who created the trust and s.15(1)(b): the purposes for which the property subject to the trust is held

These two factors will often give rise to the same considerations. Upon an application under LPA, s.30 for sale of a property subject to a trust, the court would usually order sale (thereby giving effect to the trust for sale) unless there was a collateral or secondary purpose to the trust which still subsisted, for example the provision of a matrimonial home. A similar approach is taken under TLATA, although there is no longer any trust for sale. Where a marriage or other relationship has come to an end, then the court will generally order sale.

8–010

In *Jones v Challenger*,[32] the parties (a married couple) purchased for £375 a lease of a property in Glamorgan upon trust for themselves as joint tenants. The purchase monies were provided equally and therefore they were beneficial joint tenants. At the time of purchase, the lease had about 10 years to run. They soon separated and divorced. Mrs Jones, who had left the property, subsequently remarried and applied under LPA, s.30 for an order that Mr Challenger concur with her in the sale of the property, alternatively that the property should be sold by order of the court. The judge at first instance refused to order sale on the grounds that the application was "premature". Mrs Jones successfully appealed. Devlin L.J. stated that with the end of the marriage, the purpose of providing a matrimonial home dissolved and the primacy of the duty to sell was restored. The court retained a discretion, for example, to postpone any order for sale to allow Mr Challenger to find alternative accommodation or to raise monies in order to purchase Mrs Jones' interest. He had not sought such an order, however, and therefore the only way in which the discretion could be properly exercised was by making an order for sale (at 183).

Where the purpose of the trust was to provide a home for one of the co-owners and that purpose is capable of enduring, then the court is not likely to order sale. Also, where there has been inequitable conduct on the part of the party seeking sale of the property the court is less likely to order sale.

In *Re Buchanan-Wollaston's Conveyance*[33] land had been conveyed to four people as joint tenants. Shortly afterwards they entered into a deed of covenant by which they mutually agreed that any transaction in connection with one part of the land needed the unanimous agreement of all the parties and that any question arising with reference to the remainder of the land was to be determined by a majority vote. The Court of Appeal refused to order sale upon the application of one party under LPA, s.30. The applicant had entered into a contract which restricted the power of the trustees to sell the land. Where the applicant

8–011

---

[32] [1961] 1 Q.B. 176.
[33] [1939] 1 Ch. 738.

had not acted in accordance with the contract it would not be right to order a sale.

In *Abbey National Plc v Moss and Ors*[34] the Court of Appeal had to consider an appeal against a decision of the lower court ordering sale of the Appellant's property. The Appellant, Mrs Moss, purchased a property in Enfield jointly with her husband in 1971. Mr and Mrs Moss's daughter and son-in-law, Mr and Mrs Leto, also lived in the property. Mr Moss died in 1981 and in 1982 Mrs Moss transferred the property into the joint names of herself and her daughter for nil consideration. The judge found that Mrs Moss agreed to this on the basis that when she died, survivorship would make the transfer of the property to her daughter much simpler, on condition that the property would never be sold in her lifetime. Mr and Mrs Leto subsequently borrowed £30,000 on the security of the property. The judge found that Mrs Moss's signatures on the mortgage documents were forgeries and blamed Mrs Leto. In 1988 Mrs Moss and Mrs Leto fell out and Mrs Leto threw her mother out of the house and issued an application under s.30 for an order for sale of the property. Those proceedings never came to trial. Mrs Moss obtained an order allowing her to return to her home and Mr and Mrs Leto left the country. They stopped making payments under the mortgage and in 1989 the Respondent bank sought possession of the property.

Peter Gibson L.J. held that it was impossible to say that the collateral purpose, *viz.* that Mrs Moss should continue to live in the property during her life, had come to an end (although it would have been otherwise if the collateral purpose had been that Mrs Leto and Mrs Moss would live together in the property) (at 317–318).[35]

Section 15(1)(c) The welfare of any minor who occupies or might reasonably be expected to occupy any land subject to the trust as his home

8–012   One of the most important aspects of TLATA is that the court is required, when considering its powers under s.14, to take into consideration the welfare of any minor who occupies or might reasonably be expected to occupy any land subject to the trust as his home.[36]

Prior to the implementation of TLATA the courts would often order sale of the property even though one partner and the children of the family remained in occupation.[37] In *Williams v Williams*,[38] however, a

---

[34] [1994] 1 F.L.R. 307

[35] See also *Stott v Radcliffe* [1982] 126 S.J. 310 where a Mr Stott formed a relationship with the defendant, Mrs Radcliffe. A property was acquired by them initially in Mr Stott's sole name but subsequently transferred into joint names on a beneficial tenancy in common in equal shares. Mr Stott told Mrs Radcliffe that he intended to leave his share to her in his will but never got round to it. He died and his half share vested in his wife, Mrs Stott. She sought an order for sale under LPA, s.30. The Court refused on the basis that the house had been bought as their home and was intended to remain a home for the survivor.

[36] S.15(1)(c).

[37] Eg. *Jones v Challenger* [1961] 1 Q.B. 176 at 183–84 and *Burke v Burke* [1974] 1 W.L.R. 1063 at 1067.

[38] [1976] 1 Ch. 278.

case which concerned a married couple, the Court of Appeal criticised such an approach where a house had been bought as a home for a family. Lord Denning M.R. went so far as to say that,

> "The court, in executing the trust should regard the primary object as being to provide a home and not a sale. Steps should be taken to preserve it as a home for the remaining partner and children, but giving the outgoing partner such compensation, by way of a charge or being bought out, as is reasonable in the circumstances."

Similar views were expressed in relation to a family home purchased by an unmarried couple in *Re Evers' Trust*.[39] The parties, who were both divorced, began cohabiting in 1974. A child was born in 1976 and soon after that the mother's two children from her previous marriage came to live with them. A property was purchased in 1978 in the parties' joint names as beneficial joint tenants in equity. In 1979 they separated and the father applied for an order for sale of the property under LPA, s.30. His application and subsequent appeal against an order refusing sale were dismissed.

The Court of Appeal held that the underlying purpose of the trust was to provide a home for all five of them for the indefinite future.[40] As the mother was prepared to accept full responsibility for paying the interest on the mortgage and keeping up the capital repayments and the father had a secure home with his mother, there was no justification for ordering a sale at the present time.[41] The application was therefore dismissed. The Court suggested that a further application might be made by the father, for example, upon the mother's re-marriage or on it becoming financially possible for the mother to buy the father out.[42]

Section 15(1)(d) The interests of any secured creditor or beneficiary

Prior to the implementation of TLATA, the courts would order a sale of **8–013** property upon application by a secured creditor unless there were exceptional circumstances. This was the same approach as that taken in relation to applications by a trustee in bankruptcy.[43, 44]

As stated above (at 8–008 and 8–009) the implementation of s.15 heralded a change in the law. Under s.15 of TLATA the interest of the chargee is one of the four specific factors which the court must consider when exercising its discretion. There is no suggestion that it is to be given any more importance than the interests of the children residing in the

---

[39] [1980] 1 W.L.R. 1327.
[40] At 1333E–F.
[41] At 1334 A–C.
[42] 1334E.
[43] See below at 8–016.
[44] See *Lloyds Bank v Byrne* [1993] 1 F.L.R. 369 and *Barclays Bank Plc v Hendricks* [1996] 1 F.L.R. 258 although *c.f. Abbey National Plc v Moss* [1994] 1 F.L.R. 307.

house: see s.15(1)(c).[45] It is therefore open to the courts to depart from the "exceptional circumstances" requirement propounded in cases such as *Lloyds Bank v Byrne* (above) and take a more flexible approach. In the relatively few decided cases since the advent of TLATA, however, a more flexible approach has not yet emerged.[46]

8–014   In *Bank of Ireland Home Mortgages Ltd v Bell and Anor* ([2001] 2 F.L.R. 809) the Court of Appeal had to consider the question of whether the court ought to order sale upon application by a secured creditor, having regard to the matters set out in s.15 of TLATA. Mrs Bell, the defendant, and a Bulgarian by origin, had married Mr Bell in 1979 and they had one son, born on August 27, 1981. They decided to purchase a property at a price of £189,000. Mrs Bell worked as a technical translator and made frequent trips to Bulgaria. While she was away in Bulgaria she had a telephone conversation with her husband during the course of which she gathered that about £150,000 would have to be borrowed for the purchase of the property and that the monthly repayments would cost about £1,500. She was shocked at this news.

A mortgage offer was made by the bank of £150,770 which appeared to be signed by both Mr and Mrs Bell. On November 17, 1988 the sale of the property to Mr and Mrs Bell jointly, was completed. In 1989 an application was made to the bank to reschedule the payments and agreement was reached on this by a letter of acceptance, again purportedly from Mr and Mrs Bell, dated July 26, 1989. By 1991 arrears were mounting and in early 1991 Mr Bell left to work in Czechoslovakia. He never returned.

On May 1, 1992 the bank gave formal notice of default, the arrears being about £10,000. Possession proceedings were commenced on June 9, 1992 and the District Judge made a possession order. On March 2, 1993 leave to appeal out of time was granted to Mrs Bell. She filed a defence in which she denied knowledge of the charge or being a party to it.

8–015   Some six years later, in February 1999, the matter came on for trial before the circuit judge who refused to make an order for sale. The bank successfully appealed to the Court of Appeal against the judge's refusal to order sale of the property. The Court of Appeal found that the judge had erred in the exercise of his discretion in refusing to order a sale.

Peter Gibson L.J. held:

(1) The judge had failed to consider that there was no equity which would be released for Mrs Bell on sale and that the bank in effect would take all the proceeds on sale; (at 815 [26]);

---

[45] *Mortgage Corporation v Shaire* [2001] 3 W.L.R. 639 at 654E.
[46] See, for example, *TSB v Marshall* [1998] 2 F.L.R. 769, a decision of His Honour Judge Wroath in the Newport, Isle of Wight County Court; *c.f.* Neuberger J. in *Mortgage Corporation v Shaire* at 656F disagreeing with the conclusion in *TSB v Marshall*. See also *Re McA* [2002] 2 F.L.R. 274 at 299, para.115 *per* Munby J.: "Section 15 may have given the court a somewhat greater flexibility except where the application is made by a trustee in bankruptcy but the Court of Appeal's subsequent decision in *Bank of Ireland Home Mortgages Ltd v Bell and Anor* [2001] 2 F.L.R. 809 shows that it has hardly revolutionised things."

(2) The fact that the property was purchased as a family home ceased to be operative when Mr Bell left the family. By the time of the appeal, Mr and Mrs Bell were divorced. The purpose of providing a family home was not a matter to which the judge could properly have regard (at 815 [27]);

(3) The judge had referred to the occupation of the property by Mrs Bell and her son. On the assumption that he was referring to s.15(1)(b) — the purposes for which the property is held, the Court of Appeal said that again, that was not an operative purpose of the trust since the departure of Mr Bell. If the judge was having regard to s.15(1)(c), the welfare of a minor occupying the property, the son at the time of the trial was nearly 18 and that should only have been a very slight consideration (at 816 [28]);

(4) The judge had referred to Mrs Bell's poor health. But, the Court of Appeal held that this would be a reason for postponing a sale, rather then refusing it (at 816[29]);

(5) The judge had referred to Lloyd's Bank being a second chargee. But, the Court of Appeal held that this was not a relevant consideration (at 816 [30]).

In *First National Bank v Achampong* ([2004] 1 F.C.R. 18) the court had to consider whether to make an order for sale under s.14 of TLATA. Mr Justice Blackburne (sitting with Lady Justice Arden in the Court of Appeal), in making an order for sale, stated that prominent among the considerations was that otherwise the bank would be kept waiting indefinitely for any payment out of its share of the property. His Lordship found it difficult to attach much if any weight to the position of infant grandchildren residing in the property in the absence of any evidence as to how their welfare might be affected if an order for sale was made (at para.65).

Applications by the Trustee in Bankruptcy

Where an application for an order for sale is made under s.14 of TLATA **8–016** by a trustee in bankruptcy the matters which are to be considered by the court are not those contained within s.15, but those set out in s.335A of the Insolvency Act 1986.[47]

Section 335A of the Insolvency Act 1986 provides:

---

[47] S.15(4). By s.305(2) of the Insolvency Act 1986, the Trustee in Bankruptcy has a duty to get in, realise and distribute the bankrupt's estate in accordance with the provisions of Chapter IV of the Act. The "bankrupt's estate" comprises inter alia all property belonging to or vested in the bankrupt at the commencement of the bankruptcy (s.283(1)). Where the value of an interest in a dwelling-house is less than a prescribed amount, the court shall dismiss any application for sale by the trustee (s.313A).

(2) On such an application (ie. an application for sale under section 14 of TLATA) the court shall make such order as it thinks just and reasonable having regard to –

    (a) the interests of the bankrupt's creditors;

    (b) where the application is made in respect of land which includes a dwelling house which is or has been the home of the bankrupt or the [bankrupt's spouse or civil partner, former spouse or former civil partner] –

        (i) the conduct of the [spouse, civil partner, former spouse or former civil partner], so far as contributing to the bankruptcy,

        (ii) the needs and financial resources of the spouse or former spouse, and

        (iii) the needs of any children, and

    (c) all the circumstances of the case other than the needs of the bankrupt.

(3) Where such an application is made after the end of the period of one year beginning with the first vesting under Chapter IV of this Part of the bankrupt's estate in a trustee, the court shall assume, unless the circumstances of the case are exceptional, that the interests of the bankrupt's creditors outweigh all other considerations.

Before the insertion of the words "spouse, civil partner, former spouse or former civil partner,"[48] it was generally accepted that the same principles would apply where the parties were unmarried. Given that the section now specifically includes reference to civil partners and not any other co-habitee, there is certainly an argument that the factors set out in s.335A do not apply where the bankrupt is either not married or has entered into a civil partnership. It is suggested, nevertheless, that where a trustee in bankruptcy applies for sale of a dwelling house which includes the home of a co-habitee, the factors set out in s.335A should be considered.

8–017   It is therefore instructive to consider the decided cases relating to applications for sale by the trustee in bankruptcy and married couples. Unless the circumstances of the case are exceptional, there will be an order for sale.[49] The reference to "exceptional" circumstances in s.335A(3) gives legislative effect to the principle which had begun to emerge before the coming into force of the new insolvency legislation.[50]

---

[48] By the Civil Partnership Act 2004, s.261(1), Sch.27, para.118(a).

[49] S.335A(3). See also dicta of Nourse L.J. in *Re Citro* [1991] Ch. 142 at 159. His Lordship referred to s.336(5) of the Insolvency Act 1986 (now repealed (which required the court to "assume, unless the circumstances of the case are exceptional, that the interests of the bankrupt's creditors outweigh all other considerations" and applied only to the rights of occupation of those who are or have been married. His Lordship stated that the case law will apply to unmarried couples as a difference in the basic tests applicable to the two classes of case would have been most undesirable.

[50] See Robert Walker L.J. in *Judd v Brown* [1999] 1 F.L.R. 1191 at 1195.

Re Citro[51] was a case in which two brothers had become bankrupt and the only substantial asset of each was his interest in the matrimonial home. One brother's marriage had come to an end but the other brother's marriage had not. The trustee in bankruptcy applied to the court under s.30 of the Law of Property Act 1925 for declarations as to the beneficial interests in the brothers' properties, for possession and sale of them. The judge at first instance, Hoffmann J., declared that the beneficial interest in the property was owned by the trustee and the brothers' wives in equal shares and made orders for possession and sale. His Lordship, having considered all the circumstances, including that the half shares would be insufficient for the wives to obtain alternative accommodation in the area and the educational problems of the children, postponed the sale of the property until the youngest child in each case attained the age of 16. The Court of Appeal allowed the appeal by the trustee in bankruptcy and substituted a period of postponement not exceeding six months.

Nourse L.J. set out the relevant authorities and summarised the   **8–018** principles as follows:

> Where a spouse who has a beneficial interest in the matrimonial home has become bankrupt under debts which cannot be paid without the realisation of that interest, the voice of the creditors will usually prevail over the voice of the other spouse and a sale of the property ordered within a short period. The voice of the other spouse will only prevail in exceptional circumstances. No distinction is to be made between a case where the property is still being enjoyed as the matrimonial home and one where it is not.
>
> What then are exceptional circumstances? As the cases show, it is not uncommon for a wife with young children to be faced with eviction in circumstances where the realisation of her beneficial interest will not produce enough to buy a comparable home in the same neighbourhood, or indeed elsewhere. And, if she has to move elsewhere, there may be problems over schooling and so forth. Such circumstances, while engendering a natural sympathy in all who hear of them, cannot be described as exceptional. They are the melancholy consequences of debt and improvidence with which every civilised society has been familiar.[52]

In the majority of reported decisions concerning applications by a trustee in bankruptcy, pre-1996, the voice of the bankrupt's creditors was found to prevail over that of the wife and children.[53]

---

[51] [1991] Ch. 142.

[52] *Ibid. at 157.*

[53] See *In re Solomon (A Bankrupt), Ex p. Trustee of the Property of the Bankrupt v Solomon* [1967] Ch. 573; *Boydell v Gillespie* (1970) 216 E.G. 1505; *In re Turner (A Bankrupt), Ex p. Trustee of the Property of the Bankrupt v Turner (A Bankrupt)* (1974) 1 W.L.R. 1556; *In re Densham (A Bankrupt), Ex p. Trustee of the Property of the Bankrupt v The Bankrupt* [1975] 1 W.L.R. 1519 where an order for sale was made even though there were young children of the marriage and *In re Bailey (A Bankrupt) (No. 25 of 1975)* [1977] 1 W.L.R. 278 where the Court held that the interests of the children should only incidentally be taken into consideration.

A case in which the voice of the creditors was not allowed to prevail, however, is *In re Holliday*.[54] The parties married in 1962 and had three children born in 1965, 1968 and 1973. They purchased a property as joint legal and beneficial owners in 1970. In 1974 the marriage failed and the husband left the wife and went to live with another woman. On March 3, 1976 the wife gave notice of her intention to bring an application for ancillary relief. On the same day the husband filed his own petition in the local county court and was at once adjudicated bankrupt. The trustee in bankruptcy applied for sale of the matrimonial home. The wife applied to annul the adjudication. Her application was unsuccessful at first instance and an order for sale within a short period was made. The wife appealed.

8–019   The Court of Appeal allowed the wife's appeal against the order for sale in part, holding that the voice of the wife and the children should prevail and that there should be no sale of the property for a substantial period. The factors that the Court took into consideration were:

    (a) it was highly unlikely that postponement of payment of the debts would cause any great hardship to any of the creditors;

    (b) it would have been difficult, if not impossible for the wife to secure another suitable home in the area;

    (c) it would be upsetting for the childrens' education to move from their present schools;

    (d) none of the creditors had thought fit themselves to present a bankruptcy petition and it was quite impossible to know whether any one of them would have done so if the husband himself had not (*per* Sir David Cairns at 425).

In the case of *Re Citro*[55] however, Nourse L.J. stated that in his view the *"special feature"* in *Re Holliday* which gave rise to exceptional circumstances was the observation of the Court that it was highly unlikely that postponement of payment of the debts would cause any great hardship to any of the creditors. There was sufficient equity in the property to cover the bankrupt's debts. Had it not been for that feature, Nourse L.J. could not see how the circumstances in *Re Holliday* could fairly have been treated as exceptional.

Post-implementation of TLATA and s.335A of the Insolvency Act 1986

8–020   There has been little change in approach taken by the courts since the implementation of TLATA and s.335A of the Insolvency Act 1986 in cases concerning applications by a trustee in bankruptcy.

The court must look at all the circumstances and conclude whether or not they are exceptional.[56]

---

[54] [1981] Ch. 405.
[55] [1991] Ch. 142 at 157.
[56] *Per* Jonathan Parker J. in *Claughton v Charalambous* [1999] 1 F.L.R. 740 at 745A.

"Exceptional circumstances"

In *Judd v Brown*[57] the trustee in bankruptcy applied in respect of the bankruptcies of two brothers, for possession and sale of certain freehold property. The wife of one of the brothers had been diagnosed as suffering from cancer. She had undergone extensive surgery and was undergoing a course of treatment. Her oncologist had expressed the opinion that it was important that she have security in order to aid her recovery. Harman J. found that a "sudden and serious attack" of cancer, "when recovery from the attack is directly related to the order sought is ... properly to be described as an exceptional event." His Lordship also had regard to the fact that matters could be resolved in a comparatively short time, differentiating the case from one where a person suffers a long term illness of indeterminate duration and refused to make an order for possession and sale of the matrimonial homes.

In *Re Raval*,[58] Mrs Raval suffered from paranoid schizophrenia. The evidence of the doctor treating Mrs Raval was that a move to an address far from her current accommodation and would interfere which her children's schooling, her husband's employment and the current social support that she received from her neighbours and sister would constitute an adverse life event which could cause a relapse in her condition. A move to accommodation too small for her family's needs could also constitute an adverse life event. On the application of the trustee in bankruptcy, the Registrar made an order for sale but suspended possession for six months on the basis that the circumstances of the case were exceptional. On appeal, the High Court agreed that the circumstances were exceptional and found that having regard to all the circumstances of the case, it would be appropriate to suspend the order for possession for one year for suitable alternative accommodation to be found.

Claughton v Charalambous[59] concerned an application for a trustee in **8–021** bankruptcy for sale of the former matrimonial home. The wife, Mrs Charamlambous, was approximately 60 years of age and suffered from chronic renal failure and chronic osteoarthritis. She would walk only with the aid of a Zimmer frame and required a wheelchair. The property in which she was residing was fitted with a stair lift. The judge at first instance considered each of the matters set out in s.335A of the Insolvency Act 1986 and having regard to the circumstances of the case, made an order for sale but suspended it so long as Mrs Charalambous should continue to live in the property. On appeal, the order of the judge at first instance was upheld.

---

[57] [1998] 2 F.L.R. 360.
[58] [1998] 2 F.L.R. 718.
[59] [1999] 1 F.L.R. 740.

In *Harrington v Bennett*,[60] however, the High Court found that there were no exceptional circumstances where (i) the equity (if any) would be consumed by the trustee's fees (ii) the bankrupt had made an "unusual" application for sale by him (iii) the bankrupt had kept up the mortgage payments (iv) the delay might cause the building society to exercise its power of sale.

---

[60] [2000] B.P.I.R. 630.

CHAPTER 9

PRACTICE AND PROCEDURE

INTRODUCTION

This chapter provides a summary of the practical issues which often arise   **9–001**
when bringing a claim under the Trusts of Land and Appointment of
Trustees Act 1996. It covers: –

  (i)   Funding, including public funding, conditional fee agreements
        and private funding;
 (ii)   Initial steps, including restrictions and injunctions;
(iii)   Evidence and witness statements;
 (iv)   Pre-action procedure;
  (v)   Issuing the claim;
 (vi)   Part 36 and costs; and
(vii)   Appeals.

FUNDING

There are three principle ways in which a claim under TLATA can be
funded:

  (i)   funding provided by the Legal Services Commission;
 (ii)   funding under a conditional fee agreement and
(iii)   privately.

Each of these methods of funding will be considered in turn.

(i) Funding provided by the Legal Services Commission

Does the client qualify for funding from the Legal Services Commission?

At first glance it may seem that the Administration of Justice Act 1999   **9–002**
("the 1999 Act") precludes funding for all matters of trust law. The Lord
Chancellor has authorised funding for applications under s.14 of the
Trusts of Land and Appointment of Trustees Act 1996 ("the 1996 Act").[1]
Funding is authorised where:

---

[1] This direction from April 2001 is set out in Part C of the LSC Funding Manual.

"the matters of trust law concern implied, resulting or constructive trusts, trusts arising when a person dies intestate or where matters of trust law arise in cases under Section 14 of the Trusts for Land and Appointment of Trustees Act 1996 *concerning the ownership or possession of the client's home.*"

The LSC Funding Manual sets out detailed guidance concerning LSC funding and should be consulted before advising a client. The Funding Manual is updated at intervals and can be found on the LSC website at *www.legalservices.gov.uk*. As with all applications for funding, the client's financial resources will be taken into account. Part D of the Funding Manual sets out the financial eligibility criteria. When considering making an application for funding, the advisor should bear in mind that:

(i)   Generally, the prospects of success of the claim must be at least moderate (i.e. be at least over 50 per cent).
(ii) If the prospects of success are borderline or unclear, cases may receive funding for Legal Representation if the case concerns the preservation of the home of the client or his children, or has a significant wider public interest. However, it is unlikely that a s.14 application would fall within the latter category.
(iii) A single certificate can be granted to cover a s.14 application and an application under Sch.1 of the Children Act 1989. *A single application should be made or any existing certificate amended. Advisors should have regard to the guidance set out in W v W [2004] 2 F.L.R. 231.*
(iv) Married couples will not be granted funding to make an application unless no divorce or judicial separation is intended and one of the parties wants a jointly owned property to be sold or seeks a declaration as to the rights of occupation.

Advising the client

9–003   The basic premise that funded clients are not required to make a payment towards funded services, is subject to a number of qualifications, most notably the statutory charge. It is obviously important that a client is made aware of the implications of this from the outset and the advisor is likely to be assisted by the Funding Manual.

Property recovered or preserved by the client

9–004   Property recovered or preserved in the proceedings or any settlement or compromise of proceedings will be subject to the statutory charge of monies by the LSC in funding the proceedings.
    The amount payable by the funded party will be a "reasonable one", having regard to the *financial resources* of the parties to the proceedings *and their conduct* in connection with the dispute to which the proceedings

relate. In determining financial resources the LSC will not take into account clothes, household furniture or the tools and implements of that party's trade.

The statutory charge will not apply[2]:

(i) To any periodical payments of maintenance;

(ii) To the client's clothes, household furniture or tools of the trade, save in so far as the number or quality is exceptional;

(iii) To interim payments in Inheritance Act proceedings;

(iv) To one half of a redundancy payment or any payment ordered by the Employment Appeals Tribunal (save as to costs);

(v) *Where the statutory charge is in favour of the supplier*, to the client's main or only dwelling;

(vi) To any sum, payment or benefit which, by virtue of any provision of or made under an Act of Parliament, cannot be assigned or charged;

(vii) Where the ONLY assistance was Legal Help or Help at Court and the property was not recovered or preserved in family proceedings after a certificate has been granted, to the former matrimonial home which is the client's *main or only residence*. However, where the property is recovered or preserved in family proceedings after a certificate has been granted, the Statutory Charge will apply and will include those sums expended on the Legal Help and Help at Court.

Where a statutory charge would be in favour of the supplier of the funded services (and only in this circumstance), the LSC may grant that supplier authority to waive all or part of the statutory charge where its enforcement would cause grave hardship or distress to the client or would be unreasonably difficult because of the nature of the property.[3]

The costs of a detailed assessment will not be included in the charge, although the cost of drawing up the bill for detailed assessment will be.

Enforcement of the statutory charge may be postponed[4] where: **9–005**

(i) The court order or agreement relates to property to be used as a *home by the client or his dependents* or, where the proceedings were family proceedings, to money to pay for such a home; *and*

(ii) The LSC is satisfied that the property in question will provide appropriate security for the statutory charge; *and*

(iii) As soon as possible the LSC registers a charge under the Land Registration Act 2002 or takes equivalent steps to protect its interest; *and*

---

[2] Community Legal Service (Financial) Regs 2000, reg.44.
[3] Reg.46(1).
[4] Regs 52–53.

    (iv) It appears to the LSC that *it would be unreasonable for the client to pay the amount of the charge.*

Interest will accrue on any statutory charge for which enforcement is postponed and the decision to postpone enforcement may be reviewed at any time.

Costs protection for funded clients

9–006 Section 11 of the 1999 Act, in conjunction with the Community Legal Services (Costs) Protection Regulations 2000, provides some costs protection for funded clients who are unsuccessful in the proceedings. The effect of this is considered below. However, applications under the 1996 Act arising out of family relationships are specifically designated as "family proceedings".[5]

The scope of costs protection in s.14 applications will therefore be limited, as costs protection does not apply to:

    (i) Help at Court;
    (ii) Legal Help (save where the client later receives Legal Representation or General Family Help or Help with Mediation other than in family proceedings);
    (iii) General Family Help and Help with mediation in family proceedings;
    (iv) Legal Representation in family proceedings.[6]

Costs orders against funded clients and the LSC

9–007 Where an order for costs is made against a funded client who has the benefit of costs protection, the Community Legal Service (Costs) Regulations 2000 will apply. The Regulations state[7]:

    (i) In determining a client's financial resources the first £100,000 of the value of the client's interest in the *main or only dwelling in which he resides* shall not be taken into account;
    (ii) The client's clothes, household furniture and tools of the trade shall not be taken into account unless exceptional in quantity or quality;
    (iii) The client's partners resources shall be taken into account unless the partner has a contrary interest in the dispute in respect of which the funded services are provided;
    (iv) Where a party is acting in a representative, fiduciary or official capacity, his personal resources shall not be taken into account.

---

[5] Community Legal Services (Cost Protection) Regs 2000, reg.2) in the Community Legal Services (Cost Protection) Regs 2000 and applications brought by co-habitees will fall within this definition.
[6] reg.3.
[7] Community Legal Service (Costs) Regs 2000, reg.4.

Similarly if the party is acting as litigation friend for a child or patient, the litigation friend's personal resources shall not be taken into account.

(ii) Conditional Fee Agreements

When bringing a claim under TLATA, it may be possible to obtain **9–008** funding by way of a conditional fee agreement ("CFA"). It should be noted, however, that it is not possible to enter into CFAs in "family proceedings",[8] i.e. proceedings under any one or more of the following:

(a) the Matrimonial Causes Act 1973;
(b) the Adoption Act 1976;
(c) the Domestic Proceedings and Magistrates' Courts Act 1978;
(d) Part III of the Matrimonial and Family Proceedings Act 1984;
(e) Parts I, II and IV of the Children Act 1989;
(f) Part IV of the Family Law Act 1996; and
(g) the inherent jurisdiction of the High Court in relation to children.[9]

The Courts and Legal Services Act 1990 (as amended) ("the CLSA") contains the relevant provisions governing conditional fee agreements ("CFAs"). Section 58(2) of the CLSA defines a CFA as:

"(a) an agreement with a person providing advocacy or litigation services which provides for his fees and expenses, or any part or them, to be payable only in specified circumstances; and
(b) a conditional fee agreement provides for a success fee if it provides for the amount of any fees to which it applies to be increased, in specified circumstances, above the amount which would be payable if it were not payable only in specified circumstances."

In order to be enforceable the CFA must:

(a) be in writing;
(b) not relate to proceedings which cannot be the subject of an enforceable conditional fee agreement; and
(c) it must comply with such requirements (if any) as may be prescribed by the Lord Chancellor.[10]

If the CFA is unenforceable then a claimant is under no obligation to pay **9–009** his solicitor anything. On the application of the indemnity principle, the

---

[8] Courts and Legal Services Act 1990 (as amended), s.58A.
[9] S.58A(2) of the Courts and Legal Services Act 1990 (as amended).
[10] S.58(3).

claimant's solicitor is therefore precluded from recovering from the defendant any sum in relation to costs, as the claimant himself does not owe the same to his own solicitor. When advising as to the funding options available to the client one of the factors that the solicitor should consider is whether the client may be eligible and should apply for public funding.[11] If public funding is available to the client then it will be preferable to obtain public funding since any costs order made against the client will not be enforceable without leave of the court.

When the client is represented under a CFA the solicitor should explain:

(a) the circumstances in which the client may be liable for their own costs and for the other party's costs;

(b) the client's right to assessment of costs, wherever the solicitor intends to seek payment of any or all of their costs from the client; and

(c) any interest the solicitor may have in recommending a particular policy or other funding.[12]

The effect of a breach of the Code was considered in *Garbutt v Edwards*.[13] The Court of Appeal held that failure to give an estimate as to likely costs did not necessarily render the performance of the retainer unenforceable. The thrust of the test to be applied is "whether or not the solicitor will be in a position to enforce the Agreement against his own client".

Advantages of obtaining funding under a CFA

9–010   Where the client is funded pursuant to a CFA then notification of funding has to be served on his or her opponent, pursuant to CPR 44.15. If, for example, the opponent both denies that the client has any interest in the property and the size of that interest, then service of notification of funding is likely to focus his or her mind. The uplift will necessarily be far greater where it is denied that the client has any interest at all. Service of such a notice can therefore place pressure on the opponent to accept that the client has some interest in the property. It is also advisable to consider informing one's opponent that the client has entered into a CFA prior to service of the notice, in order to obtain an early concession that the client has an interest in the property.

(iii) Private funding

9–011   In claims under TLATA the client will often be privately paying. If so, it is very important to stress the potential costs implications to them,

---

[11] The Solicitors' Costs Information and Client Care Code 1999 as amended by the Solicitors Practice (Client Care) Amendment Rules (2005) reg.4 (j)).

[12] The Solicitors' Costs Information and Client Care Code 1999 as amended by the Solicitors Practice (Client Care) Amendment Rules (2005) reg.5(d)) ("the Code").

[13] [2005] EWCA Civ 1206.

particularly where there is a relatively small amount of equity in the property in dispute and bearing in mind the potentially serious costs implications set out in Part 36 (see below, paras 9–037 *et seq.*).

INITIAL STEPS

Often it will be necessary to take swift action to protect a client's position   **9–012**
in relation to property, particularly where they are not on the title as a proprietor.

Restrictions

Where a client wishes to assert a beneficial interest in a property, con-   **9–013**
sideration should be given to registering a restriction on the Register. An application to enter a restriction on the Land Register should be made on form RX1 (see Appendix I "Precedents"), copies of which can be downloaded from the Land Registry's website (*www.landreg.gov.uk*). Where an applicant does not have the consent of the registered proprietor s/he will need to satisfy the Land Registry that s/he has a "sufficient interest" in the making of an entry and a declaration must be made at the point of application setting out the way in which the applicant is entitled to apply for the restriction.

The precise wording sought should be entered at s.10 of form RX1 and should be in one of the standard forms contained in Sch.4 of the Land Registration Rules 2003.[14]

Form A is likely to be the appropriate form to be used by an applicant who has a beneficial interest in a property:

> "(Restriction on disposition by sole proprietor). No disposition by a sole proprietor of the registered estate (except a trust corporation) under which capital money arises is to be registered unless author-ised by an order of the court."

When considering making an application to enter a restriction, advisers should satisfy themselves that there is a beneficial interest to be protected. An application for a restriction without reasonable cause which results in a person suffering loss or damage may result in an action for damages against the applicant.

Interim injunctions

Where it is apparent that the property which is the subject of dispute is   **9–014**
about to be sold, an interim injunction can be sought to prevent the sale (*Dance v Goldingham* (1873) 8 Ch. App. 902 and *Wheelwright v Walker*

---

[14] In exceptional circumstances an applicant may apply for a non-standard restriction, the form of which must be approved by the Land Registry.

(No. 2) (1883) 31 W.R. 912) or to prevent the dissipation of the proceeds of sale. The court's jurisdiction to grant injunctions arises under the Supreme Court Act 1981, s.37(1) in the High Court and the County Courts Act 1984, s.38 (as amended) in the County Court. The jurisdiction of the County Court to grant freezing injunctions and search orders is limited by County Courts Remedies Regulations 1991 (SI 1991/1222).

CPR 25 contains the relevant provisions governing applications for interim remedies, including interim injunctions. An application for an injunction should be made in accordance with CPR Part 23 and the Part 23 Practice Direction as modified by the provisions set out in CPR Part 25.

The leading authority remains *American Cyanamid Co. v Ethicon Ltd* ([1975] A.C. 396, HL). Lord Diplock stated that the court must consider the following factors:

> (1) Whether there is a *serious question to be tried*. That is, that the claim is not frivolous or vexatious (at 407). If the claimant is able to satisfy this requirement the court will then go on to consider —
>
> (2) Whether the *balance of convenience* lies in favour of granting or refusing the interlocutory relief sought. As to that the court should consider (a) whether, if the claimant were to succeed at the trial in establishing his right to a permanent injunction he would be adequately compensated by an award of damages for the loss he would have sustained as a result of the defendant's continuing to do what was sought to be enjoined between the time of the application and the time of the trial. If damages in the measure recoverable at common law would be adequate remedy and the defendant would be in a financial position to pay them, no interlocutory injunction should normally be granted, however strong the claimant's claim appeared to be at that stage. If damages would not be an adequate remedy then the court should consider (b) whether, on the contrary hypothesis that the defendant were to succeed at trial in establishing his right to do that which was sought to be enjoined, he would be adequately compensated under the plaintiff's undertaking as to damages for the loss he would have sustained by being prevented from doing so between the time of the application and the time of the trial. (c) Where there is doubt as to the adequacy of the respective remedies in damages available to either party or to both the question of the balance of convenience arises. His Lordship refused to even attempt to list all the various matters which may need to be taken into consideration in deciding where the balance lies as these vary from case to case (at 408).
>
> (3) Where other factors appear to be evenly balanced it is a counsel of prudence to take such measures as are calculated to preserve

the status quo. There may be many other special factors to be taken into consideration in the particular circumstances of individual cases (at 408).

(4) Finally, the court should consider whether there are any other special factors to be taken into consideration in the particular circumstances of individual cases (at 409).

It is normally a requirement of the grant of any injunction that the applicant give a cross-undertaking in damages (*American Cyanamid v Ethicon* at 404). (For mandatory interim injunctions see *Zockoll Group Ltd v Mercury Comminications Ltd* [1998] F.S.R. 354 CA).   **9–015**

It may, alternatively, be possible to deal with the matter by way of undertakings given by the proposed defendant to the court, or even agreement between the parties that the property or proceeds of sale will not be disposed of pending resolution of the dispute. It is preferable to obtain an undertaking to the court rather than simple agreement as the former is punishable as a contempt of court whereas the latter is merely a contractually enforceable agreement.

EVIDENCE

It is always important to try to obtain a copy of the original conveyancing file. Where the property has been purchased in the sole name of one party, the conveyancing file may well cast light on the reason for this. Where the property has been purchased in joint names but without any express declaration of trust, the conveyancing file may also assist.   **9–016**

The TR1 requires the parties to state whether the property is held as a joint tenancy or as tenants in common in equal or other shares. Where the joint tenancy box has been ticked, even though there has been a far greater contribution to the purchase price by one party than the other, the question will arise as to the precise nature of the advice that the couple received upon purchasing the property. In this situation, it is also essential that a copy of the conveyancing file be obtained.

A copy of the mortgage application form should be obtained where possible.

Where a client asserts that he has made direct financial contributions to the purchase price, it is important to obtain evidence in support of this. Often, this will take the form of bank statements. In cases where the parties have lived together for some time, it will be necessary to obtain bank statements from many years ago.

Where a client asserts that he/she was engaged to the other party, it will be necessary to obtain evidence as to the existence of an engagement ring. This can take the form of a receipt for the purchase of the ring or the ring itself or a photograph of it. Often, one party will deny that the ring was purchased with the intention of ever getting married. It is advisable to be prepared for this situation and obtain detailed instructions from the

client as to the circumstances of the engagement, whether there was a
party and whether there any witnesses who can confirm the engagement.

WITNESS STATEMENTS

9–017   It is particularly important in disputes under s.14 of TLATA to ensure
that a full and detailed account of a client's case is obtained at the outset.
It is advisable to set out their position in a witness statement as soon as
reasonably practicable. Where a claim is based upon a limb one-type
constructive trust, i.e. where there is some "agreement, arrangement or
understanding" (see *Lloyds Bank Plc v Rosset* [1991] 1 A.C. 107 *per* Lord
Bridge at 132), as much detail as is possible should be obtained and set
out in the witness statement concerning the circumstances of the agreement. The following is a summary of the types of matters to be covered:

  – when the conversation took place; this may sometimes be linked
    to birthdays/anniversaries/other special occasions
  – where it took place;
  – were any witnesses present (even if they are friends or relatives
    of the client);
  – was anything set down in writing which might support the
    account.

Where the claim is based upon a limb two-type constructive trust (see
Lord Bridge in *Rosset*, above at 132) that is, where there have been direct
contributions to the purchase price, it is important to set out in precise
detail the nature of those contributions.

   In many cases, there will be evidence of both an agreement and contributions to the purchase price and so it will be necessary to address each
of these matters. In a case where the property has been purchased in the
sole name of one of the parties, it is important to set out the reasons why
the property was not purchased in the parties' joint names.

PRE-ACTION PROCEDURE

Pre-action Protocol

9–018   The relevant procedural principles when making applications under the
Trusts of Land and Appointment of Trustees Act 1996 are found in the
Civil Procedure Rules.

   As yet, there is no pre-action protocol in respect of claims made under
the Trusts of Land and Appointment of Trustee Act 1996. Nevertheless,
the court will still expect the parties, in accordance with the overriding
objective and ensuring that the parties are on an equal footing, saving
expense and dealing with the case in ways which are proportionate to the

amount of money involved, the complexity of the issues and the financial position of each party (CPR 1.1(2)(a)(b) and (c)) to act reasonably in exchanging information and documents relevant to the claim and generally in trying to avoid the necessity for the start of proceedings (Practice Direction — Protocols para.4.1). A copy of the Practice Direction — Protocols is set out at Appendix II.

The aim of the pre-action protocols is to:

(1) encourage the exchange of early and full information about the prospective legal claim;
(2) to enable the parties to avoid litigation by agreeing a settlement of the claim before commencement of the proceedings, and
(3) to support the efficient management of proceedings where litigation cannot be avoided (Practice Direction — Protocols para.1.4).

One of the matters to be addressed, pursuant to the Practice Direction — Protocols, is whether or not the parties wish to enter into mediation or another alternative method of dispute resolution. It is suggested that in claims brought under TLATA where the circumstances are often analogous to those in ancillary relief proceedings, mediation will often be an option worthy of pursuit. Claims can be listed for trial relatively quickly after the issue of proceedings and sometimes with only one case management conference in advance of the final hearing. Unlike ancillary relief proceedings, therefore, there is limited opportunity for detailed negotiations. Often, a simple "round table" meeting at a solicitor's office can be a very useful opportunity to attempt to reach settlement or to at least narrow the issues.

Venue

The county court has jurisdiction under s.14 of TLATA whatever the amount involved and whatever the value of any fund or asset connected with the proceedings.[15]

9–019

If the claim is issued in the county court, it should be issued out of the court for the district in which the defendant resides or carries out business or the court for the district where the property is situated.

A claim should be started in the High Court, however, if by reason of (1) the financial value or the claim and the amount in dispute, and/or (2) the complexity of the facts, legal issues, remedies or procedures involved, and/or (3) the importance of the outcome of the claim to the public in general, the claimant believes that the claim ought to be dealt with by a High Court Judge (CPR 7A PD, para.2.4). Therefore, where the value of the claim is unusually high, for example, if there is more than one

---

[15] High Court and County Courts Jurisdiction Order 1991, SI 1991/724, art.2, as amended by SI 1996/3141.

property involved or there are complex issues raised, for example, fraud or undue influence, it will be more appropriate to issue in the High Court.

If the claim is issued in the High Court the application may be made to the Central Office in London or any District Registry.

The requirements for transfer between county courts and between the county court and High Court are set out in CPR 30.

Chancery or Family Division?

9–020   Where a claim is issued in the High Court, the decision will have to be taken whether to issue in the Chancery or Family Division. It is suggested that it would be more appropriate to issue a claim in the Family Division where: (i) there are children involved/there is also a Sch.1 of the Children Act application; (ii) where the parties were engaged; (iii) where the parties lived together for a considerable length of time as if they were husband and wife.

It would be more appropriate to issue in the Chancery Division where the case is stronger on an application of the strict law or where there are ancillary issues (for example where rescission or rectification of a deed is sought on the grounds of fraud, mistake or undue influence).

The Chancery Guide provides additional practical information not already contained in the CPR and Practice Directions.[16]

Jurisdiction and proper law

9–021   It is a fundamental rule of English private international law that the law governing the determination of rights to and interests in real property is the law of the jurisdiction in which the property is situated: this is known as the *lex situs*.[17] The question of where such claims should be litigated is perhaps more difficult.

The starting point in considering where claims to beneficial interests should be litigated is the traditional reluctance of the courts in England and Wales to purport to make exorbitant orders relating to property located overseas. This was known as the '*Mocambique* rule' following the decision of the House of Lords in *British South Africa Co. v Companhia de Mocambique*.[18] In that case, Lord Halsbury said[19]:

> "if the matter relates to an estate in land or to a right annexed to such an estate, in such a case, inasmuch as property of the kind is to be held according to the laws of the country where it is situated, and as the right of granting it is vested in the ruler of the country, controversies relating to such property can only be decided in the state in which it depends".

[16] The Chancery Guide 2005 can be accessed from the Court Service at *www.hmcourts-service.co.uk*
[17] *G v G (Matrimonial Property: Rights of Extended Family)* [2006] 1 F.L.R. 62 *per* Baron J. at para 75.
[18] [1893] A.C. 602.
[19] At 631

The traditional approach has however in no small measure been modified by provisions of European law. In particular, Council Regulation (EC) No. 44/2001.[20] Whereas the earlier convention had been given effect in English law by the Civil Jurisdiction and Judgments Act 1982, the Judgments Regulation is directly applicable (see Art.76)] provides at Art.22 that in the case of "proceedings which have as their object rights *in rem* in immovable property or tenancies of immovable property", exclusive jurisdiction is conferred upon "the courts of the Member State in which the property is situated". A similar restriction arises where the proceedings have as their object the validity of entries in a public register.[21] Under Art.25 of the Regulation, where proceedings are brought in the courts of a Member State which are "principally concerned with a matter over which the courts of another Member State have exclusive jurisdiction by virtue of Article 22" that court "shall declare of its own motion that it has no jurisdiction."

Plainly, at least where the land in question is situated within a member state of the European Union, the courts whichever territory the property is situated in will therefore have exclusive jurisdiction over any proceedings relating to the ownership of and interests in that property, at least to the extent that the rights in issue are properly described as rights *in rem* or the essential object of the proceedings is (for instance) the rectification of the Land Register.

Where the land in question is not situated within a member state, slightly different considerations arise, dependent on the domicile of the defendant. If the defendant is not domiciled within a member state, according to Art.4 of the Judgments Regulation, jurisdiction is a matter for the law of the forum. In the case of English law, there is little practical difference between the *Mocambique* rule and Art.22 in the light of the decision of the ECJ in *Webb v Webb*[22] and the Court of Appeal in *Ashurst v Pollard*[23]; that is to say, claims which are properly characterised as claims *in personam* (albeit that the consequences of such a claim succeeding might involve the sale of the property) do not offend either traditional English jurisdiction rules, or Art.22, but claims which are properly described as actions *in rem* must be brought in the forum where the property is located.

Where a defendant is domiciled in another member state but the land in question is not located in a member state of the EU, on the face of it the combination of Art.22 (the wording of which would suggest limits the scope of that article to land in a member state) and Art.2 means that (say) even though the land in question is in New York, and the claim concerns an action *in rem*, the domicile of the defendant in (say) Poland means that the claim must be litigated there. It may be that the true construction of

[20] This regulation, commonly known as the "Judgments Regulation", replaced the "Brussels I" convention.
[21] See Art.22(3).
[22] [1994] Q.B. 696.
[23] [2001] Ch. 595.

Art.22 is that whether or not the land in question is located in a member state of the EU, the courts of the jurisdiction where the land is situated enjoy exclusive jurisdiction in relation to actions *in rem* concerning that property[24].

It is not of course the case that all claims regarding beneficial interests in real property are by definition rights *in rem* or that such rights will always be the object of the proceedings. In *Webb v Webb*[25] the ECJ held that a claim to a beneficial interest could be a claim *in personam* in which case of course neither the *Mocambique* rule nor Art.22 of the Judgments Regulation would be offended by the exercise of jurisdiction in England. In *Ashurst v Pollard*[26] Jonathan Parker L.J. held that whether the object of the proceedings was properly regarded as a claim *in rem* or a claim *in personam* would depend on the relevant circumstances of the case, given that the policy of Art.22 was the 'proper administration of justice'.[27]

In practice, cross-border claims regarding beneficial interests in land tend to arise in one of two ways. First, in the course of litigation before a foreign court, an issue may arise as to whether a party has a beneficial interest in a property in England. To the extent that the object of the foreign proceedings is a claim *in rem*, only the English courts are competent, under the Regulation, to declare the beneficial interests in, and make consequential orders (such as orders for sale) relating to and English property. Second, in the case of litigation concerning the beneficial interests in an English property, the parties may also own property overseas in which the beneficial interests may fall to be determined. Pursuant to Art.22, the English court has no jurisdiction to entertain proceedings seeking declarations of beneficial interests in real property outside the jurisdiction (again, insofar as these claims relate to matters *in rem*, and pursuant to Art.25 the court is obliged to stay any such proceedings of its own motion in any event.

Whilst this may lead, in certain cases, to a duplication of proceedings in the courts of different countries, the provisions of Regulation 44/2001 seem plain and unambiguous: questions regarding rights *in rem* relating to a property in country A should be determined in country A; not in country B no matter how convenient it may be to do otherwise.[28]

Issuing the Claim

CPR Part 7 or Part 8?

9–022   Practice Direction 8B provides that where before April 26, 1999 a claim or application in the High Court would have been brought by originating

---

[24] See e.g. *In re Polly Peck International (No. 2)* [1998] 3 All E.R. 812 CA.
[25] [1994] Q.B. 696.
[26] [2001] Ch 595.
[27] See also *Prazic v Prazic* [2006] EWCA Civ 497.
[28] That said, where there is a "related action" in a different country, the action commenced second in time *may* be stayed on the basis of *lis alibi pendens*: see Art.28.

summons the claimant must use the Part 8 procedure (Practice Direction 8B, para.A.1 and A.2). As claims under TLATA were, before the inception of the Civil Procedure Rules, commenced by way of originating summons, it would seem that Part 8 is the correct procedure to use.

There are, however, several disadvantages to using the Part 8 procedure:

(1) Cases brought under TLATA often concern complex issues of both fact and law. It may be difficult for both the defendant and the court to identify those issues unless they are set out clearly in particulars of claim.

(2) The defendant may object to the use of the Part 8 procedure. If he does so and the court determines that the claim should continue as if under Part 7 the claimant may lose the opportunity to set out its case in particulars of claim, although the defendant will be given the opportunity to file a defence.

It is suggested, therefore, that in many cases it will be more appropriate to use the Part 7 procedure rather than Part 8. In view of Practice Direction 8B, the agreement of the defendant should be obtained to the use of the Part 7 procedure before issuing the claim.

Part 7

Proceedings under Part 7 are started when the court issues a claim form   **9–023** at the request of the claimant (CPR 7.2 (1)). A claim form is issued on the date entered on the form by the court (CPR 7.2 (2)). The relevant form is **N1**. An example of form **N1** together with Particulars of Claim is set out at Appendix I.

Part 16 sets out the contents of the claim form:

The claim form must —

(a) contain a concise statement of the nature of the claim;
(b) specify the remedy which the claimant seeks;
(c) where the claimant is making a claim for money, contain a statement of value in accordance with rule 16.3; and
(d) contain such other matters as may be set out in a practice direction. (CPR 16.2)

Part 22 requires the claim form and, where they are not included in the claim form, the particulars of claim, to be verified by a statement of truth (see also CPR 7 PD para.7.1).

The form of the statement of truth is:

"[I believe][the claimant believes] that the facts stated in [this claim form][these particulars of claim] are true."

The claimant has three options: (1) serve a claim form containing the particulars of claim; (2) serve a claim form accompanied by particulars of claim or (3) serve a claim form to be followed by the particulars of claim within 14 days after service of the claim form (CPR 7.4) in which event the claim form must contain a statement to that effect (CPR 16.2(2)). It is suggested that generally it is more appropriate to set out the particulars of claim in a separate document rather than include them in the claim form, in order to ensure that the claim is set out in sufficient detail.

After a claim form has been issued it must be served on the defendant. The general rule is that the claim form must be served within four months after the date of issue (CPR 7.5 (2)). When particulars of claim are served on a defendant, whether they are contained in the claim form, served with it or served subsequently, they must be accompanied by a form for defending the claim; a form for admitting the claim and a form for acknowledging service (CPR 7.8(1)).

Responding to Particulars of Claim

9–024   Upon receipt of the particulars of claim, the defendant has three options: (i) file or serve an admission; (ii) file a defence or (iii) file an acknowledgment of service (CPR 9.2).

Where the defendant admits either the whole or part of the claimant's case he should make a formal admission in writing in accordance with CPR 14. This should be done either in the defence or by letter.

Where the defendant intends to defend the claim he can file an acknowledgment of service in accordance with CPR Part 10. Where he is served with a claim form that states that particulars of claim are to follow, he must serve his acknowledgment of service 14 days after service of the particulars of claim (CPR 10.3 (1)(a)). In any other case, he must serve his acknowledgment of service 14 days after service of the claim form (CPR 10.3(1)(b)). The relevant form is form **N9** (see Appendix I).

Alternatively, the defendant can simply file his defence. The time for filing the defence is 14 days after service of the particulars of claim or, if the defendant has filed an acknowledgment of service, 28 days after service of the particulars of claim. By filing an acknowledgment of service, therefore, the defendant doubles the period of time available to him to file his defence (CPR15.4(1)).

The defendant and claimant can, however, agree that the period for filing a defence shall be extended by up to 28 days (CPR 15.5(1)). Where they do so they must inform the court in writing (CPR 15.5 (2)).

If an extension for a period longer than 28 days is required, then it is suggested that the defendant should make an application to the court in accordance with CPR Part 23 requesting an extension. The application should set out the reasons why it has not been possible to file a defence in time.

9–025   The defendant will often wish to make a counterclaim, for example, for a declaration that he is the sole legal and beneficial owner of the property.

If he does wish to make a counterclaim he should do so at the time of filing his defence. The defence and counterclaim should normally form one document with the counterclaim following on from the defence (CPR 15 PD para.3.1 and CPR 20 PD para.6.1).

Where a defendant files a defence the court will usually serve an allocation questionnaire on each party in form **N150** (CPR 26.3(1)). The party must complete the allocation questionnaire and file it no later than the date specified in it, which shall be at least 14 days after the date when it is deemed to be served on the party in question (CPR 26.3 (6)). When completing the allocation questionnaire, the party in question can request a stay to allow for settlement of the case (CPR 26.4(1)). It is suggested that often in TLATA cases this may be a useful device. The opportunity can then be taken for a "round table" meeting or other form of mediation. At the time of completing the allocation questionnaire, the parties should attempt to agree directions which can be put before the court (CPR 26 PD para.2.3(2)). A fee is payable by a claimant upon filing his allocation questionnaire.

Unless the court stays the claim then upon receipt of the allocation questionnaires it will proceed to allocate the matter to a track (CPR 26.5(1)). There are three tracks: the small claims track, the fast track and the multi track. Small claims are generally those with a value of not more than £5,000 (special provisions apply in respect of claims for personal injuries and housing disrepair). Fast track claims are those for which the small claims track is not the normal track and which have a financial value of not more than £15,000 and only if the court considers that the trial is likely to last no longer than one day and any oral expert evidence is limited (CPR 26.6). The multi-track is the normal track for any claim which does not fall within the small claims or fast track (CPR 26.6(6)).

Most claims under TLATA have a financial value higher than £15,000   **9–026** and often last longer than one day and will therefore be allocated to the multi-track. If the court cannot decide which track is the appropriate track for the claim the court may hold an allocation hearing if it thinks that it is necessary (CPR 26.5(4)). When it has allocated a claim to a track the court will serve notice of allocation on each party in form **N155** (or **N154** if allocated to the fast track)(CPR 26.9).

Any case that is not issued out of a Civil Trial Centre will be transferred to one upon allocation to the multi-track (CPR 26 PD para.10.2).

Part 8

Part 8 applies where the claimant seeks the court's decision on a question   **9–027** which is unlikely to involve a substantial dispute of fact (CPR 8.1(2)(a)) or a rule or practice direction requires or permits the use of the Part 8 procedure (CPR 8.1(2)(b)/8.1(6)).

In circumstances where there is unlikely to be a substantial dispute of fact and the principal issue is one of law, it would be appropriate to issue a claim form under Part 8 rather than Part 7.

The claim form is form **N208** (see Appendix I; see also **N208A** "Notes for Claimant" and **N208C** "Notes for Defendant"). The claim form must state:

(a) that this Part applies;
(b) (i) the question which the claimant wants the court to decide; or
    (ii) the remedy which the claimant is seeking and the legal basis for the claim to that remedy;
(c) if the claim is being made under an enactment, what that enactment is;
(d) if the claimant is claiming in a representative capacity, what that capacity is; and
(e) if the defendant is sued in a representative capacity, what that representative capacity is. (CPR 8.2 "Contents of the Claim Form").

9–028
The claim form must be verified by a statement of truth (CPR 22.1(1)(a)). The statement of truth must be signed by the party or his litigation friend or the legal representative of the party or litigation friend (CPR 22 PD para.3.2). It is suggested that if the legal representative is in any doubt that the client does not have an honest belief in the truth of the facts set out in the claim form he should require the client to sign the statement of truth himself. Proceedings for contempt can be brought against a person if he makes, or causes to be made, a false statement in a document verified by a statement of truth (CPR 32.14(1)).

After the Claim Form has been issued, it must be served on the defendant (CPR 7.5 (1)). The general rule is that a claim form must be served within four months after the date of issue, as with the Part 7 claim form (CPR 7.5(2)).

A specimen Part 8 Claim Form appears at Appendix I.

If the claimant wishes to rely on written evidence he must file it when he files his claim form (CPR 8.5(1)). The claimant's evidence must be served on the defendant with the claim form (CPR 8.5 2)). The claimant may, within 14 days of service of the defendant's evidence on him, file further written evidence in reply (CPR 8.5 (5)).

The claimant may rely on matters set out in his claim form as evidence under CPR 8.5(7) if the claim form is verified by a statement of truth (CPR 8.5 (7)). It is therefore open to the claimant to set out his entire case in the form **N208**. It is suggested, however, that in most cases it is better to simply state in the claim form that Part 8 applies; the question which the claimant wants the court to decide or the remedy he is seeking and the legal basis for the claim to that remedy; that the claim is being made under the Trusts of Land and Appointment of Trustees Act 1996 and if the defendant is sued in a representative capacity, what that capacity is

(CPR 8.2). The factual background should be set out in detail in a separate witness statement.

The witness statement should also be supported by a statement of truth (CPR 22.1(c)). The witness statement must be signed by the maker of the statement (CPR 22.1 (6)(b)). The claim form, together with any evidence in support should then be lodged at court, with as many copies as there are defendants, together with the relevant court fee.

The defendant must file an acknowledgment of service in form **N210**   **9–029** not more than 14 days after service of the claim form and serve the acknowledgment of service on the claimant and any other party (CPR 8.3(1)). It should be noted that the acknowledgment of service is to be served on the claimant and any other party, in contrast to CPR Part 7 which only requires the filing of the acknowledgment of service. By para.5.6 of PD 8 a defendant's time limit for filing and serving the acknowledgment of service can be extended by agreement by not more than 14 days after the defendant files his acknowledgment of service. The agreement must be filed by the defendant at the same time that he files his acknowledgment of service (CPR 8 PD para.5.6(2)(a)).

The acknowledgment of service must state — (a) whether the defendant contests the claim and if the defendant seeks a different remedy from that set out in the claim form, what that remedy is (CPR 8.3 (2)). The acknowledgment of service must be signed by the defendant or his legal representative and include the defendant's address for service (CPR 10.5).

A specimen form **N210** appears at Appendix I. Form **N210**, section D allows the defendant to object to the claimant issuing under Part 8. If the defendant considers that the claim ought more properly have been brought under CPR Part 7 because it involves a substantial dispute of fact, then he should tick this box and state his reasons for objecting (CPR 8.8(1)).

It is suggested that where the defendant objects to the use of the Part 8 procedure and avers that the claim should have been commenced by a claim form issued under Part 7 then it is advisable to file and serve a Defence and Counterclaim which sets out the Defendant's position in detail. If the court does then direct that the matter continue as if begun under Part 7 the defendant's position is clear, whereas the claimant is left with his Part 8 Claim form together with witness statement in support. It is for this reason that careful consideration should be given at the outset as to whether to commence the claim by way of Part 7 or Part 8.

The acknowledgment of service should be supported by a statement of truth (CPR 22.1 (1)(d)) signed by either the defendant, his solicitor or litigation friend.

CPR 8.7 states:

"Where the Part 8 procedure is used, Part 20 (counterclaims and other additional claims) applies, except that a party may not make a Part 20 claim (as defined by rule 20.2) without the court's permission."

9–030   When the court receives the acknowledgment of service and any written evidence it will give directions as to the future management of the case (CPR 8.8(2)). The court may at any stage order the claim to continue as if the claimant had not used the Part 8 procedure and, if it does so, the court may give any directions it considers appropriate (CPR 8.1(3)). The claimant has 14 days for filing evidence in reply but this period may be extended by agreement for not more than 28 days from the service of the defendant's evidence (CPR 8 PD para.5.6(3)).

Once the defendant has filed his acknowledgment of service the court file will be referred to the judge for directions for the disposal of the claim (See Form **N208C** — notes for defendant). The District Judge or Master will then give appropriate directions. Where the Part 8 procedure has been used, the claim will be automatically treated as allocated to the multi-track and therefore Part 26 — "Case Management — Preliminary Stage" does not apply (CPR 8.9(c)).

Application for strike out/summary judgment

9–031   (Appendix: CPR Part 3 and CPR Part 24)

Consideration should always be given to whether there are grounds for applying to strike out a statement of case under CPR Part 3 and/or for applying for summary judgment in respect of the claim under CPR Part 24. Where, for example, there is an express declaration of trust, the claimant may consider applying to the court for summary judgment for a declaration that the parties hold the property upon trust for themselves as set out in the declaration, an order for sale and any consequential remedies and/or for strike out of any defence.

CPR Part 3.4 provides that the court may strike out a statement of case if it appears that:

(a) that the statement of case discloses no reasonable grounds for bringing or defending the claim;

(b) that the statement of case is an abuse of the court's process or is otherwise likely to obstruct the just disposal of the proceedings; or

(c) that there has been a failure to comply with a rule, practice direction or court order.

9–032 CPR Part 24 provides that the court may give summary judgment against a claimant or defendant on the whole of a claim or on a particular issue if —

(a) it considers that —

  (i) that claimant has no real prospect of succeeding on the claim or issue; or

  (ii) that defendant has no real prospect of successfully defending the claim or issue; and

(b) there is no other compelling reason why the case or issue should be disposed of at trial.[29]

Multi-track

As stated above, most claims brought under TLATA will be allocated to the multi-track. Claims commenced by under the Part 8 procedure are automatically treated as allocated to multi-track (CPR 8.9(c)).   **9–033**

On allocation to the multi-track, the court will give directions or fix a case management conference (CMC) or pre-trial review (CPR 29.2). The parties should always attempt to agree directions. If the court considers that they are suitable, it may approve them without listing the matter for a CMC (CPR 29.4). Even if the matter is listed for a CMC, the court will be greatly assisted if an effort has been made to agree directions.

Common directions include:

(i) a direction for the filing of any reply or amended statement of case;

(ii) a direction for the service of any request for further information;

(iii) the appointment of a single joint expert. It will invariably be necessary to obtain a valuation of the property in question. Attempts should be made to agree on the instruction of a single expert to carry out a valuation;

(iv) standard disclosure. Disclosure will either be by list in Form **N265** or by service of copy documents (check whether list still has to be filed/served (see CPR 31);

(v) exchange of witness statements by way of simultaneous exchange (see CPR 29 PD para.4.8);

(vi) list the matter for trial, together with a time estimate; or

(vii) list the matter for a further CMC, together with a time estimate.

If the matter is listed for trial, then there should be a direction requiring the trial bundle to be prepared by the claimant and agreed by the other parties to be lodged at court not more than seven days and not less than three days before the start of the trial (CPR 39.5). The timetable of directions should refer to calendar dates (CPR 29 PD para.4.7(a)).   **9–034**

It is also necessary to consider whether a case summary would be useful for the court (CPR 29 PD para.5.6(3)). The case summary is prepared by the claimant and should set out a brief chronology of the claim and the issues before the court in no more than 500 words (29 PD para.5.7(1)). It is suggested that in all but the most straightforward cases, a case summary should be provided.

---

[29] Note, however, that the court may not give summary judgment against a defendant in proceedings for possession of residential premises against a mortgagor or a tenant or person holding over after the end of his tenancy whose occupancy is protected within the meaning of the Rent Act 1977 or the Housing Act 1988 (CPR 24.3(2)(a).

The CMC should be attended by a legal representative who is familiar with the case and has sufficient authority to deal with any issues that are likely to arise, including settlement of the case (CPR 29.3(2)). In claims under TLATA, where the CMC is a useful opportunity for negotiations, it is better if either the file handler or, if counsel has been instructed, counsel attends the CMC.

9–035   At the CMC, consideration should also be given to whether the case should be tried by a High Court judge or someone who specialises in TLATA claims. Often, cases under TLATA are allocated to judges with experience of chancery matters. If the case involves children, however, then it might be considered more appropriate to allocate it to a judge with family law experience. The court may fix a trial date at the CMC or it might list the matter for a further CMC. (NB The court will fix the trial date or trial period as soon as practicable (CPR 29.2 (2)).

When the court fixes the trial date or trial period it will give notice to the parties of the date or period and specify the date by which the parties must file a pre-trial checklist (CPR 29.2 (3)), unless it dispenses with the need for pre-trial checklists (CPR 29.6(1)). The completed pre-trial checklist in form **N170** should be lodged at court on a date specified by the court which will be at least eight weeks before the trial (29 PD para.8.1). A costs estimate should also be filed with the pre-trial checklist (CPR 43 PD para.6). Upon receiving the parties' pre-trial check-lists, the court may decide to list the matter for a pre-trial review (CPR 29.7).

The trial

9–036   It should be noted that in trials conducted under the CPR the witness statement generally stands as the party's evidence in chief (CPR 32.5(2). The party may only give oral evidence of any matters not dealt with in his witness statement with the permission of the court (CPR 32.5(3)). It is therefore very important to ensure that the witness statement sets out the client's case in detail.

The trial bundle should be paginated continuously throughout (CPR 39 PD para.3.5), a requirement which is often overlooked. If there are over 100 pages, numbered dividers should separate different types of document. Identical bundles should be supplied to all parties (CPR 39 PD para.3.10) and it is important to remember to supply a bundle for the use of the witnesses at trial.

COSTS AND PART 36 OFFERS

9–037   Costs implications in claims brought under TLATA are very important. Unlike in ancillary relief proceedings, the losing party is likely to end up paying both his own costs and those of the successful party which can often be very significant. Where the case is being dealt with on the multi-track it is not unusual for one party's costs to be at least £10,000. It is therefore very important to address the issue of costs at the outset and to ensure that the client is fully aware at all stages of the costs implications of their actions. The general rule is that costs follow the event (see *Daniels v Commissioner of Police for the Metropolis* [2005] EWCA Civ 1312; LTL 20/10/05; *The Times*, October 28, 2005).

CPR rule 44.3 contains provisions regarding the court's discretion and circumstances to be taken into account when exercising its discretion as to costs and provides:

"(1) The court has discretion as to —

  (a) whether costs are payable by one party to another; ...

    (2) If the court decides to make an order about costs –

      (a) the general rule is that the unsuccessful party will be ordered to pay the costs of the successful pary; but

      (b) the court may make a different order. ...

    (3) The general rule does not apply to the following proceedings —

      (a) proceedings in the Court of Appeal on an application or appeal made in connection with proceedings in the Family Division; or

      (b) proceedings in the Court of Appeal from a judgment, direction, decision or order given or made in probate proceedings or family proceedings.

    (4) In deciding what order (if any) to make about costs, the court must have regard to all the circumstances, including —

      (a) the conduct of all the parties;

      (b) whether a party has succeeded on part of his case, even if he has not been wholly successful; and

      (c) any payment into court or admissible offer to settle made by a party which is drawn to the court's attention (whether or not made in accordance with Part 36).

    (5) The conduct of the parties includes —-

      (a) conduct before, as well as during, the proceedings and in particular ...

      (b) whether it was reasonable for a party to raise, pursue or contest a particular allegation or issue; and

> (c) the manner in which a party has pursued or defended his case or a particular allegation or issue; and
>
> (d) whether a claimant who has succeeded in his claim, in whole or in part, exaggerated his claim."

9–038   CPR Part 36 contains the relevant provisions governing offers to settle and payments into court.

Both claimant and defendant can make a Part 36 offer to settle any claim. The general rule is that an offer by a defendant to settle a money claim will not automatically have the cost consequences set out in CPR 36.20(2) unless it is made by way of a Part 36 payment (see CPR 36.3(1) "A defendant's offer to settle a money claim requires a Part 36 payment). The court does, however, retain a discretion to order that an offer which is not made in accordance with Part 36 shall have the costs consequences specified in CPR 36.20(2) (see 36.1(2) and 44.3(4)(c)).

An offer to settle a money claim should usually be treated as having the same effect as a payment into court if the offer is expressed in clear terms, is open for acceptance for at least 21 days and otherwise accords with the substance of a Calderbank offer,[30] is a genuine offer and if the defendant is good for the money when the offer is made.[31]

A Part 36 offer must be in writing and state whether it relates to the whole or part of the claim or to a specific issue and if so, which part or issue (CPR 36.5 (3)).

A Part 36 offer may be accepted not less than 21 days before the start of the trial without needing the court's permission if the claimant gives the defendant written notice of acceptance not later than 21 days after the offer was made (CPR 36.11 (1)). After the expiry of 21 days it is necessary to obtain the court's permission to accept a payment into court unless the parties agree the liability for costs (CPR 36.11(2)). It is also necessary to obtain the permission of the court where the defendant's Part 36 offer or Part 36 payment is made less than 21 days before the start of the trial (CPR 36.11(2)(a)). The judge has an unfettered discretion in considering whether to permit applications to accept Part 36 offers after that time.[32]

The costs implications of failing to beat a Part 36 offer are severe. Where the claimant fails to do better than the defendant's Part 36 offer, unless it considers it unjust to do so, the court will order the claimant to pay any costs incurred by the defendant after the latest date on which the offer could have been accepted without needing the permission of the court (CPR 36.20).

---

[30] *Calderbank v Calderbank* [1975] F.L.R. Rep.113.
[31] *Trustees of Stokes Pension Fund v Western Power Distribution (South West) Plc* [2005] EWCA Civ 854; LTL 11/7/2005; [2005] 1 W.L.R. 3595; [2005] 3 All E.R. 775; *The Times, July 28, 2005; Independent*, July 15, 2005.
[32] *Capital Bank Plc v Stickland* [2004] EWCA Civ 1677 applying *Cumper v Pothecary* [1941] 2 K.B. 58.

Where the claimant does better than his Part 36 offer, i.e. the defendant **9–039** is held liable for more or the judgment against him is more advantageous to the claimant than the claimant's Part 36 offer, the following principles apply:

> "The court may order interest on the whole or part of any sum of money (excluding interest) awarded to the claimant at a rate not exceeding 10 per cent above base rate for some or all of the period starting with the latest date on which the defendant could have accepted the offer without needing the permission of the court. (CPR 36.21 (2))
>
> The court may also order that the claimant is entitled to —
>
> (a) his costs on the indemnity basis from the latest date when the defendant could have accepted the offer without needing the permission of the court; and
>
> (b) interest on those costs at a rate not exceeding 10% above base rate." (CPR 36.21 (3))

The court *will* make the orders set out above unless it considers it unjust to do so (CPR 36.21(4)).

Costs and the failure to mediate

CPR 44.3(2) provides that "if the court decides to make an order about **9–040** costs (a) the general rule is that the unsuccessful party will be ordered to pay the cost of the successful party; but (b) the court may make a different order". CPR 44.3 (4) provides that "in deciding what order (if any) to make about costs, the court must have regard to all the circumstances, including — (a) the conduct of the parties." Rule 44.3(5) provides that the conduct of the parties includes "(a) conduct before, as well as during, the proceedings and in particular the extent to which the parties followed any relevant pre-action protocol." In *Halsey v Milton Keynes General NHS Trust* ([2004] EWCA Civ 576), the Court of Appeal reiterated that the general rule is that costs should follow the event and that the burden is on the unsuccessful party to show why there should be a departure from the general rule (at para.13). Lord Justice Dyson stated:

> "The fundamental principle is that such departure is not justified unless it is shown (the burden being on the unsuccessful party) that the successful party acted unreasonably in refusing to agree to ADR."

The Court of Appeal then went on to set out guidance as to the factors that should be considered by the court in deciding whether a refusal to agree to ADR is unreasonable.[33]

Generally a without prejudice offer, made in the course of a mediation or other settlement meeting which is not accepted is not admissible, unless it is made on the basis that it is without prejudice save as to costs. Nor is anything which happens at a mediation or settlement meeting admissible.[34]

APPEALS

9–041   See Appendix II: CPR 52; see Court of Appeal website: *www.civilappeals. gov.uk*

CPR Part 52 applies to appeals to the civil division of the Court of Appeal; the High Court and County Court (CPR Part 52.1).

Routes of appeal

9–042   (See CPR Part 52 Practice Direction 2A.1 and the tables set out therein).

Generally, where the decision being appealed is a final decision in multi-track proceedings (except proceedings under CPR Part 8 if not allocated to track or if simply treated as allocated to the multi-track under CPR 8.9(c)), the appeal will be to the Court of Appeal.[35]

A decision of the High Court is appealed to the Court of Appeal. In all other cases (including final decisions under CPR Part 8 if not allocated to any track or if simply treated as allocated to the multi-track under CPR 8.9(c)), the route of appeal is:

> from a District Judge to a Circuit Judge;
> from a Circuit Judge and a Master or District Judge sitting in a District Registry to a Single Judge of the High Court.

A "final decision" is defined in CPR 52 PD para.2A.2 as a "decision of a court that would finally determine (subject to any possible appeal or detailed assessment of costs) the entire proceedings whichever way the court decided the issues before it. It is important to note that decisions made on an application for strike out or summary judgment are not treated as final decisions for this purpose.

---

[33] For a case in which it was held that the refusal of one party to participate in mediation was not unreasonable see *Hickman v Lapthorn and Fisher* [2006] EWHC 12 (Q.B.).

[34] See *Jackson v Ministry of Defence* [2006] EWCA Civ 46 at paras 11 and 12.

[35] In addition, the final decision of a Circuit Judge or Master or District Judge sitting in specialist proceedings under the Companies Acts 1985 or 1989 or to which Section I, II or III of Part 57 or any of Parts 58 to 63, is appealed to the Court of Appeal.

In addition, where proceedings under TLATA[36] have been heard by a   **9–043**
District Judge in the in the Family Division of the High Court the appeal
is to a High Court Judge of the Family Division, except where the proceedings have been brought under CPR Part 7, have been allocated to the
multi-track and relate to a final decision of the court, in which case the
appeal lies to the Court of Appeal.

Any decision by a High Court Judge in the Family Division of the
High Court in proceedings under TLATA is appealed to the Court of
Appeal.[37]

See also the routes of appeal guide at *www.hmcourts-service.gov.uk/
infoabout/coa_civil/routes_app/index.htm*

Steps to be taken by the appellant

The following is a summary of the steps which should be taken by the   **9–044**
appellant when appealing an adverse decision.

Permission to appeal should be requested at the hearing, upon the
judgment or decision being given. Permission is not often given by the
judge that has given the judgement or made the decision although where
the issue concerns a controversial point of law, permission is more likely
to be granted.

Consideration should also be given at the hearing as to whether to
request an extension of time for filing a notice of appeal in the appeal
court.[38] Consideration should also be given to the question of whether to
apply for a stay of proceedings.[39] Permission will only be granted where
the court considers that the appeal would have a real prospect of success
or there is some other compelling reason why the appeal should be
heard.[40] If permission is refused then it must be requested from the appeal
court in the appellant's notice.[41] The Appellant's Notice is in Form **N161**
(see Appendix I). If permission is refused by the appeal court without a
hearing, the person seeking permission may request the decision to be
reconsidered at a hearing (CPR 52.3(4)). Such a request must be filed
within seven days after service of the notice that permission has been
refused (CPR 52.3 (4)).

A copy of the judgment should be obtained as soon as possible. The   **9–045**
Practice Direction to CPR 52 provides that where the judgment to be
appealed has been officially recorded an approved transcript should
accompany the appellant's notice (see CPR 52 PD 5.12). This can often
take some time to obtain. It is therefore recommended that in all cases an
effort should be made by the representatives of each party to agree a note
of judgment which should be submitted to the judge for his or her

---

[36] Also under the Inheritance (Provision for Family and Dependants) Act 1975 see CPR 52
PD 3.1 table 3.
[37] CPR 52 PD3.1 table 3.
[38] CPR 52.4 (2).
[39] CPR 52.7.
[40] CPR 52.3(6).
[41] CPR 52.4.

approval. This can then accompany the appellant's notice and be replaced by the official transcript when it becomes available.[42]

The form **N161** must be filed at the appeal court within 21 days of the date of the decision of the lower court.[43]

Generally, every appeal is limited to a review of the decision of the lower court (CPR 52.11). It is important to have this in mind when drafting any grounds of appeal. The grounds of appeal should be set out in Section 7 of the form **N161**. The grounds should set out why (a) the decision of the lower court is wrong and/or (b) the decision of the lower court is unjust because of a serious procedural or other irregularity and in respect of each ground, whether the ground raises an appeal on a point of law or is an appeal against a finding of fact (CPR 52.11(3) and CPR 52 PD para.3.2).

9–046   The form **N161** should also be accompanied by a skeleton argument, although if necessary this can be filed and served 14 days after filing the appellant's notice.[44] A chronology is necessary in most appeals and it may be useful to include a list of persons who featured in the case or glossaries of technical terms.[45]

The appellant must file an appeal bundle with his or her appellant's notice which includes the documents set out in CPR 52 PD para.5.6. All documents that are extraneous to the issues to be considered must be excluded.[46] The appeal bundle must contain a certificate signed by the appellant's solicitor, counsel or other representative to the effect that he has read and understood his obligations in respect of extraneous documents and has complied with it (CPR 52 PD para.5.6(3)). It is important to ensure that the bundle is paginated consecutively (CPR 52 PD para.15.4). It is not sufficient to insert tabs and paginate each individual section consecutively. This may result in the bundle being returned by the appeal court.

Any application should also be included in the form **N161** (see CPR 52 PD para.11). This might include an application for an extension of time (CPR 52 PD para.5.2). It could also include and application to rely upon evidence which was not before the lower court.[47]

9–047   Where the appellant wishes to rely upon evidence that was not before the lower court, the the relevant considerations remain those set out in *Ladd v Marshall*.[48]

---

[42] It should be noted that for the purposes of permission to appeal the note need not be approved by the respondent or the lower court judge.

[43] The period for requesting permission was increased from 14 days to 21 days on April 6, 2006 — Civil Procedure (Amendment No. 4) Rules 2005 (SI 2005/3515) or such period as the lower court may have directed (CPR 52.4 (2)).

[44] CPR 52 PD 5.9.

[45] CPR 52 PD para.5.11.

[46] CPR 52 PD para.5.6(2).

[47] CPR 52.11(2) provides that unless the appeal court order otherwise it will not receive oral evidence or evidence which was not before the lower court.

[48] [1954] 1 W.L.R. 1489; see *Hertfordshire Investments Ltd v Bubb* [2000] 1 W.L.R. 2318 at 2325 *per* Hale L.J. and *Hamilton v Al-Fayed (Joined Party), The Times*, October 13, 2000 at para.11, *per* Lord Phillips M.R.

It may also be necessary to consider applying for a stay of proceedings, for example, where sale of a property has been ordered within a relatively short period of time. The appeal will not automatically operate as a stay of any decision of the lower court.[49] When considering whether or not to grant a stay the court will balance the risk of injustice to the parties if it grants or refuses a stay.[50]

The appellant's notice must be served on each respondent not later than seven days after it is filed (CPR 52.4 (3)).

Steps to be taken by the respondent

If the respondent merely wishes the appeal court to uphold the decision of the lower court he need not serve a respondent's notice. If he proposes to address arguments to the court, however, he must file a skeleton argument[51] at least seven days before the appeal hearing.[52]   **9–048**

If the respondent wishes the appeal court to uphold the order of the lower court for additional reasons or different reasons from those given by the lower court he must serve a respondent's notice in form **N162**. If he wishes to vary the order of the lower court he must ask for permission to appeal, within the respondent's notice.[53]

The respondent's notice must be filed within 14 days of it becoming clear that the appeal will be proceeding.[54] The respondent must file a skeleton argument within 14 days of filing the notice (if it is not included in the notice).[55] The respondent's notice should be served on the appellant not later than seven days after it is filed (CPR 52.5(6)).

Where the appeal is to the Court of Appeal the respondent must, no later than 21 days after the date he is served with notification that permission to appeal has been granted or the application for permission and the appeal are to be granted together, inform the Civil Appeals Office and the appellant in writing whether he intends to file a respondent's notice or intends to rely upon the reasons given by the lower court (CPR 52 PD para.15.6).

After permission has been granted

Where permission is granted, the appeal bundle must be served on the respondent(s) within seven days of receiving the order giving permission to appeal.[56] Where permission is granted the appellant must add certain documents including the respondent's notice and skeleton argument (if   **9–049**

---

[49] CPR 52.7.
[50] *Hammond Suddard Solicitors v Agrichem International Holdings Ltd* [2002] EWCA Civ 2065 *per* Clarke L.J. at para.22).
[51] CPR 52 PD para.7.6.
[52] CPR 52 PD para.7.7(2).
[53] CPR 52 PD 7.1 to para.7.3.
[54] CPR 52.5(4) and (5).
[55] CPR 52 PD para.7.7(1).
[56] CPR 52 PD para.6.2.

any) to the bundle.[57] The Court of Appeal will send an Appeal Questionnaire to the appellant when permission is granted or it was given by the lower court or is not required.[58] This should be completed within 14 days of receipt.[59]

Where the appeal is to the Court of Appeal and the bundle comprises more than 500 pages, exclusive of transcripts, the appellants solicitors must, after consultation with the respondent's solicitors, prepare a core bundle. The core bundle must contain the documents central to the case and not exceed 150 pages. It must be filed within 28 days of receipt of the order granting permission by the appeal court or where permission to appeal was granted by the lower court or is not needed, within 28 days of service of the appellant's notice on the respondent (CPR 52 PD paras 15.2 and 15.3).

The appeal court has broad powers. It can:

(a) affirm, set aside or vary any order or judgment made or given by the lower court;
(b) refer any claim or issue for determination by the lower court;
(c) order a new trial or hearing;
(d) make orders for the payment of interest;
(e) make a costs order.[60]

It may exercise its powers in relation to whole or part of an order of the lower court.[61]

Second appeals

9–050   Appeals against decisions of the County Court or High Court which were themselves made on appeal are rare. Permission is required from the Court of Appeal and will only be granted where the Court considers that the appeal would raise an important point of principle or practice or there is some other compelling reason for the Court of Appeal to hear it.[62]

Leapfrog procedure

9–051   Where the County Court or High Court considers that the appeal before it raises an important point of principle or practice or there is some other compelling reason, it can order the appeal to be transferred to the Court of Appeal.[63] The Master of the Rolls also has power to direct that the appeal be heard by the Court of Appeal.

---

[57] CPR 52 PD para.6.3A.
[58] CPR 52 PD para.6.4.
[59] CPR 52 PD para.6.5.
[60] CPR 52.10(2).
[61] CPR 52.10 (4).
[62] CPR 52.13.
[63] CPR 52.14 and Access to Justice Act 1999, s.57.

CHAPTER 10

ENGAGED COUPLES

The majority of this book has considered the issues surrounding joint **10–001**
ownership of property regardless of the nature of the relationship of
those who claim that joint ownership. Chapter 11 considers the property
rights and claims that can be made by those who are parents or primary
carers of children. The claims that can be made on the dissolution of
marriage or civil partnership have not been covered here but are of course
widely known and widely dealt with elsewhere in many other publica-
tions. This chapter considers claims by those who were in the transition,
perhaps from cohabitation, towards marriage or civil partnership who do
not quite make the final leap. It deals with the claims that can be made
following the termination of an engagement to marry or the termination
of a civil partnership agreement.

An engagement to marry is a well understood concept. A civil partnership agreement is an agreement between two people to register as each
other's civil partnership — it is the counterpart of an engagement to
marry. It is defined in s.73(3) of the Civil Partnership Act 2004 (CPA). A
civil partnership agreement does not have effect as a contract[1] and there is
no right of action in England and Wales for the breach of a civil partnership agreement.[2]

The rights of a person whose engagement or civil partnership agreement has been terminated to make the TLATA claims or Sch.1 of the
Children Act 1989 claims as set out elsewhere in this book, are not altered
by their change in status. However, their status does add the possibility of
making additional claims. As with any claim the parties must first prove
(or disprove) the engagement or civil partnership agreement and the
termination of that status before any claim can be considered on the
merits.

These additional claims flow from legislation in place for married **10–002**
couples that was enacted prior to the Matrimonial Causes Act 1973
(MCA). The Acts concerned are Married Women's Property Act 1882
(MWPA), the Matrimonial Causes (Property & Maintenance) Act 1958
(MCPMA), the Matrimonial Proceedings and Property Act 1970 (MPPA),
The Law Reform (Miscellaneous Provisions) Act 1970 (LRMPA) and of
course the Civil Partnership Act 2004 (CPA).

[1] S.73(1) of the CPA.
[2] S.73(2) CPA.

The MWPA was a major step forward for the rights of married women. Following the enactment, married women were finally able to acquire, hold and dispose of real property and enter into contracts in respect of their own property, all matters that had previously been the preserve of husbands.

Section 17 of the MWPA remains in force and reads as follows:

> "In any question between husband and wife as to the title to or possession of property, either party may apply by summons or otherwise in a summary way to the High Court or such county court as may be prescribed and the court may, on such an application (which may be heard in private), make such order with respect to the property as it thinks fit."

10–003   The LRMPA 1970 s.2(2) extended the provisions of the MWPA to cover not only parties who were married but also those who were engaged but did not marry and whose engagement had been terminated. In terms of civil partnership legislation, s.66 of the CPA replicates s.17 of the MWPA almost exactly. The only addition is in s.66(2), where the power to order a sale of the property is specifically included. Section 7(7) of the MCMPA gives the court the power to order a sale of property in an application under s.17 but only when the application is dealing with the title or possession of the property not simply a dispute about whether an item should be sold or not. Section 74 of the CPA extends s.66 to cover those whose civil partnership agreement has been terminated.

Section 66 of the Civil Partnership Act 2004 provides:

(1) In a question between the civil partners in a civil partnership as to title to or possession of property, either civil partner may apply to:

(a) the High Court, or
(b) such county court as may be prescribed by rules of court.

(2) On such an application, the court may make such order with respect to the property as it thinks fit (including an order for the sale of the property).

(3) Rules of court made for the purposes of this section may confer jurisdiction on county courts whatever the situation or value of the property in dispute.

Prior to the MCA the Court of Appeal used s.17 of the MWPA to exercise its jurisdiction over property in disputes between husbands and wives as it considered just and reasonable. It was recognised that this took the section too far. The section simply provides declaratory relief following an analysis of trust and common law principles (the same principles applied in an application under TLATA).[3] There is no power under the section to vary established rights to property even if those rights are perceived as unfair.[4] The section does give the power to enforce the right as the court has found them to be, e.g. by ordering a sale.

Property under this section has a wider definition that simply land or buildings. This is clear from s.17 itself with the use of the phrase "any question". It is further developed with the definition of property to be found in the MCPMA. This Act defines property to mean any real or personal property, and money, any negotiable instrument, debt or other chose in action and any other right or interest whether in possession or not.[5] An advantage of this wide definition is that it can apply to property abroad,[6] whereas the TLATA jurisdiction is limited to property within England and Wales. Section 7 of the MCPMA extended the courts power to make an order against money or property that is no longer in the possession or control of the respondent to a claim. The court can order one party to pay to the other the value of the claiming party's interest in an asset that has been disposed of or transfer to the claimant assets into which the original property can be traced. This definition is mirrored in the CPA in s.67. **10–004**

Section 67 provides:

(1) The right of a civil partner ("A") to make an application under s.66 includes the right to make such an application where A claims that the other civil partner ("B") has had in possession or under his control: **10–005**

    (a) money to which, or to a share or which, A was beneficially entitled, or

    (b) property (other than money) to which, or to an interest in which, A was beneficially entitled,

And that either the money or the other property has ceased to be in B's possession or under B's control or that A does not know whether it is still in B's possession or under B's control.

(2) For the purposes of subs.(1)(a) it does not matter whether A is beneficially entitled to the money or share:

    (a) because it represents the proceeds of property to which, or to an interest in which, A was beneficially entitled, or

    (b) for any other reason.

---

[3] See *Pettit v Pettit* [1970] A.C. 777 at 803.
[4] The MCA and CPA provide this adjustive jurisdiction for those whose relationship fails after marriage or civil partnership.
[5] S.8 MCPMA.
[6] See *Razelos v Razelos* [1969] 3 All E.R. 929.

(3) Subss (4) and (5) apply if, on such an application being made, the court is satisfied that B:

(a) has had in his possession or under his control money or other property as mentioned in subs.(1)(a) or (b), and

(b) has not made to A, in respect of that money or other property, such payment or disposition as would have been appropriate in the circumstances.

(4) The power of the court to make orders under s.66 includes power to order B to pay to A:

(a) in a case falling within subs.(1)(a), such sum in respect of the money to which the application relates, or A's share of it, as the court considers appropriate, or

(b) in a case falling within subs.(1)(b), such sum in respect of the value of the property to which the application relates, or A's interest in it as the court considers appropriate.

(5) If it appears to the court that there is any property which –

(a) represents the whole or part of the money or property, and

(b) is property in respect of which an order could (apart from this section) have been made under section 66,

the court may (either instead of or as well as making an order in accordance with subs.(4)) make and order which it could (apart from this section) have made under s.66.

(6) Any power of the court which is exercisable on an application under s.66 is exercisable in relation to an application made under that section as extended by this section.

Following the breakdown of a marriage of civil partnership the wider powers of the MCA and CPA are much more attractive than the declaratory relief achievable under s.17. In the context of married couples (and presumably civil partners although this remains untested) s.17 can prove useful if one party is shortly to be declared bankrupt. It can be a quick way to achieve a declaration of beneficial interest to protect one spouse's interest from the trustee in bankruptcy. It can also be used to achieve an order for sale of a property prior to an ancillary relief hearing (given that there is not power to make an interim order for sale under MCA or CPA).

10–006   For engaged/civil partnership agreement couples concerned about their interest in say the property occupied during the course of the relationship, the declaratory relief mirrors that provided under the trust/TLATA proceedings but does not have the more discretionary powers to delay sale that are found in TLATA. The place where s.17 may be useful is, given the wide definition of property, in respect of property other than real property in relation to which a party seeks to make a claim.

Section 17 is occasionally used within ancillary relief proceedings as a backstop jurisdiction to deal with disputes about household contents that cannot be agreed within the main body of the ancillary relief and so can be used where similar disputes arise between engaged couples and even cohabitants. In the case of *Hammond v Mitchell*[7] involving a cohabiting couple Waite J. said that if it was necessary to bring cases of disputed ownership of household chattels into adjudication, the proper course was to claim for a declaration or inquiry as to the beneficial interest supported by appropriate affidavit evidence on lines similar to the procedure for resolving disputes under s.17 of the MWPA.

Issues arising in relation to specific types of property; endowment   **10–007** policies, bank accounts and also household contents are dealt with in Chapter 7, above.

Any such claim must be made within 3 years of the date of the termination of the engagement. Section 74(4) CPA provides that any application under s.66 or 67 must be made within three years of the termination of the civil partnership agreement.

Section 74(5) CPA provides that a party to a civil partnership agreement who makes a gift of property to the other party on the condition that the property is returned if the civil partnership agreement is terminated is not prevented from recovering that property because he (the giver of the gift) was the one who terminated the agreement.

Applications under s.17 of the MWPA or s.66 of the CPA can be made   **10–008** to the High Court (Family Division) or to a county court. The procedure is set out in the Family Proceedings Rules 1991, rr.3.6–3.7. The High Court requires and originating summons and a county court requires an originating application both in Form M23 (see Appendix I) which must be support by affidavit.[8] If the application is to be made in a county court it should the court in the district where the applicant or respondent resides or where proceedings for dissolution of marriage or civil partnership have been issued.[9] Details of the land concerned and any mortgage must be provided[10] and the mortgagee must be served.[11] The respondent must file an affidavit in answer to the application within 28 days and if he does not do so a district judge can give directions.[12] A district judge can also grant an injunction if necessary.[13] The application is, in effect, treated as if it were an application for ancillary relief under MCA but because it is not an ancillary relief claim the FPR 2.52–2.77, as amended, do not apply. The unamended rules apply. FPR 3.7 deals with the specific circumstances in which an application can be issued in the Principal Registry of the Family Division.

---

[7] [1992] 1 F.L.R. 229.
[8] FPR 3.6(1).
[9] FPR 3.6(3).
[10] FPR 3.6(4).
[11] FPR 3.6(6).
[12] FPR 3.6(7) and (8).
[13] FPR 3.6(9).

One further jurisdiction under which a claim can be made is the Matrimonial Proceedings and Property Act 1970, s.37. As with s.17 of the MWPA, this was extended to cover formerly engaged couples by s.2 of the Law Reform (Miscellaneous Provisions) Act 1970. Section 37 provides that a substantial contribution in money or money's worth to the improvement of property in which either or both parties have a beneficial interest can serve to acquire a share that did not previously exist or enlarge a share that does exist subject to any agreement between the parties to the contrary. The court can reflect in an order an agreement reached between the parties as to the effect of the contribution or order such solution as is just in the circumstances.

Section 37 provides:

10–009   It is hereby declared that where a husband or wife contributes in money or money's worth to the improvement of real or personal property in which or in the proceeds of sale of which either or both of them has or have a beneficial interest, the husband or wife so contributing shall, if the contribution is of a substantial nature and subject to any agreement between them to the contrary express or implied, be treated as having then acquired by virtue of his or her contribution a share or an enlarged share, as the case may be, in that beneficial interest of such an extent as may have been then agreed, or in default of such agreement, as may seem in all the circumstances just to any court before which the question of the existence or extent of the beneficial interest of the husband or wife arises (whether in proceedings between them or in any other proceedings).

The provisions of s.37 of MPPA are mirrored exactly (save as to the format) in the CPA by s.65. This section also applies where a civil partnership agreement is terminated s.74(2).

This section may prove useful for those falling within its jurisdiction if no beneficial interest in a property can be proved by constructive or resulting trust or using any estoppel argument but where a significant contribution — say to a whole sale refurbishment of a property after purchase can be proved and it would be unjust to allow it to go uncompensated. The procedure for an application under MPPA is not dealt with in FPR. It is suggested that a free standing application could adopt the same rules as for an MWPA application but it is most likely that an application will be made at the same time as a TLATA application where the facts are fully pleaded and as such the applications could be combined.

CHAPTER 11

SCHEDULE 1 TO THE CHILDREN ACT 1989

Section 15 and Sch.1 of the Children Act 1989 provide a separate but **11–001**
complementary statutory regime to the Trusts of Land and Appointment
of Trustees Act 1996 covering property rights for unmarried people but
only in connection with financial provision for children. It provides the
court with the jurisdiction to make financial orders (both in terms of
property and maintenance) against the absent parent of a child for the
benefit of the child.

Schedule 1 can be used as a stand alone application in a situation
where the person with care of the child (see below for those who are
entitled to apply) has no property rights. It can also be combined with an
application under TLATA as an alternative or additional solution for the
court where the person with care of the child has limited property rights.

THE STATUTORY REGIME

Schedule 1 did not create new law. It has its legislative history within the **11–002**
Poor Laws and the Bastardy Acts under which a putative father could be
ordered to pay a weekly sum to the mother of a "bastard child". Schedule
1 is essentially a re-enactment of the provisions of earlier statutes that
gave the court jurisdiction in a variety of different circumstances to make
orders for financial relief in relation to children. Those statutes were, in
particular, the Affiliation Proceedings Act 1957, the Guardianship of
Minors Acts 1971 and 1973, the Children Act 1975 and ss.15 and 16 of
the Family Law Reform Act 1987.

The legislative history is dealt with by Ward J. (as he then was) in his
judgments in *H v O*[1] and *A v A (A Minor: Financial Provision)*[2]

WHO MAY APPLY

An order can be made under Sch.1 on the application of any person who **11–003**
is a parent, guardian or a special guardian of a child or by any person in

---

[1] [1992] 1 F.L.R. 282.
[2] [1994] 1 F.L.R. 657.

whose favour a residence order is in force.[3] The application must be made against a parent of the child. Parent is defined in Sch.1 to include a party to a marriage or civil partnership whether or not the marriage or civil partnership is subsisting, in relation to whom the child concerned is a child of the family.[4] This means that the court is not restricted to biological parents but can make an order against a step-parent or civil partner provided the child is a child of the family. Where there has been a marriage or civil partnership the procedure for financial relief upon dissolution under the Matrimonial Causes Act 1973 or the Civil Partnership Act 2004 is likely to be the most appropriate jurisdiction under which to consider the needs of the child concerned.

Schedule 1 does not restrict applications to parents, guardians, special guardians and those with a residence order. Paragraph 2 allows children who are over the age of 18 to make an application against a parent provided that the applicant is or will be receiving instruction at an educational establishment or undergoing training for a trade, profession or vocation or there are special circumstances justifying an order.[5] The orders that the court can make under para.2 are restricted to periodical payments and a lump sum.[6] An application cannot be made if there was already a periodical payments order in force in relation to the child immediately before the child reached the age of 16,[7] and an order can only be made if the parents of the child live in separate households.[8]

ORDERS THE COURT CAN MAKE

11–004   Where an application has been made the court can make a variety of orders under Sch.1, para.1 (2):

> (2) The orders referred to in subparagraph (1) are:
>
>> (a) an order requiring either or both parents of a child –
>>
>>> (i) to make to the applicant for the benefit of the child; or
>>> (ii) to make to the child himself,
>>
>> such periodical payments, for such term, as may be specified in the order;
>>
>> (b) an order requiring either or both parents of a child –
>>
>>> (i) to secure to the applicant for the benefit of the child; or
>>> (ii) to secure to the child himself,

---

[3] Sch.1, para.1(1).
[4] Sch.1, para.16 and Children Act 1989, s.105 for definition of child of the family.
[5] Sch.1, para.2(1).
[6] Sch.1, para.2(2).
[7] Sch.1, para.2(3) as defined in para 2(6).
[8] Sch.1 para 2(4).

such periodical payments, for such term, as may be so specified;

(c) an order requiring either or both parents of a child —

    (i) to pay to the applicant for the benefit of the child; or

    (ii) to pay to the child himself,

such lump sum as may be so specified;

(d) an order requiring a settlement to be made for the benefit of the child, and to the satisfaction of the court, or property —

    (i) to which either parent is entitled (either in possession or in reversion); and

    (ii) which is specified in the order;

(e) an order requiring either or both parents of a child —

    (i) to transfer to the application, for the benefit of the child; or

    (ii) to transfer to the child himself,

such property to which the parent is, or the parents are, entitled (either in possession or in reversion) as may be specified in the order.

11–005 The power of the court to make an order may be exercised at any time.[9] An order for periodical payments or secured periodical payments under para.1(2)(a) or (b) can be varied or discharged upon application by the payer or the payee.[10] In addition to the power to vary periodical payments the court also has the power to make a second or subsequent order for periodical payments, secured periodical payments or for a lump sum under para.1(2)(c) provided that the child concerned has not reached the age of 18.[11]

As with the powers under para.1 the powers under para.2 (where the child is the applicant) are exercisable at any time[12] can be varied in the case of periodical payments[13] and further orders can be made from time to time.[14]

In contrast to the power to make more than one lump sum order or order for periodical payments, only one order can be made under paragraph 1(2)(d) or (e) for the settlement or transfer of property[15] against the same person in respect of the same child.

11–006 The provision allowing only one transfer or settlement of property order was considered in *Phillips v Peace*.[16] The mother's first bite at the

[9] Sch.1, para.1(3).
[10] Sch.1, para.1(4) and Sch.1, paras 6 and 6A.
[11] Sch.1, para.1(5)(a).
[12] Sch.1, para.2(7)
[13] Sch.1, para.2(5)
[14] Sch.1, para.2(8).
[15] Sch.1, para.1(5)(b).
[16] [2005] 2 F.L.R. 1212.

cherry is discussed in detail below. This reference is to her attempt in January 2005 to seek further financial provision following the original order made in January 1996. In the first round of litigation the father had been ordered to settle £90,000 in trust for the purchase of a home for the child with the property to revert to the father. He was ordered to pay a lump sum of £24,300. He fulfilled these obligations. Subsequently the father was required to pay £143.50 per week in child support and there was litigation surrounding the question of school fees. In this final application, the mother applied for, amongst other things, £400,000 in order to purchase a further property to house herself, the child and a further child whose father was unknown. The court dismissed her application for housing provision finding that there was no inconsistency between the power to make an order "at any time" and the prohibition on there being only one settlement or transfer of property. The words "transfer" and "settlement" were to be read conjunctively so that only one order adjusting property rights could be made.

The court also made it clear that a second or subsequent lump sum order could be made but a lump sum order was not meant to revert to the payer. It is an order meant to meet past expenditure or current/future needs. The court's power could not be misused so as to circumvent the restriction on only making one property order by ordering a lump sum that could revert to the payer. An order to pay a lump sum that reverts to the payer is akin to a property order.[17] The comparison is made in the judgement with the Matrimonial Causes Act 1973 where a property adjustment order is part of a once and for all settlement of a claim.

The court has jurisdiction to exercise its powers under the Schedule in the absence of an application in the event of the making, varying or discharging of a residence order[18] or a special guardianship order,[19, 20] or when the child concerned is a ward of court.[21] It also has power to revoke or vary an existing order for financial relief made under another enactment when a residence order or special guardianship order is made.[22]

11–007 Applications under Sch.1 can be made to the High Court or County Court for the full range of financial relief or to the magistrates court for a more limited range of financial relief,[23] covering simply orders for periodical payments under para.1(2)(a) and lump sum under para.1(2)(c) which in any event is limited in the magistrates court to £1,000.[24]

Without prejudice to the power to order the payment of lump sum under para.1(2)(c) a lump sum order may be made for the purpose of meeting any liabilities or expenses incurred in connection with the birth of the child or in maintaining the child and reasonably incurred before

[17] *Per* Singer J. paras 27–30.
[18] Under Children Act 1989, s.8.
[19] Under Children Act 1989, s.14A.
[20] Sch.1, para.1(6).
[21] Sch.1, para.1(7).
[22] Sch.1, para.8.
[23] Sch.1, para.1(a) and 1(b).
[24] Sch.1, para.5(2).

the making of the order.[25] A lump sum can be paid in instalments and the instalments can be varied.[26]

Paragraph 9 of the Schedule gives the court the power to make interim orders for periodical payments and directions where an application has been made under paras 1 or 2. Such payments can be backdated to the date of the application[27] and cease to have effect on the final resolution of the proceedings or earlier if so specified by the court.[28]

Where one parent of a child lives within the jurisdiction of England and Wales and the child lives outside England and Wales with the other parent, a guardian or special guardian or with a person in whose favour a residence order has been made the court only has power to make an order for secured or unsecured periodical payments against the parent living in England and Wales (this includes the power to vary any such order).[29]

PERIODICAL PAYMENT ORDERS

Duration

An order made under Schedule 1 for periodical payments in respect of a child can commence with the date of the making of an application. The order must not in the first instance extend beyond the child's 17th birthday unless the court thinks it right in the circumstances of the case to specify a later date and shall not in any event extend beyond the child's 18th birthday[30] unless the child is, or will be, or, if an order were made without complying with that paragraph, would be receiving instruction at an educational establishment or undergoing training for a trade, profession or vocation, whether or not while in gainful employment or there are special circumstances which justify the making of an order without complying with that paragraph.[31] Special circumstances are undefined but can include physical and other handicap. This jurisdiction exists even though the Child Support legislation provides that a child support assessment (which may be in force in respect of the same child) cannot continue after the child's 19th birthday.[32]

11–008

Child Support legislation

When considering periodical payments it is essential to understand the interaction between the judicial powers in Sch.1 to make periodical payment orders and the administrative powers under Child Support Act

11–009

[25] Sch.1, para.5.
[26] Sch.1, para.5(6).
[27] Sch.1, para.9(2).
[28] Sch.1, para.9(3).
[29] Sch.1, para.14.
[30] Sch.1, para.3(1).
[31] Sch.1, para.3(2).
[32] *C v F (Disabled Child: Maintenance Order)* [1998] 2 F.L.R. 1.

1991 as amended by the Child Support Act 1995 and the Child Support, Pensions and Social Security Act 2000 (CSA 1991). The CSA 1991 sets out the duty of each parent to maintain a qualifying child[33] and the power (exercised by the Child Support Agency) of the Secretary of State to make a maintenance calculation against a non-resident parent in respect of a qualifying child. A detailed analysis of the provisions of the CSA 1991 as amended and the workings of the Child Support Agency is beyond the scope of this book. However, for the purpose of consideration of the powers of the court under Sch.1 it is essential to consider the restriction placed upon those powers by s.8 of the CSA 1991.

Provided the Secretary of State has jurisdiction (under the terms of the CSA 1991) and even though no application is made to him the court cannot hear an application for child periodical payments[34] and make an order except in the following circumstances where:

(a) the order reflects an agreement as to maintenance provision reached between the parties,[35]

(b) a maintenance calculation is in force with respect to the child and the non-resident parent's net weekly income exceeds the maximum figures (currently £2,000 net per week) and the court is satisfied that it is appropriate for the non-resident parent to make further payments in addition to the child support maintenance payable under the calculation (referred to as a "top up order"),[36]

(c) where the child is, will be or (if the order were to be made) would be receiving instruction at an educational establishment or undergoing training for a trade, profession or vocation (whether or not while in gainful employment) and the order is made solely for the purposes of meeting some or all of the expenses incurred in connection with the provision of instruction or training,[37]

(d) where a disability living allowance is paid to or in respect of the child or no such allowance is paid but the child is disabled and the order is made solely for the purpose of meeting some of all of any expenses attributable to the child's disability.[38]

It remains possible for the court to vary an existing periodical payments order under s.8(3A) of the CSA 1991 provided that a maintenance calculation has not been made. With a child periodical payments order made on or after March 3, 2003 it is possible for either parent to give notice of termination of that order and make an application to the Child Support Agency.

---

[33] S.1 of the Child Support Act 1991, as amended.
[34] S.8(3) CSA 1991.
[35] S.8(5) of the CSA 1991.
[36] S.8(6) of the CSA 1991.
[37] S.8(7) of the CSA 1991
[38] S.8(8) of the CSA 1991 with disability being defined in s.8(9).

Phillips v Peace[39] in its first incarnation highlighted the problem with   **11–010**
the relationship between Sch.1 and the child support legislation. In that
case the father worked very successfully in the financial world and owned
and controlled a company that dealt in shares. He had a home worth
c.£2.6m and cars worth £36,000, £54,000 and £100,000. An assessment
had been made by the Child Support Agency and the conclusion of the
application using the child support formula then in place was that the
father had no actual income and was not therefore liable for any child
maintenance payments (this was prior to the amendments brought about
by the Child Support Act 1995, including departure directions for use
where there are assets capable of producing an income or where a persons
lifestyle is inconsistent with their income). The assessment seemed plainly
wrong given the father's asset base, his potential income and his admission that he was considering arranging for his company to pay him a
salary of £50,000 per annum. The mother sought to use Sch.1 as the way
round the unsatisfactory CSA assessment.

Johnson J. reminded himself that the provisions of the Child Support
Act, s.8(3) prohibit the court from making an order for periodical payments in most circumstances and that he should not exercise his discretion under Sch.1 so as to circumvent s.8(3). The mother sought a lump
sum order or a series of lump sum orders to provide her with money to
live off in the light of the nil CSA assessment. Johnson J. concluded at
235B that

> "the undoubted power which I have to make a lump sum award
> should not be exercised in such a way as to provide for the regular
> support of the child, which would ordinarily have been provided by
> an order for periodic payments."

It is therefore clear that Sch.1 cannot be used to circumvent the Child
Support legislation.

In the case of *Re G (Children Act 1989, Sch.1)*[40]:   In this case the father   **11–011**
was declared bankrupt shortly before the hearing of the mother's Sch.1
application. Singer J. concluded he could and should make a Sch.1 order
notwithstanding the father's bankruptcy. He noted that he was told that
as a matter of practice, a Child Support Agency assessment would be
taken into account in the exercise of the court's discretion when considering an income payments order within the bankruptcy. He drew an
analogy between that situation and the consideration that the bankruptcy
court may give to the liability under a lump sum order as falling within
the category of reasonable demands upon the bankrupt's income.[41]
Singer J. does not attempt to resolve this comment with Johnson J.'s view

[39] [1996] 2 F.L.R. 230.
[40] [1996] 2 F.L.R 171.
[41] At 176.

in *Philips v Peace* that lump sum orders under Sch.1 should not fill in where the Child Support Agency fails and would perhaps (it is suggested) find it difficult so to do.

Variation

11–012   Schedule 1, para.6 sets out the wide powers of the court to vary orders for periodical payments including secured periodical payments. The court must take into account all of the circumstances of the case including any change in any of the matters to which the court was required to have regard when making the order.[42] The application for variation of payments made on behalf of a child who has reached 16 can be made by the child him/herself.[43] A child can also apply for the revival of an order that ceased to have effect when that child was 16 provided that the application is made on or before the date that the child reaches 18[44] but the court will only revive such an order where the child is, will be or (if an order were made) would be receiving instruction at an educational establishment or undergoing training for a trade, profession or vocation, whether or not while in gainful employment or there are special circumstances justifying such a revival.[45]

Maintenance agreements

11–013   Schedule 1 paras 10 and 11 deal with alterations to maintenance agreements. These are agreements in writing made with respect to a child, between the father and the mother of the child that contain provision with respect to the making or securing of payments, or the disposition or use of any property for the maintenance or education of the child. The court has the power upon the application by either party to vary the agreement by reason of a change in circumstances (even if it was foreseen) or on the ground that the agreement does not contain proper financial provision for the child.[46]

Property transfer/settlement orders

11–014   It is interesting to note that the Schedule itself does not expressly prevent the direct transfer of property to the applicant in perpetuity. The only proviso in para.1(2)(e) is that any transfer is for the benefit of the child. The Schedule does not require that any such property transferred reverts back to the transferor at the conclusion of the child's minority but the interpretation placed upon that paragraph is that because any transfer is for the benefit of the child that need no longer exists once the child has grown up. For that reason in the vast majority of cases where a transfer

---

[42] Sch.1, para.6(1).
[43] Sch.1, para.6(4).
[44] Sch.1, para.6(5).
[45] Sch.1, para.6(6).
[46] Sch.1, para.10(3).

(or settlement) of property order is made the property reverts back to the provider at the end of a particular term often linked to the child's age and/or stage of education.

It is perhaps worth a brief comparison with provisions under the Matrimonial Causes Act 1973 where an order transferring property under s.24 can be made in favour of the party to the marriage, a child of the family or such person as may be specified for the benefit of a child of the family. Allowing such an order under Sch.1 in favour of the applicant would bring parity between married parents and unmarried parents which may be viewed by some as a step too far and not what was intended by the Sch.1 legislation.[47] Given the innocence of children in their status at birth, parity between children of married parents and children of unmarried parents may be a more palatable way to analyse the situation for those who object to parity of provision between married and unmarried parents.

The question of how to treat a property provided under a Sch.1 order   **11–015** at the end of the children's minority was consider by Johnson J. in *T v S (Financial Provision for Children)*.[48] In this case the unmarried parents had five children. The mother applied for financial provision and the judge at first instance concluded that the available financial resources were £74,000. The district judge ordered that some of those monies were to be used as a lump sum payment to cover arrears of school fees and that the balance would be used to purchase a small property. She ordered that the property should be held by trustees with a power of sale, the exercise of which should be postponed until the youngest child reached 21 or ceased full time secondary education. In the event of sale the benefit would then pass to the children.

On appeal, Johnson J. concluded that rather than reverting to the children the property should revert to the father. Johnson J. considered with care the question of provision for children during their minority and otherwise. He was referred to a number of cases decided under the Matrimonial Causes Act 1973 in the context of married couples. He considered that the purpose of the Schedule was similar to the purpose of previous matrimonial legislation and that was to make proper financial provision for children as children or dependants.[49] Johnson J. recognised the difficulty that the mother was placed in:

"The sadness here is that, after a long and seemingly happy relationship, this mother of five children, never having been married to their father, has no rights against him of her own. She has no rights

---

[47] The law relating to cohabitants is being considered by the Law Commission in their consultation paper "*Cohabitation: The Financial Consequences of Relationship Breakdown*", No. 179.

[48] [1994] 2 F.L.R. 883.

[49] At 888.

to be supported by him in the short, still less in the long term; no right in herself to have even a roof over her head."[50]

He was concerned to stick to the principle and the letter of the statute and felt that, in addition to his principle objection to the district judge's order, allowing the capital to revert to the children may well give the mother a windfall to which she was not entitled. No argument seems to have been made in this case that the mother had any interest in the property and that some or all of it should revert to her at the appropriate time. The case therefore stresses that the role of the court under Sch.1 is to assess the needs of the child or children during their minority and dependency and not further.

11–016   The question of direct provision for children was also considered by Ward J. (as he then was) in *A v A (A Minor: Financial Provision)*.[51] This case was decided in December 1993 and did not refer to Johnson J.'s judgment in *T v S* that had been decided in the previous July. Ward reached the same conclusion that there is a distinct trend against making lump sum payments or property adjustment orders in favour of adult children who have ceased their full-time education.[52] The court concluded that there was no need or requirement to support a child beyond the child's minority but there was a need for security during minority that could be met by the settlement of a property. The fact that the father had purchased a property for occupation by the child and her mother was not an exceptional circumstance so as to justify the transfer of the property to the child absolutely. This was the situation even in the circumstances of a case where the father was so rich that he could have transferred the property in perpetuity and not even been aware that he had done so. The duty of the father was to provide maintenance and support through to completion of education and there was no further duty to advance capital.

FACTORS FOR THE COURT TO CONSIDER

The statutory criteria under paragraph 4

11–017   Paragraph 4 of Sch.1 sets out the particular factors to which the court shall have regard when considering an application for financial provision for a child. The court must have regard to all of the circumstances of the particular case.[53] When an application is made under para.1 or 2 the court must consider in respect of any parent of the child in question if the application is made under para.1 of the Schedule,[54] the mother

---

[50] At 889.
[51] As above, [1994] 1 F.L.R. 657.
[52] At 661D.
[53] Sch.1, para.4(1).
[54] Sch.1, para.4(4)(a)

and father of the child if the application is made under para.2 of the Schedule,[55] the person applying for the order[56] and any other person in whose favour the court proposes to make an order[57] the following matters:

(a) the income, earning capacity, property and other financial resources each of those person(s) has or is likely to have in the foreseeable future;[58] and

(b) the financial needs, obligations and responsibilities which each of those person(s) has or is likely to have in the foreseeable future;[59]

and in addition the court must consider:

(a) the financial needs of the child;[60]

(b) the income, earning capacity (if any), property and other financial resources of the child;[61]

(c) any physical or mental disability of the child;[62]

(d) the manner in which the child was being, or was expected to be, educated or trained.[63]

In deciding whether to exercise its powers under para.1 against a person who is not the mother or father of the child the court shall in addition have regard to: **11–018**

(a) whether that person had assumed responsibility for the maintenance of the child, and, if so, the extent to which and basis on which he assumed that responsibility and the length of the period during which he met that responsibility;

(b) whether he did so knowing that the child was not his child;

(c) the liability of any other person to maintain the child.[64]

Standard of living

The question of the standard of living, while featuring as a criterion to be considered in the context of ancillary relief under s.25 of the Matrimonial Causes Act 1973 does not feature specifically in the criteria for consideration under para.4. However, even without specific reference within the Schedule (save for it falling under the auspices "all of the circum-   **11–019**

---

[55] Sch.1, para.4(4)(b)
[56] Sch.1, para.4(4)(c)
[57] Sch.1, para.4(4)(d)
[58] Sch.1, para.4(1)(a)
[59] Sch.1, para.4(1)(b)
[60] Sch.1, para.4(1)(c)
[61] Sch.1, para.4(1)(d)
[62] Sch.1, para.4(1)(e)
[63] Sch.1, para.4(1)(f)
[64] Sch.1, para.4(2)

stances of the case") this has been considered in various authorities. In *A v A (A Minor: Financial Provision)*[65] Ward J. (as he then was) thought that the way that the respondent father had treated his other children was relevant and concluded that "what he has provided for her cannot be dissimilar from the ... other establishments he maintains..."

In *Phillips v Peace*[66] when dealing with the consideration of standard of living Johnson J. said:

> "C is of course the child of her father and I bear in mind the way of life and the standard of living that I would expect a child of the father to enjoy in the joint home of her father and mother. Equally C is the child of her mother and I bear in mind the way of the life and the standard of living that she might expect to enjoy had she lived with her mother and a husband or partner of the mother of ordinary means."[67]

11–020   In the case of *J v C (Child: Financial Provision)*[68] the father won £1.4 million on the National Lottery which dramatically changed his standard of living. Hale J. (as she then was) said:

> "the child is entitled to be brought up in circumstances which bear some sort of relationship with the father's current resources and the father's present standard of living. Parents are responsible for their children throughout their dependency. The fact that such riches as they have came after the break-up of the relationship cannot affect that."

The judgment also makes the public policy point that where resources allow a child should be supported by family obligations rather than turning to public funds.

In *F v G (Child: Financial Provision)*[69] the court considered that the omission of standard of living from para.4 of Sch.1 does not render its consideration inappropriate or impermissible and that in a case where the lifestyle of the parties was a factor that would impact to an extent on the outcome, standard of living must be among the totality of the circumstances which the court is to hold in view.[70] The extent to which the unit of primary carer and child have become accustomed to a particular level of lifestyle can impact on the court's evaluation of the child's needs viewed against his history and the judge sought to award the mother a

---

[65] As above [1994] 1 F.L.R. 657)
[66] Above [1996] 2 F.L.R. 230.
[67] At 237B.
[68] [1999] 1 F.L.R. 152.
[69] [2005] 1 F.L.R. 261.
[70] *Per* Singer J. para.33.

sum that would mitigate the disparity between the father's spending power and the house in which the child would grow up.[71]

Other children

The circumstances where there are other children in the household were   **11–021**
also considered in *A v A (A Minor: Financial Provision)*.[72] In this case the mother had three children. It had been concluded that two of the children were not children of the respondent so that the court was only considering specific provision for one child. Ward J. concluded that a large proportion of expenditure (on housing, etc.) would have to be provided regardless of how many children were in the house. It was his view that taking total expenditure and dividing it by the total number living in the house was not going to allow for the fact that a majority of that expenditure would have to be met in housing one child and that the addition of two others added very little extra.[73]

These comments were approved in *J v C*[74] where Hale J said:

> "The other point on behalf of the father is that he is not responsible for T's two half-sisters. Of course I accept that. However, T does need to live with them. In practical terms she needs to live with her mother and her mother has to provide for them and so I have to take that into account. In human terms she needs to grow up with her sisters. It would clearly be greatly to her benefit for her to do so. In taking that view I draw some support from A v A where there were two other children who were not the responsibility of the father. Ward J. held that this was immaterial because their needs did not greatly affect the cost of keeping a roof over the head of the relevant child and her carer."[75]

The recent case of *H v M (Child: Financial Provision)*[76] considered the question of the presence of other children in the primary carer's home. In *H v M*, the mother was receiving some support from the father of her other children by way of periodical payments of £14,000 p.a. and school fees. The father argued that the mother should seek additional support from the father of that other child or that in the alternative he should not pay a disproportionate burden of the costs of the household. The court concluded that the provision that the mother received would be taken into account but the provision that the father should pay in the instant case should not be reduced on the basis that the mother ought to seek more from the other child's father. The court also considered that the

---

[71] *Per* Singer J. paras 35 and 38.
[72] Above [1994] 1 F.L.R. 657.
[73] At 666F.
[74] As above [1999] 1 F.L.R. 152.
[75] At 160E.
[76] Unreported decision of Peter Hughes WC sitting as a Deputy High Court Judge in February 2006.

father could not reasonably complain if the other child indirectly bene-fited from the provision he was ordered to make. The father has applied and been given leave to appeal to the Court of Appeal on this issue. At the time of writing the matter has not yet been heard.

The welfare principle

11–022   The welfare principle is, of course, a central part of the structure of the Children Act 1989. It is enshrined in s.1 as the paramount consideration when a court determines any questions with respect to the upbringing of a child or the administration of a child's property of the application of any income arising from it.[77]

The extent to which this principle applies to financial proceedings has developed from the early comment of Ward J. in *A v A (A Minor: Financial Provision)*[78] where he expressed surprise that welfare played no express part in considerations under Sch.1 but felt that it must be one of the circumstances to be taken into account.

11–023   Johnson J. noted in *Phillips v Peace*[79] that in exercising its powers the court would attach importance to the welfare of the child but that it was not the paramount consideration.

The question of the significance of the welfare of the child was further considered in *J v C (Child: Financial Provision)*.[80] It is clear from the statute that the child's welfare is the paramount consideration when matters concerning the child's upbringing are under consideration and s.105(1) of the Children Act provides that upbringing does not include maintenance. In her judgment Hale J. clarified that if welfare is neither the paramount nor the first consideration in cases of this kind it must be one of the relevant circumstances to be taken into account.[81]

This was approved and the application of the welfare principle amplified by Thorpe L.J. in *Re P (Child: Financial Provision)*[82] to, in the generality of cases, being a constant influence on the discretionary outcome.[83]

---

[77] Children Act 1989, s.1:
   "(1) When a court determines any question with respect to –
      (a) the upbringing of a child; or
      (b) the administration of a child's property or the application of any income arising from it,
   the child's welfare shall be the court's paramount consideration.
   S.105 "upbringing", in relation to any child, includes the care of the child but not his maintenance..."
[78] Above, [1994] 1 F.L.R. 657 at 667F.
[79] Above, [1996] 2 F.L.R. 230 at 233C.
[80] Above [1999] 1 F.L.R. 152.
[81] At 156G.
[82] [2003] 2 F.L.R. 865.
[83] *Per* Thorpe L.J. at para.44.

No order principle

In the first reported authority concerning financial matters after the   **11–024**
implementation of the Children Act 1989, *K v H (Child Maintenance)*,[84]
the court considered the application of the "no order" principle in s.1(5)
of the Children Act 1989.[85]

The unmarried parents in this case were in agreement that the father
should pay £20 per week and had been making these payments on a
voluntary basis for the previous year. Both parties wanted the magistrates' court to make an order but the justices refused having considered
the provision of s.1(5) and decided that court intervention was not
necessary. Sir Stephen Brown P. held that the justices had misdirected
themselves as to the relevance and effect of s.1(5) in the context of an
application solely for financial provision and that it was not correct to
consider that s.1(5) was applicable to an application under s.15 and Sch.1
of the Act. The President also noted that while the parents were in
agreement at that point in time that could not be guaranteed and that any
question of arrears or variation were better dealt with in the context of a
court order. It was clearly in the interest of the child that proper provision should be made for his financial needs.

Conduct

In a case where findings had been made against the mother, her mis-   **11–025**
conduct did not affect the child's claim for maintenance[86] and when
considering orders for financial provision there was no great significance
to be attached to whether the pregnancy was planned or not or indeed to
the length or quality of the parents relationship.[87] However, on this last
point Suger J. in *F v G (Child: Financial Provision*[88] suggested that the
longer the period of settled cohabitation the more weight should be
attached to it.[89]

Recent authorities

Re P (Child: Financial Provision).[90]

The leading case in this is area is *Re P*, a decision of the Court of Appeal   **11–026**
(Thorpe and May L.J.J. and Bodey J.). The father against whom the
application was made was described as "*fabulously rich*". The first
instance judge said that the father conceded "that he could without

---

[84] [1993] 2 F.L.R. 61.
[85] Children Act 1989, s.1:
    (5) Where a court is considering whether or not to make one or more orders under this
       Act with respect to a child, it shall not make the order or any of the orders unless it
       considers that doing so would be better for the child than making no order at all...
[86] *A v A (A Minor: Financial Provision)* [1994] 1 F.L.R. 657.
[87] *J v C (Child: Financial Provision)* [1999] 1 F.L.R. 152.
[88] [2005] F.L.R. 261.
[89] At para.34.
[90] [2003] 2 F.L.R. 865.

financial embarrassment raise and pay any sum which the court may order ... he is in a position he says to pay a lump sum in excess of £10 million if ordered to do so".[91] The mother had never really worked. She came from a wealthy background and had to a great extent been supported by her father. The parties had never cohabited during the course of their relationship. At first instance the court awarded the mother the sum of £450,000 for the purchase of a property to be held in trust, £30,000 for furnishings and periodical payments of £35,360 per annum to be reduced by £9,333 when the child reached seven years old. The mother appealed to the Court of Appeal. The appeal was allowed and the mother was awarded a housing fund of £1 million, a lump sum of £100,000 for internal redecoration and periodical payments of £70,000 per annum (less state benefits).

One of the key features of the case when it came to the quantification of the maintenance award was the development of the concept of the "carer's allowance". This is not a wholly new idea. The historic authorities had considered the question of the amount of maintenance to be awarded with particular reference to the child's needs over those of the carer (usually the mother). The case of *Haroutunian v Jennings*[92] was decided in 1977 by the then President of the Family Division Sir George Baker sitting with Balcombe J. It was an application in the Magistrates Court for an affiliation order under the Affiliation Proceedings Act 1957 that was appealed by way of case stated to the Family Division. The magistrates having ordered the payment of £20 per week as being within the father's means and had made the clear point in their judgment that "It was not our intention that this amount should be disguised maintenance of the mother." Baker P. considered the court's power under s.3 of the Affiliation Act 1957 and the Guardianship of Minors Act 1971 as amended by the Guardianship Act 1973 s.9(2).[93]

11–027   The court made the following comments on the question of quantification of maintenance:

"The maintenance must be not only for food, clothing, heat, light and housing and so on but for care for a young child. And the fact that the money goes to the child and may eventually find its way into the pocket of the mother paying her for caring for the child seems to

---

[91] *Per* Thorpe L.J. at para.2.
[92] [1980] 1 F.L.R. 62.
[93] Affiliation Act 1957 s.3(2):
  "Where the court has adjudged the defendant to be the putative father of the child it may also if it thinks fit in all the circumstances of the case proceed to make against him an order (referred to in this Act as 'an affiliation order') for the payment by him of (a) a sum of money weekly for the maintenance and education of the child."
  Guardianship of Minors Act 1971 as amended by the Guardianship Act 1973 s.9(2):
  "Where the court makes an order under subsection (1) of this section giving custody of the minor to the mother, the court may make a further order requiring the father to pay to the mother such weekly or other periodical sum towards the maintenance of the minor as the court thinks reasonable having regard to the means of the father."

me to be something which the father cannot pray in aid to bring down the amount of the order."[94] and

"There is no reason why the maintenance for a child under the Affiliation Proceedings Act of 1957 should not include a proper sum towards the services rendered by the mother to that child."[95]

The concept of maintenance providing the child with a roof over its head and the care of an adult was compared with the principles under the Fatal Accidents Act and while the comparison with the concept of damages has lost popularity the principle that maintenance can include a sum towards the services rendered by the mother to the child has been further developed in more recent authorities to be the concept of a "carer's allowance".

The court in *A v A (A Minor: Financial Provision)*[96] considered the maintenance element of the claim as part of the financial needs of the child, comparing the mother's work carried out for free with the child's need to remunerate full-time staff to care for her 24 hours a day in the absence of her mother.[97]   **11–028**

When considering the quantification of this principle Ward J. went on to say:

"I bear in mind a broad range of imprecise information from the extortionate demands (but excellent service) of Norland nannies to au pair girls and mother's helps, from calculations in personal injury and fatal accident claims and from the notice-boards in the employment agencies I pass daily. I allow £8,000 under this head. It is almost certainly much less that the father would have to pay were he to be employing staff, but to allow more would be — or would be seen to be — paying maintenance to the former mistress who has no claim in her own right to be maintained."[98]

Both of these earlier authorities approach the issue not on the basis of an allowance for the mother but as funding for the child to enable the mother to care for the child.

Hale J. confirmed the need to concentrate on provision for the children alone when she said in *J v C (Child: Financial Provision)*[99] that one had to guard against unreasonable claims made on the child's behalf with the disguised element of proving for the mother's benefit rather than that child's.[1]

---

[94] *Per* Baker P. at 62V.
[95] *Per* Balcombe J. at 66I.
[96] As above, [1994] 1 F.L.R. 657.
[97] *Per* Ward J. at 665G.
[98] *Per* Ward J. at 665H.
[99] As above, [1999] 1 F.L.R. 152.
[1] At 159H.

11–029   Against the background of these authorities the Court of in *Re P*[2] found that a generous approach to the calculation of the mother's allowance was not only permissible but also realistic. Thorpe L.J. specifically considered the "Norland nanny" comment of Ward J. in *A v A* set out above and found himself unable to agree with that approach and further, unable to agree with the comparison with personal injury or fatal accident act claims. Thorpe L.J. promoted the need for a broad brush assessment to be carried out by family judges with expertise and experience in the specialist field of ancillary relief.[3] He commented that:

> "the mother's entitlement to an allowance as the primary carer (an expression which I stress) may be checked but not diminished by the absence of any direct claim in law"[4]

The court in *Re P* strove to strike a balance between under- and over-provision for the mother and sought to achieve it in two ways. First the court noted that whilst the mother should not be burdened with unnecessary financial anxiety or have to resort to parsimony when the other parent was able to live lavishly, there could be no slack to enable her to fund a pension or an endowment policy or otherwise put money away for a rainy day and that whatever is provided is there to be spent at the expiration of the year for which it is provided. Second, it was suggested as appropriate in some circumstances for the mother to keep relatively detailed accounts of her outgoings and expenditure in the first and succeeding years of receipt of maintenance.[5] As to the first point there is nothing within Sch.1 that requires the sum awarded to be spent at the end of each year and there may be circumstances where it is appropriate to save or budget over a period that is longer than one year. The suggestion also begs the question what happens in any year when there is an under spend.

As to the second point, whilst seemingly sensible in the first instance it is suggested that the idea of the child's carer keeping receipts and accounting for expenditure is problematic. It ties the parties to litigation together in a way that may not be appropriate, it may continue to fuel resentment built up during litigation and possibly promote further litigation which cannot be in the best interests of any child. Neither point gives the mother any incentive to reduce her expenditure.

11–030   Thorpe L.J. from para.45 onwards in *Re P* sets out the method by which, in his view, Sch.1 cases involving parents on the spectrum from affluent to fabulously rich should be dealt with. While the figures may be different there is much to commend this approach to all such cases regardless of the wealth of the parties involved. The first step is for the court to decide the type of home that the respondent should provide for

---

[2] As above.
[3] *Per* Thorpe L.J. at para.43.
[4] *Per* Thorpe L.J. at para.48.
[5] *Per* Thorpe L.J. at para.49.

the benefit of the child. This consideration should include the value, the size, and the location, all of which will have a bearing upon the second consideration, which will be the reasonable capital costs (provided by way of lump sum) for furnishing and redecorating such a property. The home will also then inform the third consideration being the appropriate level of maintenance to be considered with a broad brush. The need for the home will ordinarily be transient during the child's minority and the appropriate legal mechanism is therefore a settlement of property order. Thorpe L.J. commented that given the way the property was normally to be held the respondent must have some right of veto over an unsuitable investment.

In his judgment Bodey J. sets out a useful checklist of criteria to be considered in claims under Sch.1 in the light of para.4 of the Schedule and the authorities at that stage.[6]

In *F v G (Child: Financial Provision)*[7] the court considered how to deal   **11–031**
with the concept that there should be no slack in the maintenance provided by the absent parent as required by *Re P* when a primary carer is earning an income. In this case the mother was earning £37,000 p.a. net and the father was earning £450,000 p.a. net. Should the appropriate level of periodical payments be assessed and then reduced by the amount that the primary carer is earning? If this were to occur then the primary carer has no incentive to work and is unable to make any provision for the future because the appropriate budget has been assessed without scope for her to save or provide for the future in any way. Singer J. solved the question in *F v G* by ordering the mother (primary carer) to pay for the costs of employing a nanny from her own income (costing £24,000 p.a.), allowing her to use the rest of her income as she wished and approaching the assessment of the maintenance award on the basis that she should receive the full primary carer's allowance.[8]

There have been two recent cases in this area both as yet unreported. *Re S (A Child)*,[9] a decision of the Court of Appeal, and *H v M (Child: Financial Provision)*, a decision of Peter Hughes Q.C. sitting as a Deputy High Court Judge in February 2006. The father in *H v M* has been given leave to appeal to the Court of Appeal and at the time of writing the appeal has not yet been heard.

In *Re S* Bennett J. at first instance made an assessment of the father's net worth at £4 million against a background of poor disclosure and in the absence of professional valuations of properties. The applicant mother lived with the child in Knightsbridge in central London where the child attended school. At first instance, Bennett J. had had to decide between the mother's case focussed on Knightsbridge seeking property costing between £1.6 million and £2 million and the father's cases

---

[6] *Per* Bodey J. at paras 76 and 77.
[7] [2005] 1 F.L.R. 261.
[8] *Per* Singer J. at paras 47–53/
[9] [2006] EWCA Civ 479 March 15, 2006, *The Times*, April 17, 2006. Full judgment available on Lawtel.

focussed on Fulham/Parsons Green in South West London with property costing between £500,000–£550,000. He concluded that the appropriate figure was £800,000 for housing inclusive of costs of purchase.

11–032   The Court of Appeal granted the mother permission to appeal on the basis of her challenge to the quantum of the property fund. Counsel for the mother at the appeal advanced an argument based on what he called the four S's — "security, stress, schooling and stability", supporting the mother's case for staying in Knightsbridge where she and the child had always lived and where the child attended school[10] and also on the basis that Bennett J. had inappropriately used the award in *Re P*[11] as a bench mark.

Thorpe L.J. describes himself as troubled by two points. One was the possible misinterpretation of the effect of *Re P* and the second was as to the extent of the judge's focus on the daughter's needs as opposed to the needs of her mother. Bennett J. had recognised correctly according to Thorpe L.J. that the father in *Re P* was at about 9.75 on the scale of worldly riches from 1 to 10 but that *Re P* had not created a ceiling to these awards. However, Bennett J. is criticised for his comment that the award in *Re P* was proportionate to the father's wealth and so must the award be in the current case. Thorpe L.J. considered this was the wrong approach. *Re P* does not provide a benchmark.[12] It is clear that each case must be considered on it's own facts and within its own discretionary sphere.

11–033   As to the second concern of Thorpe L.J., Bennett J. had criticised a number of the mother's reasons for seeking to remain in the Knightsbridge area and was, according to Thorpe L.J., perfectly entitled to hold that the reasons were selfish and an example of the mother's egocentricity. However, Thorpe L.J. felt that Bennett J. should have asked himself what were the daughter's needs as distinct from the mother's and what would the consequence be for her of a loss of the familiar — a home in Knightsbridge, the school in Knightsbridge and friends in Knightsbridge. He says:

> "Perhaps, given the extent of the father's fortune, the judge needed to ask the question: was it necessary for the daughter to move from the familiar, as well as asking, would a move from the familiar risk harm to the daughter's welfare?"[13]

In this case, the Court of Appeal reiterated a call made back in 1994 by Ward J. in *A v A*[14] for the separate representation of children in these cases where, given the bitter dispute between parents, there is a need for an advocate to constantly urge the needs and interest of the child upon the proceedings.[15]

[10] *Per* Thorpe L.J. at paras 7–8.
[11] As above.
[12] *Per* Thorpe L.J. at paras 12–14.
[13] *Per* Thorpe L.J. at para.15.
[14] As above.
[15] *Per* Thorpe L.J. para.17.

The appeal was allowed but the Court of Appeal sought further evidence as to property prices before concluding the appropriate quantum of the housing fund.

The idea that *Re P* should not be a bench mark was further confirmed **11–034** by a recent decision of District Judge Million in the Principal Registry of The Family Division in June 2006 where he ordered the provision of a housing fund of £2 million for a mother and child (to include purchase and refurbishment costs). The mother in that case had sought in the first instance for the father to pay for the rental of a property rather than a purchase. The District Judge considered that in some case rental rather than purchase may be appropriate but not in this particular case.

H v M (Child: Financial Provision) considered a number of issues including the enforceability of an agreement reached outside proceedings, how to treat a primary carers income and pre-existing capital and what to do in circumstances where the primary carer has another child living in their household who is not the child of the respondent.

When considering a pre-existing agreement the court concluded that such an agreement could not oust the statutory jurisdiction of the court but it was integral to the circumstances of the case. It is suggested that it would be difficult to contemplate that a court would give primacy to an agreement over and above the interests of the child. Schedule 1 already gives the court the power to vary maintenance agreements,[16] so the underlying policy of Sch.1 must be that the court should be free to depart from any agreement unless it is satisfied that it makes satisfactory provision. Therefore any agreement would be taken into account but within the wide context of the para.4 criteria. The father has been given leave to appeal to the Court of Appeal on this point and at the time of writing the appeal has not yet been heard.

On the question of the primary carer's own earned income the court expressly agreed with the approach of Singer J in *F v G*[17] in relation to the treatment of the income of primary carers who work. Although the mother in *H v M* was no longer working she had been employed as an international banker with a significant earning capacity. The court considered that if the mother were to work she should meet the extra child care costs associated with that decision and should be able to use any surplus funds for her own lifestyle choices or for her own future. The court also found it appropriate to allow the mother the retain her pre-existing capital (she owned a flat in Paris worth c. £117,000) because the flat represented some level of security for the mother. By doing this the court sought to recognise the responsibility and sacrifice of the unmarried parent as Thorpe L.J. tried to do in *Re P*.

The court also called for a consideration of the rules under which Sch.1 cases proceed through the courts and made a call for the concept of mediation and the introduction of a type of Financial Dispute Resolution

[16] Sch.1 para.10(2) and 10(3) and see above.
[17] As set out above.

hearing in line with the Family Proceedings Rules governing ancillary relief applications under Matrimonial Causes Act 1973.

Funding for legal costs

11–035   In *W v J (Child: Variation of Financial Provision)*[18] Bennett J. considered a mother's application under Sch.1 (or under the court's inherent jurisdiction) to vary a periodical payments order made by consent so as to cover her estimated legal costs in relation to a contested dispute as to residence, leave to remove from the jurisdiction and financial provision for the child. The court considered that "for the benefit of the child" was not wide enough to cover the provision of legal fees and that the court had no power under the inherent jurisdiction to make such an order. This is in contrast to the provision under the Matrimonial Causes Act 1973 which extends the concept of maintenance (pending suit) to cover legal costs to be incurred.

In *Re S (Child: Financial Provision)*[19] the Court of Appeal distinguished *W v J*.[20] In *Re S* a Sudanese mother applied to effectively sequestrate the Sudanese father's only asset in the UK using Sch.1 so as to provide her with money to travel to Sudan for contact with the parties' child whom the father had unlawfully retained in Sudan and to continue the legal process. The mother had instituted legal proceedings for the return of the child both in this jurisdiction and in Sudan. The English court had made orders in the mother's favour on habitual residence issues but did not order return on the basis that the Sudanese court was seized of the matter and competent to determine the issue. *W v J* was distinguished on the basis that the application for money to cover litigation costs in that case had been designed benefit the mother's taste for litigation and not to benefit the child and whilst the decision was right on those extreme facts should not necessarily go beyond those facts. The term "for the benefit of the child" should be given a wide construction and could cover an application for funding to enable one parent to recover a child because such an order could be said, in broad terms and on appropriate facts, to be for the child's benefit.[21]

The question of the funding of legal costs appears to remain open in an appropriate case. There seem to be two possible avenues to make an order that would cover legal costs. One would be by way of an interim periodical payments order in line with orders that can be made within the context of matrimonial proceedings and the other would be the lump sum route. The difficulty with interim periodical payments is that this would apply to very few cases given the inter-relationship between the CSA 1991 and Sch.1 discussed above and the restrictions on the court's power to make a periodical payments order at any time. The lump sum alternative

---

[18] [2004] 2 F.L.R. 300.
[19] [2005] 2 F.L.R. 94.
[20] As above.
[21] *Per* Wall L.J. at para.28.

may fall foul of the restrictions in *Philips v Peace*[22] ensuring that Sch.1 is not used as a back door to receive income by way of lump sum and so alleviate the problems of CSA 1991. This could be resolved if legal costs are considered as expenditure of a capital rather than income nature.

Procedure

Applications under Sch.1 are governed by Part IV of the Family Proceedings Rules 1991 and can be made to the High Court, County Court and Magistrates Court. The application is made by way of Form C1, Form C10 and Form C10A (statement of means) at the appropriate court. The Respondent must answer any application with Form C7 and Form C10A.   **11–036**

The Court of Appeal in *W v W (Joinder of Trusts of Land Act and Child Act Applications)*[23] recognised the need for sensible management of cases brought under both statutory regimes (TLATA and Sch.1). In this case there was no dispute between the unmarried parents of two children as to their respective interests in a jointly owned property but it is suggested that the principles apply equally well to a case where property rights are in issue. Proceedings were commenced by the mother to defer the realisation of the father's share of the property until the youngest child reached the age of 18 or completed full time education. The father sought an immediate order for sale. These stances altered dramatically when a residence order under s.8 of the Children Act 1989 was granted in favour of the father. The father then sought to delay any sale and the mother sought an immediate realisation of her interest. In addition to the TLATA application the father issued an application under Schedule 1 seeking a transfer of the mother's interest in the property to him during the children's minority. At a directions hearing the court refused his application to have the two applications heard together and adjourned his Sch.1 application generally with liberty to restore within four weeks of the determination of the mother's TLATA claim otherwise it would be dismissed. The court went on to order a sale of the property. The father appealed and applied for a restoration of his Sch.1 application on the basis that following the order for sale he did not have sufficient funds to rehouse himself and the children. The Court of Appeal held that it made case management sense for an application under TLATA and an application under Sch.1 involving the same property and parties should, unless there were special reasons why not, be heard together.[24]

Thorpe L.J. considered that leading status should be given to the Sch.1 application as that statute confers more extensive powers upon the court to make adjustive orders between the co-owners.[25] When considering which application should take the lead it should be remembered that   **11–037**

[22] [1996] 2 F.L.R. 230 as set out above.
[23] [2004] 2 F.L.R. 321.
[24] *Per* Thorpe L.J. at para.5.
[25] *Per* Thorpe L.J. at para.5

these comments were made in the context of a TLATA application to delay sale rather than to quantify a beneficial interest. It is very often the case that the beneficial interest of co-owners needs quantifying before an adjustive order can be considered otherwise the court simply does not know whether any adjustment is appropriate or necessary.

Thorpe L.J. commented on the desirability for judicial continuity in cases involving children when saying that it would be highly desirable for the judge who deals with any s.8 of the Children Act 1989 applications should deal with any financial application.[26]

Care is needed when arguing a combined case. In *A v A (A Minor: Financial Provision)*[27] the mother lived in a property with her three children (only one of which was a child of the respondent to the proceedings) that had been purchased by the father through an offshore company over which he had control. The mother argued that the property was purchased with the intention that it be and remain the family home. She sought a declaration that the beneficial interest in the property was hers and that the legal interest should be transferred to her. She also sought orders under Sch.1 in respect of the property. Ward J. (as he then was) was concerned at the dichotomy of the position presented by the mother. He noted that to succeed in her Sch.1 application she had to establish that property concerned was one that the father was entitled to in possession or reversion but she was in fact claiming that she was entitled to the entirety of the beneficial and legal ownership of the property on various trust principles. Ward J. ventured that in such circumstances in may be appropriate for a next friend to be appointed to represent the interests of the child.[28]

11–038   In the light of those comments it is important any dual case is run very carefully. It is not impossible to run a case with the type of obviously dichotomy of the *A v A*[29] argument but the TLATA case must be clearly pleaded and the Sch.1 claim must be put in the alternative. If the claim under TLATA is for the entirety of the equity the Sch.1 claim is issued to be considered by the court if the TLATA claim is not accepted. If the TLATA claim is for a certain percentage of the equity the Sch.1 claim is either in the alternative if the TLATA claim fails or it is added so as to ensure that the claimant/applicant and the child are suitably housed using that person's share of the equity as defined by the TLATA judgment and using the absent parent's share of the equity under Sch.1. Ward J.'s call in *A v A*[30] for separate representation of children when a dual case is being run has not been followed up save in the recent case of *Re S (a child)*.[31]

[26] *Per* Thorpe L.J. at para.17
[27] As above [1994] 1 F.L.R. 657.
[28] *Per* Ward J. at 662A.
[29] As above.
[30] As above.
[31] Unreported [2006] EWCA Civ 479.

Appendix I

PRECEDENTS

A1–001

Transfer of whole **of registered title(s)**	**Land Registry** # TR1

If you need more room than is provided for in a panel, use continuation sheet CS and attach to this form

1. Stamp Duty

Place "X" in the appropriate box or boxes and complete the appropriate certificate.

☐ It is certified that this instrument falls within category ☐ in the Schedule to the Stamp Duty (Exempt Instruments) Regulations 1987

☐ It is certified that the transaction effected does not form part of a larger transaction or of a series of transactions in respect of which the amount or value or the aggregate amount or value of the consideration exceeds the sum of £ ☐

☐ It is certified that this is an instrument on which stamp duty is not chargeable by virtue of the provisions of section 92 of the Finance Act 2001

2. Title Number(s) of the Property *Leave blank if not yet registered.*

3. Property

4. Date

5. Transferor *Give full names and company's registered number if any.*

6. Transferee **for entry on the register** *Give full name(s) and company's registered number, if any. For Scottish companies use an SC prefix and for limited liability partnerships use an OC prefix before the registered number, if any. For foreign companies give territory in which incorporated.*

Unless otherwise arranged with Land Registry headquarters, a certified copy of the Transferee's constitution (in English or Welsh) will be required if it is a body corporate but is not a company registered in England and Wales or Scotland under the Companies Acts.

7. Transferee's intended **address(es) for service (including postcode) for entry on the register** *You may give up to three addresses for service **one** of which **must** be a postal address but does not have to be within the UK. The other addresses can be any combination of a postal address, a box number at a UK document exchange or an electronic address.*

8. **The Transferor transfers the Property to the Transferee**

9. Consideration *Place "X" in the appropriate box. State clearly the currency unit if other than sterling. If none of the boxes applies, insert an appropriate memorandum in the additional provisions panel.*

☐ The Transferor has received from the Transferee for the Property the sum of *In words and figures.*

☐ *Insert other receipt as appropriate.*

☐ The transfer is not for money or anything which has a monetary value

10. The Transferor transfers with *Place "X" in the appropriate box and add any modifications.*

☐ full title guarantee ☐ limited title guarantee

11. Declaration of trust *Where there is more than one Transferee, place "X" in the appropriate box.*

☐ The Transferees are to hold the Property on trust for themselves as joint tenants

☐ The Transferees are to hold the Property on trust for themselves as tenants in common in equal shares

☐ The Transferees are to hold the Property *Complete as necessary.*

12. Additional provisions *Insert here any required or permitted statements, certificates or applications and any agreed covenants, declarations, etc.*

13. Execution *The Transferor must execute this transfer as a deed using the space below. If there is more than one Transferor, all must execute. Forms of execution are given in Schedule 9 to the Land Registration Rules 2003. If the transfer contains Transferee's covenants or declarations or contains an application by the Transferee (e.g. for a restriction), it must also be executed by the Transferee (all of them, if there is more than one).*

A1–002

Application to enter
a restriction

Land Registry
RX1

If you need more room than is provided for in a panel, use continuation sheet CS and attach to this form.

1. **Administrative area and postcode** if known
2. **Title number(s)**
3. If you have already made this application by **outline application**, insert reference number:
4. **Property** *Insert address or other description.* The restriction applied for is to affect *Place "X" in the appropriate box and complete as necessary.* ☐ the whole of each registered estate ☐ the part(s) of the registered estate(s) shown on the attached plan by *State reference e.g. "edged red".* ☐ the registered charge(s) dated   in favour of referred to in the Charges Register

5. **Application and fee** *A fee calculator for all types of applications can be found on Land Registry's website at www.landregistry.gov.uk/fees* **Restriction** Fee paid £ **Fee payment method:** *Place "X" in the appropriate box.* I wish to pay the appropriate fee payable under the current Land Registration Fee Order: ☐ by cheque or postal order, amount £ _____ made payable to "Land Registry". ☐ by Direct Debit under an authorised agreement with Land Registry.	FOR OFFICIAL USE ONLY Record of fee paid Particulars of under/over payment Fees debited £ Reference number

6. **Documents lodged with this application** *If this application is accompanied by either Form AP1 or FR1 please only complete the corresponding panel on Form AP1 or DL. Number the documents in sequence; copies should also be numbered and listed as separate documents, alternatively you may prefer to use Form DL. If you supply the original document and a certified copy, we shall assume that you request the return of the original; if a certified copy is not supplied, we may retain the original document and it may be destroyed.*

7. **The applicant is:** *Please provide the full name of the person applying for the restriction.* **The application has been lodged by:** Land Registry Key No. (if appropriate) Name (if different from the applicant) Address/DX No. Reference E-mail	FOR OFFICIAL USE ONLY Codes Dealing Status
Telephone No. Fax No.	

8. Where you would like us to deal with someone else *We shall deal only with the applicant, or the person lodging the application if different, unless you place "X" against one or more of the statements below and give the necessary details.*

☐ Send title information document to the person shown below

☐ Raise any requisitions or queries with the person shown below

☐ Return original documents lodged with this form (see note in panel 6) to the person shown below
If this applies only to certain documents, please specify.

Name
Address/DX No.

Reference
E-mail

Telephone No.	Fax No.

9. Entitlement to apply for a restriction *Place "X" in the appropriate box.*

☐ The applicant is the registered proprietor of the registered estate/charge referred to in panel 4.

☐ The applicant is the person **entitled** to be registered as proprietor of the registered estate/charge referred to in panel 4. **Complete panel 12.**

☐ The consent of the registered proprietor of the registered estate/charge referred to in panel 4 accompanies this application or the applicant's conveyancer certifies that he holds this consent. **Complete panel 11.**

☐ The consent of the person **entitled** to be registered as proprietor of the registered estate/charge referred to in panel 4 accompanies this application or the applicant's conveyancer certifies that he holds this consent. **Complete panels 11 and 12.**

☐ Evidence that the applicant has sufficient interest in the making of the entry of the restriction applied for in panel 10 accompanies this application. **Complete panel 13.**

10. The applicant applies to enter the following restriction against the registered estate/charge referred to in panel 4: *Please set out the form of restriction required. Schedule 4 to the Land Registration Rules 2003 contains standard forms of restrictions. Use this form to apply for a standard form of restriction (as set out in Schedule 4 to the Land Registration Rules 2003) or, where appropriate, a restriction in another form. If the restriction is not a standard form of restriction, the registrar must be satisfied that the terms of the proposed restriction are reasonable and that applying the proposed restriction would be straightforward and not place an unreasonable burden on him. If the restriction requires notice to be given to a person, requires a person's consent or certificate or is a standard form restriction that refers to a named person, include that person's address for service.*

11. Evidence of consent *Please complete this panel if instructed to do so in panel 9. Place "X" in the appropriate box.*

☐ The [registered proprietor of][person entitled to be registered as the proprietor of] the registered estate/charge referred to in panel 4 consents to the entry of the restriction and that person or their conveyancer has completed panel 15.

☐ I am the applicant's conveyancer and certify that I hold the consent referred to in panel 9.

☐ The consent referred to in panel 9 is contained on page___of the document numbered ___ referred to in [panel 6][Form AP1][Form DL].

12. Evidence of entitlement to be registered as proprietor *Please complete this panel if instructed to do so in panel 9. Place "X" in the appropriate box.*

☐ I am the applicant's conveyancer and certify that I am satisfied that the applicant/person consenting to this application is entitled to be registered as proprietor and that I hold the originals of the documents that contain evidence of that person's entitlement, or an application for registration of that person as proprietor is pending at Land Registry.

☐ Evidence that the applicant/person consenting to this application is entitled to be registered as proprietor is contained in the document(s) numbered ___ referred to in [panel 6][Form AP1][Form DL].

13. Evidence that the applicant has sufficient interest *Please complete this panel if instructed to do so in panel 9.*

State brief details of the applicant's interest in the making of the entry of the restriction applied for in panel 10.

Evidence of this interest is contained in the document(s) numbered referred to in [panel 6] [Form AP1][Form DL].

14. Signature of applicant
or their conveyancer .... Date ....

15. Consent
Consent to the entry of the restriction specified in panel 10 is given by:

Names *BLOCK LETTERS*	Signatures
1.	1.
2.	2.
3.	3.

Witness statement of the Claimant   **A1–003**
Miss Catherine Smith
First Witness Statement
Dated this day of   200

IN THE IPSWICH COUNTY COURT   <u>CLAIM NO</u>
BETWEEN:

MISS CATHERINE SMITH   <u>Claimant</u>

-and-

MR JONATHAN TAYLOR   <u>Defendant</u>

WITNESS STATEMENT OF CATHERINE SMITH

---

1. I was born on 22nd June 1974 and am therefore 31 years old. The Defendant was born in 3rd March 1970 and so he is 35 years old. I have one child, Chloe Jane Taylor who was born on 13th March 2002 and is therefore 3 ½ years old. The Defendant is Chloe's father. Chloe and I are currently living at Flat 3, Constable Road, Ipswich, Suffolk as guests of my friend Victoria Green.

2. I met the Defendant in July 1995. I had just graduated from Aberystwyth University with a degree in English and I had returned to live with my parents in Enfield. I was 22 years old and the Defendant was 26 years old.

3. In September 1995 I started my Post Graduate Certificate in Education (PGCE) at North London Polytechnic. I was training to be a primary school teacher. The Defendant was working for Genius Insurance in their London office. He was living in a rented flat in Barnet and I think that he was earning about £21,000. As our relationship developed I spent a couple of nights a week at his flat usually at the weekends.

4. At about the same time that I started my PGCE the Defendant was transferred from the Genius Insurance London office to their Ipswich office – this involved a promotion as well. He started working in Ipswich in November 1995 and lived in a flat sorted out by the company.

5. The Defendant and I talked about how our relationship was going to work out with me in Enfield and him in Ipswich. We very much wanted to be together but we both thought that it was sensible for me to finish my course and then I could move to Ipswich and apply for a job there. In the meantime we would buy a property in Ipswich that would be our home and we would spend our weekends there

together. The Defendant said that it would be much better to buy a property together rather than renting somewhere. This was perfect as my mother and father didn't like the Defendant staying with me at their house.

6. As agreed I spent every weekend in Ipswich and we looked at a number of houses together – I think we looked at about eight in all. I collected the local newspapers each weekend and suggested properties and the Defendant made the appointments with the estate agents.

7. When we looked at 1 Gainsborough Road we both knew that it was perfect. He said to me "I like that – why don't we buy it". The purchase price was agreed at £79,950. The Defendant was able to pay the deposit of £8,000 as he had been given some money by his parents. I had savings of about £5,000 at the time but we agreed that I should keep those as I was still studying and might need them. I did pay £500 to the solicitors who dealt with the purchase. We took out a mortgage for the rest of the purchase price of £71,950 with Suffolk Building Society.

8. I told him that I was concerned because I had no income and was still studying but he said "Don't worry about that, my salary will cover the mortgage for us." Because I had no income, the mortgage had to be in his sole name and so did the property. It is clear to me that we agreed that we would own the property jointly.

9. I graduated from my PGCE course and got a job in a primary school in Ipswich to start in September 1996. I was earning about £16,000. I moved in to the property in August 1996. By this time the Defendant was earning about £26,000 per annum.

10. When I moved in the Defendant was paying the mortgage and I bought all of the food for us. I also gave the Defendant £25 per week to cover my contribution to the outgoings on the property. This carried on until January 1999.

11. When I moved in the house was in a bit of a state. I organised and paid for redecorating. I repainted the sitting room and bedrooms and my father put up some shelves for us. The total cost was about £1,500. The money for this came from my savings. I also used my savings to purchase a three piece suite for about £1,000.

12. In January 1999 we finally got round to setting up a joint bank account with the Colchester Building Society. We each paid our salaries into this account and the mortgage and all of the outgoings for the property were paid for out of this account.

13. In about February 1999 the Defendant was sacked by Genius Insurance because they accused him of not fulfilling his targets properly. This was a very worrying time for us. The Defendant did

not accept the reasons why he was sacked and he claimed unfair dismissal. His claim was successful and in December 1999 he was paid £15,000 by Genius as compensation.

14. Because the Defendant was not earning it became my responsibility to meet all of the expenses on the house including the mortgage, outgoings and all of our food bills. I used up the rest of my savings and my salary to do this.

15. The Defendant tried to find a new job but with the unfair dismissal claim hanging over him this was difficult so he decided to set up his own business as an Independent Financial Advisor.

16. When he received his £15,000 he used some of it to carry out so advertising for his business. He also spent £10,000 on a conservatory for the property. I wasn't keen on this idea – I thought that we should save this money but the Defendant thought that it would add value to the property.

17. By the middle of 2000 the Defendant was earning about £12,000 from this business but the earnings were very on and off and the main responsibility for paying the mortgage rested upon me.

18. On 24th December 2000 the Defendant gave me a ring and we agreed to get married. He had just received a good commission on a deal so he could afford a ring. We didn't fix a date for actually getting married but I was very pleased to be engaged. I know that the Defendant says that we were not engaged and I find this very upsetting. He gave me a ring and we talked about marriage. It was clear to me and our family and friends that we were engaged. We celebrated on Christmas Day with our families and went out for a drink with some friends on Boxing Day. We were definitely engaged.

19. In June 2001 I realised that I was pregnant. I was very pleased but our relationship was hitting a rocky patch at the time and the Defendant suggested that the baby was not his. He moved out for a short period but we got back together after about a month. Chloe was born in March 2002. I stopped working in December 2001 and I returned to work 3 days per week in September 2002.

20. We patched up our relationship and we were still engaged. We had further problems in 2004 and the Defendant started alleging that I was having an affair – this was and is not true. He also wanted me to work full time but I wanted to keep working for 3 days to spend time with Chloe. I couldn't take this any more and I moved out of the property in September 2004.

21. Since I moved out Chloe and I have been put up by my friend Victoria Green who is a fellow teacher with me. She is not charging me rent at the moment but I am contributing to the general outgoings.

22. I want to be able to purchase my own property as a home for myself
     and Chloe. I cannot do this until I receive the monies due to me from
     the property.

23. I estimate that the property is now worth about £205,000. The
     mortgage is about £68,000 and so the equity is about £130,000 if the
     costs of sale are taken into account. I ask for a declaration that I
     have a 50% beneficial interest in the property, an order that the
     property be sold and the proceeds of sale divided equally.

Statement of Truth

I believe that the contents of this witness statement are true.

Signed..
          Miss Catherine Smith

Dated...

	In the	
Claim Form		
		for court use only
Click here to clear your data after printing	Claim No.	
	Issue date	

Claimant

SEAL

Defendant(s)

Brief details of claim

Value

			£
Defendant's name and address		Amount claimed	
		Court fee	
		Solicitor's costs	
		Total amount	

The court office at

is open between 10 am and 4 pm Monday to Friday. When corresponding with the court, please address forms or letters to the Court Manager and quote the claim number.

N1 Claim form (CPR Part 7) (01.02)   *Printed on behalf of The Court Service*

	Claim No.	

Does, or will, your claim include any issues under the Human Rights Act 1998? ☐ Yes ☐ No

Particulars of Claim (attached)(to follow)

Statement of Truth
*(I believe)(The Claimant believes) that the facts stated in these particulars of claim are true.
* I am duly authorised by the claimant to sign this statement

Full name

Name of claimant's solicitor's firm

signed   position or office held
*(Claimant)(Litigation friend)(Claimant's solicitor)   (if signing on behalf of firm or company)
*delete as appropriate

Claimant's or claimant's solicitor's address to which documents or payments should be sent if different from overleaf including (if appropriate) details of DX, fax or e-mail.

IN THE IPSWICH COUNTY COURT   **CLAIM NO:**   **A1–005**

BETWEEN:

MISS CATHERINE SMITH   <u>Claimant</u>

-and-

MR JONATHAN TAYLOR   <u>Defendant</u>

PARTICULARS OF CLAIM

---

1.   In or about July 1995 the Claimant and the Defendant began a relationship. The Claimant was then residing with her parents in Enfield and the Defendant was residing in private rented accommodation in Barnet.

2.   The Claimant had graduated from university in June 1995 and in September 1995 commenced her Post Graduate Certificate in Education ("PGCE") in order to qualify as a primary school teacher. The Defendant was working for an insurance company in London and earned approximately £21,000 per annum.

3.   In about November 1995 the Defendant was transferred to work in Ipswich and the Claimant and Defendant decided that they would like to purchase a property together in Ipswich.

4.   It was expressly agreed between the Claimant and the Defendant that the new house would be shared equally between them in various conversations prior to deciding upon the purchase of the new property at 1 Gainsborough Road, Ipswich, IP3 2DK, title number IP2 3456 ("the property").

PARTICULARS

(a)   When the Defendant informed the Claimant about his transfer to Ipswich in or about 15th November 1995 he said to her, "We should buy a property together, rather than renting somewhere."

(b)   Having looked at the property with the Claimant, the Defendant said to her, "I like that, why don't we buy it."

(c)   When the Claimant raised the fact that she was still studying and consequently had little income, the Defendant said, "Don't worry about that, my salary will cover the mortgage for us."

5.   The property was purchased for £79,950. The deposit of £8,000 was provided by the Defendant. £71,950 was provided by way of mortgage advanced by the Suffolk Building Society into the Defendant's sole name and secured upon the property.

6.   The purchase of the property completed in January 1996.

A1–006

| Click here to reset form | Click here to print form |

Response Pack

You should read the 'notes for defendant' attached to the claim form which will tell you when and where to send the forms

Included in this pack are:

- either **Admission Form N9A** (if the claim is for a specified amount) or **Admission Form N9C** (if the claim is for an unspecified amount or is not a claim for money)
- either **Defence and Counterclaim Form N9B** (if the claim is for a specified amount) or **Defence and Counterclaim Form N9D** (if the claim is for an unspecified amount or is not a claim for money)
- **Acknowledgment of service** (see below)

Complete

If you admit the claim or the amount claimed and/or you want time to pay	the admission form
If you admit part of the claim	the admission form and the defence form
If you dispute the whole claim or wish to make a claim (a counterclaim) against the claimant	the defence form
If you need 28 days (rather than 14) from the date of service to prepare your defence, or wish to contest the court's jurisdiction	the acknowledgment of service
If you do nothing, judgment may be entered against you	

Acknowledgment of Service

Defendant's full name if different from the name given on the claim form

In the	
Claim No.	
Claimant (including ref.)	
Defendant	

Address to which documents about this claim should be sent (including reference if appropriate)

	if applicable
	fax no.
	DX no.
	Ref. no.
Tel. no. Postcode	e-mail

Tick the appropriate box

1. I intend to defend all of this claim ☐

2. I intend to defend part of this claim ☐

3. I intend to contest jurisdiction ☐

(My) (Defendant's) date of birth is [D D M M Y Y Y Y]

If you file an acknowledgment of service but do not file a defence within 28 days of the date of service of the claim form, or particulars of claim if served separately, judgment may be entered against you.

If you do not file an application to dispute the jurisdiction of the court within 14 days of the date of filing this acknowledgment of service, it will be assumed that you accept the court's jurisdiction and judgment may be entered against you.

Signed		Position or office held		

(Defendant)(Defendant's solicitor)(Litigation friend)   (if signing on behalf of firm or company)

Date

The court office at

is open between 10 am and 4 pm Monday to Friday. When corresponding with the court, please address forms or letters to the Court Manager and quote the claim number.

N9 Response Pack (04.06)   HMCS

IN THE IPSWICH COUNTY COURT   **CLAIM NO:**   **A1–007**

BETWEEN:

MISS CATHERINE SMITH   <u>Claimant</u>

-and-

MR JONATHAN TAYLOR   <u>Defendant</u>

DEFENCE AND PART 20 CLAIM

DEFENCE

1. Paragraph 1 of the Particulars of Claim herein is admitted.

2. Paragraph 2 of the Particulars of Claim is admitted, save that the Defendant will contend that he was earning around £26,000 p.a. The figure of £21,000 represented his approximate net income at that time.

3. Save that it is admitted that the Defendant was transferred to work in Ipswich in November 1995, Paragraph 3 of the Particulars of Claim is expressly and specifically denied. The Defendant will contend that he alone decided to purchase a property in Ipswich. Save to the extent that she was the Defendant's girlfriend and took an interest in the property which her boyfriend proposed to buy, the Claimant had no involvement or connection with the purchase, either pursuant to an agreement arrangement or understanding that the property would be purchased together, or otherwise.

5. Paragraph 4 of the Particulars of Claim is denied. No conversations of any sort took place in which it was agreed, suggested or contemplated that the Claimant would have any proprietary interest in the property. Without prejudice to the generality of the foregoing, the Defendant will say in response to the particulars pleaded at paragraph 4 of the Particulars of Claim:

    (a) The Defendant and the Claimant discussed the issue of the Defendant's accommodation on a number of occasions prior to the Defendant taking up his new post in November 1995. The thrust of those discussions was always that the Defendant intended to rent a room or a flat for the initial period with a view to purchasing a property as soon as was practicable, once he had familiarised himself with the Ipswich area.

    (b) The Claimant went to view the property externally without the Claimant four days before the Claimant and the Defendant visited the property with the selling agent. The Claimant accompanied the Defendant on such viewing not in the character of a prospective purchaser but in the character of the

Defendant's girlfriend. It was understood by the Claimant and the Defendant that the Claimant would stay with the Defendant from time to time; the Claimant's interest and concern in the process of the selection and purchase of a house by the Defendant had no greater significance than that. The Defendant revisited the property in the week after he had seen it with the Claimant. It was only then that he decided to make an offer for the property. The Defendant will aver that at the relevant time it was not known whether the Claimant would obtain employment in Ipswich upon completion of her studies. The Claimant did not engage in any discussions as to the general location of the property, such as the area in which the Defendant should purchase a property, whether in Ipswich itself or in an outlying village, transport connections, local amenities and so forth.

(c) The Claimant and the Defendant did discuss their finances prior to the purchase. The Claimant pointed out that the cost of travelling from London to Ipswich each weekend would consume a very large proportion of her available income, which was very low at that time as the Claimant was still a student. The Defendant pointed out that even after he had paid the mortgage and other costs of living in the property, his salary would still provide a level of disposable income with which could be used to fund a reasonable social life for the Defendant and the Claimant. The Defendant expressly denies the conversation alleged at paragraph 5(c) of the Particulars of Claim.

6. Paragraph 5, 6 and 7 of the Particulars of Claim are admitted.

7. As to paragraph 8 of the Particulars of Claim, the Defendant responds as follows:
    (a) it is admitted that the Claimant provided the Defendant with approximately £500 which he used towards the payment of the legal fees connected to the purchase. The Defendant will contend that this payment was expressly understood to be in the manner of a loan, which the Defendant needed as he had miscalculated the amount which he would need to spend on removal costs, provision of certain fixtures and fittings (e.g. kitchen shelves and a bathroom cabinet) domestic appliances (such as a refrigerator and a washing machine) and so forth. The Defendant had previously lived in rented property and did not own any items such as a kettle or a toaster. It is specifically denied that the Claimant relied upon the agreement alleged in the Particulars of Claim or any other agreement in providing the sum of £500. It is a pure accident of fortune that the Claimant paid for the legal expenses rather than, for instance, any electrical items. Such actions do not and should not be taken to evidence any common intention that the beneficial interest in the property was to be shared;
    (b) The Claimant purchased some but not all of the food for herself and the Defendant. The Defendant will contend that the Claimant is a vegetarian and that she refused to buy meat products.

The Defendant used to buy his own meat. The Defendant and the Claimant shared the burden of grocery shopping. Sometimes it was convenient for the Claimant to pay, sometimes not.

(c) The payment of £25 per week was agreed by the Claimant and the Defendant to be 'sort of rent'.

(d) Paragraph 8(d) of the Particulars of Claim is admitted, although the Claimant is put to strict proof of the amount spent. It is denied that such expenditure evidences any intention or understanding on the part of the parties that the Claimant had or should have an interest. More specifically, the Defendant will contend: The Claimant took it upon herself to redecorate certain rooms (namely the kitchen, bathroom, living room and main bedroom) because she thought the decor (which the Defendant had not altered since acquiring the property) was 'vile'. The Claimant's father came to visit the property one weekend and offered to put up some shelves that the Defendant had proposed to put up himself as the Defendant unexpectedly needed to work over the weekend. The Claimant was not asked to decorate the property by the Defendant, nor was it understood that in so doing the Claimant would acquire an interest in the property. The Defendant will aver that the Claimant only decorated the rooms in which she herself spent any appreciable periods of time. The dining room was used by the Defendant as a study and was never decorated by the Defendant. The second bedroom was not decorated by the Claimant until shortly before the birth of Chloe in 2002. The Defendant admits that any soft furnishings purchased in or about 1996/7 by the Claimant are her property absolutely.

(e) The Defendant denies that the purchase by the Claimant of soft furnishings evidences any agreement arrangement or understanding that the Claimant should have a proprietary interest in the property.

8.   Paragraph 9 of the Particulars of Claim is admitted.

9.   Save that it is averred that in September 1996 the Defendant was earning approximately £26,000 net per annum, paragraph 10 of the Particulars of Claim is admitted.

10. It is not admitted that in about January 1999 the Claimant and Defendant opened a joint account with the Colchester Savings Bank Plc as alleged at paragraph 11 of the Particulars of Claim, and the Claimant is put to strict proof of the matters therein alleged. The Defendant will contend that he had opened a bank account in his sole name under account number 25368852 with the Colchester Savings Bank Plc upon first moving to Ipswich in late 1995. The mortgage repayments and utility bills were paid out of that account. In about February 1999 the account in the Defendant's sole name was converted into a joint account bearing the same account number because in the difficult financial circumstances which then existed, it was agreed that as a short term measure the Claimant's income

would be used to meet necessary household expenses. The Defendant refers further in this regard to paragraph 16 below.

15. Paragraph 12 of the Particulars of Claim is admitted.

16. Paragraph 13 of the Particulars of Claim is denied. The Defendant's personal bank account was converted into a joint bank account in the circumstances pleaded at paragraph 14 above. The Claimant arranged for her salary was paid into that account. The Claimant faced the prospect of becoming homeless in the event that the Defendant could not pay the mortgage and agreed with the Defendant in early 1999 that she would make available her salary to the Defendant in order to ensure that the property was not repossessed. The said arrangement in no way was intended or understood by the parties to create or evidence a proprietary interest in the property in favour of the Claimant. By the end of 1999 the Defendant had secured alternative employment at a salary comparable to that which he had enjoyed in his previous employment, and indicated that the Claimant should make use of the debit card linked to the joint account (into which the Defendant's salary was paid) until she felt she had been fairly compensated for the period in which hers was the sole income in the household. In a conversation in about June 2001 the Defendant pointed out that the amount the Claimant had spent on items for herself in the preceding 18 months such as clothes, personal electrical equipment (such as a laptop computer) books and a weekend away with a friend visiting a health farm, was approximately double the amount which had been used from the Claimant's income to defray household expenditure during the Defendant's period of unemployment in 1999. The Claimant admitted this by saying 'I think we're about quits now.'

17. It is denied that the parties became engaged to be married on 24th December 2000 as alleged at paragraph 14 of the Particulars of Claim or at all. In November 2000 the Defendant asked the Claimant what she would like for Christmas. The period of slightly less than two years between December 1998 about September 2000 had been difficult financially for both parties and the Defendant was pleased that the difficult period appeared to be at an end. He asked whether the Claimant would prefer a substantial present for Christmas or a long haul holiday and the Claimant indicated she would like a ring. The ring was selected by the Claimant and the Defendant together on Christmas Eve 2000. It was wrapped by the Defendant and given to the Claimant the next day at the Claimant's parents' house where the parties had agreed to spend Christmas Day. To the Defendant's surprise, the Claimant placed the ring on the third finger of her left hand. When selecting the ring at the jewellers the Claimant had tried the ring on the third finger of her right hand. The Claimant's family took the ring as a sign of the parties' engagement, and to avoid humiliating the Claimant before her family the Defendant did not correct their misapprehension. At no time did the Defendant ever ask the Claimant to marry him. The

parties never made enquiries as to wedding venues, or agreed to set a date, or undertook any other activity consistent with being engaged. The Claimant told the Defendant, after she became pregnant with Chloe in the summer of 2001, that she felt more comfortable wearing a ring of some sort on the third finger of her left hand.

18. Paragraph 15 of the Particulars of Claim is admitted.

19. Paragraph 16 of the Particulars of Claim is admitted.

20. The Defendant denies that the Claimant is entitled to an order for the sale of the property as alleged at paragraph 17 of the Particulars of Claim or at all.

22. As to paragraph 18 of the Particulars of Claim, if, which is denied, there was any understanding arrangement or agreement between the parties concerning the existence of a beneficial interest in the property in favour of the Claimant, the Defendant will contend that the Claimant has placed no reliance upon such. The Claimant is put to strict proof of the matters pleaded in Paragraph 18.

23. It is specifically and expressly denied that there is in the circumstances to be inferred a common intention of the Claimant and the Defendant that the Defendant should hold the property upon trust of land for the Claimant and himself as alleged in the Particulars of Claim or at all.

24. In the premises it is denied that the Claimant is entitled to the relief claimed or any.

PART 20 CLAIM

25. The Defendant repeats paragraphs 1 to 23 inclusive above.

26. It was never agreed or understood between the Claimant and the Defendant that the Claimant would have any beneficial interest in the property. Without prejudice to the generality of the foregoing, the Defendant will contend:
    (i)   Defendant purchased the property at a time when the relationship between the parties was in its relevant infancy, at a time when the parties neither knew whether their relationship would survive the strains imposed by living some 80 miles apart from each other, nor whether the Claimant would obtain employment in the area in which the property was located. There was no intention at that time and in those circumstances which was common to the parties to the effect that the Claimant would have any interest in the property.
    (ii) Such payments as have been made by the Claimant towards the cost of purchasing or running the property have been either been in the manner of a loan, and have subsequently been

reimbursed to the Claimant, or have been in the manner of a contribution by the Claimant towards the cost of living in the Defendant's property, and have been applied by the Defendant accordingly.

(iii) The Claimant never made any contribution towards repairs or renewals in relation to the property. For instance, whenever the boiler broke down (which frequently occurred in the winter of 1996/7) it was always the Defendant's responsibility to ensure that it was fixed. Whenever the fuses were blown, or the drains, gutters or toilet became blocked, or floorboards became loose, it was always the responsibility of the Defendant to make good the defect.

(iv) Before the Claimant secured employment in or about the summer of 1996, she had discussed with the Defendant the possibility of living with the Defendant and claiming housing benefit. The Claimant cannot now be heard to assert an interest in the property in circumstances where she had proposed to claim a financial benefit which should only have been made available to her if she did not have any interest in the property.

27. If, which is denied, the Claimant is found to have made a financial contribution to the purchase of the property, the Defendant denies that such payment evidences a common intention that the parties should each enjoy a beneficial interest in the property, and avers that it was plainly understood by both that the Claimant did not enjoy any interest in the property.

28. Further or alternatively, if the Claimant has construed the arrangements in place between the parties from November 1996 onwards as indicating an intention of the Defendant's part that she should enjoy a beneficial interest in the property, such construction is unreasonable and the Claimant cannot rely upon such construction in support of her claim to a proprietary interest.

29. In the circumstances, the Claimant has no beneficial interest in the property

AND the Defendant claims:

1. A declaration that the Defendant is the sole beneficial owner of the freehold property and the net proceeds of sale thereof.
2. An order that the Defendant pay the costs of this application.

Dated this   day of   200

Statement of Truth

*[I believe] [The Defendant believes] that the facts stated in this Statement of Case are true.
*I am duly authorised by the Defendant to sign this statement.

Full name...
Name of Defendant's solicitor's firm......................................
Signed..
*[Defendant][Defendant's solicitor]
*delete as appropriate

Address for receiving documents
Insert address

Solicitors for the Defendant

A1–008

Claim Form
(CPR Part 8)

In the	SHEFFIELD COUNTY COURT
Claim No.	

Claimant

Miss Helen Jones
2 Field Crescent,
Sheffield
S12 3AP

SEAL

Defendant(s)

Mr. Neil Alan Green
12 Kensington Gardens,
Sheffield
S30 5DF

Does your claim include any issues under the Human Rights Act 1998?　　☐ Yes　　☒ No

Details of claim *(see also overleaf)*

The Claimant brings this claim under the Trusts of Land and Appointment of Trustees Act 1996 in respect of the property known as 12 Kensington Gardens, Sheffield S30 5DF, title number SYK67890 ("the property").

The Claimant seeks the following:

(1) a declaration that she has a beneficial interest in the property;
(2) an order for sale of the property;
(3) a declaration that the net proceeds of sale be divided equally between the Claimant and Defendant or in such shares as the court may deem fit;
(4) further or other relief and
(5) costs.

	£
Defendant's name and address	
Mr. Neil Alan Green 12 Kensington Gardens, Sheffield, S30 5DF	

	£
Court fee	
Solicitor's costs	
Issue date	

The court office at

is open between 10 am and 4 pm Monday to Friday. When corresponding with the court, please address forms or letters to the Court Manager and quote the case number.

N208 Claim form (CPR Part 8) (October 2000)

Crown Copyright. Reproduced by Sweet & Maxwell Ltd.

Claim No.	

Details of claim *(continued)*

See witness statement attached.

Statement of Truth

I believe that the facts stated in these particulars of claim are true.

Full name   Helen Jones

Name of claimant's solicitor's firm   Fairwood's

signed

Claimant

Fairwood's Solicitors
13 Park View,
Sheffield
S1 3ER
DX: SHEFFIELD 23456

Claimant's or claimant's solicitor's address to
which documents should be sent if different
from overleaf. If you are prepared to accept
service by DX, fax or e-mail, please add details.

Witness statement of the Claimant
Miss H. Jones
First Witness Statement
Exhibit HJ1
Dated this day of 2006

IN THE SHEFFIELD COUNTY COURT   **CLAIM NO:**

BETWEEN:

MISS HELEN JONES   Claimant

-and-

MR NEIL ALAN GREEN   Defendant

WITNESS STATEMENT OF THE CLAIMANT

I, HELEN JONES of 2 Field Crescent, Sheffield S12 3AP make this statement in support of my application under the Trusts of Land and Appointment of Trustees Act 1996 for a declaration that I have a beneficial interest in the property known as 12 Kensington Gardens, Sheffield, S30 5DF, title number SYK67890 ("the property"), an order for sale of the property and a declaration that the net proceeds of sale be divided equally between myself and the Defendant or in such shares as the court may deem fit.

1. I met the Defendant in 1997 through one of my friends whilst I was still at school. I was just 16 and he was 18. When he left school he had started working as a carpet fitter. I left school and started work at the Travel Lodge in Sheffield city centre. I was working full time. At this point we were both living with our respective parents.

2. In about 1999, however, the Defendant fell out with his parents over him staying out late at night and returning home in a drunken state. At this point we therefore decided that we would rent a property together and we began to live together. We rented a property in Hood Green, Sheffield from a private landlord pursuant to an assured shorthold tenancy. We each contributed to the rent and bills more or less equally.

3. In September 2001 I discovered that I was pregnant. I carried on working until December 2001 but had to stop due to difficulties with my pregnancy. At about this time we decided that we would purchase a property together.

4. Both the Defendant and I agreed that we would purchase the property together as it was to be a family home for ourselves and our new baby. I went with the Defendant to most of the appointments

with the bank and the solicitors regarding the purchase of the property and we were both told them that we wanted to buy the property together.

5. When the documents came back, however, my name was not on them. I was surprised but didn't think anything more about it because I was having a difficult pregnancy and was due to give birth very soon. The purchase of the property completed on about 12th April 2002. The purchase price was approximately £42,000. Neil's father supplied the deposit of about £4,000. The mortgage with the Halifax was for £38,000.

6. I gave birth to Samuel Neil Green ("Sammy") on 22nd June 2002. After Sammy's birth I stayed at home to look after him whilst Neil went out to work. I did all the cooking, cleaning and housework. I did a significant amount of decorating at the property including painting and wallpapering it from top to bottom. I did all this because I believed that the property was our family home. I can honestly say that if we had still been renting or I did not think that the property was not as much mine as it was Neil's I would not have done half the work I did on it.

7. I was in receipt of Family Tax Credits. The only account that we had was our joint account. The Tax Credits would go into that, as well as Neil's wage.

8. On 10th September 2003 I went back to work part time. My salary was paid weekly into our joint account. The monies in the joint bank account were pooled to pay for all the outgoings including the mortgage, utility bills, food etc. I refer the court to the bank statements for the joint bank account, exhibited hereto marked "HJ1".

9. In late 2004 Neil became depressed and less interested in working and in January 2005 he just stopped work. At that time, therefore, I started to work full time in order to pay the bills and mortgage. From January to June 2005 when we separated Neil did not contribute anything to the household finances, including the mortgage. I funded everything myself.

10. Neil had been violent towards me throughout the relationship but at this point the violence increased and in June 2005 I had to attend the Casualty department of the Royal Hallamshire Hospital due to the injuries he had caused me. I took Sammy and went to live at my Grandma's and never returned.

11. I now seek a declaration that that I have a beneficial interest in the property known as 12 Kensington Gardens, Sheffield, S30 5DF, an order for sale of the property, a declaration that the net proceeds of sale be divided equally between myself and the Defendant or in such shares as the court may deem fit and costs.

Statement of Truth

I believe that the contents of this witness statement are true.

Signed...

       Miss Helen Jones

Dated..

Acknowledgment of Service
(Part 8 claim)

click here to clear all text after printing

You should read the 'notes for defendant' attached to the claim form which will tell you how to complete this form, and when and where to send it.

In the	
Claim No.	
Claimant (including ref)	
Defendant	

Tick and complete sections A - E as appropriate.
In all cases you must complete sections F and G

Section A

☐ **I do not** intend to contest this claim

Give details of any order, direction, etc. you are seeking from the court.

Section B

☐ I intend to contest this claim

Give brief details of any different remedy you are seeking.

Section C

☐ I intend to dispute the court's jurisdiction
(Please note, any application must be filed within 14 days of the date on which you file this acknowledgment of service)

The court office at

is open between 10 am and 4 pm Monday to Friday. When corresponding with the court, please address forms or letters to the Court Manager and quote the claim number.

N210 Acknowledgment of Service (CPR Part 8) (3.01)   *Printed on behalf of The Court Service*

Claim No.	

Section D

☐   I object to the claimant issuing under this procedure

My reasons for objecting are:

Section E

☐   I intend to rely on written evidence

My written evidence:

☐   is filed with this form

☐   will be filed within 14 days as agreed with the other party(ies). A copy of the written agreement is attached to this form

Section F

Full name of defendant filing
this acknowledgment   _____

Section G

Signed (To be signed by you or by your solicitor or litigation friend)	*(I believe)(The defendant believes) that the facts stated in this form are true. *I am duly authorised by the defendant to sign this statement *delete as appropriate	**Position or office held** (if signing on behalf of firm or company)	

Date

Give an address to which notices about this case can be sent to you			if applicable	
			Ref. no.	
			fax no.	
	Postcode		DX no.	
Tel. no.			e-mail	

Listing questionnaire
(Pre-trial checklist) [Click here to clear all fields]

In the

To be completed by, or on behalf of.

Claim No.

Last date for filing
with court office

who is [1ˢᵗ][2ⁿᵈ][3ʳᵈ][   ][Claimant][Defendant]
[Part 20 claimant][Part 20 defendant] in this claim

Date(s) fixed for trial
or trial period

This form must be **completed** and **returned** to the court no later than the date given above. If not, your statement of case may be struck out or some other sanction imposed.

If the claim has settled, or settles before the trial date, you must let the court know immediately.

Legal representatives only: You must **attach** estimates of costs incurred to date, and of your likely overall costs. In substantial cases, these should be provided in compliance with CPR Part 43.

For multi-track claims only, you must also **attach** a proposed timetable for the trial itself.

A Confirmation of compliance with directions

1. I confirm that I have complied with those directions already given which require action by me.   ☐Yes ☐No

If you are unable to give confirmation, state which directions you have still to comply with and the date by which this will be done.

Directions	Date

2. I believe that additional directions are necessary before the trial takes place.   ☐Yes ☐No

If Yes, you should attach an application and a draft order.

*Include in your application all directions needed to enable the claim **to be tried on the date, or within the trial period, already fixed.** These should include any issues relating to experts and their evidence, and any orders needed in respect of directions still requiring action by any other party.*

3. Have you agreed the additional directions you are seeking with the other party(ies)?   ☐Yes ☐No

B Witnesses

1. How many witnesses (including yourself) will be giving evidence on your behalf at the trial? *(Do not include experts - see Section C)*

Continued over ↻

Witnesses continued

2. If the trial date is not yet fixed, are there any days within the trial period you or your witnesses would wish to avoid if possible? *(Do not include experts - see Section C)*

Please give details

Name of witness	Dates to be avoided, if possible	Reason

Please specify any special facilities or arrangements needed at court for the party or any witness (e.g. witness with a disability).

3. Will you be providing an interpreter for any of your witnesses?   ☐ Yes ☐ No

C Experts

You are reminded that you may not use an expert's report or have your expert give oral evidence unless the court has given permission. If you do not have permission, you must make an application (see section A2 above)

1. Please give the information requested for your expert(s)

Name	Field of expertise	Joint expert?	Is report agreed?	Has permission been given for oral evidence?
		☐ Yes ☐ No	☐ Yes ☐ No	☐ Yes ☐ No
		☐ Yes ☐ No	☐ Yes ☐ No	☐ Yes ☐ No
		☐ Yes ☐ No	☐ Yes ☐ No	☐ Yes ☐ No

2. Has there been discussion between experts?   ☐ Yes ☐ No

3. Have the experts signed a joint statement?   ☐ Yes ☐ No

4. If your expert is giving oral evidence and the trial date is not yet fixed, is there any day within the trial period which the expert would wish to avoid, if possible?   ☐ Yes ☐ No

If Yes, please give details

Name	Dates to be avoided, if possible	Reason

D Legal representation

1. Who will be presenting your case at the trial?   ☐ You ☐ Solicitor ☐ Counsel

2. If the trial date is not yet fixed, is there any day within the trial
period that the person presenting your case would wish to avoid,
if possible?   ☐Yes ☐No

If Yes, please give details

Name	Dates to be avoided, if possible	Reason

E The trial

1. Has the estimate of the time needed for trial changed?   ☐Yes ☐No

If Yes, say how long you estimate the whole trial will take, including
both parties' cross-examination and closing arguments   ☐days ☐hours ☐minutes

2. If different from original estimate have you agreed with the other
party(ies) that this is now the **total** time needed?   ☐Yes ☐No

3. Is the timetable for trial you have attached agreed with the
other party(ies)?   ☐Yes ☐No

Fast track cases only
The court will normally give you 3 weeks notice of the date fixed for a fast track trial unless, in
exceptional circumstances, the court directs that shorter notice will be given.

Would you be prepared to accept shorter notice of the date
fixed for trial?   ☐Yes ☐No

F Document and fee checklist
Tick as appropriate

I attach to this questionnaire -

☐An application and fee for additional directions   ☐A proposed timetable for trial

☐A draft order   ☐An estimate of costs

☐Listing fee

Signed _____

[Counsel][Solicitor][for the][1ˢᵗ][2ⁿᵈ][3ʳᵈ][ ]
[Claimant][Defendant]
[Part 20 claimant][Part 20 defendant]

Date _____

Please enter your [firm's] name, reference number and full postal address including (if appropriate) details of DX, fax or e-mail

Postcode

| Tel. no. | | DX no. | | E-mail | |
| Fax no. | | Ref. no. | | | |

3 of 3

A1–012

Appellant's notice
(All appeals except small claims track appeals)

Click here to reset form	Click here to print form
For Court use only	
Appeal Court Ref. No.	
Date filed	

Notes for guidance are available which will help you complete this form. Please read them carefully before you complete each section.

SEAL

Section 1 Details of the claim or case you are appealing against

Claim or Case no. [_____]

Name(s) of the ☐ Claimant(s)   ☐ Applicant(s)   ☐ Petitioner(s)

[ ]

Name(s) of the ☐ Defendant(s)   ☐ Respondent(s)

[ ]

Details of the party appealing ('The Appellant')

Name

[ ]

Address (including postcode)

	Tel No.	
	Fax	
	E-mail	

Details of the Respondent to the appeal

Name

[ ]

Address (including postcode)

	Tel No.	
	Fax	
	E-mail	

Details of additional parties (if any) are attached   ☐ Yes   ☐ No

N161 Appellant's notice (07.06)   HMCS

Section 2   Details of the appeal

From which court is the appeal being brought?

☐ The County Court at

☐ High Court District Registry at

☐ The Royal Courts of Justice

☐ Other (please specify)

What is the name of the Judge whose decision you want to appeal?

What is the status of the Judge whose decision you want to appeal?

☐ District Judge or Deputy   ☐ Circuit Judge or Recorder

☐ Master or Deputy   ☐ High Court Judge or Deputy

What is the date of the decision you wish to appeal?

To which track, if any, was the claim or case allocated?

☐ Fast track

☐ Multi track

☐ Not allocated to a track

Nature of the decision you wish to appeal

☐ Case management decision   ☐ Grant or refusal of interim relief

☐ Final decision   ☐ A previous appeal decision

Section 3　Legal representation

Are you legally represented?

☐ Yes ☐ No

If 'Yes', please give details of your solicitor below

Your solicitor's name

Your solicitor's address (including postcode)

Tel No.	
Fax	
E-mail	
DX	
Ref.	

Are you, the Appellant, in receipt of a Legal Aid Certificate or a Community Legal Service Fund (CLSF) certificate?

☐ Yes ☐ No

Is the respondent legally represented?

☐ Yes ☐ No

If 'Yes', please give details of the respondent's solicitor below

The respondent's solicitor's address (including postcode)

Tel No.	
Fax	
E-mail	
DX	
Ref.	

Section 4　Permission to appeal

Do you need permission to appeal?

☐ Yes ☐ No

Has permission to appeal been granted ?

☐ Yes   ☐ No

Date of order granting permission

Name of Judge granting permission

I

the Appellant('s solicitor) seek permission to appeal.

Section 5   Other information required for the appeal

Please set out the order (or part of the order) you wish to appeal

Does your appeal include any issues arising from the
Human Rights Act 1998?   ☐ Yes   ☐ No

Are you asking for a stay of execution of any
judgment against you?   ☐ Yes   ☐ No
                                                            If 'Yes' you must complete
                                                            Part A of Section 8

Have you lodged this notice with the court within
21 days of the date on which the Judge made the   ☐ Yes   ☐ No
decision you wish to appeal?   If 'No' you must complete
                                                            Part B of Section 8

Are you making any other applications?   ☐ Yes   ☐ No
                                                            If 'Yes' you must complete
                                                            Part C of Section 8

Section 6   Grounds for appeal and arguments in support

Please state, in numbered paragraphs, **on a separate sheet** attached to this notice and entitled 'Grounds
of Appeal' (also in the top right hand corner add your claim or case number and full name), why you are
saying that the Judge who made the order you are appealing was wrong.

☐   The arguments (known as a 'Skeleton Argument') in support of the 'Grounds of Appeal will follow
     within 14 days of filing this Appellant's Notice

OR

☐   The arguments (known as a 'Skeleton Argument') in support of the 'Grounds of Appeal' are set out
     on a separate sheet and attached to this notice.

Section 7   What are you asking the Appeal Court to do?

I am asking the appeal court to:-
(please tick the appropriate box)

☐ set aside the order which I am appealing

☐ vary the order which I am appealing and substitute the following order. Set out in the following space
the order you are asking for:-

[blank box]

☐ order a new trial

Section 8   Other applications

Complete this section **only** if you are asking for orders **in addition** to the order asked for in Section 7.

Part A
I apply for a stay of execution because:

[blank box]

Part B
☐ I do not need an extension of time for filing my appeal notice because it has been filed within the
extended time granted by the Judge whose decision I am appealing.

OR

☐ I apply for an extension of time for filing my appeal notice because (set out the reasons for the delay.
You must also set out in Section 9 what steps you have taken since the decision you are appealing).

Part C
I apply for an order that:

[blank box]

because

[blank box]

Section 9   Evidence in support

In support of my application(s) in Section 8, I wish to rely upon the following evidence:

Statement of Truth

I believe (The appellant believes) that the facts stated in this section are true.

Full name

Name of appellant's solicitor's firm

signed   position or office held

Appellant ('s solicitor)   (if signing on behalf of firm or company)

Section 10 | Supporting documents

To support your appeal you should file with this notice all relevant documents listed below. To show which documents you are filing, please tick the appropriate boxes.

If you do not have a document that you intend to use to support your appeal complete the box over the page.

☐ two additional copies of your appellant's notice for the appeal court;

☐ one copy of your appellant's notice for each of the respondents;

☐ one copy of your skeleton argument for each copy of the appellant's notice that is filed;

☐ a sealed *(stamped by the court)* copy of the order being appealed;

☐ a copy of any order giving or refusing permission to appeal, together with a copy of the judge's reasons for allowing or refusing permission to appeal;

☐ any witness statements or affidavits in support of any application included in the appellant's notice;

☐ a copy of the order allocating the case to a track *(if any)*; and

☐ a copy of the legal aid or CLSF certificate *(if legally represented)*.

A bundle of documents for the appeal hearing containing copies of all the papers listed below:-

☐ a sealed copy *(stamped by the court)* of your appellant's notice;

☐ a sealed copy *(stamped by the court)* of the order being appealed;

☐ a copy of any order giving or refusing permission to appeal, together with a copy of the judge's reasons for allowing or refusing permission to appeal;

☐ any affidavit or witness statement filed in support of any application included in the appellant's notice;

☐ a copy of the skeleton argument;

☐ a transcript or note of judgment, and in cases where permission to appeal was given by the lower court or is not required those parts of any transcript of evidence which are directly relevant to any question at issue on the appeal;

☐ the claim form and statements of case (where relevant to the subject of the appeal);

☐ any application notice (or case management documentation) relevant to the subject of the appeal;

☐ in cases where the decision appealed was itself made on appeal (eg from district judge to circuit judge), the first order, the reasons given and the appellant's notice used to appeal from that order;

☐ in the case of judicial review or a statutory appeal, the original decision which was the subject of the application to the lower court;

☐ in cases where the appeal is from a Tribunal, a copy of the Tribunal's reasons for the decision, a copy of the decision reviewed by the Tribunal and the reasons for the original decision and any document filed with the Tribunal setting out the grounds of appeal from that decision;

☐ any other documents which are necessary to enable the appeal court to reach a decision; and

☐ such other documents as the court may direct.

Reasons why you have not supplied a document and date when you expect it to be available:-

Title of document and reason not supplied	Date when it will be supplied

Signed [   ] Appellant('s Solicitor)

[Click here to reset form] [Click here to print form]

A1–013

Respondent's Notice

In the	

Notes for guidance are available which will help
you complete this form. Please read them
carefully before you complete each section.

Appeal Court Reference No.	

For Court use only	
Date filed	

Seal

Click hear to clear all fields

Section 1 Details of the claim or case

Name of court _____   Case or claim number _____

Name or title of case or claim _____

In the case or claim, were you the
(*tick appropriate box*)

☐ claimant   ☐ applicant   ☐ petitioner

☐ defendant   ☐ respondent   ☐ other *(please specify)* _____

Section 2 Your (respondent's) name and address

Your (respondent's) name _____

Your solicitor's name _____ *(if you are legally represented)*

Your (your solicitor's) address

	Your reference or contact name	
	Your contact telephone number	
	DX number	

Details of other respondents are attached ☐ Yes   ☐ No

Section 3 Time estimate for appeal hearing

Do not complete if appealing to the Court of Appeal

	Days	Hours	Minutes
How long do you estimate it will take to put your case to the appeal court at the hearing?			

Who will represent you at the appeal hearing?   ☐ Yourself   ☐ Solicitor   ☐ Counsel

N162 Respondent's Notice (10.00)   *Printed on behalf of The Court Service*

Section 4	Details of the order(s) or part(s) of order(s) you want to appeal

Name of Judge

Date of order(s)

If only part of an order is appealed, write out that part (or those parts)

Section 5	Permission to file a respondent's notice

Has permission to appeal been granted?

Yes ☐   complete box **A**

No ☐   complete box **B**

if you are asking for permission or it is not required

A

Date of order granting permission _____

Name of judge _____

Name of court _____

B

☐ I do not need permission

☐ I _____
respondent('s solicitor) seek permission to appeal the order(s) at **section 4** above.

Are you making any other applications?   Yes ☐   No ☐
If Yes, complete section 9

Is the respondent in receipt of legal aid certificate or a
community legal service fund (CLSF) certificate?   Yes ☐   No ☐

Does your appeal include any issues arising from the Human Rights Act 1998?   Yes ☐   No ☐

2

Section 6	Grounds for appeal or for upholding the order

I (the respondent)

☐ appeal(s) the order   ☐ wish(es) the appeal court to uphold the order on different or additional grounds

because:-

Section 7	Arguments in support of grounds

My skeleton argument is:-

☐ set out below   ☐ attached   ☐ will follow within 21 days of receiving the appellant's
                                            skeleton arguments

I (the respondent) will rely on the following arguments at the hearing of the appeal:-

APPENDIX I

| Section 8 | What decision are you asking the appeal court to make? |

I (the respondent) am (is) asking that:-

(tick appropriate box)

- ☐ the order(s) at **section 4** be set aside
- ☐ the order(s) at **section 4** be varied and the following order(s) substituted :-

- ☐ a new trial be ordered
- ☐ the appeal court makes the following additional orders :-

- ☐ the appeal court upholds the order but for the following different or additional reasons

5

Section 9	Other applications

I wish to make an application for additional orders ☐ in this section

☐ in the Part 23 application
form (N244) attached

Part A
I apply (the respondent applies) for an order (a draft of which is attached) that :-

because :-

Part B
I (the respondent) wish(es) to rely on :

☐ evidence in Part C
☐ witness statement (affidavit)

6

Part C

I (the respondent) wish(es) to rely on the following evidence in support of this application:-

---

Statement of Truth

I believe (the respondent believes) that the facts stated in Section 9 are true.

Full name

Name of respondent's solicitor's firm

signed _____   position or office held _____

Respondent ('s solicitor)   (if signing on behalf of firm or company)

Section 10	Supporting documents

Please tick the papers you are filing in your bundle:-

☐ your respondent's notice and any skeleton arguments (if separate);

☐ any witness statements or affidavits in support of any application included in section 5 or 9 of your notice or in a separate Part 23 application notice;

☐ any other affidavit or witness statement filed in support of your arguments;

☐ a copy of the legal aid or CLSF certificate (if legally represented); and

☐ any other documents directed by the court to be filed in your appeal *(give details).*

Reasons why you have not supplied a document and date when you expect it to be available:-

Signed _____ Respondent/'s Solicitor

A1–014

Click here to clear your fields

Application for an order   Form C1

Children Act 1989

The court	To be completed by the court
	Date issued
	Case number
The full name(s) of the child(ren)	Child(ren)'s number(s)

Important Note
You should only answer question 7 if you are asking the court to make one of the following orders:
a Contact Order, a Residence Order, a Prohibited Steps Order, a Specific Issue Order or a Parental Responsibility Order.

1   About you (the person completing this form known as 'the applicant')

State:
- *your title, full name, address, telephone number, date of birth and relationship to each child above*
- *your solicitor's name, address, reference, telephone, FAX and DX numbers.*

2   The child(ren) and the order(s) you are applying for

For each child state:
- *the full name, date of birth and sex*
- *the type of order(s) you are applying for (for example, residence order, contact order, supervision order).*

3 Other cases which concern the child(ren)

If there have ever been, or there are pending, any court cases which concern:
*   *a child whose name you have put in paragraph 2*
*   *a full, half or step brother or sister of a child whose name you have put in paragraph 2*
*   *a person in this case who is or has been, involved in caring for a child whose name you have put in paragraph 2*

attach a copy of the relevant order and give:
*   *the name of the court*
*   *the name and contact address (if known) of the children's guardian, if appointed*
*   *the name and contact address (if known) of the children and family reporter, if appointed*
*   *the name and contact address (if known) of the welfare officer, if appointed*
*   *the name and contact address (if known) of the solicitor appointed for the child(ren).*

4 The respondent(s)

Appendix 3 Family Proceedings Rules 1991; Schedule 2 Family Proceedings Courts (Children Act 1989) Rules 1991

For each respondent state:
*   *the title, full name and address*
*   *the date of birth (if known) or the age*
*   *the relationship to each child.*

C1

5 Others to whom notice is to be given

Appendix 3 Family Proceedings Rules 1991; Schedule 2 Family Proceedings Courts (Children Act 1989) Rules 1991

For each person state:
- *the title, full name and address*
- *the date of birth (if known) or the age*
- *the relationship to each child.*

6 The care of the child(ren)

For each child in paragraph 2 state:
- *the child's current address and how long the child has lived there*
- *whether it is the child's usual address and who cares for the child there*
- *the child's relationship to the other children (if any).*

7 Domestic abuse, violence or harm

Do you believe that the child(ren) named above have suffered or are at risk of suffering any harm from any of the following:
- *any form of domestic abuse*
- *violence within the household*
- *child abduction*
- *other conduct or behaviour*

by any person who is or has been involved in caring for the child(ren) or lives with, or has contact with, the child(ren)?

Please tick the box which applies   Yes ☐   No ☐

If you tick the Yes box, you must also fill in Supplemental Information Form (form C1A). You can obtain a copy of this from a court office if one has not been enclosed with the papers served on you.

C1

8 Social Services

For each child in paragraph 2 state:
- *whether the child is known to the Social Services. If so, give the name of the social worker and the address of the Social Services department.*
- *whether the child is, or has been, on the Child Protection Register. If so, give details of registration.*

9 The education and health of the child(ren)

For each child state:
- *the name of the school, college or place of training which the child attends*
- *whether the child is in good health. Give details of any serious disabilities or ill health.*
- *whether the child has any special needs.*

10 The parents of the child(ren)

For each child state:
- *the full name of the child's parents*
- *whether the parents are, or have been, married to each other or civil partners of each other*
- *whether the parents live together. If so, where.*
- *whether, to your knowledge, either of the parents have been involved in a court case concerning a child. If so, give the date and the name of the court.*

C1

11 The family of the child(ren) (other children)

For any other child not already mentioned in the family (for example, a brother or half sister) state:
- *the full name and address*
- *the date of birth (if known) or age*
- *the relationship of the child to you.*

12 Other adults

State:
- *the full name of any other adults (for example, lodgers) who live at the same address as any child named in paragraph 2*
- *whether they live there all the time*
- *whether, to your knowledge, the adult has been involved in a court case concerning a child. If so, give the date and the name of the court.*

13 Your reason(s) for applying and any plans for the child(ren)

State briefly your reasons for applying and what you want the court to order.
- ***Do not** give a full statement if you are applying for an order under Section 8 of Children Act 1989. You may be asked to provide a full statement later.*
- ***Do not** complete this section if this form is accompanied by a supplementary form.*

14 Attending the court

State:
- *whether you will need an interpreter at court. If so, please indicate what language interpreter you will use. If you require an interpreter you must notify the court immediately so that one can be arranged.*
- *whether you have a disability for which you require special assistance or special facilities. If so, please say what your needs are. The court staff will get in touch with you about your requirements.*

15 Parenting Information – Arrangements after Separation

	Yes	No
Have you received a Parenting Plan booklet? *(If No, you may obtain a copy from a court office,* *a citizen's advice bureau or other family advice service.)*	☐	☐
Have you agreed to a Parenting Plan? *(If Yes, please include a copy of the Plan when you send* *your application to the court)*	☐	☐
If you did agree a Parenting Plan, has the Plan *broken down?*	☐	☐

If Yes, please explain briefly why the Plan broke down –

Signed   Date
(Applicant)

CI

| Supplement for an application for financial provision for a child or variation of financial provision for a child | Form C10 |

Paragraph 4 Schedule 1 Children Act 1989

The court	To be completed by the court
	Date issued
	Case number
The full name(s) of the child(ren)	Child(ren)'s number(s)

1 About the application

State whether you are seeking

- *an order for a lump sum; a transfer of property; a settlement of property; periodical payments; secured periodical payments*

or • *a variation of an order for periodical payments; secured periodical payments; payment of a lump sum by instalments.*

Note: *Applications concerning transfer of property, settlement of property or secured periodical payments can only be heard in the High Court or a county court.*

2 Previous court orders and written agreements

If a written agreement or court order has been made a copy should be attached to this application.

If not available state • *the date*

- *the terms*
- *the parties*
- *the court.*

3 The Child Support Agency

Assessment for maintenance

State whether the Agency has made an assessment for the maintenance of the child(ren):   ☐ Yes ☐ No

If Yes, state whether you are applying for additional child maintenance

- • *because the Child Support Agency will no longer deal with your claim.*

  You should explain why the Agency will not deal with the claim.

or • *on top of payments made through the Child Support Agency.*

  You should explain why you need additional maintenance and confirm that the Child Support

  Agency's assessment is the maximum amount obtainable.

Written agreement for maintenance

State whether there is a written maintenance agreement: ☐ Yes ☐ No

If No, state whether you are applying for payment:

☐ for [a] stepchild[ren]

☐ in addition to child support maintenance already paid under a Child Support Agency assessment

  ☐ to meet expenses arising from the disability of [a] child[ren]

  ☐ to meet expenses incurred by [a] child[ren] in being educated or training for work

  ☐ when either the child[ren] OR the person with care of the child[ren] OR
  the absent parent of the child[ren] is not habitually resident in the United Kingdom

  ☐ for any other reason *(specify)*:

C10

4 About the order

State the terms of the order you ask the Court to make and in particular
* *the amount you would like the court to order*
* *whether you would like that amount paid weekly or monthly (if you are not applying for a lump sum)*
* *why you require the payments, or would like the court to vary an existing order.*

5 The collection of payment

If payments are not to be collected and paid to you by the Child Support Agency, give full details of how you would like payments collected. Possible ways are:

☐ **Directly to a bank, building society or post office account**
Give the full name and address, sorting code and the number of the account into which payment is to be made.

☐ **By an attachment of earnings order**
This is a court order which is sent to the employer of the person who is to pay.

☐ **If you would like the court to direct that money is paid in some other way**
please say what method you would like.
And if you do not mind how the money is paid, please say so. The Court will decide how it should be paid.

Signed   Date
(Applicant)

You should now complete a Statement of Means, Form C10A

C10

Click here to clear your text after printing

Statement of Means
Schedule 1 Children Act 1989

Form C10A

The court

To be completed by the court

Date issued

The full name(s) of the child(ren)

Case number

Child(ren)'s number(s)

Warning   **The Court will require to see written evidence of unemployment or sickness; or wage or salary slips, bank statements, and other papers giving details of your means. This evidence should be attached to this form or brought with you when you attend the hearing.**

1   About you

State •   *your title, full name, address, telephone number and date of birth*
•   *whether you are married, in a civil partnership, single or other*
•   *whether you are the applicant or the respondent.*

2   Your dependants

State for each dependant •   *the dependant's title, full name and age*
•   *whether the dependant is a spouse, civil partner, partner, child or other*
•   *whether the dependant is wholly or partially financially dependent on you*
•   *whether the dependant lives with you.*

3   Your employment

State whether you are employed, self-employed, unemployed or other.
If you are employed, state •   *your employment*
•   *your employer's name, address and daytime telephone number.*

4   Your buildings and land

List all buildings and land you own, whether in your name alone or jointly, stating for each
- *the address*
- *the name(s) of the owner(s)*
- *the current value.*

5   Your financial assets

List each bank, building society and post office account, stating for each
- *the name and address where the account is held*
- *the account number*
- *the current balance.*

List all investments and securities (for example, shares, insurance policies) stating for each one the name and quantity and current value.

List all pension schemes, stating for each one the scheme name and the company.

6   Other possessions of value

List all possessions of value (for example, jewellery, antiques, collectable items), stating for each:
- *what they are*
- *the current value.*

C10A

7 Your income

State whether
Weekly (W) or
Monthly (M)

If employed, state your usual take home pay		£	

If self employed, state
- your drawings — £
- your gross turnover — £
- your profit after expenses — £
- whether you expect your turnover to increase, decrease or remain the same:
- the date of the accounts showing the above gross turnover and profit after expenses — Year ending [19   ][20   ]

In all cases, state any of the following which you receive
- Income support — £
- Child benefits — £
- Child Support Agency — £
- Other state benefits (specify source) — £
   £
   £
- Pension(s) (specify source) — £
   £
   £
- Contributions from others in the home (total) — £
- Other income (specify source and amount) — £
   £
   £
   £

Total income: £ _____

8 Court Orders

Enclose a copy of any order

Court	Case Number	Amount outstanding (£)	Amount of payment (£)	Weekly (W) or Monthly (M)

C10A

3

9 Your expenses

	Amount of payments	Weekly (W) or Monthly (M)	Total debt	Amount of arrears
Mortgage				
1st				
2nd				
Rent				
Council tax				
Gas				
Electricity				
Telephone				
Water charges				
Credit Card				
Loans				
Storecards				
HP Payments				
TV rental and licence				
Mail Order				
Food				
Clothing				
Public transport				
Car expenses				
School meals				
Child minding				
Maintenance				
Child Support Agency				
Other payments (give details)				
Total Payments				

Signed: Date:

[Applicant] [Respondent]

C10A

Rule 3.6(1)   **Form M23**   A1–015

ORIGINATING SUMMONS UNDER SECTION 17 OF THE MARRIED WOMEN'S PROPERTY ACT 1882 [OR SECTION 1 OF THE MATRIMONIAL HOMES ACT 1983]

In the High Court of Justice
   Family Division
      [District Registry]
In the Matter of an Application by,
      under section 17 of the Married Women's Property Act 1882 [or section 1 of the Matrimonial Homes Act 1983]

Between   Applicant
And   Respondent

Let   of   attend before District Judge   in chambers at the Principal Registry, Somerset House, London, WC2R ILP, [or
as the case may be] on   day, the   day of   19 ,
at   o'clock,   on   the   hearing   of   an   application
by   for   an   order in the following terms:–
[*here set out the terms of order sought*]

Dated this   day of   19 .

    This summons was taken out by
    [Solicitor for] the above-named applicant
    To the Respondent

TAKE NOTICE THAT:–
1. A copy of the affidavit to be used in support of the application is delivered herewith.

2. You must complete the accompanying acknowledgment of service and send it so as to reach the court within eight days after you receive this summons.

3. If you wish to dispute the claim made by the applicant you must file an affidavit in answer within 14 days after the time allowed for sending the acknowledgment of service.

4. If you intend to instruct a solicitor to act for you, you should at once give him all the documents served on you, so that he may take the necessary steps on your behalf.

A1–016 **TYPICAL DIRECTIONS**

IN THE IPSWICH COUNTY COURT   CLAIM NO: IP 06 01977
BETWEEN:

MISS CATHERINE SMITH   <u>Claimant</u>

-and-

MR JONATHAN TAYLOR   <u>Defendant</u>

ORDER

UPON HEARING Counsel for the Claimant and Counsel for the Defendant

IT IS ORDERED THAT

1. This claim shall be heard together with the Claimant's application for financial provision under Children Act 1989, Schedule 1, proceeding under case number IP C 02423 ('the Schedule 1 application').

2. The parties do seek to agree the value of 1 Gainsborough Road, Ipswich, IP3 2DK. In the event that the parties have not agreed the value of the said property by 4.00pm on 11th January 2007, the following directions shall apply:
    a. The parties shall agree by 25th January 2007 upon the identity of a suitable surveyor to act as valuer who shall be jointly instructed as a single joint expert; in default thereof the President of the Royal Institute of Chartered Surveyors shall appoint a surveyor for the purposes of such valuation.
    b. The parties shall agree the letter of instruction to the valuer so appointed by no later than 1st February 2007 (or, if later, 7 days after notification of the identity of the surveyor appointed by the President of the Royal Institute of Chartered Surveyors
    c. The surveyor so instructed shall file and serve his report by no later than 4.00 pm on 22nd February 2007
    d. The surveyor so instructed ensure that he is available to give evidence, if so required, on the first day of the hearing listed at paragraph 8 below. For the avoidance of doubt, the surveyor so instructed shall not be required to give evidence unless directed to do so by the court. The court shall consider further the question of whether either party requires the attendance of the surveyor so instructed at the hearing referred to at para 7 below.
    e. The costs of the report referred to above shall in the first instance be borne by the parties in equal shares. Those costs will form part of the costs of the case and may form part of the costs

which any party may be ordered to pay at the conclusion of the proceedings.

3. The Claimant and the Defendant do give disclosure by way of lists of documents by no later than 4.00pm on 1st March 2007. Any party seeking to inspect or request copies of any documents so disclosed must do so by no later than 4.00pm on 15th March 2007.

4. The Claimant shall file witness statements in relation to all witnesses upon whose evidence she proposes to rely at trial by no later than 4.00pm on 29th March 2007. The Claimant shall refer in her witness statement to all facts and matters upon which she proposes to rely in relation to the Schedule 1 application.

5. The Defendant shall file witness statements in relation to all witnesses upon whose evidence he proposes to rely at trial by no later than 4.00pm on 12th April 2007.

6. The parties are each responsible for ensuring that any witnesses upon whose evidence he or she proposes to rely are available to give evidence and be cross examined at the final hearing listed at paragraph 8 below, unless notified by the other party not less than one week before such hearing that the attendance of any such witness is not required

7. This claim and the Schedule 1 application shall be listed for a further Directions/Case Management Conference (to be conducted as though it was a Financial Dispute Resolution appointment) to be heard by a District Judge of this court on 24th May 2007 at 10.30 am with a time estimate of 1 hour, in relation to which the following directions shall apply:
   a. The parties shall attend at court from 9.30 am for the purposes of negotiations
   b. The parties are responsible for preparing a separate bundle for the use of the Judge at such hearing containing all without prejudice offers made
   c. The bundle referred to at paragraph (b) above shall be filed at court by no later than 4.00pm on 22nd May 2007
   d. The parties are responsible for ensuring that the bundle referred to at para (b) above is returned by the Judge at the conclusion of the said hearing
   e. The District Judge conducting the said hearing shall thereafter have no further involvement in the case in relation to any contested matter

8. This claim shall be listed for final hearing together with the Schedule 1 application before a Circuit Judge sitting in Chambers at 10.30am on 20th June 2007 with a time estimate of two days.

9. For the purposes of the Practice Direction of 27th July 2006 relating to the preparation of Court Bundles, the Claimant shall for the

avoidance of doubt be treated as the Applicant in relation to both this claim and the Schedule 1 proceeding under case number IP C 02423.

10. Costs in the Case.

DRAFT ORDER   A1–017

IN THE IPSWICH COUNTY COURT   CLAIM NO: IP 06 01977
BETWEEN:

MISS CATHERINE SMITH   <u>Claimant</u>

-and-

MR JONATHAN TAYLOR   <u>Defendant</u>

ORDER

BEFORE HIS HONOUR JUDGE WRIGHT QC

Sitting at Ipswich County Court on 20th & 21st July 2007

IT IS DECLARED THAT:

The Defendant holds the property at 1 Gainsborough Road, Ipswich, IP3 2DK, title number IP2 3456 ("the property") upon trust for himself and for the Claimant subject to the mortgage secured thereon in shares 70% as to the Defendant and 30% as to the Claimant

AND IT IS ORDERED THAT

1.   The property be placed on the market forthwith and be sold for the best price which can be obtained within a reasonable period of time. In relation to such sale the following consequential directions shall apply.
     i.   The Defendant shall have the conduct of the sale
     ii.   The proceeds of sale shall be applied as follows:
           1.   in discharge of the mortgage secured thereon in favour of Suffolk Building Society
           2.   in payment of reasonable estate agents' and solicitors' fees and
           3.   in payment of the balance to the Claimant and the Defendant in proportions 30% to the Claimant and 70% to the Defendant
     iii. Until the completion of the sale ordered hereby the Defendant shall be responsible for the maintenance of the property and the payment of the running costs (including but not limited to buildings and contents insurance premia, payments of mortgage interest (but not capital), council tax and utility bills)

2. The Defendant do pay the Claimant's costs of this claim (including costs reasonably incidental thereto to be assessed on the standard basis if not agreed.

Appendix II

STATUTORY PROVISIONS

Children Act 1989 (c.41)

(1989 c. 41)

Part II

Orders With Respect to Children in Family Proceedings

Financial relief

15.—(1) Schedule 1 (which consists primarily of the re-enactment, with consequential amendments and minor modifications, of provisions of the Guardianship of Minors Acts 1971 and 1973, the [1975 c. 72.] Children Act 1975 and of sections 15 and 16 of the [1987 c. 42.] Family Law Reform Act 1987) makes provision in relation to financial relief for children.

(2) The powers of a magistrates' court under section 60 of the Magistrates' Courts Act 1980 to revoke, revive or vary an order for the periodical payment of money shall not apply in relation to an order made under Schedule 1.

SCHEDULES

SCHEDULE 1

Section 15(1).

Financial Provision for Children

Orders for financial relief against parents

1.—(1) On an application made by a parent or guardian of a child, or by any person in whose favour a residence order is in force with respect to a child, the court may—

(a) in the case of an application to the High Court or a county court, make one or more of the orders mentioned in sub-paragraph (2);
(b) in the case of an application to a magistrates' court, make one or both of the orders mentioned in paragraphs (a) and (c) of that sub-paragraph.

(2) The orders referred to in sub-paragraph (1) are—

    (a) an order requiring either or both parents of a child—

        (i) to make to the applicant for the benefit of the child; or
        (ii) to make to the child himself,

        such periodical payments, for such term, as may be specified in the order;

    (b) an order requiring either or both parents of a child—

        (i) to secure to the applicant for the benefit of the child; or
        (ii) to secure to the child himself,

        such periodical payments, for such term, as may be so specified;

    (c) an order requiring either or both parents of a child—

        (i) to pay to the applicant for the benefit of the child; or
        (ii) to pay to the child himself,

        such lump sum as may be so specified;

    (d) an order requiring a settlement to be made for the benefit of the child, and to the satisfaction of the court, of property—

        (i) to which either parent is entitled (either in possession or in reversion); and
        (ii) which is specified in the order;

    (e) an order requiring either or both parents of a child—

        (i) to transfer to the applicant, for the benefit of the child; or
        (ii) to transfer to the child himself,

        such property to which the parent is, or the parents are, entitled (either in possession or in reversion) as may be specified in the order.

(3) The powers conferred by this paragraph may be exercised at any time.

(4) An order under sub-paragraph (2)(a) or (b) may be varied or discharged by a subsequent order made on the application of any person by or to whom payments were required to be made under the previous order.

(5) Where a court makes an order under this paragraph—

    (a) it may at any time make a further such order under sub-paragraph (2)(a), (b) or (c) with respect to the child concerned if he has not reached the age of eighteen;
    (b) it may not make more than one order under sub-paragraph (2)(d) or (e) against the same person in respect of the same child.

(6) On making, varying or discharging a residence order the court may exercise any of its powers under this Schedule even though no application has been made to it under this Schedule.

Orders for financial relief for persons over eighteen

2.—(1) If, on an application by a person who has reached the age of eighteen, it appears to the court—

  (a) that the applicant is, will be or (if an order were made under this paragraph) would be receiving instruction at an educational establishment or undergoing training for a trade, profession or vocation, whether or not while in gainful employment; or
  (b) that there are special circumstances which justify the making of an order under this paragraph,

the court may make one or both of the orders mentioned in sub-paragraph (2).

  (2) The orders are—

  (a) an order requiring either or both of the applicant's parents to pay to the applicant such periodical payments, for such term, as may be specified in the order;
  (b) an order requiring either or both of the applicant's parents to pay to the applicant such lump sum as may be so specified.

  (3) An application may not be made under this paragraph by any person if, immediately before he reached the age of sixteen, a periodical payments order was in force with respect to him.

  (4) No order shall be made under this paragraph at a time when the parents of the applicant are living with each other in the same household.

  (5) An order under sub-paragraph (2)(a) may be varied or discharged by a subsequent order made on the application of any person by or to whom payments were required to be made under the previous order.

  (6) In sub-paragraph (3) "periodical payments order" means an order made under—

  (a) this Schedule;
  (b) section 6(3) of the [1969 c. 46.] Family Law Reform Act 1969;
  (c) section 23 or 27 of the [1973 c. 18.] Matrimonial Causes Act 1973;
  (d) Part I of the [1978 c. 22.] Domestic Proceedings and Magistrates' Courts Act 1978,

for the making or securing of periodical payments.

  (7) The powers conferred by this paragraph shall be exercisable at any time.

  (8) Where the court makes an order under this paragraph it may from time to time while that order remains in force make a further such order.

Duration of orders for financial relief

3.—(1) The term to be specified in an order for periodical payments made under paragraph 1(2)(a) or (b) in favour of a child may begin with the date of the making of an application for the order in question or any later date but—

> (a) shall not in the first instance extend beyond the child's seventeenth birthday unless the court thinks it right in the circumstances of the case to specify a later date; and
> (b) shall not in any event extend beyond the child's eighteenth birthday.

(2) Paragraph (b) of sub-paragraph (1) shall not apply in the case of a child if it appears to the court that—

> (a) the child is, or will be or (if an order were made without complying with that paragraph) would be receiving instruction at an educational establishment or undergoing training for a trade, profession or vocation, whether or not while in gainful employment; or
> (b) there are special circumstances which justify the making of an order without complying with that paragraph.

(3) An order for periodical payments made under paragraph 1(2)(a) or 2(2)(a) shall, notwithstanding anything in the order, cease to have effect on the death of the person liable to make payments under the order.

(4) Where an order is made under paragraph 1(2)(a) or (b) requiring periodical payments to be made or secured to the parent of a child, the order shall cease to have effect if—

> (a) any parent making or securing the payments; and
> (b) any parent to whom the payments are made or secured,

live together for a period of more than six months.

*Matters to which court is to have regard in making orders
for financial relief*

4.—(1) In deciding whether to exercise its powers under paragraph 1 or 2, and if so in what manner, the court shall have regard to all the circumstances including—

> (a) the income, earning capacity, property and other financial resources which each person mentioned in sub-paragraph (3) has or is likely to have in the foreseeable future;

    (b)   the financial needs, obligations and responsibilities which each person mentioned in sub-paragraph (3) has or is likely to have in the foreseeable future;

    (c)   the financial needs of the child;

    (d)   the income, earning capacity (if any), property and other financial resources of the child;

    (e)   any physical or mental disability of the child;

    (f)   the manner in which the child was being, or was expected to be, educated or trained.

(2) In deciding whether to exercise its powers under paragraph 1 against a person who is not the mother or father of the child, and if so in what manner, the court shall in addition have regard to—

    (a)   whether that person had assumed responsibility for the maintenance of the child and, if so, the extent to which and basis on which he assumed that responsibility and the length of the period during which he met that responsibility;

    (b)   whether he did so knowing that the child was not his child;

    (c)   the liability of any other person to maintain the child.

(3) Where the court makes an order under paragraph 1 against a person who is not the father of the child, it shall record in the order that the order is made on the basis that the person against whom the order is made is not the child's father.

(4) The persons mentioned in sub-paragraph (1) are—

    (a)   in relation to a decision whether to exercise its powers under paragraph 1, any parent of the child;

    (b)   in relation to a decision whether to exercise its powers under paragraph 2, the mother and father of the child;

    (c)   the applicant for the order;

    (d)   any other person in whose favour the court proposes to make the order.

Provisions relating to lump sums

5.—(1) Without prejudice to the generality of paragraph 1, an order under that paragraph for the payment of a lump sum may be made for the purpose of enabling any liabilities or expenses—

    (a)   incurred in connection with the birth of the child or in maintaining the child; and

    (b)   reasonably incurred before the making of the order,

to be met.

(2) The amount of any lump sum required to be paid by an order made by a magistrates' court under paragraph 1 or 2 shall not exceed £1000 or

such larger amount as the Secretary of State may from time to time by order fix for the purposes of this sub-paragraph.

(3) The power of the court under paragraph 1 or 2 to vary or discharge an order for the making or securing of periodical payments by a parent shall include power to make an order under that provision for the payment of a lump sum by that parent.

(4) The amount of any lump sum which a parent may be required to pay by virtue of sub-paragraph (3) shall not, in the case of an order made by a magistrates' court, exceed the maximum amount that may at the time of the making of the order be required to be paid under sub-paragraph (2), but a magistrates' court may make an order for the payment of a lump sum not exceeding that amount even though the parent was required to pay a lump sum by a previous order under this Act.

(5) An order made under paragraph 1 or 2 for the payment of a lump sum may provide for the payment of that sum by instalments.

(6) Where the court provides for the payment of a lump sum by instalments the court, on an application made either by the person liable to pay or the person entitled to receive that sum, shall have power to vary that order by varying—

(a)   the number of instalments payable;
(b)   the amount of any instalment payable;
(c)   the date on which any instalment becomes payable.

Variation etc. of orders for periodical payments

6.—(1) In exercising its powers under paragraph 1 or 2 to vary or discharge an order for the making or securing of periodical payments the court shall have regard to all the circumstances of the case, including any change in any of the matters to which the court was required to have regard when making the order.

(2) The power of the court under paragraph 1 or 2 to vary an order for the making or securing of periodical payments shall include power to suspend any provision of the order temporarily and to revive any provision so suspended.

(3) Where on an application under paragraph 1 or 2 for the variation or discharge of an order for the making or securing of periodical payments the court varies the payments required to be made under that order, the court may provide that the payments as so varied shall be made from such date as the court may specify, not being earlier than the date of the making of the application.

(4) An application for the variation of an order made under paragraph 1 for the making or securing of periodical payments to or for the benefit of a child may, if the child has reached the age of sixteen, be made by the child himself.

(5) Where an order for the making or securing of periodical payments made under paragraph 1 ceases to have effect on the date on which the child reaches the age of sixteen, or at any time after that date but before

or on the date on which he reaches the age of eighteen, the child may apply to the court which made the order for an order for its revival.

(6) If on such an application it appears to the court that—

(a) the child is, will be or (if an order were made under this sub-paragraph) would be receiving instruction at an educational establishment or undergoing training for a trade, profession or vocation, whether or not while in gainful employment; or

(b) there are special circumstances which justify the making of an order under this paragraph,

the court shall have power by order to revive the order from such date as the court may specify, not being earlier than the date of the making of the application.

(7) Any order which is revived by an order under sub-paragraph (5) may be varied or discharged under that provision, on the application of any person by whom or to whom payments are required to be made under the revived order.

(8) An order for the making or securing of periodical payments made under paragraph 1 may be varied or discharged, after the death of either parent, on the application of a guardian of the child concerned.

Variation of orders for secured periodical payments after death of parent

7.—(1) Where the parent liable to make payments under a secured periodical payments order has died, the persons who may apply for the variation or discharge of the order shall include the personal representatives of the deceased parent.

(2) No application for the variation of the order shall, except with the permission of the court, be made after the end of the period of six months from the date on which representation in regard to the estate of that parent is first taken out.

(3) The personal representatives of a deceased person against whom a secured periodical payments order was made shall not be liable for having distributed any part of the estate of the deceased after the end of the period of six months referred to in sub-paragraph (2) on the ground that they ought to have taken into account the possibility that the court might permit an application for variation to be made after that period by the person entitled to payments under the order.

(4) Sub-paragraph (3) shall not prejudice any power to recover any part of the estate so distributed arising by virtue of the variation of an order in accordance with this paragraph.

(5) Where an application to vary a secured periodical payments order is made after the death of the parent liable to make payments under the order, the circumstances to which the court is required to have regard under paragraph 6(1) shall include the changed circumstances resulting from the death of the parent.

(6) In considering for the purposes of sub-paragraph (2) the question when representation was first taken out, a grant limited to settled land or

to trust property shall be left out of account and a grant limited to real estate or to personal estate shall be left out of account unless a grant limited to the remainder of the estate has previously been made or is made at the same time.

(7) In this paragraph "secured periodical payments order" means an order for secured periodical payments under paragraph 1(2)(b).

Financial relief under other enactments

8.—(1) This paragraph applies where a residence order is made with respect to a child at a time when there is in force an order ("the financial relief order") made under any enactment other than this Act and requiring a person to contribute to the child's maintenance.

(2) Where this paragraph applies, the court may, on the application of—

 (a) any person required by the financial relief order to contribute to the child's maintenance; or
 (b) any person in whose favour a residence order with respect to the child is in force,

make an order revoking the financial relief order, or varying it by altering the amount of any sum payable under that order or by substituting the applicant for the person to whom any such sum is otherwise payable under that order.

Interim orders

9.—(1) Where an application is made under paragraph 1 or 2 the court may, at any time before it disposes of the application, make an interim order—

 (a) requiring either or both parents to make such periodical payments, at such times and for such term as the court thinks fit; and
 (b) giving any direction which the court thinks fit.

(2) An interim order made under this paragraph may provide for payments to be made from such date as the court may specify, not being earlier than the date of the making of the application under paragraph 1 or 2.

(3) An interim order made under this paragraph shall cease to have effect when the application is disposed of or, if earlier, on the date specified for the purposes of this paragraph in the interim order.

(4) An interim order in which a date has been specified for the purposes of sub-paragraph (3) may be varied by substituting a later date.

Alteration of maintenance agreements

10.—(1) In this paragraph and in paragraph 11 "maintenance agreement" means any agreement in writing made with respect to a child, whether before or after the commencement of this paragraph, which—

(a) is or was made between the father and mother of the child; and

(b) contains provision with respect to the making or securing of payments, or the disposition or use of any property, for the maintenance or education of the child,

and any such provisions are in this paragraph, and paragraph 11, referred to as "financial arrangements".

(2) Where a maintenance agreement is for the time being subsisting and each of the parties to the agreement is for the time being either domiciled or resident in England and Wales, then, either party may apply to the court for an order under this paragraph.

(3) If the court to which the application is made is satisfied either—

(a) that, by reason of a change in the circumstances in the light of which any financial arrangements contained in the agreement were made (including a change foreseen by the parties when making the agreement), the agreement should be altered so as to make different financial arrangements; or

(b) that the agreement does not contain proper financial arrangements with respect to the child,

then that court may by order make such alterations in the agreement by varying or revoking any financial arrangements contained in it as may appear to it to be just having regard to all the circumstances.

(4) If the maintenance agreement is altered by an order under this paragraph, the agreement shall have effect thereafter as if the alteration had been made by agreement between the parties and for valuable consideration.

(5) Where a court decides to make an order under this paragraph altering the maintenance agreement—

(a) by inserting provision for the making or securing by one of the parties to the agreement of periodical payments for the maintenance of the child; or

(b) by increasing the rate of periodical payments required to be made or secured by one of the parties for the maintenance of the child,

then, in deciding the term for which under the agreement as altered by the order the payments or (as the case may be) the additional payments attributable to the increase are to be made or secured for the benefit of the child, the court shall apply the provisions of sub-paragraphs (1) and (2) of paragraph 3 as if the order were an order under paragraph 1(2)(a) or (b).

(6) A magistrates' court shall not entertain an application under sub-paragraph (2) unless both the parties to the agreement are resident in England and Wales and at least one of the parties is resident in the commission area (within the meaning of the Justices of the [1979 c. 55.] Peace Act 1979) for which the court is appointed, and shall not have power to make any order on such an application except—

   (a) in a case where the agreement contains no provision for peri-odical payments by either of the parties, an order inserting provision for the making by one of the parties of periodical payments for the maintenance of the child;
   (b) in a case where the agreement includes provision for the making by one of the parties of periodical payments, an order increasing or reducing the rate of, or terminating, any of those payments.

(7) For the avoidance of doubt it is hereby declared that nothing in this paragraph affects any power of a court before which any proceedings between the parties to a maintenance agreement are brought under any other enactment to make an order containing financial arrangements or any right of either party to apply for such an order in such proceedings.

   11.—(1) Where a maintenance agreement provides for the continua-tion, after the death of one of the parties, of payments for the main-tenance of a child and that party dies domiciled in England and Wales, the surviving party or the personal representatives of the deceased party may apply to the High Court or a county court for an order under paragraph 10.

(2) If a maintenance agreement is altered by a court on an application under this paragraph, the agreement shall have effect thereafter as if the alteration had been made, immediately before the death, by agreement between the parties and for valuable consideration.

(3) An application under this paragraph shall not, except with leave of the High Court or a county court, be made after the end of the period of six months beginning with the day on which representation in regard to the estate of the deceased is first taken out.

(4) In considering for the purposes of sub-paragraph (3) the question when representation was first taken out, a grant limited to settled land or to trust property shall be left out of account and a grant limited to real estate or to personal estate shall be left out of account unless a grant limited to the remainder of the estate has previously been made or is made at the same time.

(5) A county court shall not entertain an application under this para-graph, or an application for leave to make an application under this paragraph, unless it would have jurisdiction to hear and determine pro-ceedings for an order under section 2 of the [1975 c. 63.] Inheritance (Provision for Family and Dependants) Act 1975 in relation to the deceased's estate by virtue of section 25 of the [1984 c. 28.] County Courts Act 1984 (jurisdiction under the Act of 1975).

(6) The provisions of this paragraph shall not render the personal representatives of the deceased liable for having distributed any part of the estate of the deceased after the expiry of the period of six months referred to in sub-paragraph (3) on the ground that they ought to have

taken into account the possibility that a court might grant leave for an application by virtue of this paragraph to be made by the surviving party after that period.

(7) Sub-paragraph (6) shall not prejudice any power to recover any part of the estate so distributed arising by virtue of the making of an order in pursuance of this paragraph.

Enforcement of orders for maintenance

12.—(1) Any person for the time being under an obligation to make payments in pursuance of any order for the payment of money made by a magistrates' court under this Act shall give notice of any change of address to such person (if any) as may be specified in the order.

(2) Any person failing without reasonable excuse to give such a notice shall be guilty of an offence and liable on summary conviction to a fine not exceeding level 2 on the standard scale.

(3) An order for the payment of money made by a magistrates' court under this Act shall be enforceable as a magistrates' court maintenance order within the meaning of section 150(1) of the [1980 c. 43.] Magistrates' Courts Act 1980.

Direction for settlement of instrument by conveyancing counsel

13. Where the High Court or a county court decides to make an order under this Act for the securing of periodical payments or for the transfer or settlement of property, it may direct that the matter be referred to one of the conveyancing counsel of the court to settle a proper instrument to be executed by all necessary parties.

Financial provision for child resident in country outside England and Wales

14.—(1) Where one parent of a child lives in England and Wales and the child lives outside England and Wales with—

    (a) another parent of his;
    (b) a guardian of his; or
    (c) a person in whose favour a residence order is in force with respect to the child,

the court shall have power, on an application made by any of the persons mentioned in paragraphs (a) to (c), to make one or both of the orders mentioned in paragraph 1(2)(a) and (b) against the parent living in England and Wales.

(2) Any reference in this Act to the powers of the court under paragraph 1(2) or to an order made under paragraph 1(2) shall include a

reference to the powers which the court has by virtue of sub-paragraph (1) or (as the case may be) to an order made by virtue of sub-paragraph (1).

Local authority contribution to child's maintenance

15.—(1) Where a child lives, or is to live, with a person as the result of a residence order, a local authority may make contributions to that person towards the cost of the accommodation and maintenance of the child.

(2) Sub-paragraph (1) does not apply where the person with whom the child lives, or is to live, is a parent of the child or the husband or wife of a parent of the child.

Interpretation

16.—(1) In this Schedule "child" includes, in any case where an application is made under paragraph 2 or 6 in relation to a person who has reached the age of eighteen, that person.

(2) In this Schedule, except paragraphs 2 and 15, "parent" includes any party to a marriage (whether or not subsisting) in relation to whom the child concerned is a child of the family; and for this purpose any reference to either parent or both parents shall be construed as references to any parent of his and to all of his parents.

A2–002   # Law Reform (Miscellaneous Provisions) Act 1970

(C. 33)

LEGAL CONSEQUENCES OF TERMINATION OF CONTRACT TO MARRY

s.2 Property of engaged couples.

(1) Where an agreement to marry is terminated, any rule of law relating to the rights of husbands and wives in relation to property in which either or both has or have a beneficial interest, including any such rule as explained by section 37 of the Matrimonial Proceedings and Property Act 1970, shall apply, in relation to any property in which either or both of the parties to the agreement had a beneficial interest while the agreement was in force, as it applies in relation to property in which a husband or wife has a beneficial interest.

(2) Where an agreement to marry is terminated, section 17 of the Married Women's Property Act 1882 and section 7 of the Matrimonial Causes (Property and Maintenance) Act 1958 (which sections confer power on a judge of the High Court or a county court to settle disputes between husband and wife about property) shall apply, as if the parties were married, to any dispute between, or claim by, one of them in relation to property in which either or both had a beneficial interest while the agreement was in force; but an application made by virtue of this section to the judge under the said section 17, as originally enacted or as extended by the said section 7, shall be made within three years of the termination of the agreement.

Notes:

Words of enactment omitted under authority of Statute Law Revision Act 1948 (c. 62), s.3

Law of Property Act 1925   A2–003

(15 GEO. 5, C. 20.)

An Act to consolidate the enactments relating to Conveyancing and the Law of Property in England and Wales.

[9TH APRIL, 1925]

Instruments required to be in writing

53.—(1) Subject to the provision hereinafter contained with respect to the creation of interests in land by parol—

(a) no interest in land can be created or disposed of except by writing signed by the person creating or conveying the same, or by his agent thereunto lawfully authorised in writing, or by will, or by operation of law;

(b) a declaration of trust respecting any land or any interest therein must be manifested and proved by some writing signed by some person who is able to declare such trust or by his will;

(c) a disposition of an equitable interest or trust subsisting at the time of the disposition, must be in writing signed by the person disposing of the same, or by his agent thereunto lawfully authorised in writing or by will.

(2) This section does not affect the creation or operation of resulting, implied or constructive trusts.

Abolition of technicalities in regard to conveyances and deeds

60.—(1) A conveyance of freehold land to any person without words of limitation, or any equivalent expression, shall pass to the grantee the fee simple or other the whole interest which the grantor had power to convey in such land, unless a contrary intention appears in the conveyance.

(2) A conveyance of freehold land to a corporation sole by his corporate designation without the word "successors" shall pass to the corporation the fee simple or other the whole interest which the grantor had power to convey in such land, unless a intention appears in the conveyance.

(3) In a voluntary conveyance a resulting trust for the grantor shall not be implied merely by reason that the property is not expressed to be conveyed for the use or benefit of the grantee.

(4) The foregoing provisions of this section apply only to conveyances and deeds executed after the commencement of this Act:

Provided that in a deed executed after the thirty-first day of December, eighteen hundred and eighty-one, it is sufficient—

(a) In the limitation of an estate in fee simple, to use the words "in fee simple", without the word "heirs";

(b) In the limitation of an estate tail, to use the words "in tail" without the words "heirs of the body"; and

(c) In the limitation of an estate in tail male or in tail female, to use the words "in tail male" or "in tail female", as the case requires, without the words "heirs male of the body", or "heirs female of the body."

A2–004   **Law of Property (Miscellaneous Provisions) Act 1989**

(c. 34)

2.—(1) A contract for the sale or other disposition of an interest in land can only be made in writing and only by incorporating all the terms which the parties have expressly agreed in one document or, where contracts are exchanged, in each.

(2) The terms may be incorporated in a document either by being set out in it or by reference to some other document.

(3) The document incorporating the terms or, where contracts are exchanged, one of the documents incorporating them (but not necessarily the same one) must be signed by or on behalf of each party to the contract.

(4) Where a contract for the sale or other disposition of an interest in land satisfies the conditions of this section by reason only of the rectification of one or more documents in pursuance of an order of a court, the contract shall come into being, or be deemed to have come into being, at such time as may be specified in the order.

(5) This section does not apply in relation to—

(a)   a contract to grant such a lease as is mentioned in section 54(2) of the [1925 c. 20.] Law of Property Act 1925 (short leases);
(b)   a contract made in the course of a public auction; or
(c)   a contract regulated under the [1986 c. 60.] Financial Services Act 1986;

and nothing in this section affects the creation or operation of resulting, implied or constructive trusts.

(6) In this section—

"disposition" has the same meaning as in the Law of Property Act 1925;
"interest in land" means any estate, interest or charge in or over land or in or over the proceeds of sale of land.

(7) Nothing in this section shall apply in relation to contracts made before this section comes into force.

(8) Section 40 of the Law of Property Act 1925 (which is superseded by this section) shall cease to have effect.

Matrimonial Proceedings and Property Act 1970

(c. 45)   A2–005

Part II

Miscellaneous Provisions

Provisions Relating to Property of Married Persons

s.37 Contributions by spouse in money or money's worth to the improvement of property

It is hereby declared that where a husband or wife contributes in money or money's worth to the improvement of real or personal property in which or in the proceeds of sale of which either or both of them has or have a beneficial interest, the husband or wife so contributing shall, if the contribution is of a substantial nature and subject to any agreement between them to the contrary express or implied, be treated as having then acquired by virtue of his or her contribution a share or an enlarged share, as the case may be, in that beneficial interest of such an extent as may have been then agreed or, in default of such agreement, as may seem in all the circumstances just to any court before which the question of the existence or extent of the beneficial interest of the husband or wife arises (whether in proceedings between them or in any other proceedings).

Notes:

Words of enactment omitted under authority of Statute Law Revision Act 1948 (c. 62), s.3A dagger appended to a marginal note means that it is no longer accurate.
S.37 applied by Law Reform (Miscellaneous Provisions) Act 1970 (c. 33), s.2(1).

s.39 Extension of s.17 of Married Women's Property Act 1882.

An application may be made to the High Court or a county court under section 17 of the Married Women's Property Act 1882 (powers of the court in disputes between husband and wife about property) (including that section as extended by section 7 of the Matrimonial Causes (Property and Maintenance) Act 1958) by either of the parties to a marriage notwithstanding that their marriage has been dissolved or annulled so long as the application is made within the period of three years beginning with the date on which the marriage was dissolved or annulled; and references in the said section 17 and the said section 7 to a husband or a wife shall be construed accordingly.

Notes:

Words of enactment omitted under authority of Statute Law Revision Act 1948 (c. 62), s.3A dagger appended to a marginal note means that it is no longer accurate.

A2–006   **Married Women's Property Act 1882**

(c.75)

s.17 Questions between husband and wife as to property to be decided in a summary way.

In any question between husband and wife as to the title to or possession of property, either party, [. . .][1] may apply by summons or otherwise in a summary way [to the High Court or such county court as may be prescribed and the court may, on such an application (which may be heard in private), make such order with respect to the property as it thinks fit.][2] [In this section "prescribed" means prescribed by rules of court and rules made for the purposes of this section may confer jurisdiction on county courts whatever the situation or value of the property in dispute.[3]

Notes:

Act amended by Married Women's Property Act 1907 (c. 18); Preamble omitted under authority of Statute Law Revision Act 1898 (c. 22); Words of enactment omitted under authority of Statute Law Revision Act 1948 (c. 62), s.3; This Act is not necessarily in the form in which it has effect in Northern Ireland; s.11 amended by Family Law Reform Act 1969 (c. 46), s.19(1)
S.17 extended by Matrimonial Causes (Property and Maintenance) Act 1958 (c. 35), s.7; applied by Law Reform (Miscellaneous Provisions) Act 1970 (c. 33), s.2(2); amended by Matrimonial Proceedings and Property Act 1970 (c. 45), s.39 and extended with modifications by SI 1977/344, r.106 (as substituted by SI 1986/634, r.21)

Trusts of Land and Appointment of Trustees Act 1996   A2–007

(c. 47)

An Act to make new provision about trusts of land including provision phasing out the Settled Land Act 1925; abolishing the doctrine of conversion and otherwise amending the law about trusts for sale of land; to amend the law about the appointment and retirement of trustees of any trust; and for connected purposes.

[JULY 24, 1996]

BE IT ENACTED by the Queen's most Excellent Majesty, by and with the advice and consent of the Lords Spiritual and Temporal, and Commons, in this present Parliament assembled, and by the authority of the same, as follows:—

---

[1] Words repealed by Statute Law (Repeals) Act 1969 (c. 52), Sch.1, Pt. III
[2] Words substituted by Matrimonial and Family Proceedings Act 1984 (c. 42), ss.43, 48(2)
[3] Words substituted by Matrimonial and Family Proceedings Act 1984 (c. 42), ss.43, 48(2)

PART I

TRUSTS OF LAND

Introductory

s.1 Meaning of "trust of land".

(1) In this Act—

    (a) "trust of land" means (subject to subsection (3)) any trust of property which consists of or includes land; and

    (b) "trustees of land" means trustees of a trust of land.

(2) The reference in subsection (1)(a) to a trust—

    (a) is to any description of trust (whether express, implied, resulting or constructive), including a trust for sale and a bare trust, and

    (b) includes a trust created, or arising, before the commencement of this Act.

(3) The reference to land in subsection (1)(a) does not include land which (despite section 2) is settled land or which is land to which the Universities and College Estates Act 1925 applies.

Settlements and Trusts for Sale as Trusts of Land

s.2 Trusts in place of settlements.

(1) No settlement created after the commencement of this Act is a settlement for the purposes of the Settled Land Act 1925, and no settlement shall be deemed to be made under that Act after that commencement.

(2) Subsection (1) does not apply to a settlement created on the occasion of an alteration in any interest in, or of a person becoming entitled under, a settlement which—

    (a) is in existence at the commencement of this Act, or

    (b) derives from a settlement within paragraph (a) or this paragraph.

(3) But a settlement created as mentioned in subsection (2) is not a settlement for the purposes of the Settled Land Act 1925 if provision to the effect that it is not is made in the instrument, or any of the instruments, by which it is created.

(4) Where at any time after the commencement of this Act there is in the case of any settlement which is a settlement for the purposes of the Settled Land Act 1925 no relevant property which is, or is deemed to be subject to the settlement, the settlement permanently ceases at that time to be a settlement for the purposes of that Act.

In this subsection "relevant property" means land and personal chattels to which section 67(1) of the Settled Land Act 1925 (heirlooms) applies.

(5) No land held on charitable, ecclesiastical or public trusts shall be or be deemed to be settled land after the commencement of this Act, even if it was or was deemed to be settled land before that commencement.

(6) Schedule 1 has effect to make provision consequential on this section (including provision to impose a trust in circumstances in which, apart from this section, there would be a settlement for the purposes of the Settled Land Act 1925 (and there would not otherwise be a trust)).

s.3 Abolition of doctrine of conversion.

(1) Where land is held by trustees subject to a trust for sale, the land is not to be regarded as personal property; and where personal property is subject to a trust for sale in order that the trustees may acquire land, the personal property is not to be regarded as land.

(2) Subsection (1) does not apply to a trust created by a will if the testator died before the commencement of this Act.

(3) Subject to that, subsection (1) applies to a trust whether it is created, or arises, before or after that commencement.

s.4 Express trusts for sale as trusts of land.

(1) In the case of every trust for sale of land created by a disposition there is to be implied, despite any provision to the contrary made by the disposition, a power for the trustees to postpone sale of the land; and the trustees are not liable in any way for postponing sale of the land, in the exercise of their discretion, for an indefinite period.

(2) Subsection (1) applies to a trust whether it is created, or arises, before or after the commencement of this Act.

(3) Subsection (1) does not affect any liability incurred by trustees before that commencement.

s.5 Implied trusts for sale as trusts of land.

(1) Schedule 2 has effect in relation to statutory provisions which impose a trust for sale of land in certain circumstances so that in those circumstances there is instead a trust of the land (without a duty to sell).

(2) Section 1 of the Settled Land Act 1925 does not apply to land held on any trust arising by virtue of that Schedule (so that any such land is subject to a trust of land).

Functions of Trustees of Land

s.6 General powers of trustees.

(1) For the purpose of exercising their functions as trustees, the trustees of land have in relation to the land subject to the trust all the powers of an absolute owner.

(2) Where in the case of any land subject to a trust of land each of the beneficiaries interested in the land is a person of full age and capacity who is absolutely entitled to the land, the powers conferred on the trustees by subsection (1) include the power to convey the land to the beneficiaries even though they have not required the trustees to do so; and where land is conveyed by virtue of this subsection—

> (a) the beneficiaries shall do whatever is necessary to secure that it vests in them, and
> (b) if they fail to do so, the court may make an order requiring them to do so.

(3) The trustees of land have power to acquire land under the power conferred by section 8 of the Trustee Act 2000.

(5) In exercising the powers conferred by this section trustees shall have regard to the rights of the beneficiaries.

(6) The powers conferred by this section shall not be exercised in contravention of, or of any order made in pursuance of, any other enactment or any rule of law or equity.

(7) The reference in subsection (6) to an order includes an order of any court or of the Charity Commissioners.

(8) Where any enactment other than this section confers on trustees authority to act subject to any restriction, limitation or condition, trustees of land may not exercise the powers conferred by this section to do any act which they are prevented from doing under the other enactment by reason of the restriction, limitation or condition.

[

(9) The duty of care under section 1 of the Trustee Act 2000 applies to trustees of land when exercising the powers conferred by this section.

]¹

s.7 Partition by trustees.

(1) The trustees of land may, where beneficiaries of full age are absolutely entitled in undivided shares to land subject to the trust, partition the land, or any part of it, and provide (by way of mortgage or otherwise) for the payment of any equality money.

(2) The trustees shall give effect to any such partition by conveying the partitioned land in severalty (whether or not subject to any legal mort-

---

¹ Added by Trustee Act (2000 c.29), Sch 2 (II) Para 45 (3).

gage created for raising equality money), either absolutely or in trust, in accordance with the rights of those beneficiaries.

(3) Before exercising their powers under subsection (2) the trustees shall obtain the consent of each of those beneficiaries.

(4) Where a share in the land is affected by an incumbrance, the trustees may either give effect to it or provide for its discharge from the property allotted to that share as they think fit.

(5) If a share in the land is absolutely vested in a minor, subsections (1) to (4) apply as if he were of full age, except that the trustees may act on his behalf and retain land or other property representing his share in trust for him.

[

(6) Subsection (1) is subject to sections 21 (part-unit: interests) and 22 (part-unit: charging) of the Commonhold and Leasehold Reform Act 2002.

$]^2$

s.8 Exclusion and restriction of powers.

(1) Sections 6 and 7 do not apply in the case of a trust of land created by a disposition in so far as provision to the effect that they do not apply is made by the disposition.

(2) If the disposition creating such a trust makes provision requiring any consent to be obtained to the exercise of any power conferred by section 6 or 7, the power may not be exercised without that consent.

(3) Subsection (1) does not apply in the case of charitable, ecclesiastical or public trusts.

(4) Subsections (1) and (2) have effect subject to any enactment which prohibits or restricts the effect of provision of the description mentioned in them.

s.9 Delegation by trustees.

(1) The trustees of land may, by power of attorney, delegate to any beneficiary or beneficiaries of full age and beneficially entitled to an interest in possession in land subject to the trust any of their functions as trustees which relate to the land.

(2) Where trustees purport to delegate to a person by a power of attorney under subsection (1) functions relating to any land and another person in good faith deals with him in relation to the land, he shall be presumed in favour of that other person to have been a person to whom the functions could be delegated unless that other person has knowledge at the time of the transaction that he was not such a person.

And it shall be conclusively presumed in favour of any purchaser whose interest depends on the validity of that transaction that other person dealt in good faith and did not have such knowledge if that other

---

[2] Added by Commonhold and Leasehold Reform Act (2002 c.15), Sch.5, para.8.

person makes a statutory declaration to that effect before or within three months after the completion of the purchase.

(3) A power of attorney under subsection (1) shall be given by all the trustees jointly and (unless expressed to be irrevocable and to be given by way of security) may be revoked by any one or more of them; and such a power is revoked by the appointment as a trustee of a person other than those by whom it is given (though not by any of those persons dying or otherwise ceasing to be a trustee).

(4) Where a beneficiary to whom functions are delegated by a power of attorney under subsection (1) ceases to be a person beneficially entitled to an interest in possession in land subject to the trust—

(a) if the functions are delegated to him alone, the power is revoked,

(b) if the functions are delegated to him and to other beneficiaries to be exercised by them jointly (but not separately), the power is revoked if each of the other beneficiaries ceases to be so entitled (but otherwise function exercisable in accordance with the power are so exercisable by the remaining beneficiary or beneficiaries), and

(c) if the functions are delegated to him and to other beneficiaries to be exercised by them separately (or either separately or jointly), the power is revoked in so far as it relates to him.

(5) A delegation under subsection (1) may be for any period or indefinite.

(6) A power of attorney under subsection (1) cannot be an enduring power within the meaning of the Enduring Powers of Attorney Act 1985

(7) Beneficiaries to whom functions have been delegated under subsection (1) are, in relation to the exercise of the functions, in the same position as trustees (with the same duties and liabilities); but such beneficiaries shall not be regarded as trustees for any other purposes (including, in particular, the purposes of any enactment permitting the delegation of functions by trustees or imposing requirements relating to the payment of capital money).

(9) Neither this section nor the repeal by this Act of section 29 of the Law of Property Act 1925 (which is superseded by this section) affects the operation after the commencement of this Act of any delegation effected before that commencement.

s.9A Duties of trustees in connection with delegation etc.

[

9A.—Duties of trustees in connection with delegation etc.

(1) The duty of care under section 1 of the Trustee Act 2000 applies to trustees of land in deciding whether to delegate any of their functions under section 9.

(2) Subsection (3) applies if the trustees of land—

(a)   delegate any of their functions under section 9, and
(b)   the delegation is not irrevocable.

(3) While the delegation continues, the trustees—

(a)   must keep the delegation under review,
(b)   if circumstances make it appropriate to do so, must consider whether there is a need to exercise any power of intervention that they have, and
(c)   if they consider that there is a need to exercise such a power, must do so.

(4)

"Power of intervention" includes—

(a)   a power to give directions to the beneficiary;
(b)   a power to revoke the delegation.

(5) The duty of care under section 1 of the 2000 Act applies to trustees in carrying out any duty under subsection (3).
(6) A trustee of land is not liable for any act or default of the beneficiary, or beneficiaries, unless the trustee fails to comply with the duty of care in deciding to delegate any of the trustees' functions under section 9 or in carrying out any duty under subsection (3).
(7) Neither this section nor the repeal of section 9(8) by the Trustee Act 2000 affects the operation after the commencement of this section of any delegation effected before that commencement.

Consents and Consultation

s.10 Consents.

(1) If a disposition creating a trust of land requires the consent of more than two persons to the exercise by the trustees of any function relating to the land, the consent of any two of them to the exercise of the function is sufficient in favour of a purchaser.
(2) Subsection (1) does not apply to the exercise of a function by trustees of land held on charitable, ecclesiastical or public trusts.
(3) Where at any time a person whose consent is expressed by a disposition creating a trust of land to be required to the exercise by the trustees of any function relating to the land is not of full age—

(a)   his consent is not, in favour of a purchaser, required to the exercise of the function, but
(b)   the trustees shall obtain the consent of a parent who has parental responsibility for him (within the meaning of the Children Act 1989 or of a guardian of his.

s.11 Consultation with beneficiaries.

(1) The trustees of land shall in the exercise of any function relating to land subject to the trust—

    (a) so far as practicable, consult the beneficiaries of full age and beneficially entitled to an interest in possession in the land, and

    (b) so far as consistent with the general interest of the trust, give effect to the wishes of those beneficiaries, or (in case of dispute) of the majority (according to the value of their combined interests).

(2) Subsection (1) does not apply—

    (a) in relation to a trust created by a disposition in so far as provision that it does not apply is made by the disposition.

    (b) in relation to a trust created or arising under a will made before the commencement of this Act, or

    (c) in relation to the exercise of the power mentioned in <u>section 6(2)</u>

(3) Subsection (1) does not apply to a trust created before the commencement of this Act by a disposition, or a trust created after that commencement by reference to such a trust, unless provision to the effect that it is to apply is made by a deed executed—

    (a) in a case in which the trust was created by one person and he is of full capacity, by that person, or

    (b) in a case in which the trust was created by more than one person, by such of the persons who created the trust as are alive and of full capacity.

(4) A deed executed for the purposes of subsection (3) is irrevocable.

Right of Beneficiaries to Occupy Trust Land

s.12 The right to occupy.

(1) A beneficiary who is beneficially entitled to an interest in possession in land subject to a trust of land is entitled by reason of his interest to occupy the land at any time if at that time—

    (a) the purposes of the trust include making the land available for his occupation (or for the occupation of beneficiaries of a class of which he is a member or of beneficiaries in general), or

    (b) the land is held by the trustees so as to be so available.

(2) Subsection (1) does not confer on a beneficiary a right to occupy land if it is either unavailable or unsuitable for occupation by him.

(3) This section is subject to section 13

s.13 Exclusion and restriction of right to occupy

(1) Where two or more beneficiaries are (or apart from this subsection would be) entitled under section 12 to occupy land, the trustees of land may exclude or restrict the entitlement of any one or more (but not all) of them.

(2) Trustees may not under subsection (1)—

    (a)   unreasonably exclude any beneficiary's entitlement to occupy land, or

    (b)   restrict any such entitlement to an unreasonable extent.

(3) The trustees of land may from time to time impose reasonable conditions on any beneficiary in relation to his occupation of land by reason of his entitlement under section 12

(4) The matters to which trustees are to have regard in exercising the powers conferred by this section include—

    (a)   the intentions of the person or persons (if any) who created the trust.

    (b)   the purposes for which the land is held, and

    (c)   the circumstances and wishes of each of the beneficiaries who is (or apart from any previous exercise by the trustees of those powers would be) entitled to occupy the land under section 12

(5) The conditions which may be imposed on a beneficiary under subsection (3) include, in particular, conditions requiring him—

    (a)   to pay any outgoings or expenses in respect of the land, or

    (b)   to assume any other obligation in relation to the land or to any activity which is or is proposed to be conducted there.

(6) Where the entitlement of any beneficiary to occupy land under section 12 has been excluded or restricted, the conditions which may be imposed on any other beneficiary under subsection (3) include, in particular, conditions requiring him to—

    (a)   make payments by way of compensation to the beneficiary whose entitlement has been excluded or restricted, or

    (b)   forgo any payment or other benefit to which he would otherwise be entitled under the trust so as to benefit that beneficiary.

(7) The powers conferred on trustees by this section may not be exercised—

    (a)   so as prevent any person who is in occupation of land (whether or not by reason of an entitlement under section 12 from continuing to occupy the land, or

    (b)   in a manner likely to result in any such person ceasing to occupy the land, unless he consents or the court has given approval.

(8) The matters to which the court is to have regard in determining whether to give approval under subsection (7) include the matters mentioned in subsection (4)(a) to (c)

Powers of Court

s.14 Applications for order.

(1) Any person who is a trustee of land or has an interest in property subject to a trust of land may make an application to the court for an order under this section

(2) On an application for an order under this section the court may make any such order—

> (a) relating to the exercise by the trustees of any of their functions (including an order relieving them of any obligation to obtain the consent of, or to consult, any person in connection with the exercise of any of their functions), or
>
> (b) declaring the nature or extent of a person's interest in property subject to the trust,

as the court thinks fit.

(3) The court may not under this section make any order as to the appointment or removal of trustees.

(4) The powers conferred on the court by this section are exercisable on an application whether it is made before or after the commencement of this Act.

s.15 Matters relevant in determining applications.

(1) The matters to which the court is to have regard in determining an application for an order under section 14 include—

> (a) the intentions of the person or persons (if any) who created the trust,
>
> (b) the purposes for which the property subject to the trust is held,
>
> (c) the welfare of any minor who occupies or might reasonably be expected to occupy any land subject to the trust as his home, and
>
> (d) the interests of any secured creditor of any beneficiary.

(2) In the case of an application relating to the exercise in relation to any land of the powers conferred on the trustees by section 13 the matters to which the court is to have regard also include the circumstances and wishes of each of the beneficiaries who is (or apart from any previous exercise by the trustees of those powers would be) entitled to occupy the land under section 12.

(3) In the case of any other application, other than one relating to the exercise of the power mentioned in section 6(2), the matters to which the court is to have regard also include the circumstances and wishes of any beneficiaries of full age and entitled to an interest in possession in property subject to the trust or (in case of dispute) of the majority (according to the value of their combined interests).

(4) This section does not apply to an application if section 335A of the Insolvency Act 1986 (which is inserted by Schedule 3 and relates to applications by a trustee of a bankrupt) applies to it.

Purchaser Protection

s.16 Protection of purchasers.

(1) A purchaser of land which is or has been subject to a trust need not be concerned to see that any requirement imposed on the trustees by section 6(5), 7(3) or 11(1) has been complied with.

(2) Where—

(a) trustees of land who convey land which (immediately before it is conveyed) is subject to the trust contravene section 6(6) or (8) but

(b) the purchaser of the land from the trustees has no actual notice of the contravention,

the contravention does not invalidate the conveyance.

(3) Where the powers of trustees of land are limited by virtue of section 8—

(a) the trustees shall take all reasonable steps to bring the limitation to the notice of any purchaser of the land from them, but

(b) the limitation does not invalidate any conveyance by the trustees to a purchaser who has no actual notice of the limitation.

(4) Where trustees of land convey land which (immediately before it is conveyed) is subject to the trust to persons believed by them to be beneficiaries absolutely entitled to the land under the trust and of full age and capacity—

(a) the trustees shall execute a deed declaring that they are discharged from the trust in relation to that land, and

(b) if they fail to do so, the court may make an order requiring them to do so.

(5) A purchaser of land to which a deed under subsection (4) relates is entitled to assume that, as from the date of the deed, the land is not subject to the trust unless he has actual notice that the trustees were mistaken in their belief that the land was conveyed to beneficiaries

absolutely entitled to the land under the trust and of full age and capacity.

(6) Subsections (2) and (3) do not apply to land held on charitable, ecclesiastical or public trusts.

(7) This section does not apply to registered land.

Supplementary

s.17 Application of provisions to trusts of proceeds of sale [...].

(2) Section 14 applies in relation to a trust of proceeds of sale of land and trustees of such a trust as in relation to a trust of land and trustees of land.

(3) In this section "trust of proceeds of sale of land" means (subject to subsection (5)) any trust of property (other than a trust of land) which consists of or includes—

    (a) any proceeds of a disposition of land held in trust (including settled land), or

    (b) any property representing any such proceeds.

(4) The references in subsection (3) to a trust—

    (a) are to any description of trust (whether express, implied, resulting or constructive), including a trust for sale and a bare trust, and

    (b) include a trust created, or arising, before the commencement of this Act.

(5) A trust which (despite section 2 is a settlement for the purposes of the Settled Land Act 1925 cannot be a trust of proceeds of sale of land.

(6) In subsection (3)—

    (a) "disposition" includes any disposition made, or coming into operation, before the commencement of this Act, and

    (b) the reference to settled land includes personal chattels to which section 67(1) of the Settled Land Act 1925 (heirlooms) applies.

s.18 Application of Part to personal representatives.

(1) The provisions of this Part relating to trustees, other than sections 10, 11 and 14, apply to personal representatives, but with appropriate modifications and without prejudice to the functions of personal representatives for the purposes of administration.

(2) The appropriate modifications include–

    (a) the substitution of references to persons interested in the due administration of the estate for references to beneficiaries, and

(b)   the substitution of references to the will for references to the disposition creating the trust.

(3) Section 3(1) does not apply to personal representatives if the death occurs before the commencement of this Act.

PART II

APOINTMENT AND RETIREMENT OF TRUSTEES

s.19 Appointment and retirement of trustee at instance of beneficiaries.

(1) This section applies in the case of a trust where–

(a)   there is no person nominated for the purpose of appointing new trustees by the instrument, if any creating the trust, and
(b)   the beneficiaries under the trust are of full age and capacity and (taken together) are absolutely entitled to the property subject to the trust.

(2) The beneficiaries may give a direction or directions of either or both of the following descriptions–

(a)   a written direction to a trustee or trustees to retire from the trust, and
(b)   a written direction to the trustees or trustee for the time being for, if there are none, to the personal representative of the last person who was a trustee) to appoint by writing to be a trustee or trustees the person or persons specified in the direction

(3) Where–

(a)   a trustee has been given a direction under subsection (2)(a)
(b)   reasonable arrangements have been made for the protection of any rights of his in connection with the trust,
(c)   after he has retired there will be either a trust corporation or at least two persons to act as trustees to perform the trust, and
(d)   either another person is to be appointed to be a new trustee on his retirement (whether in compliance with a direction under subsection (2)(b) or otherwise) or the continuing trustees by deed consent to his retirement,

he shall make a deed declaring his retirement and shall be deemed to have retired and be discharged from the trust.

(4) Where a trustee retires under subsection (3) he and the continuing trustees (together with any new trustee) shall (subject to any arrangements for the protection of his rights) do anything necessary to vest the

trust property in the continuing trustees (or the continuing and new trustees).

(5) This section has effect subject to the restrictions imposed by the Trustee Act 1925 on the number of trustees

s.20 Appointment of substitute for incapable trustee.

(1) This section applies where–

(a) a trustee is incapable by reason of mental disorder of exercising his functions as trustee.

(b) there is no person who is both entitled and willing and able to appoint a trustee in place of him under section 36(1) of the Trustee Act 1925 and

(c) the beneficiaries under the trust are of full age and capacity and (taken together) are absolutely entitled to the property subject to the trust.

(2) The beneficiaries may give to–

(a) a receiver of the trustee.

(b) an attorney acting for him under the authority of a power of attorney created by an instrument which is registered under section 6 of the Enduring Powers of Attorney Act 1985, or

(c) a person authorised for the purpose by the authority having jurisdiction under Part VII of the Mental Health Act 1983,

a written direction to appoint by writing the person or persons specified in the direction to be a trustee or trustees in place of the incapable trustee.

s.21 Supplementary.

(1) For the purposes of section 19 or 20 a direction is given by beneficiaries if–

(a) a single direction is jointly given by all of them.

(b) (subject to subsection (2)) a direction is given by each of them (whether solely or jointly with one or more, but not all, of the others),

and none of them by writing withdraws the direction given by him before it has been complied with.

(2) Where more than one direction is given each must specify for appointment or retirement the same person or persons.

(3) Subsection (7) of section 36 of the Trustee Act 1925 (powers of trustees appointed under that section applies to a trustee appointed under section 19 or 20 as if he were appointed under that section.

(4) A direction under section 19 or 20 must not specify a person or persons for appointment if the appointment of that person or those persons would be in contravention of section 35(1) of the Trustee Act

1925 or section 24(1) of the Law of Property Act 1925 (requirements as to identity of trustees).

(5) Section 19 and 20 do not apply in relation to a trust created by a disposition in so far as provision that they do not apply is made by the disposition.

(6) Section 19 and 20 do not apply in relation to a trust created before the commencement of this Act by a disposition in so far as provision to the effect that they do not apply is made by a deed executed–

(a) in a case in which the trust was created by one person and he is of full capacity, by that person, or

(b) in a case in which the trust was created by more than one person, by such of the persons who created the trust as are alive and of full capacity.

(7) A deed executed for the purposes of subsection (6) is irrevocable.

(8) Where a deed is executed for the purposes of subsection (6)–

(a) it does not affect anything done before its execution to comply with a direction under section 19 or 20; but

(b) a direction under section 19 or 20 which has been given but not complied with before its execution shall cease to have effect.

PART III

Supplementary

s.22 Meaning of "beneficiary".

(1) In this Act "beneficiary", in relation to a trust, means any person who under the trust has an interest in property subject to the trust (including a person who has such an interest as a trustee or a personal representative).

(2) In this Act references to a beneficiary who is beneficially entitled do not include a beneficiary who has an interest in property subject to the trust only by reason of being a trustee or personal representative.

(3) For the purposes of this Act a person who is a beneficiary only by reason of being an annuitant is not to be regarded as entitled to an interest in possession in land subject to the trust.

s.23 Other interpretation provisions.

(1) In this Act "purchaser" has the same meaning as in Part I of the Law of Property Act 1925.

(2) Subject to that, where an expression used in this Act is given a meaning by the Law of Property Act 1925 it has the same meaning as in that Act unless the context otherwise requires.

(3) In this Act "the court" means–

    (a) the High Court, or

    (b) a county court.

s.24 Application to Crown.

(1) Subject to subsection (2), this Act binds the Crown.

(2) This Act (except so far as it relates to undivided shares and joint ownership) does not affect or alter the descent, devolution or nature of the estates and interests of or in–

    (a) land for the time being vested in Her Majesty in right of the Crown or of the Duchy of Lancaster, or

    (b) land for the time being belonging to the Duchy of Cornwall and held in right or respect of the Duchy.

s.25 Amendments repeals etc.

(1) The enactments mentioned in Schedule 3 have effect subject to the amendments specified in that Schedule (which are minor or consequential on other provisions of this Act).

(2) The enactments mentioned in Schedule 4 are repealed to the extent specified in the third column of that Schedule.

(3) Neither section 2(5) nor the repeal by this Act of section 29 of the Settled Land Act 1925 applies in relation to the deed of settlement set out in the Schedule to the Chequers Estate Act 1917 or the trust instrument set out in the Schedule to the Chevening Estate Act 1959.

(4) The amendments and repeals made by this Act do not affect any entailed interest created before the commencement of this Act.

(5) The amendments and repeals made by this Act in consequence of section 3–

    (a) do not affect a trust created by a will if the testator died before the commencement of this Act, and

    (b) do not affect personal representatives of a person who died before that commencement;

and the repeal of section 22 of the Partnership Act 1890 does not apply in any circumstances involving the personal representatives of a partner who died before that commencement.

s.26 Power to make consequential provision.

(1) The Lord Chancellor may by order made by statutory instrument make any such supplementary, transitional or incidental provision as appears to him to be appropriate for any of the purposes of this Act or in consequence of any of the provisions of this Act.

(2) An order under subsection (1) may, in particular, include provision modifying any enactment contained in a public general or local Act which is passed before, or in the same Session as, this Act.

(3) A statutory instrument made in the exercise of the power conferred by this section is subject to annulment in pursuance of a resolution of either House of Parliament.

s.27 Short title, commencement and extent.

(1) This Act may be cited as the Trusts of Land and Appointment of Trustees Act 1996.

(2) This Act comes into force on such day as the Lord Chancellor appoints by order made by statutory instrument.

(3) Subject to subsection (4), the provisions of this Act extend only to England and Wales.

(4) The repeal in section 30(2) of the Agriculture Act 1970 extends only to Northern Ireland.

SCHEDULE 1

PROVISIONS CONSEQUENTIAL ON SECTION 2

Minors

Para.1

(1) Where after the commencement of this Act a person purports to convey a legal estate in land to a minor or two or more minors alone the conveyance–

    (a) is not effective to pass the legal estate, but

    (b) operates as a declaration that the land is held in trust for the minor or minors (or if he purports to convey it to the minor or minors in trust for any persons for those persons).

(2) Where after the commencement of this Act a person purports to convey a legal estate in land to–

    (a) a minor or two or more minors and

    (b) another person who is or other persons who are of full age

the conveyance operates to vest the land in the other person or persons in trust for the minor or minors and the other person or persons (or if he purports to convey it to them in trust for any persons, for those persons).

(3) Where immediately before the commencement of this Act a conveyance is operating (by virtue of section 27 of the Settled Land Act 1925 as an agreement to execute a settlement in favour of a minor or minors.

    (a) the agreement ceases to have effect on the commencement of this Act, and

(b) the conveyance subsequently operates instead as a declaration that the land is held in trust for the minor or minors.

Para.2

Where after the commencement of this Act a legal estate in land would, by reason of intestacy or in any other circumstances not dealt with in paragraph 1, vest in a person who is a minor if he were a person of full age, the land is held in trust for the minor.

Para.3

Where, by virtue of an instrument coming into operation after the commencement of this Act, land becomes charged voluntarily (or in consideration of marriage [or the formation of a civil partnership]) or by way of family arrangement, whether immediately or after an interval, with the payment of–

(a) a rentcharge for the life of a person or a shorter period, or
(b) capital, annual or periodical sums for the benefit of a person,

the instrument operates as a declaration that the land is held in trust for giving effect to the charge.

Para.4

(1) This paragraph applies in the case of land held on charitable, ecclesiastical or public trusts (other than land to which the Universities and College Estates Act 1925 applies).
(2) Where there is a conveyance of such land–

(a) if neither section 37(1) nor section 39(1) of the Charities Act 1993 applies to the conveyance, it shall state that the land is held on such trusts, and
(b) if neither section 37(2) nor section 39(2) of that Act has been complied with in relation to the conveyance and a purchaser has notice that the land is held on such trusts, he must see that any consents or orders necessary to authorise the transaction have been obtained.

(3) Where any trustees or the majority of any set of trustees have power to transfer or create any legal estate in the land, the estate shall be transferred or created by them in the names and on behalf of the persons in whom it is vested

Para.5

(1) Where a person purports by an instrument coming into operation after the commencement of this Act to grant to another person an entailed interest in real or personal property, the instrument–

(a) is not effective to grant an entailed interest, but

(b) operates instead as a declaration that the property is held in trust absolutely for the person to whom an entailed interest in the property was purportedly granted.

(2) Where a person purports by an instrument coming into operation after the commencement of this Act to declare himself a tenant in tail of real or personal property, the instrument is not effective to create an entailed interest.

Para.6

Where a settlement ceases to be a settlement for the purposes of the Settled Land Act 1925 because no relevant property (within the meaning of section 2(4) is or is deemed to be, subject to the settlement, any property which is or later becomes subject to the settlement is held in trust for the persons interested under the settlement.

SCHEDULE 2

AMENDMENTS OF STATUTORY PROVISIONS IMPOSING TRUST FOR SALE

Mortgaged Property held by Trustees after Redemption Barred

Para.1

(1) Section 31 of the Law of Property Act 1925 (implied trust for sale of mortgaged property where right of redemption is barred) is amended as follows

(2) In subsection (1), for the words "on trust for sale" substitute

"in trust—

(a) to apply the income from the property in the same manner as interest paid on the mortgage debt would have been applicable and

(b) if the property is sold, to apply the net proceeds of sale, after payment of costs and expenses, in the same manner as repayment of the mortgage debt would have been applicable.
"

(3) In subsection (2) for the words from the beginning to "this subsection" substitute—

"

(2) Subsection (1) of this section
"

(4) Omit subsection (3)

(5) For subsection (4) substitute–

"

(4) Where–

(a) the mortgage money is capital money for the purposes of the Settled Land Act 1925;

(b) land other than any forming the whole or part of the property mentioned in subsection (1) of this section is, or is deemed to be, subject to the settlement; and

(c) the tenant for life or statutory owner requires the trustees to execute with respect to land forming the whole or part of that property a vesting deed such as would have been required in relation to the land if it had been acquired on a purchase with capital money.

the trustees shall execute such a vesting deed

"

(6) In accordance with the amendments made by sub-paragraphs (2) to (5), in the sidenote of section 31 for the words "Trust for sale" substitute "Trust".

(7) The amendments made by this paragraph–

(a) apply whether the right of redemption is discharged before or after the commencement of this Act, but

(b) are without prejudice to any dealings or arrangements made before the commencement of this Act.

Land Purchased by Trustees of Personal Property etc.

Para.2

(1) Section 32 of the Law of Property Act 1925 (implied trust for sale of land acquired by trustees of personal property or of land held on trust for sale) is omitted.

(2) The repeal made by this paragraph applies in relation to land purchased after the commencement of this Act whether the trust or will in pursuance of which it is purchased comes into operation before or after the commencement of this Act.

Dispositions to Tenants in Common

Para.3

(1) Section 34 of the Law of Property Act 1925 is amended as follows.

(2) In subsection (2) (conveyance of land in undivided shares to operate as conveyance to grantees on trust for sale), for the words from "upon the statutory trusts" to "those shares" substitute "in trust for the persons interested in the land"

(3) In subsection (3) (devise etc. of land in undivided shares to operate as devise etc. to trustees of will etc. on trust for sale)–

(a)   omit the words from "the trustees (if any)" to "then to" and the words "in each case" and

(b)   for the words "upon the statutory trusts hereinafter mentioned" substitute "in trust for the persons interested in the land".

(4) After that subsection insert–

"(3A) In subsections (2) and (3) of this section references to the persons interested in the land include persons interested as trustees or personal representatives (as well as persons beneficially interested)."

(5) Omit subsection (4) (settlement of undivided shares in land to operate only as settlement of share of profits of sale and rents and profits).

(6) The amendments made by this paragraph apply whether the disposition is made, or comes into operation, before or after the commencement of this Act.

Joint Tenancies

Para.4

(1) Section 36 of the Law of Property Act 1925 is amended as follows.

(2) In subsection (1) (implied trust for sale applicable to land held for persons as joint tenants), for the words "on trust for sale" substitute "in trust"

(3) In subsection (2) (severance of beneficial joint tenancy)–

(a)   in the proviso for the words "under the trust for sale affecting the land the net proceeds of sale, and the net rents and profits until sale, shall be held upon the trusts" substitute "the land shall be held in trust on terms", and

(b)   in the final sentence, for the words "on trust for sale" substitute "in trust".

(4) The amendments made by this paragraph apply whether the legal estate is limited, or becomes held in trust, before or after the commencement of this Act.

Intestacy

Para 5

(1) Section 33 of the Administration of Estates Act 1925 (implied trust for sale on intestacy) is amended as follows.
(2) For subsection (1) substitute–

"

(1) On the death of a person intestate as to any real or personal estate, that estate shall be held in trust by his personal representatives with the power to sell it.
"

(3) In subsection (2), for the words from the beginning to "pay all" substitute

"

(2) The personal representatives shall pay out of–

(a) the ready money of the deceased (so far as not disposed of by his will, if any); and
(b) any not money arising from disposing of any other part of his estate (after payment of costs).
all
"

(4) In subsection (4) for the words from "including" to "retained" substitute "and any part of the estate of the deceased which remains"
(5) The amendments made by this paragraph apply whether the death occurs before or after the commencement of this Act.

Reverter of Sites

Para.6

(1) Section 1 of the Reverter of Sites Act 1987 (right of reverter replaced by trust for sale) is amended as follows.
(2) In subsection (2)–

(a) after "a trust" insert "for the persons who (but for this Act) would from time to time be entitled to the ownership of the land by virtue of its reverter with a power, without consulting them" and
(b) for the words "upon trust" onwards substitute "in trust for those persons; but they shall not be entitled by reason of their interest to occupy the land."

(3) In subsection (3), for the words "trustees for sale" substitute "trustees"

(4) In subsection (4); for the words "on trust for sale" substitute "in trust"

(5) In accordance with the amendments made by this paragraph, in the sidenote, for "trust for sale" substitute "trust".

(6) The amendments made by this paragraph apply whether the trust arises before or after the commencement of this Act.

Trusts Deemed to Arise in 1926

Para.7

Where at the commencement of this Act any land is held on trust for sale, or on the statutory trusts, by virtue of Schedule 1 to the Law of Property Act 1925 (transitional provisions), it shall after that commencement be held in trust for the persons interested in the land; and references in that Schedule to trusts for sale or trustees for sale or to the statutory trusts shall be construed accordingly.

SCHEDULE 3

MINOR AND CONSEQUENTIAL AMENDMENTS

The Law of Property Act 1922 (c. 16)

Para.1

In paragraph 17(3) and (4) of Schedule 15 to the Law of Property Act 1922 for the words "held on trust for sale" substitute "subject to a trust of land".

The Settled Land Act 1925 (c. 18)

Para.2

(1) The Settled Land Act 1925 is amended as follows.

(2) In section 1(1)(ii)(c) after the word "fee" insert "(other than a fee which as a fee simple absolute by virtue of section 7 of the Law of Property Act 1925)"

(3) In section 3; for the words "not held upon trust for sale which has been subject to a settlement" substitute "which has been subject to a settlement which as a settlement for the purposes of this Act"

(4) In section 7(5), for the words "trustee for sale" substitute "trustee of land"

(5) In section 12(1); for the words "trustee for sale" substitute "trustee of land".

(6) In section 17.

(a) in subsection (1)–

  (i)   for the words "trust for sale", in the first three places, substitute "trust of land" and

  (ii) for the words "held on trust for sale" substitute "subject to a trust of land".

(b) in subsection (2)(c), for the words "a conveyance on trust for sale" substitute "land". and

(c) in subsection (3), for the words "any trust for sale" substitute "a trust of land".

(7) In section 18(2)(b); for the words "trustee for sale" substitute "trustee of land"

(8) In section 20(1)(viii), for the words "an immediate binding trust for sale" substitute "a trust of land"

(9) In section 30(1)–

(a) in paragraph (iii) for the words "power of or upon trust for sale of" substitute "a power or duty to sell", and

(b) in paragraph (iv)–

  (i)   for the words "future power of sale, or under a future trust for sale of" substitute "a future power or duty to sell", and

  (ii) for the words "or trust" substitute "or duty".

(10) In section 33(1), for the words "any power of sale, or trust for sale" substitute "a power or duty to sell".

(11) In section 36–

(a) for the words–

  (i)   "upon the statutory trusts" in subsection (2), and

  (ii) "on the statutory trusts" in subsection (3),

  substitute "in trust for the persons interested in the land",

(b) in subsection (4) for the words "trust for sale" substitute "trust of land".

(c) for subsection (6) substitute–

  "(6) In subsections (2) and (3) of this section references to the persons interested in the land include persons interested as trustees or personal representatives (as well as persons beneficially interested)."

; and

(d) in accordance with the amendments made by paragraphs (a) to
     (c) in the sidenote, for the words "trust for sale of the land"
     substitute "trust of land"

(12) In section 110(5), for the words "trustee for sale" substitute
"trustee of land"
(13) In section 117(1)–

(a) in paragraph (ix), for the words "not being" substitute "but
     does not (except in the phrase "trust of land") include", and
(b) in paragraph (xxx), for the words "trustees for sale" and
     "power to postpone a sale" have the same meanings" substitute
     "has the same meaning".

The Trustee Act 1925 (c. 19)

Para.3

(1) The Trustee Act 1925 as amended as follows.
(2) In section 12–

(a) in subsection (1), for the words "a trust for sale or a power of
     sale of property is vested in a trustee" substitute "a trustee has a
     duty or power to sell property", and
(b) in subsection (2), for the word "trust", in both places, substitute
     "duty"

(3) In section 14(2), for paragraph (a) substitute–

   "(a) proceeds of sale or other capital money arising under a trust of
        land;"

[…]
(5) In section 20(3)(c), for the words "property held upon trust for
sale" substitute "land subject to a trust of land or personal property held
on trust for sale"
(6) In section 24–

(a) for the words "the proceeds of sale of land directed to be sold,
     or in any other" substitute "any",
(b) for the words "trust for sale" substitute "trust",
(c) for the words "trustees for sale" substitute "trustees", and
(d) for the words "trust or" substitute "duty or".

(7) In section 27(1), for the words "or of a disposition on trust for sale"
substitute "trustees of land, trustees for sale of personal property"
(8) In section 32, for subsection (2) substitute–

"(2) This section does not apply to capital money arising under the Settled Land Act 1925"

(9) In section 34(2), for the words "on trust for sale of land" substitute "creating trusts of land".

(10) In section 35–

(a)   for subsection (1) substitute–

"(1) Appointments of new trustees of land and of new trustees of any trust of the proceeds of sale of the land shall, subject to any order of the court, be effected by separate instruments, but in such manner as to secure that the same persons become trustees of land and trustees of the trust of the proceeds of sale.",

(b)   for subsection (3) substitute–

"(3) Where new trustees of land are appointed, a memorandum of the persons who are for the time being the trustees of the land shall be endorsed on or annexed to the conveyance by which the land was vested in trustees of land, and that conveyance shall be produced to the persons who are for the time being the trustees of the land by the persons in possession of it in order for that to be done when the trustees require its production"

, and

(c)   in accordance with the amendments made by paragraphs (a) and (b), in the sidenote, for the words "dispositions on trust for sale of land" substitute "and trustees of land".

(11) In section 36(6), for the words before paragraph (a) substitute–

"(6) Where, in the case of any trust, there are not more than three trustees"

(12) In section 37(1)(c), for the word "individuals" substitute "persons"

(13) In section 39(1), for the word "individuals" substitute "persons"

(14) In section 40(2), for the words "the statutory power" substitute "section 39 of this Act or section 19 of the Trusts of Land and Appointment of Trustees Act 1996"

The Law of Property Act 1925 (c. 20)

Para.4

(1) The Law of Property Act 1925 is amended as follows.

(2) In section 2–

(a)   in subsection (1), in paragraph (ii)–

    (i)   for the words "trustees for sale" substitute "trustees of land", and

    (ii)   for the words "the statutory requirements respecting the payment of capital money arising under a disposition upon trust for sale" substitute "the requirements of section 27 of this Act respecting the payment of capital money arising on such a conveyance".

(b)   after that subsection insert–

"(1A) An equitable interest in land subject to a trust of land which remains in, or is to revert to, the settlor shall (subject to any contrary intention) be overreached by the conveyance if it would be so overreached were it an interest under the trust."

, and

(c)   in subsection (2)–

    (i)   for the words "a trust for sale" substitute "a trust of land".

    (ii)   for the words "under the trust for sale or the powers conferred on the trustees for sale" substitute "by the trustees", and

    (iii)   for the words "to the trust for sale" substitute "to the trust".

(3) In section 3(1)(c), for the words "Where the legal estate affected is neither settled land nor vested in trustees for sale" substitute "in any other case".

(4) In section 16–

(a)   in subsection (2), for the words "pursuant to a trust for sale" substitute "by trustees of land", and

(b)   in subsection (6), for the words "trustee for sale" substitute "trustee of land".

(5) In section 18–

(a)   in subsection (1)–

    (i)   after the word "settled" insert "or held subject to a trust of land", and

    (ii)   for the words "trustee for sale" substitute "trustee of land", and

(b)   in subsection (2)(b), for the words "of the land or of the proceeds of sale" substitute "or trust".

(6) In section 22(2)–

(a) for the words "held on trust for sale" substitute "subject to a trust of land", and

(b) for the words "under the trust for sale or under the powers vested in the trustees for sale" substitute "by the trustees".

and, in accordance with the amendments made by paragraphs (a) and (b), in the sidenote of section 22, for the words "on trust for sale" substitute "in trust".

(7) For section 24 substitute–

"Trusts of land
   24—Appointment of trustees of land
   (1) The persons having power to appoint new trustees of land shall be bound to appoint the same persons (if any) who are for the time being trustees of any trust of the proceeds of sale of the land.
   (2) A purchaser shall not be concerned to see that subsection (1) of this section has been complied with.
   (3) This section applies whether the trust of land and the trust of proceeds of sale are created, or arise, before or after the commencement of this Act."

(8) In section 27–

(a) for subsection (1) substitute–

"(1) A purchaser of a legal estate from trustees of land shall not be concerned with the trusts affecting the land, the net income of the land or the proceeds of sale of the land whether or not those trusts are declared by the same instrument as that by which the trust of land is created."

, and

(b) in subsection (2)–
     (i)   for the words "trust for sale" substitute "trust",
     (ii) for the words "the settlement of the net proceeds" substitute "any trust affecting the net proceeds of sale of the land if it is sold", and
     (iii) for the words "trustees for sale" substitute "trustees"

(9) In section 33–

(a) for the words "trustees for sale" substitute "trustees of land", and

(b) for the words "on trust for sale" substitute "land in trust".

(10) In section 39(4), for the words "trusts for sale" substitute "trusts"
(11) In section 42–

(a) in subsection (1)(a) for the words "trust for sale" substitute "trust of land", and

(b) in subsection (2)–

    (i) in paragraph (a), for the words "a conveyance on trust for sale" substitute "land", and

    (ii) in paragraph (b), for the words "on trust for sale" substitute "in trust".

(12) In section 66(2), for the words "trustee for sale" substitute "trustee of land".

(13) In section 102(1)–

(a) for the words "share in the proceeds of sale of the land and in the rents and profits thereof until sale" substitute "interest under the trust to which the land is subject", and

(b) for the words "trustees for sale" substitute "trustees".

(14) In section 131, after the words "but for this section" insert "(and paragraph 5 of Schedule 1 to the Trusts of Land and Appointment of Trustees Act 1996"

(15) In section 137

(a) in subsection (2)(ii), for the words "the proceeds of sale of land" onwards substitute "land subject to a trust of land, or the proceeds of the sale of such land, the persons to be served with notice shall be the trustees", and

(b) in subsection (5), for the words "held on trust for sale" substitute "subject to a trust of land".

(16) In section 153(6)(ii), for the words "in trust for sale" substitute "as a trustee of land".

The Land Registration Act 1925 (c. 21)

Para.5

[. . .]³

The Administration of Estates Act 1925 (c. 23)

Para.6

(1) The Administration of Estates Act 1925 is amended as follows.

(2) In section 39(1)–

---

³ Repealed by Land Registration Act (2002 c.9), Sch.13, para.1.

    (a) in paragraph (i), at the beginning insert "as respects the personal estate,".

    (b) for paragraph (ii) substitute–

"

    (ii) as respects the real estate, all the functions conferred on them by Part I of the Trusts of Land and Appointment of Trustees Act 1996

"

, and

    (c) in paragraph (iii), for the words "conferred by statute on trustees for sale, and" substitute "necessary".

(3) In section 41(6), for the words "trusts for sale" substitute "trusts".

(4) In section 51(3)–

    (a) after the word "married" insert "and without issue".

    (b) before the word "settlement", in both places, insert "trust or", and

    (c) for the words "an entailed interest" substitute "a life interest".

(5) In section 55(1), after paragraph (vi) insert–

    "(via) "Land" has the same meaning as in the Law of Property Act 1925."

The Green Belt (London and Home Counties) Act 1938 (C.XCIII)

Para.7

In section 19(1) of the Green Belt (London and Home Counties) Act 1938

    (a) for the words "trustee for sale within the meaning of the Law of Property Act 1925" substitute "trustee of land", and

    (b) for the words "of a trustee for sale" substitute "of a trustee of land"

The Settled Land and Trustee Acts (Court's General Powers)
Act 1943 (c. 25)

Para.8

In section 1 of the Settled Land and Trustee Acts (Court's General Powers) Act 1943–

(a) in subsection (1)–

   (i) for the words "trustees for sale of land" substitute "trustees of land", and
   (ii) for the words "land held on trust for sale" substitute "land subject to a trust of land", and

(b) in subsections (2) and (3) for the words "trust for sale" substitute "trust of land"

The Historic Buildings and Ancient Monuments Act 1953 (c. 49)

Para.9

In sections 8(3), 8A(3) and 8 B(3) of the Historic Buildings and Ancient Monuments Act 1953 for the words from "held on" to "thereof" substitute "subject to a trust of land, are conferred by law on the trustees of land in relation to the land and to the proceeds of its sale"

The Leasehold Reform Act 1967 (c. 88)

Para.10

In the Leasehold Reform Act 1967–

(a) in section 6(1) for the words "the statutory trusts arising by virtue of sections 34 to 36" substitute "a trust arising under section 34 or section 36"
(b) in section 24(1)(a), for the words "held on trust for sale" substitute "subject to a trust of land", and
(c) in paragraph 7 of Schedule 2–

   (i) in sub-paragraph (1), for the words "a disposition on trust for sale" substitute "trust of land", and
   (ii) in sub-paragraph (3), for the words "held on trust for sale" substitute "subject to a trust of land"

The Agriculture Act 1970 (c. 40)

Para.11

In section 33(2) of the Agriculture Act 1970–

(a) for the words "held under a trust for sale" substitute "subject to a trust of land" and

(b) for the words "the trustees for sale" substitute "the trustees of land"

The Land Charges Act 1972 (c. 61)

Para.12

(1) The Land Charges Act 1972 as amended as follows.
(2) In section 2(4)(iii)(b), for the words "trust for sale" substitute "trust of land".
(3) In section 6, after subsection (1) insert–

"(1A) No writ or order affecting an interest under a trust of land may be registered under subsection (1) above."

The Land Compensation Act 1973 (c. 26)

Para.13

In subsection (2) of section 10 of the Land Compensation Act 1973, for the words "held on trust for sale" substitute "subject to a trust of land" and, in accordance with that amendment, in the sidenote of that section, for the words "trusts for sale" substitute "trusts of land".

The Local Land Charges Act 1975 (c. 76)

Para.14

In section 11(2) of the Local Land Charges Act 1975 for the words "held on trust for sale" substitute "subject to a trust of land"

The Rentcharges Act 1977 (c. 30)

Para.15

(1) The Rentcharges Act 1977 is amended as follows
(2) In section 2(3) for paragraphs (a) and (b) substitute–

"

(a) in the case of which paragraph 3 of Schedule 1 to the Trusts of Land and Appointment of Trustees Act 1996 (trust in case of family charges) applies to the land on which the rent is charged.

(b) in the case of which paragraph (a) above would have effect but for the fact that the land on which the rent is charged is settled land or subject to a trust of land.

"

(3) In section 10(2)(b), for the words "trust for sale" substitute "trust of land"

The Interpretation Act 1978 (c. 30)

Para.16

In Schedule 1 to the Interpretation Act 1978, after the definition of "The Treasury" insert–

"

"Trust of land" and "trustees of land", relation on England and Wales, have the same meanings as in the Trusts of Land and Appointment of Trustees Act 1996."

The Ancient Monuments and Archaeological Areas Act 1979 (c. 46)

Para.17

In the Ancient Monuments and Archaeological Areas Act 1979–

(a) in section 12(3), for the words "trust for sale" substitute "trust of land", and

(b) in section 18(4), for paragraph (b) substitute–

"(b) as trustees of land;"

The Limitation Act 1980 (c. 58)

Para.18

In paragraph 9 of Schedule 1 to the Limitation Act 1980, for the words "held on trust for sale" substitute "subject to a trust of land"

The Highways Act 1980 (c. 66)

Para.19

In section 87(4)(b) of the Highways Act 1980, for the words from "and section 28" to "apply" substitute "applies"

The Wildlife and Countryside Act 1981 (c. 69)

Para.20

[. . .]⁴

The Health and Social Services and Social Security Adjudications Act 1983 (c. 41)

Para.21

In section 22 of the Health and Social Services and Social Security Adjudications Act 1983—

    (a)   in subsection (5)—

        (i)   for the words "a joint tenant in the proceeds of sale of land held upon trust for sale" substitute "an equitable joint tenant in land", and

        (ii) for the words "those proceeds" substitute "the land",

    (b)   in subsection (6)—

        (i)   for the words "a joint tenant in the proceeds of sale of land held upon trust for sale" substitute "an equitable joint tenant in land",

        (ii) for the words "proceeds is" substitute "land is", and

        (iii) for the words "interests in the proceeds" substitute "interests in the land", and

    (c)   in subsection (8), for the words "an interest in the proceeds of sale of land" substitute "the interest of an equitable joint tenant in land".

---

⁴ Also the heading preceeding it by Countryside and Rights of Way Act (2000 c.37), Sch.16 (III), para.1.

The Telecommunications Act 1984 (c. 12)

Para.22

In paragraph 4(10) of Schedule 2 to the Telecommunications Act 1984, for the words "trusts for sale" substitute "trusts of land".

The Insolvency Act 1986 (c. 45)

Para.23

At the beginning of Chapter V of Part IX of the Insolvency Act 1986, insert—

"Rights under trusts of land
335A.—Rights under trusts of land
(1) Any application by a trustee of a bankrupt's estate under section 14 of the Trusts of Land and Appointment of Trustees Act 1996 powers of court in relation to trusts of land) for an order under that section for the sale of land shall be made to the court having jurisdiction in relation to the bankruptcy.
(2) On such an application the court shall make such order as it thinks just and reasonable having regard to—

    (a) the interests of the bankrupt's creditors,
    (b) where the application is made in respect of land which includes a dwelling house which is or has been the home of the bankrupt or the bankrupt's spouse or former spouse—

        (i)   the conduct of the spouse or former spouse, so far as contributing to the bankruptcy,
        (ii) the needs and financial resources of the spouse or former spouse, and
        (iii) the needs of any children; and

    (c) all the circumstances of the case other than the needs of the bankrupt.

(3) Where such an application is made after the end of the period of one year beginning with the first vesting under Chapter IV of this Part of the bankrupt's estate in a trustee, the court shall assume, unless the circumstances of the case are exceptional, that the interests of the bankrupt's creditors outweigh all other considerations.
(4) The powers conferred on the court by this section are exercisable on an application whether it is made before or after the commencement of this section."

The Patronage (Benefices) Measure 1986 (No. 3)

Para.24

In section 33 of the Patronage (Benefices) Measure 1986—

    (a) in subsection (1), for the words from "held by any trustee" to "capable of sale" substitute "subject to a trust of land", and

    (b) in subsection (2), for the words "section 26(1) and (2) of the Law of Property Act 1925 (consents to the execution of a trust for sale)" substitute "section 10 of the Trusts of Land and Appointment of Trustees Act 1996 (consents)"

The Family Law Reform Act 1987 (c. 42)

Para.25

In section 19(2) of the Family Law Reform Act 1987, for the words "which is used to create" substitute "purporting to create"

The Charities Act 1993 (c. 10)

Para.26

In section 23 of the Charities Act 1993

    (a) in subsection (1)(b), for the words "trust for sale" substitute "trust",

    (b) in subsection (5) for the words "trustee for sale" substitute "trustee",

    (c) in subsection (7) for the words "trustees for sale" substitute "trustees", and

    (d) in subsection (9), for the words "trust for sale" substitute "trust".

The Leasehold Reform, Housing and Urban Development Act 1993 (c. 28)

Para.27

(1) The Leasehold Reform, Housing and Urban Development Act 1993 is amended as follows.

(2) In Schedule 2—

(a) in paragraph 5(1) and (2), for the words "held on trust for sale" substitute "subject to a trust of land" (and, accordingly, in the heading immediately preceding paragraph 5 for the words "on trust for sale" substitute "in trust").

(b) in paragraph 6, for the words "as mentioned in paragraph 5(2)(b) above" substitute "by the landlord on the termination of a new lease granted under Chapter II or section 93(4) (whether the payment is made in pursuance of an order under section 61 or in pursuance of an agreement made in conformity with paragraph 5 of Schedule 14 without an application having been made under that section", and

(c) in paragraphs 7(2)(b) and 8(3)(b) and (4)(c) for "5(2)(b)" substitute "6".

(3) In Schedule 14—

(a) in paragraph 7(1), for the words "disposition on trust for sale" substitute "trust of land", and

(b) in paragraph 9(a) for the words "held on trust for sale" substitute "subject to a trust of land".

Schedule 4

Repeals

Para.1

Schedule 4

Repeals

Chapter	Short title	Extent of repeal
3 & 4 Will.4 c. 74.	The Fines and Recoveries Act 1833.	In section 1, the words ", and any undivided share thereof", in both places.
7 Will.4 & 1 Vict. c. 26.	The Wills Act 1837.	In section 1, the words "and to any undivided share thereof,". Section 32.
53 & 54 Vict. c. 39.	The Partnership Act 1890.	Section 22.
12 & 13 Geo.5 c. 16.	The Law of Property Act 1922.	In section 188— in subsection (1), the words "but not an undivided share in land;" and the words "but not an undivided share thereof", and subsection (30).

15 & 16 Geo.5 c. 18.	The Settled Land Act 1925.	Section 27.
		Section 29.
15 & 16 Geo.5 c. 19.	The Trustee Act 1925.	In section 10(2)– in the first paragraph, the words "by trustees or" and the words "the trustees, or", and in the second paragraph, the words from the beginning to "mortgage; and". In section 19(1), the words "building or", in the second place. In section 68– in subsection (6), the words, "but not an undivided share in land" and the words, "but not an undivided share thereof", and in subsection (19), the word "binding", the words, "and with or without power at discretion to postpone the sale" and the definition of "trustees for sale".
15 & 16 Geo.5 c. 20.	The Law of Property Act 1925.	In section 3– subsections (1)(b) and (2), and in subsection (5), the words "trustees for sale or other". In section 7(3), the second paragraph. In section 18– in subsection (1), the words from, "and personal estate" to "payable", in the second place, and the words "or is capable of being", and in subsection (2), the words "of the settlement or the trustees for sale", in both places. Section 19.

		Section 23 (and the heading immediately preceding it).
		Sections 25 and 26.
		Sections 28 to 30.
		Section 31(3).
		Section 32.
		In section 34– in subsection (3), the words from "the trustees (if any)" to "then to" and the words "in each case", and subsection (4).
		Section 35.
		Section 42(6).
		In section 60, paragraphs (b) and (c) of the proviso to subsection (4).
		In section 130, subsections (1) to (3) and (6) (and the words "Creation of" in the sidenote).
		Section 201(3).
		In section 205(1)– in paragraph (ix), the words "but not an undivided share in land;" and the words "but not an undivided share thereof", in paragraph (x), the words "or in the proceeds of sale thereof", and in paragraph (xxix), the word "binding", the words, "and with or without a power at discretion to postpone the sale" and the words "and "power"" onwards.

15 & 16 Geo.5 c. 21.	The Land Registration Act 1925.	In section 3– in paragraph (viii), the words "but not an undivided share in land;", in paragraph (xi), the words "or in the proceeds of sale thereof", in paragraph (xiv), the words, "but not an undivided share thereof", and paragraphs (xxviii) and (xxix).
15 & 16 Geo.5 c. 23.	The Administration of Estates Act 1925.	In section 3(1)(ii), the words "money to arise under a trust for sale of land, nor". In section 39(1)(i), the words from, "and such power" to "legal mortgage". In section 51– in subsection (3), the word "settled", and subsection (4). In section 55(1)– in paragraph (vii), the words "or in the proceeds of sale thereof", in paragraph (xxiv), the word " "land" ", and paragraph (xxvii).
15 & 16 Geo.5 c. 24.	The Universities and College Estates Act 1925.	In section 43(iv), the words, "but not an undivided share in land".
16 & 17 Geo.5 c. 11.	The Law of Property (Amendment) Act 1926.	In the Schedule, the entries relating to section 3 of the Settled Land Act 1925 and sections 26, 28 and 35 of the Law of Property Act 1925.
17 & 18 Geo.5 c. 36.	The Landlord and Tenant Act 1927.	In section 13– in subsection (1), the words from "(either" to "Property Act, 1925)", in subsection (2), the words, "trustee for sale, or personal representative", and in subsection (3), the words, "and "settled land" " onwards.

22 & 23 Geo.5 c. 27.	The Law of Property (Entailed Interests) Act 1932.	Section 1.
2 & 3 Geo.6 c. 72.	The Landlord and Tenant (War Damage) Act 1939.	Section 3(c).
9 & 10 Geo.6 c. 73.	The Hill Farming Act 1946.	Section 11(2).
12 & 13 Geo.6 c. 74.	The Coast Protection Act 1949.	In section 11(2)(a)– the words, "by that section as applied by section twenty-eight of the Law of Property Act, 1925, in relation to trusts for sale,", and the words, "by that section as applied as aforesaid,".
2 & 3 Eliz.2 c. 56.	The Landlord and Tenant Act 1954.	In the Second Schedule, in paragraph 6– the words, "by that section as applied by section twenty-eight of the Law of Property Act, 1925, in relation to trusts for sale,", and the words, "by that section as applied as aforesaid,".
7 & 8 Eliz.2 c. 72.	The Mental Health Act 1959.	In Schedule 7, in Part I, the entries relating to sections 26 and 28 of the Law of Property Act 1925.
1964 No. 2.	The Incumbents and Churchwardens (Trusts) Measure 1964.	In section 1, in the definition of "land", the words "nor an undivided share in land".
1967 c. 10.	The Forestry Act 1967.	In Schedule 2, paragraph 1(4).
1967 c. 88.	The Leasehold Reform Act 1967.	In section 6(5)– the words, "or by that section as applied by section 28 of the Law of Property Act 1925 in relation to trusts for sale,", the words "or by that section as applied as aforesaid", and the words "or by trustees for sale".

		In Schedule 2, in paragraph 9(1)– the words, "or by that section as applied by section 28 of the Law of Property Act 1925 in relation to trusts for sale", and the words "or by that section as applied as aforesaid".
1969 c. 10.	The Mines and Quarries (Tips) Act 1969.	In section 32(2)(a) and (b), the words, "by that section as applied by section 28 of the Law of Property Act 1925 in relation to trusts for sale".
1970 c. 40.	The Agriculture Act 1970.	In section 30– in subsection (1), the words "(including those provisions as extended to trusts for sale by section 28 of the Law of Property Act 1925)", and in subsection (2), the words "the words from "(including those provisions" to "Law of Property Act 1925)" and".
1972 c. 61.	The Land Charges Act 1972.	In section 17(1), the definition of "trust for sale".
1976 c. 31.	The Legitimacy Act 1976.	Section 10(4).
1976 c. 36.	The Adoption Act 1976.	Section 46(5).
1977 c. 42.	The Rent Act 1977.	In Schedule 2, in Part I, in paragraph 2(b), the words "or, if it is held on trust for sale, the proceeds of its sale are".
1980 c. 58.	The Limitation Act 1980.	In section 18– in subsection (1), the words, "including interests in the proceeds of the sale of land held upon trust for sale,", and

		in subsections (3) and (4), the words "(including a trust for sale)" and the words "or in the proceeds of sale".
		In section 38(1)– in the definition of "land", the words, "including an interest in the proceeds of the sale of land held upon trust for sale,", and the definition of "trust for sale".
		In Schedule 1, in Part I, in paragraph 9– the words "or in the proceeds of sale", the words "or the proceeds", and the words "or the proceeds of sale".
1981 c. 54.	The Supreme Court Act 1981.	In section 128, in the definition of "real estate", in paragraph (b), the words "money to arise under a trust for sale of land, nor".
1983 c. 41.	The Health and Social Services and Social Security Adjudications Act 1983.	Section 22(3).
1984 c. 28.	The County Courts Act 1984.	In Schedule 2, in Part II, in paragraph 2– in sub-paragraph (1), the entry relating to section 30 of the Law of Property Act 1925, sub-paragraph (2), and in sub-paragraph (3), "30(2),".
1984 c. 51.	The Inheritance Tax Act 1984.	In section 237(3), the words "and undivided shares in land held on trust for sale, whether statutory or not,".
1986 c. 5.	The Agricultural Holdings Act 1986.	In section 89(1), the words "or the Law of Property Act 1925".

1986 c. 45.	The Insolvency Act 1986.	In section 336– subsection (3), and in sub-section (4), the words "or (3)" and the words "or section 30 of the Act of 1925".
1988 c. 50.	The Housing Act 1988.	In Schedule 1, in Part III, in paragraph 18(1)(b), the words "or, if it is held on trust for sale, the proceeds of its sale are".
1989 c. 34.	The Law of Property (Miscellaneous Provisions) Act 1989.	In sections 1(6) and 2(6), the words "or in or over the proceeds of sale of land".
1990 c. 8.	The Town and Country Planning Act 1990.	In section 328– in subsection (1)(a), the words "and by that section as applied by section 28 of the Law of Property Act 1925 in relation to trusts for sale", and in subsection (2)(a), the words "and by that section as so applied".
1991 c. 31.	The Finance Act 1991.	Section 110(5)(b).
1993 c. 10.	The Charities Act 1993.	Section 37(6). Section 39(5).
1993 c. 28.	The Leasehold Reform, Housing and Urban Development Act 1993.	In section 93A(4)– the words, "or by that section as applied by section 28 of the Law of Property Act 1925 in relation to trusts for sale", the words, "or by that section as so applied,", and the words "or by trustees for sale". In Schedule 2, paragraph 5(2)(b) and the word "and" immediately preceding it.
1994 c. 36.	The Law of Property (Miscellaneous Provisions) Act 1994.	In section 16– subsection (2), and in subsection (3), the words; "and subsection (2)" onwards.

1995 c. 8.	The Agricultural Tenancies Act 1995.	In section 33– in subsections (1) and (2), the words from "(either" to "Property Act 1925)", and in subsection (4), the definition of "settled land" and the word "and" immediately preceding it.
1996 c. 53.	The Housing Grants, Construction and Regeneration Act 1996.	Section 55(4)(b). Section 73(3)(b). In section 98(2)(a), the words "or to the proceeds of sale of the dwelling".

Statutory Instrument 1991 No. 1247 (L.20)

A2–008

THE FAMILY PROCEEDINGS RULES 1991

STATUTORY INSTRUMENTS

1991 No. 1247 (L.20)

Family Proceedings

Supreme Court of England and Wales

County Courts

THE FAMILY PROCEEDINGS RULES 1991

Made	*1st May 1991*
Laid before Parliament	*17th July 1991*
Coming into force	*14th October 1991*

Married Women's Property Act 1882

3.6—(1) Subject to paragraph (2) below, an application under section 17 of the Married Women's Property Act 1882[1] (in this and the next following rule referred to as "section 17") shall be made—

(a) in the High Court, by originating summons, which may be issued out of the principal registry or any district registry, or

(b) in a county court, by originating application, in Form M23 and shall be supported by affidavit.

(2) An order under section 17 may be made in any ancillary relief proceedings upon the application of any party thereto in Form M11 by notice of application or summons.

(3) An application under section 17 to a county court shall be filed—

(a) subject to sub-paragraph (b), in the court for the district in which the applicant or respondent resides, or

(b) in the divorce county court in which any pending matrimonial cause has been commenced by or on behalf of either the applicant or the respondent, or in which any matrimonial cause is intended to be commenced by the applicant.

(4) Where the application concerns the title to or possession of land, the originating summons or application shall—

(a) state whether the title to the land is registered or unregistered and, if registered, the Land Registry title number; and

(b) give particulars, so far as known to the applicant, of any mortgage of the land or any interest therein.

(5) The application shall be served on the respondent, together with a copy of the affidavit in support and an acknowledgement of service in Form M6.

(6) Where particulars of a mortgage are given pursuant to paragraph (4), the applicant shall file a copy of the originating summons or application, which shall be served on the mortgagee; and any person so served may apply to the court in writing, within 14 days after service, for a copy of the affidavit in support; and within 14 days of receiving such affidavit may file an affidavit in answer and shall be entitled to be heard on the application.

(7) If the respondent intends to contest the application, he shall, within 14 days after the time allowed for sending the acknowledgement of service, file an affidavit in answer to the application setting out the grounds on which he relies, and lodge in the court office a copy of the affidavit for service on the applicant.

(8) If the respondent fails to comply with paragraph (7), the applicant may apply for directions; and the district judge may give such directions as he thinks fit, including a direction that the respondent shall be debarred from defending the application unless an affidavit is filed within such time as the district judge may specify.

(9) A district judge may grant an injunction in proceedings under section 17 if, but only so far as, the injunction is ancillary or incidental to any relief sought in those proceedings.

(10) Rules 2.62(4) to (6) and 2.63 to 2.66 shall apply, with the necessary modifications, to an application under section 17 as they apply to an application for ancillary relief.

(11) Subject to the provisions of this rule, these rules shall apply, with the necessary modifications, to an application under section 17 as if the application were a cause, the originating summons or application a petition, and the applicant a petitioner.

Exercise in principal registry of county court jurisdiction under section 17 of Married Women's Property Act 1882

3.7—(1) Where any proceedings for divorce, nullity or judicial separation which are either pending in the principal registry, or are intended to be commenced there by the applicant, are or will be treated as pending in a divorce county court, an application under section 17 by one of the parties to the marriage may be made to the principal registry as if it were a county court.

(2) In relation to proceedings commenced or intended to be commenced in the principal registry under paragraph (1) of this rule or transferred from the High Court to the principal registry by an order made under section 38 of the Act of 1984—

    (a)   section 42 of the Act of 1984 and the rules made thereunder shall have effect, with the necessary modifications, as they have effect in relation to proceedings commenced in or transferred to the principal registry under that section; and

    (b)   CCR Order 4, rule 8 and rule 3.6(3) (which relate to venue) shall not apply.

(3) Rule 1.4(1) shall apply, with the necessary modifications, to proceedings in, or intended to be commenced in, the principal registry under paragraph (1) of this rule as it applies to matrimonial proceedings.

PART IV

PROCEEDINGS UNDER THE CHILDREN ACT 1989

Interpretation and application

4.1—(1) In this Part of these rules, unless a contrary intention appears– a section or schedule referred to means the section or schedule so numbered in the Act of 1989;

    "a section 8 order" has the meaning assigned to it by section 8(2);

    "application" means an application made under or by virtue of the Act of 1989 or under these rules, and "applicant" shall be construed accordingly;

    "child", in relation to proceedings to which this Part applies–

        (a)   means, subject to sub-paragraph (b), a person under the age of 18 with respect to whom the proceedings are brought, and

(b)   where the proceedings are under Schedule 1, also includes a person who has reached the age of 18;

"directions appointment" means a hearing for directions under rule 4.14(2);

"emergency protection order" means an order under section 44;

"guardian ad litem" means a guardian ad litem, appointed under section 41, of the child with respect to whom the proceedings are brought;

"leave" includes permission and approval;

"note" includes a record made by mechanical means;

"parental responsibility" has the meaning assigned to it by section 3;

"recovery order" means an order under section 50;

"specified proceedings" has the meaning assigned to it by section 41(6) and rule 4.2(2); and

"welfare officer" means a person who has been asked to prepare a welfare report under section 7.

(2) Except where the contrary intention appears, the provisions of this Part apply to proceedings in the High Court and the county courts–

(a)   on an application for a section 8 order;

(b)   on an application for a care order or a supervision order;

(c)   on an application under section 4(1)(a), 4(3), 5(1), 6(7), 13(1), 16(6), 33(7), 34(2), 34(3), 34(4), 34(9), 36(1), 38(8)(b), 39(1), 39(2), 39(3), 39(4), 43(1), 43(12), 44, 45, 46(7), 48(9), or 50(1);

(d)   under Schedule 1, except where financial relief is also sought by or on behalf of an adult,

(e)   on an application under paragraph 19(1) of Schedule 2;

(f)   on an application under paragraph 6(3), 15(2) or 17(1) of Schedule 3;

(g)   on an application under paragraph 11(3) or 16(5) of Schedule 14; or

(h)   under section 25.

Application

4.4—(1) Subject to paragraph (4), an applicant shall–

(a)   file the application in respect of each child in the appropriate form in Appendix 1 to these rules or, where there is no such form, in writing, together with sufficient copies for one to be served on each respondent, and

(b)   serve a copy of the application, endorsed in accordance with paragraph (2)(b), on each respondent such number of days prior to the date fixed under paragraph (2)(a) as is specified for that application in column (ii) of Appendix 3 to these rules.

(2) On receipt of the documents filed under paragraph (1)(a) the proper officer shall–

(a) fix the date for a hearing or a directions appointment, allowing sufficient time for the applicant to comply with paragraph (1)(b),

(b) endorse the date so fixed upon the copies of the application filed by the applicant, and

(c) return the copies to the applicant forthwith.

(3) The applicant shall, at the same time as complying with paragraph (1)(b), give written notice of the proceedings, and of the date and place of the hearing or appointment fixed under paragraph (2)(a), to the persons set out for the relevant class of proceedings in column (iii) of Appendix 3 to these rules.

(4) An application for—

(a) a prohibited steps order, or a specific issue order, under section 8,

(b) an emergency protection order,

(c) a warrant under section 48(9), or

(d) a recovery order,

may be made ex parte in which case the applicant shall—

(i) file the application in respect of each child in the appropriate form in Appendix 1 to these rules—

(a) where the application is made by telephone, within 24 hours after the making of the application, or

(b) in any other case, at the time when the application is made, and

(ii) in the case of an application for a prohibited steps order, or a specific issue order, under section 8 or an emergency protection order, serve a copy of the application on each respondent within 48 hours after the making of the order.

(5) Where the court refuses to make an order on an ex parte application it may direct that the application be made inter partes.

(6) In the case of proceedings under Schedule 1, the application under paragraph (1) shall be accompanied by a statement setting out the financial details which the applicant believes to be relevant to the application and containing a declaration that it is true to the maker's best knowledge and belief, together with sufficient copies for one to be served on each respondent.

Withdrawal of application

4.5—(1) An application may be withdrawn only with leave of the court.

(2) Subject to paragraph (3), a person seeking leave to withdraw an application shall file and serve on the parties a written request for leave setting out the reasons for the request.

(3) The request under paragraph (2) may be made orally to the court if the parties and either the guardian ad litem or the welfare officer are present.

(4) Upon receipt of a written request under paragraph (2) the court shall–

    (a) if–

        (i)   the parties consent in writing,
        (ii) the guardian ad litem has had an opportunity to make representations, and
        (iii) the court thinks fit,

grant the request, in which case the proper officer shall notify the parties, the guardian ad litem and the welfare officer of the granting of the request, or

    (b) direct that a date be fixed for the hearing of the request in which case the proper officer shall give at least 7 days' notice to the parties, the guardian ad litem and the welfare officer, of the date fixed.

Transfer from magistrates' court to county court and from county court to High Court

4.6—(1) Where an application is made, in accordance with the provisions of any Order made under Part I of Schedule 11 to the Act of 1989, to a county court for an order transferring proceedings from a magistrates' court following the refusal of the magistrates' court to order such a transfer, the applicant shall–

    (a) file the application in Form CHA58, together with a copy of the certificate issued by the magistrates' court, and
    (b) serve a copy of the documents mentioned in sub-paragraph (a) personally on all parties to the proceedings which it is sought to have transferred,

within 2 days after receipt by the applicant of the certificate.

(2) Within 2 days after receipt of the documents served under paragraph (1)(b), any party other than the applicant may file written representations.

(3) The court shall, not before the fourth day after the filing of the application under paragraph (1), unless the parties consent to earlier consideration, consider the application and either–

    (a) grant the application, whereupon the proper officer shall inform the parties of that decision, or
    (b) direct that a date be fixed for the hearing of the application, whereupon the proper officer shall fix such a date and give not less than 1 day's notice to the parties of the date so fixed.

(4) Where proceedings are transferred from a magistrates' court to a county court in accordance with the provisions of any Order under Part I

of Schedule 11 to the Act of 1989, the county court shall consider whether to transfer those proceedings to the High Court in accordance with that Order and either—

(a) determine that such an order need not be made,
(b) make such an order,
(c) order that a date be fixed for the hearing of the question whether such an order should be made, whereupon the proper officer shall give such notice to the parties as the court directs of the date so fixed, or
(d) invite the parties to make written representations, within a specified period, as to whether such an order should be made; and upon receipt of the representations the court shall act in accordance with sub-paragraph (a), (b) or (c).

(5) The proper officer shall notify the parties of an order transferring the proceedings from a county court or from the High Court made in accordance with the provisions of any Order under Part I of Schedule 11 to the Act of 1989.

Parties

4.7—(1) The respondents to proceedings to which this Part applies shall be those persons set out in the relevant entry in column (iv) of Appendix 3 to these rules.

(2) In proceedings to which this Part applies, a person may file a request in writing that he or another person—

(a) be joined as a party, or
(b) cease to be a party.

(3) On considering a request under paragraph (2) the court shall, subject to paragraph (4)—

(a) grant it without a hearing or representations, save that this shall be done only in the case of a request under paragraph (2)(a), whereupon the proper officer shall inform the parties and the person making the request of that decision, or
(b) order that a date be fixed for the consideration of the request, whereupon the proper officer shall give notice of the date so fixed, together with a copy of the request—

(i)   in the case of a request under paragraph (2)(a), to the applicant, and
(ii) in the case of a request under paragraph (2)(b), to the parties, or

(c) invite the parties or any of them to make written representations, within a specified period, as to whether the request should be granted; and upon the expiry of the period the court shall act in accordance with sub-paragraph (a) or (b).

(4) Where a person with parental responsibility requests that he be joined under paragraph (2)(a), the court shall grant his request.

(5) In proceedings to which this Part applies the court may direct–

    (a) that a person who would not otherwise be a respondent under these rules be joined as a party to the proceedings, or

    (b) that a party to the proceedings cease to be a party.

Service

4.8—(1) Subject to the requirement in rule 4.6(1)(b) of personal service, where service of a document is required under this Part (and not by a provision to which section 105(8) (Service of notice or other document under the Act) applies) it may be effected–

    (a) if the person to be served is not known by the person serving to be acting by solicitor–

        (i) by delivering it to him personally, or

        (ii) by delivering it at, or by sending it by first-class post to, his residence or his last known residence, or

    (b) if the person to be served is known by the person serving to be acting by solicitor–

        (i) by delivering the document at, or sending it by first-class post to, the solicitor's address for service,

        (ii) where the solicitor's address for service includes a numbered box at a document exchange, by leaving the document at that document exchange or at a document exchange which transmits documents on every business day to that document exchange, or

        (iii) by sending a legible copy of the document by facsimile transmission to the solicitor's office.

(2) In this rule "first-class post" means first-class post which has been pre-paid or in respect of which pre-payment is not required.

(3) Where a child who is a party to proceedings to which this Part applies is required by these rules or other rules of court to serve a document, service shall be effected by–

    (a) the solicitor acting for the child, or

    (b) where there is no such solicitor, the guardian ad litem, or

    (c) where there is neither such a solicitor nor a guardian ad litem, the court.

(4) Service of any document on a child shall, subject to any direction of the court, be effected by service on–

    (a) the solicitor acting for the child, or

    (b) where there is no such solicitor, the guardian ad litem, or

    (c) where there is neither such a solicitor nor a guardian ad litem, with leave of the court, the child.

(5) Where the court refuses leave under paragraph (4)(c) it shall give a direction under paragraph (8).

(6) A document shall, unless the contrary is proved, be deemed to have been served–

    (a) in the case of service by first-class post, on the second business day after posting, and

    (b) in the case of service in accordance with paragraph (1)(b)(ii), on the second business day after the day on which it is left at the document exchange.

(7) At or before the first directions appointment in, or hearing of, proceedings to which this Part applies the applicant shall file a statement that service of–

    (a) a copy of the application has been effected on each respondent, and

    (b) notice of the proceedings has been effected under rule 4.4(3); and the statement shall indicate–

        (i) the manner, date, time and place of service, or

        (ii) where service was effected by post, the date, time and place of posting.

(8) In proceedings to which this Part applies, the court may direct that a requirement of these rules or other rules of court to serve a document shall not apply or shall be effected in such manner as the court directs.

Answer to application

4.9—(1) Within 14 days of service of an application for a section 8 order, each respondent shall file, and serve on the parties, an answer to the application in Form CHA1OA.

(2) Within 14 days after service of an application under Schedule 1, each respondent shall file, and serve on the parties, an answer to the application in Form CHA13A.

(3) Following service of an application to which this Part applies, other than an application under rule 4.3 or for a section 8 order, a respondent may, subject to paragraph (4), file a written answer, which shall be served on the other parties.

(4) An answer under paragraph (3) shall, except in the case of an application under section 25, 31, 34, 38, 43, 44, 45, 46, 48 or 50, be filed, and served, not less than 2 days before the date fixed for the hearing of the application.

Directions

4.14—(1) In this rule, "party" includes the guardian ad litem and, where a request or a direction concerns a report under section 7, the welfare officer.

(2) In proceedings to which this Part applies the court may, subject to paragraph (3), give, vary or revoke directions for the conduct of the proceedings, including–

(a) the timetable for the proceedings;
(b) varying the time within which or by which an act is required, by these rules or by other rules or court, to be done;
(c) the attendance of the child;
(d) the appointment of a guardian ad litem, whether under section 41 or otherwise, or of a solicitor under section 41(3);
(e) the service of documents;
(f) the submission of evidence including experts' reports;
(g) the preparation of welfare reports under section 7;
(h) the transfer of the proceedings to another court;
(i) consolidation with other proceedings.

(3) Directions under paragraph (2) may be given, varied or revoked either–

(a) of the court's own motion having given the parties notice of its intention to do so, and an opportunity to attend and be heard or to make written representations,
(b) on the written request of a party specifying the direction which is sought, filed and served on the other parties, or
(c) on the written request of a party specifying the direction which is sought, to which the other parties consent and which they or their representatives have signed.

(4) In an urgent case the request under paragraph (3)(b) may, with the leave of the court, be made–

(a) orally, or
(b) without notice to the parties, or
(c) both as in sub-paragraph (a) and as in sub-paragraph (b).

(5) On receipt of a written request under paragraph (3)(b) the proper officer shall fix a date for the hearing of the request and give not less than 2 days' notice to the parties of the date so fixed.

(6) On considering a request under paragraph (3)(c) the court shall either–

(a) grant the request, whereupon the proper officer shall inform the parties of the decision, or
(b) direct that a date be fixed for the hearing of the request, whereupon the proper officer shall fix such a date and give not less than 2 days' notice to the parties of the date so fixed.

(7) A party may apply for an order to be made under section 11(3) or, if he is entitled to apply for such an order, under section 38(1) in accordance with paragraph (3)(b) or (c).

(8) Where a court is considering making, of its own motion, a section 8 order, or an order under section 31, 34 or 38, the power to give directions under paragraph (2) shall apply.

(9) Directions of a court which are still in force immediately prior to the transfer of proceedings to which this Part applies to another court shall continue to apply following the transfer, subject to any changes of terminology which are required to apply those directions to the court to which the proceedings are transferred, unless varied or discharged by directions under paragraph (2).

(10) The court or the proper officer shall take a note of the giving, variation or revocation of a direction under this rule and serve, as soon as practicable, a copy of the note on any party who was not present at the giving, variation or revocation.

Timing of proceedings

4.15—(1) Where these rules or other rules of court provide a period of time within which or by which a certain act is to be performed in the course of proceedings to which this Part applies, that period may not be extended otherwise than by direction of the court under rule 4.14.

(2) At the–

(a) transfer to a court of proceedings to which this Part applies,
(b) postponement or adjournment of any hearing or directions appointment in the course of proceedings to which this Part applies, or
(c) conclusion of any such hearing or directions appointment other than one at which the proceedings are determined, or so soon thereafter as is practicable,

the court or the proper officer shall–

(i) fix a date upon which the proceedings shall come before the court again for such purposes as the court directs, which date shall, where paragraph (a) applies, be as soon as possible after the transfer, and
(ii) give notice to the parties, the guardian ad litem or the welfare officer of the date so fixed.

Attendance at directions appointment and hearing

4.16—(1) Subject to paragraph (2), a party shall attend a directions appointment of which he has been given notice in accordance with rule 4.14(5) unless the court otherwise directs.

(2) Proceedings or any part of them shall take place in the absence of any party, including the child, if–

(a) the court considers it in the interests of the child, having regard to the matters to be discussed or the evidence likely to be given, and
(b) the party is represented by a guardian ad litem or solicitor;

and when considering the interests of the child under sub-paragraph (a) the court shall give the guardian ad litem, the solicitor for the child and, if he is of sufficient understanding, the child an opportunity to make representations.

(3) Subject to paragraph (4), where at the time and place appointed for a hearing or directions appointment the applicant appears but one or more of the respondents do not, the court may proceed with the hearing or appointment.

(4) The court shall not begin to hear an application in the absence of a respondent unless–

    (a) it is proved to the satisfaction of the court that he received reasonable notice of the date of the hearing; or

    (b) the court is satisfied that the circumstances of the case justify proceeding with the hearing.

(5) Where, at the time and place appointed for a hearing or directions appointment one or more of the respondents appear but the applicant does not, the court may refuse the application or, if sufficient evidence has previously been received, proceed in the absence of the applicant.

(6) Where at the time and place appointed for a hearing or directions appointment neither the applicant nor any respondent appears, the court may refuse the application.

(7) Unless the court otherwise directs, a hearing of, or directions appointment in, proceedings to which this Part applies shall be in chambers.

Documentary evidence

4.17—(1) Subject to paragraphs (4) and (5), in proceedings to which this Part applies a party shall file and serve on the parties, any welfare officer and any guardian ad litem of whose appointment he has been given notice under rule 4.10(5)-

    (a) written statements of the substance of the oral evidence which the party intends to adduce at a hearing of, or a directions appointment in, those proceedings, which shall–

        (i)   be dated,

        (ii) be signed by the person making the statement, and

        (iii) contain a declaration that the maker of the statement believes it to be true and understands that it may be placed before the court; and

    (b) copies of any documents, including experts' reports, upon which the party intends to rely at a hearing of, or a directions appointment in, those proceedings,

at or by such time as the court directs or, in the absence of a direction, before the hearing or appointment.

(2) A party may, subject to any direction of the court about the timing of statements under this rule, file and serve on the parties a statement which is supplementary to a statement served under paragraph (1).

(3) At a hearing or a directions appointment a party may not, without the leave of the court–

(a) adduce evidence, or
(b) seek to rely on a document,

in respect of which he has failed to comply with the requirements of paragraph (1).

(4) In proceedings for a section 8 order a party shall–

(a) neither file nor serve any document other than as required or authorised by these rules, and
(b) in completing a form prescribed by these rules, neither give information, nor make a statement, which is not required or authorised by that form,

without the leave of the court.

(5) In proceedings for a section 8 order no statement or copy may be filed under paragraph (1) until such time as the court directs.

Amendment

4.19—(1) Subject to rule 4.17(2), a document which has been filed or served in proceedings to which this Part applies, may not be amended without the leave of the court which shall, unless the court otherwise directs, be requested in writing.

(2) On considering a request for leave to amend a document the court shall either–

(a) grant the request, whereupon the proper officer shall inform the person making the request of that decision, or
(b) invite the parties or any of them to make representations, within a specified period, as to whether such an order should be made.

(3) A person amending a document shall file it and serve it on those persons on whom it was served prior to amendment; and the amendments shall be identified.

Oral evidence

4.20—(1) The court or the proper officer shall keep a note of the substance of the oral evidence given at a hearing of, or directions appointment in, proceedings to which this Part applies.

Hearing

4.21—(1) The court may give directions as to the order of speeches and evidence at a hearing, or directions appointment, in the course of proceedings to which this Part applies.

(2) Subject to directions under paragraph (1), at a hearing of, or directions appointment in, proceedings to which this Part applies, the parties and the guardian ad litem shall adduce their evidence in the following order–

(a) the applicant,
(b) any party with parental responsibility for the child,
(c) other respondents,
(d) the guardian ad litem,
(e) the child, if he is a party to the proceedings and there is no guardian ad litem.

(3) After the final hearing of proceedings to which this Part applies, the court shall deliver its judgment as soon as is practicable.

(4) When making an order or when refusing an application, the court shall state any findings of fact and the reasons for the court's decision.

(5) An order made in proceedings to which this Part applies shall be recorded, by the court or the proper officer, either in the appropriate form in Appendix 1 to these rules or, where there is no such form, in writing.

(6) Subject to paragraph (7), a copy of an order made in accordance with paragraph (5) shall, as soon as practicable after it has been made, be served by the proper officer on the parties to the proceedings in which it was made on any person with whom the child is living.

(7) Within 48 hours after the making ex parte of–

(a) a prohibited steps order or specific issue order under section 8, or
(b) an order under section 44, 48(4), 48(9) or 50,

the applicant shall serve a copy of the order in the appropriate form in Appendix 1 to these Rules on–

(i) each party,
(ii) any person who has actual care of the child or who had such care immediately prior to the making of the order, and
(iii) in the case of an order referred to in sub-paragraph (b), the local authority in whose area the child lives or is found.

(8) At a hearing of, or directions appointment in, an application which takes place outside the hours during which the court office is normally open, the court or the proper officer shall take a note of the substance of the proceedings.

Notes:

1 1882 c. 75; s.17 was amended by s.43 of the Matrimonial and Family Proceedings Act 1984 (c. 42) and repealed in part by the Statute Law (Repeals) Act 1969 (c. 52).

Family Proceedings: Court Bundles
(Universal Practice to be Applied in all Courts other than the Family Proceedings Court)

A2–009

President's Direction

[27ᵀᴴ JULY 2006]

1 The President of the Family Division has issued this practice direction to achieve consistency across the country in all family courts (other than the Family Proceedings Court) in the preparation of court bundles and in respect of other related matters.

Application of the practice direction
2.1 Except as specified in paragraph 2.4, and subject to specific directions given in any particular case, the following practice applies to:

    (a)   all hearings of whatever nature (including but not limited to hearings in family proceedings, CPR Part 7 and Part 8 claims and appeals) before a judge of the Family Division of the High Court wherever the court may be sitting;

    (b)   all hearings in family proceedings in the Royal Courts of Justice ("RCJ");

    (c)   all hearings in the Principal Registry of the Family Division ("PRFD") at First Avenue House; and

    (d)   all hearings in family proceedings in all other courts except for Family Proceedings Courts.

2.2 "Hearings" includes all appearances before a judge or district judge, whether with or without notice to other parties and whether for directions or for substantive relief.

2.3 This practice direction applies whether a bundle is being lodged for the first time or is being re-lodged for a further hearing (see paragraph 9.2).

2.4 This practice direction does not apply to:

    (a)   cases listed for one hour or less at a court referred to in paragraph 2.1(c) or 2.1(d); or

    (b)   the hearing of any urgent application if and to the extent that it is impossible to comply with it.

2.5 The Designated Family Judge responsible for any court referred to in paragraph 2.1(c) or 2.1(d) may, after such consultation as is appropriate (but in the case of hearings in the PRFD at First Avenue House only with the agreement of the Senior District Judge), direct that in that court this practice direction shall apply to all family proceedings irrespective of the length of hearing.

Responsibility for the preparation of the bundle

3.1 A bundle for the use of the court at the hearing shall be provided by the party in the position of applicant at the hearing (or, if there are cross-applications, by the party whose application was first in time) or, if that person is a litigant in person, by the first listed respondent who is not a litigant in person.

3.2 The party preparing the bundle shall paginate it. If possible the contents of the bundle shall be agreed by all parties.

Contents of the bundle

4.1 The bundle shall contain copies of all documents relevant to the hearing, in chronological order from the front of the bundle, paginated and indexed, and divided into separate sections (each section being separately paginated) as follows:

(a) preliminary documents (see paragraph 4.2) and any other case management documents required by any other practice direction;

(b) applications and orders;

(c) statements and affidavits (which must be dated in the top right corner of the front page);

(d) care plans (where appropriate);

(e) experts' reports and other reports (including those of a guardian, children's guardian or litigation friend); and

(f) other documents, divided into further sections as may be appropriate.

Copies of notes of contact visits should normally not be included in the bundle unless directed by a judge.

4.2 At the commencement of the bundle there shall be inserted the following documents ("the preliminary documents"):

(i) an up to date summary of the background to the hearing confined to those matters which are relevant to the hearing and the management of the case and limited, if practicable, to one A4 page;

(ii) a statement of the issue or issues to be determined (1) at that hearing and (2) at the final hearing;

(iii) a position statement by each party including a summary of the order or directions sought by that party (1) at that hearing and (2) at the final hearing;

(iv) an up to date chronology, if it is a final hearing or if the summary under (i) is insufficient;

(v) skeleton arguments, if appropriate, with copies of all authorities relied on; and

(vi) a list of essential reading for that hearing.

4.3 Each of the preliminary documents shall state on the front page immediately below the heading the date when it was prepared and the date of the hearing for which it was prepared.

4.4 The summary of the background, statement of issues, chronology, position statement and any skeleton arguments shall be cross-referenced to the relevant pages of the bundle.

4.5 The summary of the background, statement of issues, chronology and reading list shall in the case of a final hearing, and shall so far as practicable in the case of any other hearing, each consist of a single document in a form agreed by all parties. Where the parties disagree as to the content the fact of their disagreement and their differing contentions shall be set out at the appropriate places in the document.

4.6 Where the nature of the hearing is such that a complete bundle of all documents is unnecessary, the bundle (which need not be repaginated) may comprise only those documents necessary for the hearing, but

(i) the summary (paragraph 4.2(i)) must commence with a statement that the bundle is limited or incomplete; and
(ii) the bundle shall if reasonably practicable be in a form agreed by all parties.

4.7 Where the bundle is re-lodged in accordance with paragraph 9.2, before it is re-lodged:

(a) the bundle shall be updated as appropriate; and
(b) all superseded documents (and in particular all outdated summaries, statements of issues, chronologies, skeleton arguments and similar documents) shall be removed from the bundle.

Format of the bundle

5.1 The bundle shall be contained in one or more A4 size ring binders or lever arch files (each lever arch file being limited to 350 pages).

5.2 All ring binders and lever arch files shall have clearly marked on the front and the spine:

(a) the title and number of the case;
(b) the court where the case has been listed;
(c) the hearing date and time;
(d) if known, the name of the judge hearing the case; and
(e) where there is more than one ring binder or lever arch file, a distinguishing letter (A, B, C etc).

Timetable for preparing and lodging the bundle

6.1 The party preparing the bundle shall, whether or not the bundle has been agreed, provide a paginated index to all other parties not less than 4 working days before the hearing (in relation to a case management conference to which the provisions of the Public Law Protocol [2003] 2 FLR 719 apply, not less than 5 working days before the case management conference).

6.2 Where counsel is to be instructed at any hearing, a paginated bundle shall (if not already in counsel's possession) be delivered to counsel by the person instructing that counsel not less than 3 working days before the hearing.

6.3 The bundle (with the exception of the preliminary documents if and insofar as they are not then available) shall be lodged with the court not less than 2 working days before the hearing, or at such other time as may be specified by the judge.

6.4 The preliminary documents shall be lodged with the court no later than 11 am on the day before the hearing and, where the hearing is before a judge of the High Court and the name of the judge is known, shall at the same time be sent by e-mail to the judge's clerk.

Lodging the bundle

7.1 The bundle shall be lodged at the appropriate office. If the bundle is lodged in the wrong place the judge may:

   (a) treat the bundle as having not been lodged; and
   (b) take the steps referred to in paragraph 12.

7.2 Unless the judge has given some other direction as to where the bundle in any particular case is to be lodged (for example a direction that the bundle is to be lodged with the judge's clerk) the bundle shall be lodged:

   (a) for hearings in the RCJ, in the office of the Clerk of the Rules, Room TM 9.09, Royal Courts of Justice, Strand, London WC2A 2LL (DX 44450 Strand);
   (b) for hearings in the PRFD at First Avenue House, at the List Office counter, 3rd floor, First Avenue House, 42/49 High Holborn, London, WC1V 6NP (DX 396 Chancery Lane); and
   (c) for hearings at any other court, at such place as may be designated by the Designated Family Judge or other judge at that court and in default of any such designation at the court office of the court where the hearing is to take place.

7.3 Any bundle sent to the court by post, DX or courier shall be clearly addressed to the appropriate office and shall show the date and place of the hearing on the outside of any packaging as well as on the bundle itself.

Lodging the bundle – additional requirements for cases being heard at First Avenue House or at the RCJ

8.1 In the case of hearings at the RCJ or First Avenue House, parties shall:

   (a) if the bundle or preliminary documents are delivered personally, ensure that they obtain a receipt from the clerk accepting it or them; and
   (b) if the bundle or preliminary documents are sent by post or DX, ensure that they obtain proof of posting or despatch.

The receipt (or proof of posting or despatch, as the case may be) shall be brought to court on the day of the hearing and must be produced to the court if requested. If the receipt (or proof of posting or despatch) cannot

be produced to the court the judge may (i) treat the bundle as having not been lodged and (ii) take the steps referred to in paragraph 12.
8.2 For hearings at the RCJ:

(a) bundles or preliminary documents delivered after 11 am on the day before the hearing will not be accepted by the Clerk of the Rules and shall be delivered:

    (i) in a case where the hearing is before a judge of the High Court, directly to the clerk of the judge hearing the case;

    (ii) in a case where the hearing is before a Circuit Judge, Deputy High Court Judge or Recorder, directly to the messenger at the Judge's entrance to the Queen's Building (with telephone notification to the personal assistant to the Designated Family Judge, 020 7947 7155, that this has been done).

(b) upon learning before which judge a hearing is to take place, the clerk to counsel, or other advocate, representing the party in the position of applicant shall no later than 3pm the day before the hearing:

    (i) in a case where the hearing is before a judge of the High Court, telephone the clerk of the judge hearing the case;

    (ii) in a case where the hearing is before a Circuit Judge, Deputy High Court Judge or Recorder, telephone the personal assistant to the Designated Family Judge;

to ascertain whether the judge has received the bundle (including the preliminary documents) and, if not, shall organise prompt delivery by the applicant's solicitor.

Removing and re-lodging the bundle

9.1 Following completion of the hearing the party responsible for the bundle shall retrieve it from the court immediately or, if that is not practicable, shall collect it from the court within five working days. Bundles which are not collected in due time may be destroyed.
9.2 The bundle shall be re-lodged for the next and any further hearings in accordance with the provisions of this practice direction and in a form which complies with paragraph 4.7.

Time estimates

10.1 In every case a time estimate (which shall be inserted at the front of the bundle) shall be prepared which shall so far as practicable be agreed by all parties and shall:

(a) specify separately (i) the time estimated to be required for judicial pre-reading and (ii) the time required for hearing all evidence and submissions and (iii) the time estimated to be required for preparing and delivering judgment; and

(b) be prepared on the basis that before they give evidence all witnesses will have read all relevant filed statements and reports.

10.2 Once a case has been listed, any change in time estimates shall be notified immediately by telephone (and then immediately confirmed in writing):

    (a) in the case of hearings in the RCJ, to the Clerk of the Rules;

    (b) in the case of hearings in the PRFD at First Avenue House, to the List Officer at First Avenue House; and

    (c) in the case of hearings elsewhere, to the relevant listing officer.

Taking cases out of the list

11 As soon as it becomes known that a hearing will no longer be effective, whether as a result of the parties reaching agreement or for any other reason, the parties and their representatives shall immediately notify the court by telephone and by letter. The letter, which shall wherever possible be a joint letter sent on behalf of all parties with their signatures applied or appended, shall include:

    (a) a short background summary of the case;

    (b) the written consent of each party who consents and, where a party does not consent, details of the steps which have been taken to obtain that party's consent and, where known, an explanation of why that consent has not been given;

    (c) a draft of the order being sought; and

    (d) enough information to enable the court to decide (i) whether to take the case out of the list and (ii) whether to make the proposed order.

Penalties for failure to comply with the practice direction

12 Failure to comply with any part of this practice direction may result in the judge removing the case from the list or putting the case further back in the list and may also result in a "wasted costs" order in accordance with CPR Part 48.7 or some other adverse costs order.

Commencement of the practice direction and application of other practice directions

13 This practice direction replaces President's Direction (Family Proceedings: Court Bundles) [2000] 1 FLR 536 and shall have effect from 2 October 2006.

14 Any reference in any other practice direction to President's Direction (Family Proceedings: Court Bundles) [2000] 1 FLR 536 shall be read as if substituted by a reference to this practice direction.

15 This practice direction should where appropriate be read in conjunction with President's Direction (Human Rights Act 1998) [2000] 2 FLR 429 and with Practice Direction (Care Cases: Judicial Continuity and Judicial Case Management) appended to the Public Law Protocol [2003] 2 FLR 719. In particular, nothing in this practice direction is to be read as removing or altering any obligation to comply with the requirements of the Public Law Protocol.

This Practice Direction is issued:

(i)   in relation to family proceedings, by the President of the Family Division, as the nominee of the Lord Chief Justice, with the agreement of the Lord Chancellor; and

(ii) to the extent that it applies to proceedings to which section 5 of the Civil Procedure Act 1997 applies, by the Master of the Rolls as the nominee of the Lord Chief Justice, with the agreement of the Lord Chancellor.

The Right Honourable	The Right Honourable
Sir Mark Potter	Sir Anthony Clarke
President of the Family Division &	Master of the Rolls &
Head of Family Justice	Head of Civil Justice

CPR Part 1

OVERRIDING OBJECTIVE   A2–010

CONTENTS OF THIS PART

Rule 1.1 The overriding objective
Rule 1.2 Application by the court of the overriding objective
Rule 1.3 Duty of the parties
Rule 1.4 Court's duty to manage cases

1.1 The overriding objective

(1) These Rules are a new procedural code with the overriding objective of enabling the court to deal with cases justly.

(2) Dealing with a case justly includes, so far as is practicable –

(a)   ensuring that the parties are on an equal footing;
(b)   saving expense;
(c)   dealing with the case in ways which are proportionate –

  (i)   to the amount of money involved;
  (ii) to the importance of the case;
  (iii) to the complexity of the issues; and
  (iv) to the financial position of each party;

(d)   ensuring that it is dealt with expeditiously and fairly; and
(e)   allotting to it an appropriate share of the court's resources, while taking into account the need to allot resources to other cases.

1.2 Application by the court of the overriding objective

The court must seek to give effect to the overriding objective when it –

(a) exercises any power given to it by the Rules; or
(b) interprets any rule subject to rule 76.2.

1.3 Duty of the parties

The parties are required to help the court to further the overriding objective.

1.4 Court's duty to manage cases

(1) The court must further the overriding objective by actively managing cases.
(2) Active case management includes –

(a) encouraging the parties to co-operate with each other in the conduct of the proceedings;
(b) identifying the issues at an early stage;
(c) deciding promptly which issues need full investigation and trial and accordingly disposing summarily of the others;
(d) deciding the order in which issues are to be resolved;
(e) encouraging the parties to use an alternative dispute resolution$^{(GL)}$ procedure if the court considers that appropriate and facilitating the use of such procedure;
(f) helping the parties to settle the whole or part of the case;
(g) fixing timetables or otherwise controlling the progress of the case;
(h) considering whether the likely benefits of taking a particular step justify the cost of taking it;
(i) dealing with as many aspects of the case as it can on the same occasion;
(j) dealing with the case without the parties needing to attend at court;
(k) making use of technology; and
(l) giving directions to ensure that the trial of a case proceeds quickly and efficiently.

CPR Part 3

A2–011   THE COURT'S CASE MANAGEMENT POWERS

CONTENTS OF THIS PART

Rule 3.5   Judgment without trial after striking out
Rule 3.6   Setting aside judgment entered after striking out
Rule 3.7   Sanctions for non-payment of certain fees
Rule 3.7A
Rule 3.7B Sanctions for dishonouring cheque
Rule 3.8   Sanctions have effect unless defaulting party obtains relief
Rule 3.9   Relief from sanctions
Rule 3.10 General power of the court to rectify matters where there has
been an error of procedure
Rule 3.11 Power of the court to make civil restraint orders

3.1 The court's general powers of management

(1) The list of powers in this rule is in addition to any powers given to the court by any other rule or practice direction or by any other enactment or any powers it may otherwise have.

(2) Except where these Rules provide otherwise, the court may –

    (a)   extend or shorten the time for compliance with any rule, practice direction or court order (even if an application for extension is made after the time for compliance has expired);

    (b)   adjourn or bring forward a hearing;

    (c)   require a party or a party's legal representative to attend the court;

    (d)   hold a hearing and receive evidence by telephone or by using any other method of direct oral communication;

    (e)   direct that part of any proceedings (such as a counterclaim) be dealt with as separate proceedings;

    (f)   stay$^{(GL)}$ the whole or part of any proceedings or judgment either generally or until a specified date or event;

    (g)   consolidate proceedings;

    (h)   try two or more claims on the same occasion;

    (i)   direct a separate trial of any issue;

    (j)   decide the order in which issues are to be tried;

    (k)   exclude an issue from consideration;

    (l)   dismiss or give judgment on a claim after a decision on a preliminary issue;

    (ll) order any party to file and serve an estimate of costs;

    (m) take any other step or make any other order for the purpose of managing the case and furthering the overriding objective.

(3) When the court makes an order, it may –

    (a)   make it subject to conditions, including a condition to pay a sum of money into court; and

    (b)   specify the consequence of failure to comply with the order or a condition.

(4) Where the court gives directions it may take into account whether or not a party has complied with any relevant pre-action protocol$^{(GL)}$.

(5) The court may order a party to pay a sum of money into court if that party has, without good reason, failed to comply with a rule, practice direction or a relevant pre-action protocol.

(6) When exercising its power under paragraph (5) the court must have regard to –

    (a) the amount in dispute; and
    (b) the costs which the parties have incurred or which they may incur.

(6A) Where a party pays money into court following an order under paragraph (3) or (5), the money shall be security for any sum payable by that party to any other party in the proceedings, subject to the right of a defendant under rule 37.2 to treat all or part of any money paid into court as a Part 36 payment.

(Rule 36.2 explains what is meant by a Part 36 payment)

(7) A power of the court under these Rules to make an order includes a power to vary or revoke the order.

3.2 Court officer's power to refer to a judge

Where a step is to be taken by a court officer –

    (a) the court officer may consult a judge before taking that step;
    (b) the step may be taken by a judge instead of the court officer.

3.3 Court's power to make order of its own initiative

(1) Except where a rule or some other enactment provides otherwise, the court may exercise its powers on an application or of its own initiative.

(Part 23 sets out the procedure for making an application)

(2) Where the court proposes to make an order of its own initiative –

    (a) it may give any person likely to be affected by the order an opportunity to make representations; and
    (b) where it does so it must specify the time by and the manner in which the representations must be made.

(3) Where the court proposes –

    (a) to make an order of its own initiative; and
    (b) to hold a hearing to decide whether to make the order,
        it must give each party likely to be affected by the order at least 3 days' notice of the hearing.

(4) The court may make an order of its own initiative, without hearing the parties or giving them an opportunity to make representations.
(5) Where the court has made an order under paragraph (4) –

(a) a party affected by the order may apply to have it set aside^(GL), varied or stayed^(GL); and

(b) the order must contain a statement of the right to make such an application.

(6) An application under paragraph (5)(a) must be made –

(a) within such period as may be specified by the court; or

(b) if the court does not specify a period, not more than 7 days after the date on which the order was served on the party making the application.

(7) If the court of its own initiative strikes out a statement of case or dismisses an application, (including an application for permission to appeal or for permission to apply for judicial review) and it considers that the claim or application is totally without merit –

(a) the court's order must record that fact; and

(b) the court must at the same time consider whether it is appropriate to make a civil restraint order.

3.4 Power to strike out a statement of case

(1) In this rule and rule 3.5, reference to a statement of case includes reference to part of a statement of case.

(2) The court may strike out^(GL) a statement of case if it appears to the court –

(a) that the statement of case discloses no reasonable grounds for bringing or defending the claim;

(b) that the statement of case is an abuse of the court's process or is otherwise likely to obstruct the just disposal of the proceedings; or

(c) that there has been a failure to comply with a rule, practice direction or court order.

(3) When the court strikes out a statement of case it may make any consequential order it considers appropriate.

(4) Where –

(a) the court has struck out a claimant's statement of case;

(b) the claimant has been ordered to pay costs to the defendant; and

(c) before the claimant pays those costs, he starts another claim against the same defendant, arising out of facts which are the same or substantially the same as those relating to the claim in which the statement of case was struck out,

the court may, on the application of the defendant, stay^(GL) that other claim until the costs of the first claim have been paid.

(5) Paragraph (2) does not limit any other power of the court to strike out$^{(GL)}$ a statement of case.

(6) If the court strikes out a claimant's statement of case and it considers that the claim is totally without merit –

    (a)   the court's order must record that fact; and
    (b)   the court must at the same time consider whether it is appropriate to make a civil restraint order.

3.5 Judgment without trial after striking out

(1) This rule applies where –

    (a)   the court makes an order which includes a term that the statement of case of a party shall be struck out if the party does not comply with the order; and
    (b)   the party against whom the order was made does not comply with it.

(2) A party may obtain judgment with costs by filing a request for judgment if –

    (a)   the order referred to in paragraph (1)(a) relates to the whole of a statement of case; and
    (b)   where the party wishing to obtain judgment is the claimant, the claim is for –

        (i)   a specified amount of money;
        (ii)   an amount of money to be decided by the court;
        (iii)   delivery of goods where the claim form gives the defendant the alternative of paying their value; or
        (iv)   any combination of these remedies.

(3) Where judgment is obtained under this rule in a case to which paragraph (2)(b)(iii) applies, it will be judgment requiring the defendant to deliver goods, or (if he does not do so) pay the value of the goods as decided by the court (less any payments made).

(4) The request must state that the right to enter judgment has arisen because the court's order has not been complied with.

(5) A party must make an application in accordance with Part 23 if he wishes to obtain judgment under this rule in a case to which paragraph (2) does not apply.

3.6 Setting aside judgment entered after striking out

(1) A party against whom the court has entered judgment under rule 3.5 may apply to the court to set the judgment aside.

(2) An application under paragraph (1) must be made not more than 14 days after the judgment has been served on the party making the application.

(3) If the right to enter judgment had not arisen at the time when judgment was entered, the court must set aside$^{(GL)}$ the judgment.

(4) If the application to set aside$^{(GL)}$ is made for any other reason, rule 3.9 (relief from sanctions) shall apply.

3.7 Sanctions for non-payment of certain fees

(1) This rule applies where –

    (a)   an allocation questionnaire or a pre-trial check list (listing questionnaire) is filed without payment of the fee specified by the relevant Fees Order;

    (b)   the court dispenses with the need for an allocation questionnaire or a pre-trial check list or both;

    (c)   these Rules do not require an allocation questionnaire or a pre-trial check list to be filed in relation to the claim in question; or

    (d)   the court has made an order giving permission to proceed with a claim for judicial review.

(Rule 26.3 provides for the court to dispense with the need for an allocation questionnaire and rules 28.5 and 29.6 provide for the court to dispense with the need for a pre-trial check list)

(Rule 54.12 provides for the service of the order giving permission to proceed with a claim for judicial review)

(2) The court will serve a notice on the claimant requiring payment of the fee specified in the relevant Fees Order if, at the time the fee is due, the claimant has not paid it or made an application for exemption or remission.

(3) The notice will specify the date by which the claimant must pay the fee.

(4) If the claimant does not –

    (a)   pay the fee; or

    (b)   make an application for an exemption from or remission of the fee, by the date specified in the notice –

        (i)   the claim will automatically be struck out without further order of the court; and

        (ii)   the claimant shall be liable for the costs which the defendant has incurred unless the court orders otherwise.

(Rule 44.12 provides for the basis of assessment where a right to costs arises under this rule)

(5) Where an application for exemption from or remission of a fee is refused, the court will serve notice on the claimant requiring payment of the fee by the date specified in the notice.

(6) If the claimant does not pay the fee by the date specified in the notice –

    (a)   the claim will automatically be struck out without further order of the court; and

    (b)   the claimant shall be liable for the costs which the defendant has incurred unless the court orders otherwise.

(7) If –

    (a) a claimant applies to have the claim reinstated; and
    (b) the court grants relief,
          the relief shall be conditional on the claimant either paying the fee or filing evidence of exemption from payment or remission of the fee within the period specified in paragraph (8).

(8) The period referred to in paragraph (7) is –

    (a) if the order granting relief is made at a hearing at which the claimant is present or represented, 2 days from the date of the order;
    (b) in any other case, 7 days from the date of service of the order on the claimant.

3.7A

(1) This rule applies where a defendant files a counterclaim without –

    (a) payment of the fee specified by the relevant Fees Order; or
    (b) making an application for an exemption from or remission of the fee.

(2) The court will serve a notice on the defendant requiring payment of the fee specified in the relevant Fees Order if, at the time the fee is due, the defendant has not paid it or made an application for exemption or remission.

(3) The notice will specify the date by which the defendant must pay the fee.

(4) If the defendant does not –

    (a) pay the fee; or
    (b) make an application for an exemption from or remission of the fee,
          by the date specified in the notice, the counterclaim will automatically be struck out without further order of the court.

(5) Where an application for exemption from or remission of a fee is refused, the court will serve notice on the defendant requiring payment of the fee by the date specified in the notice.

(6) If the defendant does not pay the fee by the date specified in the notice, the counterclaim will automatically be struck out without further order of the court.

(7) If –

    (a) the defendant applies to have the counterclaim reinstated; and
    (b) the court grants relief,
          the relief will be conditional on the defendant either paying the fee or filing evidence of exemption from payment or remission of the fee within the period specified in paragraph (8).

(8) The period referred to in paragraph (7) is –

    (a) if the order granting relief is made at a hearing at which the defendant is present or represented, 2 days from the date of the order;

    (b) in any other case, 7 days from the date of service of the order on the defendant.

3.7B Sanctions for dishonouring cheque

(1) This rule applies where any fee is paid by cheque and that cheque is subsequently dishonoured.

(2) The court will serve a notice on the paying party requiring payment of the fee which will specify the date by which the fee must be paid.

(3) If the fee is not paid by the date specified in the notice –

    (a) where the fee is payable by the claimant, the claim will automatically be struck out without further order of the court;

    (b) where the fee is payable by the defendant, the defence will automatically be struck out without further order of the court,

and the paying party shall be liable for the costs which any other party has incurred unless the court orders otherwise.

(Rule 44.12 provides for the basis of assessment where a right to costs arises under this rule)

(4) If –

    (a) the paying party applies to have the claim or defence reinstated; and

    (b) the court grants relief,
        the relief shall be conditional on that party paying the fee within the period specified in paragraph (5).

(5) The period referred to in paragraph (4) is –

    (a) if the order granting relief is made at a hearing at which the paying party is present or represented, 2 days from the date of the order;

    (b) in any other case, 7 days from the date of service of the order on the paying party.

(6) For the purposes of this rule, 'claimant' includes a Part 20 claimant and 'claim form' includes a Part 20 claim.

3.8 Sanctions have effect unless defaulting party obtains relief

(1) Where a party has failed to comply with a rule, practice direction or court order, any sanction for failure to comply imposed by the rule, practice direction or court order has effect unless the party in default applies for and obtains relief from the sanction.

(Rule 3.9 sets out the circumstances which the court may consider on an application to grant relief from a sanction)

(2) Where the sanction is the payment of costs, the party in default may only obtain relief by appealing against the order for costs.

(3) Where a rule, practice direction or court order –

    (a) requires a party to do something within a specified time, and
    (b) specifies the consequence of failure to comply,
        the time for doing the act in question may not be extended by agreement between the parties.

3.9 Relief from sanctions

(1) On an application for relief from any sanction imposed for a failure to comply with any rule, practice direction or court order the court will consider all the circumstances including –

    (a) the interests of the administration of justice;
    (b) whether the application for relief has been made promptly;
    (c) whether the failure to comply was intentional;
    (d) whether there is a good explanation for the failure;
    (e) the extent to which the party in default has complied with other rules, practice directions, court orders and any relevant preaction protocol[(GL)];
    (f) whether the failure to comply was caused by the party or his legal representative;
    (g) whether the trial date or the likely trial date can still be met if relief is granted;
    (h) the effect which the failure to comply had on each party; and
    (i) the effect which the granting of relief would have on each party.

(2) An application for relief must be supported by evidence.

3.10 General power of the court to rectify matters where there has been an error of procedure

Where there has been an error of procedure such as a failure to comply with a rule or practice direction –

    (a) the error does not invalidate any step taken in the proceedings unless the court so orders; and
    (b) the court may make an order to remedy the error.

3.11 Power of the court to make civil restraint orders

A practice direction may set out –

    (a) the circumstances in which the court has the power to make a civil restraint order against a party to proceedings;
    (b) the procedure where a party applies for a civil restraint order against another party; and
    (c) the consequences of the court making a civil restraint order.

PRACTICE DIRECTION

STRIKING OUT A STATMENT OF CASE

THIS PRACTICE DIRECTION SUPPLEMENTS CPR RULE 3.4

INTRODUCTORY

1.1 Rule 1.4(2)(c) includes as an example of active case management the summary disposal of issues which do not need full investigation at trial.
1.2 The rules give the court two distinct powers which may be used to achieve this. Rule 3.4 enables the court to strike out the whole or part of a statement of case which discloses no reasonable grounds for bringing or defending a claim (rule 3.4(2)(a)), or which is an abuse of the process of the court or otherwise likely to obstruct the just disposal of the proceedings (rule 3.4(2)(b)) Rule 24.2 enables the court to give summary judgment against a claimant or defendant where that party has no real prospect of succeeding on his claim or defence. Both those powers may be exercised on an application by a party or on the court's own initiative.
1.3 This practice direction sets out the procedure a party should follow if he wishes to make an application for an order under rule 3.4.
1.4 The following are examples of cases where the court may conclude that particulars of claim (whether contained in a claim form or filed separately) fall within rule 3.4(2)(a):

(1) those which set out no facts indicating what the claim is about, for example 'Money owed £5000',
(2) those which are incoherent and make no sense,
(3) those which contain a coherent set of facts but those facts, even if true, do not disclose any legally recognisable claim against the defendant.

1.5 A claim may fall within rule 3.4(2)(b) where it is vexatious, scurrilous or obviously ill-founded.
1.6 A defence may fall within rule 3.4(2)(a) where:

(1) it consists of a bare denial or otherwise sets out no coherent statement of facts, or
(2) the facts it sets out, while coherent, would not even if true amount in law to a defence to the claim.

1.7 A party may believe he can show without a trial that an opponent's case has no real prospect of success on the facts, or that the case is bound to succeed or fail, as the case may be, because of a point of law (including the construction of a document). In such a case the party concerned may make an application under rule 3.4 or Part 24 (or both) as he thinks appropriate.

1.8 The examples set out above are intended only as illustrations.

1.9 Where a rule, practice direction or order states 'shall be struck out or dismissed' or 'will be struck out or dismissed' this means that the striking out or dismissal will be automatic and that no further order of the court is required.

CLAIMS WHICH APPEAR TO FALL WITHIN RULE 3.4(2)(A) OR (B)

2.1 If a court officer is asked to issue a claim form which he believes may fall within rule 3.4(2)(a) or (b) he should issue it, but may then consult a judge (under rule 3.2) before returning the claim form to the claimant or taking any other step to serve the defendant. The judge may on his own initiative make an immediate order designed to ensure that the claim is disposed of or (as the case may be) proceeds in a way that accords with the rules.

2.3 The judge may allow the claimant a hearing before deciding whether to make such an order.

2.4 Orders the judge may make include:

    (1)   an order that the claim be stayed until further order,

    (2)   an order that the claim form be retained by the court and not served until the stay is lifted,

    (3)   an order that no application by the claimant to lift the stay be heard unless he files such further documents (for example a witness statement or an amended claim form or particulars of claim) as may be specified in the order.

2.5 Where the judge makes any such order or, subsequently, an order lifting the stay he may give directions about the service on the defendant of the order and any other documents on the court file.

2.6 The fact that a judge allows a claim referred to him by a court officer to proceed does not prejudice the right of any party to apply for any order against the claimant.

DEFENCES WHICH APPEAR TO FALL WITHIN RULE 3.4(2)(A) OR (B)

3.1 A court officer may similarly consult a judge about any document filed which purports to be a defence and which he believes may fall within rule 3.4(2)(a) or (b).

3.2 If the judge decides that the document falls within rule 3.4(2)(a) or (b) he may on his own initiative make an order striking it out. Where he does so he may extend the time for the defendant to file a proper defence.

3.3 The judge may allow the defendant a hearing before deciding whether to make such an order.

3.4 Alternatively the judge may make an order under rule 18.1 requiring the defendant within a stated time to clarify his defence or to give additional information about it. The order may provide that the defence will be struck out if the defendant does not comply.

3.5 The fact that a judge does not strike out a defence on his own initiative does not prejudice the right of the claimant to apply for any order against the defendant.

GENERAL PROVISIONS

4.1 The court may exercise its powers under rule 3.4(2)(a) or (b) on application or on its own initiative at any time.

4.2 Where a judge at a hearing strikes out all or part of a party's statement of case he may enter such judgment for the other party as that party appears entitled to.

APPLICATIONS FOR ORDERS UNDER RULE 3.4(2)

5.1 Attention is drawn to Part 23 (General Rules about Applications) and to the practice direction that supplements it. The practice direction requires all applications to be made as soon as possible and before allocation if possible.

5.2 While many applications under rule 3.4(2) can be made without evidence in support, the applicant should consider whether facts need to be proved and, if so, whether evidence in support should be filed and served.

APPLICATIONS FOR SUMMARY JUDGMENT

6.1 Applications for summary judgment may be made under Part 24. Attention is drawn to that Part and to the practice direction that supplements it.

VEXATIOUS LITIGANTS

7.1 This Practice Direction applies where a 'civil proceedings order' or an 'all proceedings order' (as respectively defined under section 42(1A) of the Supreme Court Act, 1981) is in force against a person ('the litigant').
7.2 An application by the litigant for permission to begin or continue, or to make any application in, any civil proceedings shall be made by application notice issued in the High Court and signed by the litigant.
7.3 The application notice must state:

    (1) the title and reference number of the proceedings in which the civil proceedings order or the all proceedings order, as the case may be, was made,

    (2) the full name of the litigant and his address,

    (3) the order the applicant is seeking, and

    (4) briefly, why the applicant is seeking the order.

7.4 The application notice must be filed together with any written evidence on which the litigant relies in support of his application.
7.5 Either in the application notice or in written evidence filed in support of the application, the previous occasions on which the litigant made an application for permission under section 42(1A) of the said Act must be listed.
7.6 The application notice, together with any written evidence, will be placed before a High Court judge who may:

    (1) without the attendance of the applicant make an order giving the permission sought;

    (2) give directions for further written evidence to be supplied by the litigant before an order is made on the application;

    (3) make an order dismissing the application without a hearing; or

    (4) give directions for the hearing of the application.

7.7 Directions given under paragraph 7.6(4) may include an order that the application notice be served on the Attorney General and on any person against whom the litigant desires to bring the proceedings for which permission is being sought.
7.8 Any order made under paragraphs 6 or 7 will be served on the litigant at the address given in the application notice. CPR Part 6 will apply.
7.9 A person may apply to set aside the grant of permission if:

(1) the permission allowed the litigant to bring or continue proceedings against that person or to make any application against him, and

(2) the permission was granted other than at a hearing of which that person was given notice under paragraph 7.

7.10 Any application under paragraph 7.9 must be made in accordance with CPR Part 23.

CPR Part 7

HOW TO START PROCEEDINGS – THE CLAIM FORM   A2–013

CONTENTS OF THIS PART

7.1 Where to start proceedings

Restrictions on where proceedings may be started are set out in the relevant practice direction.

7.2 How to start proceedings

(1) Proceedings are started when the court issues a claim form at the request of the claimant.

(2) A claim form is issued on the date entered on the form by the court.

(A person who seeks a remedy from the court before proceedings are started or in relation to proceedings which are taking place, or will take place, in another jurisdiction must make an application under Part 23)

(Part 16 sets out what the claim form must include)

(The costs practice direction sets out the information about a funding arrangement to be provided with the claim form where the claimant intends to seek to recover an additional liability)

('Funding arrangements' and 'additional liability' are defined in rule 43.2)

7.3 Right to use one claim form to start two or more claims

A claimant may use a single claim form to start all claims which can be conveniently disposed of in the same proceedings.

7.4 Particulars of claim

(1) Particulars of claim must –

    (a) be contained in or served with the claim form; or
    (b) subject to paragraph (2) be served on the defendant by the claimant within 14 days after service of the claim form.

(2) Particulars of claim must be served on the defendant no later than the latest time for serving a claim form.

(Rule 7.5 sets out the latest time for serving a claim form)

(3) Where the claimant serves particulars of claim separately from the claim form in accordance with paragraph (1)(b), he must, within 7 days of service on the defendant, file a copy of the particulars together with a certificate of service.

(Part 16 sets out what the particulars of claim must include)

(Part 22 requires particulars of claim to be verified by a statement of truth)

(Rule 6.10 makes provision for a certificate of service)

7.5 Service of a claim form

(1) After a claim form has been issued, it must be served on the defendant.
(2) The general rule is that a claim form must be served within 4 months after the date of issue.
(3) The period for service is 6 months where the claim form is to be served out of the jurisdiction.

7.6 Extension of time for serving a claim form

(1) The claimant may apply for an order extending the period within which the claim form may be served.
(2) The general rule is that an application to extend the time for service must be made –

   (a) within the period for serving the claim form specified by rule
       7.5; or

   (b) where an order has been made under this rule, within the period
       for service specified by that order.

(3) If the claimant applies for an order to extend the time for service of
the claim form after the end of the period specified by rule 7.5 or by an
order made under this rule, the court may make such an order only if –

   (a) the court has been unable to serve the claim form; or

   (b) the claimant has taken all reasonable steps to serve the claim
       form but has been unable to do so; and

   (c) in either case, the claimant has acted promptly in making the
       application.

(4) An application for an order extending the time for service –

   (a) must be supported by evidence; and

   (b) may be made without notice.

7.7 Application by defendant for service of claim form

(1) Where a claim form has been issued against a defendant, but has not
yet been served on him, the defendant may serve a notice on the claimant
requiring him to serve the claim form or discontinue the claim within a
period specified in the notice.

(2) The period specified in a notice served under paragraph (1) must be at
least 14 days after service of the notice.

(3) If the claimant fails to comply with the notice, the court may, on the
application of the defendant –

   (a) dismiss the claim; or

   (b) make any other order it thinks just.

7.8 Form for defence etc. must be served with particulars of claim

(1) When particulars of claim are served on a defendant, whether they are
contained in the claim form, served with it or served subsequently, they
must be accompanied by –

   (a) a form for defending the claim;

   (b) a form for admitting the claim; and

   (c) a form for acknowledging service.

(2) Where the claimant is using the procedure set out in Part 8 (alternative
procedure for claims) –

   (a) paragraph (1) does not apply; and

   (b) a form for acknowledging service must accompany the claim
       form.

7.9 Fixed date and other claims

A practice direction –

    (a) may set out the circumstances in which the court may give a fixed date for a hearing when it issues a claim;

    (b) may list claims in respect of which there is a specific claim form for use and set out the claim form in question; and

    (c) may disapply or modify these Rules as appropriate in relation to the claims referred to in paragraphs (a) and (b).

7.10 Production Centre for claims

(1) There shall be a Production Centre for the issue of claim forms and other related matters.

(2) The relevant practice direction makes provision for –

    (a) which claimants may use the Production Centre;

    (b) the type of claims which the Production Centre may issue;

    (c) the functions which are to be discharged by the Production Centre;

    (d) the place where the Production Centre is to be located; and

    (e) other related matters.

(3) The relevant practice direction may disapply or modify these Rules as appropriate in relation to claims issued by the Production Centre.

7.11 Human Rights

(1) A claim under section 7(1)(a) of the Human Rights Act 19981 in respect of a judicial act may be brought only in the High Court.

(2) Any other claim under section 7(1)(a) of that Act may be brought in any court.

7.12 Electronic issue of claims

(1) A practice direction may make provision for a claimant to start a claim by requesting the issue of a claim form electronically.

(2) The practice direction may, in particular –

    (a) specify –

        (i) the types of claim which may be issued electronically; and

        (ii) the conditions which a claim must meet before it may be issued electronically;

    (b) specify –

        (i) the court where the claim will be issued; and

        (ii) the circumstances in which the claim will be transferred to another court;

    (c) provide for the filing of other documents electronically where a claim has been started electronically;

(d) specify the requirements that must be fulfilled for any document
     filed electronically; and
(e) provide how a fee payable on the filing of any document is to be
     paid where that document is filed electronically.

(3) The practice direction may disapply or modify these Rules as
appropriate in relation to claims started electronically.

PRACTICE DIRECTION   A2–014

HOW TO START PROCEEDINGS – THE CLAIM FORM

THIS PRACTICE DIRECTION SUPPLEMENTS CPR PART 7

GENERAL

1 Subject to the following provisions of this practice direction, proceedings which both the High Court and the county courts have jurisdiction to deal with may be started in the High Court or in a county court.

WHERE TO START PROCEEDINGS

2.1 Proceedings (whether for damages or for a specified sum) may not be started in the High Court unless the value of the claim is more than £15,000.
2.2 Proceedings which include a claim for damages in respect of personal injuries must not be started in the High Court unless the value of the claim is £50,000 or more (paragraph 9 of the High Court and County Courts Jurisdiction Order 1991 (S.I. 1991/724 as amended) describes how the value of a claim is to be determined).
2.3 A claim must be issued in the High Court or a county court if an enactment so requires.
2.4 Subject to paragraphs 2.1 and 2.2 above, a claim should be started in the High Court if by reason of:

(1) the financial value of the claim and the amount in dispute, and/
     or

(2) the complexity of the facts, legal issues, remedies or procedures involved, and/or

(3) the importance of the outcome of the claim to the public in general, the claimant believes that the claim ought to be dealt with by a High Court judge.

(CPR Part 30 and the practice direction supplementing Part 30 contain provisions relating to the transfer to the county court of proceedings started in the High Court and vice-versa.)

2.5 A claim relating to Chancery business (which includes any of the matters specified in paragraph 1 of Schedule 1 to the Supreme Court Act 1981) may, subject to any enactment, rule or practice direction, be dealt with in the High Court or in a county court. The claim form should, if issued in the High Court, be marked in the top right hand corner 'Chancery Division' and, if issued in the county court, be marked 'Chancery Business'.

(For the equity jurisdiction of county courts, see section 23 of the County Courts Act 1984.)

2.6 A claim relating to any of the matters specified in sub-paragraphs (a) and (b) of paragraph 2 of Schedule 1 to the Supreme Court Act 1981 must be dealt with in the High Court and will be assigned to the Queen's Bench Division.

2.7 Practice directions applying to particular types of proceedings, or to proceedings in particular courts, will contain provisions relating to the commencement and conduct of those proceedings.

2.8 A claim in the High Court for which a jury trial is directed will, if not already being dealt with in the Queen's Bench Division, be transferred to that Division.

2.9 The following proceedings may not be started in a county court unless the parties have agreed otherwise in writing:

(1) a claim for damages or other remedy for libel or slander, and

(2) a claim in which the title to any toll, fair, market or franchise is in question.

2.10

(1) The normal rules apply in deciding in which court and specialist list a claim that includes issues under the Human Rights Act 1998 should be started. They also apply in deciding which procedure to use to start the claim; this Part or CPR Part 8 or CPR Part 54 (judicial review).

(2) The exception is a claim for damages in respect of a judicial act, which should be commenced in the High Court. If the claim is made in a notice of appeal then it will be dealt with according to the normal rules governing where that appeal is heard.

(A county court cannot make a declaration of incompatibility in accordance with section 4 of the Human Rights Act 1998. Legislation may direct that such a claim is to be brought before a specified tribunal)

THE CLAIM FORM

3.1 A claimant must use practice form N1 or practice form N208 (the Part 8 claim form) to start a claim (but see paragraphs 3.2 and 3.4 below).
3.2 Rule 7.9 deals with fixed date claims and rule 7.10 deals with the Production Centre for the issue of claims; there are separate practice directions supplementing rules 7.9 and 7.10.
3.3 If a claimant wishes his claim to proceed under Part 8, or if the claim is required to proceed under Part 8, the claim form should so state. Otherwise the claim will proceed under Part 7. But note that in respect of claims in specialist proceedings (listed in CPR Part 49) and claims brought under the RSC or CCR set out in the Schedule to the CPR (see CPR Part 50) the CPR will apply only to the extent that they are not inconsistent with the rules and practice directions that expressly apply to those claims.
3.4 Other practice directions may require special practice forms to be used to commence particular types of proceedings, or proceedings in particular courts.
3.5 Where a claim which is to be served out of the jurisdiction is one which the court has power to deal with under the Civil Jurisdiction and Judgments Act 1982, the claim form and, when they are contained in a separate document, the particulars of claim should be endorsed with a statement that the court has power under that Act to deal with the claim and that no proceedings based on the same claim are pending between the parties in Scotland, Northern Ireland or another Convention territory.[1]
3.5A Where a claim which is to be served out of jurisdiction is one which the court has power to deal with under Council Regulation (EC) No 44/2001 of 22nd December 2000 on jurisdiction and the recognition and enforcement of judgments in civil and commercial matters, the claim form and, when they are contained in a separate document, the particulars of claim must be endorsed with a statement that the court has power under that Regulation to deal with the claim and that no proceedings based on the same claim are pending between the parties in Scotland, Northern Ireland or another Regulation State.[2]
3.6 If a claim for damages or for an unspecified sum is started in the High Court, the claim form must:

   (1)   state that the claimant expects to recover more than £15,000 (or £50,000 or more if the claim is for personal injuries) or

---

[1] 'Convention territory' means the territory or territories of any Contracting State as defined by S.1(3) of the Civil Jurisdiction and Judgments Act 1982, to which the Brussels Conventions or Lugano Convention apply.
[2] 'Regulation State' means all Member States except Denmark.

(2) state that some enactment provides that the claim may only be commenced in the High Court and specify that enactment or

(3) state that the claim is to be in one of the specialist High Court lists (see CPR Parts 49 and 58–62) and specify that list.

3.7 If the contents of a claim form commencing specialist proceedings complies with the requirements of the specialist list in question the claim form will also satisfy paragraph 3.6 above.

3.8 If a claim for damages for personal injuries is started in the county court, the claim form must state whether or not the claimant expects to recover more than £1000 in respect of pain, suffering and loss of amenity.

3.9 If a claim for housing disrepair which includes a claim for an order requiring repairs or other work to be carried out by the landlord is started in the county court, the claim form must state:

(1) whether or not the cost of the repairs or other work is estimated to be more than £1000, and

(2) whether or not the claimant expects to recover more than £1000 in respect of any claim for damages.[3]

If either of the amounts mentioned in (1) and (2) is more than £1000, the small claims track will not be the normal track for that claim.

(The Costs Practice Direction supplementing Parts 43 to 48 contains details of the information required to be filed with a claim form to comply with rule 44.15 (providing information about funding arrangements))

TITLE OF PROCEEDINGS

4.1 The claim form and every other statement of case, must be headed with the title of the proceedings. The title should state:

(1) the number of proceedings,

(2) the court or Division in which they are proceeding,

(3) the full name of each party,

(4) his status in the proceedings (i.e. claimant/defendant).

(Paragraph 2.6 of the Practice Direction to Part 16 sets out what is meant by a full name in respect of each type of claimant.)

4.2 Where there is more than one claimant and/or more than one defendant, the parties should be described in the title as follows:

(1) AB

(2) CD

(3) EF   Claimants

[3] See rules 16.3(4) and 26.6.

and

    (1) GH
    (2) IJ
    (3) KL   Defendants

START OF PROCEEDINGS

5.1 Proceedings are started when the court issues a claim form at the request of the claimant (see rule 7.2) but where the claim form as issued was received in the court office on a date earlier than the date on which it was issued by the court, the claim is 'brought' for the purposes of the Limitation Act 1980 and any other relevant statute on that earlier date.

5.2 The date on which the claim form was received by the court will be recorded by a date stamp either on the claim form held on the court file or on the letter that accompanied the claim form when it was received by the court.

5.3 An enquiry as to the date on which the claim form was received by the court should be directed to a court officer.

5.4 Parties proposing to start a claim which is approaching the expiry of the limitation period should recognise the potential importance of establishing the date the claim form was received by the court and should themselves make arrangements to record the date.

5.5 Where it is sought to start proceedings against the estate of a deceased defendant where probate or letters of administration have not been granted, the claimant should issue the claim against 'the personal representatives of A.B. deceased'. The claimant should then, before the expiry of the period for service of the claim form, apply to the court for the appointment of a person to represent the estate of the deceased.

PARTICULARS OF CLAIM

6.1 Where the claimant does not include the particulars of claim in the claim form, particulars of claim may be served separately:

    (1)   either at the same time as the claim form, or

    (2)   within 14 days after service of the claim form provided that the service of the particulars of claim is within 4 months after the date of issue of the claim form[4] (or 6 months where the claim form is to be served out of the jurisdiction[5]).

---

[4] See rules 7.4(2) and 7.5(2).
[5] See rule 7.5(3).

6.2 If the particulars of claim are not included in or have not been served with the claim form, the claim form must contain a statement that particulars of claim will follow[6].

(These paragraphs do not apply where the Part 8 procedure is being used. For information on matters to be included in the claim form or the particulars of claim, see Part 16 (statements of case) and the practice direction which supplements it.)

STATEMENT OF TRUTH

7.1 Part 22 requires the claim form and, where they are not included in the claim form, the particulars of claim, to be verified by a statement of truth.
7.2 The form of the statement of truth is as follows:

'[I believe][the claimant believes] that the facts stated in [this claim form] [these particulars of claim] are true.'

7.3 Attention is drawn to rule 32.14 which sets out the consequences of verifying a statement of case containing a false statement without an honest belief in its truth.

(For information regarding statements of truth see Part 22 and the practice direction which supplements it.)

EXTENSION OF TIME

8.1 An application under rule 7.6 (for an extension of time for serving a claim form under rule 7.6(1)) must be made in accordance with Part 23 and supported by evidence.
8.2 The evidence should state:

    (1)   all the circumstances relied on,
    (2)   the date of issue of the claim,
    (3)   the expiry date of any rule 7.6 extension, and
    (4)   a full explanation as to why the claim has not been served.

(For information regarding (1) written evidence see Part 32 and the practice direction which supplements it and (2) service of the claim form see Part 6 and the practice direction which supplements it.)

---

[6] See rule 16.2(2).

CPR Part 8

ALTERNATIVE PROCEDURE FOR CLAIMS   A2–015

CONTENTS OF THIS PART

8.1 Types of claim in which Part 8 procedure may be followed

(1) The Part 8 procedure is the procedure set out in this Part.
(2) A claimant may use the Part 8 procedure where –

  (a)   he seeks the court's decision on a question which is unlikely to involve a substantial dispute of fact; or
  (b)   paragraph (6) applies.

(3) The court may at any stage order the claim to continue as if the claimant had not used the Part 8 procedure and, if it does so, the court may give any directions it considers appropriate.
(4) Paragraph (2) does not apply if a practice direction provides that the Part 8 procedure may not be used in relation to the type of claim in question.
(5) Where the claimant uses the Part 8 procedure he may not obtain default judgment under Part 12.
(6) A rule or practice direction may, in relation to a specified type of proceedings –

  (a)   require or permit the use of the Part 8 procedure; and
  (b)   disapply or modify any of the rules set out in this Part as they apply to those proceedings.

(Rule 8.9 provides for other modifications to the general rules where the Part 8 procedure is being used)

8.2 Contents of the claim form

Where the claimant uses the Part 8 procedure the claim form must state –

  (a)   that this Part applies;

(b) (i) the question which the claimant wants the court to decide; or

    (ii) the remedy which the claimant is seeking and the legal basis for the claim to that remedy;

(c) if the claim is being made under an enactment, what that enactment is;

(d) if the claimant is claiming in a representative capacity, what that capacity is; and

(e) if the defendant is sued in a representative capacity, what that capacity is.

(Part 22 provides for the claim form to be verified by a statement of truth)
(Rule 7.5 provides for service of the claim form)
(The costs practice direction sets out the information about a funding arrangement to be provided with the claim form where the claimant intends to seek to recover an additional liability)
('Funding arrangement' and 'additional liability' are defined in rule 43.2)

8.2A Issue of claim form without naming defendants

(1) A practice direction may set out circumstances in which a claim form may be issued under this Part without naming a defendant.
(2) The practice direction may set out those cases in which an application for permission must be made by application notice before the claim form is issued.
(3) The application notice for permission –

(a) need not be served on any other person; and

(b) must be accompanied by a copy of the claim form that the applicant proposes to issue.

(4) Where the court gives permission it will give directions about the future management of the claim.

8.3 Acknowledgment of service

(1) The defendant must –

(a) file an acknowledgment of service in the relevant practice form not more than 14 days after service of the claim form; and

(b) serve the acknowledgment of service on the claimant and any other party.

(2) The acknowledgment of service must state –

(a) whether the defendant contests the claim; and

(b) if the defendant seeks a different remedy from that set out in the claim form, what that remedy is.

(3) The following rules of Part 10 (acknowledgment of service) apply –

(a) rule 10.3(2) (exceptions to the period for filing an acknowl-
     edgment of service); and
(b) rule 10.5 (contents of acknowledgment of service).

(4) Omitted

(The costs practice direction sets out the information about a funding
arrangement to be provided with the acknowledgment of service where
the defendant intends to seek to recover an additional liability)
('Funding arrangement' and 'additional liability' are defined in rule 43.2)

8.4 Consequence of not filing an acknowledgment of service

(1) This rule applies where –

(a) the defendant has failed to file an acknowledgment of service;
     and
(b) the time period for doing so has expired.

(2) The defendant may attend the hearing of the claim but may not take
part in the hearing unless the court gives permission.

8.5 Filing and serving written evidence

(1) The claimant must file any written evidence on which he intends to
rely when he files his claim form.
(2) The claimant's evidence must be served on the defendant with the
claim form.
(3) A defendant who wishes to rely on written evidence must file it when
he files his acknowledgment of service.
(4) If he does so, he must also, at the same time, serve a copy of his
evidence on the other parties.
(5) The claimant may, within 14 days of service of the defendant's evidence on him, file further written evidence in reply.
(6) If he does so, he must also, within the same time limit, serve a copy of
his evidence on the other parties.
(7) The claimant may rely on the matters set out in his claim form as
evidence under this rule if the claim form is verified by a statement of
truth.

8.6 Evidence – general

(1) No written evidence may be relied on at the hearing of the claim
unless –

(a) it has been served in accordance with rule 8.5; or
(b) the court gives permission.

(2) The court may require or permit a party to give oral evidence at the
hearing.
(3) The court may give directions requiring the attendance for cross-
examination$^{(GL)}$ of a witness who has given written evidence.

(Rule 32.1 contains a general power for the court to control evidence)

8.7 Part 20 claims

Where the Part 8 procedure is used, Part 20 (counterclaims and other additional claims) applies except that a party may not make a Part 20 claim (as defined by rule 20.2) without the court's permission.

8.8 Procedure where defendant objects to use of the Part 8 procedure

(1) Where the defendant contends that the Part 8 procedure should not be used because –

>   (a)   there is a substantial dispute of fact; and
>   (b)   the use of the Part 8 procedure is not required or permitted by a rule or practice direction, he must state his reasons when he files his acknowledgment of service.

(Rule 8.5 requires a defendant who wishes to rely on written evidence to file it when he files his acknowledgment of service)

(2) When the court receives the acknowledgment of service and any written evidence it will give directions as to the future management of the case.

(Rule 8.1(3) allows the court to make an order that the claim continue as if the claimant had not used the Part 8 procedure)

8.9 Modifications to the general rules

Where the Part 8 procedure is followed –

>   (a)   provision is made in this Part for the matters which must be stated in the claim form and the defendant is not required to file a defence and therefore –
>
>   (i)   Part 16 (statements of case) does not apply;
>   (ii)   Part 15 (defence and reply) does not apply;
>   (iii) any time limit in these Rules which prevents the parties from taking a step before a defence is filed does not apply;
>   (iv)   the requirement under rule 7.8 to serve on the defendant a form for defending the claim does not apply;
>
>   (b)   the claimant may not obtain judgment by request on an admission and therefore –
>
>   (i)   rules 14.4 to 14.7 do not apply; and
>   (ii)   the requirement under rule 7.8 to serve on the defendant a form for admitting the claim does not apply; and
>
>   (c)   the claim shall be treated as allocated to the multi-track and therefore Part 26 does not apply.

PRACTICE DIRECTION   A2–016

ALTERNATIVE PROCEDURE FOR CLAIMS

THIS PRACTICE DIRECTION SUPPLEMENTS CPR PART 8

TYPES OF CLAIM IN WHICH PART 8 PROCEDURE MAY BE USED

1.1 A claimant may use the Part 8 procedure where he seeks the court's decision on a question which is unlikely to involve a substantial dispute of fact.

1.2 A claimant may also use the Part 8 procedure if a practice direction permits or requires its use for the type of proceedings in question.

1.3 The practice directions referred to in paragraph 1.2 above may in some respects modify or disapply the Part 8 procedure and, where that is so, it is those practice directions that must be complied with.

1.4 The types of claim for which the Part 8 procedure may be used include:

   (1) a claim by or against a child or patient which has been settled before the commencement of proceedings and the sole purpose of the claim is to obtain the approval of the court to the settlement,

   (2) a claim for provisional damages which has been settled before the commencement of proceedings and the sole purpose of the claim is to obtain a consent judgment, and

   (3) provided there is unlikely to be a substantial dispute of fact, a claim for a summary order for possession against named or unnamed defendants occupying land or premises without the licence or consent of the person claiming possession.

1.5 Where it appears to a court officer that a claimant is using the Part 8 procedure inappropriately, he may refer the claim to a judge for the judge to consider the point.

1.6 The court may at any stage order the claim to continue as if the claimant had not used the Part 8 procedure and, if it does so, the court will allocate the claim to a track and give such directions as it considers appropriate[1].

---

[1] Rule 8.1(3).

ISSUING THE CLAIM

2.1 Part 7 and the practice direction which supplements it contain a number of rules and directions applicable to all claims, including those to which Part 8 applies. Those rules and directions should be applied where appropriate.

2.2 Where a claimant uses the Part 8 procedure, the claim form (practice form N208) should be used and must state the matters set out in rule 8.2 and, if paragraphs 1.2 or 1.3 apply, must comply with the requirements of the practice direction in question. In particular, the claim form must state that Part 8 applies; a Part 8 claim form means a claim form which so states.

(The Costs Practice Direction supplementing Parts 43 to 48 contains details of the information required to be filed with a claim form to comply with rule 44.15 (providing information about funding arrangements))

RESPONDING TO THE CLAIM

3.1 The provisions of Part 15 (defence and reply) do not apply where the claim form is a Part 8 claim form.

3.2 Where a defendant who wishes to respond to a Part 8 claim form is required to file an acknowledgment of service, that acknowledgment of service should be in practice form N210[2] but can, alternatively, be given in an informal document such as a letter.

3.3 Rule 8.3 sets out provisions relating to an acknowledgment of service of a Part 8 claim form.

3.4 Rule 8.4 sets out the consequence of failing to file an acknowledgment of service.

3.5 The provisions of Part 12 (obtaining default judgment) do not apply where the claim form is a Part 8 claim form.

3.6 Where a defendant believes that the Part 8 procedure should not be used because there is a substantial dispute of fact or, as the case may be, because its use is not authorised by any rule or practice direction, he must state his reasons in writing when he files his acknowledgment of service[3]. If the statement of reasons includes matters of evidence it should be verified by a statement of truth.

---

[2] Rule 8.3(1)(a).
[3] Rule 8.8(1).

MANAGING THE CLAIM

4.1 The court may give directions immediately a Part 8 claim form is issued either on the application of a party or on its own initiative. The directions may include fixing a hearing date where:

(1) there is no dispute, such as in child and patient settlements, or

(2) where there may be a dispute, such as in claims for mortgage possession or appointment of trustees, but a hearing date could conveniently be given.

4.2 Where the court does not fix a hearing date when the claim form is issued, it will give directions for the disposal of the claim as soon as practicable after the defendant has acknowledged service of the claim form or, as the case may be, after the period for acknowledging service has expired.

4.3 Certain applications may not require a hearing.

4.4 The court may convene a directions hearing before giving directions.

EVIDENCE

5.1 A claimant wishing to rely on written evidence should file it when his Part 8 claim form is issued[4] (unless the evidence is contained in the claim form itself).

5.2 Evidence will normally be in the form of a witness statement or an affidavit but a claimant may rely on the matters set out in his claim form provided that it has been verified by a statement of truth.

(For information about (1) statements of truth see Part 22 and the practice direction that supplements it, and (2) written evidence see Part 32 and the practice direction that supplements it.)

5.3 A defendant wishing to rely on written evidence, should file it with his acknowledgment of service[5].

5.4 Rule 8.5 sets out the times and provisions for filing and serving written evidence.

5.5 A party may apply to the court for an extension of time to serve and file evidence under Rule 8.5 or for permission to serve and file additional evidence under Rule 8.6(1).

(For information about applications see Part 23 and the practice direction that supplements it)

---

[4] Rule 8.5.
[5] Rule 8.5(3).

5.6

(1) The parties may, subject to the following provisions, agree in writing on an extension of time for serving and filing evidence under Rule 8.5(3) or Rule 8.5(5).

(2) An agreement extending time for a defendant to file evidence under Rule 8.5(3) –

    (a) must be filed by the defendant at the same time as he files his acknowledgement of service; and

    (b) must not extend time by more than 14 days after the defendant files his acknowledgement of service.

(3) An agreement extending time for a claimant to file evidence in reply under Rule 8.5(5) must not extend time to more than 28 days after service of the defendant's evidence on the claimant.

CPR Part 9

A2–017 RESPONDING TO PARTICULARS OF CLAIM – GENERAL

CONTENTS OF THIS PART

Rule 9.1 Scope of this Part
Rule 9.2 Defence, admission or acknowledgment of service

9.1 Scope of this Part

(1) This Part sets out how a defendant may respond to particulars of claim.
(2) Where the defendant receives a claim form which states that particulars of claim are to follow, he need not respond to the claim until the particulars of claim have been served on him.

9.2 Defence, admission or acknowledgment of service

When particulars of claim are served on a defendant, the defendant may –

    (a) file or serve an admission in accordance with Part 14;

    (b) file a defence in accordance with Part 15, (or do both, if he admits only part of the claim); or

    (c) file an acknowledgment of service in accordance with Part 10.

(Paragraph 10.6 of the Practice Direction to Part 16 contains provision about the content of the admission, defence or acknowledgment of service).

CPR Part 10

ACKNOWLEDGEMENT OF SERVICE

A2–018

CONTENTS OF THIS PART

10.1 Acknowledgment of service

(1) This Part deals with the procedure for filing an acknowledgment of service.

(2) Where the claimant uses the procedure set out in Part 8 (alternative procedure for claims) this Part applies subject to the modifications set out in rule 8.3.

(3) A defendant may file an acknowledgment of service if –

(a) he is unable to file a defence within the period specified in rule 15.4; or

(b) he wishes to dispute the court's jurisdiction.

(Part 11 sets out the procedure for disputing the court's jurisdiction)

10.2 Consequence of not filing an acknowledgment of service

If –

(a) a defendant fails to file an acknowledgment of service within the period specified in rule 10.3; and

(b) does not within that period file a defence in accordance with Part 15 or serve or file an admission in accordance with Part 14,

the claimant may obtain default judgment if Part 12 allows it.

10.3 The period for filing an acknowledgment of service

(1) The general rule is that the period for filing an acknowledgment of service is –

(a) where the defendant is served with a claim form which states that particulars of claim are to follow, 14 days after service of the particulars of claim; and

(b) in any other case, 14 days after service of the claim form.

(2) The general rule is subject to the following rules –

(a) rule 6.22 (which specifies how the period for filing an acknowledgment of service is calculated where the claim form is served out of the jurisdiction);

(b) rule 6.16(4) (which requires the court to specify the period for responding to the particulars of claim when it makes an order under that rule); and

(c) rule 6.21(4) (which requires the court to specify the period within which the defendant may file an acknowledgment of service calculated by reference to Practice Direction 6B when it makes an order giving permission to serve a claim form out of the jurisdiction).

10.4 Notice to claimant that defendant has filed an acknowledgment of service

On receipt of an acknowledgment of service, the court must notify the claimant in writing.

10.5 Contents of acknowledgment of service

(1) An acknowledgment of service must –

(a) be signed by the defendant or his legal representative; and
(b) einclude the defendants' address for service.

(Rule 6.5 provides that an address for service must be within the jurisdiction)
(Rule 19.8A modifies this Part where a notice of claim is served under that rule to bind a person not a party to the claim).

A2–019

PRACTICE DIRECTION

ACKNOWLEDGMENT OF SERVICE

THIS PRACTICE DIRECTION SUPPLEMENTS CPR PART 10

RESPONDING TO THE CLAIM

1.1 Part 9 sets out how a defendant may respond to a claim.
1.2 Part 10 sets out the provisions for acknowledging service (but see rule 8.3 for information about acknowledging service of a claim under the Part 8 procedure).

THE FORM OF ACKNOWLEDGEMENT OF SERVICE

2 A defendant who wishes to acknowledge service of a claim should do so by using form N9.

ADDRESS FOR SERVICE

3.1 The defendant must include in his acknowledgment of service an address for the service of documents[1].

3.2 Where the defendant is represented by a legal representative[2] and the legal representative has signed the acknowledgment of service form, the address must be the legal representative's business address; otherwise the address for service that is given should be as set out in rule 6.5 and the practice direction which supplements Part 6.

Signing the Acknowledgment of Service

4.1 An acknowledgment of service must be signed by the defendant or by his legal representative.

4.2 Where the defendant is a company or other corporation, a person holding a senior position in the company or corporation may sign the acknowledgment of service on the defendant's behalf, but must state the position he holds.

4.3 Each of the following persons is a person holding a senior position:

    (1) in respect of a registered company or corporation, a director, the treasurer, secretary, chief executive, manager or other officer of the company or corporation, and

    (2) in respect of a corporation which is not a registered company, in addition to those persons set out in (1), the mayor, chairman, president, town clerk or similar officer of the corporation.

4.4 Where the defendant is a partnership, the acknowledgment of service may be signed by:

    (1) any of the partners, or

    (2) a person having the control or management of the partnership business.

4.5 Children and patients may acknowledge service only by their litigation friend or his legal representative unless the court otherwise orders[3].

---

[1] See rule 6.5.
[2] See rule 2.3 for the definition of legal representative.
[3] See Part 21.

GENERAL

5.1 The defendant's name should be set out in full on the acknowledgment of service.

5.2 Where the defendant's name has been incorrectly set out in the claim form, it should be correctly set out on the acknowledgment of service followed by the words 'described as' and the incorrect name.

5.3 If two or more defendants to a claim acknowledge service of a claim through the same legal representative at the same time, only one acknowledgment of service need be used.

5.4 An acknowledgment of service may be amended or withdrawn only with the permission of the court.

5.5 An application for permission under paragraph 5.4 must be made in accordance with Part 23 and supported by evidence.

(Paragraph 8.3 of the practice direction supplementing Part 6 (Service of documents) makes provision for the service on the claimant of any notice of funding filed with an acknowledgment of service)

CPR Part 14

A2–020

Admissions

Contents of this Part

14.1 Making an admission

(1) A party may admit the truth of the whole or any part of another party's case.

(2) He may do this by giving notice in writing (such as in a statement of case or by letter).

(3) Where the only remedy which the claimant is seeking is the payment of money, the defendant may also make an admission in accordance with –

    (a)   rule 14.4 (admission of whole claim for specified amount of money);

    (b)   rule 14.5 (admission of part of claim for specified amount of money);

    (c)   rule 14.6 (admission of liability to pay whole of claim for unspecified amount of money); or

    (d)   rule 14.7 (admission of liability to pay claim for unspecified amount of money where defendant offers a sum in satisfaction of the claim).

(4) Where the defendant makes an admission as mentioned in paragraph (3), the claimant has a right to enter judgment except where –

    (a)   the defendant is a child or patient; or

    (b)   the claimant is a child or patient and the admission is made under rule 14.5 or 14.7.

(Rule 21.10 provides that, where a claim is made by or on behalf of a child or patient or against a child or patient, no settlement, compromise or payment shall be valid, so far as it relates to that person's claim, without the approval of the court)

(5) The court may allow a party to amend or withdraw an admission.

(Rule 3.1(3) provides that the court may attach conditions when it makes an order)

14.2 Period for making an admission

(1) The period for returning an admission under rule 14.4 or for filing it under rules 14.5, 14.6 or 14.7 is –

    (a)   where the defendant is served with a claim form which states that particulars of claim will follow, 14 days after service of the particulars; and

    (b)   in any other case, 14 days after service of the claim form.

(2) Paragraph (1) is subject to the following rules –

    (a)   rule 6.22 (which specifies how the period for filing or returning an admission is calculated where the claim form is served out of the jurisdiction); and

(b) rule 6.16(4) (which requires the court to specify the period for responding to the particulars of claim when it makes an order under that rule).

(3) A defendant may return an admission under rule 14.4 or file it under rules 14.5, 14.6 or 14.7 after the end of the period for returning or filing it specified in paragraph (1) if the claimant has not obtained default judgment under Part 12.
(4) If he does so, this Part shall apply as if he had made the admission within that period.

14.3 Admission by notice in writing – application for judgment

(1) Where a party makes an admission under rule 14.1(2) (admission by notice in writing), any other party may apply for judgment on the admission.
(2) Judgment shall be such judgment as it appears to the court that the applicant is entitled to on the admission.

14.4 Admission of whole of claim for specified amount of money

(1) This rule applies where –

(a) the only remedy which the claimant is seeking is the payment of a specified amount of money; and
(b) the defendant admits the whole of the claim.

(2) The defendant may admit the claim by returning to the claimant an admission in the relevant practice form.
(3) The claimant may obtain judgment by filing a request in the relevant practice form and, if he does so –

(a) if the defendant has not requested time to pay, the procedure in paragraphs (4) to (6) will apply;
(b) if the defendant has requested time to pay, the procedure in rule 14.9 will apply.

(4) The claimant may specify in his request for judgment –

(a) the date by which the whole of the judgment debt is to be paid; or
(b) the times and rate at which it is to be paid by instalments.

(5) On receipt of the request for judgment the court will enter judgment.
(6) Judgment will be for the amount of the claim (less any payments made) and costs –

(a) to be paid by the date or at the rate specified in the request for judgment; or
(b) if none is specified, immediately.

(Rule 14.14 deals with the circumstances in which judgment under this rule may include interest)

14.5 Admission of part of a claim for a specified amount of money

(1) This rule applies where –

    (a) the only remedy which the claimant is seeking is the payment of a specified amount of money; and

    (b) the defendant admits part of the claim.

(2) The defendant may admit part of the claim by filing an admission in the relevant practice form.

(3) On receipt of the admission, the court will serve a notice on the claimant requiring him to return the notice stating that –

    (a) he accepts the amount admitted in satisfaction of the claim;

    (b) he does not accept the amount admitted by the defendant and wishes the proceedings to continue; or

    (c) if the defendant has requested time to pay, he accepts the amount admitted in satisfaction of the claim, but not the defendant's proposals as to payment.

(4) The claimant must –

    (a) file the notice; and

    (b) serve a copy on the defendant,

within 14 days after it is served on him.

(5) If the claimant does not file the notice within 14 days after it is served on him, the claim is stayed$^{(GL)}$ until he files the notice.

(6) If the claimant accepts the amount admitted in satisfaction of the claim, he may obtain judgment by filing a request in the relevant practice form and, if he does so –

    (a) if the defendant has not requested time to pay, the procedure in paragraphs (7) to (9) will apply;

    (b) if the defendant has requested time to pay, the procedure in rule 14.9 will apply.

(7) The claimant may specify in his request for judgment –

    (a) the date by which the whole of the judgment debt is to be paid; or

    (b) the time and rate at which it is to be paid by instalments.

(8) On receipt of the request for judgment, the court will enter judgment.

(9) Judgment will be for the amount admitted (less any payments made) and costs –

(a) to be paid by the date or at the rate specified in the request for judgment; or

(b) if none is specified, immediately.

(If the claimant files notice under paragraph (3) that he wishes the proceedings to continue, the procedure which then follows is set out in Part 26)

14.6 Admission of liability to pay whole of claim for unspecified amount of money

(1) This rule applies where –

(a) the only remedy which the claimant is seeking is the payment of money;

(b) the amount of the claim is not specified; and

(c) the defendant admits liability but does not offer to pay a specified amount of money in satisfaction of the claim.

(2) The defendant may admit the claim by filing an admission in the relevant practice form.

(3) On receipt of the admission, the court will serve a copy on the claimant.

(4) The claimant may obtain judgment by filing a request in the relevant practice form.

(5) If the claimant does not file a request for judgment within 14 days after service of the admission on him, the claim is stayed$^{(GL)}$ until he files the request.

(6) On receipt of the request for judgment the court will enter judgment.

(7) Judgment will be for an amount to be decided by the court and costs.

14.7 Admission of liability to pay claim for unspecified amount of money where defendant offers a sum in satisfaction of the claim

(1) This rule applies where –

(a) the only remedy which the claimant is seeking is the payment of money;

(b) the amount of the claim is not specified; and

(c) the defendant –

(i) admits liability; and

(ii) offers to pay a specified amount of money in satisfaction of the claim.

(2) The defendant may admit the claim by filing an admission in the relevant practice form.

(3) On receipt of the admission, the court will serve a notice on the claimant requiring him to return the notice stating whether or not he accepts the amount in satisfaction of the claim.

(4) If the claimant does not file the notice within 14 days after it is served on him, the claim is stayed$^{(GL)}$ until he files the notice.

(5) If the claimant accepts the offer he may obtain judgment by filing a request in the relevant practice form and if he does so –

    (a) if the defendant has not requested time to pay, the procedure in paragraphs (6) to (8) will apply;

    (b) if the defendant has requested time to pay, the procedure in rule 14.9 will apply.

(6) The claimant may specify in his request for judgment –

    (a) the date by which the whole of the judgment debt is to be paid; or

    (b) the times and rate at which it is to be paid by instalments.

(7) On receipt of the request for judgment, the court will enter judgment.
(8) Judgment will be for the amount offered by the defendant (less any payments made) and costs –

    (a) to be paid on the date or at the rate specified in the request for judgment; or

    (b) if none is specified, immediately.

(9) If the claimant does not accept the amount offered by the defendant, he may obtain judgment by filing a request in the relevant practice form.
(10) Judgment under paragraph (9) will be for an amount to be decided by the court and costs.

14.8 Allocation of claims in relation to outstanding matters

Where the court enters judgment under rule 14.6 or 14.7 for an amount to be decided by the court it will –

    (a) give any directions it considers appropriate; and

    (b) if it considers it appropriate, allocate the case.

14.9 Request for time to pay

(1) A defendant who makes an admission under rules 14.4, 14.5 or 14.7 (admission relating to a claim for a specified amount of money or offering to pay a specified amount of money) may make a request for time to pay.
(2) A request for time to pay is a proposal about the date of payment or a proposal to pay by instalments at the times and rate specified in the request.
(3) The defendant's request for time to pay must be served or filed (as the case may be) with his admission.
(4) If the claimant accepts the defendant's request, he may obtain judgment by filing a request in the relevant practice form.
(5) On receipt of the request for judgment, the court will enter judgment.
(6) Judgment will be –

    (a) where rule 14.4 applies, for the amount of the claim (less any payments made) and costs;

(b) where rule 14.5 applies, for the amount admitted (less any payments made) and costs; or

(c) where rule 14.7 applies, for the amount offered by the defendant (less any payments made) and costs; and

(in all cases) will be for payment at the time and rate specified in the defendant's request for time to pay.

(Rule 14.10 sets out the procedure to be followed if the claimant does not accept the defendant's request for time to pay)

14.10 Determination of rate of payment

(1) This rule applies where the defendant makes a request for time to pay under rule 14.9.

(2) If the claimant does not accept the defendant's proposals for payment, he must file a notice in the relevant practice form.

(3) Where the defendant's admission was served direct on the claimant, a copy of the admission and the request for time to pay must be filed with the claimant's notice.

(4) When the court receives the claimant's notice, it will enter judgment for the amount admitted (less any payments made) to be paid at the time and rate of payment determined by the court.

14.11 Determination of rate of payment by court officer

(1) A court officer may exercise the powers of the court under rule 14.10(4) where the amount outstanding (including costs) is not more than £50,000.

(2) Where a court officer is to determine the time and rate of payment, he must do so without a hearing.

14.12 Determination of rate of payment by judge

(1) Where a judge is to determine the time and rate of payment, he may do so without a hearing.

(2) Where a judge is to determine the time and rate of payment at a hearing, the proceedings must be transferred automatically to the defendant's home court if –

(a) the only claim is for a specified amount of money;

(b) the defendant is an individual;

(c) the claim has not been transferred to another defendant's home court under rule 13.4 (application to set aside[GL] or vary default judgment – procedure) or rule 26.2 (automatic transfer);

(d) the claim was not started in the defendant's home court; and

(e) the claim was not started in a specialist list.

(Rule 2.3 explains which court is a defendant's home court)

(3) If there is to be a hearing to determine the time and rate of payment, the court must give each party at least 7 days' notice of the hearing.

14.13 Right of re-determination

(1) Where –

    (a) a court officer has determined the time and rate of payment under rule 14.11; or

    (b) a judge has determined the time and rate of payment under rule 14.12 without a hearing, either party may apply for the decision to be re-determined by a judge.

(2) An application for re-determination must be made within 14 days after service of the determination on the applicant.

(3) Where an application for re-determination is made, the proceedings must be transferred to the defendant's home court if –

    (a) the only claim (apart from a claim for interest or costs) is for a specified amount of money;

    (b) the defendant is an individual;

    (c) the claim has not been transferred to another defendant's home court under rule 13.4 (application to set aside[GL] or vary default judgment – procedure) or rule 26.2 (automatic transfer);

    (d) the claim was not started in the defendant's home court; and

    (e) the claim was not started in a specialist list.

(Rule 2.3 explains which court is a defendant's home court)

14.14 Interest

(1) Judgment under rule 14.4 (admission of whole of claim for specified amount of money) shall include the amount of interest claimed to the date of judgment if –

    (a) the particulars of claim include the details required by rule 16.4;

    (b) where interest is claimed under section 35A of the Supreme Court Act 1981[1] or section 69 of the County Courts Act 1984[2], the rate is no higher than the rate of interest payable on judgment debts at the date when the claim form was issued; and

    (c) the claimant's request for judgment includes a calculation of the interest claimed for the period from the date up to which interest was stated to be calculated in the claim form to the date of the request for judgment.

(2) In any case where judgment is entered under rule 14.4 and the conditions in paragraph (1) are not satisfied judgment shall be for an amount of interest to be decided by the court.

(3) Where judgment is entered for an amount of interest to be decided by the court, the court will give directions for the management of the case.

---

[1] 1981 c.54. Section 35A was inserted by the Adminstration of Justice Act 1982 (c.53), s.15(1), Sch.1, Pt.I.

[2] 1984 c.28. Schedule 69 was amended by the Courts and Legal Services Act 1990 (c.41), s.125(3), Sch.18, para.46.

PRACTICE DIRECTION

ADMISSIONS

THIS PRACTICE DIRECTION SUPPLEMENTS CPR PART 14

ADMISSIONS GENERALLY

1.1 Rules 14.1 and 14.2 deal with the manner in which a defendant may make an admission of a claim or part of a claim.

1.2 Rules 14.3, 14.4, 14.5, 14.6 and 14.7 set out how judgment may be obtained on a written admission.

FORMS

2.1 When particulars of claim are served on a defendant the forms for responding to the claim that will accompany them will include a form[3] for making an admission.

2.2 If the defendant is requesting time to pay he should complete as fully as possible the statement of means contained in the admission form, or otherwise give in writing the same details of his means as could have been given in the admission form.

RETURNING OR FILING THE ADMISSION

3.1 If the defendant wishes to make an admission in respect of the whole of a claim for a specified amount of money, the admission form or other written notice of the admission should be completed and returned to the claimant within 14 days of service of the particulars of claim[4].

3.2 If the defendant wishes to make an admission in respect of a part of a claim for a specified amount of money, or in respect of a claim for an unspecified amount of money, the admission form or other written notice of admission should be completed and filed with the court within 14 days of service of the particulars of claim[5].

3.3 The defendant may also file a defence under rule 15.2.

---

[3] Practice forms N9A (specified amount) or N9C (unspecified amount).
[4] Rules 14.2 and 14.4.
[5] Rules 14.2, 14.5, 14.6 and 14.7.

REQUEST FOR TIME TO PAY

4.1 A defendant who makes an admission in respect of a claim for a specified sum of money or offers to pay a sum of money in respect of a claim for an unspecified sum may, in the admission form, make a request for time to pay[6].

4.2 If the claimant accepts the defendant's request, he may obtain judgment by filing a request for judgment contained in Form N225A[7]; the court will then enter judgment for payment at the time and rate specified in the defendant's request[8].

4.3 If the claimant does not accept the request for time to pay, he should file notice to that effect by completing Form N225A; the court will then enter judgment for the amount of the admission (less any payments made) at a time and rate of payment decided by the court (see rule 14.10).

DETERMINING THE RATE OF PAYMENT

5.1 In deciding the time and rate of payment the court will take into account:

   (1) the defendant's statement of means set out in the admission form or in any other written notice of the admission filed,

   (2) the claimant's objections to the defendant's request set out in the claimant's notice[9], and

   (3) any other relevant factors.

5.2 The time and rate of payment may be decided:

   (1) by a judge with or without a hearing, or

   (2) by a court officer without a hearing provided that –

      (a) the only claim is for a specified sum of money, and

      (b) the amount outstanding is not more than £50,000 (including costs).

5.3 Where a decision has been made without a hearing whether by a court officer or by a judge, either party may apply for the decision to be re-determined by a judge[10].

5.4 If the decision was made by a court officer the re-determination may take place without a hearing, unless a hearing is requested in the application notice.

5.5 If the decision was made by a judge the re-determination must be made at a hearing unless the parties otherwise agree.

5.6 Rule 14.13(2) describes how to apply for a re-determination.

---

[6] Rule 14.9.
[7] Rule 14.9(4).
[8] Rule 14.9(5) and (6).
[9] Practice form N225A.
[10] Rule 14.13(1).

VARYING THE RATE OF PAYMENT

6.1 Either party may, on account of a change in circumstances since the date of the decision (or re-determination as the case may be) apply to vary the time and rate of payment of instalments still remaining unpaid.
6.2 An application to vary under paragraph 6.1 above should be made in accordance with Part 23.

CPR Part 15

A2–022

DEFENCE AND REPLY

CONTENTS OF THIS PART

15.1 Part not to apply where claimant uses Part 8 procedure

This Part does not apply where the claimant uses the procedure set out in Part 8 (alternative procedure for claims).

15.2 Filing a defence

A defendant who wishes to defend all or part of a claim must file a defence.

(Part 14 contains further provisions which apply where the defendant admits a claim)

15.3 Consequence of not filing a defence

If a defendant fails to file a defence, the claimant may obtain default judgment if Part 12 allows it.

15.4 The period for filing a defence

(1) The general rule is that the period for filing a defence is –

(a) 14 days after service of the particulars of claim; or
(b) if the defendant files an acknowledgment of service under Part 10, 28 days after service of the particulars of claim.

(Rule 7.4 provides for the particulars of claim to be contained in or served with the claim form or served within 14 days of service of the claim form)

(2) The general rule is subject to the following rules –

(a) rule 6.23 (which specifies how the period for filing a defence is calculated where the claim form is served out of the jurisdiction);
(b) rule 11 (which provides that, where the defendant makes an application disputing the court's jurisdiction, he need not file a defence before the hearing);
(c) rule 24.4(2) (which provides that, if the claimant applies for summary judgment before the defendant has filed a defence, the defendant need not file a defence before the summary judgment hearing); and
(d) rule 6.16(4) (which requires the court to specify the period for responding to the particulars of claim when it makes an order under that rule).

15.5 Agreement extending the period for filing a defence

(1) The defendant and the claimant may agree that the period for filing a defence specified in rule 15.4 shall be extended by up to 28 days.
(2) Where the defendant and the claimant agree to extend the period for filing a defence, the defendant must notify the court in writing.

15.6 Service of copy of defence

A copy of the defence must be served on every other party.

(Part 16 sets out what a defence must contain)

(The costs practice direction sets out the information about a funding arrangement to be provided with the defence where the defendant intends to seek to recover an additional liability)

('Funding arrangement' and 'additional liability' are defined in rule 43.2)

15.7 Making a counterclaim

Part 20 applies to a defendant who wishes to make a counterclaim.

15.8 Reply to defence

If a claimant files a reply to the defence, he must –

(a) file his reply when he files his allocation questionnaire; and
(b) serve his reply on the other parties at the same time as he files it.

(Rule 26.3(6) requires the parties to file allocation questionnaires and specifies the period for doing so)

(Part 22 requires a reply to be verified by a statement of truth)

15.9 No statement of case after a reply to be filed without court's permission

A party may not file or serve any statement of case after a reply without the permission of the court.

15.10 Claimant's notice where defence is that money claimed has been paid

(1) Where –

(a) the only claim (apart from a claim for costs and interest) is for a specified amount of money; and
(b) the defendant states in his defence that he has paid to the claimant the amount claimed, the court will send notice to the claimant requiring him to state in writing whether he wishes the proceedings to continue.

(2) When the claimant responds, he must serve a copy of his response on the defendant.
(3) If the claimant fails to respond under this rule within 28 days after service of the court's notice on him the claim shall be stayed$^{(GL)}$.
(4) Where a claim is stayed under this rule any party may apply for the stay$^{(GL)}$ to be lifted.

(If the claimant files notice under this rule that he wishes the proceedings to continue, the procedure which then follows is set out in Part 26)

15.11 Claim stayed if it is not defended or admitted

(1) Where –

(a) at least 6 months have expired since the end of the period for filing a defence specified in rule 15.4;
(b) no defendant has served or filed an admission or filed a defence or counterclaim; and
(c) the claimant has not entered or applied for judgment under Part 12 (default judgment), or Part 24 (summary judgment), the claim shall be stayed$^{(GL)}$.

(2) Where a claim is stayed$^{(GL)}$ under this rule any party may apply for the stay to be lifted.

PRACTICE DIRECTION

DEFENCE AND REPLY

THIS PRACTICE DIRECTION SUPPLEMENTS CPR PART 15

DEFENDING THE CLAIM

1.1 The provisions of Part 15 do not apply to claims in respect of which the Part 8 procedure is being used.

1.2 In relation to specialist proceedings (see CPR Part 49) in respect of which special provisions for defence and reply are made by the rules and practice directions applicable to those claims, the provisions of Part 15 apply only to the extent that they are not inconsistent with those rules and practice directions.

1.3 Form N9B (specified amount) or N9D (unspecified amount or non-money claims) may be used for the purpose of defence and is included in the response pack served on the defendant with the particulars of claim.

1.4 Attention is drawn to rule 15.3 which sets out a possible consequence of not filing a defence.

(Part 16 (statements of case) and the practice direction which supplements it contain rules and directions about the contents of a defence.)

(The Costs Practice Direction supplementing Parts 43 to 48 contains details of the information required to be filed with a defence to comply with rule 44.15 (providing information about funding arrangements))

STATEMENT OF TRUTH

2.1 Part 22 requires a defence to be verified by a statement of truth.

2.2 The form of the statement of truth is as follows:

'[I believe][the defendant believes] that the facts stated in this defence are true.'

2.3 Attention is drawn to rule 32.14 which sets out the consequences of verifying a statement of case containing a false statement without an honest belief in its truth.

(For information about statements of truth see Part 22 and the practice direction which supplements it.)

GENERAL

3.1 Where a defendant to a claim serves a counterclaim under Part 20, the defence and counterclaim should normally form one document with the counterclaim following on from the defence.

3.2 Where a claimant serves a reply and a defence to counterclaim, the reply and defence to counterclaim should normally form one document with the defence to counterclaim following on from the reply.

3.2A Rule 15.8(a) provides that a claimant must file any reply with his allocation questionnaire. Where the date by which he must file his allocation questionnaire is later than the date by which he must file his defence to counterclaim (because the time for filing the allocation questionnaire under rule 26.3(6) is more than 14 days after the date on which it is deemed to be served), the court will normally order that the defence to counterclaim must be filed by the same date as the reply. Where the court does not make such an order the reply and defence to counterclaim may form separate documents.

3.3 Where a claim has been stayed under rules 15.10(3) or 15.11(1) any party may apply for the stay to be lifted[1].

3.4 The application should be made in accordance with Part 23 and should give the reason for the applicant's delay in proceeding with or responding to the claim.

(Paragraph 8.3 of the practice direction supplementing Part 6 (Service of documents) makes provision for the service on the claimant of any notice of funding filed with a defence.)

---

[1] Rules 15.10(4) and 15.11(2).

CPR Part 16

STATEMENTS OF CASE   A2–024

CONTENTS OF THIS PART

16.1 Part not to apply where claimant uses Part 8 procedure

This Part does not apply where the claimant uses the procedure set out in Part 8 (alternative procedure for claims).

16.2 Contents of the claim form

(1) The claim form must –

    (a)   contain a concise statement of the nature of the claim;
    (b)   specify the remedy which the claimant seeks;
    (c)   where the claimant is making a claim for money, contain a statement of value in accordance with rule 16.3;
    (cc) where the claimant's only claim is for a specified sum, contain a statement of the interest accrued on that sum; and
    (d)   contain such other matters as may be set out in a practice direction.

(1A) In civil proceedings against the Crown, as defined in rule 66.1(2), the claim form must also contain –

    (a)   the names of the government departments and officers of the Crown concerned; and
    (b)   brief details of the circumstances in which it is alleged that the liability of the Crown arose.

(2) If the particulars of claim specified in rule 16.4 are not contained in, or are not served with the claim form, the claimant must state on the claim form that the particulars of claim will follow.
(3) If the claimant is claiming in a representative capacity, the claim form must state what that capacity is.
(4) If the defendant is sued in a representative capacity, the claim form must state what that capacity is.

(5) The court may grant any remedy to which the claimant is entitled even if that remedy is not specified in the claim form.

(Part 22 requires a claim form to be verified by a statement of truth)

(The costs practice direction sets out the information about a funding arrangement to be provided with the statement of case where the defendant intends to seek to recover an additional liability)

('Funding arrangement' and 'additional liability' are defined in rule 43.2)

16.3 Statement of value to be included in the claim form

(1) This rule applies where the claimant is making a claim for money.
(2) The claimant must, in the claim form, state –

    (a) the amount of money which he is claiming;
    (b) that he expects to recover –

        (i) not more than £5,000;
        (ii) more than £5,000 but not more than £15,000; or
        (iii) more than £15,000; or

    (c) that he cannot say how much he expects to recover.

(3) In a claim for personal injuries, the claimant must also state in the claim form whether the amount which he expects to recover as general damages for pain, suffering and loss of amenity is –

    (a) not more than £1,000; or
    (b) more than £1,000.

(4) In a claim which includes a claim by a tenant of residential premises against his landlord where the tenant is seeking an order requiring the landlord to carry out repairs or other work to the premises, the claimant must also state in the claim form –

    (a) whether the estimated costs of those repairs or other work is –

        (i) not more than £1,000; or
        (ii) more than £1,000; and

    (b) whether the financial value of any other claim for damages is –

        (i) not more than £1,000; or
        (ii) more than £1,000.

(5) If the claim form is to be issued in the High Court it must, where this rule applies –

    (a) state that the claimant expects to recover more than £15,000;
    (b) state that some other enactment provides that the claim may be commenced only in the High Court and specify that enactment;

(c) if the claim is a claim for personal injuries state that the claimant expects to recover £50,000 or more; or

(d) state that the claim is to be in one of the specialist High Court lists and state which list.

(6) When calculating how much he expects to recover, the claimant must disregard any possibility –

(a) that he may recover –

(i) interest;
(ii) costs;

(b) that the court may make a finding of contributory negligence against him;

(c) that the defendant may make a counterclaim or that the defence may include a set-off; or

(d) that the defendant may be liable to pay an amount of money which the court awards to the claimant to the Secretary of State for Social Security under section 6 of the Social Security (Recovery of Benefits) Act 1997[1].

(7) The statement of value in the claim form does not limit the power of the court to give judgment for the amount which it finds the claimant is entitled to.

16.4 Contents of the particulars of claim

(1) Particulars of claim must include –

(a) a concise statement of the facts on which the claimant relies;

(b) if the claimant is seeking interest, a statement to that effect and the details set out in paragraph (2);

(c) if the claimant is seeking aggravated damages$^{(GL)}$ or exemplary damages$^{(GL)}$, a statement to that effect and his grounds for claiming them;

(d) if the claimant is seeking provisional damages, a statement to that effect and his grounds for claiming them; and

(e) such other matters as may be set out in a practice direction.

(2) If the claimant is seeking interest he must –

(a) state whether he is doing so –

(i) under the terms of a contract;
(ii) under an enactment and if so which; or
(iii) on some other basis and if so what that basis is; and

(b) if the claim is for a specified amount of money, state –

(i) the percentage rate at which interest is claimed;
(ii) the date from which it is claimed;

[1] 1997 c.27.

(iii) the date to which it is calculated, which must not be later than the date on which the claim form is issued;

(iv) the total amount of interest claimed to the date of calculation; and

(v) the daily rate at which interest accrues after that date.

(Part 22 requires particulars of claim to be verified by a statement of truth)

16.5 Content of defence

(1) In his defence, the defendant must state –

(a) which of the allegations in the particulars of claim he denies;

(b) which allegations he is unable to admit or deny, but which he requires the claimant to prove; and

(c) which allegations he admits.

(2) Where the defendant denies an allegation –

(a) he must state his reasons for doing so; and

(b) if he intends to put forward a different version of events from that given by the claimant, he must state his own version.

(3) A defendant who –

(a) fails to deal with an allegation; but

(b) has set out in his defence the nature of his case in relation to the issue to which that allegation is relevant,
shall be taken to require that allegation to be proved.

(4) Where the claim includes a money claim, a defendant shall betaken to require that any allegation relating to the amount of money claimed be proved unless he expressly admits the allegation.

(5) Subject to paragraphs (3) and (4), a defendant who fails to deal with an allegation shall be taken to admit that allegation.

(6) If the defendant disputes the claimant's statement of value under rule 16.3 he must –

(a) state why he disputes it; and

(b) if he is able, give his own statement of the value of the claim.

(7) If the defendant is defending in a representative capacity, he must state what that capacity is.

(8) If the defendant has not filed an acknowledgment of service under Part 10, he must give an address for service.

(Part 22 requires a defence to be verified by a statement of truth)

(Rule 6.5 provides that an address for service must be within the jurisdiction)

16.6 Defence of set-off

Where a defendant –

    (a) contends he is entitled to money from the claimant; and
    (b) relies on this as a defence to the whole or part of the claim,
        the contention may be included in the defence and set off
        against the claim, whether or not it is also a Part 20 claim.

16.7 Reply to defence

(1) A claimant who does not file a reply to the defence shall not be taken to admit the matters raised in the defence.
(2) A claimant who –

    (a) files a reply to a defence; but
    (b) fails to deal with a matter raised in the defence, shall be taken to
        require that matter to be proved.

(Part 22 requires a reply to be verified by a statement of truth)

16.8 Court's power to dispense with statements of case

If a claim form has been –

    (a) issued in accordance with rule 7.2; and
    (b) served in accordance with rule 7.5,
        the court may make an order that the claim will continue
        without any other statement of case.

PRACTICE DIRECTION

A2–025

STATEMENTS OF CASE

THIS PRACTICE DIRECTION SUPPLEMENTS CPR PART 16

GENERAL

1.1 The provisions of Part 16 do not apply to claims in respect of which the Part 8 procedure is being used.

1.2 Where special provisions about statements of case are made by the rules and practice directions applying to particular types of proceedings, the provisions of Part 16 and of this practice direction apply only to the extent that they are not inconsistent with those rules and practice directions.

1.3 Examples of types of proceedings with special provisions about statements of case include –

    (1) defamation claims (Part 53);
    (2) possession claims (Part 55); and
    (3) probate claims (Part 57).

1.4 If exceptionally a statement of case exceeds 25 pages (excluding schedules) an appropriate short summary must also be filed and served.

THE CLAIM FORM

2.1 Rule 16.2 refers to matters which the claim form must contain. Where the claim is for money, the claim form must also contain the statement of value referred to in rule 16.3.

2.2 The claim form must include an address at which the claimant resides or carries on business. This paragraph applies even though the claimant's address for service is the business address of his solicitor.

2.3 Where the defendant is an individual, the claimant should (if he is able to do so) include in the claim form an address at which the defendant resides or carries on business. This paragraph applies even though the defendant's solicitors have agreed to accept service on the defendant's behalf.

2.4 Any address which is provided for the purpose of these provisions must include a postcode, unless the court orders otherwise. Postcode information may be obtained from www.royalmail.com or the Royal Mail Address Management Guide.

2.5 If the claim form does not show a full address, including postcode, at which the claimant(s) and defendant(s) reside or carry on business, the claim form will be issued but will be retained by the court and will not be served until the claimant has supplied a full address, including postcode, or the court has dispensed with the requirement to do so. The court will notify the claimant.

2.6 The claim form must be headed with the title of the proceedings, including the full name of each party. The full name means, in each case where it is known:

    (a) in the case of an individual, his full unabbreviated name and title by which he is known;
    (b) in the case of an individual carrying on business in a name other than his own name, the full unabbreviated name of the individual, together with the title by which he is known, and the full

trading name (for example, John Smith 'trading as' or 'T/as' 'JS Autos');

(c) in the case of a partnership (other than a limited liability partnership (LLP)) –

    (i) where partners are being sued in the name of the partnership, the full name by which the partnership is known, together with the words '(A Firm)'; or

    (ii) where partners are being sued as individuals, the full unabbreviated name of each partner and the title by which he is known;

(d) in the case of a company or limited liability partnership registered in England and Wales, the full registered name, including suffix (plc, limited, LLP, etc), if any;

(e) in the case of any other company or corporation, the full name by which it is known, including suffix where appropriate.

(RSC O81 contains rules about claims made by or against partners in their firm name).

(For information about how and where a claim may be started see Part 7 and the practice direction which supplements it.)

PARTICULARS OF CLAIM

3.1 If practicable, the particulars of claim should be set out in the claim form.

3.2 Where the claimant does not include the particulars of claim in the claim form, particulars of claim may be served separately:

    (1) either at the same time as the claim form, or

    (2) within 14 days after service of the claim form[2] provided that the service of the particulars of claim is not later than 4 months from the date of issue of the claim form[3] (or 6 months where the claim form is to be served out of the jurisdiction[4]).

3.3 If the particulars of claim are not included in or have not been served with the claim form, the claim form must also contain a statement that particulars of claim will follow[5].

3.4 Particulars of claim which are not included in the claim form must be verified by a statement of truth, the form of which is as follows:

'[I believe][the claimant believes] that the facts stated in these particulars of claim are true.'

---

[2] See rule 7.4(1)(b).
[3] See rules 7.4(2) and 7.5(2).
[4] See rule 7.5(3).
[5] See rule 16.2(2).

3.5 Attention is drawn to rule 32.14 which sets out the consequences of verifying a statement of case containing a false statement without an honest belief in its truth.

3.6 The full particulars of claim must include:

    (1) the matters set out in rule 16.4, and

    (2) where appropriate, the matters set out in practice directions relating to specific types of claims.

3.7 Attention is drawn to the provisions of rule 16.4(2) in respect of a claim for interest.

3.8 Particulars of claim served separately from the claim form must also contain:

    (1) the name of the court in which the claim is proceeding,

    (2) the claim number,

    (3) the title of the proceedings, and

    (4) the claimant's address for service.

MATTERS WHICH MUST BE INCLUDED IN THE PARTICULARS OF CLAIM IN CERTAIN TYPES OF CLAIM

Personal Injury Claims

4.1 The particulars of claim must contain:

    (1) the claimant's date of birth, and

    (2) brief details of the claimant's personal injuries.

4.2 The claimant must attach to his particulars of claim a schedule of details of any past and future expenses and losses which he claims.

4.3 Where the claimant is relying on the evidence of a medical practitioner the claimant must attach to or serve with his particulars of claim a report from a medical practitioner about the personal injuries which he alleges in his claim.

4.4 In a provisional damages claim the claimant must state in his particulars of claim:

    (1) that he is seeking an award of provisional damages under either section 32A of the Supreme Court Act 1981 or section 51 of the County Courts Act 1984,

    (2) that there is a chance that at some future time the claimant will develop some serious disease or suffer some serious deterioration in his physical or mental condition, and

    (3) specify the disease or type of deterioration in respect of which an application may be made at a future date.

(Part 41 and the practice direction which supplements it contain information about awards for provisional damages.)

Fatal Accident Claims

5.1 In a fatal accident claim the claimant must state in his particulars of claim:

(1) that it is brought under the Fatal Accidents Act 1976,
(2) the dependants on whose behalf the claim is made,
(3) the date of birth of each dependant, and
(4) details of the nature of the dependency claim.

5.2 A fatal accident claim may include a claim for damages for bereavement.

5.3 In a fatal accident claim the claimant may also bring a claim under the Law Reform (Miscellaneous Provisions) Act 1934 on behalf of the estate of the deceased.

(For information on apportionment under the Law Reform (Miscellaneous Provisions) Act 1934 and the Fatal Accidents Act 1976 or between dependants see Part 37 and the practice direction which supplements it.)

Hire Purchase Claims

6.1 Where the claim is for the delivery of goods let under a hire-purchase agreement or conditional sale agreement to a person other than a company or other corporation, the claimant must state in the particulars of claim:

(1) the date of the agreement,
(2) the parties to the agreement,
(3) the number or other identification of the agreement,
(4) where the claimant was not one of the original parties to the agreement, the means by which the rights and duties of the creditor passed to him,
(5) whether the agreement is a regulated agreement, and if it is not a regulated agreement, the reason why,
(6) the place where the agreement was signed by the defendant,
(7) the goods claimed,
(8) the total price of the goods,
(9) the paid-up sum,
(10) the unpaid balance of the total price,
(11) whether a default notice or a notice under section 76(1) or 98(1) of the Consumer Credit Act 1974 has been served on the defendant, and if it has, the date and method of service,
(12) the date when the right to demand delivery of the goods accrued,
(13) the amount (if any) claimed as an alternative to the delivery of goods, and
(14) the amount (if any) claimed in addition to –

(a) the delivery of the goods, or

(b) any claim under (13) above,

with the grounds of each claim.

(if the agreement is a regulated agreement the procedure set out in the practice direction relating to consumer credit act claims (which supplements Part 7) should be used).

6.2 Where the claim is not for the delivery of goods, the claimant must state in his particulars of claim:

(1) the matters set out in paragraph 6.1(1) to (6) above,

(2) the goods let under the agreement,

(3) the amount of the total price,

(4) the paid-up sum,

(5) the amount (if any) claimed as being due and unpaid in respect of any instalment or instalments of the total price, and

(6) the nature and amount of any other claim and how it arises.

OTHER MATTERS TO BE INCLUDED IN PARTICULARS OF CLAIM

7.1 Where a claim is made for an injunction or declaration in respect of or relating to any land or the possession, occupation, use or enjoyment of any land the particulars of claim must:

(1) state whether or not the injunction or declaration relates to residential premises, and

(2) identify the land (by reference to a plan where necessary).

7.2 Where a claim is brought to enforce a right to recover possession of goods the particulars of claim must contain a statement showing the value of the goods.

7.3 Where a claim is based upon a written agreement:

(1) a copy of the contract or documents constituting the agreement should be attached to or served with the particulars of claim and the original(s) should be available at the hearing, and

(2) any general conditions of sale incorporated in the contract should also be attached (but where the contract is or the documents constituting the agreement are bulky this practice direction is complied with by attaching or serving only the relevant parts of the contract or documents).

7.4 Where a claim is based upon an oral agreement, the particulars of claim should set out the contractual words used and state by whom, to whom, when and where they were spoken.

7.5 Where a claim is based upon an agreement by conduct, the particulars of claim must specify the conduct relied on and state by whom, when and where the acts constituting the conduct were done.

7.6 In a claim issued in the High Court relating to a Consumer Credit Agreement, the particulars of claim must contain a statement that the action is not one to which section 141 of the Consumer Credit Act 1974 applies.

MATTERS WHICH MUST BE SPECIFICALLY SET OUT IN THE PARTICULARS OF CLAIM IF RELIED ON

8.1 A claimant who wishes to rely on evidence:

    (1) under section 11 of the Civil Evidence Act 1968 of a conviction of an offence, or

    (2) under section 12 of the above-mentioned Act of a finding or adjudication of adultery or paternity,

    must include in his particulars of claim a statement to that effect and give the following details:

        (1) the type of conviction, finding or adjudication and its date,

        (2) the court or Court-Martial which made the conviction, finding or adjudication, and

        (3) the issue in the claim to which it relates.

8.2 The claimant must specifically set out the following matters in his particulars of claim where he wishes to rely on them in support of his claim:

    (1) any allegation of fraud,

    (2) the fact of any illegality,

    (3) details of any misrepresentation,

    (4) details of all breaches of trust,

    (5) notice or knowledge of a fact,

    (6) details of unsoundness of mind or undue influence,

    (7) details of wilful default, and

    (8) any facts relating to mitigation of loss or damage.

GENERAL

9.1 Where a claim is for a sum of money expressed in a foreign currency it must expressly state:

    (1) that the claim is for payment in a specified foreign currency,

    (2) why it is for payment in that currency,

(3) the Sterling equivalent of the sum at the date of the claim, and

(4) the source of the exchange rate relied on to calculate the Sterling equivalent.

9.2 A subsequent statement of case must not contradict or be inconsistent with an earlier one; for example a reply to a defence must not bring in a new claim. Where new matters have come to light the appropriate course may be to seek the court's permission to amend the statement of case.

9.3 In clinical negligence claims, the words 'clinical negligence' should be inserted at the top of every statement of case.

THE DEFENCE

General

10.1 Rule 16.5 deals with the contents of the defence.

10.2 A defendant should deal with every allegation in accordance with rule 16.5(1) and (2).

10.3 Rule 16.5(3), (4) and (5) sets out the consequences of not dealing with an allegation.

10.4 Where the defendant is an individual, and the claim form does not contain an address at which he resides or carries on business, or contains an incorrect address, the defendant must provide such an address in the defence.

10.5 Where the defendant's address for service is not where he resides or carries on business, he must still provide the address required by paragraph 11.4.

10.6 Any address which is provided for the purpose of these provisions must include a postcode, unless the court orders otherwise. Postcode information may be obtained from www.royalmail.com or the Royal Mail Address Management Guide.

10.7 Where a defendant to a claim or counterclaim is an individual, he must provide his date of birth (if known) in the acknowledgment of service, admission, defence, defence and counterclaim, reply or other response.

Statement of truth

11.1 Part 22 requires a defence to be verified by a statement of truth.

11.2 The form of the statement of truth is as follows:

'[I believe][the defendant believes] that the facts stated in the defence are true.'

11.3 Attention is drawn to rule 32.14 which sets out the consequences of verifying a statement of case containing a false statement without an honest belief in its truth.

MATTERS WHICH MUST BE INCLUDED IN THE DEFENCE

Personal injury claims

12.1 Where the claim is for personal injuries and the claimant has attached a medical report in respect of his alleged injuries, the defendant should:

    (1) state in his defence whether he –

        (a) agrees,
        (b) disputes, or
        (c) neither agrees nor disputes but has no knowledge of,

    the matters contained in the medical report,

    (2) where he disputes any part of the medical report, give in his defence his reasons for doing so, and

    (3) where he has obtained his own medical report on which he intends to rely, attach it to his defence.

12.2 Where the claim is for personal injuries and the claimant has included a schedule of past and future expenses and losses, the defendant should include in or attach to his defence a counter-schedule stating:

    (1) which of those items he –

        (a) agrees,
        (b) disputes, or
        (c) neither agrees nor disputes but has no knowledge of, and

    (2) where any items are disputed, supplying alternative figures where appropriate.

Other matters

13.1 The defendant must give details of the expiry of any relevant limitation period relied on.

13.2 Rule 37.3 and paragraph 2 of the practice direction which supplements Part 37 contains information about a defence of tender.

13.3 A party may:

    (1) refer in his statement of case to any point of law on which his claim or defence, as the case may be, is based,

    (2) give in his statement of case the name of any witness he proposes to call, and

    (3) attach to or serve with this statement of case a copy of any document which he considers is necessary to his claim or defence, as the case may be (including any expert's report to be filed in accordance with Part 35).

(The Costs Practice Direction supplementing Parts 43 to 48 contains details of the information required to be filed with certain statements of case to comply with rule 44.15 (providing information about funding arrangements))

COMPETITION ACT 1998

14. A party who wishes to rely on a finding of the Office of Fair Trading as provided by section 58 of the Competition Act 1998 must include in his statement of case a statement to that effect and identify the Office's finding on which he seeks to rely.

HUMAN RIGHTS

15.1 A party who seeks to rely on any provision of or right arising under the Human Rights Act 1998 or seeks a remedy available under that Act –

(1) must state that fact in his statement of case; and
(2) must in his statement of case –

  (a) give precise details of the Convention right which it is alleged has been infringed and details of the alleged infringement;
  (b) specify the relief sought;
  (c) state if the relief sought includes –
    (i) a declaration of incompatibility in accordance with section 4 of that Act, or
    (ii) damages in respect of a judicial act to which section 9(3) of that Act applies;
  (d) where the relief sought includes a declaration of incompatibility in accordance with section 4 of that Act, give precise details of the legislative provision alleged to be incompatible and details of the alleged incompatibility;
  (e) where the claim is founded on a finding of unlawfulness by another court or tribunal, give details of the finding; and
  (f) where the claim is founded on a judicial act which is alleged to have infringed a Convention right of the party as provided by section 9 of the Human Rights Act 1998, the judicial act complained of and the court or tribunal which is alleged to have made it.

(The practice direction to Part 19 provides for notice to be given and parties joined in the circumstances referred to in (c), (d) and (f))

15.2 A party who seeks to amend his statement of case to include the matters referred to in paragraph 15.1 must, unless the court orders otherwise, do so as soon as possible.

(Part 17 provides for the amendment of a statement of case)

CPR Part 24

SUMMARY JUDGMENT

CONTENTS OF THIS PART

Rule 24.1 Scope of this Part
Rule 24.2 Grounds for summary judgment
Rule 24.3 Types of proceedings in which summary judgment is available
Rule 24.4 Procedure
Rule 24.5 Evidence for the purposes of a summary judgment hearing
Rule 24.6 Court's powers when it determines a summary judgment application

24.1 Scope of this Part

This Part sets out a procedure by which the court may decide a claim or a particular issue without a trial.

(Part 53 makes special provision about summary disposal of defamation claims in accordance with the Defamation Act 1996)[1]

24.2 Grounds for summary judgment

The court may give summary judgment against a claimant or defendant on the whole of a claim or on a particular issue if –

(a) it considers that –

  (i) that claimant has no real prospect of succeeding on the claim or issue; or
  (ii) that defendant has no real prospect of successfully defending the claim or issue; and

(b) there is no other compelling reason why the case or issue should be disposed of at a trial.

[1] 1196c.31.

(Rule 3.4 makes provision for the court to strike out$^{(GL)}$ a statement of case or part of a statement of case if it appears that it discloses no reasonable grounds for bringing or defending a claim)

24.3 Types of proceedings in which summary judgment is available

(1) The court may give summary judgment against a claimant in any type of proceedings.

(2) The court may give summary judgment against a defendant in any type of proceedings except –

    (a) proceedings for possession of residential premises against –

        (i) a mortgagor; or

        (ii) a tenant or a person holding over after the end of his tenancy whose occupancy is protected within the meaning of the Rent Act 1977[2] or the Housing Act 1988[3] and;

    (b) proceedings for an admiralty claim in rem.

    (c) Omitted

24.4 Procedure

(1) A claimant may not apply for summary judgment until the defendant against whom the application is made has filed –

    (a) an acknowledgement of service; or

    (b) a defence,
        unless –

        (i) the court gives permission; or

        (ii) a practice direction provides otherwise.

(Rule 10.3 sets out the period for filing an acknowledgment of service and rule 15.4 the period for filing a defence)

(1A) In civil proceedings against the Crown, as defined in rule 66.1(2), a claimant may not apply for summary judgment until after expiry of the period for filing a defence specified in rule 15.4.

(2) If a claimant applies for summary judgment before a defendant against whom the application is made has filed a defence, that defendant need not file a defence before the hearing.

(3) Where a summary judgment hearing is fixed, the respondent (or the parties where the hearing is fixed of the court's own initiative) must be given at least 14 days' notice of –

    (a) the date fixed for the hearing; and

    (b) the issues which it is proposed that the court will decide at the hearing.

---

[2] 1977 c.42.
[3] 1988 c.50.

(4) A practice direction may provide for a different period of notice to be given.

(Part 23 contains the general rules about how to make an application)

(Rule 3.3 applies where the court exercises its powers of its own initiative)

24.5 Evidence for the purposes of a summary judgment hearing

(1) If the respondent to an application for summary judgment wishes to rely on written evidence at the hearing, he must –

  (a) file the written evidence; and
  (b) serve copies on every other party to the application,
       at least 7 days before the summary judgment hearing.

(2) If the applicant wishes to rely on written evidence in reply, he must –

  (a) file the written evidence; and
  (b) serve a copy on the respondent,
       at least 3 days before the summary judgment hearing.

(3) Where a summary judgment hearing is fixed by the court of its own initiative –

  (a) any party who wishes to rely on written evidence at the hearing must –

      (i)   file the written evidence; and
      (ii) unless the court orders otherwise, serve copies on every other party to the proceedings,

      at least 7 days before the date of the hearing;
  (b) any party who wishes to rely on written evidence at the hearing in reply to any other party's written evidence must –

      (i)   file the written evidence in reply; and
      (ii) unless the court orders otherwise serve copies on every other party to the proceedings,

      at least 3 days before the date of the hearing.

(4) This rule does not require written evidence –

  (a) to be filed if it has already been filed; or
  (b) to be served on a party on whom it has already been served.

24.6 Court's powers when it determines a summary judgment application

When the court determines a summary judgment application it may –

  (a) give directions as to the filing and service of a defence;
  (a) give further directions about the management of the case.

(Rule 3.1(3) provides that the court may attach conditions when it makes an order)

A2–027

PRACTICE DIRECTION

THE SUMMARY DISPOSAL OF CLAIMS

THIS PRACTICE DIRECTION SUPPLEMENTS CPR PART 24

APPLICATIONS FOR SUMMARY JUDGMENT UNDER PART 24

1.1 Attention is drawn to Part 24 itself and to:
Part 3, in particular rule 3.1(3)and (5),
Part 22, Part 23, in particular rule 23.6,
Part 32, in particular rule 32.6(2).

1.2 In this paragraph, where the context so admits, the word 'claim' includes:

(1) a part of a claim, and
(2) an issue on which the claim in whole or part depends.

1.3 An application for summary judgment under rule 24.2 may be based on:

(1) a point of law (including a question of construction of a document),
(2) the evidence which can reasonably be expected to be available at trial or the lack of it, or
(3) a combination of these.

1.4 Rule 24.4(1) deals with the stage in the proceedings at which an application under Part 24 can be made (but see paragraph 7.1 below).

PROCEDURE FOR MAKING AN APPLICATION

2

(1) Attention is drawn to rules 24.4(3) and 23.6.

(2) The application notice must include a statement that it is an application for summary judgment made under Part 24.

(3) The application notice or the evidence contained or referred to in it or served with it must –

    (a) identify concisely any point of law or provision in a document on which the applicant relies, and/or

    (b) state that it is made because the applicant believes that on the evidence the respondent has no real prospect of succeeding on the claim or issue or (as the case may be) of successfully defending the claim or issue to which the application relates,

and in either case state that the applicant knows of no other reason why the disposal of the claim or issue should await trial.

(4) Unless the application notice itself contains all the evidence (if any) on which the applicant relies, the application notice should identify the written evidence on which the applicant relies. This does not affect the applicant's right to file further evidence under rule 24.5(2).

(5) The application notice should draw the attention of the respondent to rule 24.5(1).

(6) Where the claimant has failed to comply with any relevant pre-action protocol, an action for summary judgment will not normally be entertained before the defence has been filed or, alternatively, the time for doing so has expired.

THE HEARING

3

(1) The hearing of the application will normally take place before a Master or a district judge.

(2) The Master or district judge may direct that the application be heard by a High Court Judge (if the case is in the High Court) or a circuit judge (if the case is in a county court).

THE COURT'S APPROACH

4 Where it appears to the court possible that a claim or defence may succeed but improbable that it will do so, the court may make a conditional order, as described below.

ORDERS THE COURT MAY MAKE

5.1 The orders the court may make on an application under Part 24 include:

    (1) judgment on the claim,
    (2) the striking out or dismissal of the claim,
    (3) the dismissal of the application,
    (4) a conditional order.

5.2 A conditional order is an order which requires a party:

    (1) to pay a sum of money into court, or
    (2) to take a specified step in relation to his claim or defence, as the case may be, and provides that that party's claim will be dismissed or his statement of case will be struck out if he does not comply.

(Note – the court will not follow its former practice of granting leave to a defendant to defend a claim, whether conditionally or unconditionally.)

ACCOUNTS AND INQUIRIES

6 If a remedy sought by a claimant in his claim form includes, or necessarily involves, taking an account or making an inquiry, an application can be made under Part 24 by any party to the proceedings for an order directing any necessary accounts or inquiries to be taken or made.

(The Accounts practice direction supplementing Part 40 contains further provisions as to orders for accounts and inquiries.)

SPECIFIC PERFORMANCE

7.1

    (1) If a remedy sought by a claimant in his claim form includes a claim –

        (a) for specific performance of an agreement (whether in writing or not) for the sale, purchase, exchange, mortgage or charge of any property, or for the grant or assignment of a lease or tenancy of any property, with or without an alternative claim for damages, or
        (b) for rescission of such an agreement, or

(c)   for the forfeiture or return of any deposit made under such an agreement,

the claimant may apply under Part 24 for judgment.

(2)   The claimant may do so at any time after the claim form has been served, whether or not the defendant has acknowledged service of the claim form, whether or not the time for acknowledging service has expired and whether or not any particulars of claim have been served.

7.2   The application notice by which an application under paragraph 7.1 is made must have attached to it the text of the order sought by the claimant.

7.3   The application notice and a copy of every affidavit or witness statement in support and of any exhibit referred to therein must be served on the defendant not less than 4 days before the hearing of the application. (Note – the 4 days replaces for these applications the 14 days specified in rule 24.4(3). Rule 24.5 cannot, therefore apply.)

(This paragraph replaces RSC Order 86, rules 1 and 2 but applies to county court proceedings as well as to High Court proceedings.)

SETTING ASIDE ORDER FOR SUMMARY JUDGMENT

8.1   If an order for summary judgment is made against a respondent who does not appear at the hearing of the application, the respondent may apply for the order to be set aside or varied (see also rule 23.11).

8.2   On the hearing of an application under paragraph 8.1 the court may make such order as it thinks just.

COSTS

9.1   Attention is drawn to Part 45 (fixed costs).

9.2   Attention is drawn to the Costs Practice Direction and in particular to the court's power to make a summary assessment of costs.

9.3   Attention is also drawn to rule 44.13(1) which provides that if an order does not mention costs no party is entitled to costs relating to that order.

CASE MANAGEMENT

10   Where the court dismisses the application or makes an order that does not completely dispose of the claim, the court will give case management directions as to the future conduct of the case.

CPR Part 29

A2–028   THE MULTI-TRACK

CONTENTS OF THIS PART

29.1 Scope of this Part

This Part contains general provisions about management of cases allocated to the multi-track and applies only to cases allocated to that track.

(Part 27 sets out the procedure for claims allocated to the small claims track)

(Part 28 sets out the procedure for claims allocated to the fast track)

29.2 Case management

(1) When it allocates a case to the multi-track, the court will –

(a)   give directions for the management of the case and set a time-table for the steps to be taken between the giving of directions and the trial; or

(b)   fix –

(i)   a case management conference; or

(ii) a pre-trial review,

or both, and give such other directions relating to the management of the case as it sees fit.

(2) The court will fix the trial date or the period in which the trial is to take place as soon as practicable.

(3) When the court fixes the trial date or the trial period under paragraph (2), it will –

    (a)   give notice to the parties of the date or period; and

    (b)   specify the date by which the parties must file a pre-trial check list.

29.3 Case management conference and pre-trial review

(1) The court may fix –

    (a)   a case management conference; or

    (b)   a pre-trial review, at any time after the claim has been allocated.

(2) If a party has a legal representative, a representative –

    (a)   familiar with the case; and

    (b)   with sufficient authority to deal with any issues that are likely to arise, must attend case management conferences and pre-trial reviews.

(Rule 3.1(2)(c) provides that the court may require a party to attend the court)

29.4 Steps taken by the parties

If –

    (a)   the parties agree proposals for the management of the proceedings (including a proposed trial date or period in which the trial is to take place); and

    (b)   the court considers that the proposals are suitable,

it may approve them without a hearing and give directions in the terms proposed.

29.5 Variation of case management timetable

(1) A party must apply to the court if he wishes to vary the date which the court has fixed for –

    (a)   a case management conference;

    (b)   a pre-trial review;

    (c)   the return of a pre-trial check list under rule 29.6;

    (d)   the trial; or

    (e)   the trial period.

(2) Any date set by the court or these Rules for doing any act may not be varied by the parties if the variation would make it necessary to vary any of the dates mentioned in paragraph (1).

(Rule 2.11 allows the parties to vary a date by written agreement except where the rules provide otherwise or the court orders otherwise)

29.6 Pre-trial check list (listing questionnaire)

(1) The court will send the parties a pre-trial check list (listing questionnaire) for completion and return by the date specified in directions given under rule 29.2(3) unless it considers that the claim can proceed to trial without the need for a pre-trial check list.
(2) Each party must file the completed pre-trial check list by the date specified by the court.
(3) If no party files the completed pre-trial checklist by the date specified, the court will order that unless a completed pre-trial checklist is filed within 7 days from service of that order, the claim, defence and any counterclaim will be struck out without further order of the court.
(4) If –

  (a) a party files a completed pre-trial checklist but another party does not;
  (b) a party has failed to give all the information requested by the pre-trial checklist; or
  (c) the court considers that a hearing is necessary to enable it to decide what directions to give in order to complete preparation of the case for trial,

the court may give such directions as it thinks appropriate.

29.7 Pre-trial review

If, on receipt of the parties' pre-trial check lists, the court decides –

  (a) to hold a pre-trial review; or
  (b) to cancel a pre-trial review which has already been fixed,
       it will serve notice of its decision at least 7 days before the date fixed for the hearing or, as the case may be, the cancelled hearing.

29.8 Setting a trial timetable and fixing or confirming the trial date or week

As soon as practicable after –

  (a) each party has filed a completed pre-trial check list;
  (b) the court has held a listing hearing under rule 29.6(3); or
  (c) the court has held a pre-trial review under rule 29.7,
       the court will –

(i)   set a timetable for the trial unless a timetable has already been fixed, or the court considers that it would be inappropriate to do so;

(ii) fix the date for the trial or the week within which the trial is to begin (or, if it has already done so, confirm that date); and

(iii) notify the parties of the trial timetable (where one is fixed under this rule) and the date or trial period.

29.9 Conduct of trial

Unless the trial judge otherwise directs, the trial will be conducted in accordance with any order previously made.

PRACTICE DIRECTION

A2–029

The Multi-Track

This Practice Direction supplements CPR Part 29

GENERAL

1.1 Attention is drawn in particular to the following Parts of the Civil Procedure Rules:

Part 1   The overriding objective
Part 3   The court's case management powers
Part 26 Case management – preliminary stage
Part 31 Disclosure and inspection of documents
Part 32 to 34 Evidence
Part 35 Experts and assessors
and to the practice directions which relate to those Parts.

CASE MANAGEMENT IN THE ROYAL COURTS OF JUSTICE

2.1 This part of the practice direction applies to claims begun by claim form issued in the Central Office or Chancery Chambers in the Royal Courts of Justice.

2.2 A claim with an estimated value of less than £50,000 will generally, unless:

    (a) it is required by an enactment to be tried in the High Court,
    (b) it falls within a specialist list, or
    (c) it falls within one of the categories specified in 2.6 below or is otherwise within the criteria of article 7(5) of the High Court and County Courts Jurisdiction Order 1991,
    be transferred to a county court.

2.3 Paragraph 2.2 is without prejudice to the power of the court in accordance with Part 30 to transfer to a county court a claim with an estimated value that exceeds £50,000.

2.4 The decision to transfer may be made at any stage in the proceedings but should, subject to paragraph 2.5, be made as soon as possible and in any event not later than the date for the filing of pre-trial check lists (listing questionnaires).

2.5 If an application is made under rule 3.4 (striking out) or under Part 24 (summary judgment) or under Part 25 (interim remedies), it will usually be convenient for the application to be dealt with before a decision to transfer is taken.

2.6 Each party should state in his allocation questionnaire whether he considers the claim should be managed and tried at the Royal Courts of Justice and, if so, why. Claims suitable for trial in the Royal Courts of Justice include:

    (1) professional negligence claims,
    (2) Fatal Accident Act claims,
    (3) fraud or undue influence claims,
    (4) defamation claims,
    (5) claims for malicious prosecution or false imprisonment,
    (6) claims against the police,
    (7) contentious probate claims.

Such claims may fall within the criteria of article 7(5) of the High Court and County Courts Jurisdiction Order 1991.

2.7 Attention is drawn to the practice direction on transfer (Part 30).

CASE MANAGEMENT — GENERAL PROVISIONS

3.1

    (1) Case management of a claim which is proceeding at the Royal Courts of Justice will be undertaken there.

    (2)

        (a) Case management of any other claim which has been allocated to the multi-track will normally be undertaken at a Civil Trial Centre.

      (b) The practice direction supplementing Part 26 provides for what will happen in the case of a claim which is issued in or transferred to a court which is not a Civil Trial Centre.

3.2 The hallmarks of the multi-track are:

    (1) the ability of the court to deal with cases of widely differing values and complexity, and

    (2) the flexibility given to the court in the way it will manage a case in a way appropriate to its particular needs.

3.3

    (1) On allocating a claim to the multi-track the court may give directions without a hearing, including fixing a trial date or a period in which the trial will take place,

    (2) Alternatively, whether or not it fixes a trial date or period, it may either –

        (a) give directions for certain steps to be taken and fix a date for a case management conference or a pre-trial review to take place after they have been taken, or

        (b) fix a date for a case management conference.

    (3) Attention is drawn to rule 29.2(2) which requires the court to fix a trial date or period as soon as practicable.

3.4 The court may give or vary directions at any hearing which may take place on the application of a party or of its own initiative.

3.5 When any hearing has been fixed it is the duty of the parties to consider what directions the court should be asked to give and to make any application that may be appropriate to be dealt with then.

3.6 The court will hold a hearing to give directions whenever it appears necessary or desirable to do so, and where this happens because of the default of a party or his legal representative it will usually impose a sanction.

3.7 When the court fixes a hearing to give directions it will give the parties at least 3 days' notice of the hearing unless rule 29.7 applies (7 days' notice to be given in the case of a pre-trial review).

3.8 Where a party needs to apply for a direction of a kind not included in the case management timetable which has been set (for example to amend his statement of case or for further information to be given by another party) he must do so as soon as possible so as to minimise the need to change that timetable.

3.9 Courts will make arrangements to ensure that applications and other hearings are listed promptly to avoid delay in the conduct of cases.

3.10

    (1) Case management will generally be dealt with by:

        (a) a Master in cases proceeding in the Royal Courts of Justice,

        (b) a district judge in cases proceeding in a District Registry of the High Court, and

(c) a district judge or a Circuit Judge in cases proceeding in a county court.

(2) A Master or a district judge may consult and seek the directions of a judge of a higher level about any aspect of case management.

(3) A member of the court staff who is dealing with the listing of a hearing may seek the directions of any judge about any aspect of that listing.

CASE MANAGEMENT – CONSIDERATION OF PERIODICAL PAYMENTS

3A Attention is drawn to Practice Direction 41B supplementing Part 41 and in particular to the direction that in a personal injury claim the court should consider and indicate to the parties as soon as practicable whether periodical payments or a lump sum is likely to be the more appropriate form for all or part of an award of damages for future pecuniary loss.

DIRECTIONS ON ALLOCATION

4.1 Attention is drawn to the court's duties under Rule 29.2.

4.2 The court will seek to tailor its directions to the needs of the case and the steps which the parties have already taken to prepare the case of which it is aware. In particular it will have regard to the extent to which any pre-action protocol has or (as the case may be) has not been complied with.

4.3 At this stage the court's first concern will be to ensure that the issues between the parties are identified and that the necessary evidence is prepared and disclosed.

4.4 The court may have regard to any document filed by a party with his allocation questionnaire containing further information, provided that the document states either that its contents has been agreed with every other party or that it has been served on every other party, and when it was served.

4.5 On the allocation of a claim to the multi-track the court will consider whether it is desirable or necessary to hold a case management conference straight away, or whether it is appropriate instead to give directions on its own initiative.

4.6 The parties and their advisers are encouraged to try to agree directions and to take advantage of rule 29.4 which provides that if:

(1) the parties agree proposals for the management of the proceedings (including a proposed trial date or period in which the trial is to take place), and

(2) the court considers that the proposals are suitable,

it may approve them without a hearing and give directions in the terms proposed.

4.7

(1) To obtain the court's approval the agreed directions must –

    (a) set out a timetable by reference to calendar dates for the taking of steps for the preparation of the case,

    (b) include a date or a period (the trial period) when it is proposed that the trial will take place,

    (c) include provision about disclosure of documents, and

    (d) include provision about both factual and expert evidence.

(2) The court will scrutinise the timetable carefully and in particular will be concerned to see that any proposed date or period for the trial and (if provided for) for a case management conference is no later than is reasonably necessary.

(3) The provision in (1)(c) above may–

    (a) limit disclosure to standard disclosure or less than that, and/or

    (b) direct that disclosure will take place by the supply of copy documents without a list, but it must in that case say either that the parties must serve a disclosure statement with the copies or that they have agreed to disclose in that way without such a statement.

(4) The provision in (1)(d) about expert evidence may be to the effect that none is required.

4.8 Directions agreed by the parties should also where appropriate contain provisions about:

    (1) the filing of any reply or amended statement of case that may be required,

    (2) dates for the service of requests for further information under the practice direction supplementing Part 18 and of questions to experts under rule 35.6 and by when they are to be dealt with,

    (3) the disclosure of evidence,

    (4) the use of a single joint expert, or in cases where it is not agreed, the exchange of expert evidence (including whether exchange is to be simultaneous or sequential) and without prejudice discussions between experts.

4.9 If the court does not approve the agreed directions filed by the parties but decides that it will give directions of its own initiative without fixing a case management conference, it will take them into account in deciding what directions to give.

4.10 Where the court is to give directions on its own initiative without holding a case management conference and it is not aware of any steps taken by the parties other than the exchange of statements of case, its general approach will be:

(1) to give directions for the filing and service of any further information required to clarify either party's case,

(2) to direct standard disclosure between the parties,

(3) to direct the disclosure of witness statements by way of simultaneous exchange,

(4) to give directions for a single joint expert on any appropriate issue unless there is a good reason not to do so,

(5) unless paragraph 4.11 (below) applies, to direct disclosure of experts' reports by way of simultaneous exchange on those issues where a single joint expert is not directed,

(6) if experts' reports are not agreed, to direct a discussion between experts for the purpose set out in rule 35.12(1) and the preparation of a statement under rule 35.12(3),

(7) to list a case management conference to take place after the date for compliance with those directions,

(8) to specify a trial period; and

(9) in such cases as the court thinks appropriate, the court may give directions requiring the parties to consider ADR. Such directions may be, for example, in the following terms:

The parties shall by [date] consider whether the case is capable of resolution by ADR. If any party considers that the case is unsuitable for resolution by ADR, that party shall be prepared to justify that decision at the conclusion of the trial, should the judge consider that such means of resolution were appropriate, when he is considering the appropriate costs order to make. The party considering the case unsuitable for ADR shall, not less than 28 days before the commencement of the trial, file with the court a witness statement without prejudice save as to costs, giving reasons upon which they rely for saying that the case was unsuitable.'

4.11 If it appears that expert evidence will be required both on issues of liability and on the amount of damages, the court may direct that the exchange of those reports that relate to liability will be exchanged simultaneously but that those relating to the amount of damages will be exchanged sequentially.

4.12

(1) If it appears to the court that it cannot properly give directions on its own initiative and no agreed directions have been filed which it can approve, the court will direct a case management conference to be listed.

(2) The conference will be listed as promptly as possible.

4.13 Where the court is proposing on its own initiative to make an order under rule 35.7 (which gives the court power to direct that evidence on a particular issue is to be given by a single expert) or under rule 35.15 (which gives the court power to appoint an assessor), the court must, unless the parties have consented in writing to the order, list a case management conference.

CASE MANAGEMENT CONFERENCES

5.1 The court will at any case management conference:

    (1) review the steps which the parties have taken in the preparation of the case, and in particular their compliance with any directions that the court may have given,

    (2) decide and give directions about the steps which are to be taken to secure the progress of the claim in accordance with the overriding objective, and

    (3) ensure as far as it can that all agreements that can be reached between the parties about the matters in issue and the conduct of the claim are made and recorded.

5.2

    (1) Rule 29.3(2) provides that where a party has a legal representative, a representative familiar with the case and with sufficient authority to deal with any issues that are likely to arise must attend case management conferences and pre-trial reviews.

    (2) That person should be someone who is personally involved in the conduct of the case, and who has the authority and information to deal with any matter which may reasonably be expected to be dealt with at such a hearing, including the fixing of the timetable, the identification of issues and matters of evidence.

    (3) Where the inadequacy of the person attending or of his instructions leads to the adjournment of a hearing, the court will expect to make a wasted costs order.

5.3 The topics the court will consider at a case management conference are likely to include:

    (1) whether the claimant has made clear the claim he is bringing, in particular the amount he is claiming, so that the other party can understand the case he has to meet,

    (2) whether any amendments are required to the claim, a statement of case or any other document,

    (3) what disclosure of documents, if any, is necessary,

    (4) what expert evidence is reasonably required in accordance with rule 35.1 and how and when that evidence should be obtained and disclosed,

    (5) what factual evidence should be disclosed,

    (6) what arrangements should be made about the giving of clarification or further information and the putting of questions to experts, and

    (7) whether it will be just and will save costs to order a split trial or the trial of one or more preliminary issues.

5.4 In all cases the court will set a timetable for the steps it decides are necessary to be taken. These steps may include the holding of a case management conference or a pre-trial review, and the court will be alert to perform its duty to fix a trial date or period as soon as it can.

5.5

(1) The court will not at this stage give permission to use expert evidence unless it can identify each expert by name or field in its order and say whether his evidence is to be given orally or by the use of his report.

(2) A party who obtains expert evidence before obtaining a direction about it does so at his own risk as to costs, except where he obtained the evidence in compliance with a pre-action protocol.

5.6 To assist the court, the parties and their legal advisers should:

(1) ensure that all documents that the court is likely to ask to see (including witness statements and experts' reports) are brought to the hearing,

(2) consider whether the parties should attend,

(3) consider whether a case summary will be useful, and

(4) consider what orders each wishes to be made and give notice of them to the other parties.

5.7

(1) A case summary:

(a) should be designed to assist the court to understand and deal with the questions before it,

(b) should set out a brief chronology of the claim, the issues of fact which are agreed or in dispute and the evidence needed to decide them,

(c) should not normally exceed 500 words in length, and

(d) should be prepared by the claimant and agreed with the other parties if possible.

5.8

(1) Where a party wishes to obtain an order not routinely made at a case management conference and believes that his application will be opposed, he should issue and serve the application in time for it to be heard at the case management conference.

(2) If the time allowed for the case management conference is likely to be insufficient for the application to be heard he should inform the court at once so that a fresh date can be fixed.

(3) A costs sanction may be imposed on a party who fails to comply with sub-paragraph (1) or (2).

5.9 At a case management conference the court may also consider whether the case ought to be tried by a High Court judge or by a judge who specialises in that type of claim and how that question will be decided. In that case the claim may need to be transferred to another court.

VARIATION OF DIRECTIONS

6.1 This paragraph deals with the procedure to be adopted:

    (1) where a party is dissatisfied with a direction given by the court,
    (2) where the parties have agreed about changes they wish made to the directions given, or
    (3) where a party wishes to apply to vary a direction.

6.2

    (1) It is essential that any party who wishes to have a direction varied takes steps to do so as soon as possible.
    (2) The court will assume for the purposes of any later application that a party who did not appeal, and who made no application to vary within 14 days of service of the order containing the directions, was content that they were correct in the circumstances then existing.

6.3

    (1) Where a party is dissatisfied with a direction given or other order made by the court he may appeal or apply to the court for it to reconsider its decision.
    (2) Unless paragraph 6.4 applies, a party should appeal if the direction was given or the order was made at a hearing at which he was present, or of which he had due notice.
    (3) In any other case he should apply to the court to reconsider its decision.
    (4) If an application is made for the court to reconsider its decision:

        (a) it will usually be heard by the judge who gave the directions or another judge of the same level,
        (b) the court will give all parties at least 3 days notice of the hearing, and
        (c) the court may confirm its directions or make a different order.

6.4 Where there has been a change in the circumstances since the order was made the court may set aside or vary a direction it has given. It may do so on application or on its own initiative.

6.5 Where the parties agree about changes they wish made to the directions given:

    (1) If rule 2.11 (variation by agreement of a date set by the court for doing any act other than those stated in the note to that rule) or rule 31.5, 31.10(8) or 31.13 (agreements about disclosure) applies the parties need not file the written agreement.
    (2)

        (a) In any other case the parties must apply for an order by consent.

    (b) The parties must file a draft of the order sought and an agreed statement of the reasons why the variation is sought.

    (c) The court may make an order in the agreed terms or in other terms without a hearing, but it may direct that a hearing is to be listed.

FAILURE TO COMPLY WITH CASE MANAGEMENT DIRECTIONS

7.1 Where a party fails to comply with a direction given by the court any other party may apply for an order that he must do so or for a sanction to be imposed or both of these.

7.2 The party entitled to apply for such an order must do so without delay but should first warn the other party of his intention to do so.

7.3 The court may take any such delay into account when it decides whether to make an order imposing a sanction or to grant relief from a sanction imposed by the rules or any other practice direction.

7.4

    (1) The court will not allow a failure to comply with directions to lead to the postponement of the trial unless the circumstances are exceptional.

    (2) If it is practical to do so the court will exercise its powers in a manner that enables the case to come on for trial on the date or within the period previously set.

    (3) In particular the court will assess what steps each party should take to prepare the case for trial, direct that those steps are taken in the shortest possible time and impose a sanction for non-compliance. Such a sanction may, for example, deprive a party of the right to raise or contest an issue or to rely on evidence to which the direction relates.

    (4) Where it appears that one or more issues are or can be made ready for trial at the time fixed while others cannot, the court may direct that the trial will proceed on the issues which are then ready, and direct that no costs will be allowed for any later trial of the remaining issues or that those costs will be paid by the party in default.

    (5) Where the court has no option but to postpone the trial it will do so for the shortest possible time and will give directions for the taking of the necessary steps in the meantime as rapidly as possible.

    (6) Litigants and lawyers must be in no doubt that the court will regard the postponement of a trial as an order of last resort. Where it appears inevitable the court may exercise its power to require a party as well as his legal representative to attend court at the hearing where such an order is to be sought.

    (7) The court will not postpone any other hearing without a very good reason, and for that purpose the failure of a party to comply on time with directions previously given will not be treated as a good reason.

PRE-TRIAL CHECK LISTS
(LISTING QUESTIONNAIRES)

8.1

(1)   The pre-trial check list (listing questionnaire) will be in Form N170.

(2)   Unless it dispenses with pre-trial check lists and orders an early trial on a fixed date, the court will specify the date for filing completed pre-trial check lists when it fixes the trial date or trial period under rule 29.2(2).

(3)   The date for filing the completed pre-trial check list will be not later than 8 weeks before the trial date or the start of the trial period.

(4)   The court will serve the pre-trial check lists on the parties at least 14 days before that date.

(5)   Although the rules do not require the parties to exchange copies of the check lists before they are filed they are encouraged to do so to avoid the court being given conflicting or incomplete information.

(6)   The file will be placed before a judge for his directions when all the check lists have been filed or when the time for filing them has expired and where a party has filed a checklist but another party has not done so.

8.2   The court's general approach will be as set out in the following paragraphs. The court may however decide to make other orders, and in particular the court will take into account the steps, if any, of which it is aware which the parties have taken to prepare the case for trial.

8.3

(1)   Where no party files a pre-trial checklist the court will order that unless a completed pre-trial checklist is filed within 7 days from service of that order, the claim, defence and any counterclaim will be struck out without further order of the court.

(2)   Where a party files a pre-trial check list but another party (the defaulting party) does not do so, the court will fix a hearing under rule 29.6(4). Whether or not the defaulting party attends the hearing, the court will normally fix or confirm the trial date and make other orders about the steps to be taken to prepare the case for trial.

8.4   Where the court decides to hold a hearing under rule 29.6(4) the court will fix a date which is as early as possible and the parties will be given at least 3 days notice of the date.

8.5 Where the court decides to hold a pre-trial review (whether or not this is in addition to a hearing under rule 29.6(4)) the court will give the parties at least 7 days notice of the date.

DIRECTIONS THE COURT WILL GIVE ON LISTING

9.1 Directions the court must give.
The court must fix the trial date or week, give a time estimate and fix the place of trial.

9.2 Other directions

   (1) The parties should seek to agree directions and may file an agreed order. The court may make an order in those terms or it may make a different order.

   (2) Agreed directions should include provision about:

      (a) evidence especially expert evidence,
      (b) a trial timetable and time estimate,
      (c) the preparation of a trial bundle, and
      (d) any other matter needed to prepare the case for trial.

   (3) The court will include such of these provisions as are appropriate in any order that it may make, whether or not the parties have filed agreed directions.

   (4) Unless a direction doing so has been given before, a direction giving permission to use expert evidence will say whether it gives permission to use oral evidence or reports or both and will name the experts concerned.

9.3 The principles set out in paragraph 6 of this practice direction about variation of directions applies equally to directions given at this stage.

THE TRIAL

10.1 The trial will normally take place at a Civil Trial Centre but it may be at another court if it is appropriate having regard to the needs of the parties and the availability of court resources.

10.2 The judge will generally have read the papers in the trial bundle and may dispense with an opening address.

10.3 The judge may confirm or vary any timetable given previously, or if none has been given set his own.

10.4 Attention is drawn to the provisions in Part 32 and the following parts of the Rules about evidence, and in particular:

   (1) to rule 32.1 (court's power to control evidence and to restrict cross-examination), and

(2) to rule 32.5(2) statements and reports to stand as evidence in chief.

10.5 In an appropriate case the judge may summarily assess costs in accordance with rule 44.7. Attention is drawn to the practice directions about costs and the steps the parties are required to take.

10.6 Once the trial of a multi-track claim has begun, the judge will normally sit on consecutive court days until it has been concluded.

CPR Part 30

TRANSFER   A2–030

CONTENTS OF THIS PART

30.1 Scope of this Part

(1) This Part deals with the transfer of proceedings between county courts, between the High Court and the county courts and within the High Court.

(2) The practice direction may make provision about the transfer of proceedings between the court and a tribunal.

(Rule 26.2 provides for automatic transfer in certain cases)

30.2 Transfer between county courts and within the High Court

(1) A county court may order proceedings before that court, or any part of them (such as a counterclaim or an application made in the proceedings), to be transferred to another county court if it is satisfied that –

    (a) an order should be made having regard to the criteria in rule 30.3; or

    (b) proceedings for –

        (i) the detailed assessment of costs; or

        (ii) the enforcement of a judgment or order,

could be more conveniently or fairly taken in that other county court.

(2) If proceedings have been started in the wrong county court, a judge of the county court may order that the proceedings –

    (a) be transferred to the county court in which they ought to have been started;

    (b) continue in the county court in which they have been started; or

    (c) be struck out.

(3) An application for an order under paragraph (1) or (2) must be made to the county court where the claim is proceeding.

(4) The High Court may, having regard to the criteria in rule 30.3, order proceedings in the Royal Courts of Justice or a district registry, or any part of such proceedings (such as a counterclaim or an application made in the proceedings), to be transferred –

    (a) from the Royal Courts of Justice to a district registry; or

    (b) from a district registry to the Royal Courts of Justice or to another district registry.

(5) A district registry may order proceedings before it for the detailed assessment of costs to be transferred to another district registry if it is satisfied that the proceedings could be more conveniently or fairly taken in that other district registry.

(6) An application for an order under paragraph (4) or (5) must, if the claim is proceeding in a district registry, be made to that registry.

(7) Where some enactment, other than these Rules, requires proceedings to be started in a particular county court, neither paragraphs (1) nor (2) give the court power to order proceedings to be transferred to a county court which is not the court in which they should have been started or to order them to continue in the wrong court.

(8) Probate proceedings may only be transferred under paragraph (4) to the Chancery Division at the Royal Courts of Justice or to one of the Chancery district registries.

30.3 Criteria for a transfer order

(1) Paragraph (2) sets out the matters to which the court must have regard when considering whether to make an order under –

    (a) section 40(2), 41(1) or 42(2) of the County Courts Act 1984[1] (transfer between the High Court and a county court);

    (b) rule 30.2(1) (transfer between county courts); or

---

[1] 1984 c.28. Section 40 was substituted by section 2(1) of the Courts and Legal Services Act 1990 (c.41). Section 41 was amended by the Matrimonial and Family Proceedings Act 1984 (c.42), Schedule 1, paragraph 31 and by section 2(2) of the Courts and Legal Services Act 1990. Section 42 was substituted by section 2(3) of the Courts and Legal Services Act 1990.

(c) rule 30.2(4) (transfer between the Royal Courts of Justice and the district registries).

(2) The matters to which the court must have regard include –

(a) the financial value of the claim and the amount in dispute, if different;
(b) whether it would be more convenient or fair for hearings (including the trial) to be held in some other court;
(c) the availability of a judge specialising in the type of claim in question;
(d) whether the facts, legal issues, remedies or procedures involved are simple or complex;
(e) the importance of the outcome of the claim to the public in general;
(f) the facilities available at the court where the claim is being dealt with and whether they may be inadequate because of any disabilities of a party or potential witness;
(g) whether the making of a declaration of incompatibility under section 4 of the Human Rights Act 1998 has arisen or may arise;
(h) in the case of civil proceedings by or against the Crown, as defined in rule 66.1(2), the location of the relevant government department or officers of the Crown and, where appropriate, any relevant public interest that the matter should be tried in London.

30.4 Procedure

(1) Where the court orders proceedings to be transferred, the court from which they are to be transferred must give notice of the transfer to all the parties.
(2) An order made before the transfer of the proceedings shall not be affected by the order to transfer.

30.5 Transfer between Divisions and to and from a specialist list

(1) The High Court may order proceedings in any Division of the High Court to be transferred to another Division.
(2) A judge dealing with claims in a specialist list may order proceedings to be transferred to or from that list.
(3) An application for the transfer of proceedings to or from a specialist list must be made to a judge dealing with claims in that list.

30.6 Power to specify place where hearings are to be held

The court may specify the place (for instance, a particular county court) where the trial or some other hearing in any proceedings is to be held and may do so without ordering the proceedings to be transferred.

30.7 Transfer of control of money in court

The court may order that control of any money held by it under rule 21.11 (control of money recovered by or on behalf of a child or patient) be transferred to another court if that court would be more convenient.

30.8 Transfer of competition law claims

(1) This rule applies if, in any proceedings in the Queen's Bench Division, (other than proceedings in the Commercial or Admiralty Courts) a district registry of the High Court or a county court, a party's statement of case raises an issue relating to the application of –

  (a) Article 81 or Article 82 of the Treaty establishing the European Community; or
  (b) Chapter I or II of Part I of the Competition Act 1998[2].

(2) Rules 30.2 and 30.3 do not apply.
(3) The court must transfer the proceedings to the Chancery Division of the High Court at the Royal Courts of Justice.
(4) If any such proceedings which have been commenced in the Queen's Bench Division or a Mercantile Court fall within the scope of rule 58.1(2), any party to those proceedings may apply for the transfer of the proceedings to the Commercial Court, in accordance with rule 58.4(2) and rule 30.5(3). If the application is refused, the proceedings must be transferred to the Chancery Division of the High Court at the Royal Courts of Justice.

A2–031

PRACTICE DIRECTION

TRANSFER

THIS PRACTICE DIRECTION SUPPLEMENTS CPR PART 30

VALUE OF A CASE AND TRANSFER

1. In addition to the criteria set out in Rule 30.3(2) attention is drawn to the financial limits set out in the High Court and County Courts Jurisdiction Order 1991, as amended.

2. Attention is also drawn to paragraph 2 of the Practice Direction on Part 29 (the multi-track).

---

[2] 1998 c.41.

DATE OF TRANSFER

3.   Where the court orders proceedings to be transferred, the order will take effect from the date it is made by the court.

PROCEDURE ON TRANSFER

4.1 Where an order for transfer has been made the transferring court will immediately send notice of the transfer to the receiving court. The notice will contain:

(1)   the name of the case, and
(2)   the number of the case.

4.2 At the same time as the transferring court notifies the receiving court it will also notify the parties of the transfer under rule 30.4(1).

PROCEDURE FOR AN APPEAL AGAINST ORDER OF TRANSFER

5.1 Where a district judge orders proceedings to be transferred and both the transferring and receiving courts are county courts, any appeal against that order should be made in the receiving court.
5.2 The receiving court may, if it is more convenient for the parties, remit the appeal to the transferring court to be dealt with there.

APPLICATIONS TO SET ASIDE

6.1 Where a party may apply to set aside an order for transfer (e.g. under rule 23.10) the application should be made to the court which made the order.
6.2 Such application should be made in accordance with Part 23 of the Rules and the practice direction which supplements it.

TRANSFER ON THE CRITERION IN RULE 30.3(2)(G)

7   A transfer should only be made on the basis of the criterion in rule 30.3(2)(g) where there is a real prospect that a declaration of incompatibility will be made.

ENTERPRISE ACT 2002

8.1 In this paragraph –

    (1) "the 1998 Act" means the Competition Act 1998;

    (2) "the 2002 Act" means the Enterprise Act 2002; and

    (3) "the CAT" means the Competition Appeal Tribunal.

8.2 Rules 30.1, 30.4 and 30.5 and paragraphs 3 and 6 apply.

TRANSFER FROM THE HIGH COURT OR A COUNTY COURT TO THE COMPETITION APPEAL TRIBUNAL UNDER SECTION 16(4) OF THE ENTERPRISE ACT 2002

8.3 The High Court or a county court may pursuant to section 16(4) of the 2002 Act, on its own initiative or on application by the claimant or defendant, order the transfer of any part of the proceedings before it, which relates to a claim to which section 47A of the 1998 Act applies, to the CAT.

8.4 When considering whether to make an order under paragraph 8.3 the court shall take into account whether –

    (1) there is a similar claim under section 47A of the 1998 Act based on the same infringement currently before the CAT;

    (2) the CAT has previously made a decision on a similar claim under section 47A of the 1998 Act based on the same infringement; or

    (3) the CAT has developed considerable expertise by previously dealing with a significant number of cases arising from the same or similar infringements.

8.5 Where the court orders a transfer under paragraph 8.3 it will immediately –

    (1) send to the CAT –

        (a) a notice of the transfer containing the name of the case; and

        (b) all papers relating to the case; and

    (2) notify the parties of the transfer.

8.6 An appeal against a transfer order made under paragraph 8.3 must be brought in the court which made the transfer order.

TRANSFER FROM THE COMPETITION APPEAL TRIBUNAL TO THE HIGH COURT UNDER SECTION 16(5) OF THE ENTERPRISE ACT 2002

8.7 Where the CAT pursuant to section 16(5) of the 2002 Act directs transfer of a claim made in proceedings under section 47A of the 1998 Act to the High Court, the claim should be transferred to the Chancery Division of the High Court at the Royal Courts of Justice.

8.8 As soon as a claim has been transferred under paragraph 8.7, the High Court must –

(1) allocate a case number; and

(2) list the case for a case management hearing before a judge.

8.9 A party to a claim which has been transferred under paragraph 8.7 may apply to transfer it to the Commercial Court if it otherwise falls within the scope of rule 58.2(1), in accordance with the procedure set out in rules 58.4(2) and 30.5(3).

CPR Part 36

OFFERS TO SETTLE AND PAYMENTS INTO COURT   A2–032

CONTENTS OF THIS PART

36.1 Scope of this Part

(1) This Part contains rules about –

    (a) offers to settle and payments into court; and
    (b) the consequences where an offer to settle or payment into court is made in accordance with this Part.

(2) Nothing in this Part prevents a party making an offer to settle in whatever way he chooses, but if that offer is not made in accordance with this Part, it will only have the consequences specified in this Part if the court so orders.

(Part 36 applies to Part 20 claims by virtue of rule 20.3)

36.2 Part 36 offers and Part 36 payments – general provisions

(1) An offer made in accordance with the requirements of this Part is called –

    (a) if made by way of a payment into court, 'a Part 36 payment';
    (b) otherwise 'a Part 36 offer'.

(Rule 36.3 sets out when an offer has to be made by way of a payment into court)

(2) The party who makes an offer is the 'offeror'.
(3) The party to whom an offer is made is the 'offeree'.
(4) A Part 36 offer or a Part 36 payment –

    (a) may be made at any time after proceedings have started; and

(b) may be made in appeal proceedings.

(5) A Part 36 offer or a Part 36 payment shall not have the consequences set out in this Part while the claim is being dealt with on the small claims track unless the court orders otherwise.

(Part 26 deals with allocation to the small claims track)

(Rule 27.2 provides that Part 36 does not apply to small claims)

36.2A Personal injury claims for future pecuniary loss

(1) This rule applies to a claim for damages for personal injury which is or includes a claim for future pecuniary loss.

(2) An offer to settle such a claim will not have the consequences set out in this Part unless it is made by way of a Part 36 offer under this rule, and where such an offer is or includes an offer to pay the whole or part of any damages in the form of a lump sum, it will not have the consequences set out in this Part unless a Part 36 payment of the amount of the lump sum offer is also made.

(3) Where both a Part 36 offer and a Part 36 payment are made under this rule –

  (a) the offer must include details of the payment, and
  (b) rules 36.11(1) and (2) and 36.13(1) and (2) apply as if there were only a Part 36 offer.

(4) A Part 36 offer to which this rule applies may contain an offer to pay, or an offer to accept –

  (a) the whole or part of the damages for future pecuniary loss in the form of –

   (i)   either a lump sum or periodical payments, or
   (ii) both a lump sum and periodical payments,

  (b) the whole or part of any other damages in the form of a lump sum.

(5) A Part 36 offer to which this rule applies –

  (a) must state the amount of any offer to pay the whole or part of any damages in the form of a lump sum;
  (b) may state what part of the offer relates to damages for future pecuniary loss to be accepted in the form of a lump sum;
  (c) may state, where part of the offer relates to other damages to be accepted in the form of a lump sum, what amounts are attributable to those other damages;
  (d) must state what part of the offer relates to damages for future pecuniary loss to be paid or accepted in the form of periodical payments and must specify –

   (i)   the amount and duration of the periodical payments,

      (ii) the amount of any payments for substantial capital purchases and when they are to be made, and

      (iii) that each amount is to vary by reference to the retail prices index (or to some other named index, or that it is not to vary by reference to any index); and

   (e) must state either that any damages which take the form of periodical payments will be funded in a way which ensures that the continuity of payment is reasonably secure in accordance with section 2(4) of the Damages Act 1996 or how such damages are to be paid and how the continuity of their payment is to be secured.

(6) Where a Part 36 payment includes a lump sum for damages for future pecuniary loss, the Part 36 payment notice may state the amount of that lump sum.

(7) Where the defendant makes a Part 36 offer to which this rule applies and which offers to pay damages in the form of both a lump sum and periodical payments, the claimant may only give notice of acceptance of the offer as a whole.

36.3 A defendant's offer to settle a money claim requires a Part 36 payment

(1) Subject to rules 36.2A(2), 36.5(5) and 36.23, an offer by a defendant to settle a money claim will not have the consequences set out in this Part unless it is made by way of a Part 36 payment.

(2) A Part 36 payment may only be made after proceedings have started.

(Rule 36.5(5) permits a Part 36 offer to be made by reference to an interim payment)

(Rule 36.10 makes provision for an offer to settle a money claim before the commencement of proceedings)

(Rule 36.23 makes provision for where benefit is recoverable under the Social Security (Recovery of Benefit) Act 1997[1]

36.4 Defendant's offer to settle the whole of a claim which includes both a money claim and a non-money claim

(1) This rule applies where a defendant to a claim which includes both a money claim and a nonmoney claim wishes –

   (a) to make an offer to settle the whole claim which will have the consequences set out in this Part; and

   (b) to make a money offer in respect of the money claim and a non-money offer in respect of the non-money claim.

(2) The defendant must –

---

[1] 1997 c.27.

(a) make a Part 36 payment or Part 36 offer made under rule 36.2A in relation to the money claim; and

(b) make a Part 36 offer in relation to the non-money claim.

(3) The Part 36 payment notice or Part 36 offer made under rule 36.2A must –

(a) identify the document which sets out the terms of the Part 36 offer made under this rule; and

(b) state that if the claimant gives notice of acceptance of the Part 36 payment or Part 36 offer made under rule 36.2A he will be treated as also accepting the Part 36 offer made under this rule.

(Rule 36.6 makes provision for a Part 36 payment notice)

(4) If the claimant gives notice of acceptance of the Part 36 payment or Part 36 offer made under rule 36.2A, he shall also be taken as giving notice of acceptance of the Part 36 offer in relation to the non-money claim.

36.5 Form and content of a Part 36 offer

(1) A Part 36 offer must be in writing.

(2) A Part 36 offer may relate to the whole claim or to part of it or to any issue that arises in it.

(3) A Part 36 offer must –

(a) state whether it relates to the whole of the claim or to part of it or to an issue that arises in it and if so to which part or issue;

(b) state whether it takes into account any counterclaim; and

(c) if it is expressed not to be inclusive of interest, give the details relating to interest set out in rule 36.22(2).

(4) A defendant may make a Part 36 offer limited to accepting liability up to a specified proportion.

(5) A Part 36 offer may be made by reference to an interim payment.

(Part 25 contains provisions relating to interim payments)

(6) A Part 36 offer made not less than 21 days before the start of the trial must –

(a) be expressed to remain open for acceptance for 21 days from the date it is made; and

(b) provide that after 21 days the offeree may only accept it if –

(i)   the parties agree the liability for costs; or

(ii) the court gives permission.

(7) A Part 36 offer made less than 21 days before the start of the trial must state that the offeree may only accept it if –

    (a) the parties agree the liability for costs; or

    (b) the court gives permission.

(Rule 36.8 makes provision for when a Part 36 offer is treated as being made)

(8) If a Part 36 offer is withdrawn it will not have the consequences set out in this Part.

36.6 Notice of a Part 36 payment

(1) A Part 36 payment may relate to the whole claim or part of it or to an issue that arises in it.

(2) A defendant who makes a Part 36 payment must file with the court a notice ('Part 36 payment notice') which –

    (a) states the amount of the payment;

    (b) states whether the payment relates to the whole claim or to part of it or to any issue that arises in it and if so to which part or issue;

    (c) states whether it takes into account any counterclaim;

    (d) if an interim payment has been made, states that the defendant has taken into account the interim payment; and

    (e) if it is expressed not to be inclusive of interest, gives the details relating to interest set out in rule 36.22(2).

(Rule 25.6 makes provision for an interim payment)

(Rule 36.4 provides for further information to be included where a defendant wishes to settle the whole of a claim which includes a money claim and a non-money claim)

(Rule 36.23 makes provision for extra information to be included in the payment notice in a case where benefit is recoverable under the Social Security (Recovery of Benefit) Act 1997)

(3) The offeror must –

    (a) serve the Part 36 payment notice on the offeree; and

    (b) file a certificate of service of the notice.

(4) Omitted

(5) A Part 36 payment may be withdrawn or reduced only with the permission of the court.

36.7 Offer to settle a claim for provisional damages

(1) A defendant may make a Part 36 payment in respect of a claim which includes a claim for provisional damages.

(2) Where he does so, the Part 36 payment notice must specify whether or not the defendant is offering to agree to the making of an award of provisional damages.

(3) Where the defendant is offering to agree to the making of an award of provisional damages the payment notice must also state –

    (a)   that the sum paid into court is in satisfaction of the claim for damages on the assumption that the injured person will not develop the disease or suffer the type of deterioration specified in the notice;

    (b)   that the offer is subject to the condition that the claimant must make any claim for further damages within a limited period; and

    (c)   what that period is.

(4) Where a Part 36 payment is –

    (a)   made in accordance with paragraph (3); and

    (b)   accepted within the relevant period in rule 36.11,
        the Part 36 payment will have the consequences set out in rule 36.13, unless the court orders otherwise.

(5) If the claimant accepts the Part 36 payment he must, within 7 days of doing so, apply to the court for an order for an award of provisional damages under rule 41.2.

(Rule 41.2 provides for an order for an award of provisional damages)

(6) The money in court may not be paid out until the court has disposed of the application made in accordance with paragraph (5).

36.8 Time when a Part 36 offer or a Part 36 payment is made and accepted

(1) A Part 36 offer is made when received by the offeree.
(2) A Part 36 payment is made when written notice of the payment into court is served on the offeree.
(3) An improvement to a Part 36 offer will be effective when its details are received by the offeree.
(4) An increase in a Part 36 payment will be effective when notice of the increase is served on the offeree.
(5) A Part 36 offer or Part 36 payment is accepted when notice of its acceptance is received by the offeror.

36.9 Clarification of a Part 36 offer or a Part 36 payment notice

(1) The offeree may, within 7 days of a Part 36 offer or payment being made, request the offeror to clarify the offer or payment notice.
(2) If the offeror does not give the clarification requested under paragraph (1) within 7 days of receiving the request, the offeree may, unless the trial has started, apply for an order that he does so.
(3) If the court makes an order under paragraph (2), it must specify the date when the Part 36 offer or Part 36 payment is to be treated as having been made.

36.10 Court to take into account offer to settle made before commencement of proceedings

(1) If a person makes an offer to settle before proceedings are begun which complies with the provisions of this rule, the court will take that offer into account when making any order as to costs.
(2) The offer must –

    (a) be expressed to be open for at least 21 days after the date it was made;
    (b) if made by a person who would be a defendant were proceedings commenced, include an offer to pay the costs of the offeree incurred up to the date 21 days after the date it was made; and
    (c) otherwise comply with this Part.

(3) Subject to paragraph (3A), if the offeror is a defendant to a money claim –

    (a) he must make a Part 36 payment within 14 days of service of the claim form; and
    (b) the amount of the payment must be not less than the sum offered before proceedings began.

(3A) In a claim to which rule 36.2A applies, if the offeror is a defendant who wishes to offer to pay the whole or part of any damages in the form of a lump sum –

    (a) he must make a Part 36 payment within 14 days of service of the claim form; and
    (b) the amount of the payment must be not less than the lump sum offered before proceedings began.

(4) An offeree may not, after proceedings have begun, accept –

    (a) an offer made under paragraph (2); or
    (b) a Part 36 payment made under paragraph (3) or (3A),
        without the permission of the court.

(5) An offer under this rule is made when it is received by the offeree.

36.11 Time for acceptance of a defendant's Part 36 offer or Part 36 payment

(1) A claimant may accept a Part 36 offer or a Part 36 payment made not less than 21 days before the start of the trial without needing the court's permission if he gives the defendant written notice of acceptance not later than 21 days after the offer or payment was made.

(Rule 36.13 sets out the costs consequences of accepting a defendant's offer or payment without needing the permission of the court)

(2) If –

(a) a defendant's Part 36 offer or Part 36 payment is made less than 21 days before the start of the trial; or

(b) the claimant does not accept it within the period specified in paragraph (1) –

   (i)   if the parties agree the liability for costs, the claimant may accept the offer or payment without needing the permission of the court;

   (ii) if the parties do not agree the liability for costs the claimant may only accept the offer or payment with the permission of the court.

(3) Where the permission of the court is needed under paragraph (2) the court will, if it gives permission, make an order as to costs.

36.12 Time for acceptance of a claimant's Part 36 offer

(1) A defendant may accept a Part 36 offer made not less than 21 days before the start of the trial without needing the court's permission if he gives the claimant written notice of acceptance not later than 21 days after the offer was made.

(Rule 36.14 sets out the costs consequences of accepting a claimant's offer without needing the permission of the court)

(2) If –

(a) a claimant's Part 36 offer is made less than 21 days before the start of the trial; or

(b) the defendant does not accept it within the period specified in paragraph (1) –

   (i)   if the parties agree the liability for costs, the defendant may accept the offer without needing the permission of the court;

   (ii) if the parties do not agree the liability for costs the defendant may only accept the offer with the permission of the court.

(3) Where the permission of the court is needed under paragraph (2) the court will, if it gives permission, make an order as to costs.

36.13 Costs consequences of acceptance of a defendant's Part 36 offer or Part 36 payment

(1) Where a Part 36 offer or a Part 36 payment is accepted without needing the permission of the court the claimant will be entitled to his costs of the proceedings up to the date of serving notice of acceptance.
(2) Where –

(a) a Part 36 offer or a Part 36 payment relates to part only of the claim; and

(b) at the time of serving notice of acceptance the claimant abandons the balance of the claim,

the claimant will be entitled to his costs of the proceedings up to the date of serving notice of acceptance, unless the court orders otherwise.

(3) The claimant's costs include any costs attributable to the defendant's counterclaim if the Part 36 offer or the Part 36 payment notice states that it takes into account the counterclaim.

(4) Costs under this rule will be payable on the standard basis if not agreed.

36.14 Costs consequences of acceptance of a claimant's Part 36 offer

Where a claimant's Part 36 offer is accepted without needing the permission of the court the claimant will be entitled to his costs of the proceedings up to the date upon which the defendant serves notice of acceptance.

36.15 The effect of acceptance of a Part 36 offer or a Part 36 payment

(1) If a Part 36 offer or Part 36 payment relates to the whole claim and is accepted, the claim will be stayed$^{(GL)}$.

(2) In the case of acceptance of a Part 36 offer which relates to the whole claim –

(a) the stay$^{(GL)}$ will be upon the terms of the offer; and
(b) either party may apply to enforce those terms without the need for a new claim.

(3) If a Part 36 offer or a Part 36 payment which relates to part only of the claim is accepted –

(a) the claim will be stayed$^{(GL)}$ as to that part; and
(b) unless the parties have agreed costs, the liability for costs shall be decided by the court.

(4) If the approval of the court is required before a settlement can be binding, any stay$^{(GL)}$ which would otherwise arise on the acceptance of a Part 36 offer or a Part 36 payment will take effect only when that approval has been given.

(5) Any stay$^{(GL)}$ arising under this rule will not affect the power of the court –

(a) to enforce the terms of a Part 36 offer;
(b) to deal with any question of costs (including interest on costs) relating to the proceedings;
(c) to order payment out of court of any sum paid into court.

(6) Where –

(a) a Part 36 offer has been accepted; and

(b) a party alleges that –

  (i) the other party has not honoured the terms of the offer; and

  (ii) he is therefore entitled to a remedy for breach of contract,

  the party may claim the remedy by applying to the court without the need to start a new claim unless the court orders otherwise.

36.16 Payment out of a sum in court on the acceptance of a Part 36 payment

Where a Part 36 payment is accepted the claimant obtains payment out of the sum in court by making a request for payment in the practice form.

36.17 Acceptance of a Part 36 offer or a Part 36 payment made by one or more, but not all, defendants

(1) This rule applies where the claimant wishes to accept a Part 36 offer or a Part 36 payment made by one or more, but not all, of a number of defendants.

(2) If the defendants are sued jointly or in the alternative, the claimant may accept the offer or payment without needing the permission of the court in accordance with rule 36.11(1) if –

  (a) he discontinues his claim against those defendants who have not made the offer or payment; and

  (b) those defendants give written consent to the acceptance of the offer or payment.

(3) If the claimant alleges that the defendants have a several liability[(GL)] to him the claimant may –

  (a) accept the offer or payment in accordance with rule 36.11(1); and

  (b) continue with his claims against the other defendants if he is entitled to do so.

(4) In all other cases the claimant must apply to the court for –

  (a) an order permitting a payment out to him of any sum in court; and

  (b) such order as to costs as the court considers appropriate.

36.18 Other cases where a court order is required to enable acceptance of a Part 36 offer or a Part 36 payment

(1) Where a Part 36 offer or a Part 36 payment is made in proceedings to which rule 21.10 applies –

  (a) the offer or payment may be accepted only with the permission of the court; and

(b) no payment out of any sum in court shall be made without a
      court order.

(Rule 21.10 deals with compromise etc. by or on behalf of a child or
patient)

(2) Where the court gives a claimant permission to accept a Part 36 offer
or payment after the trial has started –

    (a) any money in court may be paid out only with a court order;
      and
    (b) the court must, in the order, deal with the whole costs of the
      proceedings.

(3) Where a claimant accepts a Part 36 payment after a defence of tender
before claim$^{(GL)}$ has been put forward by the defendant, the money in
court may be paid out only after an order of the court.

(Rule 37.3 requires a defendant who wishes to rely on a defence of tender
before claim$^{(GL)}$ to make a payment into court)

36.19 Restriction on disclosure of a Part 36 offer or a Part 36 payment

(1) A Part 36 offer will be treated as 'without prejudice$^{(GL)}$ except as to
costs'.
(2) The fact that a Part 36 payment has been made shall not be communicated to the trial judge until all questions of liability and the amount
of money to be awarded have been decided.
(3) Paragraph (2) does not apply –

    (a) where the defence of tender before claim$^{(GL)}$ has been raised;
    (b) where the proceedings have been stayed$^{(GL)}$ under rule 36.15
      following acceptance of a Part 36 offer or Part 36 payment; or
    (c) where –

        (i)   the issue of liability has been determined before any
            assessment of the money claimed; and
        (ii) the fact that there has or has not been a Part 36 payment
            may be relevant to the question of the costs of the issue of
            liability.

36.20 Costs consequences where claimant fails to do better than a Part 36 offer or a Part 36 payment

(1) This rule applies where at trial a claimant –

    (a) fails to better a Part 36 payment;
    (b) fails to obtain a judgment which is more advantageous than a
      defendant's Part 36 offer or
    (c) in a claim to which rule 36.2A applies, fails to obtain a judg-
      ment which is more advantageous than the Part 36 offer made
      under that rule.

(2) Unless it considers it unjust to do so, the court will order the claimant to pay any costs incurred by the defendant after the latest date on which the payment or offer could have been accepted without needing the permission of the court.

(Rule 36.11 sets out the time for acceptance of a defendant's Part 36 offer or Part 36 payment)

36.21 Costs and other consequences where claimant does better than he proposed in his Part 36 offer

(1) This rule applies where at trial –

    (a) a defendant is held liable for more; or

    (b) the judgment against a defendant is more advantageous to the claimant,

        than the proposals contained in a claimant's Part 36 offer (including a Part 36 offer made under rule 36.2A).

(2) The court may order interest on the whole or part of any sum of money (excluding interest) awarded to the claimant at a rate not exceeding 10% above base rate$^{(GL)}$ for some or all of the period starting with the latest date on which the defendant could have accepted the offer without needing the permission of the court.

(3) The court may also order that the claimant is entitled to –

    (a) his costs on the indemnity basis from the latest date when the defendant could have accepted the offer without needing the permission of the court; and

    (b) interest on those costs at a rate not exceeding 10% above base rate$^{(GL)}$.

(4) Where this rule applies, the court will make the orders referred to in paragraphs (2) and (3) unless it considers it unjust to do so.

(Rule 36.12 sets out the latest date when the defendant could have accepted the offer)

(5) In considering whether it would be unjust to make the orders referred to in paragraphs (2) and (3) above, the court will take into account all the circumstances of the case including –

    (a) the terms of any Part 36 offer;

    (b) the stage in the proceedings when any Part 36 offer or Part 36 payment was made;

    (c) the information available to the parties at the time when the Part 36 offer or Part 36 payment was made; and

    (d) the conduct of the parties with regard to the giving or refusing to give information for the purposes of enabling the offer or payment into court to be made or evaluated.

(6) Where the court awards interest under this rule and also awards interest on the same sum and for the same period under any other power, the total rate of interest may not exceed 10% above base rate[GL].

36.22 Interest

(1) Unless –

    (a) a claimant's Part 36 offer which offers to accept a sum of money; or

    (b) a Part 36 payment notice,
         indicates to the contrary, any such offer or payment will be treated as inclusive of all interest until the last date on which it could be accepted without needing the permission of the court.

(2) Where a claimant's Part 36 offer or Part 36 payment notice is expressed not to be inclusive of interest, the offer or notice must state –

    (a) whether interest is offered; and

    (b) if so, the amount offered, the rate or rates offered and the period or periods for which it is offered.

36.23 Deduction of benefits

(1) This rule applies where a payment to a claimant following acceptance of a Part 36 offer or Part 36 payment into court would be a compensation payment as defined in section 1 of the Social Security (Recovery of Benefits) Act 1997[2].

(2) A defendant to a money claim may make an offer to settle the claim which will have the consequences set out in this Part, without making a Part 36 payment if –

    (a) at the time he makes the offer he has applied for, but not received, a certificate of recoverable benefit; and

    (b) he makes a Part 36 payment not more than 7 days after he receives the certificate.

(Section 1 of the 1997 Act defines 'recoverable benefit')

(3) A Part 36 payment notice must state –

    (a) the amount of gross compensation;

    (b) the name and amount of any benefit by which that gross amount is reduced in accordance with section 8 and Schedule 2 to the 1997 Act; and

    (c) that the sum paid in is the net amount after deduction of the amount of benefit.

---

[2] 1997 c.27.

(4) For the purposes of rule 36.20(1)(a), a claimant fails to better a Part 36 payment if he fails to obtain judgment for more than the gross sum specified in the Part 36 payment notice.

(4A) For the purposes of rule 36.20(1)(c), where the court is determining whether the claimant has failed to obtain a judgment which is more advantageous than the Part 36 offer made under rule 36.2A, the amount of any lump sum paid into court which it takes into account is to be the amount of the gross sum specified in the Part 36 payment notice.

(5) Where –

    (a) a Part 36 payment has been made; and

    (b) application is made for the money remaining in court to be paid out,

        the court may treat the money in court as being reduced by a sum equivalent to any further recoverable benefits paid to the claimant since the date of payment into court and may direct payment out accordingly.

PRACTICE DIRECTION

A2–033

OFFERS TO SETTLE AND PAYMENTS INTO COURT

THIS PRACTICE DIRECTION supplements CPR PART 36

PART 36 OFFERS AND PART 36 PAYMENTS

1.1 A written offer to settle a claim[3] or part of a claim or any issue that arises in it made in accordance with the provisions of Part 36 is called:

    (1) if made by way of a payment into court, a Part 36 payment[4], or

    (2) if made otherwise, a Part 36 offer[5] (including an offer under rule 36.2A).

1.2 A Part 36 offer or Part 36 payment has the costs and other consequences set out in rules 36.13, 36.14, 36.20 and 36.21.

---

[3] Includes Part 20 claims.
[4] See rule 36.2(1)(a).
[5] See rule 36.2(1)(b).

1.3 An offer to settle which is not made in accordance with Part 36 will only have the consequences specified in that Part if the court so orders and will be given such weight on any issue as to costs as the court thinks appropriate[6].

PARTIES AND PART 36 OFFERS

2.1 A Part 36 offer, subject to paragraph 3 below, may be made by any party.

2.2 The party making an offer is the 'offeror' and the party to whom it is made is the 'offeree'.

2.3 A Part 36 offer may consist of a proposal to settle for a specified sum or for some other remedy.

2.4 A Part 36 offer is made when received by the offeree[7].

2.5 An improvement to a Part 36 offer is effective when its details are received by the offeree[8].

PARTIES AND PART 36 PAYMENTS

3.1 An offer to settle for a specified sum made by a defendant[9] must, in order to comply with Part 36, be made by way of a Part 36 payment into court[10].

3.2 A Part 36 payment is made when the Part 36 payment notice is served on the claimant[11].

3.3 An increase to a Part 36 payment will be effective when notice of the increase is served on the claimant[12].

(For service of the Part 36 payment notice see rule 36.6(3) and (4).)

3.4 A defendant who wishes to withdraw or reduce a Part 36 payment must obtain the court's permission to do so.

3.5 Permission may be obtained by making an application in accordance with Part 23 stating the reasons giving rise to the wish to withdraw or reduce the Part 36 payment.

---

[6] See rule 36.1(2).
[7] See rule 36.8(1).
[8] See rule 36.8(3).
[9] Includes a respondent to a claim or issue.
[10] See rule 36.3(1).
[11] See rule 36.8(2).
[12] See rule 36.8(4).

MAKING A PART 36 PAYMENT

4.1 Except where paragraph 4.2 applies, to make a Part 36 payment in any court the defendant must –

(1) serve the Part 36 payment notice on the offeree;
(2) file at the court –

(a) a copy of the payment notice; and
(b) a certificate of service confirming service on the offeree; and

(3) send to the Court Funds Office –

(a) the payment, usually a cheque made payable to the Accountant General of the Supreme Court;
(b) a sealed copy of the claim form; and
(c) Court Funds Office form 100.

4.2 A litigant in person without a current account may, in a claim proceeding in a county court or District Registry, make a Part 36 payment by –

(1) lodging the payment in cash with the court;
(2) filing at the court –

(a) the Part 36 payment notice; and
(b) Court Funds Office form 100.

PART 36 OFFERS AND PART 36 PAYMENTS – GENERAL PROVISIONS

5.1 A Part 36 offer or a Part 36 payment notice must:

(1) state that it is a Part 36 offer or that the payment into court is a Part 36 payment, and
(2) be signed by the offeror or his legal representative[13].

5.2 The contents of a Part 36 offer must also comply with the requirements of rule 36.5(3), (5) and (6).
5.3 The contents of a Part 36 payment notice must comply with rule 36.6(2) and, if rule 36.23 applies, with rule 36.23(3).
5.3A The contents of a Part 36 offer to which rule 36.2A applies must comply with the requirements of rule 36.2A(5).
5.4 A Part 36 offer or Part 36 payment will be taken to include interest unless it is expressly stated in the offer or the payment notice that interest is not included, in which case the details set out in rule 36.22(2) must be given.
5.5 Where a Part 36 offer is made by a company or other corporation, a person holding a senior position in the company or corporation

---

[13] For the definition of legal representative see rule 2.3.

may sign the offer on the offeror's behalf, but must state the position he holds.

5.6 Each of the following persons is a person holding a senior position:

(1) in respect of a registered company or corporation, a director, the treasurer, secretary, chief executive, manager or other officer of the company or corporation, and

(2) in respect of a corporation which is not a registered company, in addition to those persons set out in (1), the mayor, chairman, president, town clerk or similar officer of the corporation.

CLARIFICATION OF PART 36 OFFER OR PAYMENT

6.1 An offeree may apply to the court for an order requiring the offeror to clarify the terms of a Part 36 offer or Part 36 payment notice (a clarification order) where the offeror has failed to comply within 7 days with a request for clarification[14].

6.2 An application for a clarification order should be made in accordance with Part 23.

6.3 The application notice should state the respects in which the terms of the Part 36 offer or Part 36 payment notice, as the case may be, are said to need clarification.

ACCEPTANCE OF A PART 36 OFFER OR PAYMENT

7.1 The times for accepting a Part 36 offer or a Part 36 payment are set out in rules 36.11 and 36.12.

7.2 The general rule is that a Part 36 offer or Part 36 payment made more than 21 days before the start of the trial may be accepted within 21 days after it was made without the permission of the court. The costs consequences set out in rules 36.13 and 36.14 will then come into effect.

7.2A Where a Part 36 payment is made as part of a Part 36 offer made under rule 36.2A, the payment is ignored for the purposes of determining the times set out in rules 36.11 and 36.13.

7.3 A Part 36 offer or Part 36 payment made less than 21 days before the start of the trial cannot be accepted without the permission of the court unless the parties agree what the costs consequences of acceptance will be.

7.4 The permission of the court may be sought:

(1) before the start of the trial, by making an application in accordance with Part 23, and

---

[14] See rule 36.9(1) and (2).

(2) after the start of the trial, by making an application to the trial judge.

7.5 If the court gives permission it will make an order dealing with costs and may order that, in the circumstances, the costs consequences set out in rules 36.13 and 36.14 will apply.

7.6 Where a Part 36 offer or Part 36 payment is accepted in accordance with rule 36.11(1) or rule 36.12(1) the notice of acceptance must be sent to the offeror and filed with the court.

7.7 The notice of acceptance:

(1) must set out –

    (a) the claim number, and
    (b) the title of the proceedings,

(2) must identify the Part 36 offer or Part 36 payment notice to which it relates, and

(3) must be signed by the offeree or his legal representative (see paragraphs 5.5 and 5.6 above).

7.8 Where:

(1) the court's approval, or
(2) an order for payment of money out of court, or
(3) an order apportioning money in court –

    (a) between the Fatal Accidents Act 1976 and the Law Reform (Miscellaneous Provisions) Act 1934, or
    (b) between the persons entitled to it under the Fatal Accidents Act 1976, is required for acceptance of a Part 36 offer or Part 36 payment, application for the approval or the order should be made in accordance with Part 23.

7.9 The court will include in any order made under paragraph 7.8 above a direction for;

(1) the payment out of the money in court, and
(2) the payment of interest.

7.10 Unless the parties have agreed otherwise:

(1) interest accruing up to the date of acceptance will be paid to the offeror, and
(2) interest accruing as from the date of acceptance until payment out will be paid to the offeree.

7.11 A claimant may not accept a Part 36 payment or Part 36 offer made under rule 36.2A which is part of a defendant's offer to settle the whole of a claim consisting of both a money and a nonmoney claim unless at the same time he accepts the offer to settle the whole of the claim. Therefore:

(1) if a claimant accepts a Part 36 payment or Part 36 offer made under rule 36.2A which is part of a defendant's offer to settle the whole of the claim, or

(2) if a claimant accepts a Part 36 offer which is part of a defendant's offer to settle the whole of the claim,

the claimant will be deemed to have accepted the offer to settle the whole of the claim[15].

(See paragraph 8 below for the method of obtaining money out of court.)

PAYMENT OUT OF COURT

8.1 To obtain money out of court following acceptance of a Part 36 payment, the claimant should –

(1) file a request for payment in Court Funds Office form 201 with the Court Funds Office; and

(2) file a copy of form 201 at the court.

8.2 he request for payment should contain the following details:

(1) where the party receiving the payment –

(a) is legally represented –
   (i) the name, business address and reference of the legal representative, and
   (ii) the name of the bank and the sort code number, the title of the account and the account number where the payment is to be transmitted, and

(2) where the party is acting in person –

(a) his name and address, and
(b) his bank account details as in (ii) above.

8.3 Where a trial is to take place at a different court to that where the case is proceeding, the claimant must also file notice of request for payment with the court where the trial is to take place.

8.4 Subject to paragraph 8.5(1) and (2), if a party does not wish the payment to be transmitted into his bank account or if he does not have a bank account, he may send a written request to the Accountant-General for the payment to be made to him by cheque.

8.5 Where a party seeking payment out of court has provided the necessary information, the payment:

(1) where a party is legally represented, must be made to the legal representative,

---

[15] See rule 36.4.

(2) if the party is not legally represented but is, or has been, in receipt of legal aid in respect of the proceedings and a notice to that effect has been filed, should be made to the Legal Aid Board by direction of the court,

(3) where a person entitled to money in court dies without having made a will and the court is satisfied –

(a) that no grant of administration of his estate has been made, and

(b) that the assets of his estate, including the money in court, do not exceed in value the amount specified in any order in force under section 6 of the Administration of Estates (Small Payments) Act 1965,

may be ordered to be made to the person appearing to have the prior right to a grant of administration of the estate of the deceased, e.g. a widower, widow, child, father, mother, brother or sister of the deceased.

FOREIGN CURRENCY

9.1 Money may be paid into court in a foreign currency:

(1) where it is a Part 36 payment and the claim is in a foreign currency, or

(2) under a court order.

9.2 The court may direct that the money be placed in an interest bearing account in the currency of the claim or any other currency.

9.3 Where a Part 36 payment is made in a foreign currency and has not been accepted within 21 days, the defendant may apply for an order that the money be placed in an interest bearing account.

9.4 The application should be made in accordance with Part 23 and should state:

(1) that the payment has not been accepted in accordance with rule 36.11, and

(2) the type of currency on which interest is to accrue.

COMPENSATION RECOVERY

10.1 Where a defendant makes a Part 36 payment in respect of a claim for a sum or part of a sum:

(1) which falls under the heads of damage set out in column 1 of Schedule 2 of the Social Security (Recovery of Benefits) Act 1997 in respect of recoverable benefits received by the claimant as set out in column 2 of that Schedule, and

    (2) where the defendant is liable to pay recoverable benefits to the Secretary of State, the defendant should obtain from the Secretary of State a certificate of recoverable benefits and file the certificate with the Part 36 payment notice.

10.2 If a defendant wishes to offer to settle a claim where he has applied for but not yet received a certificate of recoverable benefits, he may, provided that he makes a Part 36 payment not more than 7 days after he has received the certificate, make a Part 36 offer which will have the costs and other consequences set out in rules 36.13 and 36.20.

10.3 The Part 36 payment notice should state in addition to the requirements set out in rule 36.6(2):

    (1) the total amount represented by the Part 36 payment (the gross compensation),

    (2) that the defendant has reduced this sum by £   , in accordance with section 8 of and Schedule 2 to the Social Security (Recovery of Benefits) Act 1997, which was calculated as follows:

        Name of benefit

        Amount

        and

    (3) that the amount paid in, being the sum of £ is the net amount after the deduction of the amount of benefit.

10.4 On acceptance of a Part 36 payment to which this paragraph relates, a claimant will receive the sum in court which will be net of the recoverable benefits.

10.5 In establishing at trial whether a claimant has bettered or obtained a judgment more advantageous than a Part 36 payment to which this paragraph relates, the court will base its decision on the gross sum specified in the Part 36 payment notice.

GENERAL

11.1 Where a party on whom a Part 36 offer, a Part 36 payment notice or a notice of acceptance is to be served is legally represented, the Part 36 offer, Part 36 payment notice and notice of acceptance must be served on the legal representative.

11.2 In a claim arising out of an accident involving a motor vehicle on a road or in a public place:

    (1) where the damages claimed include a sum for hospital expenses, and

    (2) the defendant or his insurer pays that sum to the hospital under section 157 of the Road Traffic Act 1988, the defendant must

give notice of that payment to the court and all the other parties to the proceedings.

11.3 Money paid into court:

(1)   as a Part 36 payment which is not accepted by the claimant, or
(2)   under a court order,

will be placed after 21 days in a basic account[16] (subject to paragraph 11.4 below) for interest to accrue.

11.4 Where money referred to in paragraph 11.3 above is paid in in respect of a child or patient it will be placed in a special investment account[17] for interest to accrue.

(A practice direction supplementing Part 21 contains information about the investment of money in court in respect of a child or patient.)

(Practice directions supplementing Part 40 contain information about adjustment of the judgment sum in respect of recoverable benefits, and about structured settlements.)

(A practice direction supplementing Part 41 contains information about provisional damages awards.)

PERSONAL INJURY CLAIMS FOR FUTURE PECUNIARY LOSS

12.1 A Part 36 offer to settle a claim for damages (whether in the form of a lump sum, periodical payments or both) for personal injury which includes a claim for future pecuniary loss must contain the details of the offer which are set out in rule 36.2A.

12.2 Section 2(4) of the Damages Act 1996 sets out the circumstances in which the continuity of periodical payments will be taken to be secure. Section 2(8) and (9) of the Act deal with the index-linking of periodical payments.

12.3 Except where otherwise stated in this Practice Direction, the rules in Part 36 will apply to offers to settle made under rule 36.2A as they apply to other Part 36 payments and to Part 36 offers.

---

[16] See rule 26 of the Court Funds Office Rules 1987.
[17] See rule 26 as above.

CPR Part 44

A2–034   GENERAL RULES ABOUT COSTS

CONTENTS OF THIS PART

44.1 Scope of this Part

This Part contains general rules about costs and entitlement to costs.

(The definitions contained in Part 43 are relevant to this Part)

44.2 Solicitor's duty to notify client

Where –

(a) the court makes a costs order against a legally represented
    party; and
(b) the party is not present when the order is made,
    the party's solicitor must notify his client in writing of the costs
    order no later than 7 days after the solicitor receives notice of
    the order.

44.3 Court's discretion and circumstances to be taken into account when exercising its discretion as to costs

(1) The court has discretion as to –

    (a)   whether costs are payable by one party to another;
    (b)   the amount of those costs; and
    (c)   when they are to be paid.

(2) If the court decides to make an order about costs –

    (a)   the general rule is that the unsuccessful party will be ordered to pay the costs of the successful party; but
    (b)   the court may make a different order.

(3) The general rule does not apply to the following proceedings –

    (a)   proceedings in the Court of Appeal on an application or appeal made in connection with proceedings in the Family Division; or
    (b)   proceedings in the Court of Appeal from a judgment, direction, decision or order given or made in probate proceedings or family proceedings.

(4) In deciding what order (if any) to make about costs, the court must have regard to all the circumstances, including –

    (a)   the conduct of all the parties;
    (b)   whether a party has succeeded on part of his case, even if he has not been wholly successful; and
    (c)   any payment into court or admissible offer to settle made by a party which is drawn to the court's attention (whether or not made in accordance with Part 36).

(Part 36 contains further provisions about how the court's discretion is to be exercised where a payment into court or an offer to settle is made under that Part)

(5) The conduct of the parties includes –

    (a)   conduct before, as well as during, the proceedings and in particular the extent to which the parties followed any relevant pre-action protocol;
    (b)   whether it was reasonable for a party to raise, pursue or contest a particular allegation or issue;
    (c)   the manner in which a party has pursued or defended his case or a particular allegation or issue; and
    (d)   whether a claimant who has succeeded in his claim, in whole or in part, exaggerated his claim.

(6) The orders which the court may make under this rule include an order that a party must pay –

(a) a proportion of another party's costs;
(b) a stated amount in respect of another party's costs;
(c) costs from or until a certain date only;
(d) costs incurred before proceedings have begun;
(e) costs relating to particular steps taken in the proceedings;
(f) costs relating only to a distinct part of the proceedings; and
(g) interest on costs from or until a certain date, including a date before judgment.

(7) Where the court would otherwise consider making an order under paragraph (6)(f), it must instead, if practicable, make an order under paragraph (6)(a) or (c).
(8) Where the court has ordered a party to pay costs, it may order an amount to be paid on account before the costs are assessed.
(9) Where a party entitled to costs is also liable to pay costs the court may assess the costs which that party is liable to pay and either –

(a) set off the amount assessed against the amount the party is entitled to be paid and direct him to pay any balance; or
(b) delay the issue of a certificate for the costs to which the party is entitled until he has paid the amount which he is liable to pay.

44.3A Costs orders relating to funding arrangements

(1) The court will not assess any additional liability until the conclusion of the proceedings, or the part of the proceedings, to which the funding arrangement relates.

('Funding arrangement' and 'additional liability' are defined in rule 43.2)

(2) At the conclusion of the proceedings, or the part of the proceedings, to which the funding arrangement relates the court may –

(a) make a summary assessment of all the costs, including any additional liability;
(b) make an order for detailed assessment of the additional liability but make a summary assessment of the other costs; or
(c) make an order for detailed assessment of all the costs.

(Part 47 sets out the procedure for the detailed assessment of costs)

44.3B Limits on recovery under funding arrangements

(1) A party may not recover as an additional liability –

(a) any proportion of the percentage increase relating to the cost to the legal representative of the postponement of the payment of his fees and expenses;
(b) any provision made by a membership organisation which exceeds the likely cost to that party of the premium of an

insurance policy against the risk of incurring a liability to pay the costs of other parties to the proceedings;

(c) any additional liability for any period in the proceedings during which he failed to provide information about a funding arrangement in accordance with a rule, practice direction or court order;

(d) any percentage increase where a party has failed to comply with —

(i) a requirement in the costs practice direction; or

(ii) a court order,

to disclose in any assessment proceedings the reasons for setting the percentage increase at the level stated in the conditional fee agreement.

(2) This rule does not apply in an assessment under rule 48.9 (assessment of a solicitor's bill to his client).

(Rule 3.9 sets out the circumstances the court will consider on an application for relief from a sanction for failure to comply with any rule, practice direction or court order)

44.4 Basis of assessment

(1) Where the court is to assess the amount of costs (whether by summary or detailed assessment) it will assess those costs –

(a) on the standard basis; or

(b) on the indemnity basis,
but the court will not in either case allow costs which have been unreasonably incurred or are unreasonable in amount.

(Rule 48.3 sets out how the court decides the amount of costs payable under a contract)

(2) Where the amount of costs is to be assessed on the standard basis, the court will –

(a) only allow costs which are proportionate to the matters in issue; and

(b) resolve any doubt which it may have as to whether costs were reasonably incurred or reasonable and proportionate in amount in favour of the paying party.

(Factors which the court may take into account are set out in rule 44.5)

(3) Where the amount of costs is to be assessed on the indemnity basis, the court will resolve any doubt which it may have as to whether costs were reasonably incurred or were reasonable in amount in favour of the receiving party.

(4) Where –

   (a) the court makes an order about costs without indicating the basis on which the costs are to be assessed; or

   (b) the court makes an order for costs to be assessed on a basis other than the standard basis or the indemnity basis, the costs will be assessed on the standard basis.

(5) Omitted

(6) Where the amount of a solicitor's remuneration in respect of non-contentious business is regulated by any general orders made under the Solicitors Act 1974[1], the amount of the costs to be allowed in respect of any such business which falls to be assessed by the court will be decided in accordance with those general orders rather than this rule and rule 44.5.

44.5 Factors to be taken into account in deciding the amount of costs

(1) The court is to have regard to all the circumstances in deciding whether costs were –

   (a) if it is assessing costs on the standard basis –

      (i) proportionately and reasonably incurred; or
      (ii) were proportionate and reasonable in amount, or

   (b) if it is assessing costs on the indemnity basis –

      (i) unreasonably incurred; or
      (ii) unreasonable in amount.

(2) In particular the court must give effect to any orders which have already been made.

(3) The court must also have regard to –

   (a) the conduct of all the parties, including in particular –

      (i) conduct before, as well as during, the proceedings; and
      (ii) the efforts made, if any, before and during the proceedings in order to try to resolve the dispute;

   (b) the amount or value of any money or property involved;
   (c) the importance of the matter to all the parties;
   (d) the particular complexity of the matter or the difficulty or novelty of the questions raised;
   (e) the skill, effort, specialised knowledge and responsibility involved;
   (f) the time spent on the case; and
   (g) the place where and the circumstances in which work or any part of it was done.

(Rule 35.4(4) gives the court power to limit the amount that a party may recover with regard to the fees and expenses of an expert)

[1] 1974 c.47.

44.6 Fixed costs

A party may recover the fixed costs specified in Part 45 in accordance with that Part.

44.7 Procedure for assessing costs

Where the court orders a party to pay costs to another party (other than fixed costs) it may either –

    (a) make a summary assessment of the costs; or

    (b) order detailed assessment of the costs by a costs officer,
        unless any rule, practice direction or other enactment provides otherwise.

(The costs practice direction sets out the factors which will affect the court's decision under this rule)

44.8 Time for complying with an order for costs

A party must comply with an order for the payment of costs within 14 days of –

    (a) the date of the judgment or order if it states the amount of those costs;

    (b) if the amount of those costs (or part of them) is decided later in accordance with Part 47, the date of the certificate which states the amount; or

    (c) in either case, such later date as the court may specify.

(Part 47 sets out the procedure for detailed assessment of costs)

44.9 Costs on the small claims track and fast track

(1) Part 27 (small claims) and Part 46 (fast track trial costs) contain special rules about –

    (a) liability for costs;

    (b) the amount of costs which the court may award; and

    (c) the procedure for assessing costs.

(2) Once a claim is allocated to a particular track, those special rules shall apply to the period before, as well as after, allocation except where the court or a practice direction provides otherwise.

44.10 Limitation on amount court may allow where a claim allocated to the fast track settles before trial

(1) Where the court –

    (a) assesses costs in relation to a claim which –

        (i) has been allocated to the fast track; and

        (ii) settles before the start of the trial; and

(b) is considering the amount of costs to be allowed in respect of a party's advocate for preparing for the trial,
it may not allow, in respect of those advocate's costs, an amount that exceeds the amount of fast track trial costs which would have been payable in relation to the claim had the trial taken place.

(2) When deciding the amount to be allowed in respect of the advocate's costs, the court shall have regard to –

(a) when the claim was settled; and
(b) when the court was notified that the claim had settled.

(3) In this rule, 'advocate' and 'fast track trial costs' have the meanings given to them by Part 46.

(Part 46 sets out the amount of fast track trial costs which may be awarded)

44.11 Costs following allocation and re-allocation

(1) Any costs orders made before a claim is allocated will not be affected by allocation.
(2) Where –

(a) a claim is allocated to a track; and
(b) the court subsequently re-allocates that claim to a different track,
then unless the court orders otherwise, any special rules about costs applying –

(i) to the first track, will apply to the claim up to the date of re-allocation; and
(ii) to the second track, will apply from the date of re-allocation.

(Part 26 deals with the allocation and re-allocation of claims between tracks)

44.12 Cases where costs orders deemed to have been made

(1) Where a right to costs arises under –

(a) rule 3.7 (defendant's right to costs where claim struck out for non-payment of fees);
(b) rule 36.13(1) (claimant's right to costs where he accepts defendant's Part 36 offer or Part 36 payment);
(c) rule 36.14 (claimant's right to costs where defendant accepts the claimant's Part 36 offer); or
(d) rule 38.6 (defendant's right to costs where claimant discontinues),

a costs order will be deemed to have been made on the standard basis.

(2) Interest payable pursuant to section 17 of the Judgments Act 1838[2] or section 74 of the County Courts Act 1984[3] on the costs deemed to have been ordered under paragraph (1) shall begin to run from the date on which the event which gave rise to the entitlement to costs occurred.

44.12A Costs-only proceedings

(1) This rule sets out a procedure which may be followed where –

    (a) the parties to a dispute have reached an agreement on all issues (including which party is to pay the costs) which is made or confirmed in writing; but

    (b) they have failed to agree the amount of those costs; and

    (c) no proceedings have been started.

(2) Either party to the agreement may start proceedings under this rule by issuing a claim form in accordance with Part 8.

(3) The claim form must contain or be accompanied by the agreement or confirmation.

(4) Except as provided in paragraph (4A), in proceedings to which this rule applies the court –

    (a) may

        (i) make an order for costs to be determined by detailed assessment; or

        (ii) dismiss the claim; and

    (b) must dismiss the claim if it is opposed.

(4A) In proceedings to which Section II of Part 45 applies, the court shall assess the costs in the manner set out in that Section.

(5) Rule 48.3 (amount of costs where costs are payable pursuant to a contract) does not apply to claims started under the procedure in this rule. (Rule 7.2 provides that proceedings are started when the court issues a claim form at the request of the claimant)

(Rule 8.1(6) provides that a practice direction may modify the Part 8 procedure)

44.13 Special situations

(1) Where the court makes an order which does not mention costs –

    (a) subject to paragraphs (1A) and (1B), the general rule is that no party is entitled to costs in relation to that order; but

---

[2] 1838 c.110. Section 17 was amended by S.I. 1998/2940.
[3] 1984 c.28. Section 74 was amended by section 2 of the Private International Law (Miscellaneous Provisions) Act 1995 (c.42).

(b) this does not affect any entitlement of a party to recover costs out of a fund held by him as trustee or personal representative, or pursuant to any lease, mortgage or other security.

(1A) Where the court makes –

(a) an order granting permission to appeal;
(b) an order granting permission to apply for judicial review; or
(c) any other order or direction sought by a party on an application without notice,
and its order does not mention costs, it will be deemed to include an order for applicant's costs in the case.

(1B) Any party affected by a deemed order for costs under paragraph (1A) may apply at any time to vary the order.
(2) The court hearing an appeal may, unless it dismisses the appeal, make orders about the costs of the proceedings giving rise to the appeal as well as the costs of the appeal.
(3) Where proceedings are transferred from one court to another, the court to which they are transferred may deal with all the costs, including the costs before the transfer.
(4) Paragraph (3) is subject to any order of the court which ordered the transfer.

44.14 Court's powers in relation to misconduct

(1) The court may make an order under this rule where –

(a) a party or his legal representative, in connection with a summary or detailed assessment, fails to comply with a rule, practice direction or court order; or
(b) it appears to the court that the conduct of a party or his legal representative, before or during the proceedings which gave rise to the assessment proceedings, was unreasonable or improper.

(2) Where paragraph (1) applies, the court may –

(a) disallow all or part of the costs which are being assessed; or
(b) order the party at fault or his legal representative to pay costs which he has caused any other party to incur.

(3) Where –

(a) the court makes an order under paragraph (2) against a legally represented party; and
(b) the party is not present when the order is made,
the party's solicitor must notify his client in writing of the order no later than 7 days after the solicitor receives notice of the order.

44.15 Providing information about funding arrangements

(1) A party who seeks to recover an additional liability must provide information about the funding arrangement to the court and to other parties as required by a rule, practice direction or court order.

(2) Where the funding arrangement has changed, and the information a party has previously provided in accordance with paragraph (1) is no longer accurate, that party must file notice of the change and serve it on all other parties within 7 days.

(3) Where paragraph (2) applies, and a party has already filed –

    (a)   an allocation questionnaire; or

    (b)   a pre-trial check list (listing questionnaire)

        he must file and serve a new estimate of costs with the notice.

(The costs practice direction sets out –

    •   the information to be provided when a party issues or responds to a claim form, files an allocation questionnaire, a pre-trial check list, and a claim for costs;

    •   the meaning of estimate of costs and the information required in it)

(Rule 44.3B sets out situations where a party will not recover a sum representing any additional liability)

44.16 Adjournment where legal representative seeks to challenge disallowance of any amount of percentage increase

(1) This rule applies where the Conditional Fee Agreements Regulations 2000 or the Collective Conditional Fee Agreements Regulations 2000 continues to apply to an agreement which provides for a success fee.

(2) Where –

    (a)   the court disallows any amount of a legal representative's percentage increase in summary or detailed assessment proceedings; and

    (b)   the legal representative applies for an order that the disallowed amount should continue to be payable by his client,

        the court may adjourn the hearing to allow the client to be –

    (i)   notified of the order sought; and

    (ii) separately represented.

(Regulation 3(2)(b) of the Conditional Fee Agreements Regulations 2000, which applies to Conditional Fee Agreements entered into before 1st November 2005, provides that a conditional fee agreement which provides for a success fee must state that any amount of a percentage increase disallowed on assessment ceases to be payable unless the court is satisfied that it should continue to be so payable. Regulation 5(2)(b) of the Collective Conditional Fee Agreements Regulations 2000, which applies to Collective Conditional Fee Agreements entered into before 1st

November 2005, makes similar provision in relation to collective conditional fee agreements.)

44.17 Application of costs rules

This Part and Part 45 (fixed costs), Part 46 (fast track trial costs), Part 47 (procedure for detailed assessment of costs and default provisions) and Part 48 (special cases), do not apply to the assessment of costs in proceedings to the extent that –

(a) section 11 of the Access to Justice Act 1999, and provisions made under that Act, or

(b) regulations made under the Legal Aid Act 1988[4], make different provision. (The costs practice direction sets out the procedure to be followed where a party was wholly or partially funded by the Legal Services Commission).

CPR Part 52

A2–035   APPEALS

CONTENTS OF THIS PART

---

[4] 1998 c. 34.

III   **Provisions about reopening appeals**
Rule 52.17   Reopening of final appeals

I GENERAL RULES ABOUT APPEALS

52.1 Scope and interpretation

(1) The rules in this Part apply to appeals to –

(a)   the civil division of the Court of Appeal;
(b)   the High Court; and
(c)   a county court.

(2) This Part does not apply to an appeal in detailed assessment proceedings against a decision of an authorised court officer.

(Rules 47.20 to 47.23 deal with appeals against a decision of an authorised court officer in detailed assessment proceedings)

(3) In this Part –

(a)   'appeal' includes an appeal by way of case stated;
(b)   'appeal court' means the court to which an appeal is made;
(c)   'lower court' means the court, tribunal or other person or body from whose decision an appeal is brought;
(d)   'appellant' means a person who brings or seeks to bring an appeal;
(e)   'respondent' means –

   (i)   a person other than the appellant who was a party to the proceedings in the lower court and who is affected by the appeal; and

   (ii)   a person who is permitted by the appeal court to be a party to the appeal; and

(f)   'appeal notice' means an appellant's or respondent's notice.

(4) This Part is subject to any rule, enactment or practice direction which sets out special provisions with regard to any particular category of appeal.

52.2 Parties to comply with the practice direction

All parties to an appeal must comply with the relevant practice direction.

52.3 Permission

(1) An appellant or respondent requires permission to appeal –

(a)   where the appeal is from a decision of a judge in a county court or the High Court, except where the appeal is against –

(i)   a committal order;
(ii) a refusal to grant habeas corpus; or
(iii) a secure accommodation order made under section 25 of
      the Children Act 1989[1]; or

(b) as provided by the relevant practice direction.

(Other enactments may provide that permission is required for particular appeals)

(2) An application for permission to appeal may be made –

(a) to the lower court at the hearing at which the decision to be
     appealed was made; or
(b) to the appeal court in an appeal notice.

(Rule 52.4 sets out the time limits for filing an appellant's notice at the appeal court. Rule 52.5 sets out the time limits for filing a respondent's notice at the appeal court. Any application for permission to appeal to the appeal court must be made in the appeal notice (see rules 52.4(1) and 52.5(3))

(Rule 52.13(1) provides that permission is required from the Court of Appeal for all appeals to that court from a decision of a county court or the High Court which was itself made on appeal)

(3) Where the lower court refuses an application for permission to appeal, a further application for permission to appeal may be made to the appeal court.
(4) Where the appeal court, without a hearing, refuses permission to appeal, the person seeking permission may request the decision to be reconsidered at a hearing.
(5) A request under paragraph (4) must be filed within 7 days after service of the notice that permission has been refused.
(6) Permission to appeal may be given only where –

(a) the court considers that the appeal would have a real prospect
     of success; or
(b) there is some other compelling reason why the appeal should be
     heard.

(7) An order giving permission may –

(a) limit the issues to be heard; and
(b) be made subject to conditions.

(Rule 3.1(3) also provides that the court may make an order subject to conditions)

---

[1] 1989 c.41.

(Rule 25.15 provides for the court to order security for costs of an appeal)

52.4 Appellant's notice

(1) Where the appellant seeks permission from the appeal court it must be requested in the appellant's notice.

(2) The appellant must file the appellant's notice at the appeal court within –

  (a) such period as may be directed by the lower court (which may be longer or shorter than the period referred to in sub-paragraph (b)); or

  (b) where the court makes no such direction, 21 days after the date of the decision of the lower court that the appellant wishes to appeal.

(3) Unless the appeal court orders otherwise, an appellant's notice must be served on each respondent –

  (a) as soon as practicable; and

  (b) in any event not later than 7 days,
       after it is filed.

52.5 Respondent's notice

(1) A respondent may file and serve a respondent's notice.

(2) A respondent who –

  (a) is seeking permission to appeal from the appeal court; or

  (b) wishes to ask the appeal court to uphold the order of the lower court for reasons different from or additional to those given by the lower court,
       must file a respondent's notice.

(3) Where the respondent seeks permission from the appeal court it must be requested in the respondent's notice.

(4) A respondent's notice must be filed within –

  (a) such period as may be directed by the lower court; or

  (b) where the court makes no such direction, 14 days after the date in paragraph (5).

(5) The date referred to in paragraph (4) is –

  (a) the date the respondent is served with the appellant's notice where –

    (i)   permission to appeal was given by the lower court; or
    (ii) permission to appeal is not required;

  (b) the date the respondent is served with notification that the appeal court has given the appellant permission to appeal; or

    (c) the date the respondent is served with notification that the application for permission to appeal and the appeal itself are to be heard together.

(6) Unless the appeal court orders otherwise a respondent's notice must be served on the appellant and any other respondent –

    (a) as soon as practicable; and
    (b) in any event not later than 7 days,
        after it is filed.

52.6 Variation of time

(1) An application to vary the time limit for filing an appeal notice must be made to the appeal court.
(2) The parties may not agree to extend any date or time limit set by –

    (a) these Rules;
    (b) the relevant practice direction; or
    (c) an order of the appeal court or the lower court.

(Rule 3.1(2)(a) provides that the court may extend or shorten the time for compliance with any rule, practice direction or court order (even if an application for extension is made after the time for compliance has expired))

(Rule 3.1(2)(b) provides that the court may adjourn or bring forward a hearing)

52.7 Stay(GL)

Unless –

    (a) the appeal court or the lower court orders otherwise; or
    (b) the appeal is from the Immigration Appeal Tribunal,
        an appeal shall not operate as a stay of any order or decision of the lower court.

52.8 Amendment of appeal notice

An appeal notice may not be amended without the permission of the appeal court.

52.9 Striking out(GL) appeal notices and setting aside or imposing conditions on permission to appeal

(1) The appeal court may –

    (a) strike out the whole or part of an appeal notice;
    (b) set aside (GL) permission to appeal in whole or in part;
    (c) impose or vary conditions upon which an appeal may be brought.

(2) The court will only exercise its powers under paragraph (1) where there is a compelling reason for doing so.
(3) Where a party was present at the hearing at which permission was given he may not subsequently apply for an order that the court exercise its powers under sub-paragraphs (1)(b) or (1)(c).

52.10 Appeal court's powers

(1) In relation to an appeal the appeal court has all the powers of the lower court.

(Rule 52.1(4) provides that this Part is subject to any enactment that sets out special provisions with regard to any particular category of appeal – where such an enactment gives a statutory power to a tribunal, person or other body it may be the case that the appeal court may not exercise that power on an appeal)
(2) The appeal court has power to –

(a) affirm, set aside or vary any order or judgment made or given by the lower court;
(b) refer any claim or issue for determination by the lower court;
(c) order a new trial or hearing;
(d) make orders for the payment of interest;
(e) make a costs order.

(3) In an appeal from a claim tried with a jury the Court of Appeal may, instead of ordering a new trial –

(a) make an order for damages$^{(GL)}$; or
(b) vary an award of damages made by the jury.

(4) The appeal court may exercise its powers in relation to the whole or part of an order of the lower court.

(Part 3 contains general rules about the court's case management powers)

(5) If the appeal court –

(a) refuses an application for permission to appeal;
(b) strikes out an appellant's notice; or
(c) dismisses an appeal,
      and it considers that the application, the appellant's notice or the appeal is totally without merit, the provisions of paragraph (6) must be complied with.

(6) Where paragraph (5) applies –

(a) the court's order must record the fact that it considers the application, the appellant's notice or the appeal to be totally without merit; and

(b) the court must at the same time consider whether it is appro-
     priate to make a civil restraint order.

52.11 Hearing of appeals

(1) Every appeal will be limited to a review of the decision of the lower
court unless –

(a) a practice direction makes different provision for a particular
     category of appeal; or
(b) the court considers that in the circumstances of an individual
     appeal it would be in the interests of justice to hold a re-hearing.

(2) Unless it orders otherwise, the appeal court will not receive –

(a) oral evidence; or
(b) evidence which was not before the lower court.

(3) The appeal court will allow an appeal where the decision of the lower
court was –

(a) wrong; or
(b) unjust because of a serious procedural or other irregularity in
     the proceedings in the lower court.

(4) The appeal court may draw any inference of fact which it considers
justified on the evidence.
(5) At the hearing of the appeal a party may not rely on a matter not
contained in his appeal notice unless the appeal court gives permission.

52.12 Non-disclosure of Part 36 offers and payments

(1) The fact that a Part 36 offer or Part 36 payment has been made must
not be disclosed to any judge of the appeal court who is to hear or
determine –

(a) an application for permission to appeal; or
(b) an appeal,
     until all questions (other than costs) have been determined.

(2) Paragraph (1) does not apply if the Part 36 offer or Part 36 payment is
relevant to the substance of the appeal.
(3) Paragraph (1) does not prevent disclosure in any application in the
appeal proceedings if disclosure of the fact that a Part 36 offer or Part 36
payment has been made is properly relevant to the matter to be decided.

II SPECIAL PROVISIONS APPLYING TO THE COURT OF APPEAL

52.13 Second appeals to the court

(1) Permission is required from the Court of Appeal for any appeal to that court from a decision of a county court or the High Court which was itself made on appeal.
(2) The Court of Appeal will not give permission unless it considers that –

  (a) the appeal would raise an important point of principle or practice; or
  (b) there is some other compelling reason for the Court of Appeal to hear it.

52.14 Assignment of appeals to the Court of Appeal

(1) Where the court from or to which an appeal is made or from which permission to appeal is sought ('the relevant court') considers that –

  (a) an appeal which is to be heard by a county court or the High Court would raise an important point of principle or practice; or
  (b) there is some other compelling reason for the Court of Appeal to hear it,
       the relevant court may order the appeal to be transferred to the Court of Appeal.

(The Master of the Rolls has the power to direct that an appeal which would be heard by a county court or the High Court should be heard instead by the Court of Appeal – see section 57 of the Access to Justice Act 1999)[2]

(2) The Master of the Rolls or the Court of Appeal may remit an appeal to the court in which the original appeal was or would have been brought.

52.15 Judicial review appeals

(1) Where permission to apply for judicial review has been refused at a hearing in the High Court, the person seeking that permission may apply to the Court of Appeal for permission to appeal.
(2) An application in accordance with paragraph (1) must be made within 7 days of the decision of the High Court to refuse to give permission to apply for judicial review.
(3) On an application under paragraph (1), the Court of Appeal may, instead of giving permission to appeal, give permission to apply for judicial review.

---

[2] 1999 c.22.

(4) Where the Court of Appeal gives permission to apply for judicial review in accordance with paragraph (3), the case will proceed in the High Court unless the Court of Appeal orders otherwise.

52.16 Who may exercise the powers of the Court of Appeal

(1) A court officer assigned to the Civil Appeals Office who is –

    (a)   a barrister; or

    (b)   a solicitor

        may exercise the jurisdiction of the Court of Appeal with regard to the matters set out in paragraph (2) with the consent of the Master of the Rolls.

(2) The matters referred to in paragraph (1) are –

    (a)   any matter incidental to any proceedings in the Court of Appeal;

    (b)   any other matter where there is no substantial dispute between the parties; and

    (c)   the dismissal of an appeal or application where a party has failed to comply with any order, rule or practice direction.

(3) A court officer may not decide an application for –

    (a)   permission to appeal;

    (b)   bail pending an appeal;

    (c)   an injunction$^{(GL)}$;

    (d)   a stay$^{(GL)}$ of any proceedings, other than a temporary stay of any order or decision of the lower court over a period when the Court of Appeal is not sitting or cannot conveniently be convened.

(4) Decisions of a court officer may be made without a hearing.

(5) A party may request any decision of a court officer to be reviewed by the Court of Appeal.

(6) At the request of a party, a hearing will be held to reconsider a decision of –

    (a)   a single judge; or

    (b)   a court officer,

        made without a hearing.

(6A) A request under paragraph (5) or (6) must be filed within 7 days after the party is served with notice of the decision.

(7) A single judge may refer any matter for a decision by a court consisting of two or more judges.

(Section 54(6) of the Supreme Court Act 1981[3] provides that there is no appeal from the decision of a single judge on an application for permission to appeal)

(Section 58(2) of the Supreme Court Act 1981[4] provides that there is no appeal to the House of Lords from decisions of the Court of Appeal that –

(a) are taken by a single judge or any officer or member of staff of that court in proceedings incidental to any cause or matter pending before the civil division of that court; and

(b) do not involve the determination of an appeal or of an application for permission to appeal,
and which may be called into question by rules of court. Rules 52.16(5) and (6) provide the procedure for the calling into question of such decisions)

III PROVISIONS ABOUT REOPENING APPEALS

52.17 Reopening of final appeals

(1) The Court of Appeal or the High Court will not reopen a final determination of any appeal unless –

(a) it is necessary to do so in order to avoid real injustice;
(b) the circumstances are exceptional and make it appropriate to reopen the appeal; and
(c) there is no alternative effective remedy.

(2) In paragraphs (1), (3), (4) and (6), "appeal" includes an application for permission to appeal.

(3) This rule does not apply to appeals to a county court.

(4) Permission is needed to make an application under this rule to reopen a final determination of an appeal even in cases where under rule 52.3(1) permission was not needed for the original appeal.

(5) There is no right to an oral hearing of an application for permission unless, exceptionally, the judge so directs.

(6) The judge will not grant permission without directing the application to be served on the other party to the original appeal and giving him an opportunity to make representations.

(7) There is no right of appeal or review from the decision of the judge on the application for permission, which is final.

(8) The procedure for making an application for permission is set out in the practice direction.

[3] 1981 c.54; section 54 was amended by section 59 of the Access to Justice Act 1999 (c.22).
[4] 1981 c.54; section 58 was amended by section 60 of the Access to Justice Act 1999 (c.22).

PRACTICE DIRECTION

APPEALS

THIS PRACTICE DIRECTION SUPPLEMENTS PART 52

CONTENTS OF THIS PRACTICE DIRECTION

1.1 This Practice Direction is divided into four sections:

- Section I – General provisions about appeals
- Section II – General provisions about statutory appeals and appeals by way of case stated
- Section III – Provisions about specific appeals
- Section IV – Provisions about reopening appeals

SECTION I – GENERAL PROVISIONS ABOUT APPEALS

2.1 This practice direction applies to all appeals to which Part 52 applies except where specific provision is made for appeals to the Court of Appeal.

2.2 For the purpose only of appeals to the Court of Appeal from cases in family proceedings this Practice Direction will apply with such modifications as may be required.

ROUTES OF APPEAL

2A.1 The court or judge to which an appeal is to be made (subject to obtaining any necessary permission) is set out in the tables below:

Table 1[1] addresses appeals in cases other than insolvency proceedings and those cases to which Table 3 applies;
Table 2 addresses insolvency proceedings; and
Table 3 addresses certain family cases to which CPR Part 52 may apply.
The tables do not include so-called 'leap frog' appeals either to the Court of Appeal pursuant to s. 57 of the Access to Justice Act 1999 or to the House of Lords pursuant to s 13 of the Administration of Justice Act 1969.

---

[1] Reproduced with the kind permission of Tottel Publishing, publisher of *Manual of Civil Appeals*.

(An interactive routes of appeal guide can be found on the Court of Appeal's website at http://www.hmcourts-service.gov.uk/infoabout/ coa_civil/routes_app/index.htm)

TABLE 1

In this Table references to a 'Circuit judge' include a recorder or a district judge who is exercising the jurisdiction of a circuit judge with the permission of the designated civil judge in respect of that case (see: Practice Direction 2B, paragraph 11.1(d)).

For the meaning of 'final decision' for the purposes of this table see paragraphs 2A.2 and 2A.3 below.

Court	Track/nature of claim	Judge who made decision	Nature of decision under appeal	Apeal Court
County	Unallocated	District judge	Any	Circuit judge in county court
	Small			
	Fast			
County	CPR Pt 8 (if not allocated to any track or if simply treated as allocated to the multi-track under CPR 8.9(c))	District judge	Final	Circuit judge in county court
County	Multi-track	District judge	Any decision other than a final decision	Circuit judge in county court
County	Multi-track	District judge	Final decision	Court of Appeal
County	Specialist Proceedings (under the Companies Acts 1985 or 1989 or to which sections I, II or III of Part 57 or any of Parts 59, 60, 62 or 63 apply)	District judge	Any decision other than a final decision	Circuit judge in county court
County	Specialist Proceedings (under the Companies Acts 1985 or 1989 or to which sections I, II or III Part 57 or any of Parts 59, 60, 62 or 63 apply)	District judge	Final decision	Court of Appeal
County	Unallocated	Circuit judge	Any (except final decision in specialist proceedings; see below)	Single judge of the High Court
	Small			

APPENDIX II

Court	Track/nature of claim	Judge who made decision	Nature of decision under appeal	Appeal Court
	Fast			
County	Multi-track	Circuit judge	Any decision other than a final decision	Single judge of the High Court
County	CPR Pt 8 (if not allocated to any track or if simply treated as allocated to the multi-track under CPR 8.9(c))	Circuit judge	Final	Single judge of the High Court
County	Specialist Proceedings (under the Companies Acts 1985 or 1989 or to which sections I, II or III of Part 57 or any of Parts 59, 60, 62 or 63 apply)	Circuit judge	Final	Court of Appeal
County	Multi-track	Circuit judge	Final decision	Court of Appeal
High Court	Multi-track	Master or district judge sitting in a District Registry	Any decision other than a final decision	Single judge of the High Court
High Court	CPR Pt 8 (if not allocated to any track or if simply treated as allocated to the multi-track under CPR 8.9(c))	Master or district judge sitting in a District Registry	Final	Single judge of the High Court
High Court	Multi-track	Master or district judge sitting in a District Registry	Final	Court of Appeal
High Court	Specialist Proceedings (under the Companies Acts 1985 or 1989 or to which sections I, II or III of Part 57 or any of Parts 58 to 63 apply)	Master or district judge sitting in a District Registry	Any decision other than a final decision	High Court
High Court	Specialist Proceedings (under the Companies Acts 1985 or 1989 or to which sections I, II or III of Part 57 or any of Parts 58 to 63 apply)	Master or district judge sitting in a District Registry	Final decision	Court of Appeal
High Court	Any	High Court judge	Any	Court of Appeal

TABLE 2

Insolvency proceedings Circuit

In this Table references to a 'Circuit judge' include a recorder or a district judge who is exercising the jurisdiction of a circuit judge with the permission of the designated civil judge in respect of that case (see: Practice Direction 2B, paragraph 11.1(d)).

Court	Track/nature of claim	Judge who made decision	Nature of decision under appeal	Apeal Court
County	Insolvency	District judge or circuit judge	Any	Single judge of the High Court
High Court	Insolvency	Registrar	Any	Single judge of the High Court
High Court	Insolvency	High Court judge	Any	Court of Appeal

TABLE 3

Proceedings which may be heard in the Family Division of the High Court and to which the CPR may apply. Appeal Centres

The proceedings to which this table will apply include proceedings under the Inheritance (Provision for Family and Dependants) Act 1975 and proceedings under the Trusts of Land and Appointment of Trustees Act 1996.

For the meaning of 'final decision' for the purposes of this table see paragraphs 2A.2 and 2A.3 below.

Court	Judge who made decision	Track/nature of claim	Nature of decision under appeal	Apeal Court
High Court Principal Registry of the Family Division	District judge	Proceedings under CPR Pt 8 (if not allocated to any track or if simply treated as allocated to the multi-track under CPR 8.9(c))	Any decision	High Court judge of the Family Division
High Court Principal Registry of the Family Division	District judge	Proceedings under CPR Pt 8 specifically allocated to the multi-track by an order of the court.	Any decision	High Court judge of the Family Division
High Court Principal Registry of the Family Division	District judge	Proceedings under CPR Part 7	Any decision other than a final decision	High Court judge of the Family Division

Court	Judge who made decision	Track/nature of claim	Nature of decision under appeal	Apeal Court
High Court Principal Registry of the Family Division	District judge	Proceedings under CPR Part 7 and allocated to the multi-track	Final decision	Court of Appeal
High Court Family Division	High Court Judge	Proceedings under CPR Part 7 or 8	Any	Court of Appeal

2A.2 A 'final decision' is a decision of a court that would finally determine (subject to any possible appeal or detailed assessment of costs) the entire proceedings whichever way the court decided the issues before it. Decisions made on an application to strike-out or for summary judgment are not final decisions for the purpose of determining the appropriate route of appeal (Art. 1 Access to Justice Act 1999 (Destination of Appeals) Order 2000). Accordingly:

(1) a case management decision;
(2) the grant or refusal of interim relief;
(3) a summary judgment;
(4) a striking out,
are not final decisions for this purpose.

2A.3 A decision of a court is to be treated as a final decision for routes of appeal purposes where it:

(1) is made at the conclusion of part of a hearing or trial which has been split into parts; and
(2) would, if it had been made at the conclusion of that hearing or trial, have been a final decision.
Accordingly, a judgment on liability at the end of a split trial is a 'final decision' for this purpose and the judgment at the conclusion of the assessment of damages following a judgment on liability is also a 'final decision' for this purpose.

2A.4 An order made:

(1) on a summary or detailed assessment of costs; or
(2) on an application to enforce a final decision,
is not a 'final decision' and any appeal from such an order will follow the routes of appeal set out in the tables above.

(Section 16(1) of the Supreme Court Act 1981 (as amended); section 77(1) of the County Courts Act 1984 (as amended); and the Access to Justice Act 1999 (Destination of Appeals) Order 2000 set out the provisions governing routes of appeal).

2A.5

(1) Where an applicant attempts to file an appellant's notice and the appeal court does not have jurisdiction to issue the notice, a court officer may notify the applicant in writing that the appeal court does not have jurisdiction in respect of the notice.

(2) Before notifying a person under paragraph (1) the court officer must confer –

    (a) with a judge of the appeal court; or,

    (b) where the Court of Appeal, Civil Division is the appeal court, with a court officer who exercises the jurisdiction of that Court under rule 52.16.

(3) Where a court officer in the Court of Appeal, Civil Division notifies a person under paragraph (1), rule 52.16(5) shall not apply.

GROUNDS FOR APPEAL

3.1 Rule 52.11(3) (a) and (b) sets out the circumstances in which the appeal court will allow an appeal.

3.2 The grounds of appeal should –

(1) set out clearly the reasons why rule 52.11(3)(a) or (b) is said to apply; and

(2) specify, in respect of each ground, whether the ground raises an appeal on a point of law or is an appeal against a finding of fact.

PERMISSION TO APPEAL

4.1 Rule 52.3 sets out the circumstances when permission to appeal is required.

4.2 The permission of –

(1) the Court of Appeal; or

(2) where the lower court's rules allow, the lower court, is required for all appeals to the Court of Appeal except as provided for by statute or rule 52.3.

(The requirement of permission to appeal may be imposed by a practice direction – see rule 52.3(b))

4.3 Where the lower court is not required to give permission to appeal, it may give an indication of its opinion as to whether permission should be given.

(Rule 52.1(3)(c) defines 'lower court')

4.3A

   (1) This paragraph applies where a party applies for permission to appeal against a decision at the hearing at which the decision was made.

   (2) Where this paragraph applies, the judge making the decision shall state –

       (a) whether or not the judgment or order is final;

       (b) whether an appeal lies from the judgment or order and, if so, to which appeal court;

       (c) whether the court gives permission to appeal; and

       (d) if not, the appropriate appeal court to which any further application for permission may be made.

(Rule 40.2(4) contains requirements as to the contents of the judgment or order in these circumstances.)

4.3B Where no application for permission to appeal has been made in accordance with rule 52.3(2)(a) but a party requests further time to make such an application, the court may adjourn the hearing to give that party the opportunity to do so.

Appeals from case management decisions

4.4 Case management decisions include decisions made under rule 3.1(2) and decisions about:

   (1) disclosure

   (2) filing of witness statements or experts reports

   (3) directions about the timetable of the claim

   (4) adding a party to a claim

   (5) security for costs.

4.5 Where the application is for permission to appeal from a case management decision, the court dealing with the application may take into account whether:

   (1) the issue is of sufficient significance to justify the costs of an appeal;

   (2) the procedural consequences of an appeal (e.g. loss of trial date) outweigh the significance of the case management decision;

   (3) it would be more convenient to determine the issue at or after trial.

Court to which permission to appeal application should be made

4.6 An application for permission should be made orally at the hearing at which the decision to be appealed against is made.

4.7 Where:

       (a) no application for permission to appeal is made at the hearing; or

(b) the lower court refuses permission to appeal,
an application for permission to appeal may be made to the appeal court in accordance with rules 52.3(2) and (3).

4.8 There is no appeal from a decision of the appeal court to allow or refuse permission to appeal to that court (although where the appeal court, without a hearing, refuses permission to appeal, the person seeking permission may request that decision to be reconsidered at a hearing). See section 54(4) of the Access to Justice Act and rule 52.3(2), (3), (4) and (5).

Second appeals

4.9 An application for permission to appeal from a decision of the High Court or a county court which was itself made on appeal must be made to the Court of Appeal.
4.10 If permission to appeal is granted the appeal will be heard by the Court of Appeal.

Consideration of Permission without a hearing

4.11 Applications for permission to appeal may be considered by the appeal court without a hearing.
4.12 If permission is granted without a hearing the parties will be notified of that decision and the procedure in paragraphs 6.1 to 6.6 will then apply.
4.13 If permission is refused without a hearing the parties will be notified of that decision with the reasons for it. The decision is subject to the appellant's right to have it reconsidered at an oral hearing. This may be before the same judge.
4.14 A request for the decision to be reconsidered at an oral hearing must be filed at the appeal court within 7 days after service of the notice that permission has been refused. A copy of the request must be served by the appellant on the respondent at the same time.

Permission hearing

4.14A

(1) This paragraph applies where an appellant, who is represented, makes a request for a decision to be reconsidered at an oral hearing.
(2) The appellant's advocate must, at least 4 days before the hearing, in a brief written statement –

    (a) inform the court and the respondent of the points which he proposes to raise at the hearing;
    (b) set out his reasons why permission should be granted notwithstanding the reasons given for the refusal of permission; and
    (c) confirm, where applicable, that the requirements of paragraph 4.17 have been complied with (appellant in receipt of services funded by the Legal Services Commission).

4.15 Notice of a permission hearing will be given to the respondent but he is not required to attend unless the court requests him to do so.

4.16 If the court requests the respondent's attendance at the permission hearing, the appellant must supply the respondent with a copy of the appeal bundle (see paragraph 5.6A) within 7 days of being notified of the request, or such other period as the court may direct. The costs of providing that bundle shall be borne by the appellant initially, but will form part of the costs of the permission application.

Appellants in receipt of services funded by the Legal Services Commission applying for permission to appeal

4.17 Where the appellant is in receipt of services funded by the Legal Services Commission (or legally aided) and permission to appeal has been refused by the appeal court without a hearing, the appellant must send a copy of the reasons the appeal court gave for refusing permission to the relevant office of the Legal Services Commission as soon as it has been received from the court. The court will require confirmation that this has been done if a hearing is requested to re-consider the question of permission.

Limited permission

4.18 Where a court under rule 52.3(7) gives permission to appeal on some issues only, it will –

   (1)   refuse permission on any remaining issues; or
   (2)   reserve the question of permission to appeal on any remaining issues to the court hearing the appeal.

4.19 If the court reserves the question of permission under paragraph 4.18(2), the appellant must, within 14 days after service of the court's order, inform the appeal court and the respondent in writing whether he intends to pursue the reserved issues. If the appellant does intend to pursue the reserved issues, the parties must include in any time estimate for the appeal hearing, their time estimate for the reserved issues.

4.20 If the appeal court refuses permission to appeal on the remaining issues without a hearing and the applicant wishes to have that decision reconsidered at an oral hearing, the time limit in rule 52.3(5) shall apply. Any application for an extension of this time limit should be made promptly. The court hearing the appeal on the issues for which permission has been granted will not normally grant, at the appeal hearing, an application to extend the time limit in rule 52.3(5) for the remaining issues.

4.21 If the appeal court refuses permission to appeal on remaining issues at or after an oral hearing, the application for permission to appeal on those issues cannot be renewed at the appeal hearing. See section 54(4) of the Access to Justice Act 1999.

Respondents' costs of permission applications

4.22 In most cases, applications for permission to appeal will be determined without the court requesting –

    (1) submissions from, or
    (2) if there is an oral hearing, attendance by
        the respondent.

4.23 Where the court does not request submissions from or attendance
by the respondent, costs will not normally be allowed to a respondent who volunteers submissions or attendance.

4.24 Where the court does request –

    (1) submissions from; or
    (2) attendance by the respondent,
        the court will normally allow the respondent his costs if per-
        mission is refused.

APPELLANT'S NOTICE

5.1 An appellant's notice must be filed and served in all cases. Where an
application for permission to appeal is made to the appeal court it
must be applied for in the appellant's notice.

Human Rights

5.1A

    (1) This paragraph applies where the appellant seeks –

        (a) to rely on any issue under the Human Rights Act 1998; or
        (b) a remedy available under that Act,

        for the first time in an appeal.
    (2) The appellant must include in his appeal notice the information
        required by paragraph 15.1 of the practice direction supple-
        menting Part 16.
    (3) Paragraph 15.2 of the practice direction supplementing Part 16
        applies as if references to a statement of case were to the appeal
        notice.

5.1B CPR rule 19.4A and the practice direction supplementing it shall
apply as if references to the case management conference were to
the application for permission to appeal.

(The practice direction to Part 19 provides for notice to be given and parties joined in certain circumstances to which this paragraph applies)

Extension of time for filing appellant's notice

5.2 Where the time for filing an appellant's notice has expired, the appellant must –

    (a) file the appellant's notice; and
    (b) include in that appellant's notice an application for an extension of time.

The appellant's notice should state the reason for the delay and the steps taken prior to the application being made.

5.3 Where the appellant's notice includes an application for an extension of time and permission to appeal has been given or is not required the respondent has the right to be heard on that application. He must be served with a copy of the appeal bundle (see paragraph 5.6A). However, a respondent who unreasonably opposes an extension of time runs the risk of being ordered to pay the appellant's costs of that application.

5.4 If an extension of time is given following such an application the procedure at paragraphs 6.1 to 6.6 applies.

Applications

5.5 Notice of an application to be made to the appeal court for a remedy incidental to the appeal (e.g. an interim remedy under rule 25.1 or an order for security for costs) may be included in the appeal notice or in a Part 23 application notice.

(Rule 25.15 deals with security for costs of an appeal)

(Paragraph 11 of this practice direction contains other provisions relating to applications)

Documents

5.6

    (1) This paragraph applies to every case except where the appeal –

        (a) relates to a claim allocated to the small claims track; and
        (b) is being heard in a county court or the High Court.

    (Paragraph 5.8 applies where this paragraph does not apply)

    (2) The appellant must file the following documents together with an appeal bundle (see paragraph 5.6A) with his appellant's notice –

        (a) two additional copies of the appellant's notice for the appeal court; and

(b) one copy of the appellant's notice for each of the respondents;

(c) one copy of his skeleton argument for each copy of the appellant's notice that is filed (see paragraph 5.9);

(d) a sealed copy of the order being appealed;

(e) a copy of any order giving or refusing permission to appeal, together with a copy of the judge's reasons for allowing or refusing permission to appeal;

(f) any witness statements or affidavits in support of any application included in the appellant's notice.

(g) a copy of the order allocating a case to a track (if any).

5.6A

(1) An appellant must include in his appeal bundle the following documents:

(a) a sealed copy of the appellant's notice;

(b) a sealed copy of the order being appealed;

(c) a copy of any order giving or refusing permission to appeal, together with a copy of the judge's reasons for allowing or refusing permission to appeal;

(d) any affidavit or witness statement filed in support of any application included in the appellant's notice;

(e) a copy of his skeleton argument;

(f) a transcript or note of judgment (see paragraph 5.12), and in cases where permission to appeal was given by the lower court or is not required those parts of any transcript of evidence which are directly relevant to any question at issue on the appeal;

(g) the claim form and statements of case (where relevant to the subject of the appeal);

(h) any application notice (or case management documentation) relevant to the subject of the appeal;

(i) in cases where the decision appealed was itself made on appeal (eg from district judge to circuit judge), the first order, the reasons given and the appellant's notice used to appeal from that order;

(j) in the case of judicial review or a statutory appeal, the original decision which was the subject of the application to the lower court;

(k) in cases where the appeal is from a Tribunal, a copy of the Tribunal's reasons for the decision, a copy of the decision reviewed by the Tribunal and the reasons for the original decision and any document filed with the Tribunal setting out the grounds of appeal from that decision;

(l) any other documents which the appellant reasonably considers necessary to enable the appeal court to reach its decision on the hearing of the application or appeal; and

(m) such other documents as the court may direct.

    (2) All documents that are extraneous to the issues to be considered on the application or the appeal must be excluded. The appeal bundle may include affidavits, witness statements, summaries, experts' reports and exhibits but only where these are directly relevant to the subject matter of the appeal.

    (3) Where the appellant is represented, the appeal bundle must contain a certificate signed by his solicitor, counsel or other representative to the effect that he has read and understood paragraph (2) above and that the composition of the appeal bundle complies with it.

5.7 Where it is not possible to file all the above documents, the appellant must indicate which documents have not yet been filed and the reasons why they are not currently available. The appellant must then provide a reasonable estimate of when the missing document or documents can be filed and file them as soon as reasonably practicable.

Small claims

5.8

    (1) This paragraph applies where –

        (a) the appeal relates to a claim allocated to the small claims track; and

        (b) the appeal is being heard in a county court or the High Court.

    (1A) An appellant's notice must be filed and served in Form N164.

    (2) The appellant must file the following documents with his appellant's notice –

        (a) a sealed copy of the order being appealed; and

        (b) any order giving or refusing permission to appeal, together with a copy of the reasons for that decision.

    (3) The appellant may, if relevant to the issues to be determined on the appeal, file any other document listed in paragraph 5.6 or 5.6A in addition to the documents referred to in sub paragraph (2).

    (4) The appellant need not file a record of the reasons for judgment of the lower court with his appellant's notice unless sub-paragraph (5) applies.

    (5) The court may order a suitable record of the reasons for judgment of the lower court (see paragraph 5.12) to be filed –

        (a) to enable it to decide if permission should be granted; or

        (b) if permission is granted to enable it to decide the appeal.

Skeleton arguments

5.9

(1) The appellant's notice must, subject to (2) and (3) below, be accompanied by a skeleton argument. Alternatively the skeleton argument may be included in the appellant's notice. Where the skeleton argument is so included it will not form part of the notice for the purposes of rule 52.8.

(2) Where it is impracticable for the appellant's skeleton argument to accompany the appellant's notice it must be filed and served on all respondents within 14 days of filing the notice.

(3) An appellant who is not represented need not file a skeleton argument but is encouraged to do so since this will be helpful to the court.

Content of skeleton arguments

5.10

(1) A skeleton argument must contain a numbered list of the points which the party wishes to make. These should both define and confine the areas of controversy. Each point should be stated as concisely as the nature of the case allows.

(2) A numbered point must be followed by a reference to any document on which the party wishes to rely.

(3) A skeleton argument must state, in respect of each authority cited –

(a) the proposition of law that the authority demonstrates; and

(b) the parts of the authority (identified by page or paragraph references) that support the proposition.

(4) If more than one authority is cited in support of a given proposition, the skeleton argument must briefly state the reason for taking that course.

(5) The statement referred to in sub-paragraph (4) should not materially add to the length of the skeleton argument but should be sufficient to demonstrate, in the context of the argument –

(a) the relevance of the authority or authorities to that argument; and

(b) that the citation is necessary for a proper presentation of that argument.

(6) The cost of preparing a skeleton argument which –

(a) does not comply with the requirements set out in this paragraph; or

(b) was not filed within the time limits provided by this Practice Direction (or any further time granted by the court),

will not be allowed on assessment except to the extent that the court otherwise directs.

5.11 The appellant should consider what other information the appeal court will need. This may include a list of persons who feature in the case or glossaries of technical terms. A chronology of relevant events will be necessary in most appeals.

Suitable record of the judgment

5.12 Where the judgment to be appealed has been officially recorded by the court, an approved transcript of that record should accompany the appellant's notice. Photocopies will not be accepted for this purpose. However, where there is no officially recorded judgment, the following documents will be acceptable:

Written judgments
  (1) Where the judgment was made in writing a copy of that judgment endorsed with the judge's signature.
  Note of judgment
  (2) When judgment was not officially recorded or made in writing a note of the judgment (agreed between the appellant's and respondent's advocates) should be submitted for approval to the judge whose decision is being appealed. If the parties cannot agree on a single note of the judgment, both versions should be provided to that judge with an explanatory letter. For the purpose of an application for permission to appeal the note need not be approved by the respondent or the lower court judge.

  Advocates' notes of judgments where the appellant is unrepresented
  (3) When the appellant was unrepresented in the lower court it is the duty of any advocate for the respondent to make his/her note of judgment promptly available, free of charge to the appellant where there is no officially recorded judgment or if the court so directs. Where the appellant was represented in the lower court it is the duty of his/her own former advocate to make his/her note available in these circumstances. The appellant should submit the note of judgment to the appeal court.

  Reasons for Judgment in Tribunal cases
  (4) A sealed copy of the Tribunal's reasons for the decision.

5.13 An appellant may not be able to obtain an official transcript or other suitable record of the lower court's decision within the time within which the appellant's notice must be filed. In such cases the appellant's notice must still be completed to the best of the appellant's ability on the basis of the documentation available. However it may be amended subsequently with the permission of the appeal court.

Advocates' notes of judgments

5.14 Advocates' brief (or, where appropriate, refresher) fee includes:

(1) remuneration for taking a note of the judgment of the court;
(2) having the note transcribed accurately;
(3) attempting to agree the note with the other side if represented;
(4) submitting the note to the judge for approval where appropriate;
(5) revising it if so requested by the judge,
(6) providing any copies required for the appeal court, instructing solicitors and lay client; and
(7) providing a copy of his note to an unrepresented appellant.

Transcripts or Notes of Evidence

5.15 When the evidence is relevant to the appeal an official transcript of the relevant evidence must be obtained. Transcripts or notes of evidence are generally not needed for the purpose of determining an application for permission to appeal.

Notes of evidence

5.16 If evidence relevant to the appeal was not officially recorded, a typed version of the judge's notes of evidence must be obtained.

Transcripts at public expense

5.17 Where the lower court or the appeal court is satisfied that –

(1) an unrepresented appellant; or
(2) an appellant whose legal representation is provided free of charge to the appellant and not funded by the Community Legal Service;
is in such poor financial circumstances that the cost of a transcript would be an excessive burden the court may certify that the cost of obtaining one official transcript should be borne at public expense.

5.18 In the case of a request for an official transcript of evidence or proceedings to be paid for at public expense, the court must also be satisfied that there are reasonable grounds for appeal. Whenever possible a request for a transcript at public expense should be made to the lower court when asking for permission to appeal.

Filing and service of appellant's notice

5.19 Rule 52.4 sets out the procedure and time limits for filing and serving an appellant's notice. The appellant must file the appellant's notice at the appeal court within such period as may be directed by the lower court which should not normally exceed 28 days or, where the lower court directs no such period, within 14 days of the date of the decision that the appellant wishes to appeal.

(Rule 52.15 sets out the time limit for filing an application for permission to appeal against the refusal of the High Court to grant permission to apply for judicial review)

5.20 Where the lower court judge announces his decision and reserves the reasons for his judgment or order until a later date, he should, in the exercise of powers under rule 52.4(2)(a), fix a period for filing the appellant's notice at the appeal court that takes this into account.

5.21

   (1) Except where the appeal court orders otherwise a sealed copy of the appellant's notice, including any skeleton arguments must be served on all respondents in accordance with the timetable prescribed by rule 52.4(3) except where this requirement is modified by paragraph 5.9(2) in which case the skeleton argument should be served as soon as it is filed.

   (2) The appellant must, as soon as practicable, file a certificate of service of the documents referred to in paragraph (1).

5.22 Unless the court otherwise directs a respondent need not take any action when served with an appellant's notice until such time as notification is given to him that permission to appeal has been given.

5.23 The court may dispense with the requirement for service of the notice on a respondent. Any application notice seeking an order under rule 6.9 to dispense with service should set out the reasons relied on and be verified by a statement of truth.

5.24

   (1) Where the appellant is applying for permission to appeal in his appellant's notice, he must serve on the respondents his appellant's notice and skeleton argument (but not the appeal bundle), unless the appeal court directs otherwise.

   (2) Where permission to appeal –

      (a)   has been given by the lower court; or

      (b)   is not required,

   the appellant must serve the appeal bundle on the respondents with the appellant's notice.

Amendment of Appeal Notice

5.25 An appeal notice may be amended with permission. Such an application to amend and any application in opposition will normally be dealt with at the hearing unless that course would cause unnecessary expense or delay in which case a request should be made for the application to amend to be heard in advance.

PROCEDURE AFTER PERMISSION IS OBTAINED

6.1 This paragraph sets out the procedure where:

(1) permission to appeal is given by the appeal court; or

(2) the appellant's notice is filed in the appeal court and –

   (a) permission was given by the lower court; or

   (b) permission is not required.

6.2 If the appeal court gives permission to appeal, the appeal bundle must be served on each of the respondents within 7 days of receiving the order giving permission to appeal.

(Part 6 (service of documents) provides rules on service)

6.3 The appeal court will send the parties –

   (1) notification of –

      (a) the date of the hearing or the period of time (the 'listing window') during which the appeal is likely to be heard; and

      (b) in the Court of Appeal, the date by which the appeal will be heard (the 'hear by date');

   (2) where permission is granted by the appeal court a copy of the order giving permission to appeal; and

   (3) any other directions given by the court.

6.3A

   (1) Where the appeal court grants permission to appeal, the appellant must add the following documents to the appeal bundle –

      (a) the respondent's notice and skeleton argument (if any);

      (b) those parts of the transcripts of evidence which are directly relevant to any question at issue on the appeal;

      (c) the order granting permission to appeal and, where permission to appeal was granted at an oral hearing, the transcript (or note) of any judgment which was given; and

      (d) any document which the appellant and respondent have agreed to add to the appeal bundle in accordance with paragraph 7.11.

   (2) Where permission to appeal has been refused on a particular issue, the appellant must remove from the appeal bundle all documents that are relevant only to that issue.

APPEAL QUESTIONNAIRE IN THE COURT OF APPEAL

6.4 The Court of Appeal will send an Appeal Questionnaire to the appellant when it notifies him of the matters referred to in paragraph 6.3.

6.5 The appellant must complete and file the Appeal Questionnaire within 14 days of the date of the letter of notification of the matters in paragraph 6.3. The Appeal Questionnaire must contain:

(1) if the appellant is legally represented, the advocate's time estimate for the hearing of the appeal;

(2) where a transcript of evidence is relevant to the appeal, confirmation as to what parts of a transcript of evidence have been ordered where this is not already in the bundle of documents;

(3) confirmation that copies of the appeal bundle are being prepared and will be held ready for the use of the Court of Appeal and an undertaking that they will be supplied to the court on request. For the purpose of these bundles photocopies of the transcripts will be accepted;

(4) confirmation that copies of the Appeal Questionnaire and the appeal bundle have been served on the respondents and the date of that service.

Time estimates

6.6 The time estimate included in an Appeal Questionnaire must be that of the advocate who will argue the appeal. It should exclude the time required by the court to give judgment. If the respondent disagrees with the time estimate, the respondent must inform the court within 7 days of receipt of the Appeal Questionnaire. In the absence of such notification the respondent will be deemed to have accepted the estimate proposed on behalf of the appellant.

RESPONDENT

7.1 A respondent who wishes to ask the appeal court to vary the order of the lower court in any way must appeal and permission will be required on the same basis as for an appellant.

(Paragraph 3.2 applies to grounds of appeal by a respondent.)

7.2 A respondent who wishes only to request that the appeal court upholds the judgment or order of the lower court whether for the reasons given in the lower court or otherwise does not make an appeal and does not therefore require permission to appeal in accordance with rule 52.3(1).

(Paragraph 7.6 requires a respondent to file a skeleton argument where he wishes to address the appeal court)

7.3

(1) A respondent who wishes to appeal or who wishes to ask the appeal court to uphold the order of the lower court for reasons

different from or additional to those given by the lower court must file a respondent's notice.

(2) If the respondent does not file a respondent's notice, he will not be entitled, except with the permission of the court, to rely on any reason not relied on in the lower court.

7.3A Paragraphs 5.1A, 5.1B and 5.2 of this practice direction (Human Rights and extension for time for filing appellant's notice) also apply to a respondent and a respondent's notice.

Time limits

7.4 The time limits for filing a respondent's notice are set out in rule 52.5 (4) and (5).

7.5 Where an extension of time is required the extension must be requested in the respondent's notice and the reasons why the respondent failed to act within the specified time must be included.

7.6 Except where paragraph 7.7A applies, the respondent must file a skeleton argument for the court in all cases where he proposes to address arguments to the court. The respondent's skeleton argument may be included within a respondent's notice. Where a skeleton argument is included within a respondent's notice it will not form part of the notice for the purposes of rule 52.8.

7.7

(1) A respondent who –

    (a) files a respondent's notice; but
    (b) does not include his skeleton argument within that notice,

    must file and serve his skeleton argument within 14 days of filing the notice.

(2) A respondent who does not file a respondent's notice but who files a skeleton argument must file and serve that skeleton argument at least 7 days before the appeal hearing.

(Rule 52.5(4) sets out the period for filing and serving a respondent's notice)

7.7A

(1) Where the appeal relates to a claim allocated to the small claims track and is being heard in a county court or the High Court, the respondent may file a skeleton argument but is not required to do so.

(2) A respondent who is not represented need not file a skeleton argument but is encouraged to do so in order to assist the court.

7.7B The respondent must –

(1) serve his skeleton argument on –

(a) the appellant; and

(b) any other respondent,

at the same time as he files it at the court; and

(2) file a certificate of service.

Content of skeleton arguments

7.8 A respondent's skeleton argument must conform to the directions at paragraphs 5.10 and 5.11 with any necessary modifications. It should, where appropriate, answer the arguments set out in the appellant's skeleton argument.

Applications within respondent's notices

7.9 A respondent may include an application within a respondent's notice in accordance with paragraph 5.5 above.

Filing respondent's notices and skeleton arguments

7.10

(1) The respondent must file the following documents with his respondent's notice in every case:

(a) two additional copies of the respondent's notice for the appeal court; and

(b) one copy each for the appellant and any other respondents.

(2) The respondent may file a skeleton argument with his respondent's notice and –

(a) where he does so he must file two copies; and

(b) where he does not do so he must comply with paragraph 7.7.

7.11 If the respondent wishes to rely on any documents which he reasonably considers necessary to enable the appeal court to reach its decision on the appeal in addition to those filed by the appellant, he must make every effort to agree amendments to the appeal bundle with the appellant.

7.12

(1) If the representatives for the parties are unable to reach agreement, the respondent may prepare a supplemental bundle.

(2) If the respondent prepares a supplemental bundle he must file it, together with the requisite number of copies for the appeal court, at the appeal court –

(a) with the respondent's notice; or

(b) if a respondent's notice is not filed, within 21 days after he is served with the appeal bundle.

7.13 The respondent must serve –

(1) the respondent's notice;
(2) his skeleton argument (if any); and
(3) the supplemental bundle (if any),
   on –

   (a) the appellant; and
   (b) any other respondent,

at the same time as he files them at the court.

APPEALS TO THE HIGH COURT

Application

8.1 This paragraph applies where an appeal lies to a High Court judge from the decision of a county court or a district judge of the High Court.

8.2 The following table sets out the following venues for each circuit –

(a) Appeal centres – court centres where appeals to which this paragraph applies may be filed, managed and heard. Paragraphs 8.6 to 8.8 provide for special arrangements in relation to the South Eastern Circuit.

(b) Hearing only centres – court centres where appeals to which this paragraph applies may be heard by order made at an appeal centre (see paragraph 8.10).

Circuit	Appeal Centres	Hearing Only Centres
Midland Circuit	Birmingham	Lincoln
	Nottingham	Leicester
		Northampton
		Stafford
North Eastern Circuit	Leeds	Teesside
	Newcastle	
	Sheffield	
Northern Circuit	Manchester	Carlisle
	Liverpool	
	Preston	
Wales and Chester Circuit	Cardiff	
	Swansea	
	Chester	
Western Circuit	Bristol	Truro
	Exeter	Plymouth
	Winchester	

South Eastern Circuit	Royal Courts of Justice
	Lewes
	Luton
	Norwich
	Reading
	Chelmsford
	St Albans
	Maidstone
	Oxford

Venue for appeals and filing of notices on circuits other than the South Eastern Circuit

8.3 Paragraphs 8.4 and 8.5 apply where the lower court is situated on a circuit other than the South Eastern Circuit.

8.4 The appellant's notice must be filed at an appeal centre on the circuit in which the lower court is situated. The appeal will be managed and heard at that appeal centre unless the appeal court orders otherwise.

8.5 A respondent's notice must be filed at the appeal centre where the appellant's notice was filed unless the appeal has been transferred to another appeal centre, in which case it must be filed at that appeal centre.

Venue for appeals and filing of notices on the South Eastern Circuit

8.6 Paragraphs 8.7 and 8.8 apply where the lower court is situated on the South Eastern Circuit.

8.7 The appellant's notice must be filed at an appeal centre on the South Eastern Circuit. The appeal will be managed and heard at the Royal Courts of Justice unless the appeal court orders otherwise. An order that an appeal is to be managed or heard at another appeal centre may not be made unless the consent of the Presiding Judge of the circuit in charge of civil matters has been obtained.

8.8 A respondent's notice must be filed at the Royal Courts of Justice unless the appeal has been transferred to another appeal centre, in which case it must be filed at that appeal centre.

General provisions

8.9 The appeal court may transfer an appeal to another appeal centre (whether or not on the same circuit). In deciding whether to do so the court will have regard to the criteria in rule 30.3 (criteria for a transfer order). The appeal court may do so either on application by a party or of its own initiative. Where an appeal is transferred under this paragraph, notice of transfer must be served on every person on whom the appellant's notice has been served. An appeal may not be transferred to an appeal centre on another circuit, either for management or hearing, unless the consent of the Presiding Judge of that circuit in charge of civil matters has been obtained.

8.10 Directions may be given for –

(a) an appeal to be heard at a hearing only centre; or

(b) an application in an appeal to be heard at any other venue,

instead of at the appeal centre managing the appeal.

8.11 Unless a direction has been made under 8.10, any application in the appeal must be made at the appeal centre where the appeal is being managed.

8.12 The appeal court may adopt all or any part of the procedure set out in paragraphs 6.4 to 6.6.

8.13 Where the lower court is a county court:

   (1)   subject to paragraph (1A), appeals and applications for permission to appeal will be heard by a High Court Judge or by a person authorised under paragraphs (1), (2) or (4) of the Table in section 9(1) of the Supreme Court Act 1981 to act as a judge of the High Court;

   (1A) an appeal or application for permission to appeal from the decision of a Recorder in the county court may be heard by a Designated Civil Judge who is authorised under paragraph (5) of the Table in section 9(1) of the Supreme Court Act 1981 to act as a judge of the High Court; and

   (2)   other applications in the appeal may be heard and directions in the appeal may be given either by a High Court Judge or by any person authorised under section 9 of the Supreme Court Act 1981 to act as a judge of the High Court.

8.14 In the case of appeals from Masters or district judges of the High Court, appeals, applications for permission and any other applications in the appeal may be heard and directions in the appeal may be given by a High Court Judge or by any person authorised under section 9 of the Supreme Court Act 1981 to act as a judge of the High Court.

APPEALS TO A JUDGE OF A COUNTY COURT FROM A DISTRICT JUDGE

8A.1 The Designated Civil Judge in consultation with his Presiding Judges has responsibility for allocating appeals from decisions of district judges to circuit judges.

RE-HEARINGS

9.1 The hearing of an appeal will be a re-hearing (as opposed to a review of the decision of the lower court) if the appeal is from the decision of a minister, person or other body and the minister, person or other body –

(1) did not hold a hearing to come to that decision; or

(2) held a hearing to come to that decision, but the procedure adopted did not provide for the consideration of evidence.

APPEALS TRANSFERRED TO THE COURT OF APPEAL

10.1 Where an appeal is transferred to the Court of Appeal under rule 52.14 the Court of Appeal may give such additional directions as are considered appropriate.

APPLICATIONS

11.1 Where a party to an appeal makes an application whether in an appeal notice or by Part 23 application notice, the provisions of Part 23 will apply.

11.2 The applicant must file the following documents with the notice

(1) one additional copy of the application notice for the appeal court and one copy for each of the respondents;

(2) where applicable a sealed copy of the order which is the subject of the main appeal;

(3) a bundle of documents in support which should include:

(a) the Part 23 application notice; and

(b) any witness statements and affidavits filed in support of the application notice.

DISPOSING OF APPLICATIONS OR APPEALS BY CONSENT

DISMISSAL OF APPLICATIONS OR APPEALS BY CONSENT

12.1 These paragraphs do not apply where any party to the proceedings is a child or patient.

12.2 Where an appellant does not wish to pursue an application or an appeal, he may request the appeal court for an order that his application or appeal be dismissed. Such a request must contain a statement that the appellant is not a child or patient. If such a request is granted it will usually be on the basis that the appellant pays the costs of the application or appeal.

12.3 If the appellant wishes to have the application or appeal dismissed without costs, his request must be accompanied by a consent signed by the respondent or his legal representative stating that the respondent is not a child or patient and consents to the dismissal of the application or appeal without costs.

12.4 Where a settlement has been reached disposing of the application or appeal, the parties may make a joint request to the court stating that none of them is a child or patient, and asking that the application or appeal be dismissed by consent. If the request is granted the application or appeal will be dismissed.

Allowing unopposed appeals or applications on paper

13.1 The appeal court will not normally make an order allowing an appeal unless satisfied that the decision of the lower court was wrong, but the appeal court may set aside or vary the order of the lower court with consent and without determining the merits of the appeal, if it is satisfied that there are good and sufficient reasons for doing so. Where the appeal court is requested by all parties to allow an application or an appeal the court may consider the request on the papers. The request should state that none of the parties is a child or patient and set out the relevant history of the proceedings and the matters relied on as justifying the proposed order and be accompanied by a copy of the proposed order.

Procedure for consent orders and agreements to pay periodical payments involving a child or patient

13.2 Where one of the parties is a child or patient –

   (1)   a settlement relating to an appeal or application; or
   (2)   in a personal injury claim for damages for future pecuniary loss, an agreement reached at the appeal stage to pay periodical payments,

requires the court's approval.

Child

13.3 In cases involving a child a copy of the proposed order signed by the parties' solicitors should be sent to the appeal court, together with an opinion from the advocate acting on behalf of the child.

Patient

13.4 Where a party is a patient the same procedure will be adopted, but the documents filed should also include any relevant reports prepared for the Court of Protection and a document evidencing formal approval by that court where required.

Periodical payments

13.5 Where periodical payments for future pecuniary loss have been negotiated in a personal injury case which is under appeal, the documents filed should include those which would be required in the case of a personal injury claim for damages for future pecuniary loss dealt with at first instance. Details can be found in the Practice Direction which supplements Part 21.

SUMMARY ASSESSMENT OF COSTS

14.1 Costs are likely to be assessed by way of summary assessment at the following hearings:

    (1) contested directions hearings;
    (2) applications for permission to appeal at which the respondent is present;
    (3) dismissal list hearings in the Court of Appeal at which the respondent is present;
    (4) appeals from case management decisions; and
    (5) appeals listed for one day or less.

14.2 Parties attending any of the hearings referred to in paragraph 14.1 should be prepared to deal with the summary assessment.

OTHER SPECIAL PROVISIONS REGARDING THE COURT OF APPEAL

Filing of Documents

15.1

    (1) The documents relevant to proceedings in the Court of Appeal, Civil Division must be filed in the Civil Appeals Office Registry, Room E307, Royal Courts of Justice, Strand, London, WC2A 2LL.
    (2) The Civil Appeals Office will not serve documents and where service is required by the CPR or this practice direction it must be effected by the parties.

15.1A

    (1) A party may file by email –

        (a) an appellant's notice;
        (b) a respondent's notice;
        (c) an application notice,

in the Court of Appeal, Civil Division, using the email account specified in the 'Guidelines for filing by Email' which appear on the Court of Appeal, Civil Division website at www.civilappeals.gov.uk.

(2) A party may only file a notice in accordance with paragraph (1) where he is permitted to do so by the 'Guidelines for filing by Email'.

Core Bundles

15.2 In cases where the appeal bundle comprises more than 500 pages, exclusive of transcripts, the appellant's solicitors must, after consultation with the respondent's solicitors, also prepare and file with the court, in addition to copies of the appeal bundle (as amended in accordance with paragraph 7.11) the requisite number of copies of a core bundle.

15.3

(1) The core bundle must be filed within 28 days of receipt of the order giving permission to appeal or, where permission to appeal was granted by the lower court or is not required, within 28 days of the date of service of the appellant's notice on the respondent.

(2) The core bundle –

(a) must contain the documents which are central to the appeal; and

(b) must not exceed 150 pages.

Preparation of bundles

15.4 The provisions of this paragraph apply to the preparation of appeal bundles, supplemental respondents' bundles where the parties are unable to agree amendments to the appeal bundle, and core bundles.

(1) **Rejection of bundles**. Where documents are copied unnecessarily or bundled incompletely, costs may be disallowed. Where the provisions of this Practice Direction as to the preparation or delivery of bundles are not followed the bundle may be rejected by the court or be made the subject of a special costs order.

(2) **Avoidance of duplication**. No more than one copy of any document should be included unless there is a good reason for doing otherwise (such as the use of a separate core bundle – see paragraph 15.2).

(3) **Pagination**

(a) Bundles must be paginated, each page being numbered individually and consecutively. The pagination used at trial must also be indicated. Letters and other documents should normally be included in chronological order. (An exception to consecutive page numbering arises in the case of core bundles where it may be preferable to retain the original numbering).

(b) Page numbers should be inserted in bold figures at the bottom of the page and in a form that can be clearly distinguished from any other pagination on the document.

(4) Format and presentation

(a) Where possible the documents should be in A4 format. Where a document has to be read across rather than down the page, it should be so placed in the bundle as to ensure that the text starts nearest the spine.

(b) Where any marking or writing in colour on a document is important, the document must be copied in colour or marked up correctly in colour.

(c) Documents which are not easily legible should be transcribed and the transcription marked and placed adjacent to the document transcribed.

(d) Documents in a foreign language should be translated and the translation marked and placed adjacent to the document translated. The translation should be agreed or, if it cannot be agreed, each party's proposed translation should be included.

(e) The size of any bundle should be tailored to its contents. A large lever arch file should not be used for just a few pages nor should files of whatever size be overloaded.

(f) Where it will assist the Court of Appeal, different sections of the file may be separated by cardboard or other tabbed dividers so long as these are clearly indexed. Where, for example, a document is awaited when the appeal bundle is filed, a single sheet of paper can be inserted after a divider, indicating the nature of the document awaited. For example, 'Transcript of evidence of Mr J Smith (to follow)'.

(5) Binding

(a) All documents, with the exception of transcripts, must be bound together. This may be in a lever arch file, ring binder or plastic folder. Plastic sleeves containing loose documents must not be used. Binders and files must be strong enough to withstand heavy use.

(b) Large documents such as plans should be placed in an easily accessible file. Large documents which will need to be opened up frequently should be inserted in a file larger than A4 size.

(6) Indices and labels

(a) An index must be included at the front of the bundle listing all the documents and providing the page references for each. In the case of documents such as letters, invoices or bank statements, they may be given a general description.

(b) Where the bundles consist of more than one file, an index to all the files should be included in the first file and an index included for each file. Indices should, if possible, be on a single sheet. The full name of the case should not be inserted on the index if this would waste space. Documents should be identified briefly but properly.

(7) Identification

    (a) Every bundle must be clearly identified, on the spine and on the front cover, with the name of the case and the Court of Appeal's reference. Where the bundle consists of more than one file, each file must be numbered on the spine, the front cover and the inside of the front cover.

    (b) Outer labels should use large lettering eg 'Appeal Bundle A' or 'Core Bundle'. The full title of the appeal and solicitors' names and addresses should be omitted. A label should be used on the front as well as on the spine.

(8) Staples etc. All staples, heavy metal clips etc, must be removed.

(9) Statements of case

    (a) Statements of case should be assembled in 'chapter' form – i.e claim followed by particulars of claim, followed by further information, irrespective of date.

    (b) Redundant documents, eg particulars of claim overtaken by amendments, requests for further information recited in the answers given, should generally be excluded.

(10) New Documents

    (a) Before a new document is introduced into bundles which have already been delivered to the court, steps should be taken to ensure that it carries an appropriate bundle/page number so that it can be added to the court documents. It should not be stapled and it should be prepared with punch holes for immediate inclusion in the binders in use.

    (b) If it is expected that a large number of miscellaneous new documents will from time to time be introduced, there should be a special tabbed empty loose-leaf file for that purpose. An index should be produced for this file, updated as necessary.

(11) Inter-solicitor correspondence. Since inter-solicitor correspondence is unlikely to be required for the purposes of an appeal, only those letters which will need to be referred to should be copied.

(12) Sanctions for non-compliance. If the appellant fails to comply with the requirements as to the provision of bundles of documents, the application or appeal will be referred for consideration to be given as to why it should not be dismissed for failure to so comply.

Master in the Court of Appeal, Civil Division

15.5 When the Head of the Civil Appeals Office acts in a judicial capacity pursuant to rule 52.16, he shall be known as Master. Other eligible officers may also be designated by the Master of the Rolls to exercise judicial authority under rule 52.16 and shall then be known as Deputy Masters.

Respondent to notify Civil Appeals Office whether he intends to file respondent's notice

15.6 A respondent must, no later than 21 days after the date he is served with notification that –

(1) permission to appeal has been granted; or

(2) the application for permission to appeal and the appeal are to be heard together,

inform the Civil Appeals Office and the appellant in writing whether –

(a) he proposes to file a respondent's notice appealing the order or seeking to uphold the order for reasons different from, or additional to, those given by the lower court; or

(b) he proposes to rely on the reasons given by the lower court for its decision.

(Paragraph 15.11B requires all documents needed for an appeal hearing, including a respondent's skeleton argument, to be filed at least 7 days before the hearing)

Listing and hear-by dates

15.7 The management of the list will be dealt with by the listing officer under the direction of the Master.

15.8 The Civil Appeals List of the Court of Appeal is divided as follows:

- *The applications list* – applications for permission to appeal and other applications.

- *The appeals list* – appeals where permission to appeal has been given or where an appeal lies without permission being required where a hearing date is fixed in advance. (Appeals in this list which require special listing arrangements will be assigned to the special fixtures list)

- *The expedited list* – appeals or applications where the Court of Appeal has directed an expedited hearing. The current practice of the Court of Appeal is summarised in *Unilever plc. v. Chefaro Proprietaries Ltd. (Practice Note)* [1995]1 W.L.R. 243.

- *The stand-out list* – Appeals or applications which, for good reason, are not at present ready to proceed and have been stood out by judicial direction.

- *The second fixtures list* – [see paragraph 15.9A(1) below].

- *The second fixtures list* – if an appeal is designated as a 'second fixture' it means that a hearing date is arranged in advance on the express basis that the list is fully booked for the period in question and therefore the case will be heard only if a suitable gap occurs in the list.

- *The short-warned list* – appeals which the court considers may be prepared for the hearing by an advocate other than the one originally instructed with a half day's notice, or such other period as the court may direct.

Special provisions relating to the short-warned list

15.9

(1) Where an appeal is assigned to the short-warned list, the Civil Appeals Office will notify the parties' solicitors in writing. The court may abridge the time for filing any outstanding bundles in an appeal assigned to this list.

(2) The solicitors for the parties must notify their advocate and their client as soon as the Civil Appeals Office notifies them that the appeal has been assigned to the short-warned list.

(3) The appellant may apply in writing for the appeal to be removed from the short-warned list within 14 days of notification of its assignment. The application will be decided by a Lord Justice, or the Master, and will only be granted for the most compelling reasons.

(4) The Civil Appeals Listing Officer may place an appeal from the short-warned list 'on call' from a given date and will inform the parties' advocates accordingly.

(5) An appeal which is 'on call' may be listed for hearing on half a day's notice or such longer period as the court may direct.

(6) Once an appeal is listed for hearing from the short warned list it becomes the immediate professional duty of the advocate instructed in the appeal, if he is unable to appear at the hearing, to take all practicable measures to ensure that his lay client is represented at the hearing by an advocate who is fully instructed and able to argue the appeal.

Special provisions relating to the special fixtures list

15.9A

(1) The special fixtures list is a sub-division of the appeals list and is used to deal with appeals that may require special listing arrangements, such as the need to list a number of cases before the same constitution, in a particular order, during a particular period or at a given location.

(2) The Civil Appeals Office will notify the parties' representatives, or the parties if acting in person, of the particular arrangements that will apply. The notice –

    (a) will give details of the specific period during which a case is scheduled to be heard; and

    (b) may give directions in relation to the filing of any outstanding documents.

(3) The listing officer will notify the parties' representatives of the precise hearing date as soon as practicable. While every effort will be made to accommodate the availability of counsel, the requirements of the court will prevail.

Requests for directions

15.10 To ensure that all requests for directions are centrally monitored and correctly allocated, all requests for directions or rulings (whether relating to listing or any other matters) should be made to the Civil Appeals Office. Those seeking directions or rulings must not approach the supervising Lord Justice either directly, or via his or her clerk.

Bundles of authorities

15.11

   (1) Once the parties have been notified of the date fixed for the hearing, the appellant's advocate must, after consultation with his opponent, file a bundle containing photocopies of the authorities upon which each side will rely at the hearing.

   (2) The bundle of authorities should, in general –

      (a) have the relevant passages of the authorities marked;
      (b) not include authorities for propositions not in dispute; and
      (c) not contain more than 10 authorities unless the scale of the appeal warrants more extensive citation.

   (3) The bundle of authorities must be filed –

      (a) at least 7 days before the hearing; or
      (b) where the period of notice of the hearing is less than 7 days, immediately.

   (4) If, through some oversight, a party intends, during the hearing, to refer to other authorities the parties may agree a second agreed bundle. The appellant's advocate must file this bundle at least 48 hours before the hearing commences.

   (5) A bundle of authorities must bear a certification by the advocates responsible for arguing the case that the requirements of sub-paragraphs (3) to (5) of paragraph 5.10 have been complied with in respect of each authority included.

Supplementary skeleton arguments

15.11A

   (1) A supplementary skeleton argument on which the appellant wishes to rely must be filed at least 14 days before the hearing.

   (2) A supplementary skeleton argument on which the respondent wishes to rely must be filed at least 7 days before the hearing.

   (3) All supplementary skeleton arguments must comply with the requirements set out in paragraph 5.10.

   (4) At the hearing the court may refuse to hear argument from a party not contained in a skeleton argument filed within the relevant time limit set out in this paragraph.

Papers for the appeal hearing

15.11B

(1) All the documents which are needed for the appeal hearing must be filed at least 7 days before the hearing. Where a document has not been filed 10 days before the hearing a reminder will be sent by the Civil Appeals Office.

(2) Any party who fails to comply with the provisions of paragraph (1) may be required to attend before the Presiding Lord Justice to seek permission to proceed with, or to oppose, the appeal.

Disposal of bundles of documents

15.11C

(1) Where the court has determined a case, the official transcriber will retain one set of papers. The Civil Appeals Office will destroy any remaining sets of papers not collected within 21 days of –

   (a) where one or more parties attend the hearing, the date of the court's decision;

   (b) where there is no attendance, the date of the notification of court's decision.

(2) The parties should ensure that bundles of papers supplied to the court do not contain original documents (other than transcripts). The parties must ensure that they –

   (a) bring any necessary original documents to the hearing; and

   (b) retrieve any original documents handed up to the court before leaving the court.

(3) The court will retain application bundles where permission to appeal has been granted. Where permission is refused the arrangements in sub-paragraph (1) will apply.

(4) Where a single Lord Justice has refused permission to appeal on paper, application bundles will not be destroyed until after the time limit for seeking a hearing has expired.

Availability of Reserved judgments before hand down

15.12 This section applies where the presiding Lord Justice is satisfied that the result of the appeal will attract no special degree of confidentiality or sensitivity.

15.13 A copy of the written judgment will be made available to the parties' legal advisers by 4 p.m. on the second working day before judgment is due to be pronounced or such other period as the court may direct. This can be shown, in confidence, to the parties but only for the purpose of obtaining instructions and on the strict understanding that the judgment, or its effect, is not to be disclosed to any other person. A working day is any day on which the Civil Appeals Office is open for business.

15.14 The appeal will be listed for judgment in the cause list and the judgment handed down at the appropriate time.

Attendance of advocates on the handing down of a reserved judgment

15.15 Where any consequential orders are agreed, the parties' advocates need not attend on the handing down of a reserved judgment. Where an advocate does attend the court may, if it considers such attendance unnecessary, disallow the costs of the attendance. If the parties do not indicate that they intend to attend, the judgment may be handed down by a single member of the court.

Agreed orders following judgment

15.16 The parties must, in respect of any draft agreed orders –

    (a) fax a copy to the clerk to the presiding Lord Justice; and
    (b) file four copies in the Civil Appeals Office,
        no later than 12 noon on the working day before the judgment is handed down.

15.17 A copy of a draft order must bear the Court of Appeal case reference, the date the judgment is to be handed down and the name of the presiding Lord Justice.

Corrections to the draft judgment

15.18 Any proposed correction to the draft judgment should be sent to the clerk to the judge who prepared the draft with a copy to any other party.

Application for leave to appeal

15.19 Where a party wishes to apply for leave to appeal to the House of Lords under section 1 of the Administration of Justice (Appeals) Act 1934 the court may deal with the application on the basis of written submissions.

15.20 A party must, in relation to his submission –

    (a) fax a copy to the clerk to the presiding Lord Justice; and
    (b) file four copies in the Civil Appeals Office,
        no later than 12 noon on the working day before the judgment is handed down.

15.21 A copy of a submission must bear the Court of Appeal case reference, the date the judgment is to be handed down and the name of the presiding Lord Justice.

SECTION II – GENERAL PROVISIONS ABOUT STATUTORY APPEALS AND APPEALS BY WAY OF CASE STATED

16.1 This section of this practice direction contains general provisions about statutory appeals (paragraphs 17.1–17.6) and appeals by way of case stated (paragraphs 18.1–18.20).

16.2 Where any of the provisions in this section provide for documents to be filed at the appeal court, these documents are in addition to any documents required under Part 52 or section I of this practice direction.

STATUTORY APPEALS

17.1 This part of this section –

   (1) applies where under any enactment an appeal (other than by way of case stated) lies to the court from a Minister of State, government department, tribunal or other person ('statutory appeals'); and

   (2) is subject to any provision about a specific category of appeal in any enactment or Section III of this practice direction.

Part 52

17.2 Part 52 applies to statutory appeals with the following amendments:

Filing of appellant's notice

17.3 The appellant must file the appellant's notice at the appeal court within 28 days after the date of the decision of the lower court he wishes to appeal.

17.4 Where a statement of the reasons for a decision is given later than the notice of that decision, the period for filing the appellant's notice is calculated from the date on which the statement is received by the appellant.

Service of appellant's notice

17.5 In addition to the respondents to the appeal, the appellant must serve the appellant's notice in accordance with rule 52.4(3) on the chairman of the tribunal, Minister of State, government department or other person from whose decision the appeal is brought.

Right of Minister etc. to be heard on the appeal

17.6 Where the appeal is from an order or decision of a Minister of State or government department, the Minister or department, as the case may be, is entitled to attend the hearing and to make representations to the court.

APPEALS BY WAY OF CASE STATED

18.1 This part of this section –

   (1) applies where under any enactment –

     (a) an appeal lies to the court by way of case stated; or
     (b) a question of law may be referred to the court by way of case stated; and

   (2) is subject to any provision about to a specific category of appeal in any enactment or Section III of this practice direction.

Part 52

18.2 Part 52 applies to appeals by way of case stated subject to the following amendments.

Case stated by Crown Court or Magistrates' Court

Application to state a case

18.3 The procedure for applying to the Crown Court or a Magistrates' Court to have a case stated for the opinion of the High Court is set out in the Crown Court Rules 1982 and the Magistrates' Courts Rules 1981 respectively.

Filing of appellant's notice

18.4 The appellant must file the appellant's notice at the appeal court within 10 days after he receives the stated case.

Documents to be lodged

18.5 The appellant must lodge the following documents with his appellant's notice:

   (1) the stated case;
   (2) a copy of the judgment, order or decision in respect of which the case has been stated; and
   (3) where the judgment, order or decision in respect of which the case has been stated was itself given or made on appeal, a copy of the judgment, order or decision appealed from.

Service of appellant's notice

18.6 The appellant must serve the appellant's notice and accompanying documents on all respondents within 4 days after they are filed or lodged at the appeal court.

Case stated by Minister, government department, tribunal or other person

Application to state a case

18.7 The procedure for applying to a Minister, government department, tribunal or other person ('Minister or tribunal etc.') to have a case stated for the opinion of the court may be set out in –

   (1) the enactment which provides for the right of appeal; or
   (2) any rules of procedure relating to the Minister or tribunal etc.

Signing of stated case by Minister or tribunal etc.

18.8 A case stated by a tribunal must be signed by the chairman or president of the tribunal. A case stated by any other person must be signed by that person or by a person authorised to do so.

Service of stated case by Minister or tribunal etc.

18.9 The Minister or tribunal etc. must serve the stated case on –

   (1) the party who requests the case to be stated; or
   (2) the party as a result of whose application to the court, the case was stated.

18.10 Where an enactment provides that a Minister or tribunal etc. may state a case or refer a question of law to the court by way of case stated without a request being made, the Minister or tribunal etc. must –

   (1) serve the stated case on those parties that the Minister or tribunal etc. considers appropriate; and
   (2) give notice to every other party to the proceedings that the stated case has been served on the party named and on the date specified in the notice.

Filing and service of appellant's notice

18.11 The party on whom the stated case was served must file the appellant's notice and the stated case at the appeal court and serve copies of the notice and stated case on –

   (1) the Minister or tribunal etc. who stated the case; and
   (2) every party to the proceedings to which the stated case relates, within 14 days after the stated case was served on him.

18.12 Where paragraph 18.10 applies the Minister or tribunal etc. must –

   (1) file an appellant's notice and the stated case at the appeal court; and
   (2) serve copies of those documents on the persons served under paragraph 18.10 within 14 days after stating the case.

18.13 Where –

   (1) a stated case has been served by the Minister or tribunal etc. in accordance with paragraph 18.9; and

   (2) the party on whom the stated case was served does not file an appellant's notice in accordance with paragraph 18.11,
any other party may file an appellant's notice with the stated case at the appeal court and serve a copy of the notice and the case on the persons listed in paragraph 18.11 within the period of time set out in paragraph 18.14.

18.14 The period of time referred to in paragraph 18.13 is 14 days from the last day on which the party on whom the stated case was served may file an appellant's notice in accordance with paragraph 18.11.

Amendment of stated case

18.15 The court may amend the stated case or order it to be returned to the Minister or tribunal etc. for amendment and may draw inferences of fact from the facts stated in the case.

Right of Minister etc. to be heard on the appeal

18.16 Where the case is stated by a Minister or government department, that Minister or department, as the case may be, is entitled to appear on the appeal and to make representations to the court.

Application for order to state a case

18.17 An application to the court for an order requiring a minister or tribunal etc. to state a case for the decision of the court, or to refer a question of law to the court by way of case stated must be made to the court which would be the appeal court if the case were stated.

18.18 An application to the court for an order directing a Minister or tribunal etc. to –

   (1) state a case for determination by the court; or

   (2) refer a question of law to the court by way of case stated, must be made in accordance with CPR Part 23

18.19 The application notice must contain –

   (1) the grounds of the application;

   (2) the question of law on which it is sought to have the case stated; and

   (3) any reasons given by the minister or tribunal etc. for his or its refusal to state a case.

18.20 The application notice must be filed at the appeal court and served on –

   (1) the minister, department, secretary of the tribunal or other person as the case may be; and

(2) every party to the proceedings to which the application relates, within 14 days after the appellant receives notice of the refusal of his request to state a case.

SECTION III – PROVISIONS ABOUT SPECIFIC APPEALS

20.1 This section of this Practice Direction provides special provisions about the appeals to which the following table refers. This Section is not exhaustive and does not create, amend or remove any right of appeal.

20.2 Part 52 applies to all appeals to which this section applies subject to any special provisions set out in this section.

20.3 Where any of the provisions in this section provide for documents to be filed at the appeal court, these documents are in addition to any documents required under Part 52 or sections I or II of this practice direction.

APPEALS TO THE COURT OF APPEAL	*Paragraph*
Articles 81 and 82 of the EC Treaty and Chapters I and II of Part I of the Competition Act 1998	21.10A
Civil Partnership – conditional order for dissolution or nullity	21.1
Competition Appeal Tribunal	21.10
Contempt of Court	21.4
Decree nisi of divorce	21.1
Immigration Appeal Tribunal	21.7
Lands Tribunal	21.9
Nullity of marriage	21.1
Patents Court on appeal from Comptroller	21.3
Revocation of patent	21.2
Social Security Commissioners	21.5
Special Commissioner (where the appeal is direct to the Court of Appeal)	21.8
Value Added Tax and Duties Tribunals (where the appeal is direct to the Court of Appeal)	21.6

APPEALS TO THE HIGH COURT	Paragraph
Agricultural Land Tribunal	22.7
Architects Act 1997, s. 22	22.3
Charities Act 1993	23.8A
Chiropractors Act 1994, s. 31	22.3
Clergy Pensions Measure 1961, s. 38(3)	23.2
Commons Registration Act 1965	23.9
Consumer Credit Act 1974	22.4
Dentists Act 1984, s. 20 or s. 44	22.3

Extradition Act 2003	22.6A
Friendly Societies Act 1974	23.7
Friendly Societies Act 1992	23.7
Industrial and Provident Societies Act 1965	23.2, 23.7
Industrial Assurance Act 1923	23.2, 23.7
Industrial Assurance Act 1923, s. 17	23.6
Inheritance Tax Act 1984, s. 222	23.3
Inheritance Tax Act 1984, s. 225	23.5
Inheritance Tax Act 1984, ss. 249(3) and 251	23.4
Land Registration Act 1925	23.2
Land Registration Act 2002	23.2, 23.8B
Law of Property Act 1922, para. 16 of Sched. 15	23.2
Medical Act 1983, s. 40	22.3
Medicines Act 1968, ss. 82(3) and 83	(2)22.3
Mental Health Review Tribunal	22.8
Merchant Shipping Act 1995	22.2
Nurses, Midwives and Health Visitors Act 1997, s. 12	22.3
Opticians Act 1989, s. 23	22.3
Osteopaths Act 1993, s. 31	22.3
Pensions Act 1995, s. 97	23.2
Pension Schemes Act 1993, ss. 151 and 173	23.2
Pensions Appeal Tribunal Act 1943	22.5
Pharmacy Act 1954	22.3
Social Security Administration Act 1992	22.6
Stamp Duty Reserve Tax Regulations 1986, reg. 10	23.5
Taxes Management Act 1970, ss. 53 and 100C	(4)23.4
Taxes Management Act 1970, s. 56A	23.5
Value Added Tax and Duties Tribunal	23.8
Water Resources Act 1991, s. 205	(4)23.2

APPEALS TO THE COUNTY COURT	Paragraph
Local Government (Miscellaneous Provisions) Act 1976	24.1
Housing Act 1996, ss. 204 and 204A	24.2
Immigration and Asylum Act 1999, Part II	24.3

APPEALS TO THE COURT OF APPEAL

Appeal against decree nisi of divorce or nullity of marriage or conditional dissolution or nullity order in relation to civil partnership

21.1

(1) The appellant must file the appellant's notice at the Court of Appeal within 28 days after the date on which the decree was pronounced or conditional order made.

(2) The appellant must file the following documents with the appellant's notice –

    (a) the decree or conditional order; and
    (b) a certificate of service of the appellant's notice.

(3) The appellant's notice must be served on the appropriate district judge (see sub-paragraph (6)) in addition to the persons to be served under rule 52.4(3) and in accordance with that rule.

(4) The lower court may not alter the time limits for filing of the appeal notices.

(5) Where an appellant intends to apply to the Court of Appeal for an extension of time for serving or filing the appellant's notice he must give notice of that intention to the appropriate district judge (see sub-paragraph 6) before the application is made.

(6) In this paragraph 'the appropriate district judge' means, where the lower court is –

    (a) a county court, the district judge of that court;
    (b) a district registry, the district judge of that registry;
    (c) the Principal Registry of the Family Division, the senior district judge of that division.

Appeal against order for revocation of patent

21.2

(1) This paragraph applies where an appeal lies to the Court of Appeal from an order for the revocation of a patent.

(2) The appellant must serve the appellant's notice on the Comptroller-General of Patents, Designs and Trade Marks (the 'Comptroller') in addition to the persons to be served under rule 52.4(3) and in accordance with that rule.

(3) Where, before the appeal hearing, the respondent decides not to oppose the appeal or not to attend the appeal hearing, he must immediately serve notice of that decision on –

    (a) the Comptroller; and
    (b) the appellant

(4) Where the respondent serves a notice in accordance with paragraph (3), he must also serve copies of the following documents on the Comptroller with that notice –

(a) the petition;
(b) any statements of claim;
(c) any written evidence filed in the claim.

(5) Within 14 days after receiving the notice in accordance with paragraph (3), the Comptroller must serve on the appellant a notice stating whether or not he intends to attend the appeal hearing.

(6) The Comptroller may attend the appeal hearing and oppose the appeal –

(a) in any case where he has given notice under paragraph (5) of his intention to attend; and
(b) in any other case (including, in particular, a case where the respondent withdraws his opposition to the appeal during the hearing) if the Court of Appeal so directs or permits.

Appeal from Patents Court on appeal from Comptroller

21.3 Where the appeal is from a decision of the Patents Court which was itself made on an appeal from a decision of the Comptroller-General of Patents, Designs and Trade Marks, the appellant must serve the appellant's notice on the Comptroller in addition to the persons to be served under rule 52.4(3) and in accordance with that rule.

Appeals in cases of contempt of court

21.4 In an appeal under section 13 of the Administration of Justice Act 1960 (appeals in cases of contempt of court), the appellant must serve the appellant's notice on the court from whose order or decision the appeal is brought in addition to the persons to be served under rule 52.4(3) and in accordance with that rule.

Appeals from Social Security or Child Support Commissioners

21.5

(1) This paragraph applies to appeals under the following provisions (appeals from the decision of a Social Security Commissioner or a Child Support Commissioner on a question of law) –

(a) section 6C of the Pensions Appeal Tribunals Act 1943;
(b) section 25 of the Child Support Act 1991;
(c) section 15 of the Social Security Act 1998;
(d) paragraph 9 of Schedule 7 to the Child Support, Pensions and Social Security Act 2000.

(2) The appellant must file the appellant's notice within 6 weeks after the date on which the Commissioner's decision on permission to appeal to the Court of Appeal was given in writing to the appellant.

(3) In an appeal brought under paragraph 9 of Schedule 7 to the Child Support, Pensions and Social Security Act 2000 by a party other than the Secretary of State, the appellant must serve the appellant's notice on the Secretary of State in addition to the persons to be served under rule 52.4(3) and in accordance with that rule.

(4) Where, after a Commissioner has given a decision, responsibility for the subject matter of the appeal has been transferred from a government department or the Commissioners for HM Revenue and Customs or a local authority ("the first body") to another such body ("the second body") and an appeal is brought by a party other than the second body –

(a) the second body shall be a respondent in place of the first body and the second body shall notify the court accordingly;

(b) if the appellant serves the appellant's notice or any other document on the first body, or if the court sends to the first body any communication in relation to the appeal, the first body shall forthwith send the notice, document or communication to the second body and the date on which the appellant's notice or other document was served on the first body shall be treated as the date on which it was served on the second body.

(5) This sub-paragraph applies where the appellant is the Secretary of State, the Commissioners for HM Revenue and Customs or a local authority. The appellant must serve the appellant's notice on any person appointed by the appellant to proceed with a claim, or an appeal arising out of a claim, in addition to the persons to be served under rule 52.4(3) and in accordance with that rule.

(Sub-paragraph (5) applies where the Secretary of State, the Commissioners for HM Revenue and Customs or a local authority is the appellant and that appellant appoints a person to proceed, in effect, on behalf of a respondent who is not himself able to proceed. An example is regulation 33 of the Social Security (Claims and Payments) Regulations 1987 which authorises the Secretary of State to appoint a person to proceed with the claim of another person who is unable for the time being to act.)

Appeals from Value Added Tax and Duties Tribunals

21.6

(1) An application to the Court of Appeal for permission to appeal from a value added tax and duties tribunal direct to that court must be made within 28 days after the date on which the tribunal certifies that its decision involves a point of law relating wholly or mainly to the construction of –

(a) an enactment or of a statutory instrument; or

(b) any of the Community Treaties or any Community Instrument,

which has been fully argued before and fully considered by it.

(2) The application must be made by the parties jointly filing at the Court of Appeal an appellant's notice that –

(a) contains a statement of the grounds for the application; and

(b) is accompanied by a copy of the decision to be appealed, endorsed with the certificate of the tribunal.

(3) The court will notify the appellant of its decision and –

(a) where permission to appeal to the Court of Appeal is given, the appellant must serve the appellant's notice on the chairman of the tribunal in addition to the persons to be served under rule 52.4(3) within 14 days after that notification.

(b) where permission to appeal to the Court of Appeal is refused, the period for appealing to the High Court is to be calculated from the date of the notification of that refusal.

Asylum and Immigration Appeals

21.7

(1) This paragraph applies to appeals –

(a) from the Immigration Appeal Tribunal under section 103 of the Nationality, Immigration and Asylum Act 2002 ('the 2002 Act'); and

(b) from the Asylum and Immigration Tribunal under the following provisions of the 2002 Act –
(i) section 103B (appeal from the Tribunal following reconsideration); and
(ii) section 103E (appeal from the Tribunal sitting as a panel).

(2) The appellant is not required to file an appeal bundle in accordance with paragraph 5.6A of this practice direction, but must file the documents specified in paragraphs 5.6(2)(a) to (f) together with a copy of the Tribunal's determination.

(3) The appellant's notice must be filed at the Court of Appeal within 14 days after the appellant is served with written notice of the decision of the Tribunal to grant or refuse permission to appeal.

(4) The appellant must serve the appellant's notice in accordance with rule 52.4(3) on –

(a) the persons to be served under that rule; and

(b) the Asylum and Immigration Tribunal.

(5) On being served with the appellant's notice, the Asylum and Immigration Tribunal must send to the Court of Appeal copies of the documents which were before the relevant Tribunal when it considered the appeal.

21.7A

    (1) This paragraph applies to appeals from the Asylum and Immigration Tribunal referred to the Court of Appeal under section 103C of the Nationality, Immigration and Asylum Act 2002.

    (2) On making an order referring an appeal to the Court of Appeal, the High Court shall send to the Court of Appeal copies of –

        (a) that order and any other order made in relation to the application for reconsideration; and

        (b) the application notice, written submissions and other documents filed under rule 54.29

    (3) Unless the court directs otherwise, the application notice filed under rule 54.29 shall be treated as the appellant's notice.

    (4) The respondent may file a respondent's notice within 14 days after the date on which the respondent is served with the order of the High Court referring the appeal to the Court of Appeal.

    (5) The Court of Appeal may give such additional directions as are appropriate.

Appeal from Special Commissioners

21.8

    (1) An application to the Court of Appeal for permission to appeal from the Special Commissioners direct to that court under section 56A of the Taxes Management Act 1970 must be made within 28 days after the date on which the Special Commissioners certify that their decision involves a point of law relating wholly or mainly to the construction of an enactment which has been fully argued before and fully considered before them.

    (2) The application must be made by the parties jointly filing at the Court of Appeal an appellant's notice that –

        (a) contains a statement of the grounds for the application; and

        (b) is accompanied by a copy of the decision to be appealed, endorsed with the certificate of the tribunal.

    (3) The court will notify the parties of its decision and –

        (a) where permission to appeal to the Court of Appeal is given, the appellant must serve the appellant's notice on the Clerk to the Special Commissioners in addition to the persons to be served under rule 52.4(3) within 14 days after that notification.

        (b) where permission to appeal to the Court of Appeal is refused, the period for appealing to the High Court is to be calculated from the date of the notification of that refusal.

Appeal from Lands Tribunal

21.9 The appellant must file the appellant's notice at the Court of Appeal within 28 days after the date of the decision of the tribunal.

Appeal from Competition Appeal Tribunal

21.10

(1) Where the appellant applies for permission to appeal at the hearing at which the decision is delivered by the tribunal and –

    (a) permission is given; or

    (b) permission is refused and the appellant wishes to make an application to the Court of Appeal for permission to appeal,

the appellant's notice must be filed at the Court of Appeal within 14 days after the date of that hearing.

(2) Where the appellant applies in writing to the Registrar of the tribunal for permission to appeal and –

    (a) permission is given; or

    (b) permission is refused and the appellant wishes to make an application to the Court of Appeal for permission to appeal,

the appellant's notice must be filed at the Court of Appeal within 14 days after the date of receipt of the tribunal's decision on permission.

(3) Where the appellant does not make an application to the tribunal for permission to appeal, but wishes to make an application to the Court of Appeal for permission, the appellant's notice must be filed at the Court of Appeal within 14 days after the end of the period within which he may make a written application to the Registrar of the tribunal.

Appeals relating to the application of Articles 81 and 82 of the EC Treaty and Chapters I and II of Part I of the Competition Act 1998

21.10A

(1) This paragraph applies to any appeal to the Court of Appeal relating to the application of –

    (a) Article 81 or Article 82 of the Treaty establishing the European Community; or

    (b) Chapter I or Chapter II of Part I of the Competition Act 1998.

(2) In this paragraph –

    (a) 'the Act' means the Competition Act 1998;

    (b) 'the Commission' means the European Commission;

    (c) 'the Competition Regulation' means Council Regulation (EC) No. 1/2003 of 16 December 2002 on the implementation of the rules on competition laid down in Articles 81 and 82 of the Treaty;

    (d) 'national competition authority' means –

        (i) the Office of Fair Trading; and

      (ii) any other person or body designated pursuant to Article 35 of the Competition Regulation as a national competition authority of the United Kingdom;

   (e) 'the Treaty' means the Treaty establishing the European Community.

(3) Any party whose appeal notice raises an issue relating to the application of Article 81 or 82 of the Treaty, or Chapter I or II of Part I of the Act, must –

   (a) state that fact in his appeal notice; and

   (b) serve a copy of the appeal notice on the Office of Fair Trading at the same time as it is served on the other party to the appeal (addressed to the Director of Competition Policy Coordination, Office of Fair Trading, Fleetbank House, 2–6 Salisbury Square, London EC4Y 8JX).

(4) Attention is drawn to the provisions of article 15.3 of the Competition Regulation, which entitles competition authorities and the Commission to submit written observations to national courts on issues relating to the application of Article 81 or 82 and, with the permission of the court in question, to submit oral observations to the court.

(5) A national competition authority may also make written observations to the Court of Appeal, or apply for permission to make oral observations, on issues relating to the application of Chapter I or II.

(6) If a national competition authority or the Commission intends to make written observations to the Court of Appeal, it must give notice of its intention to do so by letter to the Civil Appeals Office at the earliest opportunity.

(7) An application by a national competition authority or the Commission for permission to make oral representations at the hearing of an appeal must be made by letter to the Civil Appeals Office at the earliest opportunity, identifying the appeal and indicating why the applicant wishes to make oral representations.

(8) If a national competition authority or the Commission files a notice under sub-paragraph (6) or an application under sub-paragraph (7), it must at the same time serve a copy of the notice or application on every party to the appeal.

(9) Any request by a national competition authority or the Commission for the court to send it any documents relating to an appeal should be made at the same time as filing a notice under sub-paragraph (6) or an application under sub-paragraph (7).

(10) When the Court of Appeal receives a notice under sub-paragraph (6) it may give case management directions to the national competition authority or the Commission, including directions about the date by which any written observations are to be filed.

(11) The Court of Appeal will serve on every party to the appeal a copy of any directions given or order made –

   (a) on an application under sub-paragraph (7); or

(b) under sub-paragraph (10).

(12) Every party to an appeal which raises an issue relating to the application of Article 81 or 82, and any national competition authority which has been served with a copy of a party's appeal notice, is under a duty to notify the Court of Appeal at any stage of the appeal if they are aware that –

(a) the Commission has adopted, or is contemplating adopting, a decision in relation to proceedings which it has initiated; and

(b) the decision referred to in (a) above has or would have legal effects in relation to the particular agreement, decision or practice in issue before the court.

(13) Where the Court of Appeal is aware that the Commission is contemplating adopting a decision as mentioned in sub-paragraph (12)(a), it shall consider whether to stay the appeal pending the Commission's decision.

(14) Where any judgment is given which decides on the application of Article 81 or 82, the court shall direct that a copy of the transcript of the judgment shall be sent to the Commission. Judgments may be sent to the Commission electronically to comp-amicus@cec.eu.int or by post to the European Commission – DG Competition, B–1049, Brussels.

Appeal from Proscribed Organisations Appeal Commission

21.11

(1) The appellant's notice must be filed at the Court of Appeal within 14 days after the date when the Proscribed Organisations Appeal Commission –

(a) granted; or

(b) where section 6(2)(b) of the Terrorism Act 2000 applies, refused permission to appeal.

APPEALS TO THE HIGH COURT — QUEEN'S BENCH DIVISION

22.1 The following appeals are to be heard in the Queen's Bench Division.

Statutory Appeals

Appeals under the Merchant Shipping Act 1995

22.2

(1) This paragraph applies to appeals under the Merchant Shipping Act 1995 and for this purpose a re-hearing and an application under section 61 of the Merchant Shipping Act 1995 are treated as appeals.

(2) The appellant must file any report to the Secretary of State containing the decision from which the appeal is brought with the appellant's notice.

(3) Where a re-hearing by the High Court is ordered under sections 64 or 269 of the Merchant Shipping Act 1995, the Secretary of State must give reasonable notice to the parties whom he considers to be affected by the re-hearing.

Appeals against decisions affecting the registration of architects and health care professionals

22.3

(1) This paragraph applies to an appeal to the High Court under –

  (a) section 22 of the Architects Act 1997;

  (b) section 82(3) and 83(2) of the Medicines Act 1968;

  (c) section 12 of the Nurses, Midwives and Health Visitors Act 1997;

  (cc) article 38 of the Nursing and Midwifery Order 2001;

  (d) section 10 of the Pharmacy Act 1954;

  (e) section 40 of the Medical Act 1983;

  (f) section 29 or section 44 of the Dentists Act 1984;

  (g) sections 23 of the Opticians Act 1989;

  (h) section 31 of the Osteopaths Act 1993; and

  (i) section 31 of the Chiropractors Act 1994.

(2) Every appeal to which this paragraph applies must be supported by written evidence and, if the court so orders, oral evidence and will be by way of re-hearing.

(3) The appellant must file the appellant's notice within 28 days after the decision that the appellant wishes to appeal.

(4) In the case of an appeal under an enactment specified in column 1 of the following table, the persons to be made respondents are the persons specified in relation to that enactment in column 2 of the table and the person to be served with the appellant's notice is the person so specified in column 3.

1 Enactment	2 Respondents	3 Person to be served
Architects Act 1997, s. 22	The Architects' Registration Council of the United Kingdom	The registrar of the Council
Medicines Act 1968, s. 82(3) and s. 83(2)	The Pharmaceutical Society of Great Britain	The registrar of the Society
Nurses, Midwives and Health Visitors Act 1997, s. 12; Nursing and Midwifery Order 2001, art. 38	The Nursing and Midwifery Council	The Registrar of the Council
Pharmacy Act 1954, s. 10	The Royal Pharmaceutical Society of Great Britain	The registrar of the Society

Medical Act 1983, s. 40	The General Medical Council	The Registrar of the Council
Dentists Act 1984, s. 29 or s. 44	The General Dental Council	The Registrar of the Council
Opticians Act 1989, s. 23	The General Optical Council	The Registrar of the Council
Osteopaths Act 1993, s. 31	The General Osteopathic Council	The Registrar of the Council
Chiropractors Act 1994, s. 31	The General Chiropractic Council	The Registrar of the Council

Consumer Credit Act 1974: appeal from Secretary of State

22.4

    (1) A person dissatisfied in point of law with a decision of the Secretary of State on an appeal under section 41 of the Consumer Credit Act 1974 from a determination of the Office of Fair Trading who had a right to appeal to the Secretary of State, whether or not he exercised that right, may appeal to the High Court.

    (2) The appellant must serve the appellant's notice on –

        (a) the Secretary of State;

        (b) the original applicant, if any, where the appeal is by a licensee under a group licence against compulsory variation, suspension or revocation of that licence; and

        (c) any other person as directed by the court.

    (3) The appeal court may remit the matter to the Secretary of State to the extent necessary to enable him to provide the court with such further information as the court may direct.

    (4) If the appeal court allows the appeal, it shall not set aside or vary the decision but shall remit the matter to the Secretary of State with the opinion of the court for hearing and determination by him.

The Pensions Appeal Tribunal Act 1943

22.5

    (1) In this paragraph 'the judge' means the judge nominated by the Lord Chancellor under section 6(2) of the Pensions Appeal Tribunals Act 1943 ('the Act').

    (2) An application to the judge for permission to appeal against a decision of a Pensions Appeal Tribunal –

        (a) may not be made unless an application was made to the tribunal and was refused; and

        (b) must be made within 28 days after the date of the tribunal's refusal.

(3) The appellant's notice seeking permission to appeal from the judge must contain –

  (a) the point of law as respects which the appellant alleges that the tribunal's decision was wrong; and

  (b) the date of the tribunal's decision refusing permission to appeal.

(4) The court officer shall request the chairman of the tribunal to give the judge a written statement of the reasons for the tribunal's decision to refuse permission to appeal, and within 7 days after receiving the request, the chairman must give the judge such a statement.

(5) Where permission to appeal was given by –

  (a) the tribunal, the appellant must file and serve the appellant's notice;

  (b) the judge, the appellant must serve the appellant's notice,

  within 28 days after permission to appeal was given.

(6) Within 28 days after service of the notice of appeal on him, the chairman of the tribunal must –

  (a) state a case setting out the facts on which the decision appealed against was based;

  (b) file the case stated at the court; and

  (c) serve a copy of the case stated on the appellant and the respondent.

(7) A copy of the judge's order on the appeal must be sent by the court officer to the appellant, the respondent and the chairman of the tribunal.

The Social Security Administration Act 1992

22.6

(1) Any person who by virtue of section 18 or 58(8) of the Social Security Administration Act 1992 ('the Act') is entitled and wishes to appeal against a decision of the Secretary of State on a question of law must, within the prescribed period, or within such further time as the Secretary of State may allow, serve on the Secretary of State a notice requiring him to state a case setting out –

  (a) his decision; and

  (b) the facts on which his decision was based.

(2) Unless paragraph (3) applies the prescribed period is 28 days after receipt of the notice of the decision.

(3) Where, within 28 days after receipt of notice of the decision, a request is made to the Secretary of State in accordance with regulations made under the Act to furnish a statement of the grounds of the decision, the prescribed period is 28 days after receipt of that statement.

(4) Where under section 18 or section 58(8) of the Act, the Secretary of State refers a question of law to the court, he must state that question together with the relevant facts in a case.

(5) The appellant's notice and the case stated must be filed at the appeal court and a copy of the notice and the case stated served on –

    (a) the Secretary of State; and

    (b) every person as between whom and the Secretary of State the question has arisen,

within 28 days after the case stated was served on the party at whose request, or as a result of whose application to the court, the case was stated.

(6) Unless the appeal court otherwise orders, the appeal or reference shall not be heard sooner than 28 days after service of the appellant's notice.

(7) The appeal court may order the case stated by the Secretary of State to be returned to the Secretary of State for him to hear further evidence.

Appeals under the Extradition Act 2003

22.6A

(1) In this paragraph, 'the Act' means the Extradition Act 2003.

(2) Appeals to the High Court under the Act must be brought in the Administrative Court of the Queen's Bench Division.

(3) Where an appeal is brought under section 26 or 28 of the Act –

    (a) the appellant's notice must be filed and served before the expiry of 7 days, starting with the day on which the order is made;

    (b) the appellant must endorse the appellant's notice with the date of the person's arrest;

    (c) the High Court must begin to hear the substantive appeal within 40 days of the person's arrest; and

    (d) the appellant must serve a copy of the appellant's notice on the Crown Prosecution Service, if they are not a party to the appeal, in addition to the persons to be served under rule 52.4(3) and in accordance with that rule.

(4) The High Court may extend the period of 40 days under paragraph (3)(c) if it believes it to be in the interests of justice to do so.

(5) Where an appeal is brought under section 103 of the Act, the appellant's notice must be filed and served before the expiry of 14 days, starting with the day on which the Secretary of State informs the person under section 100(1) or (4) of the Act of the order he has made in respect of the person.

(6) Where an appeal is brought under section 105 of the Act, the appellant's notice must be filed and served before the expiry of

14 days, starting with the day on which the order for discharge is made.

(7) Where an appeal is brought under section 108 of the Act the appellant's notice must be filed and served before the expiry of 14 days, starting with the day on which the Secretary of State informs the person that he has ordered his extradition.

(8) Where an appeal is brought under section 110 of the Act the appellant's notice must be filed and served before the expiry of 14 days, starting with the day on which the Secretary of State informs the person acting on behalf of a category 2 territory, as defined in section 69 of the Act, of the order for discharge. (Section 69 of the Act provides that a category 2 territory is that designated for the purposes of Part 2 of the Act).

(9) Subject to paragraph (10), where an appeal is brought under section 103, 105, 108 or 110 of the Act, the High Court must begin to hear the substantive appeal within 76 days of the appellant's notice being filed.

(10) Where an appeal is brought under section 103 of the Act before the Secretary of State has decided whether the person is to be extradited –

(a) the period of 76 days does not start until the day on which the Secretary of State informs the person of his decision; and

(b) the Secretary of State must, as soon as practicable after he informs the person of his decision, inform the High Court –
(i) of his decision; and
(ii) of the date on which he informs the person of his decision.

(11) The High Court may extend the period of 76 days if it believes it to be in the interests of justice to do so.

(12) Where an appeal is brought under section 103, 105, 108 or 110 of the Act, the appellant must serve a copy of the appellant's notice on –

(a) the Crown Prosecution Service; and
(b) the Home Office,

if they are not a party to the appeal, in addition to the persons to be served under rule 52.4(3) and in accordance with that rule.

Appeals under section 49 of the Solicitors Act 1974

22.6B

(1) This paragraph applies to appeals from the Solicitors Disciplinary Tribunal ('the Tribunal') to the High Court under section 49(1)(b) of the Solicitors Act 1974 ('the Act'). The procedure for appeals to the Master of the Rolls under section 49(1)(a) of the Act is set out in the Master of the Rolls (Appeals and Applications) Regulations 2001.

(2) Appeals to the High Court under section 49(1)(b) of the Act must be brought in the Administrative Court of the Queen's Bench Division.

(3) The appellant's notice –

(a) must state in the heading that the appeal relates to a solicitor, or a solicitor's clerk, and is made under section 49 of the Act;

(b) must be filed within 14 days after the date on which the Tribunal's statement of its findings was filed with the Law Society in accordance with section 48(1) of the Act; and

(c) must be accompanied by copies of the order appealed against and the statement of the Tribunal's findings required by section 48(1) of the Act; and

(d) unless the court orders otherwise, must be served by the appellant on –

(i) every party to the proceedings before the Tribunal; and

(ii) the Law Society.

(4) The court –

(a) may order an appellant to give security for the costs of an appeal only if he was the applicant in the proceedings before the tribunal; and

(b) may not order any other party to give security for costs.

(5) The court may direct the Tribunal to provide it with a written statement of their opinion on the case, or on any question arising in it. If the court gives such a direction, the clerk to the Tribunal must as soon as possible –

(a) file the statement; and

(b) serve a copy on each party to the appeal.

(6) The court may give permission for any person to intervene to be heard in opposition to the appeal.

(7) An appellant may at any time discontinue his appeal by –

(a) serving notice of discontinuance on the clerk to the Tribunal and every other party to the appeal; and

(b) filing a copy of the notice.

(8) Unless the court orders otherwise, an appellant who discontinues is liable for the costs of every other party to the appeal.

Appeals by way of case stated

Reference of question of law by Agriculture Land Tribunal

22.7

(1) A question of law referred to the High Court by an Agricultural Land Tribunal under section 6 of the Agriculture (Mis-

cellaneous Provisions) Act 1954 shall be referred by way of case stated by the Tribunal.

(2) Where the proceedings before the tribunal arose on an application under section 11 of the Agricultural Holdings Act 1986, an –

  (a) application notice for an order under section 6 that the tribunal refers a question of law to the court; and

  (b) appellant's notice by which an appellant seeks the court's determination on a question of law, must be served on the authority having power to enforce the statutory requirement specified in the notice in addition to every other party to those proceedings and on the secretary of the tribunal.

(3) Where, in accordance with paragraph (2), a notice is served on the authority mentioned in that paragraph, that authority may attend the appeal hearing and make representations to the court.

Case stated by Mental Health Review Tribunal

22.8

(1) In this paragraph 'the Act' means the Mental Health Act 1983 and 'party to proceedings' means –

  (a) the person who initiated the proceedings; and

  (b) any person to whom, in accordance with rules made under section 78 of the Act, the tribunal sent notice of the application or reference or a request instead notice of reference.

(2) A party to proceedings shall not be entitled to apply to the High Court for an order under section 78(8) of the Act directing the tribunal to state a case for determination by court unless –

  (a) within 21 days after the decision of the tribunal was communicated to him in accordance with rules made under section 78 of the Act he made a written request to the tribunal to state a case; and

  (b) either the tribunal
     (i) failed to comply with that request within 21 days after it was made; or
     (ii) refused to comply with it.

(3) The period for filing the application notice for an order under section 78(8) of the Act is –

  (a) where the tribunal failed to comply with the applicant's request to state a case within the period mentioned in paragraph 2(b)(i), 14 days after the expiration of that period;

  (b) where the tribunal refused that request, 14 days after receipt by the applicant of notice of the refusal of his request.

(4) A Mental Health Review Tribunal by whom a case is stated shall be entitled to attend the proceedings for the determination of the case and make representations to the court.

(5) If the court allows the appeal, it may give any direction which the tribunal ought to have given under Part V of the Act.

APPEALS TO THE HIGH COURT — CHANCERY DIVISION

23.1 The following appeals are to be heard in the Chancery Division.

DETERMINATION OF APPEAL OR CASE STATED UNDER VARIOUS ACTS

23.2 Any appeal to the High Court, and any case stated or question referred for the opinion of that court under any of the following enactments shall be heard in the Chancery Division –

(1) paragraph 16 of Schedule 15 to the Law of Property Act 1922;
(2) the Industrial Assurance Act 1923;
(3) the Land Registration Act 1925;
(4) section 205(4) of the Water Resources Act 1991;
(5) section 38(3) of the Clergy Pensions Measure 1961;
(6) the Industrial and Provident Societies Act 1965;
(7) section 151 of the Pension Schemes Act 1993;
(8) section 173 of the Pension Schemes Act 1993;
(9) section 97 of the Pensions Act 1995;
(10) The Charities Act 1993.
(11) section 13 and 13B of the Stamp Act 1891;
(12) section 705A of the Income and Corporation Taxes Act 1988;
(13) regulation 22 of the General Commissioners (Jurisdiction and Procedure) Regulations 1994;
(14) section 53, 56A or 100C(4) of the Taxes Management Act 1970;
(15) section 222(3), 225, 249(3) or 251 of the Inheritance Tax Act 1984;
(16) regulation 8(3) or 10 of the Stamp Duty Reserve Tax Regulations 1986;
(17) the Land Registration Act 2002;
(18) regulation 74 of the European Public Limited-Liability Company Regulations 2004.

(This list is not exhaustive)

Statutory Appeals

Appeal under section 222 of the Inheritance Tax Act 1984

23.3

(1) This paragraph applies to appeals to the High Court under section 222(3) of the Inheritance Tax Act 1984 (the '1984 Act') and regulation 8(3) of the Stamp Duty Reserve Tax Regulations 1986 (the '1986 Regulations').

(2) The appellant's notice must –

    (a) state the date on which the Commissioners for HM Revenue and Customs (the 'Board') gave notice to the appellant under section 221 of the 1984 Act or regulation 6 of the 1986 Regulations of the determination that is the subject of the appeal;

    (b) state the date on which the appellant gave to the Board notice of appeal under section 222(1) of the 1984 Act or regulation 8(1) of the 1986 Regulations and, if notice was not given within the time permitted, whether the Board or the Special Commissioners have given their consent to the appeal being brought out of time, and, if they have, the date they gave their consent; and

    (c) either state that the appellant and the Board have agreed that the appeal may be to the High Court or contain an application for permission to appeal to the High Court.

(3) The appellant must file the following documents with the appellant's notice –

    (a) 2 copies of the notice referred to in paragraph 2(a);

    (b) 2 copies of the notice of appeal (under section 222(1) of the 1984 Act or regulation 8(1) of the 1986 Regulations) referred to in paragraph 2(b); and

    (c) where the appellant's notice contains an application for permission to appeal, written evidence setting out the grounds on which it is alleged that the matters to be decided on the appeal are likely to be substantially confined to questions of law.

(4) The appellant must –

    (a) file the appellant's notice at the court; and

    (b) serve the appellant's notice on the Board,

within 30 days of the date on which the appellant gave to the Board notice of appeal under section 222(1) of the 1984 Act or regulation 8(1) of the 1986 Regulations or, if the Board or the Special Commissioners have given consent to the appeal being brought out of time, within 30 days of the date on which such consent was given.

(5) The court will set a date for the hearing of not less than 40 days from the date that the appellant's notice was filed.

(6) Where the appellant's notice contains an application for permission to appeal –

(a) a copy of the written evidence filed in accordance with paragraph (3)(c) must be served on the Board with the appellant's notice; and

(b) the Board –
   (i) may file written evidence; and
   (ii) if it does so, must serve a copy of that evidence on the appellant,

within 30 days after service of the written evidence under paragraph (6)(a).

(7) The appellant may not rely on any grounds of appeal not specified in the notice referred to in paragraph (2)(b) on the hearing of the appeal without the permission of the court.

Appeals under section 53 and 100C(4) of the Taxes Management Act 1970 and section 249(3) or 251 of the Inheritance Tax Act 1984

23.4

(1) The appellant must serve the appellant's notice on –

(a) the General or Special Commissioners against whose decision, award or determination the appeal is brought; and

(b) (i) in the case of an appeal brought under section 100C(4) of the Taxes Management Act 1970 or section 249(3) of the Inheritance Tax Act 1984 by any party other than the defendant in the proceedings before the Commissioners, that defendant; or
   (ii) in any other case, the Commissioners for HM Revenue and Customs.

(2) The appellant must file the appellant's notice at the court within 30 days after the date of the decision, award or determination against which the appeal is brought.

(3) Within 30 days of the service on them of the appellant's notice, the General or Special Commissioners, as the case may be, must –

(a) file 2 copies of a note of their findings and of the reasons for their decision, award or determination at the court; and

(b) serve a copy of the note on every other party to the appeal.

(4) Any document to be served on the General or Special Commissioners may be served by delivering or sending it to their clerk.

Appeals under section 56A of the Taxes Management Act 1970, section 225 of the Inheritance Tax Act 1984 and regulation 10 of the Stamp Duty Reserve Tax Regulations 1986

23.5

(1) The appellant must file the appellant's notice –

(a) where the appeal is made following the refusal of the Special Commissioners to issue a certificate under section 56A(2)(b) of the Taxes Management Act 1970, within 28 days from the date of the release of the decision of the Special Commissioners containing the refusal;

(b) where the appeal is made following the refusal of permission to appeal to the Court of Appeal under section 56A(2)(c) of that Act, within 28 days from the date when permission is refused; or

(c) in all other cases within 56 days after the date of the decision or determination that the appellant wishes to appeal.

Appeal under section 17 of the Industrial Assurance Act 1923

23.6 The appellant must file the appellant's notice within 21 days after the date of the Commissioner's refusal or direction under section 17(3) of the Industrial Assurance Act 1923.

Appeals affecting industrial and provident societies etc.

23.7

(1) This paragraph applies to all appeals under –

(a) the Friendly Societies Act 1974;
(b) the Friendly Societies Act 1992;
(c) the Industrial Assurance Act 1923; and
(d) the Industrial and Provident Societies Act 1965

(2) At any stage on an appeal, the court may –

(a) direct that the appellant's notice be served on any person;
(b) direct that notice be given by advertisement or otherwise of –

(i) the bringing of the appeal;
(ii) the nature of the appeal; and
(iii) the time when the appeal will or is likely to be heard; or

(c) give such other directions as it thinks proper to enable any person interested in –
(i) the society, trade union, alleged trade union or industrial assurance company; or
(ii) the subject matter of the appeal,
to appear and be heard at the appeal hearing.

Appeal from Value Added Tax and Duties Tribunal

23.8

(1) A party to proceedings before a Value Added Tax and Duties Tribunal who is dissatisfied in point of law with a decision of the tribunal may appeal under section 11(1) of the Tribunals and Inquiries Act 1992 to the High Court.

(2) The appellant must file the appellant's notice –

(a) where the appeal is made following the refusal of the Value Added Tax and Duties Tribunal to grant a certificate under article 2(b) of the Value Added Tax and Duties Tribunal Appeals Order 1986, within 28 days from the date of the release of the decision containing the refusal;

(b) in all other cases within 56 days after the date of the decision or determination that the appellant wishes to appeal.

Appeal against an order or decision of the Charity Commissioners

23.8A

(1) In this paragraph –

'the Act' means the Charities Act 1993; and
'the Commissioners' means the Charity Commissioners for England and Wales.

(2) The Attorney-General, unless he is the appellant, must be made a respondent to the appeal.

(3) The appellant's notice must state the grounds of the appeal, and the appellant may not rely on any other grounds without the permission of the court.

(4) Sub-paragraphs (5) and (6) apply, in addition to the above provisions, where the appeal is made under section 16(12) of the Act.

(5) If the Commissioners have granted a certificate that it is a proper case for an appeal, a copy of the certificate must be filed with the appellant's notice.

(6) If the appellant applies in the appellant's notice for permission to appeal under section 16(13) of the Act –

(a) the appellant's notice must state –
  (i) that the appellant has requested the Commissioners to grant a certificate that it is a proper case for an appeal, and they have refused to do so;
  (ii) the date of such refusal;
  (iii) the grounds on which the appellant alleges that it is a proper case for an appeal; and
  (iv) if the application for permission to appeal is made with the consent of any other party to the proposed appeal, that fact;

(b) if the Commissioners have given reasons for refusing a certificate, a copy of the reasons must be attached to the appellant's notice;

(c) the court may, before determining the application, direct the Commissioners to file a written statement of their reasons for refusing a certificate;

(d) the court will serve on the appellant a copy of any statement filed under sub-paragraph (c).

Appeal against a decision of the adjudicator under section 111 of the Land Registration Act 2002

23.8B

(1) A person who is aggrieved by a decision of the adjudicator and who wishes to appeal that decision must obtain permission to appeal.

(2) The appellant must serve on the adjudicator a copy of the appeal court's decision on a request for permission to appeal as soon as reasonably practicable and in any event within 14 days of receipt by the appellant of the decision on permission.

(3) The appellant must serve on the adjudicator and the Chief Land Registrar a copy of any order by the appeal court to stay a decision of the adjudicator pending the outcome of the appeal as soon as reasonably practicable and in any event within 14 days of receipt by the appellant of the appeal court's order to stay.

(4) The appellant must serve on the adjudicator and the Chief Land Registrar a copy of the appeal court's decision on the appeal as soon as reasonably practicable and in any event within 14 days of receipt by the appellant of the appeal court's decision.

Appeals under regulation 74 of the European Public Limited-Liability Company Regulations 2004

23.8C

(1) In this paragraph –

(a) 'the 2004 Regulations' means the European Public Limited-Liability Company Regulations 2004;

(b) 'the EC Regulation' means Council Regulation (EC) No 2157/2001 of 8 October 2001 on the Statute for a European company (SE);

(c) 'SE' means a European public limited-liability company (Societas Europaea) within the meaning of Article 1 of the EC Regulation.

(2) This paragraph applies to appeals under regulation 74 of the 2004 Regulations against the opposition –

(a) of the Secretary of State or national financial supervisory authority to the transfer of the registered office of an SE under Article 8(14) of the EC Regulation; and

(b) of the Secretary of State to the participation by a company in the formation of an SE by merger under Article 19 of the EC Regulation.

(3) Where an SE seeks to appeal against the opposition of the national financial supervisory authority to the transfer of its registered office under Article 8(14) of the EC Regulation, it must serve the appellant's notice on both the national financial supervisory authority and the Secretary of State.

(4) The appellant's notice must contain an application for permission to appeal.

(5) The appeal will be a review of the decision of the Secretary of State and not a re-hearing. The grounds of review are set out in regulation 74(2) of the 2004 Regulations.

(6) The appeal will be heard by a High Court judge.

APPEALS BY WAY OF CASE STATED

PROCEEDINGS UNDER THE COMMONS REGISTRATION ACT 1965

23.9 A person aggrieved by the decision of a Commons Commissioner who requires the Commissioner to state a case for the opinion of the High Court under section 18 of the Commons Registration Act 1965 must file the appellant's notice within 42 days from the date on which notice of the decision was sent to the aggrieved person.

APPEALS TO A COUNTY COURT

Local Government (Miscellaneous Provisions) Act 1976

24.1 Where one of the grounds upon which an appeal against a notice under sections 21, 23 or 35 of the Local Government (Miscellaneous Provisions) Act 1976 is brought is that –

(a) it would have been fairer to serve the notice on another person; or

(b) that it would be reasonable for the whole or part of the expenses to which the appeal relates to be paid by some other person, that person must be made a respondent to the appeal, unless the court, on application of the appellant made without notice, otherwise directs.

Appeals under sections 204 and 204A of the Housing Act 1996

24.2

(1) An appellant should include appeals under section 204 and section 204A of the Housing Act 1996 in one appellant's notice.

(2) If it is not possible to do so (for example because an urgent application under section 204A is required) the appeals may be included in separate appellant's notices.

(3) An appeal under section 204A may include an application for an order under section 204A(4)(a) requiring the authority to secure that accommodation is available for the applicant's occupation.

(4) If, exceptionally, the court makes an order under section 204A(4)(a) without notice, the appellant's notice must be served on the authority together with the order. Such an order will normally require the authority to secure that accommodation is available until a hearing date when the authority can make representations as to whether the order under section 204A(4)(a) should be continued.

Appeal under Part II of the Immigration and Asylum Act 1999 (carriers' liability)

24.3

(1) A person appealing to a county court under section 35A or section 40B of the Immigration and Asylum Act 1999 ("the Act") against a decision by the Secretary of State to impose a penalty under section 32 or a charge under section 40 of the Act must, subject to paragraph (2), file the appellant's notice within 28 days after receiving the penalty notice or charge notice.

(2) Where the appellant has given notice of objection to the Secretary of State under section 35(4) or section 40A(3) of the Act within the time prescribed for doing so, he must file the appellant's notice within 28 days after receiving notice of the Secretary of State's decision in response to the notice of objection.

(3) Sections 35A and 40B of the Act provide that any appeal under those sections shall be a rehearing of the Secretary of State's decision to impose a penalty or charge, and therefore rule 52.11(1) does not apply.

SECTION IV – PROVISIONS ABOUT REOPENING APPEALS

REOPENING OF FINAL APPEALS

25.1 This paragraph applies to applications under rule 52.17 for permission to reopen a final determination of an appeal.

25.2 In this paragraph, "appeal" includes an application for permission to appeal.

25.3 Permission must be sought from the court whose decision the applicant wishes to reopen.

25.4 The application for permission must be made by application notice and supported by written evidence, verified by a statement of truth.

25.5 A copy of the application for permission must not be served on any other party to the original appeal unless the court so directs.

25.6 Where the court directs that the application for permission is to be served on another party, that party may within 14 days of the service on him of the copy of the application file and serve a written statement either supporting or opposing the application.

25.7 The application for permission, and any written statements supporting or opposing it, will be considered on paper by a single judge, and will be allowed to proceed only if the judge so directs.

A2–037

PRACTICE DIRECTION

PROTOCOLS

GENERAL

1.1 This Practice Direction applies to the pre-action protocols which have been approved by the Head of Civil Justice.

1.2 The pre-action protocols which have been approved are set out in para 5.1. Other pre-action protocols may subsequently be added.

1.3 Pre-action protocols outline the steps parties should take to seek information from and to provide information to each other about a prospective legal claim.

1.4 The objectives of pre-action protocols are:

(1) to encourage the exchange of early and full information about the prospective legal claim,

(2) to enable parties to avoid litigation by agreeing a settlement of the claim before the commencement of proceedings,

(3) to support the efficient management of proceedings where litigation cannot be avoided.

COMPLIANCE WITH PROTOCOLS

2.1 The Civil Procedure Rules enable the court to take into account compliance or non-compliance with an applicable protocol when giving directions for the management of proceedings (see CPR rules 3.1(4) and (5) and 3.9(e)) and when making orders for costs (see CPR rule 44.3(a)).

2.2 The court will expect all parties to have complied in substance with the terms of an approved protocol.

2.3 If, in the opinion of the court, non-compliance has led to the commencement of proceedings which might otherwise not have needed to be commenced, or has led to costs being incurred in the proceedings that might otherwise not have been incurred, the orders the court may make include:

(1) an order that the party at fault pay the costs of the proceedings, or part of those costs, of the other party or parties;

(2) an order that the party at fault pay those costs on an indemnity basis;

(3) if the party at fault is a claimant in whose favour an order for the payment of damages or some specified sum is subsequently made, an order depriving that party of interest on such sum and in respect of such period as may be specified, and/or awarding interest at a lower rate than that at which interest would otherwise have been awarded;

(4) if the party at fault is a defendant and an order for the payment of damages or some specified sum is subsequently made in favour of the claimant, an order awarding interest on such sum and in respect of such period as may be specified at a higher rate, not exceeding 10% above base rate (cf. CPR rule 36.21(2), than the rate at which interest would otherwise have been awarded.

2.4 The court will exercise its powers under paragraphs 2.1 and 2.3 with the object of placing the innocent party in no worse a position than he would have been in if the protocol had been complied with.

3.1 A claimant may be found to have failed to comply with a protocol by, for example:

(a) not having provided sufficient information to the defendant, or

(b) not having followed the procedure required by the protocol to be followed (e.g. not having followed the medical expert instruction procedure set out in the Personal Injury Protocol).

3.2 A defendant may be found to have failed to comply with a protocol by, for example:

(a) not making a preliminary response to the letter of claim within the time fixed for that purpose by the relevant protocol (21 days under the Personal Injury Protocol, 14 days under the Clinical Negligence Protocol),

(b) not making a full response within the time fixed for that purpose by the relevant protocol (3 months of the letter of claim under the Clinical Negligence Protocol, 3 months from the date of acknowledgement of the letter of claim under the Personal Injury Protocol),

(c) not disclosing documents required to be disclosed by the relevant protocol.

3.3 The court is likely to treat this practice direction as indicating the normal, reasonable way of dealing with disputes. If proceedings are issued and parties have not complied with this practice direction or a specific protocol, it will be for the court to decide whether sanctions should be applied.

3.4 The court is not likely to be concerned with minor infringements of the practice direction or protocols. The court is likely to look at the effect of non-compliance on the other party when deciding whether to impose sanctions.

3.5 This practice direction does not alter the statutory time limits for starting court proceedings. A claimant is required to start proceedings within those time limits and to adhere to subsequent time limits required by the rules or ordered by the court. If proceedings are for any reason started before the parties have followed the procedures in this practice direction, the parties are encouraged to agree to apply to the court for a stay of the proceedings while they follow the practice direction.

PRE-ACTION BEHAVIOUR IN OTHER CASES

4.1 In cases not covered by any approved protocol, the court will expect the parties, in accordance with the overriding objective and the matters referred to in CPR 1.1(2)(a), (b) and (c), to act reasonably in exchanging information and documents relevant to the claim and generally in trying to avoid the necessity for the start of proceedings.

4.2 Parties to a potential dispute should follow a reasonable procedure, suitable to their particular circumstances, which is intended to avoid litigation. The procedure should not be regarded as a prelude to inevitable litigation. It should normally include –

    (a) the claimant writing to give details of the claim;
    (b) the defendant acknowledging the claim letter promptly;
    (c) the defendant giving within a reasonable time a detailed written response; and
    (d) the parties conducting genuine and reasonable negotiations with a view to settling the claim economically and without court proceedings.

4.3 The claimant's letter should –

    (a) give sufficient concise details to enable the recipient to understand and investigate the claim without extensive further information;
    (b) enclose copies of the essential documents which the claimant relies on;
    (c) ask for a prompt acknowledgement of the letter, followed by a full written response within a reasonable stated period;
    (For many claims, a normal reasonable period for a full response may be one month.)
    (d) state whether court proceedings will be issued if the full response is not received within the stated period;

(e) identify and ask for copies of any essential documents, not in his possession, which the claimant wishes to see;

(f) state (if this is so) that the claimant wishes to enter into mediation or another alternative method of dispute resolution; and

(g) draw attention to the court's powers to impose sanctions for failure to comply with this practice direction and, if the recipient is likely to be unrepresented, enclose a copy of this practice direction.

4.4 The defendant should acknowledge the claimant's letter in writing within 21 days of receiving it. The acknowledgement should state when the defendant will give a full written response. If the time for this is longer than the period stated by the claimant, the defendant should give reasons why a longer period is needed.

4.5 The defendant's full written response should as appropriate –

(a) accept the claim in whole or in part and make proposals for settlement; or

(b) state that the claim is not accepted.

If the claim is accepted in part only, the response should make clear which part is accepted and which part is not accepted.

4.6 If the defendant does not accept the claim or part of it, the response should –

(a) give detailed reasons why the claim is not accepted, identifying which of the claimant's contentions are accepted and which are in dispute;

(b) enclose copies of the essential documents which the defendant relies on;

(c) enclose copies of documents asked for by the claimant, or explain why they are not enclosed;

(d) identify and ask for copies of any further essential documents, not in his possession, which the defendant wishes to see; and (The claimant should provide these within a reasonably short time or explain in writing why he is not doing so.)

(e) state whether the defendant is prepared to enter into mediation or another alternative method of dispute resolution.

4.7 The parties should consider whether some form of alternative dispute resolution procedure would be more suitable than litigation, and if so, endeavour to agree which form to adopt. Both the Claimant and Defendant may be required by the Court to provide evidence that alternative means of resolving their dispute were considered. The Courts take the view that litigation should be a last resort, and that claims should not be issued prematurely when a settlement is still actively being explored. Parties are warned that if the protocol is not followed (including this paragraph) then the Court must have regard to such conduct when determining costs.

It is not practicable in this protocol to address in detail how the parties might decide which method to adopt to resolve their particular dispute. However, summarised below are some of the options for resolving disputes without litigation:

- Discussion and negotiation.
- Early neutral evaluation by an independent third party (for example, a lawyer experienced in that field or an individual experienced in the subject matter of the claim).
- Mediation – a form of facilitated negotiation assisted by an independent neutral party.

The Legal Services Commission has published a booklet on 'Alternatives to Court', CLS Direct Information Leaflet 23 (www.clsdirect.org.uk/legalhelp/leaflet23.jsp), which lists a number of organisations that provide alternative dispute resolution services.

It is expressly recognised that no party can or should be forced to mediate or enter into any form of ADR.

4.8 Documents disclosed by either party in accordance with this practice direction may not be used for any purpose other than resolving the dispute, unless the other party agrees.

4.9 The resolution of some claims, but by no means all, may need help from an expert. If an expert is needed, the parties should wherever possible and to save expense engage an agreed expert.

4.10 Parties should be aware that, if the matter proceeds to litigation, the court may not allow the use of an expert's report, and that the cost of it is not always recoverable.

INFORMATION ABOUT FUNDING ARRANGEMENTS

4A.1 Where a person enters into a funding arrangement within the meaning of rule 43.2(1)(k) he should inform other potential parties to the claim that he has done so.

4A.2 Paragraph 4A.1 applies to all proceedings whether proceedings to which a pre-action protocol applies or otherwise.

(Rule 44.3B(1)(c) provides that a party may not recover any additional liability for any period in the proceedings during which he failed to provide information about a funding arrangement in accordance with a rule, practice direction or court order).

COMMENCEMENT

5.1 The following table sets out the protocols currently in force, the date they came into force and their date of publication:

Protocol	Coming into force	Publication
Personal Injury	26 April 1999	January 1999
Clinical Negligence	26 April 1999	January 1999
Construction and Engineering Disputes	2 October 2000	September 2000
Defamation	2 October 2000	September 2000
Professional Negligence	16 July 2001	May 2001
Judicial Review	4 March 2002	3 December 2001
Disease and Illness	8th December 2003	September 2003
Housing Disrepair	8th December 2003	September 2003

5.2 The court will take compliance or non-compliance with a relevant protocol into account where the claim was started after the coming into force of that protocol but will not do so where the claim was started before that date.

5.3 Parties in a claim started after a relevant protocol came into force, who have, by work done before that date, achieved the objectives sought to be achieved by certain requirements of that protocol, need not take any further steps to comply with those requirements. They will not be considered to have not complied with the protocol for the purposes of paragraphs 2 and 3.

5.4 Parties in a claim started after a relevant protocol came into force, who have not been able to comply with any particular requirements of that protocol because the period of time between the publication date and the date of coming into force was too short, will not be considered to have not complied with the protocol for the purposes of paragraphs 2 and 3.

DIGEST OF LEADING CASES

TLATA 1996 AND BENEFICIAL INTERESTS GENERALLY

Constructive Trusts

Lloyds Bank v Rosset [1991]
Stokes v Anderson [1991]
Grant v Edwards [1986]
Eves v Eves [1975]
Re Gorman [1992]
Hammond v Mitchell [1991]
B v B [1988]
Re Densham [1975]
Windeler v Whitehall [1990]
Lissimore v Downing [2003]
Parker v Clark [1960]
Chan Pui Chun v Leung Kam Ho [2003]
Ahmed v Gould [2005]
R v Robson (1991)
Burns v Burns [1984]
Midland Bank v Cooke [1995]
McHardy & Sons v Warren [1994]
Risch v McFee [1991]
Lightfoot v Lightfoot Brown [2005]
Leake v Bruzzi [1974]
Marsh v von Sternberg [1986]
Evans v Hayward [1995]
Re Nicholson [1974]
Huntingford v Hobbs [1993]
Savage v Dunningham [1994]
Young v Young [1984]
Re Share (Lorraine) [2002]
Carlton v Goodman [2002]
Allied Irish Banks v McWilliams [1982]
Crisp v Mullings (1976)
Bernard v Josephs [1982]
Kowalczuk v Kowalczuk [1973]

Davis v Vale [1971]
Griffiths v Griffiths [1973]
Thomas v Fuller Brown [1988]
Ungurian v Lesnoff [1990]
Hall v Hall (1982)
Le Foe v Le Foe and Woolwich Plc [2001]
Midland Bank v Dobson [1986]
Cox v Jones [2004]

Resulting Trusts

Risch v McFee [1991]
Sekhon v Alissa [1989]
Tinsley v Milligan [1994]
Lowson v Coombes [1999]
Gascoigne v Gascoigne [1918]
Tinker v Tinker [1970]
Tribe v Tribe [1996]

Quantification of Beneficial Interests

Goodman v Gallant [1986]
Harwood v Harwood [1991]
Supperstone v Hurst [2006]
Mortgage Corporation v Shaire [2001]
Clough v Killey (1996)
Oxley v Hiscock [2005]
Drake v Whipp [1996]
Savill v Goodall [1993]
Marsh v von Sternberg [1983]
Stack v Dowden [2005]

Personal Obligations Between Cohabitants

Re Pavlou [1993]
Powell v Osbourne [1993]
Smith v Clerical Medical and General Life Assurance Society and Others [1993]
Paul v Constance [1977]
Re Figgis (deceased) [1969]
Jones v Maynard [1951]

CONSTRUCTIVE TRUSTS

Case	Summary
Lloyds Bank v Rosset [1991] A.C. 107	The leading exposition of the circumstances in which a constructive trust will arise in cohabitation cases. The relevant property had been purchased on December 17, 1982 in D's sole name, but was charged with repayment of his overdraft. In 1984, the bank's demand for repayment of the overdraft was not complied with and possession proceedings were commenced against both C and D, who had by that time separated. C contended that she enjoyed a beneficial interest under a constructive trust, and thus a right to occupy the property. It was held at first instance that a common intention that C should enjoy a beneficial interest could be inferred from her involvement in the renovation process which had taken place prior to completion of the purchase. On appeal to the HL, Lord Bridge considered that the evidence simply did not warrant that inference. He identified two strands of evidence which might justify the inference of a common intention constructive trust, namely evidence of express discussions leading to some agreement arrangement or understanding ('limb one') or evidence of a contribution to the purchase price or mortgage instalments ('limb two'). A claim based on non-financial contributions alone (no matter over what period of time) or based on indirect financial contributions (whereby the claimant meets certain necessary items of recurring expenditure, leaving the defendant better able to meet the mortgage payments) is not supported by either limb.
Stokes v Anderson [1991] 1 F.L.R. 391	Perhaps the best example of a limb one case. The relevant property was initially held in the name of D and his wife W, who were in the process of divorcing. C had agreed with D that she would advance sums of money with which D would buy out W's share in the property. D's contention that the payments had been by way of loans were rejected, and the court accepted C's evidence that D had agreed that C's name "would go on the deeds when it was all sorted out". Nourse L.J. assessed the case as being, quite apart from the sums advance by C to buy out W's share, "a clear example of what in *Grant v Edwards* [1986] Ch. 638 I thought, perhaps wrongly, was the rarer class of case ... where the parties have orally declared themselves in such a way as to make plain their common intention that the claimant should have a beneficial interest in the property."
Grant v Edwards [1986] Ch. 638	C was told by her partner D that the property should be purchased in his name alone because if the property was bought in their joint names, that might operate to her prejudice in her ongoing divorce proceedings. (*c.f. Oxley v Hiscock* [2005] Fam. 211). The judge at first instance had held that there was no agreement 'as such' between the parties and therefore no interest under a constructive trust could arise. On appeal, Nourse L.J. said that the facts raised "a clear inference that there was an understanding between the plaintiff and the defendant, or a common intention, that the plaintiff was to have some sort of proprietary interest in the house; otherwise no excuse for not putting her name on to the title deeds would have been needed." Held on the facts that C's interest was 50 per cent of the property. Mustill L.J. observed that the relevant intention was the parties' intention at the time of acquisition but added "I use the expression 'on acquisition' for simplicity. In fact, the event happening between the parties which, if

Case	Summary
	followed by the relevant type of conduct on the part of the claimant, can lead to the creation of an interest in the claimant, may itself occur after acquisition. The beneficial interests may change in the course of the relationship." On the issue of detrimental reliance, Nourse L.J. observed that "If it is found to have been incurred ... expenditure will perform the two-fold function of establishing the common intention and showing that the claimant has acted upon it."
Eves v Eves [1975] 1 W.L.R. 1338	C was aged under 21 at the time of the purchase of the relevant property. D told her that the property could not be purchased in joint names for that reason. On the strength of those representations, C famously wielded a 14lb sledgehammer that was used to break up a concrete driveway. The Court of Appeal held that the mere fact of the discussions justified the inference (even if D's uncommunicated intention had been to deceive C) of a common intention that C would have an interest, which on the facts was quantified at 25 per cent.
Re Gorman [1992] 2 F.L.R. 284 Ch.D	The relevant transfer instrument provided: "It is hereby agreed and declared that the transferees are entitled to the land for their own benefit and that the survivor of them can give a valid receipt for capital moneys arising on the disposition of the land". Held (Vinelott J.), that even though the instrument had not been signed by the parties, that declaration was nonetheless evidence – on the facts, conclusive evidence – of the parties' intentions to hold as joint tenants.
Hammond v Mitchell [1991] 1 W.L.R. 1127	The relevant property was purchased in D's sole name with tax reasons being advanced by D as a reason for not purchasing the property in joint names (*c.f. Heseltine v Heseltine* [1971] 1 W.L.R. 342) D nonetheless assured C that the property would be "half yours once we are married". Waite J. held that those representations evidenced an intention that the property would be shared beneficially and said, "The primary emphasis accorded by the law in cases of this kind to express discussions between the parties ('however imperfectly remembered and however imprecise their terms') means that the tenderest exchanges of a common law courtship may assume an unforeseen significance many years later when they are brought under equity's microscope and subjected to an analysis under which many thousands of pounds of value may be liable to turn on fine questions as to whether the relevant words were spoken in earnest or in dalliance and with or without representational intent."
B v B (Real Property: Assessment of Interests) [1988] 2 F.L.R. 490	H caused W to become angry by suggesting at the time of the purchase that his name only should appear on the deeds. At trial, H suggested that W's anger was because she wanted to be seen by any third parties who had sight of the deeds as having a share in the responsibility for the house. That explanation was flatly rejected by the court as being unrealistic. Although purchased in H's name alone, W had been the driving force behind both the initial purchase and subsequent improvements, funded by H, to the property. The intention that each should have an interest was evidenced by W's provision of 'stimulus and considerable personal effort'. The way in which W reacted to the suggestion that her name should not appear on the deeds justified the inference of a common intention, not any purported agreement as to how the property should be held, as plainly W did not agree with H's proposal that the property should be in his name alone.

Case	Summary
Re Densham [1975] 1 W.L.R. 1519	The tenor of the correspondence in the solicitors' conveyancing file demonstrated a plain intention that the property should be shared beneficially, even though the property was conveyed to a single purchaser: contrast *Cowcher v Cowcher* [1972] 1 W.L.R. 425 a single letter from the legal purchaser to the solicitors acting on the purchase, which contained reference to "we" and "us", did not amount to satisfactory evidence of an intention to share the property beneficially with his wife.
Windeler v Whitehall [1990] 2 F.L.R. 505	C claimed an interest based upon what she contended were substantial works of improvement to the relevant property. Millett J. found that these were in fact relatively trivial in nature, consisting of minor building works, such as repointing, carpentry, redecoration and renovation of drains. Completion of these works by builders had been supervised by C, who let the builders in each day, made them tea and coffee and transported them around when further supplies were needed, but the works had been paid for by D. Millett J., having held that "any wife or mistress would have done the same" said, "Only a lawyer versed in the authorities but lacking all sense of proportion would consider that such conduct gave her any kind of proprietary interest in the house." C also relied on the Will executed by D leaving the bulk of his estate to C, contending that this was evidence which illustrated the common intention that C should have some interest in the property. Millett J. considered that "It was nothing of the sort. It was a recognition at that time on (D)'s part to provide for (C) if he should die unexpectedly and while circumstances remained the same. It was completely consistent with the absence of any intention on his part to make a present irrevocable disposition of an interest in his house."
Lissimore v Downing [2003] 2 F.L.R. 308	D had executed a will which on his death would leave C with an interest in the relevant property. C relied on that as evidence of a common intention or conduct necessary to found an estoppel. HHJ Norris Q.C. (sitting as a Deputy High Court Judge) considered that what D intended on his death did not impact upon the position during his life.
Parker v Clark [1960] 1 W.L.R. 286	C was the niece of the Defendants. They had agreed that C and her husband should move in to the property and effectively act as D's carers (both of whom were elderly and in poor health), in return for which the property would be left to the claimants on the death of the survivor of the defendants. That agreement was held to be specifically enforceable as a contract and relief given in terms of a contractual remedy rather than on the basis of a proprietary interest.
Chan Pui Chun v Leung Kam Ho [2003] 1 F.L.R. 23	C and D agreed (while D was in prison) that D would share "everything he had" with C if she would look after certain business ventures which were on foot during D's incarceration and organise his bail and appeal. Despite the absence of any specific promise relating to the property in which C later claimed a half interest, and some uncertainty as to whether D's promise extended to other projects undertaken by D, Jonathan Parker L.J. considered that the agreement was not so vague as to preclude the court from granting equitable relief in relation to it.
Ahmed v Gould [2005] EWCA Civ 1829	The parties (brother and sister) had agreed that C (D's sister) would buy a property which D would occupy, and that D

Case	Summary
	would be entitled to buy the property at market rate at some point in the future. Very shortly after the purchase of the property was completed by C, D paid a sum equal to around 50 per cent of the purchase price into C's bank account. He did not inform C about that. D contended that the payment either represented a contribution to the purchase price or a part payment towards the purchase of the property from C. It was held, however, that in the absence of any agreement as to the basis upon which the payment was made, it was impossible to say that there was a common intention that D was intended by both to enjoy a beneficial interest in the property. Jacob L.J. pithily observed, "You cannot create a beneficial interest by just paying money into somebody's bank account."
R v Robson (1991) 92 Cr.App.R. 1	The Court of Appeal was concerned with the beneficial interests in a property held in the name of the defendant's mother, in the context of an order for confiscation pursuant to the Drug Trafficking Offences Act 1986. The defendant had made a periodic contribution which was in fact applied by his mother towards the mortgage repayments. The Court of Appeal held that in the circumstances of that case, the mere fact of a financial contribution was not enough to establish a beneficial interest per se.
Burns v Burns [1984] Ch. 317	The property was purchased by D alone in 1963. C and D had two children together. C looked after the children, without earning an income until 1975. Thereafter C had made a series of indirect financial contributions (i.e. without contributing directly to the purchase price of the property) and non-financial contributions, though none of these was held to have demonstrated a common intention that she should have a share in the relevant property. Fox L.J. considered that C's contributions towards various household expenses (including payment of grocery bills, rates, telephone bills and purchase of domestic 'white goods' and soft furnishings) did not demonstrate a common intention of the sort which would, to put the matter in post-*Rosset* terms, suffice in terms of limb two: "What is needed is evidence of a payment or payments by the plaintiff which it can be inferred was referable to the acquisition of the house ... a payment could be said to be referable to the acquisition of the house if for example the payer either (a) pays part of the purchase price, or (b) contributes regularly to the mortgage instalments, or (c) pays off part of the mortgage, or (d) makes a substantial financial contribution to the family expenses so as to enable the mortgage instalments to be paid."
Midland Bank v Cooke [1995] 2 F.L.R. 915	The relevant property had been purchased in H's sole name, but the deposit was at least in part funded by a wedding gift made by H's parents. There had been no discussion or agreement between H and W at the time of the acquisition as to the basis upon which the property was held, or as to the extent of their respective beneficial interests. It was held that the wedding gift should be treated as having been made to H and W equally, and therefore each was regarded as having contributed half of that gift.
McHardy & Sons v Warren [1994] 2 F.L.R. 338	The relevant property was purchased with a deposit which had been a wedding gift from H's father. Dillon L.J. held that it was an "irresistible conclusion" that all three of H, W and H's father had intended that W should have a equal share in the property purchased in H's sole name.

Case	Summary
Risch v McFee [1991] 1 F.L.R. 105	A loan made from C to D was neither repaid, nor was any demand for repayment or offer of payment made. A beneficial interest was established by reason of a further advance which enabled D to repay the mortgage. It was held that although the earlier payment "started life" as a loan (*per* Balcombe L.J. at 110G) once it was established that C had a beneficial interest in the house, the loan advance would be regarded as part of her contribution.
Lightfoot v Lightfoot Brown [2005] 2 P. & C.R. 377	The parties had been married, and the relevant property was transferred to W as part of the divorce settlement. The parties reconciled (but did not remarry) and H moved back in to the property. He paid about £24,000 towards mortgage repayments and paid a lump sum of £41,000 to reduce the capital debt owed under the mortgage. The relationship between the parties broke down, and H asserted that the payments justified the inference of a common intention constructive trust. At first instance, the judge found that the mortgage repayments were paid in lieu of a maintenance award in W's favour made during the divorce proceedings which H had not paid. The £41,000 reduction was found by the judge to have been made so that the outstanding balance of the mortgage debt qualified for tax relief, and was further made without the knowledge of W. The judge therefore rejected H's claim to a beneficial interest. The Court of Appeal accepted that these were findings which were open to the judge to make on the evidence before him, and dismissed H's appeal against the finding that he had no interest in the property, despite his conduct in substantially reducing the capital debt.
Leake v Bruzzi [1974] 1 W.L.R. 1528 CA	D held the relevant property for himself and C in equal shares. After C left, D continued to pay the capital and interest elements of the mortgage to which the property was subject. Held, D should have credit in relation to one half of the capital payments he had made, although his payment of the interest payable under the mortgage should be regarded as equivalent to an occupation rent.
Marsh v von Sternberg [1986] 1 F.L.R. 526	A private landlord sought to dispose of a property which was subject to a secure tenancy. The respondent was the tenant entitled to statutory protection against eviction, and negotiated a discount attributable to the loss of that protection in the course of purchasing with the applicant the property from the landlord. Bush J. said, "Though the respondent's situation only had a financial value in a given set of circumstances and did not have a market price in the world at large, it was a financial benefit nevertheless and, in my view, it is possible to infer and I do infer that as part of their agreement or arrangement the parties regarded the realization of that financial benefit by way of discount as a contribution by the respondent to the purchase of the flat."
Evans v Hayward [1995] 2 F.L.R. 511	The discount relating to occupation of a local authority property was prayed in aid as a contribution to the purchase price of the relevant property. Staughton L.J. said that the facts as to the existence of a discount and the source from which it is derived must be taken into account "and are capable of leading to the inference that the parties have made an agreement as to how the purchase price is provided." (*c.f.* *Oxley v Hiscock* [2005] Fam. 211)
Re Nicholson [1974] 1 W.L.R. 476	The initial arrangement was that H would be responsible for mortgage repayments. W however agreed that she would repay

Case	Summary
	the mortgage from the proceeds of an inheritance the receipt of which she anticipated. It was held that the parties had intended that each would have an equal share in the property.
Huntingford v Hobbs [1993] 1 F.L.R. 736	The relevant property was bought in joint names but without a declaration as to their respective shares. The mortgage advance equated to 39 per cent of the total purchase price. D would not have been able to raise such a mortgage without C, and C had agreed to be solely responsible for the mortgage repayments and the payments of the premiums on the endowment policy. Sir Christopher Slade considered that the parties must have had a common intention that both cohabitees should have an interest in the property where the property was conveyed into the names of both, and both had accepted joint and several liability for the mortgage repayments. The mortgage advance was treated as being C's contribution to the purchase price and on sale of the property, the parties' respective interests were calculated by reference to the gross proceeds of sale without any account being taken of the mortgage debt.
Savage v Dunningham [1974] 1 Ch. 181	Plowman J. rejected the proposition that flatsharing was an area where the law of trusts was of any relevance: "the application of the law of trusts to flat-sharing agreements would give rise to all sorts of problems. The occupants of shared flats are constantly changing. People come and go for one reason or another without any thought of legal consequences and without reference to lawyers. They are not likely to have heard of s.53 of the Law of Property Act 1925."
Young v Young [1984] F.L.R. 375	The appellant paid two-thirds of the mortgage instalments for a period of about six months in the early stages of a 20-year mortgage term. May L.J. assessed the actual capital contribution to the repayment of the mortgage debt to be around £175 as opposed to the £4,000 initially contributed by the respondent. "It would, I think," he continued (at 380E), "be wholly unrealistic to decide that even a very small proportion of the equity was held beneficially for the interest of the appellant". The reduction in the capital balance of the mortgage was so small that the inference of a common intention was not justified.
Re Share (Lorraine) [2002] 2 F.L.R. 88	The property was purchased by A alone, though B had in fact paid the entire deposit and all of the mortgage repayments. A had simply been B's nominee and enjoyed no beneficial interest accordingly.
Carlton v Goodman [2002] 2 F.L.R. 259	The property was purchased in joint names but was for the use and occupation of only one purchaser. Whilst assumption of liability under the mortgage *might* be treated as a contribution to the purchase price, on the facts of that particular case it was held that there had never been any intention that the claimant should pay anything, she had not paid anything and would have been entitled as a trustee to an indemnity had she been required to pay anything. Her involvement had been so temporary and of such a limited nature that the assumption of liability under the mortgage alone could not justify the inference of a common intention that she should share the beneficial ownership of the property.
Allied Irish Banks v McWilliams [1982] N.I. 156	Murray J. was not persuaded that, in circumstances where H had not provided financially in any way (whether in terms of mortgage repayments, provision of groceries or otherwise) an assumption of personal liability under a mortgage of itself did

Case	Summary
	not evidence an intention to share the property beneficially, as the claimant would have been entitled in the event of personal liability to an indemnity from the proceeds of sale of the trust property (see 161D).
Crisp v Mullings (1976) 239 E.G. 119	The parties needed to raise a mortgage of £5,700, which D alone was unable to raise. The mortgage (and also the property) were taken in joint names, the arrangement between the parties being that D would pay the expenses of running the house (including mortgage repayments) and C would pay for groceries. D contended that since he alone had contributed to the deposit, and he alone had paid the mortgage instalments, C did not have any beneficial interest in the property, and had been a party to the transaction purely to enable to mortgage to be obtained. Russell LJ held that D's inability to raise the necessary mortgage on his own did not demonstrate that C was a mere nominee: "It is, we think, a non sequitur. On the contrary, the fact that the house for 'the family' could not be bought without the plaintiff incurring some liability, or some potential liability, would be some ground for inferring that the plaintiff was to beneficially interested."
Bernard v Josephs [1982] 1 Ch. 391	Griffiths L.J. (as he then was) gave the example of one partner (the man) purchasing the house in the first place, and the other (the woman) later using a legacy to build an extra floor to make more room for the children. "In such circumstances," said Griffiths L.J., "the obvious inference would be that the parties agreed that the woman should acquire a share in the greatly increased value of the house produced by her money."
Kowalczuk v Kowalczuk [1973] 1 W.L.R. 930	The relevant property had been bought well before H and W were married. At the date of marriage the property was legally and beneficially undoubtedly H's sole property. In those circumstances W would not be able to establish any beneficial interest unless she could point to subsequent contributions of a substantial nature in money or money's worth. On the facts of that case, W had contributed her own physical help to the repair alteration and improvement of the property. The Court of Appeal accepted (see 934E) that her contributions demonstrated an interest within the scope of s.37, and remitted the case for a determination of the extent of that interest.
Davis v Vale [1971] 1 W.L.R. 1022	The claimant wife paid for a water heater, a sink unit, fireplaces, a wall and iron gates. Had the claimant simply effected those improvements without paying for them, it is doubtful whether the necessary common intention could have been demonstrated, even bearing in mind the effect of s.37. The combination of paying for and performing the relevant improvements, however, was held to evidence a common intention that she should have an interest.
Griffiths v Griffiths [1973] 1 W.L.R. 454	The substance of the improvements was largely demonstrated by reference to the cost of the improvements and the effect of such improvements on the value of the property. Arnold J. considered that H had spent about £4,500 on improvements to the property between about 1959 and 1969, and that these had increased the value of the house from about £45,000 (had the improvements not been undertaken) to the sale price achieved of £60,000.
Thomas v Fuller Brown [1988] 1 F.L.R. 237	C (who was unemployed) undertook substantial improvements to the property owned by D. The improvements were in fact funded by D who had received an improvement grant. Slade L.J. accepted (the general proposition that improvements to

Case	Summary
	another's property in reliance upon an *implicit* promise that an interest in the land would be created following such expenditure, might suffice to give rise to an interest under a constructive trust. D relied on his personal investment of labour as evidencing a common understanding that he enjoyed an interest in the property. On the facts, however, the trial judge had concluded that the arrangements between C and D had not included any understanding that C should obtain an interest in D's property. The trial judge categorised the labours of C as equivalent to 'keep', in lieu of payment for board and lodging. The Court of Appeal refused to upset the trial judge's conclusion, even though in the absence of C's labours, D could not otherwise have afforded to have the works completed by private contractors.
Ungurian v Lesnoff [1990] 2 F.L.R. 299	C, who had given up secure accommodation and a stimulating academic career in Poland to join the Defendant undertook various works including the partitioning of certain bedrooms, removal of fireplaces and cleaning and decorating a property which, when purchased by D, was in a poor state of repair. The works were funded by D but undertaken by C and her sons. It was held that these improvements illustrated a common intention that the property was held by D on constructive trust for himself and C, though on the facts of that case D's interest under the trust was a life interest in occupation, not an interest in the equity in the property per se.
Hall v Hall (1982) 3 F.L.R. 379	The claimant relied on indirect financial contributions alone in establishing an interest under (as the court described it) a resulting trust, but the existence of a resulting trust had been conceded by the defendant and the question for the court to decide was simply the extent of the interest (per Dunn L.J. at 383E). May L.J. later describe that concession as having been wrongly made (see *Burns v Burns* [1984] Ch. 317 at 341G). The approach adopted by Lord Denning M.R. in the 1970s and early 1980s, evidenced by *Hall*, to infer the existence of a 'constructive trust of a new model' on the basis of domestic or indirect contributions to the purchase price (e.g. *Hazell v Hazell* [1972] 1 W.L.R. 301) was disapproved in *Burns v Burns* [1984] Ch. 317.
Le Foe v Le Foe and Woolwich Plc [2001] 2 F.L.R. 970	Nicholas Mostyn Q.C. (sitting as a Deputy Judge of the Family Division) considered that it was important that Lord Bridge's reference to it being "at least extremely doubtful whether anything less will do" had not been stated in absolute terms. He continued (at 980–982): "In my view what Lord Bridge of Harwich is saying is that in the second class of case to which he is adverting, namely where there is no positive evidence of an express agreement between the parties as to how the equity is to be shared, and where the court has fallen back on inferring their common intention from the course of their conduct, it will only be exceptionally that conduct other than direct contributions to the purchase price, either in cash to the deposit or by contribution to the mortgage instalments, will suffice to draw the necessary inference of a common intention to share the equity". Mr Mostyn Q.C. continued to say that he did not believe that in using the words "direct contributions" Lord Bridge of Harwich meant to exclude the situation with which he was confronted: "… namely, where there was no initial cash contribution but only an indirect contribution to the mortgage … such a state of affairs should suffice to enable the necessary inference to be drawn.

Case	Summary
	Otherwise these cases would be decided by reference to mere accidents of fortune, being the arbitrary allocation of financial responsibility as between the parties."
Midland Bank v Dobson [1986] 1 F.L.R. 171	The relevant property was held in the name of the husband alone, although he and his wife had expressly agreed that the beneficial interests should be shared equally (the Court of Appeal accepted that it could not go behind the finding of the trial judge in this regard). The wife was not, however, able to establish an interest under a constructive trust so as to defend a claim by the claimant bank for possession of the property. It had been used by the husband as security for his business borrowings and she had not in any way acted to her detriment in reliance upon that agreement. Her contributions to the household and periodic decorating were not acts done in reliance upon the agreement with her husband as regards any interest in the property; they were characterised as the sort of things that members of a family do in a house.
Cox v Jones [2004] 2 F.L.R. 1057	C, a barrister, significantly reduced her practice at the Bar in order to concentrate her energies on the joint property enterprise she was undertaking with D. That was held to be conduct which evidenced a detrimental reliance on the common intention that the beneficial interests in the relevant property should be shared.

RESULTING TRUSTS

Case	Summary
Risch v McFee [1991] 1 F.L.R. 105	What started out as a loan from C to D was neither repaid, nor was any demand for repayment or offer of payment made. A beneficial interest was established by reason of a further advance which enabled D to repay the mortgage. The Court of Appeal held that although the earlier payment 'started life' as a loan, once it was established that C had a beneficial interest in the house the loan advance would be regarded as part of her contribution.
Sekhon v Alissa [1989] 2 F.L.R. 94	Mother and daughter both contributed towards the purchase price of a property conveyed into the daughter's sole name, in respective proportions of (approximately) 60/40. The 40 per cent contributed by the daughter was in fact raised by way of a mortgage; the mother's contribution came from her savings. Hoffman J. held on the facts that neither party considered the mother's contribution to be a gift, inter alia because the finding of a gift would mean that the mother had intended to part with the entirety of her life savings.
Tinsley v Milligan [1994] 1 A.C. 340	C and D jointly purchased a house which was registered only in D's name. Although both C and D understood the beneficial interests to be shared between themselves, both made applications for various social security benefits which would not have been paid to them had the Department of Social Security been made aware that both in fact had an interest in the relevant property. On C's claim, to a 50 per cent interest in the property, after her relationship with D had broken down, D's defence was that C was not entitled to rely upon her own illegal purpose in claiming equitable relief. The House of Lords decided that C was entitled to an interest in the property by reason of the interest that arose in her favour

Case	Summary
	under a resulting trust, not by reason of any constructive trust. Lord Browne Wilkinson said, "Where the presumption of resulting trust applies, the plaintiff does not have to rely on the illegality. If he proves that the property is vested in the defendant alone but that the plaintiff provided part of the purchase money, or voluntarily transferred the property to the defendant, the plaintiff establishes his claim under a resulting trust unless either the contrary presumption of advancement displaces the presumption of resulting trust, or the defendant leads evidence to rebut the presumption of resulting trust. Therefore, in cases where the presumption of advancement does not apply, a plaintiff can establish his equitable interest without relying in any way on the underlying illegal transaction."
Lowson v Coombes [1999] Ch. 373	C and D had bought a property using joint funds but which was conveyed into D's name alone to avoid claims against C brought by his former wife. The Court of Appeal accepted that the intention to defeat the claims of C's wife was an illegal purpose, but in order to establish a resulting trust C did not need to rely upon that purpose. The provision by C of part of the purchase monies itself gave rise to the presumption of a resulting trust.
Gascoigne v Gascoigne [1918] 1 K.B. 223	C used his own funds to build a house which he then transferred into the name of D, his wife. The intention of both parties had been to defeat present and future creditors. C for instance refused to pay tax in relation to the property on the basis that it belonged to his wife. C later brought an action to recover the property which failed, on the basis that he was not entitled to rely on his own illegality in seeking to rebut the presumption of advancement which arose as between husband and wife.
Tinker v Tinker [1970] P. 136	C moved to Cornwall having purchased a garage business there. He also bought a house there, which was conveyed into his wife's name, in order to defeat potential creditors in the event that the business was not a success and he was indebted to creditors. On the breakdown of the marriage between C and D, C argued that the house belonged to him under a resulting trust. At first instance, the registrar made the finding that C had not acted dishonestly. In the Court of Appeal it was held that there was nothing objectionable about placing the house in his wife's name to protect it from the claims of creditors if the wife held the beneficial interest as well as the legal interest. If C had intended to place the property in D's name whilst retaining the beneficial interest himself, that would plainly indicate a dishonest intention. The finding of an honest intention was consistent only with an actual intention, to protect the house from the claims of creditors, that D should enjoy the beneficial interest as well as the legal interest. C's reasons for placing the house in D's name in no way went displaced the presumption of advancement: rather, the evidence tended to strengthen the effect of the presumption.
Tribe v Tribe [1996] Ch. 107	C was the majority shareholder in the company through which he conducted a clothing business. The premises from which the company traded, however, were rented by C in his own name. C's obligations under the lease included a full repairing covenant, and he was served with a schedule of dilapidations which he was not in a position to make good. In order to protect the company in the event of an attempt to any enforcement action against him arising from his liability

Case	Summary
	under the lease, C transferred the majority of his shares to his son D. The stated consideration for the transfer was £89,000, although this was never in fact paid. C was able in the event to resolve his dispute with the landlord by (inter alia) surrendering the lease, without making good the dilapidations. Subsequently, D refused to transfer the shares back to C. On C's claim for a declaration that D held the shares on trust for C, it had been contended for D that although no consideration had been paid for the shares, the presumption of advancement arose in D's favour. On the facts of the case, it was argued, the presumption could not be rebutted by C since in order to do so, he would need to rely on his own illegal purpose, namely an improper attempt to defeat his creditors. At first instance, C's claim was upheld.
	Dismissing D's appeal against the order made at first instance, Nourse L.J. held that *Tinsley v Milligan* had not decided that a claimant could not lead evidence of an illegal purpose to rebut the presumption of advancement in any circumstances. He considered that where the presumption of advancement prima facie arose, the claimant was precluded from leading evidence of his own illegality to rebut that presumption only if the illegal purpose had been carried out.

QUANTIFICATION OF BENEFICIAL INTERESTS

Case	Summary
Goodman v Gallant [1986] Fam. 106	The appellant and her husband had owned a property in equal shares. After their marriage broke down, an agreement was reached whereby the appellant and her new partner would purchase the appellant's husband's interest in the property. The property was conveyed to the appellant and her partner as joint tenants. On the breakdown of their relationship, the appellant claimed that she was beneficially entitled to three quarters of the relevant property, on the basis that she owned half of the property in any event and had joined equally with her new partner in the purchase of the other half. The Court of Appeal rejected the submission that on severance the parties were entitled to anything other than an equal share of the equity. Slade L.J. said, "in the absence of any claim for rectification or rescission, the provision in the conveyance declaring that the plaintiff and the defendant were to hold the proceeds of sale of the property 'upon trust for themselves as joint tenants' concludes the question of the respective beneficial interests of the two parties insofar as that declaration of trust, on its true construction, exhaustively declares the beneficial interests ... it is the very nature of a joint tenancy that, upon a severance, each takes an equal aliquot share according to the number of joint tenants."
Harwood v Harwood [1991] 2 F.L.R. 274	The relevant transfer containing the words "the transferees declare that the survivor of them can give a valid receipt for capital money arising on a disposition of land". Slade L.J. observed that the words used in *Re Gorman* clearly identified the transferees as the beneficiaries under the trusts of the relevant property. There was no possibility, therefore, of their holding the property as nominees for a third party. The form of declaration in *Harwood* contained no such words and was

Case	Summary
	quite consistent with the transferees' holding the property for a single third party.
Supperstone v Hurst [2006] 1 F.C.R. 352	H and W owned their house jointly in unascertained shares. H, who was in financial difficulties, entered into an Individual Voluntary Arrangement with his creditors, in the course of which both he and W made written statements indicating that the property was held in equal shares. In the course of H's subsequent bankruptcy, W asserted that she was beneficially entitled not to 50 per cent of the proceeds of sale but 85 per cent. Mr Michael Briggs Q.C. (sitting as a Deputy Judge in the Chancery Division) held that whilst the IVA statements did not amount to declarations of trust, they were compelling evidence (though not of themselves determinative) of the parties' intentions.
Mortgage Corporation v Shaire [2001] Ch. 743	Per Neuberger J.: "When determining the respective beneficial interests of two persons who are living in a house together either as man and wife or in a close relationship, the law appears to be as follows: 1. Where the parties have expressly agreed the shares in which they hold, that is normally conclusive. 2. Such an agreement can be in writing or oral. 3. Where the parties have reached such an agreement, it is open to the court to depart from that agreement only if there is very good reason for doing so, for instance a subsequent renegotiation or subsequent actions which are so inconsistent with what was agreed as to lead to the conclusion that there must have been a variation or cancellation of the agreement."
Clough v Killey (1996) 72 P. & C.R. D22	C transferred to D £12,500 from her divorce settlement which was used by D to clear an overdraft and, in part, fund improvements to the relevant property. C and D had agreed that C would have a half share in the property. At first instance, C recovered only 25 per cent and appealed against the order of the County Court Judge. In the Court of Appeal, D argued that an interest of 50 per cent was completely disproportionate to C's contribution of £12,500. Peter Gibson L.J., however, considered that even if that were correct, there was still no justification for allowing D to resile from what he had agreed with C, namely that they should share the property equally.
Oxley v Hiscock [2005] Fam. 211	C purchased the property which she occupied from the local authority under the 'right to buy' scheme. Her occupation history meant she was entitled to a significant discount on the purchase price. The balance of the purchase price was entirely met by a loan from D. Some years later, C's property was sold, and the proceeds of sale were entirely applied towards the purchase of a subsequent property, in D's name only. D provided significant further capital towards the purchase of the second property, and a small proportion of the purchase price was raised by way of a mortgage. At first instance, the trial judge found that the parties had been involved in a classic pooling of resources, and held that the parties' common intention had been to hold the property in equal shares. On appeal, it was held that the trial judge had given insufficient weight to the capital contribution made by D, and reduced the order in C's favour from a half share to 40 per cent, on the basis that where the parties had not agreed their respective shares in terms, each was entitled to such share as the court thought fit in the light of the whole course of dealing between them in relation to the property.

Case	Summary
Drake v Whipp [1996] 1 F.L.R. 826	C had contributed about 20 per cent of the purchase price, and under a purchase money resulting trust could not have recovered a greater share. The Court of Appeal however observed that her interest arose under a constructive, not a resulting trust, and so the court, in holding that her interest was 33 per cent, was not restricted to a pure arithmetic reckoning of her interest.
Savill v Goodall [1993] 1 F.L.R. 755 CA	The parties had agreed that D should pay the entire mortgage in relation to the property they held in equal shares, C having contributed more towards the initial capital payment. D failed to do so from the time he left the property. C paid the mortgage alone from that time onwards. Held, C was entitled to credit in relation to the capital element of the mortgage payments she made following D's departure (the interest element being equivalent to an occupation rent). The agreement that D would pay the mortgage had been 'the quid pro quo' for D's acquisition of a half share notwithstanding unequal contributions, and equity would not permit him to rely upon the agreement that he should have an equal share on the one hand, but deny the liability subject to which it was acquired on the other.
Marsh v von Sternberg [1986] 1 F.L.R. 526	A private landlord sought to dispose of the relevant property. The respondent was a sitting tenant entitled to statutory protection against eviction, and on purchasing the property from the landlord, negotiated a discount attributable to the loss of that protection. Bush J. inferred that the parties regarded that discount as a contribution by the respondent to the purchase of the property.
Stack v Dowden [2005] EWCA Civ 857	The relevant transfer instrument contained a declaration that the survivor of the parties was able to give a valid receipt for capital monies on the disposition of the property. Following *Huntingford*, the Court of Appeal held unanimously that of itself, that declaration could not be conclusive of the parties' beneficial interests. Nonetheless, Chadwick L.J. observed that he had little doubt (at para. 55) that the declaration would have been conclusive as to the parties' respective interest, *if* the evidence before the court had established that the parties fully understood the implications of such a declaration in terms of survivorship indicating joint tenancy and equivalent beneficial interests. If, on the other hand, the evidence from the parties established that the significance of a declaration as to survivorship had not been appreciated, it could not sensibly be held that the parties had made an express declaration in the *Goodman v Gallant* sense. In those circumstances, the reasoning in Oxley v *Hiscock* applied just as much to joint purchasers as it did to cases where the legal title was held by one party alone, with the other party enjoying an unquantified beneficial interest.

PERSONAL OBLIGATIONS BETWEEN COHABITANTS

Case	Summary
Re Pavlou [1993] 2 F.L.R. 751	The court was concerned with a claim to an equitable account between a wife and her husband's trustee in bankruptcy in relation to various improvements she had funded in relation to the property they owned as joint tenants. Millett J referred to the 'guiding principle' that neither party could take the benefit of an increase in the value of the property without making an allowance for what had been expended by the other in order to obtain it.
Powell v Osbourne [1993] 1 F.C.R. 797	C and her husband held their home together in joint names. After they separated, D moved in to the property to live with C's husband. The mortgage relating to the property was supported by an endowment policy which was charged, in the event of the death of either, with the repayment of the mortgage. On the death of C's husband, in accordance with the terms of the policy, the death benefits were paid to the deceased's personal representatives. C brought an action against the personal representatives seeking the recovery of the death benefits on the basis that they were charged with the repayment of the mortgage. Her claim was upheld: Dillon L.J. said, "If the deceased had in fact severed the joint tenancy immediately before the date of death, he would have thereupon become entitled to a half-share in the property subject to the mortgage but with the benefit of a half share in the policy monies, and, accordingly, on his death his net estate would have been left with the clear half-share of the property, half the policy monies having gone to discharge his half-share of the mortgage."
Smith v Clerical Medical and General Life Assurance Society and Others [1993] 1 F.L.R. 47	The purchasers of a property had taken out a 100 per cent mortgage at the time of acquisition. A related endowment policy was taken out and charged with the repayment of the mortgage debt. On the death of one of the joint purchasers, the property was sold and the mortgage repaid from the proceeds of sale. An issue arose as to whether the mortgage ought more properly to have been repaid from the proceeds of the endowment policy. The survivor of the purchasers contended that it was not open to the mortgage company in effect to elect whether to recover the mortgage debt from the policy or the proceeds of sale and sought in effect reimbursement of the monies used to discharge the mortgage. On an application to the court seeking a determination as to whether the death benefits under the policy should be paid to the personal representatives of the deceased or to the co-owner, the case was described by Scott L.J. as being "a simple one". He added, "The parties bought the property. They borrowed the purchase price from the building society, entered into an endowment mortgage and effected the policy with the intention that the policy proceeds should be applied in repayment of the mortgage loan. Equity will not permit either party, or the personal representatives of either party for that matter, to defeat that intention upon which both parties acted and upon the basis of which both parties entered into substantial financial commitments."
Paul v Constance [1977] 1 W.L.R. 527	D left his wife and went to live with C for a number of years before D's death. D had repeatedly told C that the funds in

Case	Summary
	D's bank account were "as much yours as they are mine". On D's death, his widow took out letters of administration and proposed to distribute the monies held within the bank account to the deceased's estate. C brought an action against the widow seeking a declaration that the monies held in the bank account were hers. She succeeded at first instance. On appeal, it was held that the judge had been entitled to find that those words constituted an express declaration of trust in equal shares. The claimant was accordingly entitled to a half share of the funds held in the account.
Re Figgis (deceased) [1969] 1 Ch. 123	H and W were married in 1915. In 1917, shortly before he went overseas on active service with the armed forces, H opened a joint bank account for himself and W. On his return from the war, H took complete control over the family finances. H and W died within six hours of each other. An issue arose between the executors of the estates of H and W respectively as to whether immediately at the date of death the funds held in the joint bank account were solely H's property or whether W had an entitlement to a half share. It was contended for H's estate that the opening of a joint account had been a simple matter of convenience and that it had never been the deceased's intention that his wife (the joint account holder) should be beneficially entitled to the funds in the account. On the facts Megarry J. rejected that contention and held that W had been intended to have a half share. It was however accepted that as a matter of law the mere fact that the account was held in joint names was not conclusive of the beneficial interests in the property.
Jones v Maynard [1951] 1 Ch. 572	In 1941 H, about to go overseas on active service, authorized W to draw on his bank account. After the war, the account was operated as though it was a joint account even though it remained in H's sole name. Funds were drawn from the account and were used for investment purposes. On H and W's separation, the account was closed. An issue arose as to the extent of W's interest in the closing balance and whether she had any entitlement to the investments made with funds drawn from the account, which were in H's sole name. H contended that he and W should receive shares in proportion to their respective contributions. That claim was rejected by Vaisey J. who held that both the joint account and the investments purchased using funds from that joint account were held in equal shares. Even though, ordinarily, personal property bought by one party using funds from a joint account remained the absolute property of that party, investments paid for out of the joint account, although made in the name of the husband alone, "were in fact made by him in his own name as a trustee as to a moiety for his wife".

Index

STOP PRESS

Morgan v Hill

On 17th October 2006 the Court of Appeal (Thorpe, Keene and Hughes LJJ) heard the father's appeal from the judgment of Peter Hughes QC in the case of M v H. Judgment was handed down on 28th November 2006. The case is dealt with at paragraphs 11-021 and 11-034 of this book.

The mother (Ms Hill) has 2 children. Her first child was born in 1997 and her second was born in 2000. The appellant father (Mr. Morgan) is the father of the second child. Ms Hill had brought proceedings against the father of her first child in 1999 and was awarded periodical payments of £80 per week (£4,160 per annum). She applied to vary these payments in 2002 and her application was compromised in 2003 and the order varied to require periodical payments of £12,000 per annum plus school fees.

Ms Hill's relationship with Mr Morgan lasted for about 2 years but broke down after the conception of the couple's child but before that child's birth. Financial negotiations began between the parties, solicitors became involved and agreement was reached when the child concerned was about 8 months old in mid 2001. The agreement in broad terms included provision of a property (half owned by Ms Hill), periodical payments (£39,000 per annum) and school fees. The agreement was never made into an order although the possibility was discussed between solicitors who concluded that it was not necessary as there had not been an application to court. Ms Hill applied under Schedule 1 for provision of property and periodical payments in January 2005. She was awarded a housing fund of £700,000, periodical payments of £60,000 per annum, school fees and a lump sum of £100,000 to clear her debts.

The appeal focussed on 2 points of principle. The first was based upon the applicability of the decision of *Edgar v Edgar* [1980] 1 WLR 1410 to Schedule 1 cases and the second being that the judge was wrong to impose financial obligations on Mr Morgan that had the effect of conferring benefit on Ms Hill's first child thus relieving the father of that child of his financial responsibilities.

The Edgar question

Mr. Morgan's case was that the trial judge should have applied the *Edgar* principles rigorously and dismissed Ms Hill's claim on the basis that she had negotiated a final and comprehensive agreement, which was effectively an order, which settled her claims, and she had had the benefit of high quality

legal advice whilst doing so. Ms Hill's case was that the *Edgar* principles should not be extended to applications brought under Schedule 1. Mr. Morgan's appeal was not successful on this point.

At paragraph 28 Thorpe LJ says, "The simple answer is to be found in paragraph 10 (3)(b). The court is empowered to alter an agreement provided it is satisfied that it "does not contain proper financial arrangements with respect to the child." The resulting alteration must however "be just having regard to all the circumstances." The agreement itself may be a very significant circumstance." Thorpe LJ concluded that the Deputy Judge was correct to reject the reliance on the *Edgar* point and to make greater provision for the child's future. At paragraph 33 he said, "Plainly whether a claim is brought under paragraph 1 or paragraph 10 of the Schedule the first hurdle that the applicant must surmount is the pre-existing agreement, which must be either demonstrated to be unenforceable given the circumstances surrounding its creation or, as the judge here found, inadequate in its extent. Thus the pre-existing agreement is the starting point of the courts assessment. It is plainly one of the circumstances of the case and the weight to be attached to it will vary from case to case. If the court conceives that the applicant is capricious or unreasonable in the attempt to depart from the terms of the agreement then the dismissal of the application will naturally follow. In upholding the judge on the facts of this particular case I do not mean in any way to depart from the approach adopted in previous cases under the Matrimonial Causes Act 1973."

It is clear that the chosen procedural routes (either paragraph 1 or 10) is not important as the same weight must be given to a pre-existing agreement under either avenue. Thorpe LJ's conclusion was supported by Keene LJ who added that "Normally, the agreement should be seen as the starting point, since there are important public policy reasons why agreements carefully negotiated and freely entered into should be treated as of great weight. But ultimately it is the interests of the child which must provide the crucial test and it is for the court to reach a determination as to what those require." (paragraph 57). Hughes LJ described an agreement as powerful and usually the best evidence of what is required as provision for a child but that the child's interest will prevail over any terms if the agreement does not make proper financial arrangements. He also noted that "To the extent that the Judge said that he should make what he considered proper provision, unless satisfied that the existing agreement already did so, that is to put the question the wrong way round, although often little will turn on the incidence of the burden of proof." (paragraph 61).

Other Children

The Deputy Judge had concluded that Ms Hill was a single mother and that Mr Morgan had known this at the time of their relationship. The Court of Appeal found that that did not prevent him from objecting to the assumption of financial responsibilities for Ms Hill's first child. Thorpe LJ specifically rejected the conclusion that it would not be right to scale down the mother's claim against Mr Morgan were she failing to seek an increase due from the other father (paragraph 37). Thorpe LJ accepted the difficulty in separating out costs for different children within a family but stated that such practical difficulties do not allow the judge to gloss over the objection in principle. "My conclusion that in principle the objection is well founded can be simply explained. The court's jurisdiction under paragraph 1 of the Schedule is, in the context of the present case, limited to making an order against the appellant as a parent of a child." (paragraph 38). Hughes LJ accepted that the first child may derive incidental benefits from living in the same house as Ms Hill and the relevant child but stressed that no order could be made that had the effect of fixing Mr Morgan with some responsibility for the first child (paragraph 65).

Thorpe LJ considered that when Mr Morgan raised the cross subsidy defence, Ms Hill should have offered to join the father of her first child to the proceedings. It was also open to Mr Morgan to have applied to join that father and therefore in this case the blame for his absence could be shared. Thorpe LJ concluded, "What is plainly objectionable in principle is for an applicant under s15 to obtain more by consecutive application than she would have obtained by simultaneous applications." (paragraph 45).

The Court of Appeal concluded that the Deputy Judge's decision in respect of housing was correct as the relevant child was unsuitably and in relation to Mr Morgan disproportionately housed. The disparity between what the first father was paying (£12,000 plus school fees) and what Mr Morgan was ordered to pay by the Deputy Judge (£60,000 plus school fees) was recognised by the Court of Appeal but Thorpe LJ narrowly concluded that the Deputy Judge was justified in ordering Mr Morgan to pay the balance (paragraph 48)

Mr. Morgan's appeal was successful on the issue of the lump sum. The Deputy Judge had ordered him to pay £100,000 as a lump sum to meet Ms Hill's debts. Although Thorpe LJ concluded that the Deputy Judge had been right to refuse to set off those debts against the value of Ms Hill's flat in Paris because that represented her only appreciating asset and financial security it was not right to order Mr Morgan to pay lump sum at that level. Thorpe LJ

decided that some of the debts must be attributed to the father of Ms Hill's first child and therefore reduced the lump sum to £50,000.

Thorpe LJ gave three pieces of general guidance for Schedule 1 claims against extremely rich fathers (although it is suggested that they could have equal application to all Schedule 1 cases). Firstly he suggested the application of ancillary relief procedure to Schedule 1 claims including the filing of Forms E, questionnaires and an FDR style appointment and noted from the Senior District Judge that the Family Procedure Rules Committee is likely to bring Children Act claims into line with ancillary relief claims. Secondly where an applicant has a claim against more than one father the court should establish the respective liabilities of those fathers at consolidated or consecutive hearing. Thirdly he called again for consideration to be given to the separate representation of children in exceptional cases where special circumstances could be demonstrated.

The judgment is due to be reported shortly.